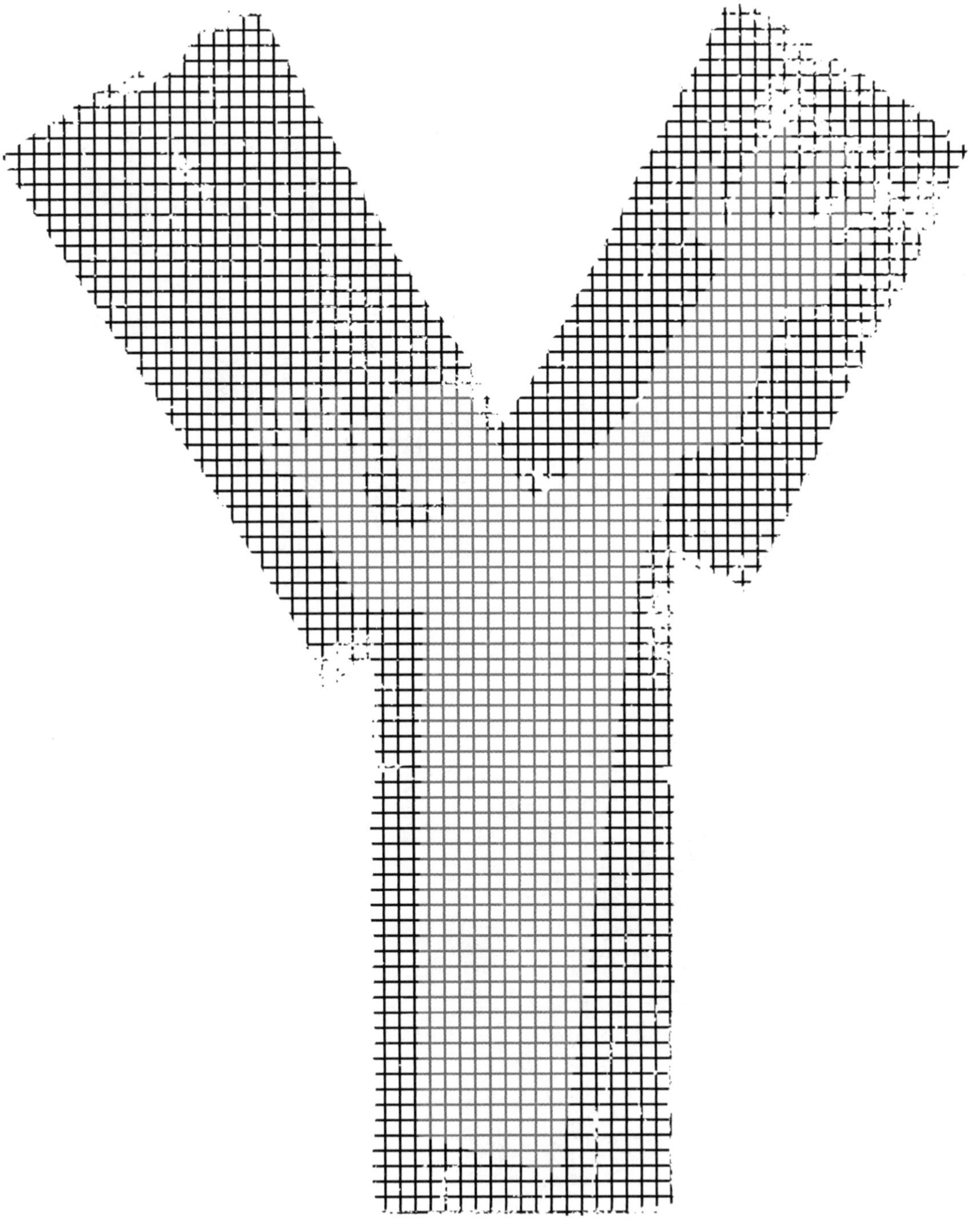
Y

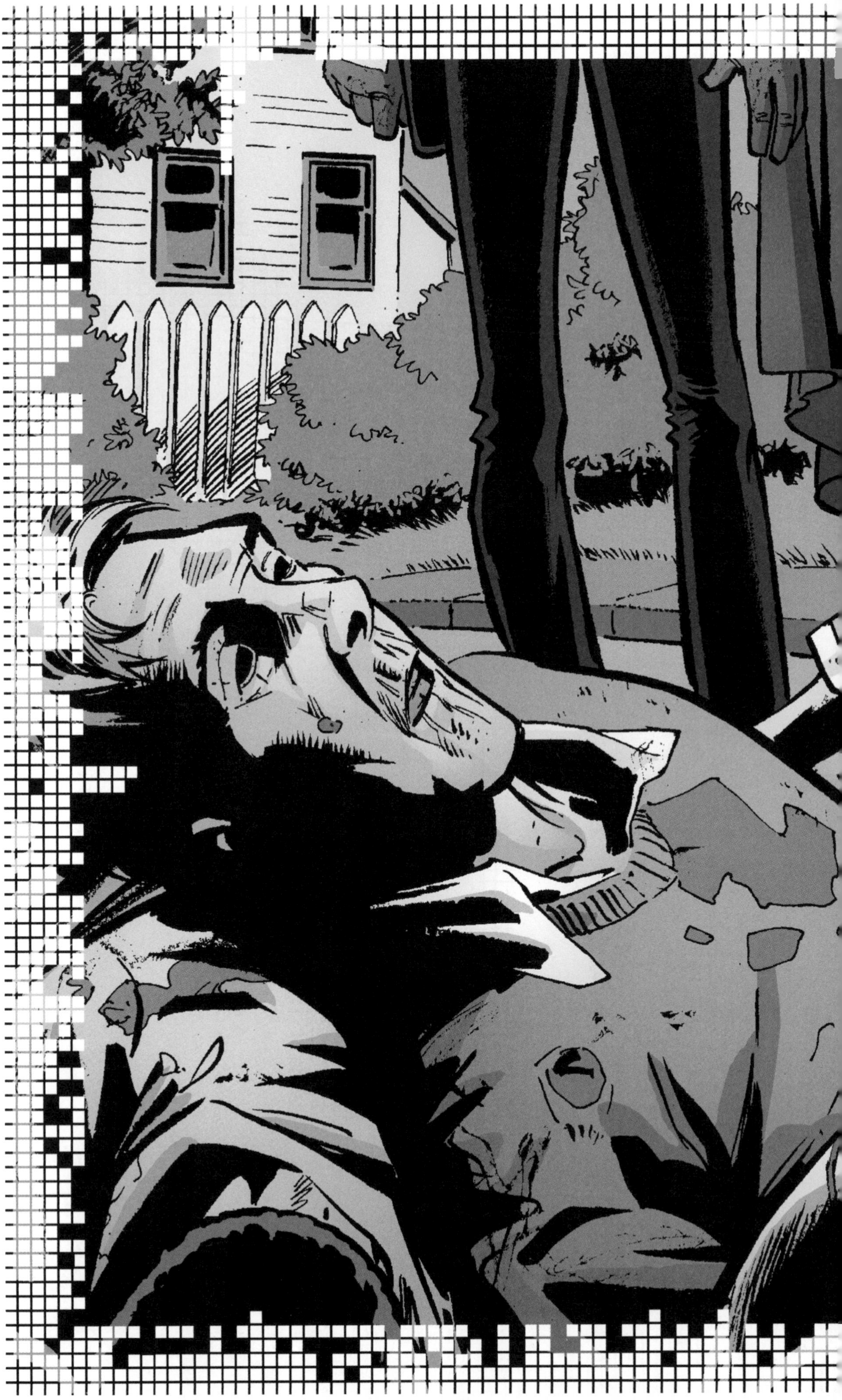

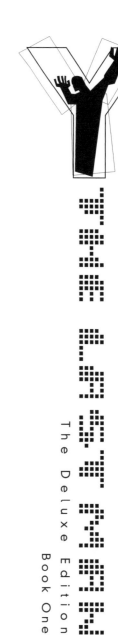

Y

THE LAST MAN

The Deluxe Edition

Book One

Brian K. Vaughan *Writer*

Pia Guerra *Penciller*

José Marzán, Jr. *Inker*

Pamela Rambo *Colorist*

Clem Robins *Letterer*

J.G. Jones *Original Series Covers*

Y: THE LAST MAN created by Brian K. Vaughan and Pia Guerra

Heidi MacDonald, Steve Bunche Editors – Original Series
Zachary Rau Assistant Editor – Original Series
Scott Nybakken Editor
Robbin Brosterman Design Director – Books
Louis Prandi Publication Design

Shelly Bond Executive Editor – Vertigo
Hank Kanalz Senior VP – Vertigo & Integrated Publishing

Diane Nelson President
Dan DiDio and Jim Lee Co-Publishers
Geoff Johns Chief Creative Officer
Amit Desai Senior VP – Marketing & Franchise Management
Amy Genkins Senior VP – Business & Legal Affairs
Nairi Gardiner Senior VP – Finance
Jeff Boison VP – Publishing Planning
Mark Chiarello VP – Art Direction & Design
John Cunningham VP – Marketing
Terri Cunningham VP – Editorial Administration
Larry Ganem VP – Talent Relations & Services
Alison Gill Senior VP – Manufacturing & Operations
Jay Kogan VP – Business & Legal Affairs, Publishing
Jack Mahan VP – Business Affairs, Talent
Nick Napolitano VP – Manufacturing Administration
Sue Pohja VP – Book Sales
Fred Ruiz VP – Manufacturing Operations
Courtney Simmons Senior VP – Publicity
Bob Wayne Senior VP – Sales

Cover illustration by
Massimo Carnevale.

Logo design by
Terry Marks.

Y: THE LAST MAN —
THE DELUXE EDITION
BOOK ONE

Published by DC Comics.
Cover and compilation
Copyright © 2008
DC Comics. All Rights
Reserved. Sketches
Copyright © 2008
Brian K. Vaughan and
Pia Guerra. All Rights
Reserved.

Originally published in
single magazine form as
Y: THE LAST MAN 1-10.
Copyright © 2002, 2003
Brian K. Vaughan and
Pia Guerra. All Rights
Reserved. All characters,
their distinctive likenesses
and related elements
featured in this publication
are trademarks of Brian K.
Vaughan and Pia Guerra.
VERTIGO is a trademark
of DC Comics. The stories,
characters and incidents
featured in this publication
are entirely fictional.
DC Comics does not read
or accept unsolicited
submissions of ideas,
stories or artwork.
DC Comics, 1700
Broadway, New York,
NY 10019 A Warner Bros.
Entertainment Company.
Printed in Canada.
Seventh Printing.
ISBN: 978-1-4012-1921-5

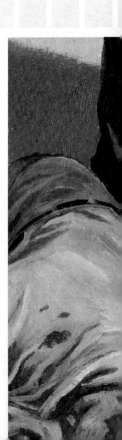

Library of Congress Cataloging-in-Publication Data

Vaughan, Brian K., author.
Y, The Last Man : Book One, Deluxe Edition / Brian K. Vaughan, Pia
Guerra, José Marzán, Jr.
pages cm
"Originally published in single magazine form as Y: The Last Man 1-10."
ISBN 978-1-4012-1921-5
1. Graphic novels. I. Guerra, Pia, illustrator. II. Marzán, José, illustrator.
III. Title.
PN6728.Y2V44 2013
741.5'973–dc23
2012046718

 SUSTAINABLE
FORESTRY
INITIATIVE

Certified Chain of Custody
Promoting Sustainable Forestry
www.sfiprogram.org
SFI-00507

This label only applies to the text section.

Y: THE LAST MAN — Contents

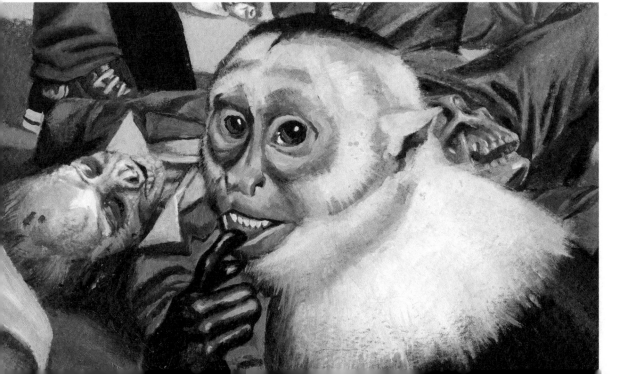

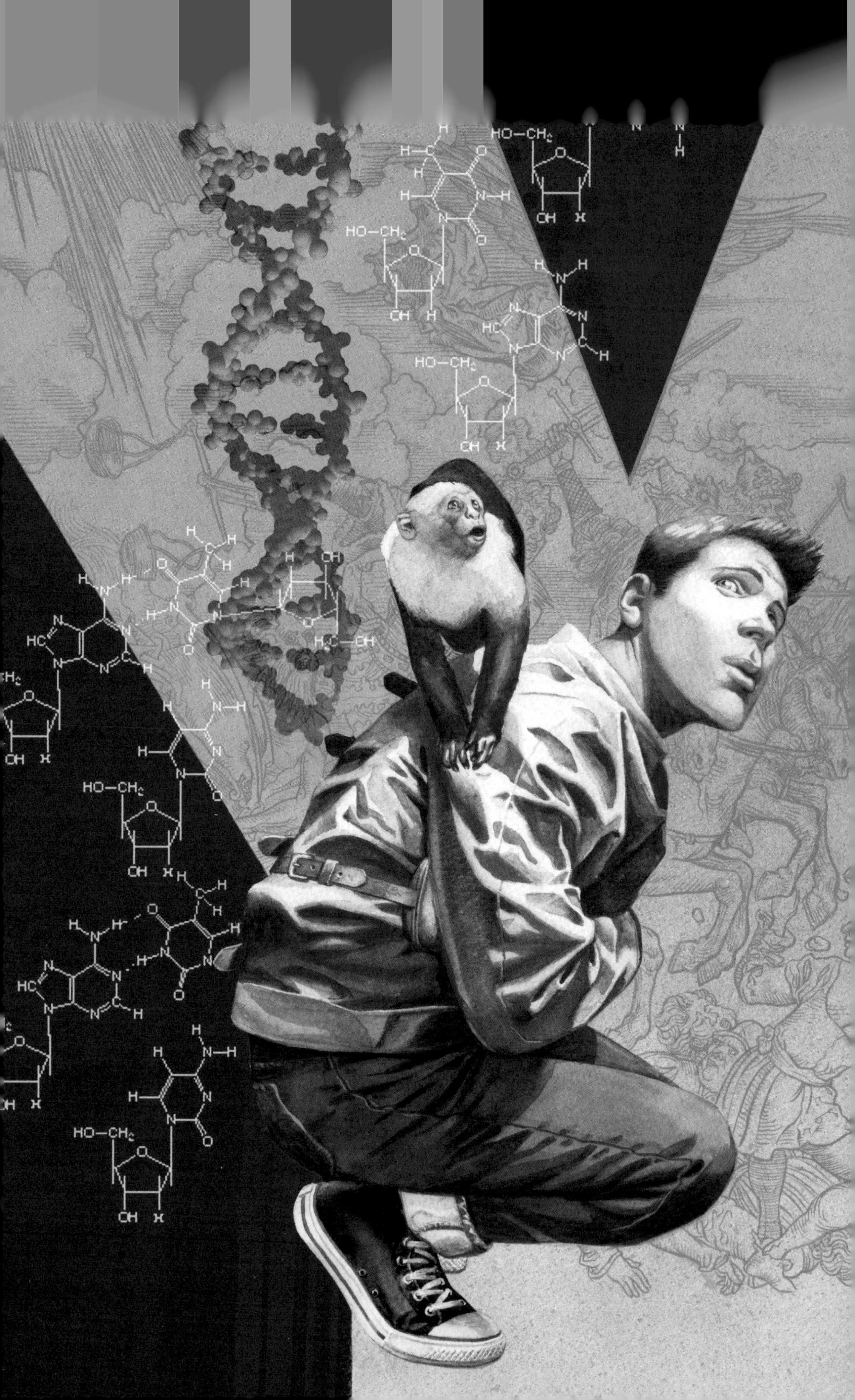

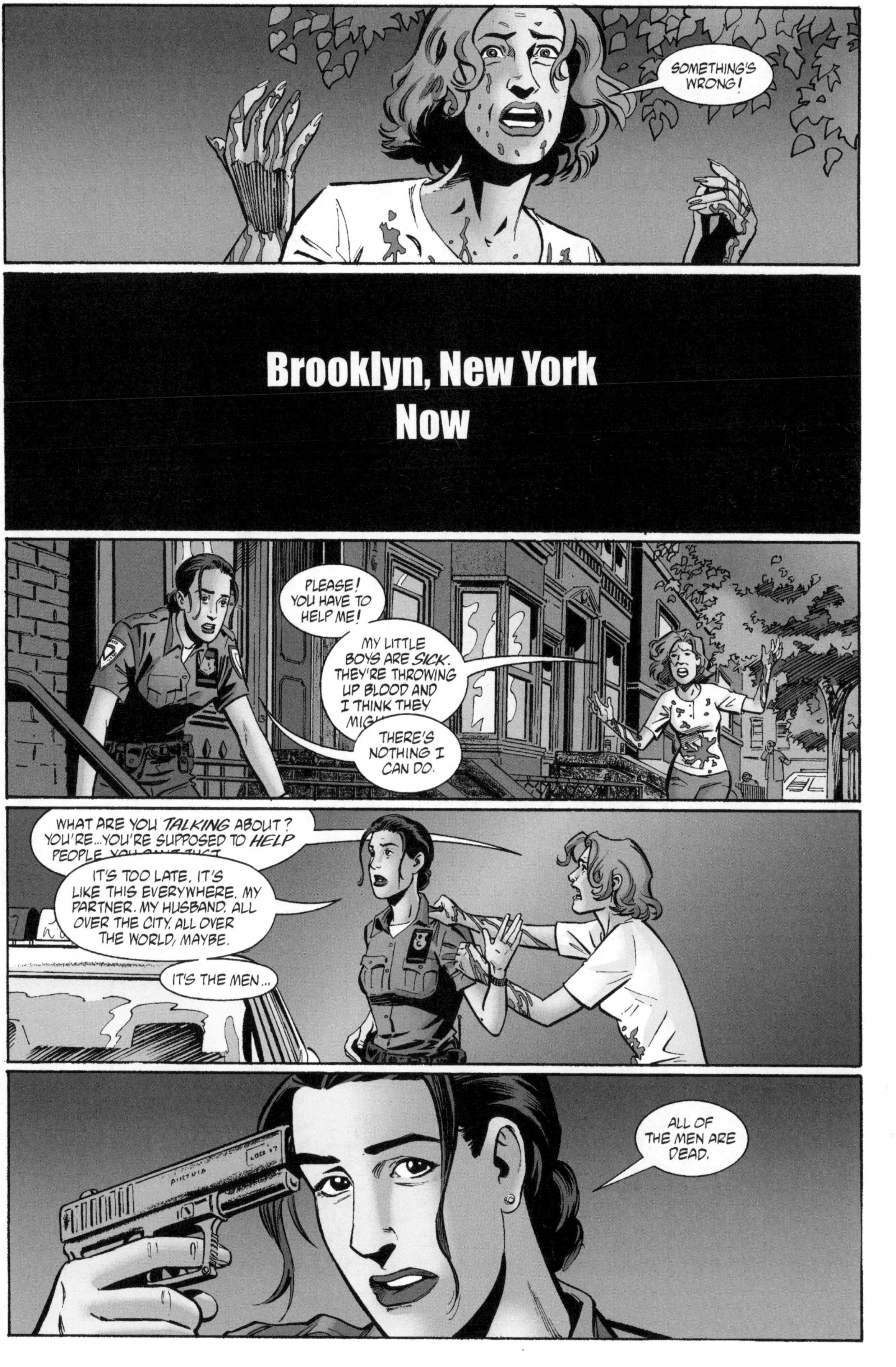
SOMETHING'S WRONG!
Brooklyn, New York
Now
PLEASE! YOU HAVE TO HELP ME!
MY LITTLE BOYS ARE SICK. THEY'RE THROWING UP BLOOD AND I THINK THEY
THERE'S NOTHING I CAN DO.
WHAT ARE YOU TALKING ABOUT? YOU'RE...YOU'RE SUPPOSED TO HELP PEOPLE.
IT'S TOO LATE. IT'S LIKE THIS EVERYWHERE. MY PARTNER. MY HUSBAND. ALL OVER THE CITY. ALL OVER THE WORLD, MAYBE.
IT'S THE MEN...
ALL OF THE MEN ARE DEAD.

Brooklyn, New York
Twenty-Nine Minutes Ago

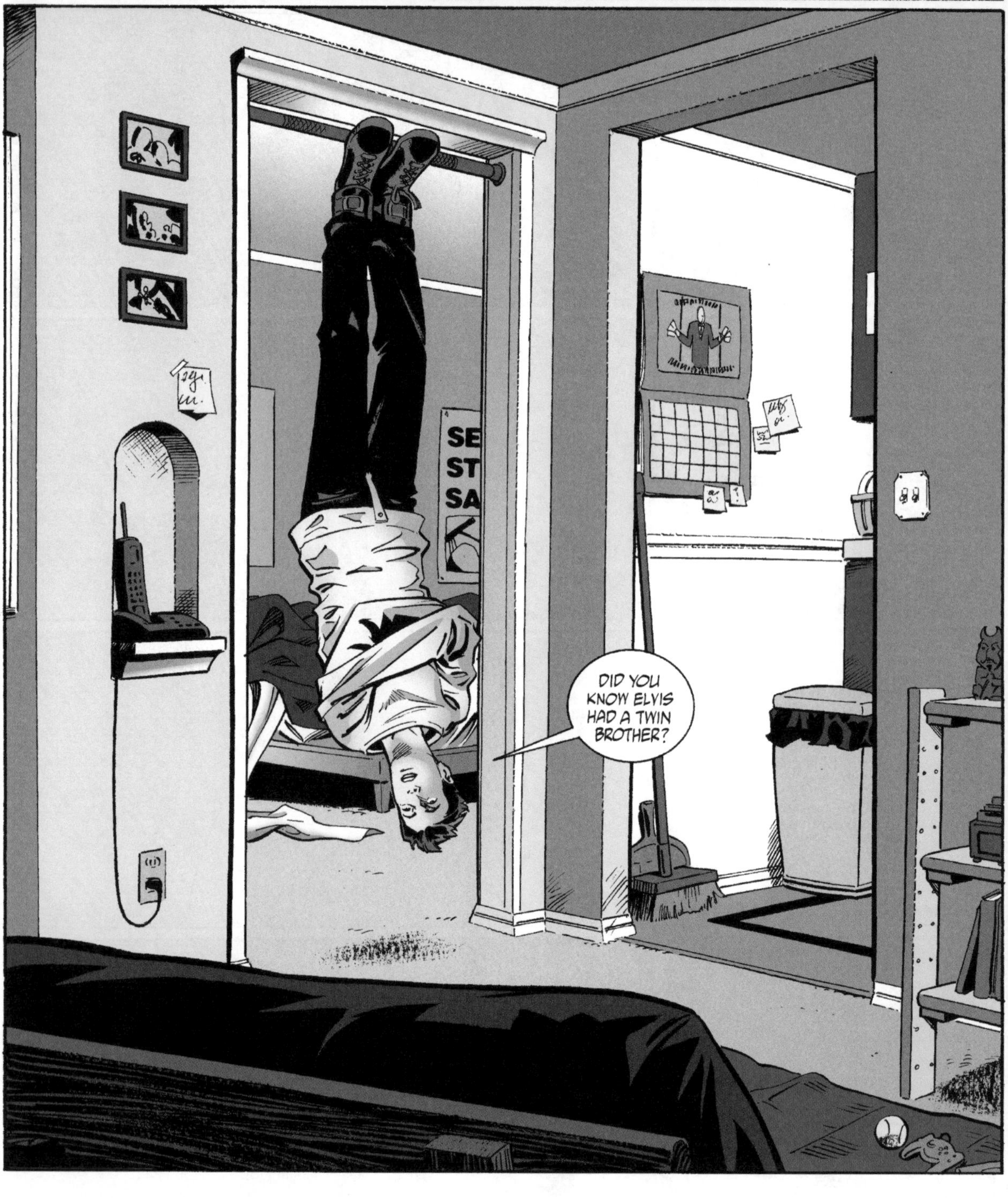
DID YOU KNOW ELVIS HAD A TWIN BROTHER?

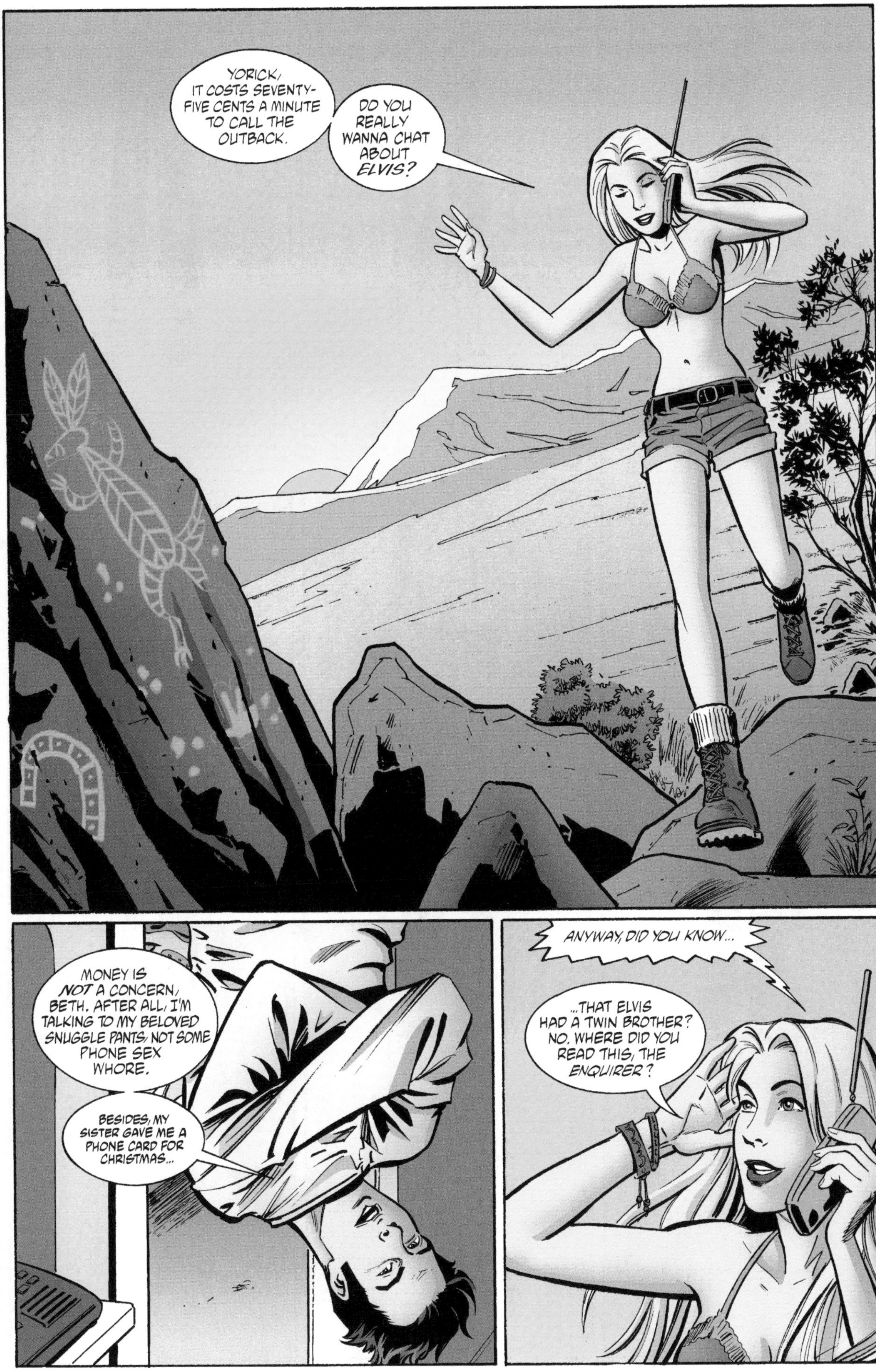
YORICK, IT COSTS SEVENTY-FIVE CENTS A MINUTE TO CALL THE OUTBACK.
DO YOU REALLY WANNA CHAT ABOUT *ELVIS?*
MONEY IS **NOT** A CONCERN, BETH. AFTER ALL, I'M TALKING TO MY BELOVED SNUGGLE PANTS, NOT SOME PHONE SEX WHORE.
BESIDES, MY SISTER GAVE ME A PHONE CARD FOR CHRISTMAS...
ANYWAY, DID YOU KNOW...
...THAT ELVIS HAD A TWIN BROTHER? NO. WHERE DID YOU READ THIS, THE *ENQUIRER?*

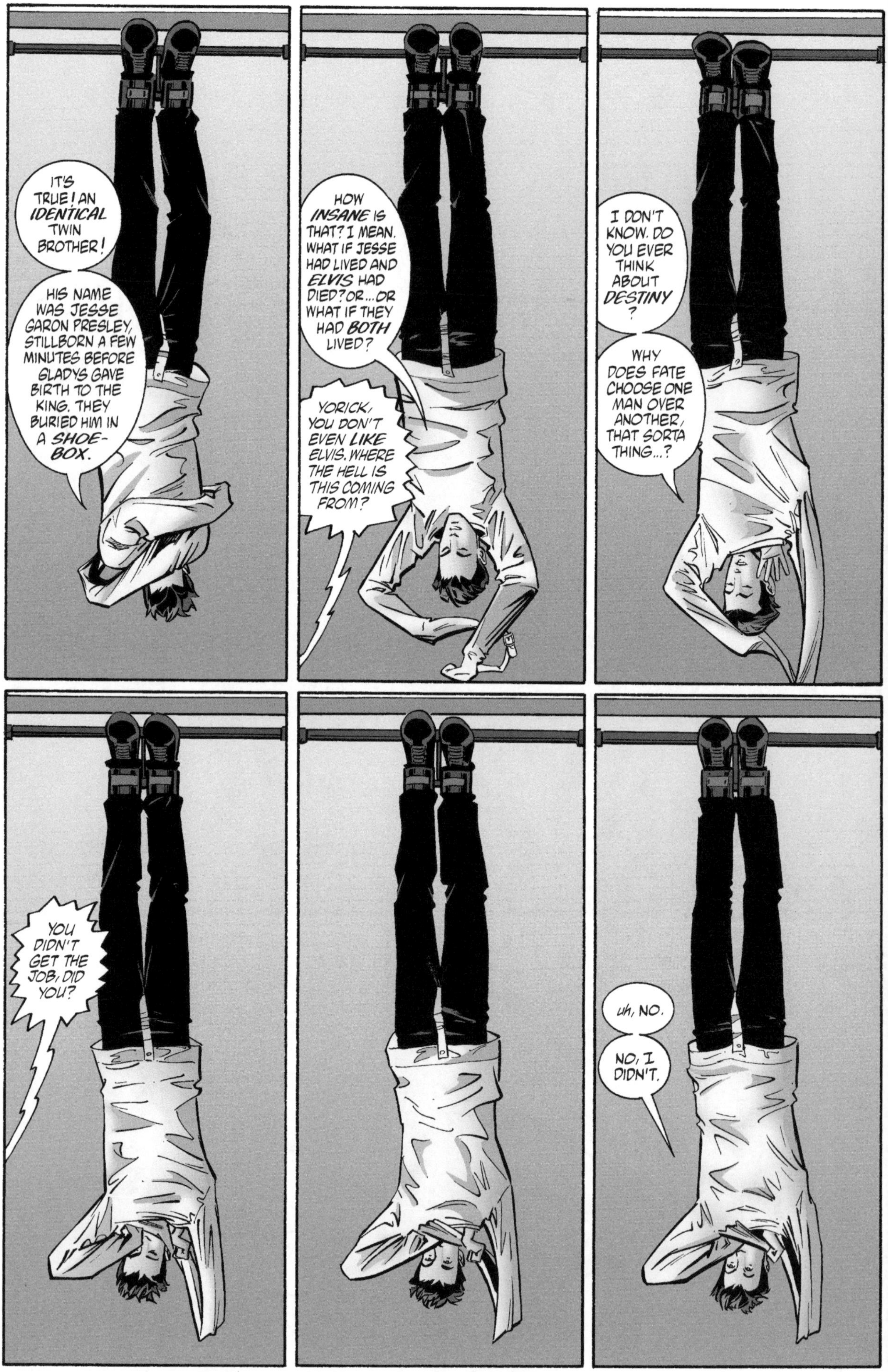
IT'S TRUE! AN IDENTICAL TWIN BROTHER!
HIS NAME WAS JESSE GARON PRESLEY, STILLBORN A FEW MINUTES BEFORE GLADYS GAVE BIRTH TO THE KING. THEY BURIED HIM IN A SHOE-BOX.
HOW INSANE IS THAT? I MEAN. WHAT IF JESSE HAD LIVED AND ELVIS HAD DIED? OR...OR WHAT IF THEY HAD BOTH LIVED?
YORICK, YOU DON'T EVEN LIKE ELVIS. WHERE THE HELL IS THIS COMING FROM?
I DON'T KNOW. DO YOU EVER THINK ABOUT DESTINY?
WHY DOES FATE CHOOSE ONE MAN OVER ANOTHER, THAT SORTA THING...?
YOU DIDN'T GET THE JOB, DID YOU?
uh, NO.
NO, I DIDN'T.

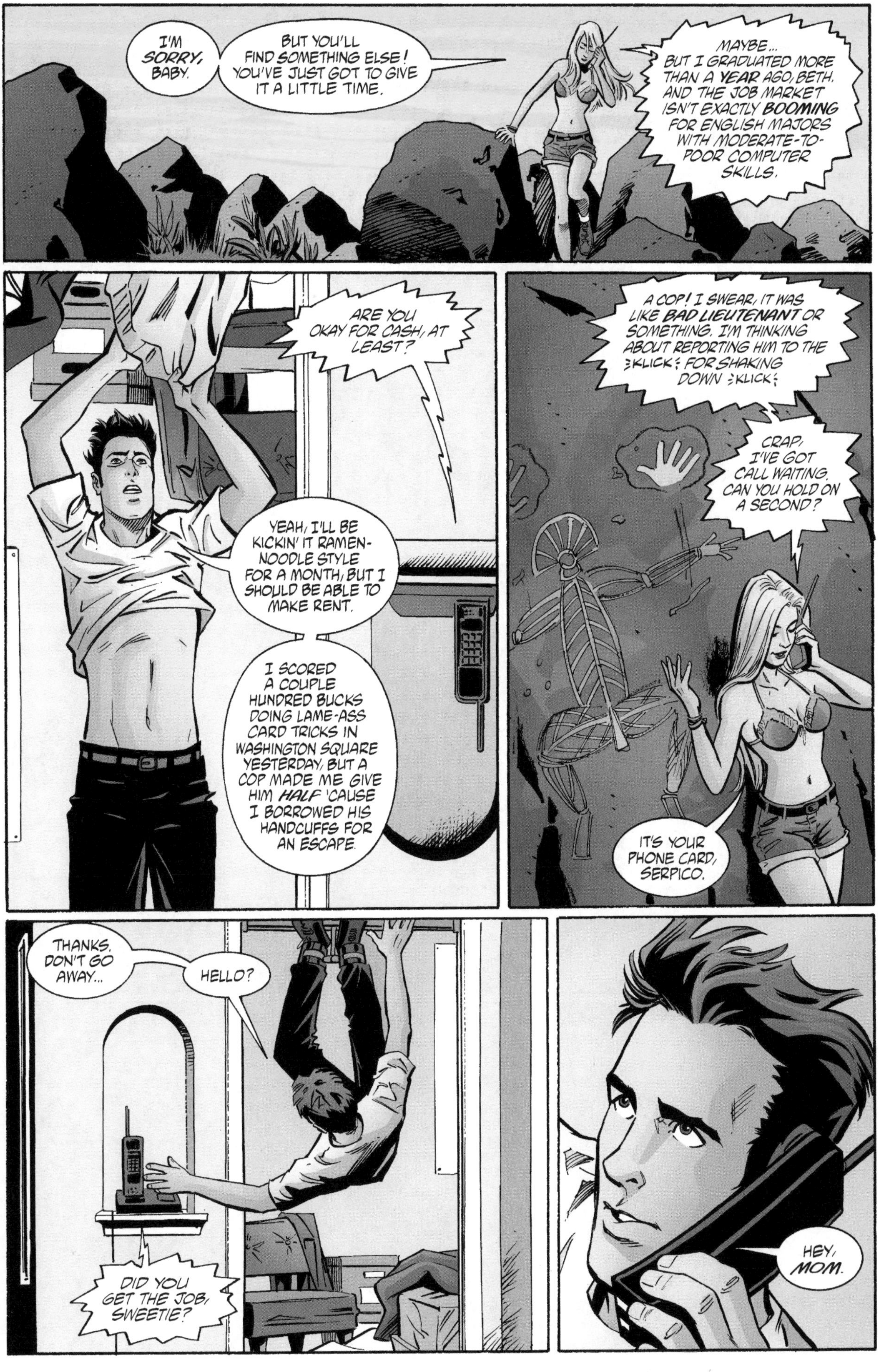
I'M SORRY, BABY.
BUT YOU'LL FIND SOMETHING ELSE! YOU'VE JUST GOT TO GIVE IT A LITTLE TIME.
MAYBE... BUT I GRADUATED MORE THAN A YEAR AGO, BETH, AND THE JOB MARKET ISN'T EXACTLY BOOMING FOR ENGLISH MAJORS WITH MODERATE-TO-POOR COMPUTER SKILLS.
ARE YOU OKAY FOR CASH, AT LEAST?
YEAH, I'LL BE KICKIN' IT RAMEN-NOODLE STYLE FOR A MONTH, BUT I SHOULD BE ABLE TO MAKE RENT.
I SCORED A COUPLE HUNDRED BUCKS DOING LAME-ASS CARD TRICKS IN WASHINGTON SQUARE YESTERDAY, BUT A COP MADE ME GIVE HIM HALF 'CAUSE I BORROWED HIS HANDCUFFS FOR AN ESCAPE.
A COP! I SWEAR, IT WAS LIKE BAD LIEUTENANT OR SOMETHING. I'M THINKING ABOUT REPORTING HIM TO THE KLICK FOR SHAKING DOWN KLICK
CRAP, I'VE GOT CALL WAITING. CAN YOU HOLD ON A SECOND?
IT'S YOUR PHONE CARD, SERPICO.
THANKS. DON'T GO AWAY...
HELLO?
DID YOU GET THE JOB, SWEETIE?
HEY, MOM.

Brooklyn, New York
Twenty-Nine Minutes Ago

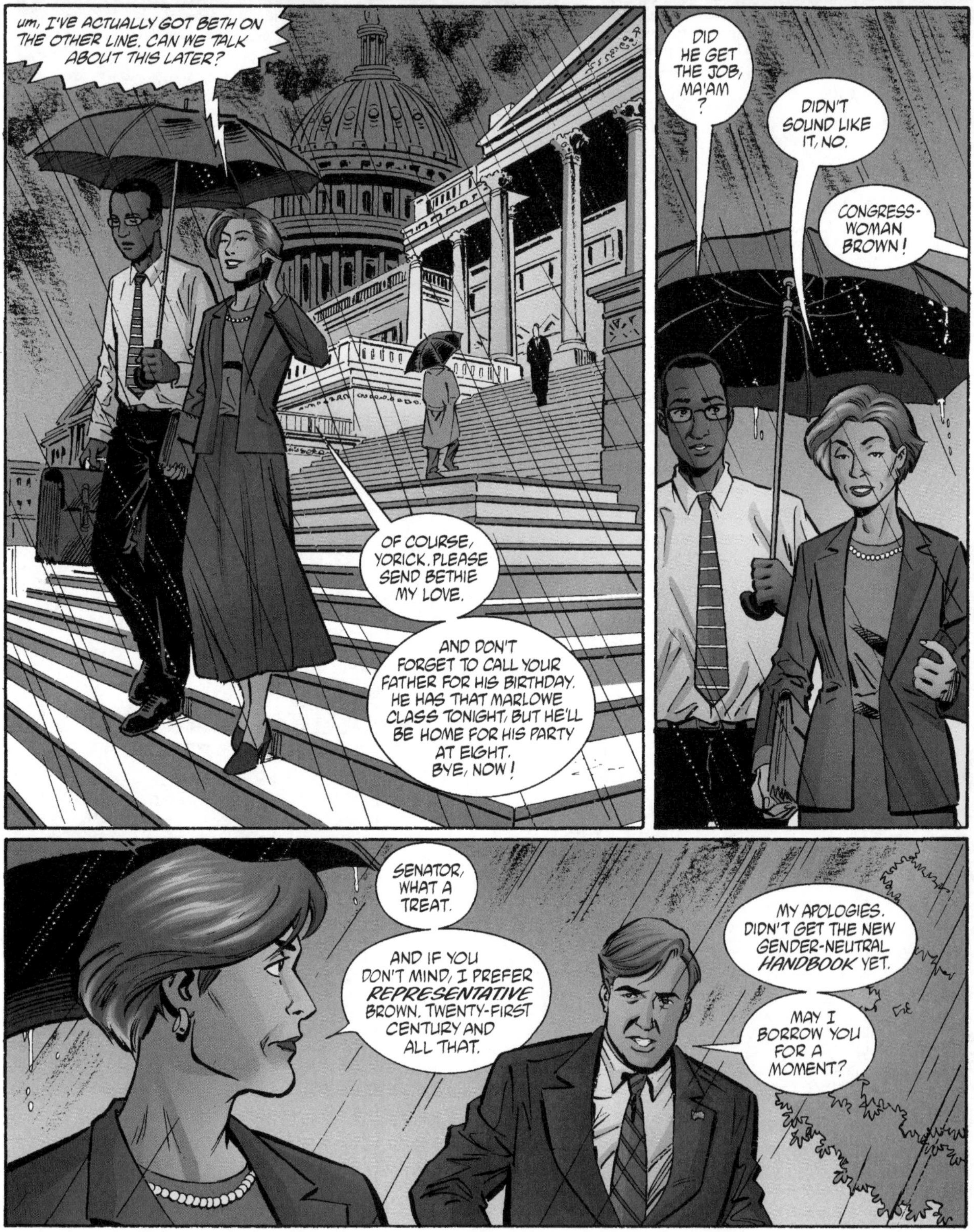
um, I'VE ACTUALLY GOT BETH ON THE OTHER LINE. CAN WE TALK ABOUT THIS LATER?
OF COURSE, YORICK. PLEASE SEND BETHIE MY LOVE.
AND DON'T FORGET TO CALL YOUR FATHER FOR HIS BIRTHDAY. HE HAS THAT MARLOWE CLASS TONIGHT, BUT HE'LL BE HOME FOR HIS PARTY AT EIGHT. BYE, NOW!
DID HE GET THE JOB, MA'AM?
DIDN'T SOUND LIKE IT, NO.
CONGRESS-WOMAN BROWN!
SENATOR, WHAT A TREAT.
AND IF YOU DON'T MIND, I PREFER REPRESENTATIVE BROWN. TWENTY-FIRST CENTURY AND ALL THAT.
MY APOLOGIES. DIDN'T GET THE NEW GENDER-NEUTRAL HANDBOOK YET.
MAY I BORROW YOU FOR A MOMENT?

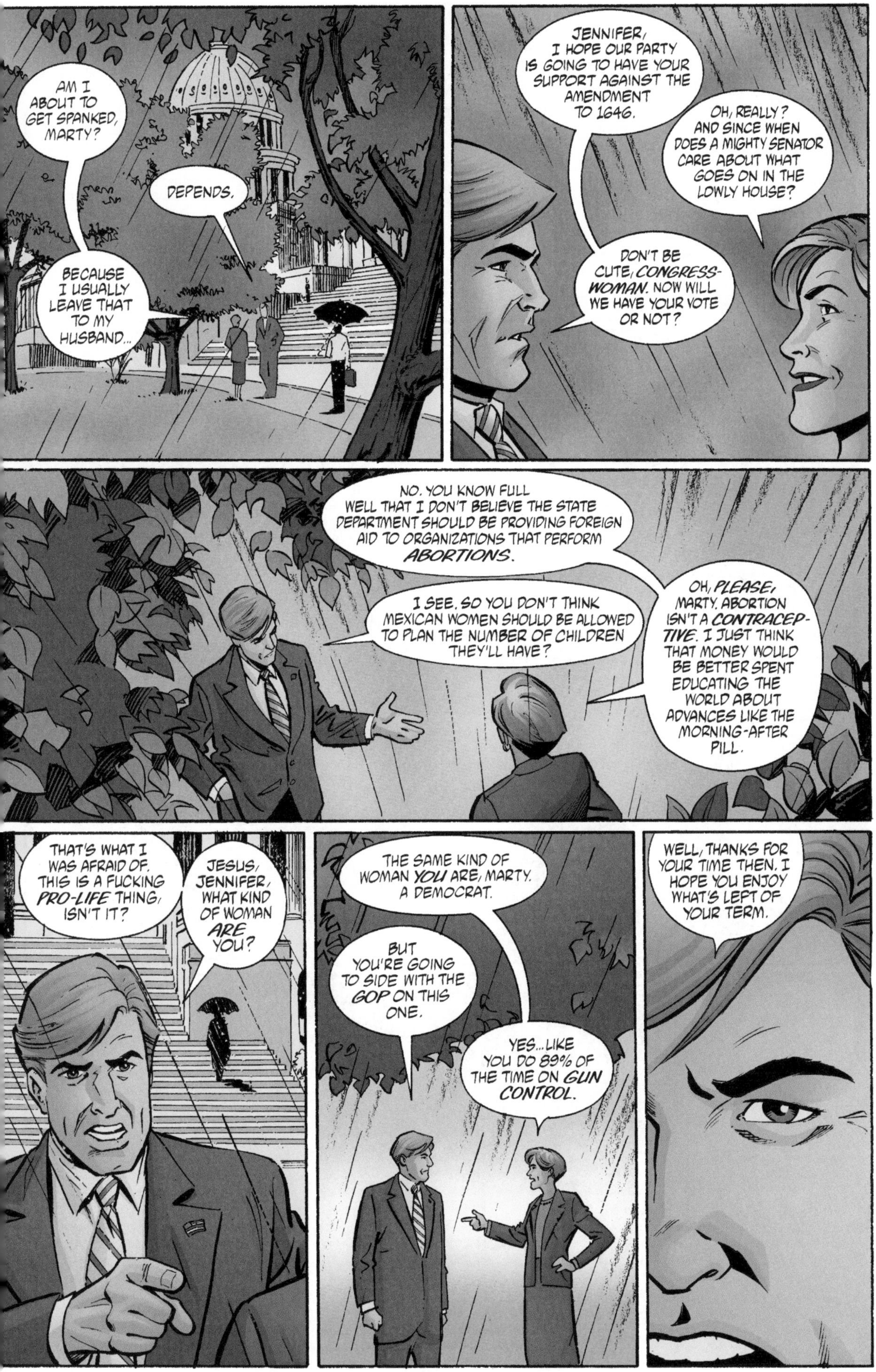

AM I ABOUT TO GET SPANKED, MARTY?
DEPENDS.
BECAUSE I USUALLY LEAVE THAT TO MY HUSBAND...
JENNIFER, I HOPE OUR PARTY IS GOING TO HAVE YOUR SUPPORT AGAINST THE AMENDMENT TO 1646.
OH, REALLY? AND SINCE WHEN DOES A MIGHTY SENATOR CARE ABOUT WHAT GOES ON IN THE LOWLY HOUSE?
DON'T BE CUTE, CONGRESS-WOMAN. NOW WILL WE HAVE YOUR VOTE OR NOT?
NO. YOU KNOW FULL WELL THAT I DON'T BELIEVE THE STATE DEPARTMENT SHOULD BE PROVIDING FOREIGN AID TO ORGANIZATIONS THAT PERFORM ABORTIONS.
I SEE. SO YOU DON'T THINK MEXICAN WOMEN SHOULD BE ALLOWED TO PLAN THE NUMBER OF CHILDREN THEY'LL HAVE?
OH, PLEASE, MARTY. ABORTION ISN'T A CONTRACEP-TIVE. I JUST THINK THAT MONEY WOULD BE BETTER SPENT EDUCATING THE WORLD ABOUT ADVANCES LIKE THE MORNING-AFTER PILL.
THAT'S WHAT I WAS AFRAID OF. THIS IS A FUCKING PRO-LIFE THING, ISN'T IT?
JESUS, JENNIFER, WHAT KIND OF WOMAN ARE YOU?
THE SAME KIND OF WOMAN YOU ARE, MARTY. A DEMOCRAT.
BUT YOU'RE GOING TO SIDE WITH THE GOP ON THIS ONE.
YES... LIKE YOU DO 89% OF THE TIME ON GUN CONTROL.
WELL, THANKS FOR YOUR TIME THEN. I HOPE YOU ENJOY WHAT'S LEFT OF YOUR TERM.

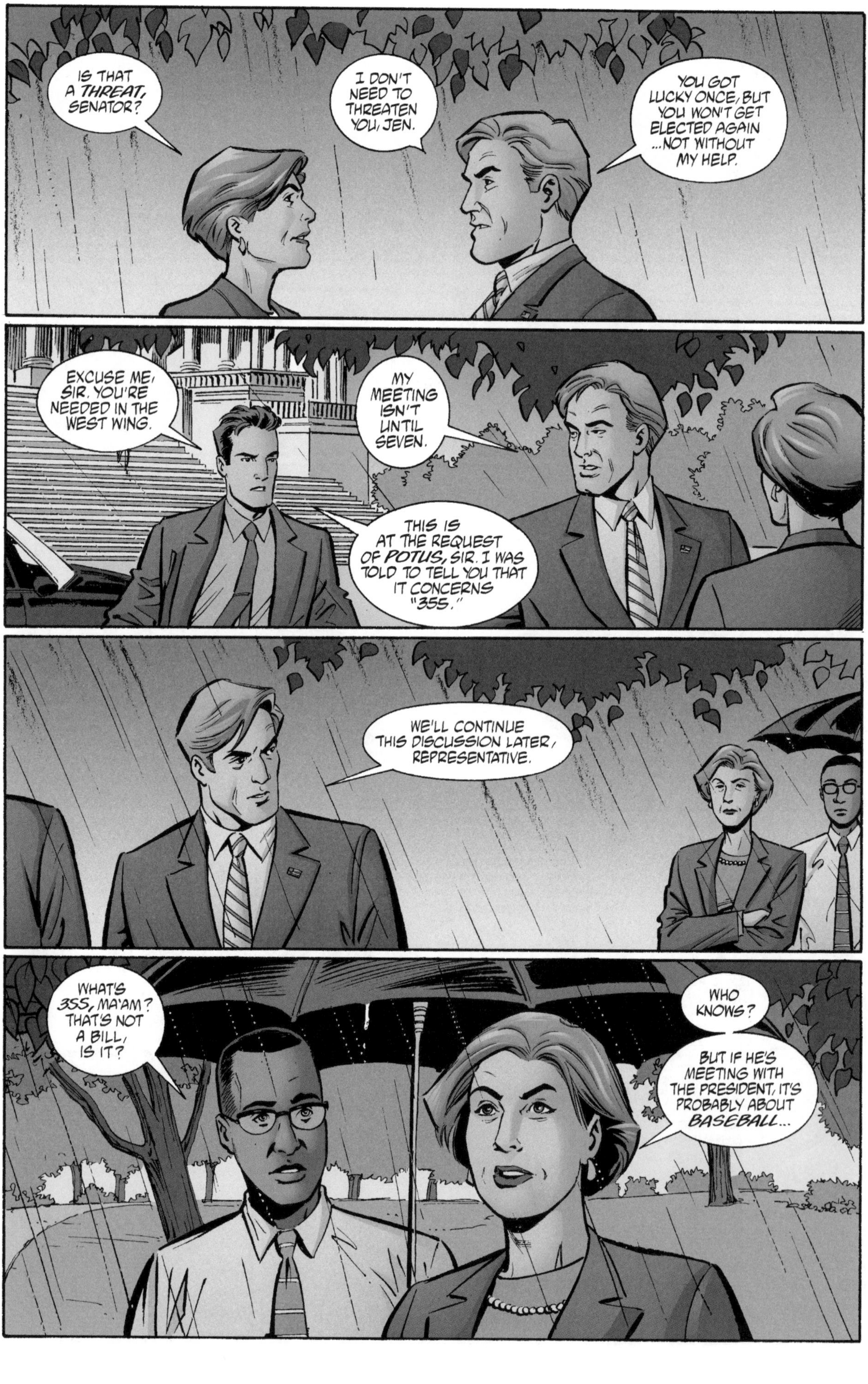
IS THAT A THREAT, SENATOR?
I DON'T NEED TO THREATEN YOU, JEN.
YOU GOT LUCKY ONCE, BUT YOU WON'T GET ELECTED AGAIN ...NOT WITHOUT MY HELP.
EXCUSE ME, SIR. YOU'RE NEEDED IN THE WEST WING.
MY MEETING ISN'T UNTIL SEVEN.
THIS IS AT THE REQUEST OF POTUS, SIR. I WAS TOLD TO TELL YOU THAT IT CONCERNS "355."
WE'LL CONTINUE THIS DISCUSSION LATER, REPRESENTATIVE.
WHAT'S 355, MA'AM? THAT'S NOT A BILL, IS IT?
WHO KNOWS?
BUT IF HE'S MEETING WITH THE PRESIDENT, IT'S PROBABLY ABOUT BASEBALL...

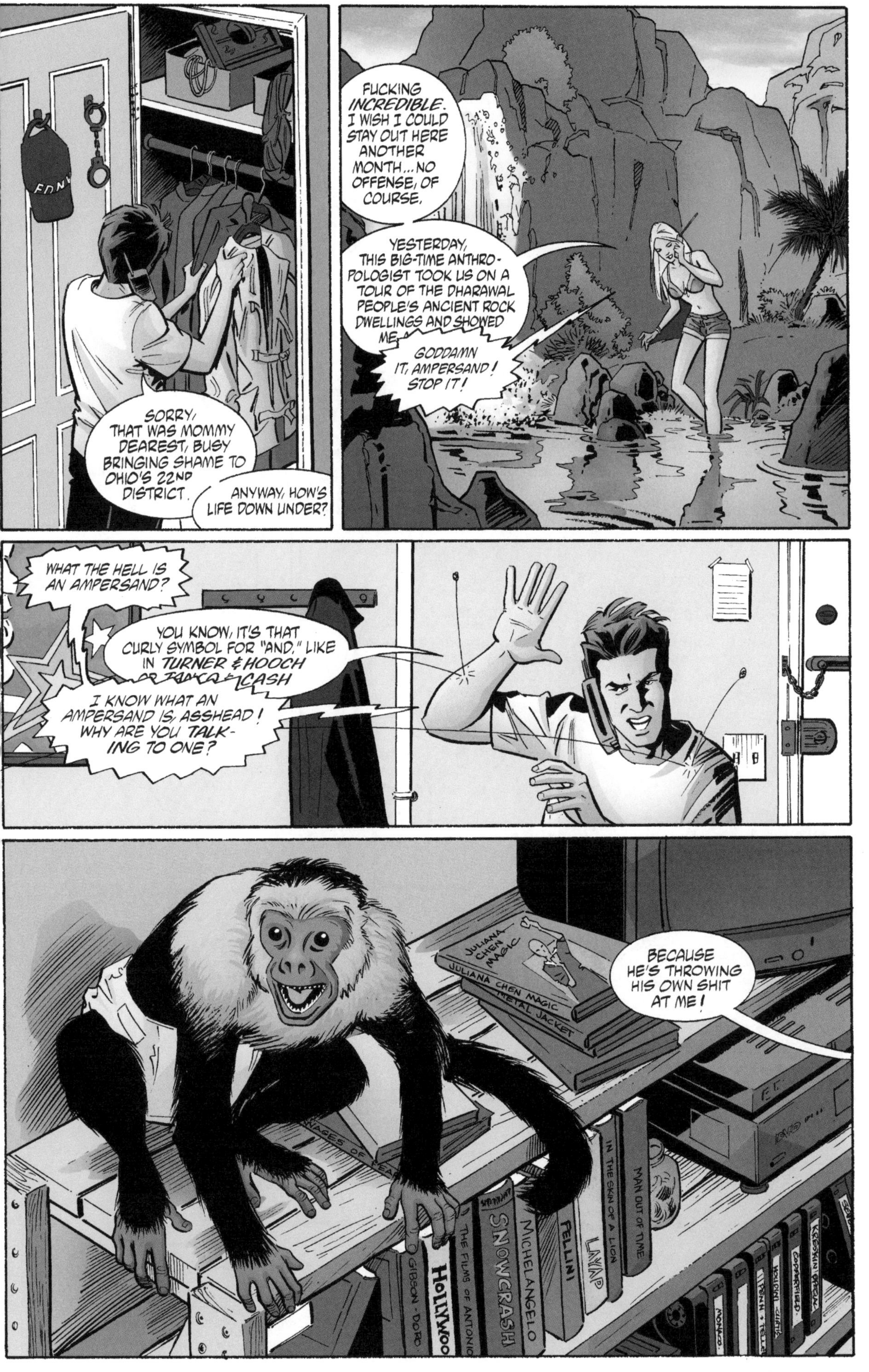
SORRY, THAT WAS MOMMY DEAREST, BUSY BRINGING SHAME TO OHIO'S 22ND DISTRICT.
ANYWAY, HOW'S LIFE DOWN UNDER?
FUCKING INCREDIBLE. I WISH I COULD STAY OUT HERE ANOTHER MONTH... NO OFFENSE, OF COURSE.
YESTERDAY, THIS BIG-TIME ANTHROPOLOGIST TOOK US ON A TOUR OF THE DHARAWAL PEOPLE'S ANCIENT ROCK DWELLINGS AND SHOWED ME
GODDAMN IT, AMPERSAND! STOP IT!
WHAT THE HELL IS AN AMPERSAND?
YOU KNOW, IT'S THAT CURLY SYMBOL FOR "AND," LIKE IN TURNER & HOOCH
I KNOW WHAT AN AMPERSAND IS, ASSHEAD! WHY ARE YOU TALKING TO ONE?
BECAUSE HE'S THROWING HIS OWN SHIT AT ME!
JULIANA CHEN MAGIC
SNOWCRASH
MICHELANGELO
FELLINI
IN THE SKIN OF A LION
MAN OUT OF TIME

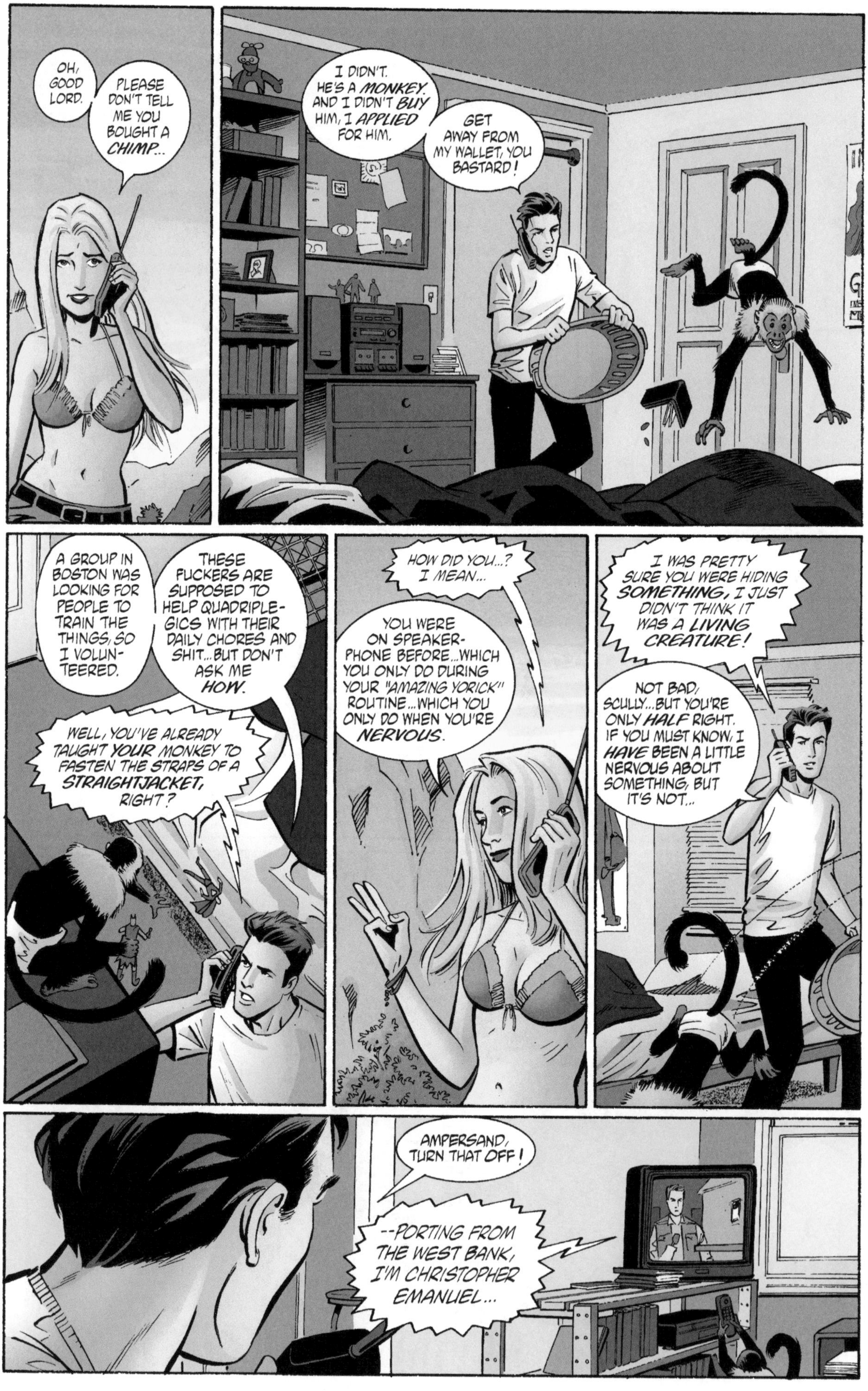
OH, GOOD LORD.
PLEASE DON'T TELL ME YOU BOUGHT A CHIMP...
I DIDN'T. HE'S A MONKEY. AND I DIDN'T BUY HIM, I APPLIED FOR HIM.
GET AWAY FROM MY WALLET, YOU BASTARD!
A GROUP IN BOSTON WAS LOOKING FOR PEOPLE TO TRAIN THE THINGS, SO I VOLUNTEERED.
THESE FUCKERS ARE SUPPOSED TO HELP QUADRIPLEGICS WITH THEIR DAILY CHORES AND SHIT...BUT DON'T ASK ME HOW.
WELL, YOU'VE ALREADY TAUGHT YOUR MONKEY TO FASTEN THE STRAPS OF A STRAIGHTJACKET, RIGHT?
HOW DID YOU...? I MEAN...
YOU WERE ON SPEAKERPHONE BEFORE...WHICH YOU ONLY DO DURING YOUR "AMAZING YORICK" ROUTINE...WHICH YOU ONLY DO WHEN YOU'RE NERVOUS.
I WAS PRETTY SURE YOU WERE HIDING SOMETHING, I JUST DIDN'T THINK IT WAS A LIVING CREATURE!
NOT BAD, SCULLY...BUT YOU'RE ONLY HALF RIGHT. IF YOU MUST KNOW, I HAVE BEEN A LITTLE NERVOUS ABOUT SOMETHING, BUT IT'S NOT...
AMPERSAND, TURN THAT OFF!
--PORTING FROM THE WEST BANK, I'M CHRISTOPHER EMANUEL...

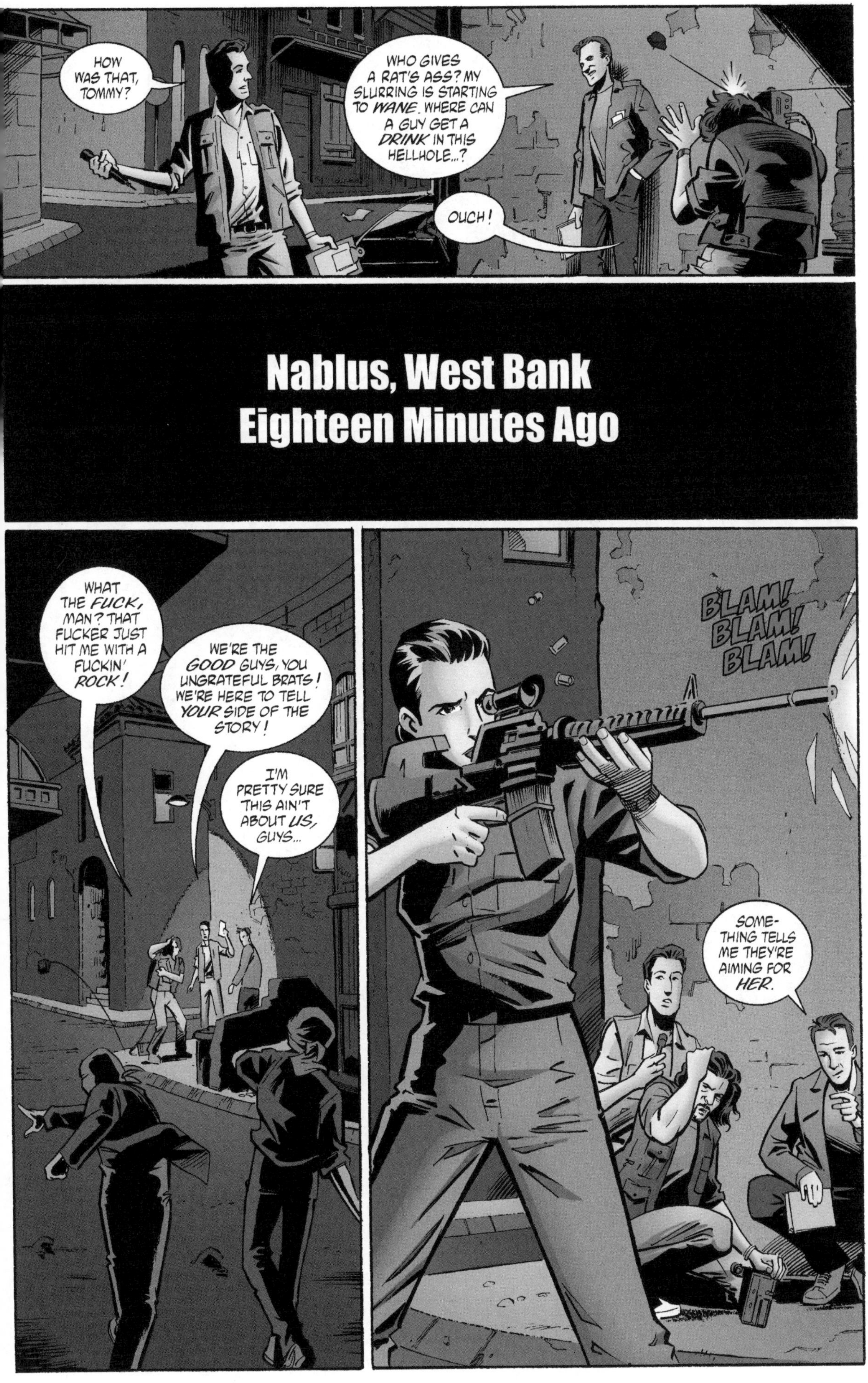
HOW WAS THAT, TOMMY?
WHO GIVES A RAT'S ASS? MY SLURRING IS STARTING TO WANE. WHERE CAN A GUY GET A DRINK IN THIS HELLHOLE...?
OUCH!
Nablus, West Bank
Eighteen Minutes Ago
WHAT THE FUCK, MAN? THAT FUCKER JUST HIT ME WITH A FUCKIN' ROCK!
WE'RE THE GOOD GUYS, YOU UNGRATEFUL BRATS! WE'RE HERE TO TELL YOUR SIDE OF THE STORY!
I'M PRETTY SURE THIS AIN'T ABOUT US, GUYS...
BLAM! BLAM! BLAM!
SOME-THING TELLS ME THEY'RE AIMING FOR HER.

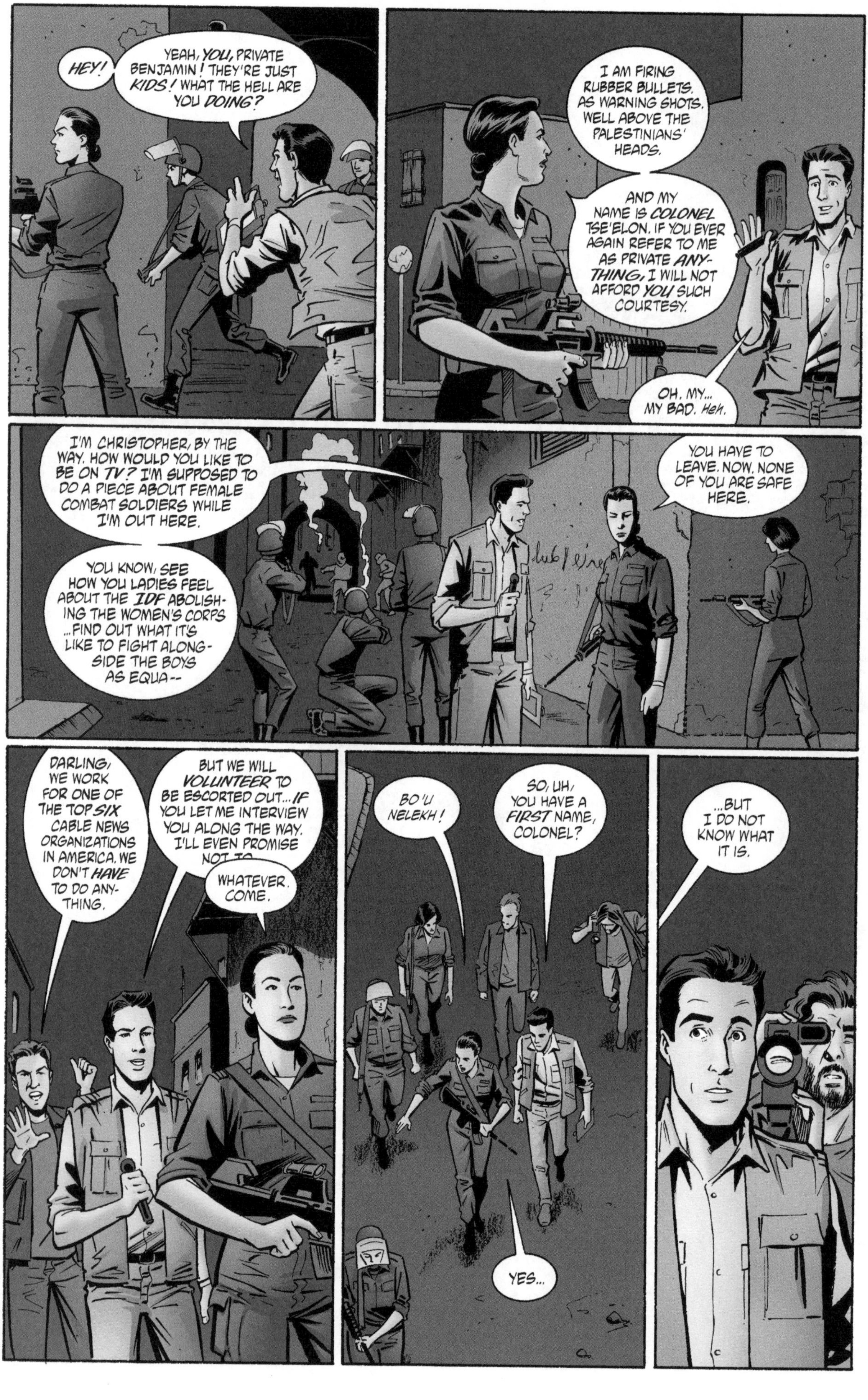
HEY!
YEAH, YOU, PRIVATE BENJAMIN! THEY'RE JUST KIDS! WHAT THE HELL ARE YOU DOING?
I AM FIRING RUBBER BULLETS. AS WARNING SHOTS. WELL ABOVE THE PALESTINIANS' HEADS.
AND MY NAME IS COLONEL TSE'ELON. IF YOU EVER AGAIN REFER TO ME AS PRIVATE ANYTHING, I WILL NOT AFFORD YOU SUCH COURTESY.
OH. MY... MY BAD. Heh.
I'M CHRISTOPHER, BY THE WAY. HOW WOULD YOU LIKE TO BE ON TV? I'M SUPPOSED TO DO A PIECE ABOUT FEMALE COMBAT SOLDIERS WHILE I'M OUT HERE.
YOU KNOW, SEE HOW YOU LADIES FEEL ABOUT THE IDF ABOLISHING THE WOMEN'S CORPS ...FIND OUT WHAT IT'S LIKE TO FIGHT ALONGSIDE THE BOYS AS EQUA--
YOU HAVE TO LEAVE. NOW. NONE OF YOU ARE SAFE HERE.
DARLING, WE WORK FOR ONE OF THE TOP SIX CABLE NEWS ORGANIZATIONS IN AMERICA. WE DON'T HAVE TO DO ANYTHING.
BUT WE WILL VOLUNTEER TO BE ESCORTED OUT... IF YOU LET ME INTERVIEW YOU ALONG THE WAY. I'LL EVEN PROMISE NOT TO
WHATEVER. COME.
BO'U NELEKH!
SO, UH, YOU HAVE A FIRST NAME, COLONEL?
YES...
...BUT I DO NOT KNOW WHAT IT IS.

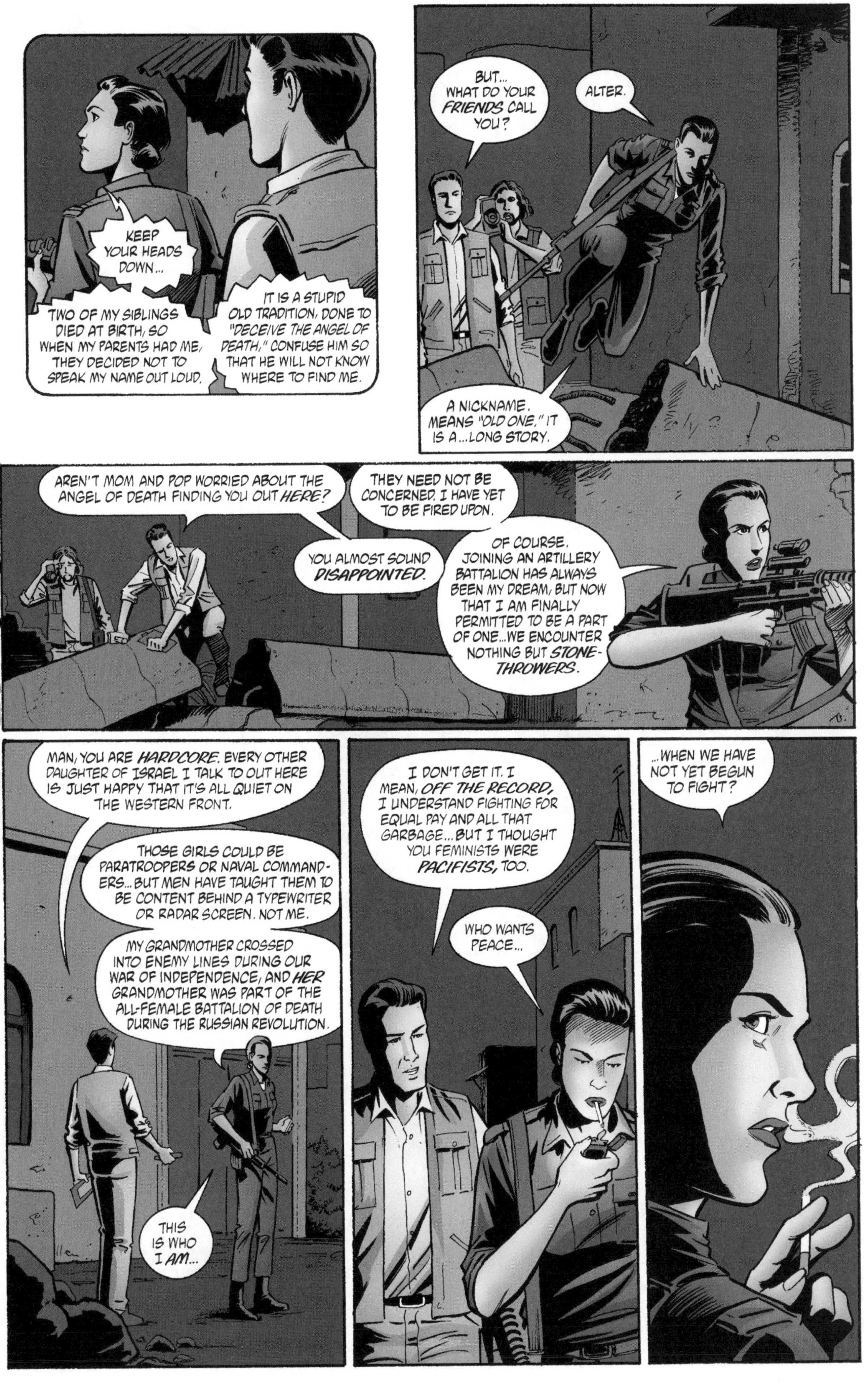
KEEP YOUR HEADS DOWN...
TWO OF MY SIBLINGS DIED AT BIRTH, SO WHEN MY PARENTS HAD ME, THEY DECIDED NOT TO SPEAK MY NAME OUT LOUD.
IT IS A STUPID OLD TRADITION, DONE TO "DECEIVE THE ANGEL OF DEATH," CONFUSE HIM SO THAT HE WILL NOT KNOW WHERE TO FIND ME.
BUT... WHAT DO YOUR FRIENDS CALL YOU?
ALTER.
A NICKNAME. MEANS "OLD ONE." IT IS A...LONG STORY.
AREN'T MOM AND POP WORRIED ABOUT THE ANGEL OF DEATH FINDING YOU OUT HERE?
THEY NEED NOT BE CONCERNED. I HAVE YET TO BE FIRED UPON.
YOU ALMOST SOUND DISAPPOINTED.
OF COURSE. JOINING AN ARTILLERY BATTALION HAS ALWAYS BEEN MY DREAM, BUT NOW THAT I AM FINALLY PERMITTED TO BE A PART OF ONE...WE ENCOUNTER NOTHING BUT STONE-THROWERS.
MAN, YOU ARE HARDCORE. EVERY OTHER DAUGHTER OF ISRAEL I TALK TO OUT HERE IS JUST HAPPY THAT IT'S ALL QUIET ON THE WESTERN FRONT.
THOSE GIRLS COULD BE PARATROOPERS OR NAVAL COMMANDERS...BUT MEN HAVE TAUGHT THEM TO BE CONTENT BEHIND A TYPEWRITER OR RADAR SCREEN. NOT ME.
MY GRANDMOTHER CROSSED INTO ENEMY LINES DURING OUR WAR OF INDEPENDENCE, AND HER GRANDMOTHER WAS PART OF THE ALL-FEMALE BATTALION OF DEATH DURING THE RUSSIAN REVOLUTION.
THIS IS WHO I AM...
I DON'T GET IT. I MEAN, OFF THE RECORD, I UNDERSTAND FIGHTING FOR EQUAL PAY AND ALL THAT GARBAGE...BUT I THOUGHT YOU FEMINISTS WERE PACIFISTS, TOO.
WHO WANTS PEACE...
...WHEN WE HAVE NOT YET BEGUN TO FIGHT?

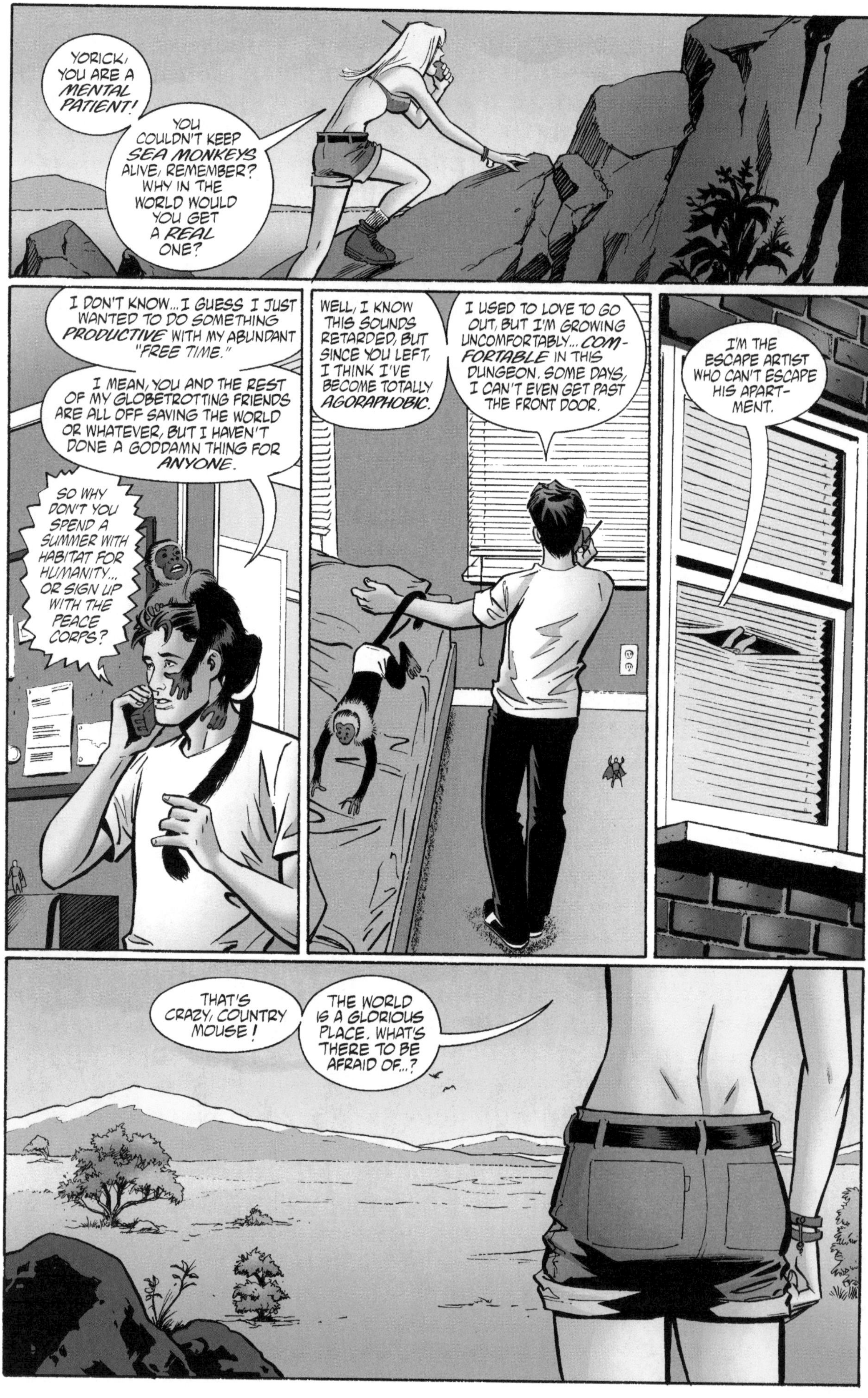
YORICK, YOU ARE A MENTAL PATIENT!
YOU COULDN'T KEEP SEA MONKEYS ALIVE, REMEMBER? WHY IN THE WORLD WOULD YOU GET A REAL ONE?
I DON'T KNOW... I GUESS I JUST WANTED TO DO SOMETHING PRODUCTIVE WITH MY ABUNDANT "FREE TIME."
I MEAN, YOU AND THE REST OF MY GLOBETROTTING FRIENDS ARE ALL OFF SAVING THE WORLD OR WHATEVER, BUT I HAVEN'T DONE A GODDAMN THING FOR ANYONE.
SO WHY DON'T YOU SPEND A SUMMER WITH HABITAT FOR HUMANITY... OR SIGN UP WITH THE PEACE CORPS?
WELL, I KNOW THIS SOUNDS RETARDED, BUT SINCE YOU LEFT, I THINK I'VE BECOME TOTALLY AGORAPHOBIC.
I USED TO LOVE TO GO OUT, BUT I'M GROWING UNCOMFORTABLY... COMFORTABLE IN THIS DUNGEON. SOME DAYS, I CAN'T EVEN GET PAST THE FRONT DOOR.
I'M THE ESCAPE ARTIST WHO CAN'T ESCAPE HIS APARTMENT.
THAT'S CRAZY, COUNTRY MOUSE!
THE WORLD IS A GLORIOUS PLACE. WHAT'S THERE TO BE AFRAID OF...?

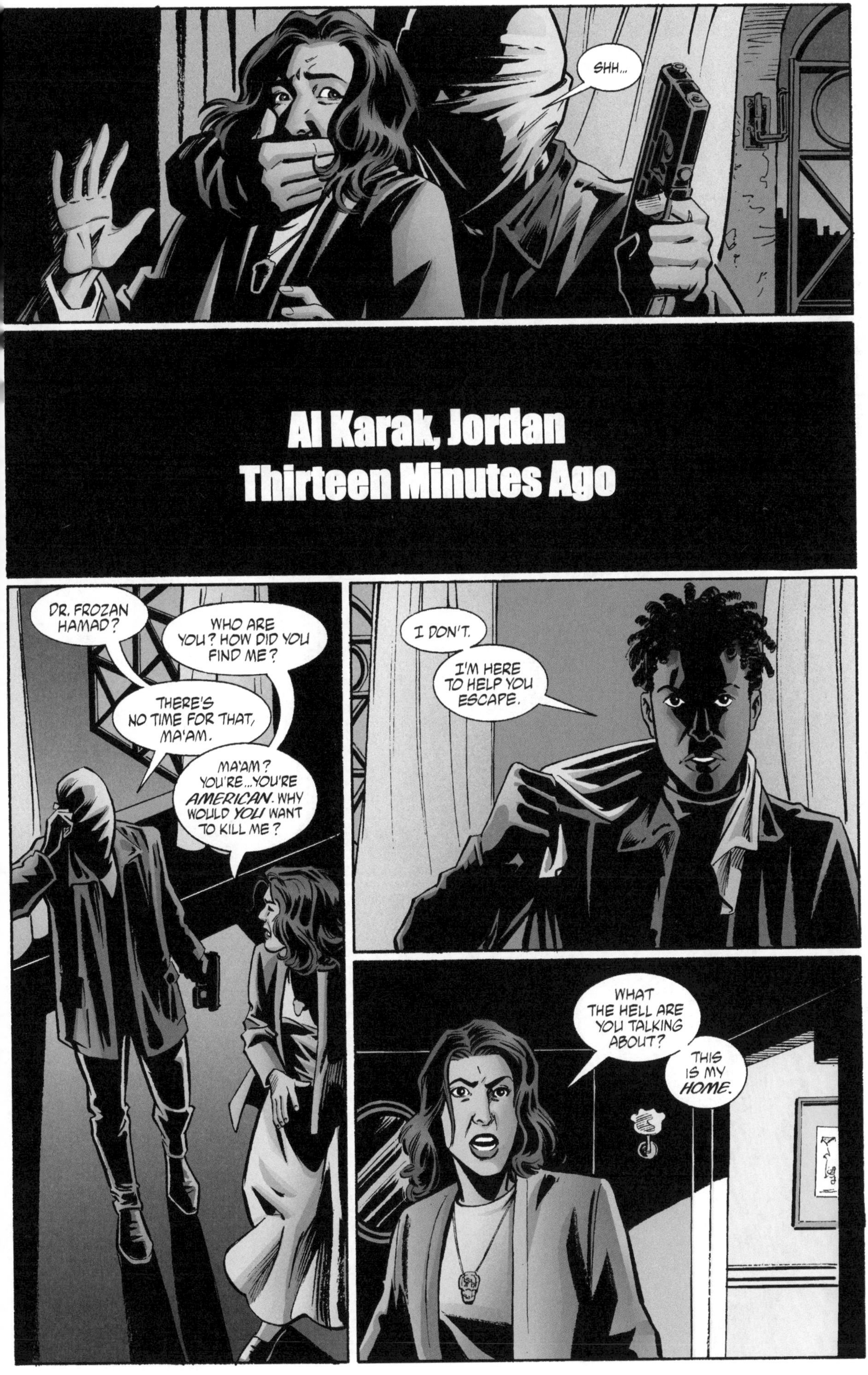
SHH...
Al Karak, Jordan
Thirteen Minutes Ago
DR. FROZAN HAMAD?
WHO ARE YOU? HOW DID YOU FIND ME?
THERE'S NO TIME FOR THAT, MA'AM.
MA'AM? YOU'RE...YOU'RE AMERICAN. WHY WOULD YOU WANT TO KILL ME?
I DON'T.
I'M HERE TO HELP YOU ESCAPE.
WHAT THE HELL ARE YOU TALKING ABOUT?
THIS IS MY HOME.

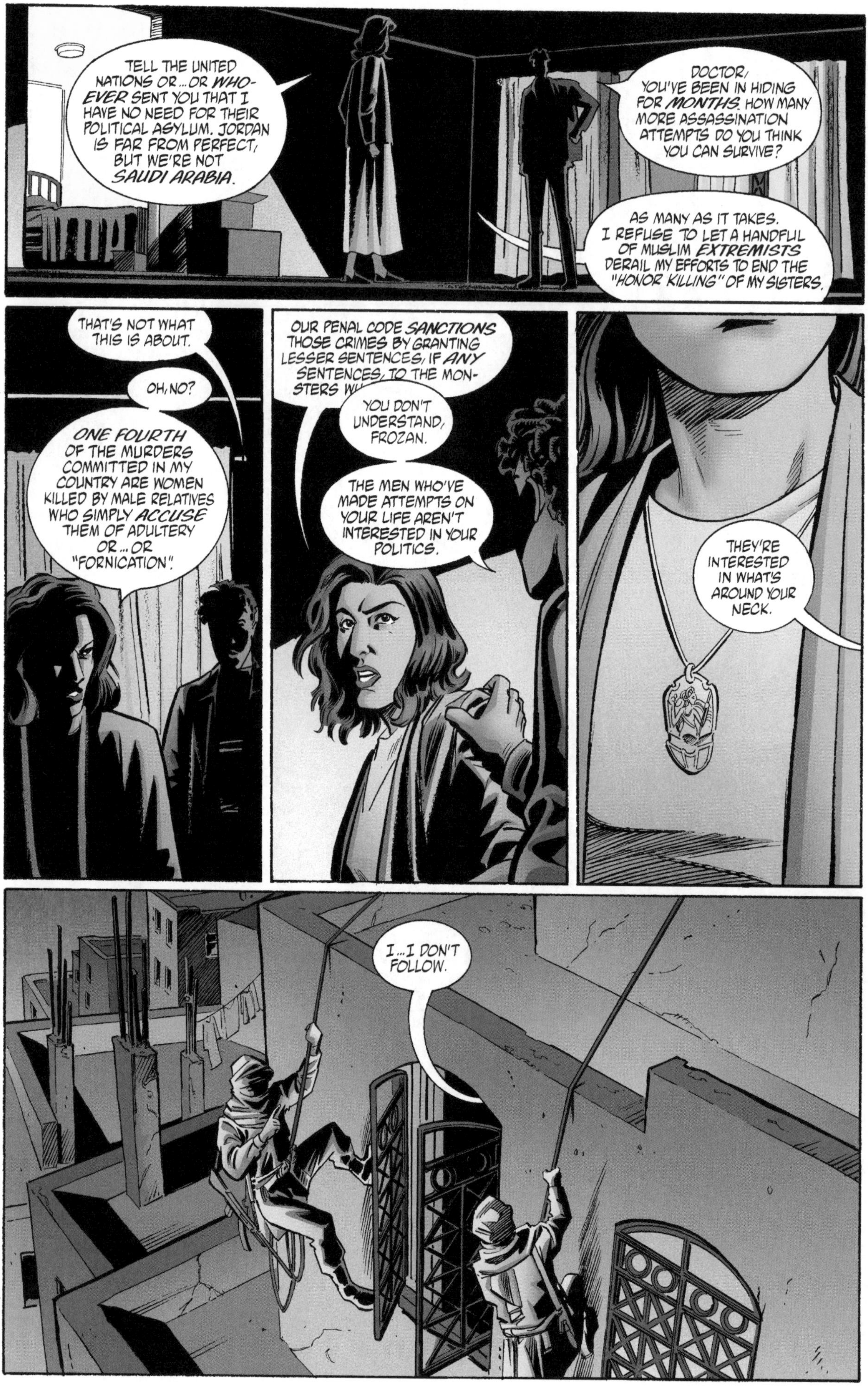
TELL THE UNITED NATIONS OR...OR WHO-EVER SENT YOU THAT I HAVE NO NEED FOR THEIR POLITICAL ASYLUM. JORDAN IS FAR FROM PERFECT, BUT WE'RE NOT SAUDI ARABIA.
DOCTOR, YOU'VE BEEN IN HIDING FOR MONTHS. HOW MANY MORE ASSASSINATION ATTEMPTS DO YOU THINK YOU CAN SURVIVE?
AS MANY AS IT TAKES. I REFUSE TO LET A HANDFUL OF MUSLIM EXTREMISTS DERAIL MY EFFORTS TO END THE "HONOR KILLING" OF MY SISTERS.
THAT'S NOT WHAT THIS IS ABOUT.
OH, NO?
ONE FOURTH OF THE MURDERS COMMITTED IN MY COUNTRY ARE WOMEN KILLED BY MALE RELATIVES WHO SIMPLY ACCUSE THEM OF ADULTERY OR...OR "FORNICATION".
OUR PENAL CODE SANCTIONS THOSE CRIMES BY GRANTING LESSER SENTENCES, IF ANY SENTENCES, TO THE MON-STERS WH
YOU DON'T UNDERSTAND, FROZAN.
THE MEN WHO'VE MADE ATTEMPTS ON YOUR LIFE AREN'T INTERESTED IN YOUR POLITICS.
THEY'RE INTERESTED IN WHAT'S AROUND YOUR NECK.
I...I DON'T FOLLOW.

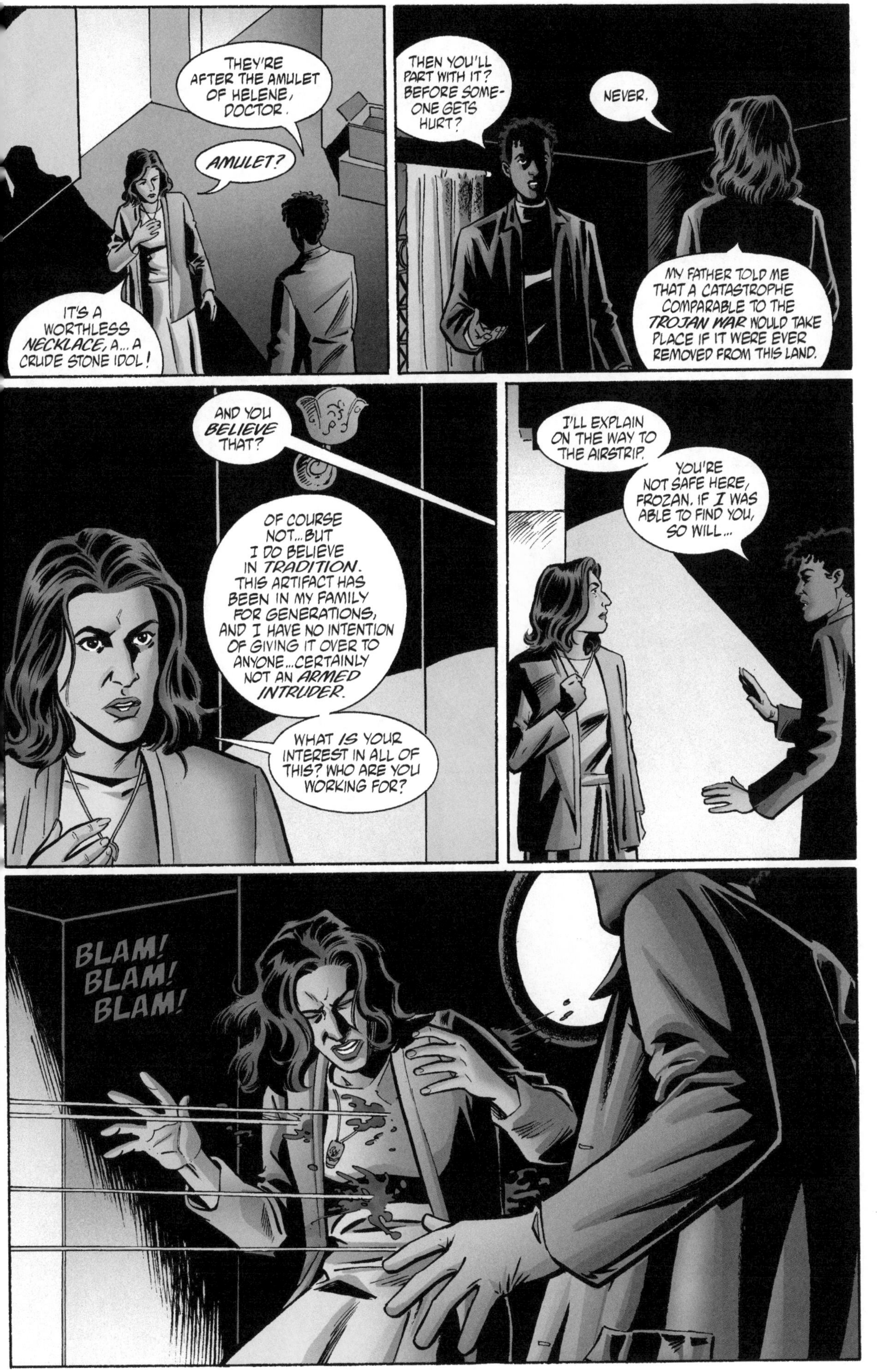
THEY'RE AFTER THE AMULET OF HELENE, DOCTOR.
AMULET?
IT'S A WORTHLESS NECKLACE, A... A CRUDE STONE IDOL!
THEN YOU'LL PART WITH IT? BEFORE SOME-ONE GETS HURT?
NEVER.
MY FATHER TOLD ME THAT A CATASTROPHE COMPARABLE TO THE TROJAN WAR WOULD TAKE PLACE IF IT WERE EVER REMOVED FROM THIS LAND.
AND YOU BELIEVE THAT?
OF COURSE NOT...BUT I DO BELIEVE IN TRADITION. THIS ARTIFACT HAS BEEN IN MY FAMILY FOR GENERATIONS, AND I HAVE NO INTENTION OF GIVING IT OVER TO ANYONE...CERTAINLY NOT AN ARMED INTRUDER.
WHAT IS YOUR INTEREST IN ALL OF THIS? WHO ARE YOU WORKING FOR?
I'LL EXPLAIN ON THE WAY TO THE AIRSTRIP.
YOU'RE NOT SAFE HERE, FROZAN. IF I WAS ABLE TO FIND YOU, SO WILL...
BLAM! BLAM! BLAM!

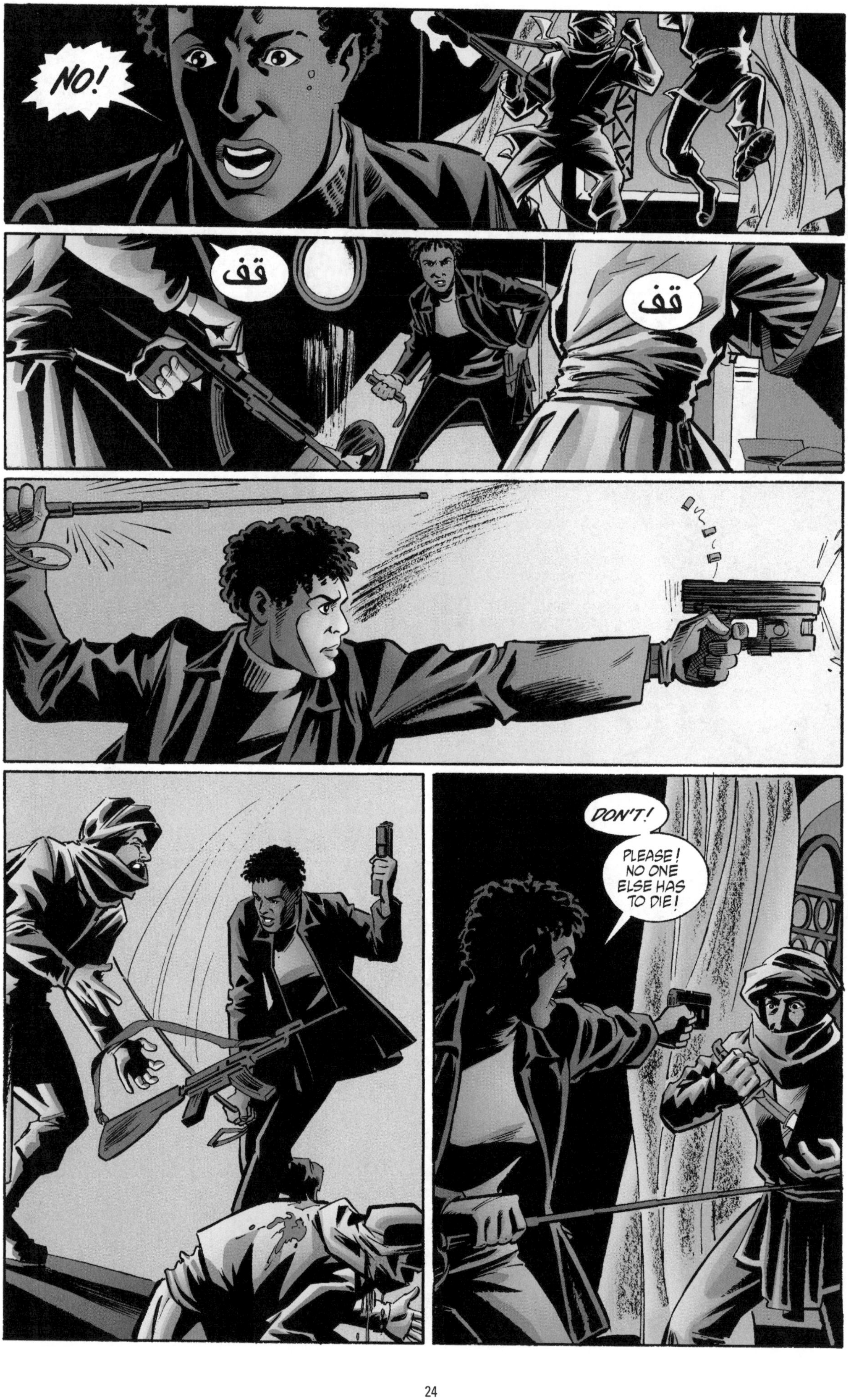
NO!
قف
قف
DON'T!
PLEASE! NO ONE ELSE HAS TO DIE!

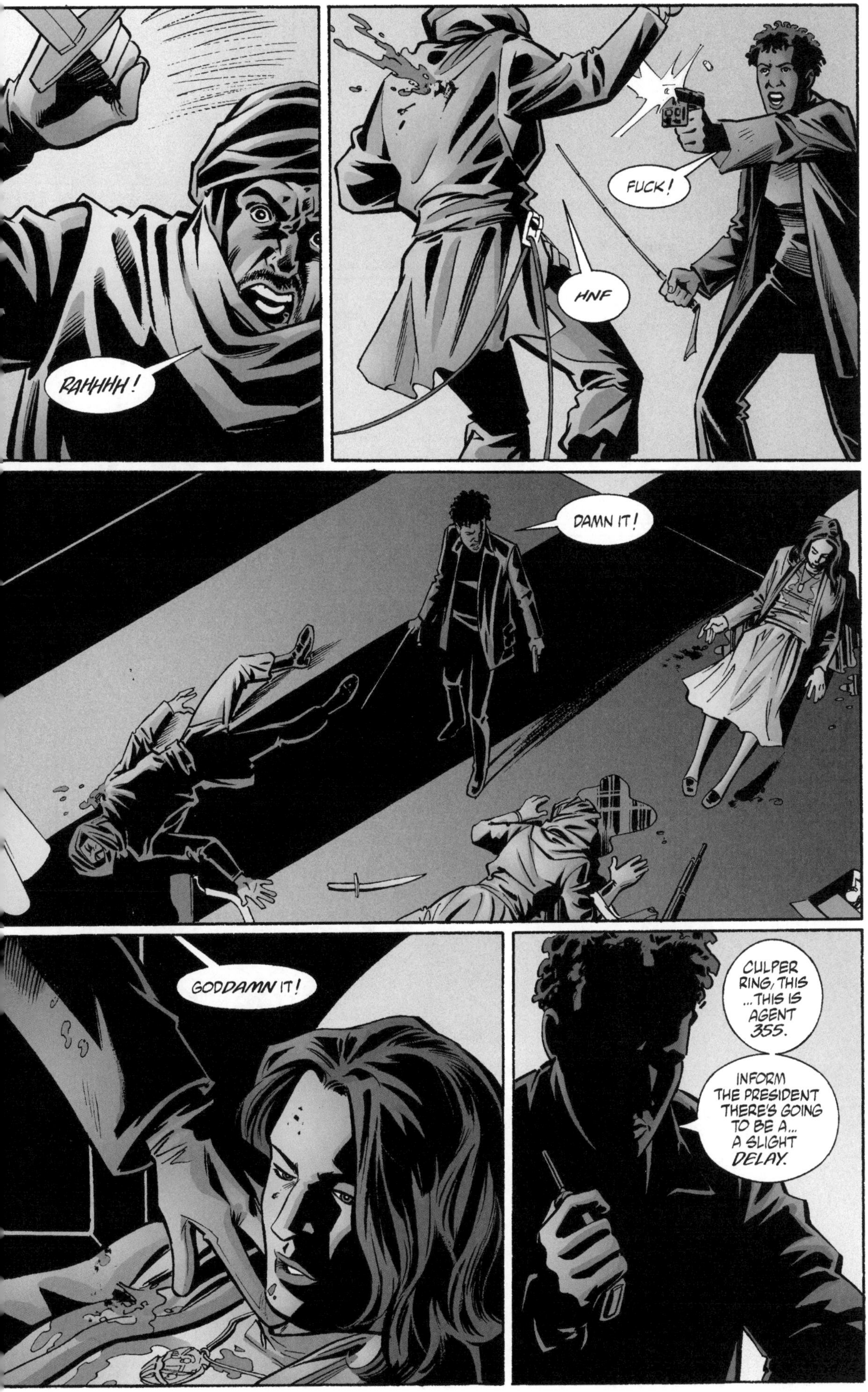
RAHHHH!
FUCK!
HNF
DAMN IT!
GODDAMN IT!
CULPER RING, THIS ...THIS IS AGENT 355.
INFORM THE PRESIDENT THERE'S GOING TO BE A... A SLIGHT DELAY.

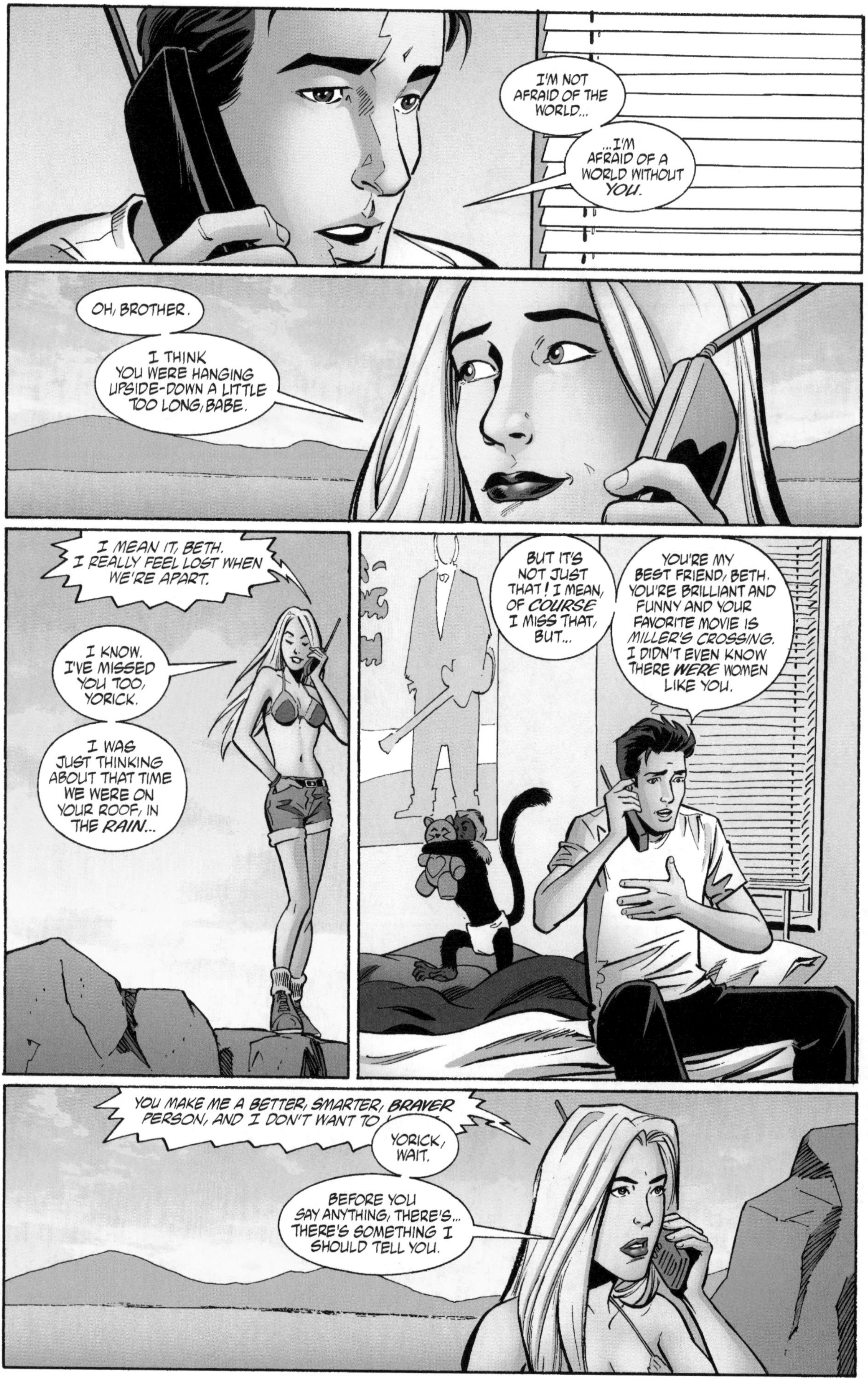
I'M NOT AFRAID OF THE WORLD...
...I'M AFRAID OF A WORLD WITHOUT YOU.
OH, BROTHER.
I THINK YOU WERE HANGING UPSIDE-DOWN A LITTLE TOO LONG, BABE.
I MEAN IT, BETH. I REALLY FEEL LOST WHEN WE'RE APART.
I KNOW. I'VE MISSED YOU TOO, YORICK.
I WAS JUST THINKING ABOUT THAT TIME WE WERE ON YOUR ROOF, IN THE RAIN...
BUT IT'S NOT JUST THAT! I MEAN, OF COURSE I MISS THAT, BUT...
YOU'RE MY BEST FRIEND, BETH. YOU'RE BRILLIANT AND FUNNY AND YOUR FAVORITE MOVIE IS MILLER'S CROSSING. I DIDN'T EVEN KNOW THERE WERE WOMEN LIKE YOU.
YOU MAKE ME A BETTER, SMARTER, BRAVER PERSON, AND I DON'T WANT TO
YORICK, WAIT.
BEFORE YOU SAY ANYTHING, THERE'S... THERE'S SOMETHING I SHOULD TELL YOU.

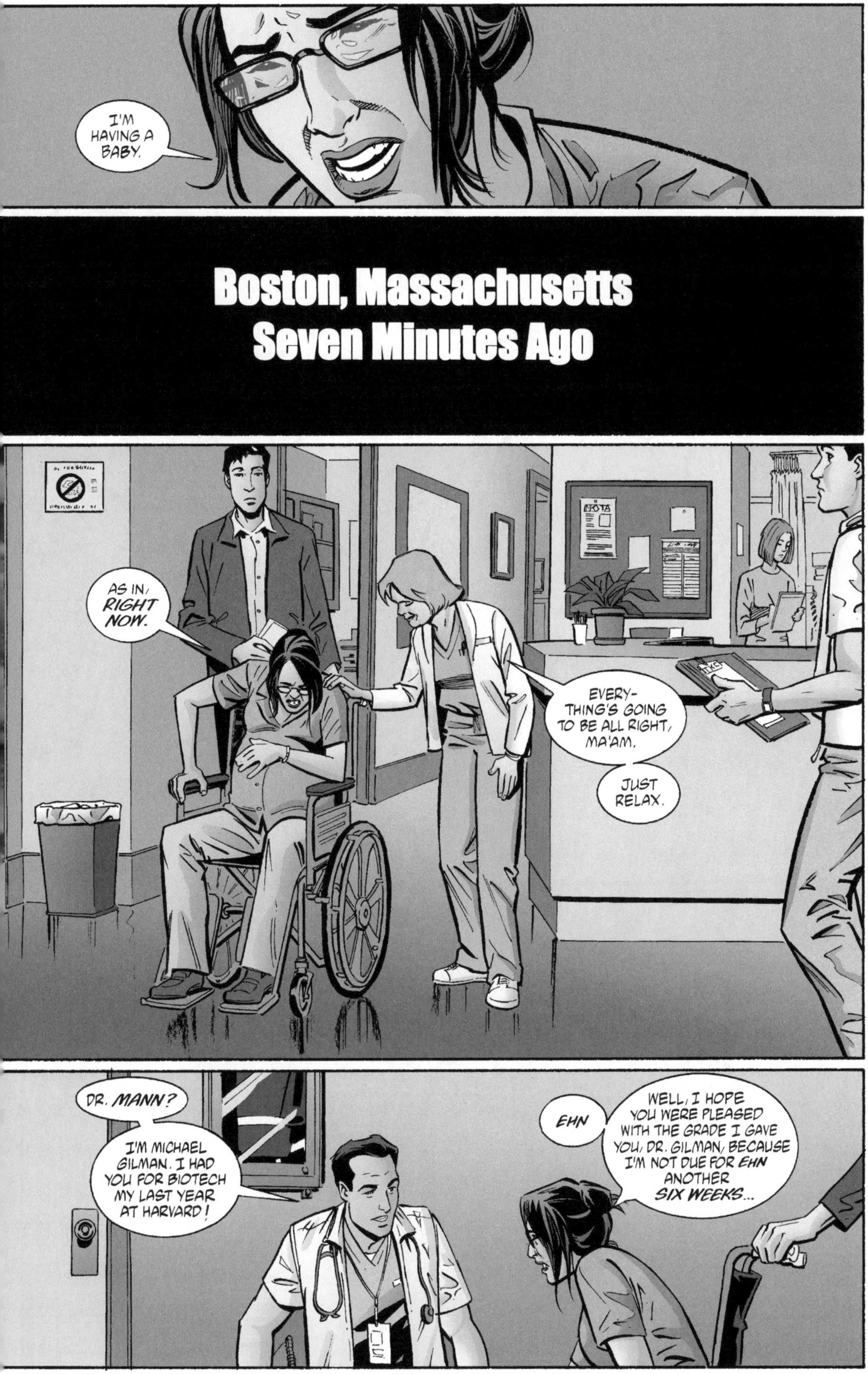

I'M HAVING A BABY.
Boston, Massachusetts
Seven Minutes Ago
AS IN, RIGHT NOW.
EVERY-THING'S GOING TO BE ALL RIGHT, MA'AM.
JUST RELAX.
DR. MANN?
I'M MICHAEL GILMAN. I HAD YOU FOR BIOTECH MY LAST YEAR AT HARVARD!
EHN
WELL, I HOPE YOU WERE PLEASED WITH THE GRADE I GAVE YOU, DR. GILMAN, BECAUSE I'M NOT DUE FOR EHN ANOTHER SIX WEEKS...

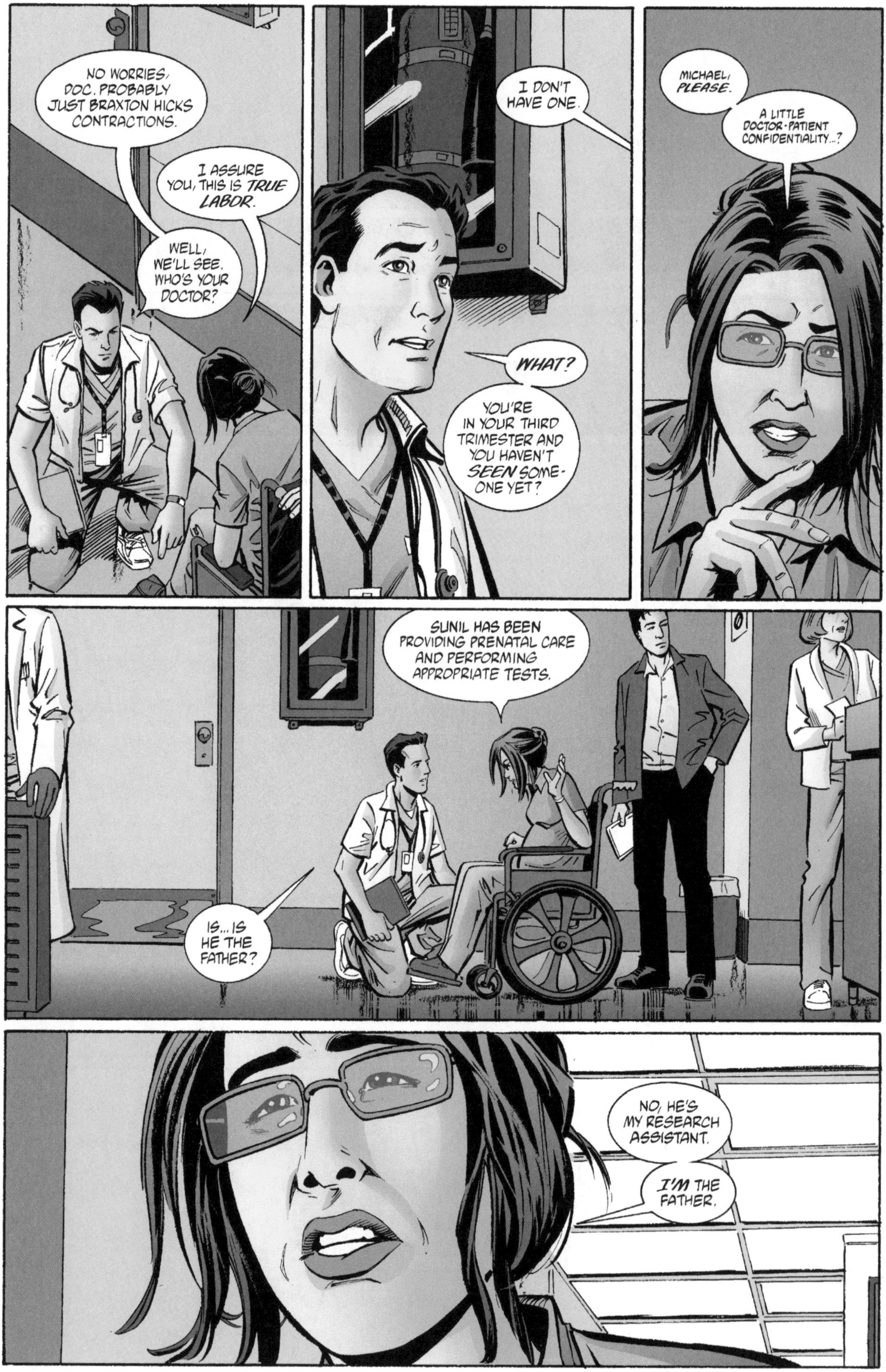
NO WORRIES, DOC. PROBABLY JUST BRAXTON HICKS CONTRACTIONS.
I ASSURE YOU, THIS IS TRUE LABOR.
WELL, WE'LL SEE. WHO'S YOUR DOCTOR?
I DON'T HAVE ONE.
WHAT?
YOU'RE IN YOUR THIRD TRIMESTER AND YOU HAVEN'T SEEN SOME-ONE YET?
MICHAEL, PLEASE.
A LITTLE DOCTOR-PATIENT CONFIDENTIALITY...?
SUNIL HAS BEEN PROVIDING PRENATAL CARE AND PERFORMING APPROPRIATE TESTS.
IS...IS HE THE FATHER?
NO, HE'S MY RESEARCH ASSISTANT.
I'M THE FATHER.

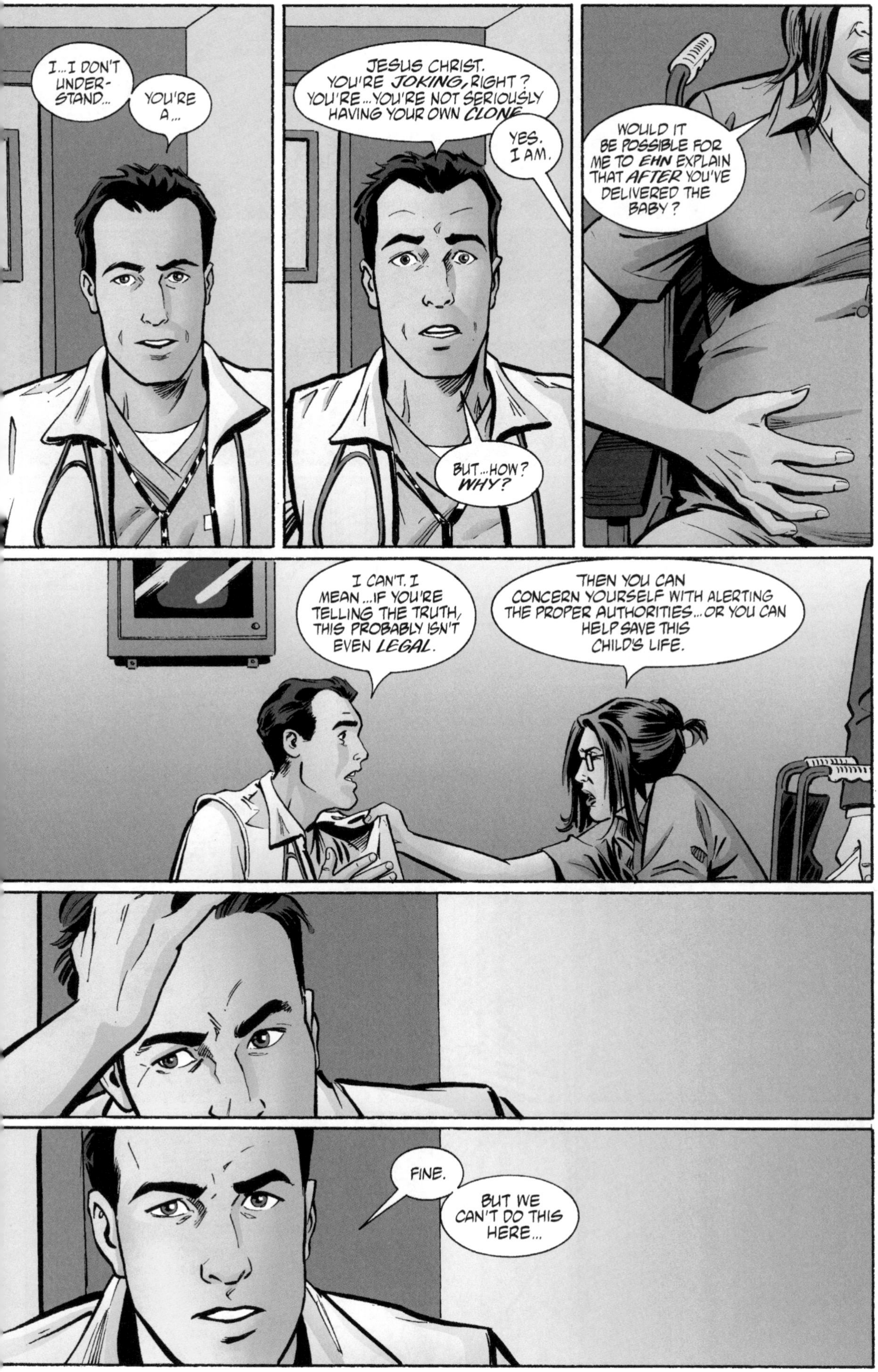
I...I DON'T UNDER-STAND...
YOU'RE A...
JESUS CHRIST. YOU'RE JOKING, RIGHT? YOU'RE...YOU'RE NOT SERIOUSLY HAVING YOUR OWN CLONE
YES. I AM.
BUT...HOW? WHY?
WOULD IT BE POSSIBLE FOR ME TO EHN EXPLAIN THAT AFTER YOU'VE DELIVERED THE BABY?
I CAN'T. I MEAN...IF YOU'RE TELLING THE TRUTH, THIS PROBABLY ISN'T EVEN LEGAL.
THEN YOU CAN CONCERN YOURSELF WITH ALERTING THE PROPER AUTHORITIES...OR YOU CAN HELP SAVE THIS CHILD'S LIFE.
FINE.
BUT WE CAN'T DO THIS HERE...

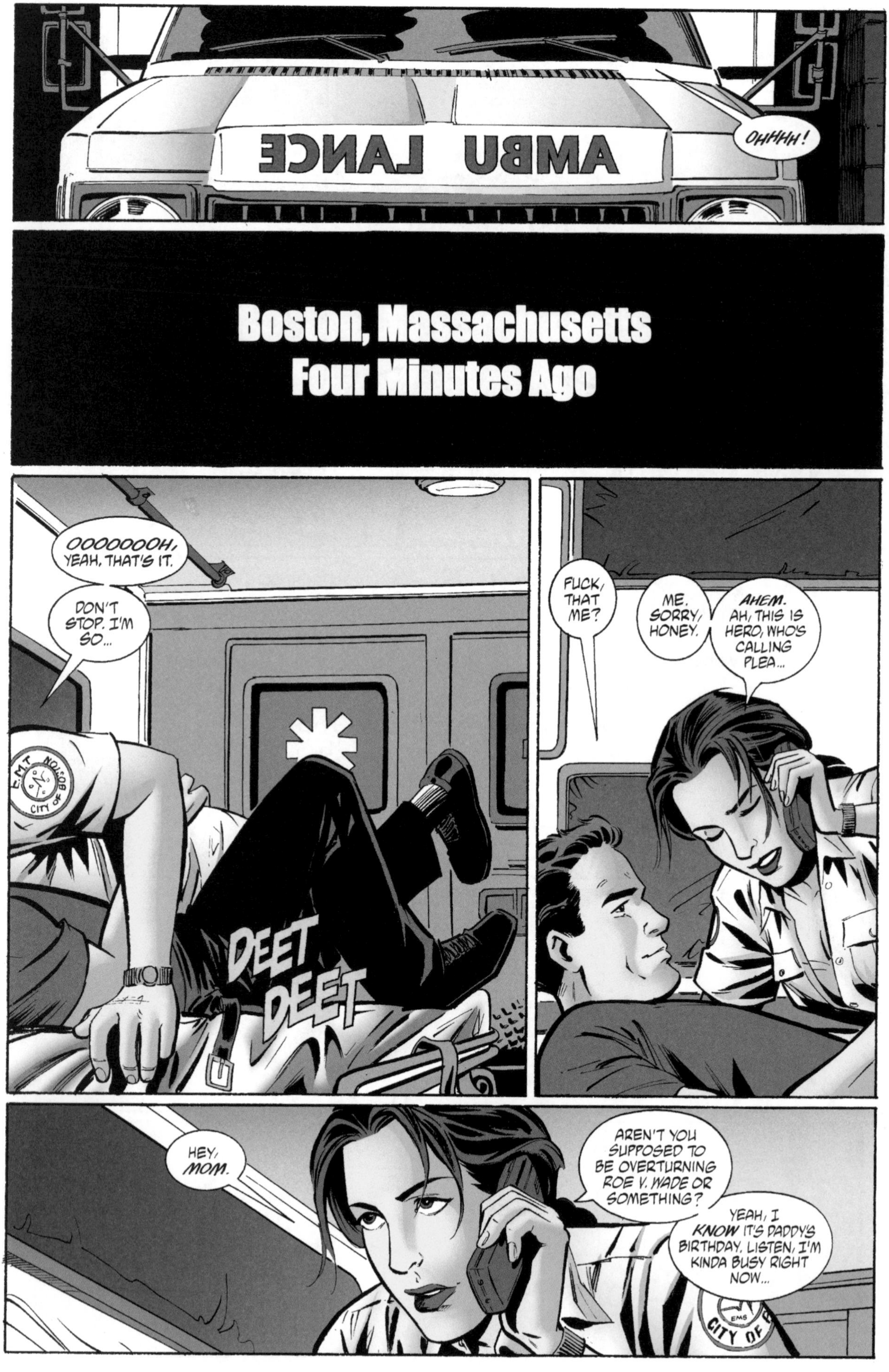
OHHHH!
Boston, Massachusetts
Four Minutes Ago
OOOOOOOH, YEAH, THAT'S IT.
DON'T STOP. I'M SO...
DEET DEET
FUCK, THAT ME?
ME. SORRY, HONEY.
AHEM. AH, THIS IS HERO, WHO'S CALLING PLEA...
HEY, MOM.
AREN'T YOU SUPPOSED TO BE OVERTURNING ROE V. WADE OR SOMETHING?
YEAH, I KNOW IT'S DADDY'S BIRTHDAY. LISTEN, I'M KINDA BUSY RIGHT NOW...

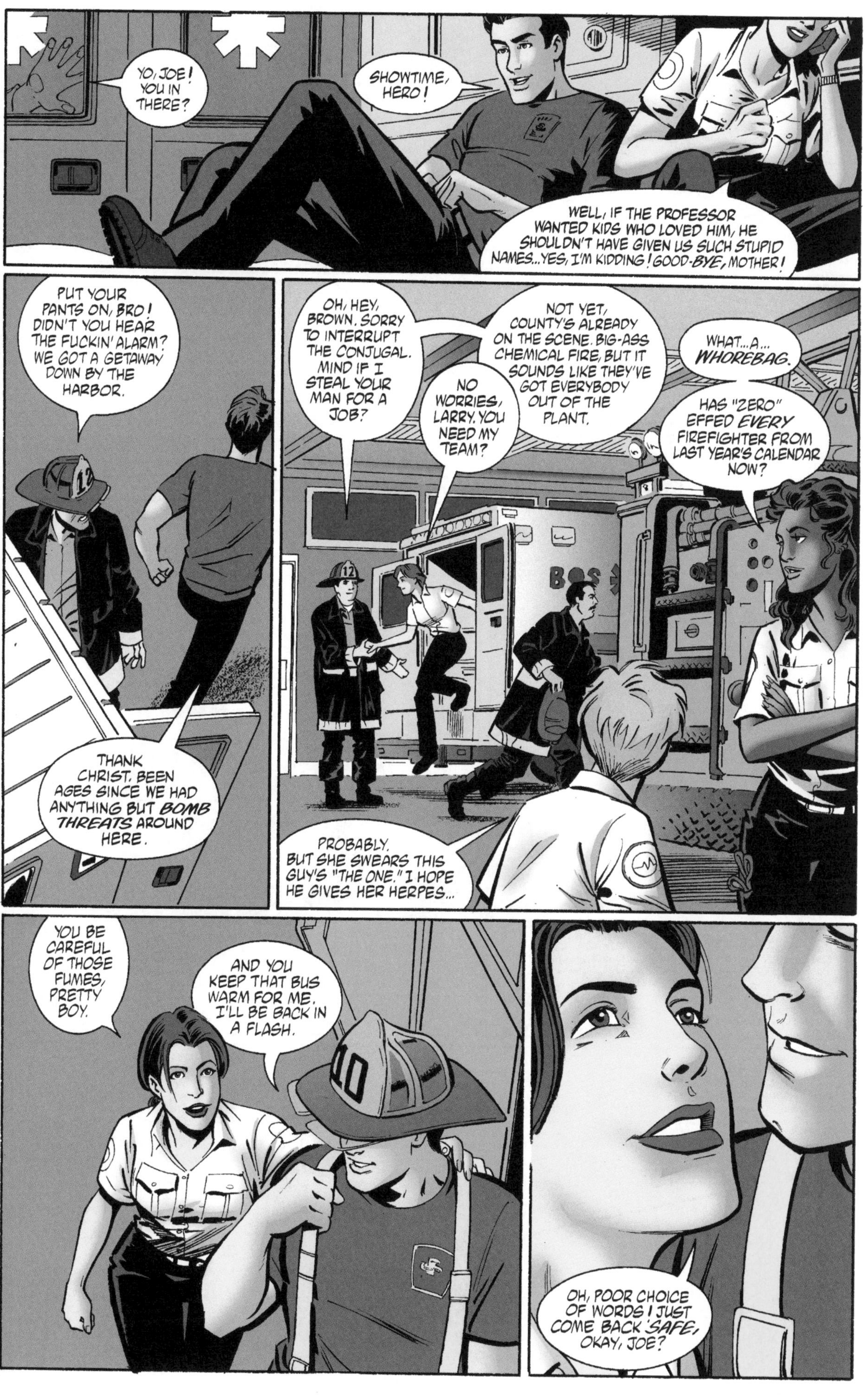
YO, JOE! YOU IN THERE?
SHOWTIME, HERO!
WELL, IF THE PROFESSOR WANTED KIDS WHO LOVED HIM, HE SHOULDN'T HAVE GIVEN US SUCH STUPID NAMES...YES, I'M KIDDING! GOOD-BYE, MOTHER!
PUT YOUR PANTS ON, BRO! DIDN'T YOU HEAR THE FUCKIN' ALARM? WE GOT A GETAWAY DOWN BY THE HARBOR.
THANK CHRIST. BEEN AGES SINCE WE HAD ANYTHING BUT BOMB THREATS AROUND HERE.
OH, HEY, BROWN. SORRY TO INTERRUPT THE CONJUGAL. MIND IF I STEAL YOUR MAN FOR A JOB?
NO WORRIES, LARRY. YOU NEED MY TEAM?
NOT YET, COUNTY'S ALREADY ON THE SCENE. BIG-ASS CHEMICAL FIRE, BUT IT SOUNDS LIKE THEY'VE GOT EVERYBODY OUT OF THE PLANT.
WHAT...A... WHOREBAG.
HAS "ZERO" EFFED EVERY FIREFIGHTER FROM LAST YEAR'S CALENDAR NOW?
PROBABLY. BUT SHE SWEARS THIS GUY'S "THE ONE." I HOPE HE GIVES HER HERPES...
YOU BE CAREFUL OF THOSE FUMES, PRETTY BOY.
AND YOU KEEP THAT BUS WARM FOR ME. I'LL BE BACK IN A FLASH.
OH, POOR CHOICE OF WORDS! JUST COME BACK SAFE, OKAY, JOE?

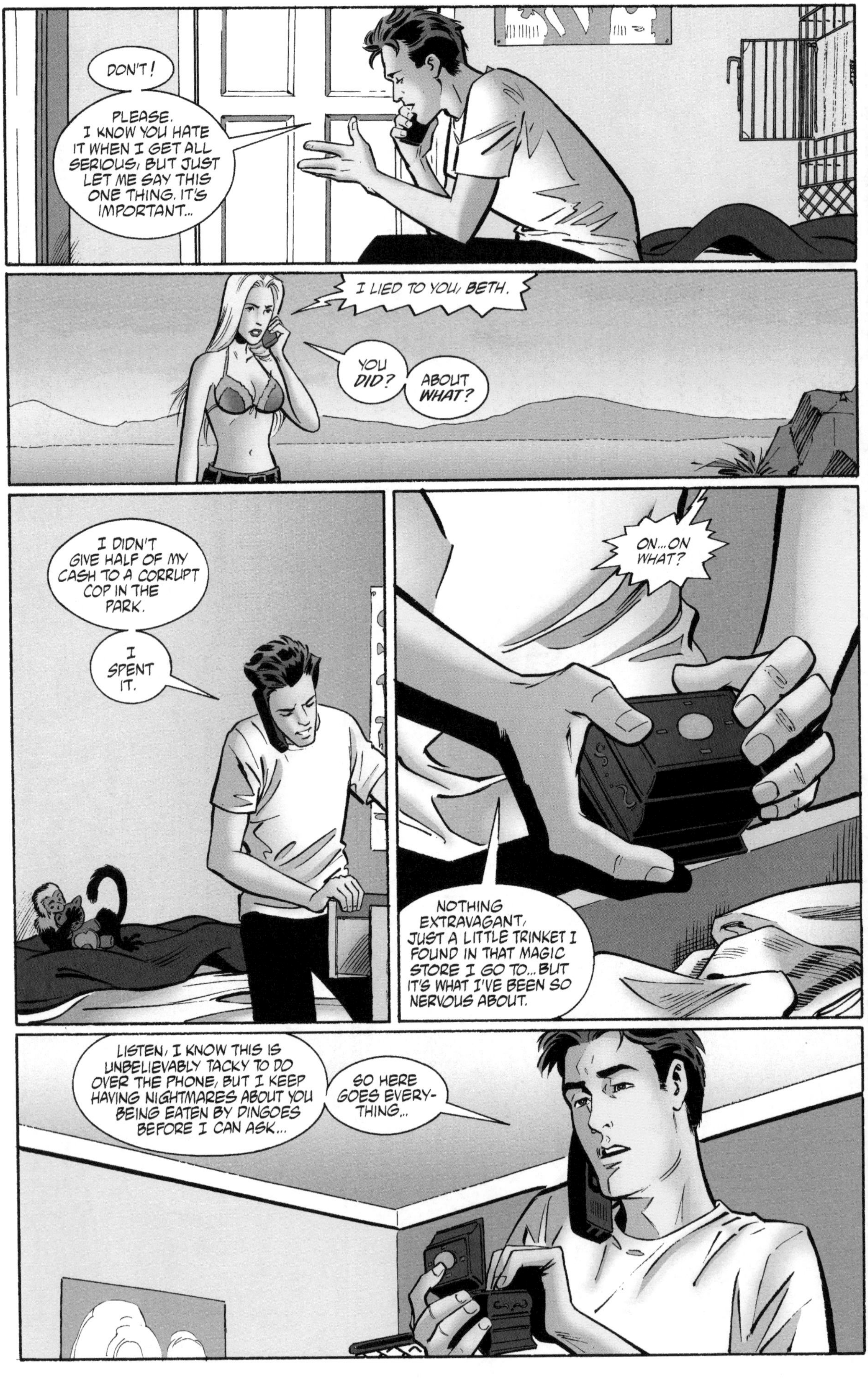
DON'T!
PLEASE. I KNOW YOU HATE IT WHEN I GET ALL SERIOUS, BUT JUST LET ME SAY THIS ONE THING. IT'S IMPORTANT...
I LIED TO YOU, BETH.
YOU DID?
ABOUT WHAT?
I DIDN'T GIVE HALF OF MY CASH TO A CORRUPT COP IN THE PARK.
I SPENT IT.
ON...ON WHAT?
NOTHING EXTRAVAGANT, JUST A LITTLE TRINKET I FOUND IN THAT MAGIC STORE I GO TO... BUT IT'S WHAT I'VE BEEN SO NERVOUS ABOUT.
LISTEN, I KNOW THIS IS UNBELIEVABLY TACKY TO DO OVER THE PHONE, BUT I KEEP HAVING NIGHTMARES ABOUT YOU BEING EATEN BY DINGOES BEFORE I CAN ASK...
SO HERE GOES EVERYTHING...

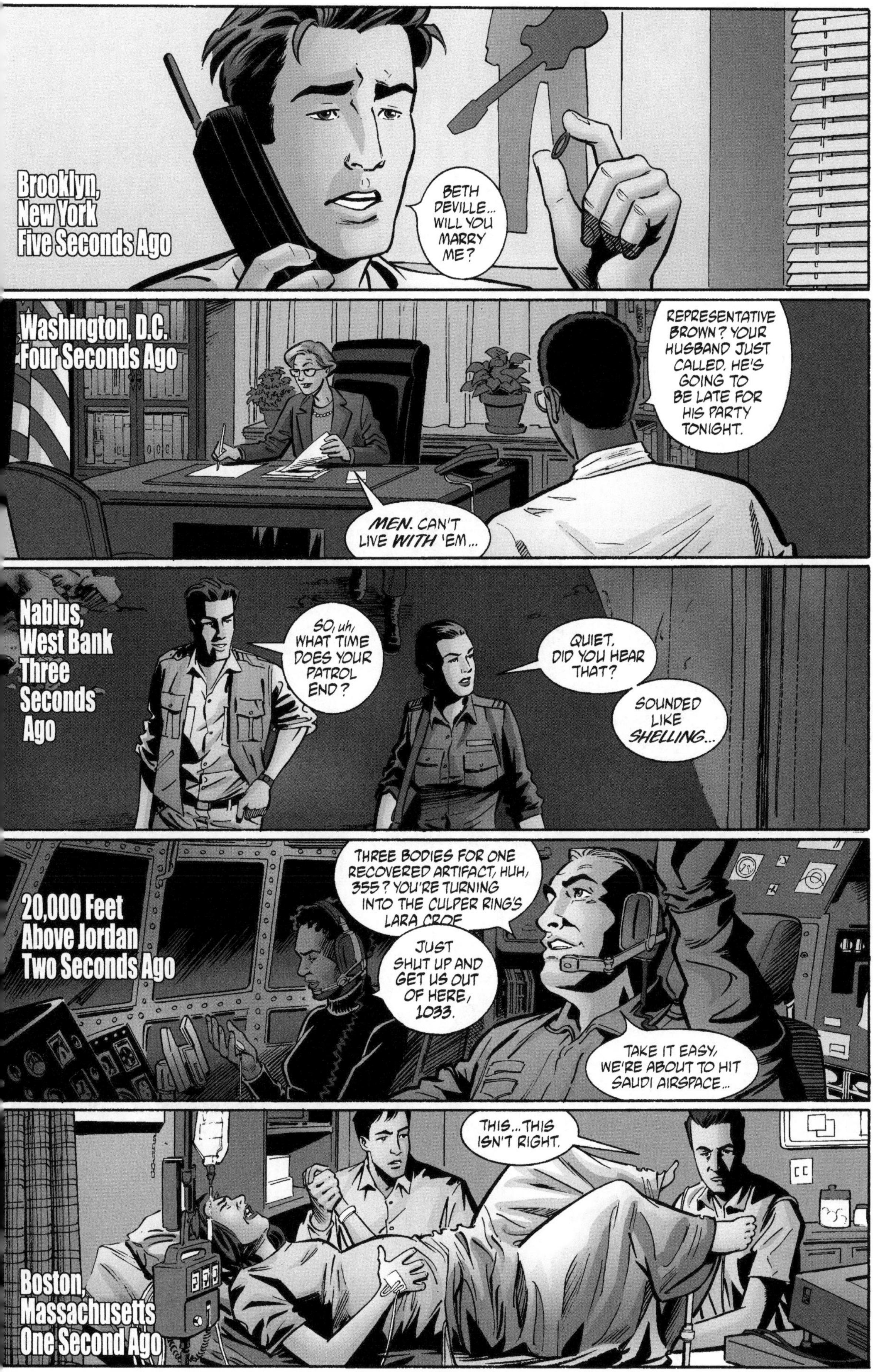

Brooklyn, New York Five Seconds Ago
BETH DEVILLE... WILL YOU MARRY ME?
Washington, D.C. Four Seconds Ago
REPRESENTATIVE BROWN? YOUR HUSBAND JUST CALLED. HE'S GOING TO BE LATE FOR HIS PARTY TONIGHT.
MEN. CAN'T LIVE WITH 'EM...
Nablus, West Bank Three Seconds Ago
SO, uh, WHAT TIME DOES YOUR PATROL END?
QUIET. DID YOU HEAR THAT?
SOUNDED LIKE SHELLING...
20,000 Feet Above Jordan Two Seconds Ago
THREE BODIES FOR ONE RECOVERED ARTIFACT, HUH, 355? YOU'RE TURNING INTO THE CULPER RING'S LARA CROF
JUST SHUT UP AND GET US OUT OF HERE, 1033.
TAKE IT EASY, WE'RE ABOUT TO HIT SAUDI AIRSPACE...
Boston, Massachusetts One Second Ago
THIS... THIS ISN'T RIGHT.

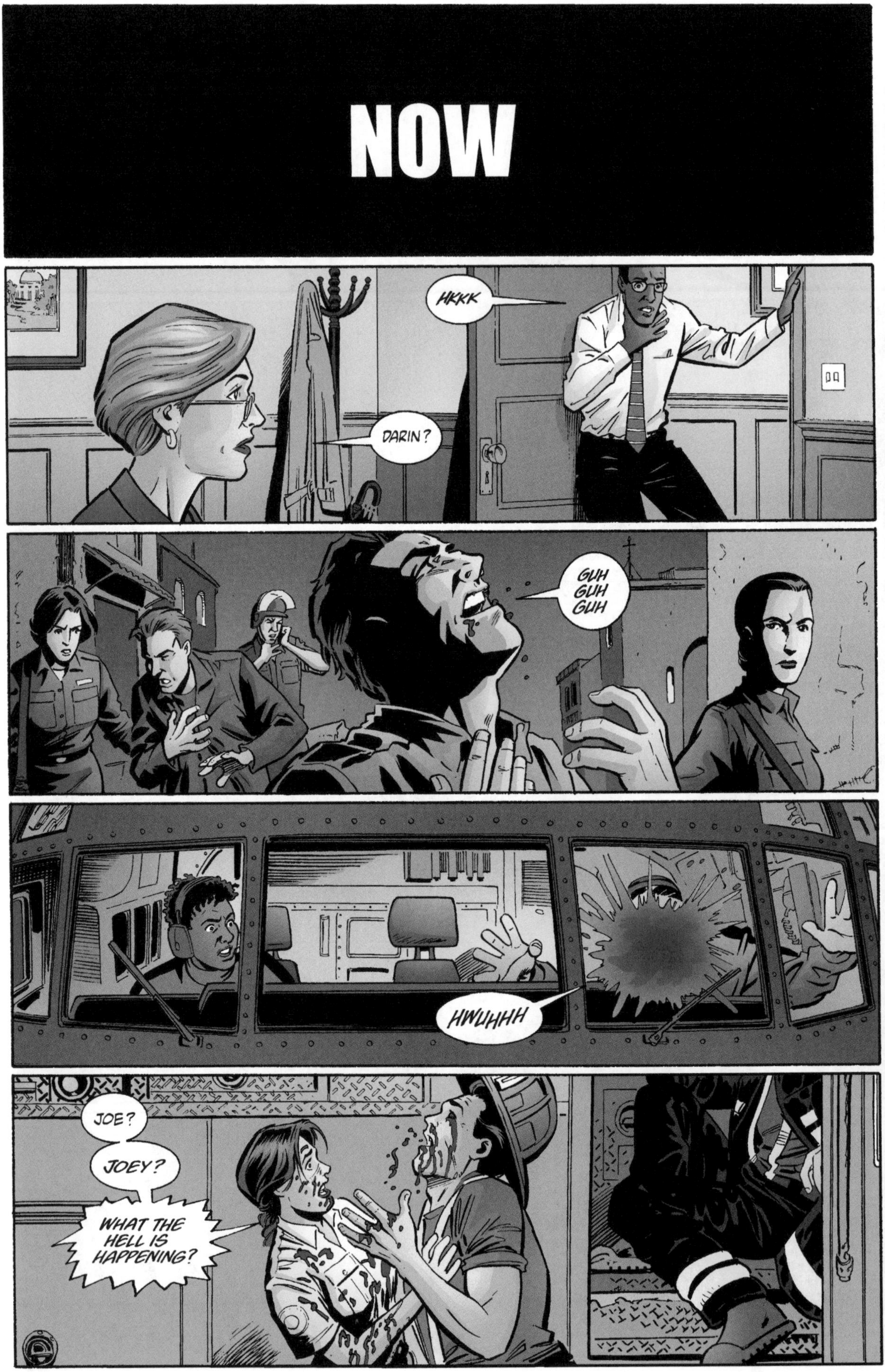
NOW
HKKK
DARIN?
GUH GUH GUH
HWUHHH
JOE?
JOEY?
WHAT THE HELL IS HAPPENING?

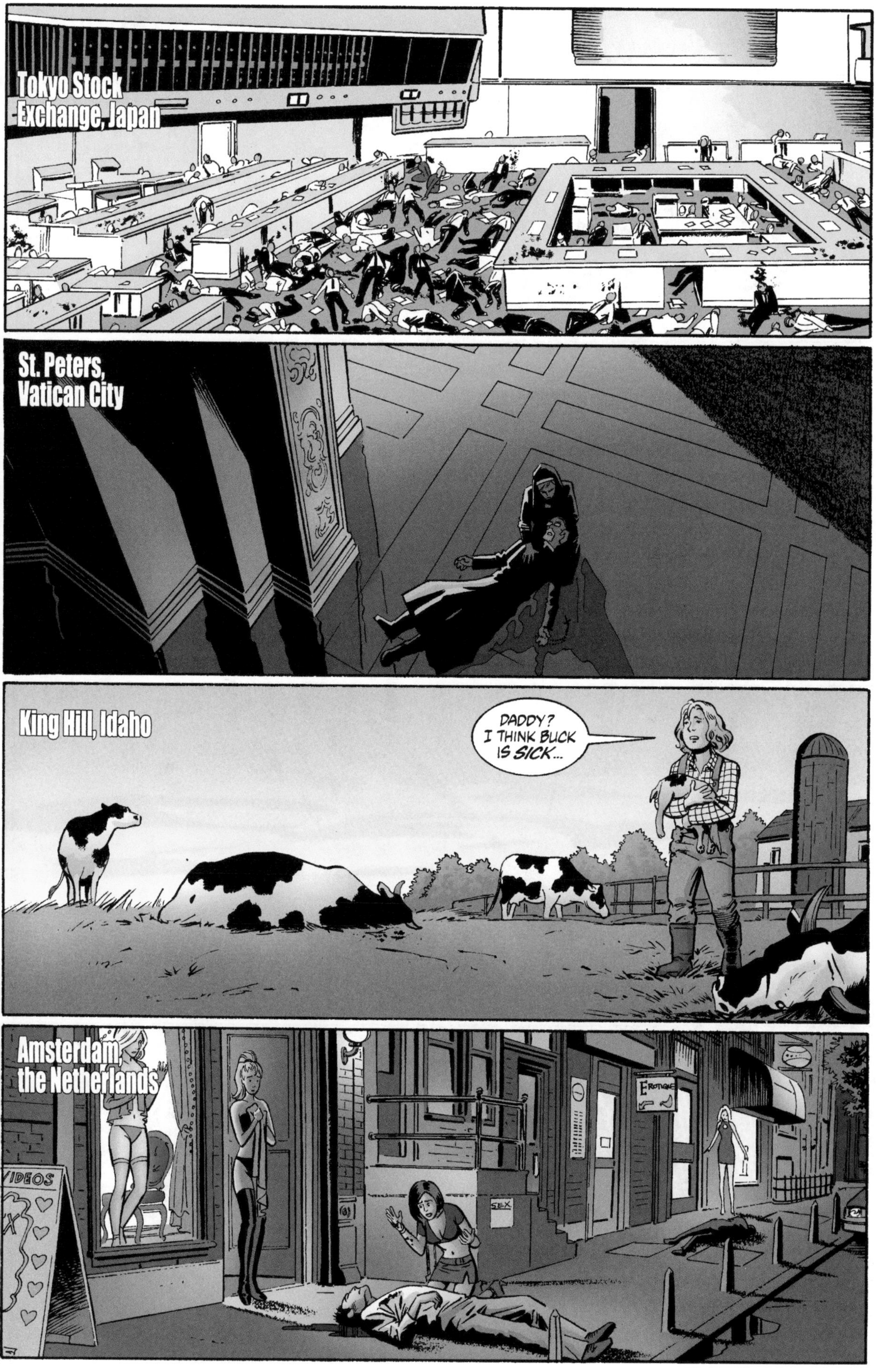
Tokyo Stock Exchange, Japan
St. Peters, Vatican City
King Hill, Idaho
DADDY? I THINK BUCK IS SICK...
Amsterdam, the Netherlands
VIDEOS
SEX

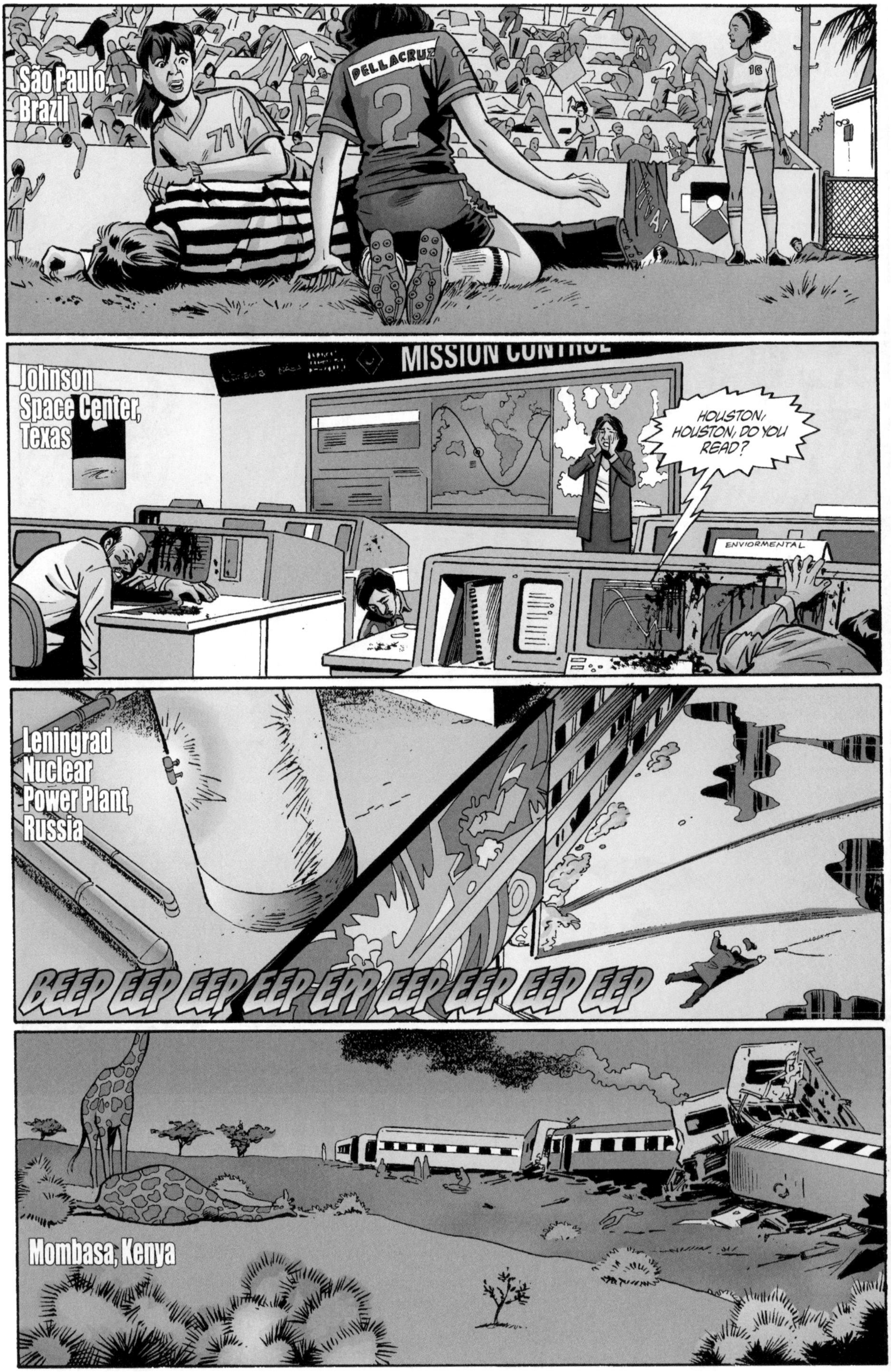
São Paulo, Brazil
PELLACRUZ
VIVA!
Johnson Space Center, Texas
MISSION CONTROL
HOUSTON, HOUSTON, DO YOU READ?
ENVIORMENTAL
Leningrad Nuclear Power Plant, Russia
BEEP EEP EEP EEP-EPP EEP EEP EEP EEP
Mombasa, Kenya

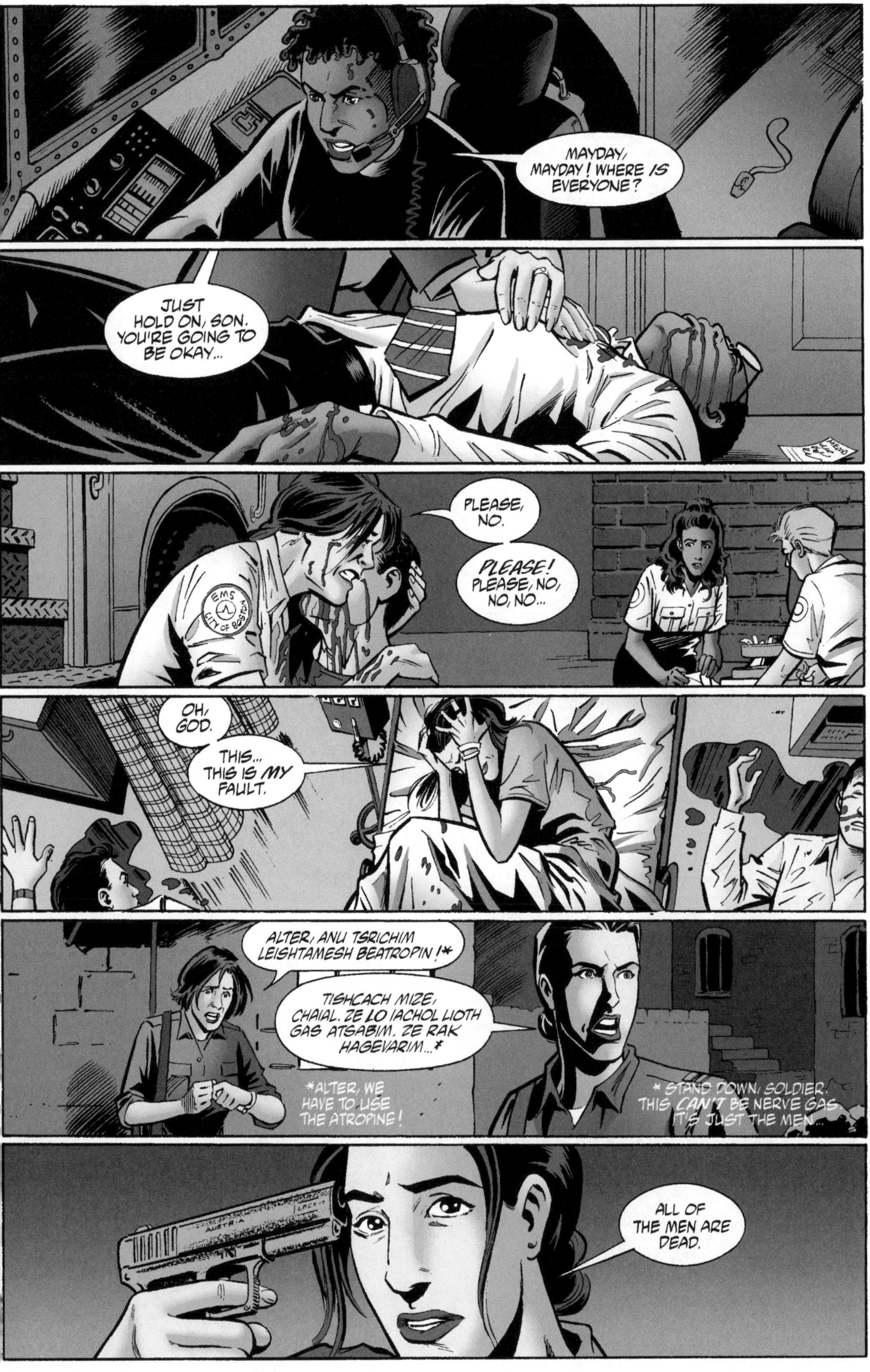
MAYDAY, MAYDAY! WHERE IS EVERYONE?
JUST HOLD ON, SON. YOU'RE GOING TO BE OKAY...
PLEASE, NO.
PLEASE! PLEASE, NO, NO, NO...
EMS CITY OF BOSTON
OH, GOD.
THIS... THIS IS MY FAULT.
ALTER, ANU TSRICHIM LEISHTAMESH BEATROPIN!*
TISHCACH MIZE, CHAIAL. ZE LO IACHOL LIOTH GAS ATSABIM. ZE RAK HAGEVARIM...*
*ALTER, WE HAVE TO USE THE ATROPINE!
* STAND DOWN, SOLDIER. THIS CAN'T BE NERVE GAS. IT'S JUST THE MEN...
ALL OF THE MEN ARE DEAD.

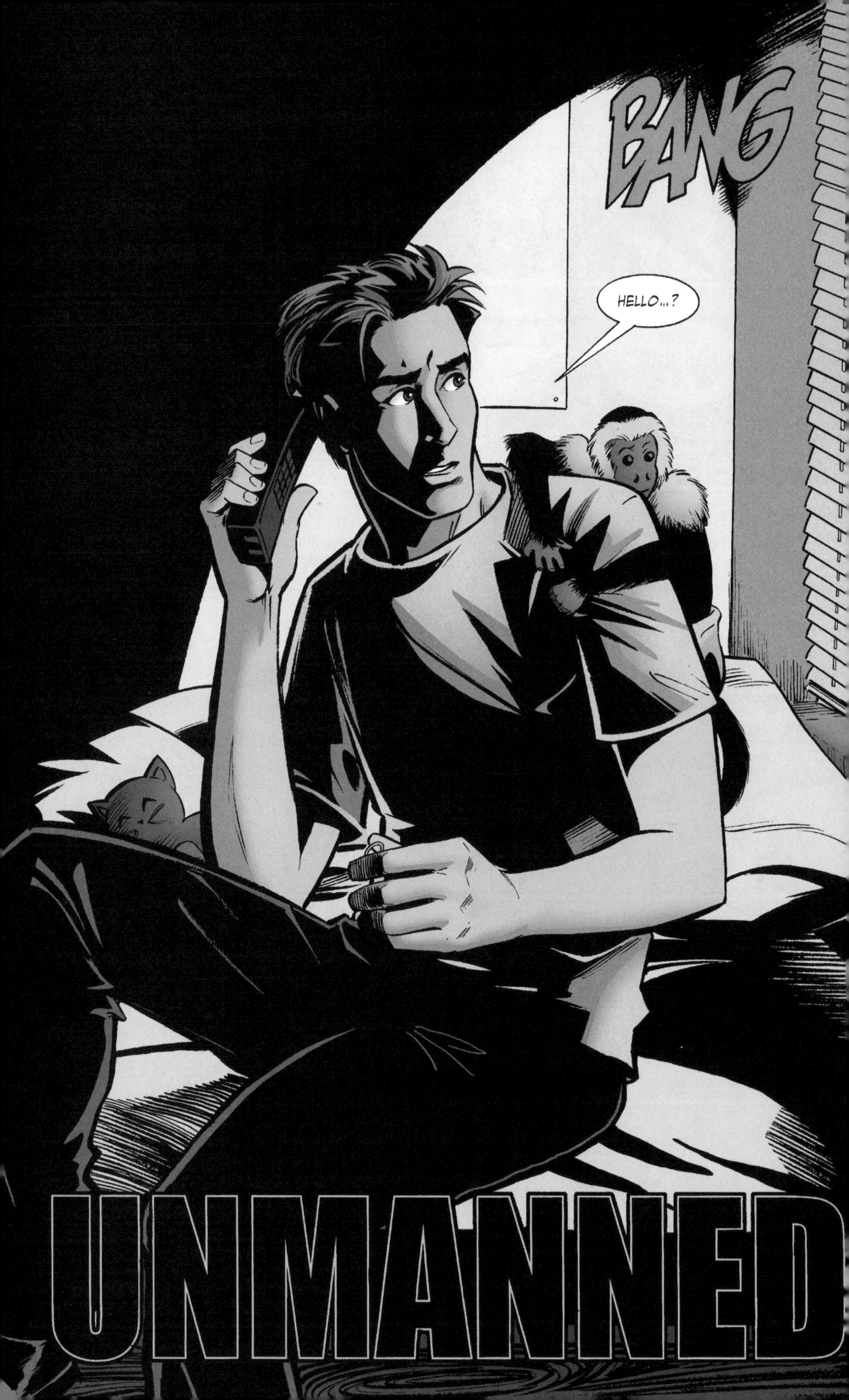
BANG
HELLO...?
UNMANNED

Welcome to the UNMANNED World

In the summer of 2002, a plague of unknown origin destroyed every last sperm, fetus, and fully developed mammal with a Y chromosome — with the apparent exception of one young man and his pet, a male Capuchin monkey.

This "gendercide" instantaneously exterminated 48% of the global population, or approximately 2.9 billion men. 495 of the Fortune 500 CEOs are now dead, as are 99% of the world's landowners.

In the United States alone, more than 95% of all commercial pilots, truck drivers, and ship captains died... as did 92% of all violent felons. Internationally, 99% of all mechanics, electricians, and construction workers are now deceased... though 51% of the planet's *agricultural* labor force is still alive.

14 nations, including Spain and Germany, have women soldiers who have served in ground combat units. *None* of the United States' nearly 200,000 female troops have ever participated in ground combat. Australia, Norway, and Sweden are the only countries that have women serving on board submarines.

In Israel, all women between the ages of 18 and 26 have performed compulsory military service in the Israeli Defense Force for at least one year and nine months. Before the Plague, at least three Palestinian suicide bombers had been women.

Worldwide, 85% of all government representatives are now dead... as are 100% of Catholic priests, Muslim imams, and Orthodox Jewish rabbis.

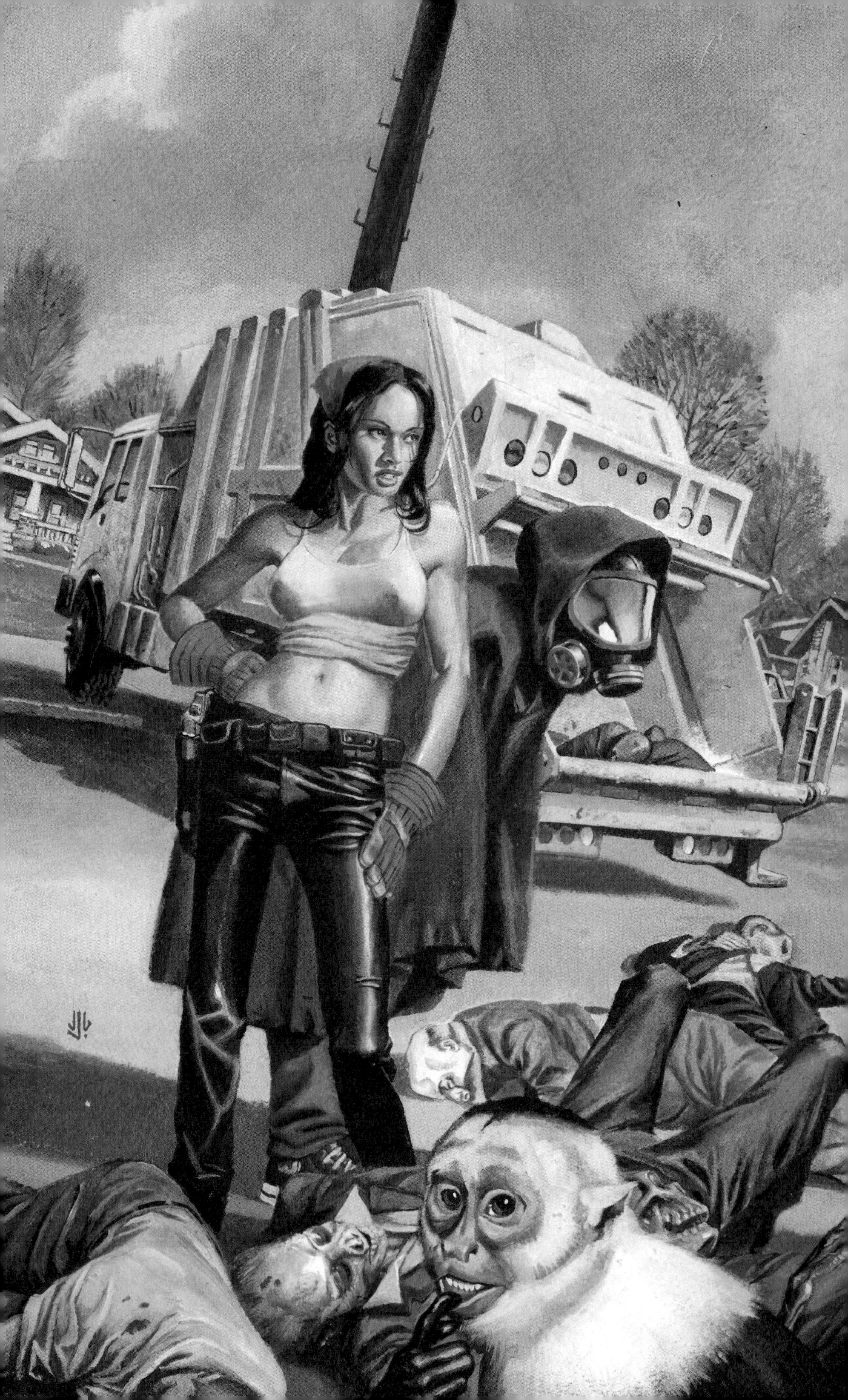

Washington, D.C.
Two Months Later

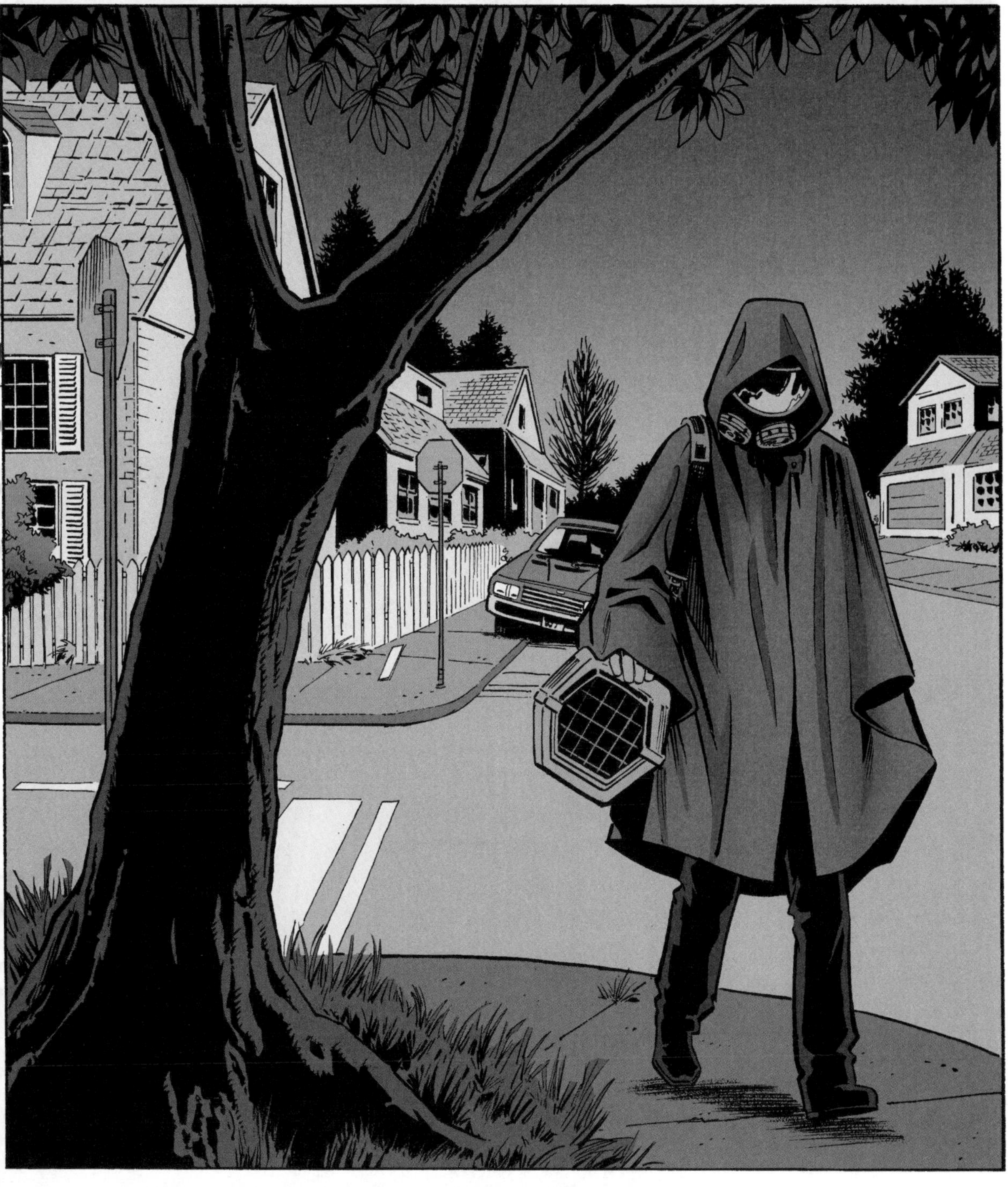

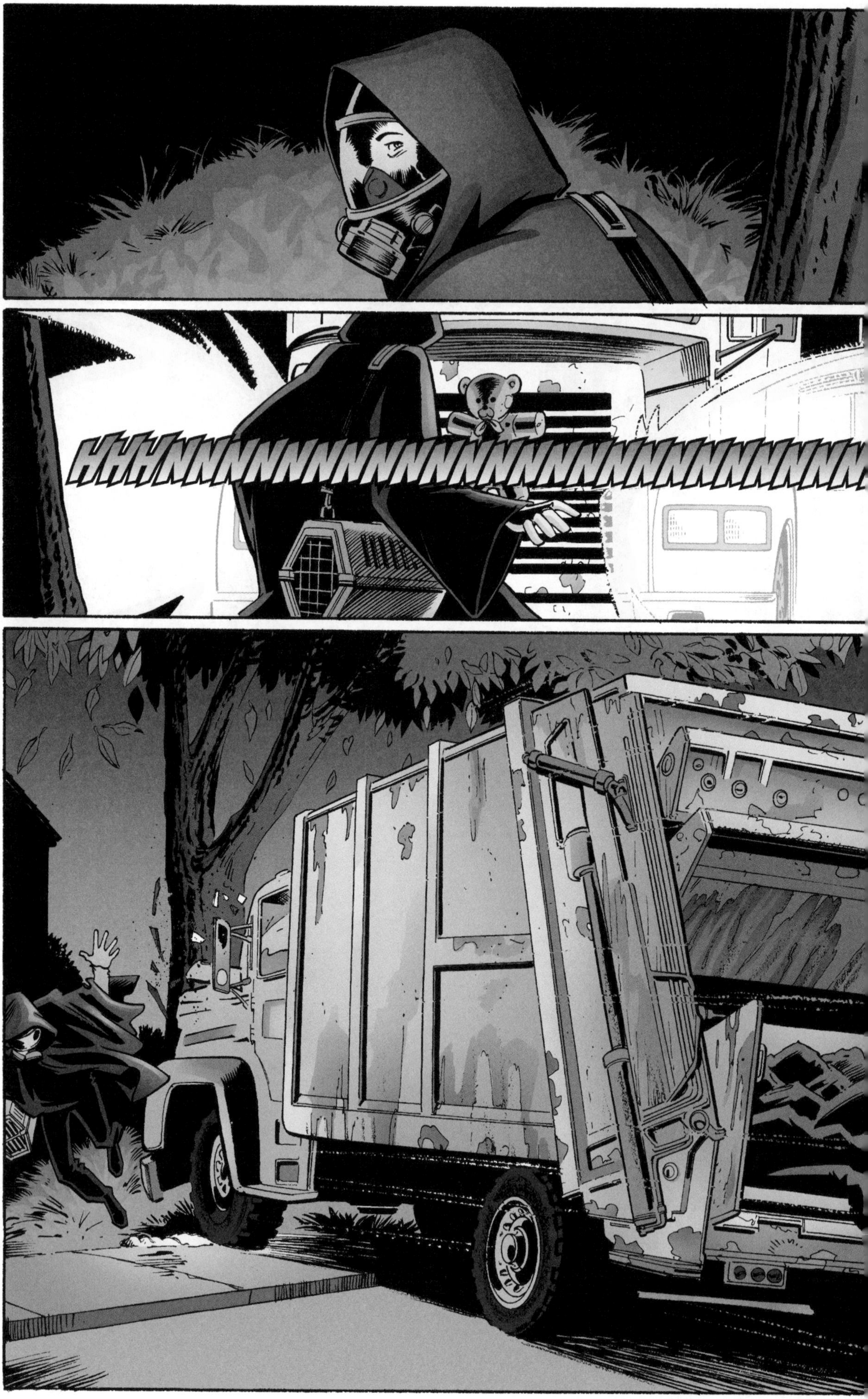
HHHNNNNNNNNNNNNNNNNNNNNNNNNNNNNN

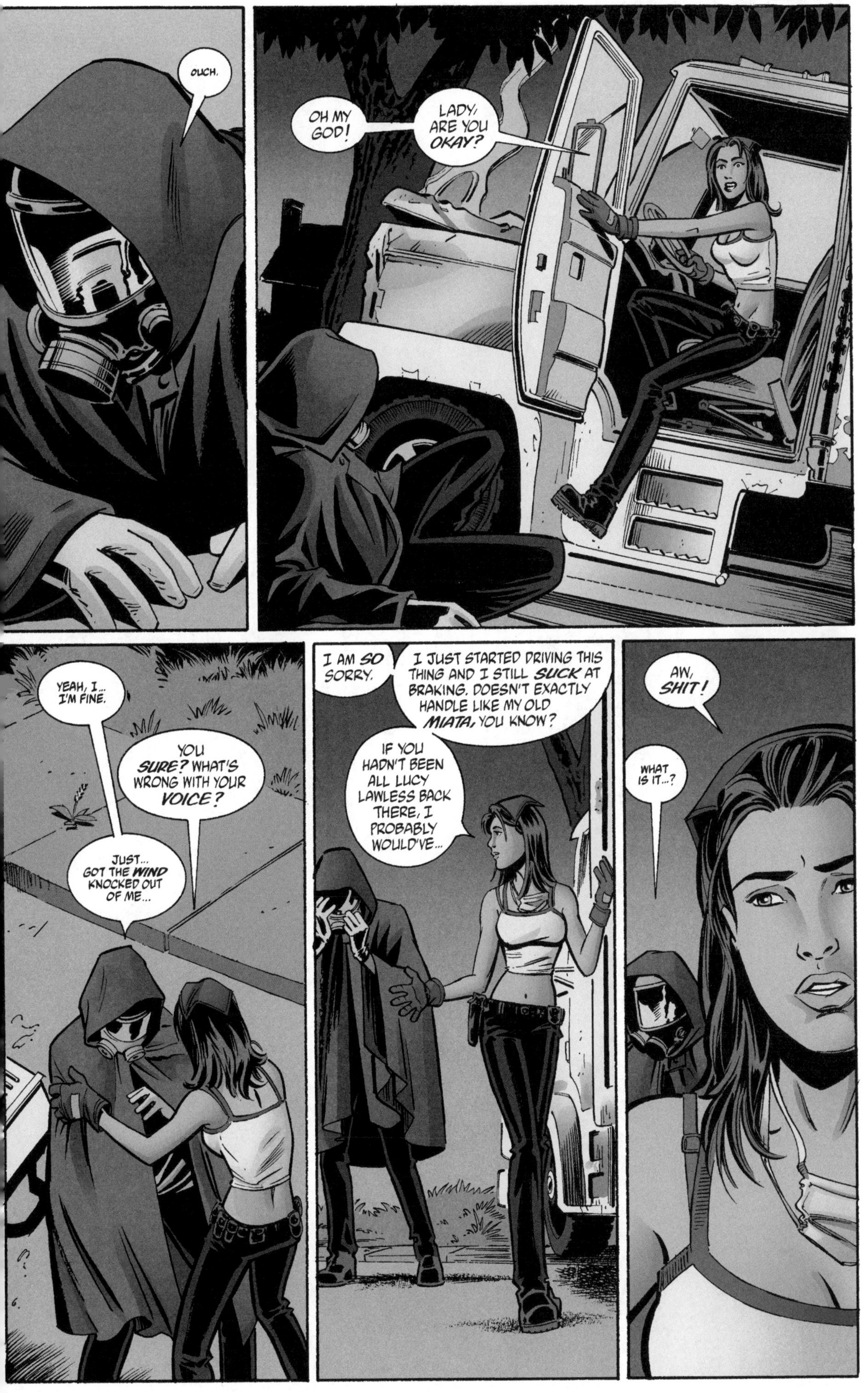
OUCH.
OH MY GOD!
LADY, ARE YOU OKAY?
YEAH, I... I'M FINE.
YOU SURE? WHAT'S WRONG WITH YOUR VOICE?
JUST... GOT THE WIND KNOCKED OUT OF ME...
I AM SO SORRY.
I JUST STARTED DRIVING THIS THING AND I STILL SUCK AT BRAKING. DOESN'T EXACTLY HANDLE LIKE MY OLD MIATA, YOU KNOW?
IF YOU HADN'T BEEN ALL LUCY LAWLESS BACK THERE, I PROBABLY WOULD'VE...
AW, SHIT!
WHAT IS IT...?

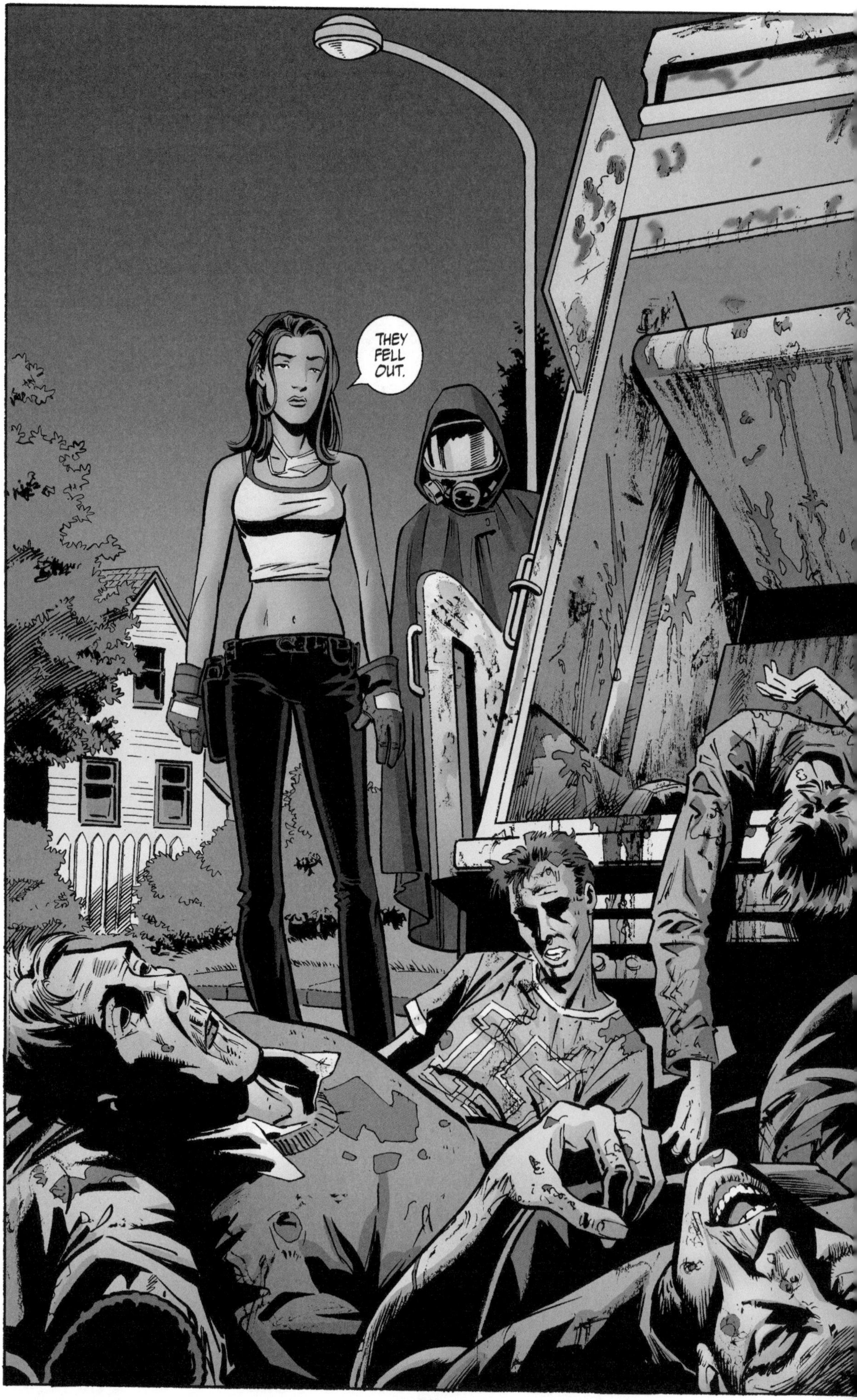
THEY FELL OUT.

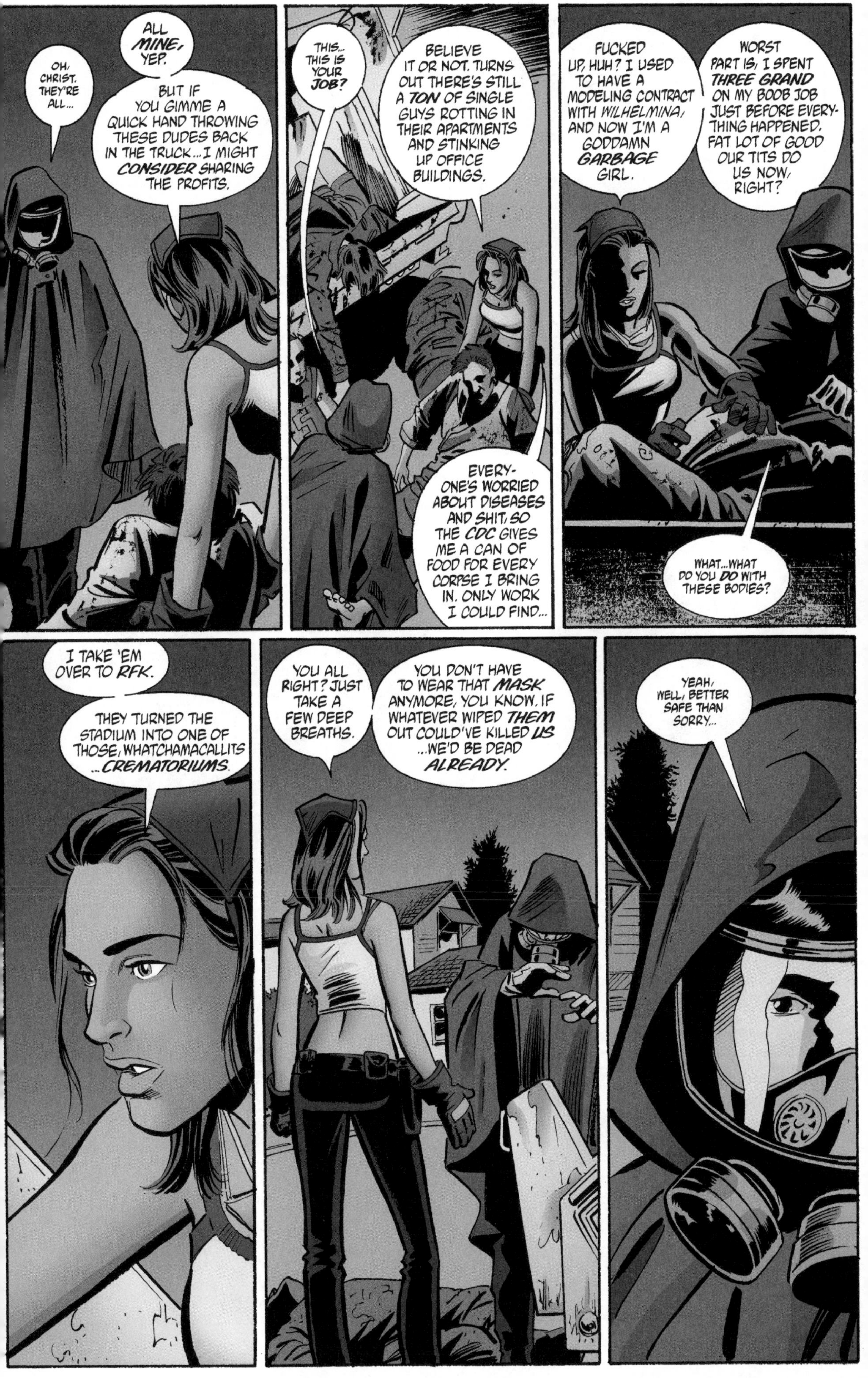
ALL MINE, YEP.
OH, CHRIST. THEY'RE ALL...
BUT IF YOU GIMME A QUICK HAND THROWING THESE DUDES BACK IN THE TRUCK... I MIGHT CONSIDER SHARING THE PROFITS.
THIS... THIS IS YOUR JOB?
BELIEVE IT OR NOT. TURNS OUT THERE'S STILL A TON OF SINGLE GUYS ROTTING IN THEIR APARTMENTS AND STINKING UP OFFICE BUILDINGS.
EVERYONE'S WORRIED ABOUT DISEASES AND SHIT, SO THE CDC GIVES ME A CAN OF FOOD FOR EVERY CORPSE I BRING IN. ONLY WORK I COULD FIND...
FUCKED UP, HUH? I USED TO HAVE A MODELING CONTRACT WITH WILHELMINA, AND NOW I'M A GODDAMN GARBAGE GIRL.
WORST PART IS, I SPENT THREE GRAND ON MY BOOB JOB JUST BEFORE EVERYTHING HAPPENED. FAT LOT OF GOOD OUR TITS DO US NOW, RIGHT?
WHAT...WHAT DO YOU DO WITH THESE BODIES?
I TAKE 'EM OVER TO RFK.
THEY TURNED THE STADIUM INTO ONE OF THOSE, WHATCHAMACALLITS ...CREMATORIUMS.
YOU ALL RIGHT? JUST TAKE A FEW DEEP BREATHS.
YOU DON'T HAVE TO WEAR THAT MASK ANYMORE, YOU KNOW. IF WHATEVER WIPED THEM OUT COULD'VE KILLED US ...WE'D BE DEAD ALREADY.
YEAH, WELL, BETTER SAFE THAN SORRY...

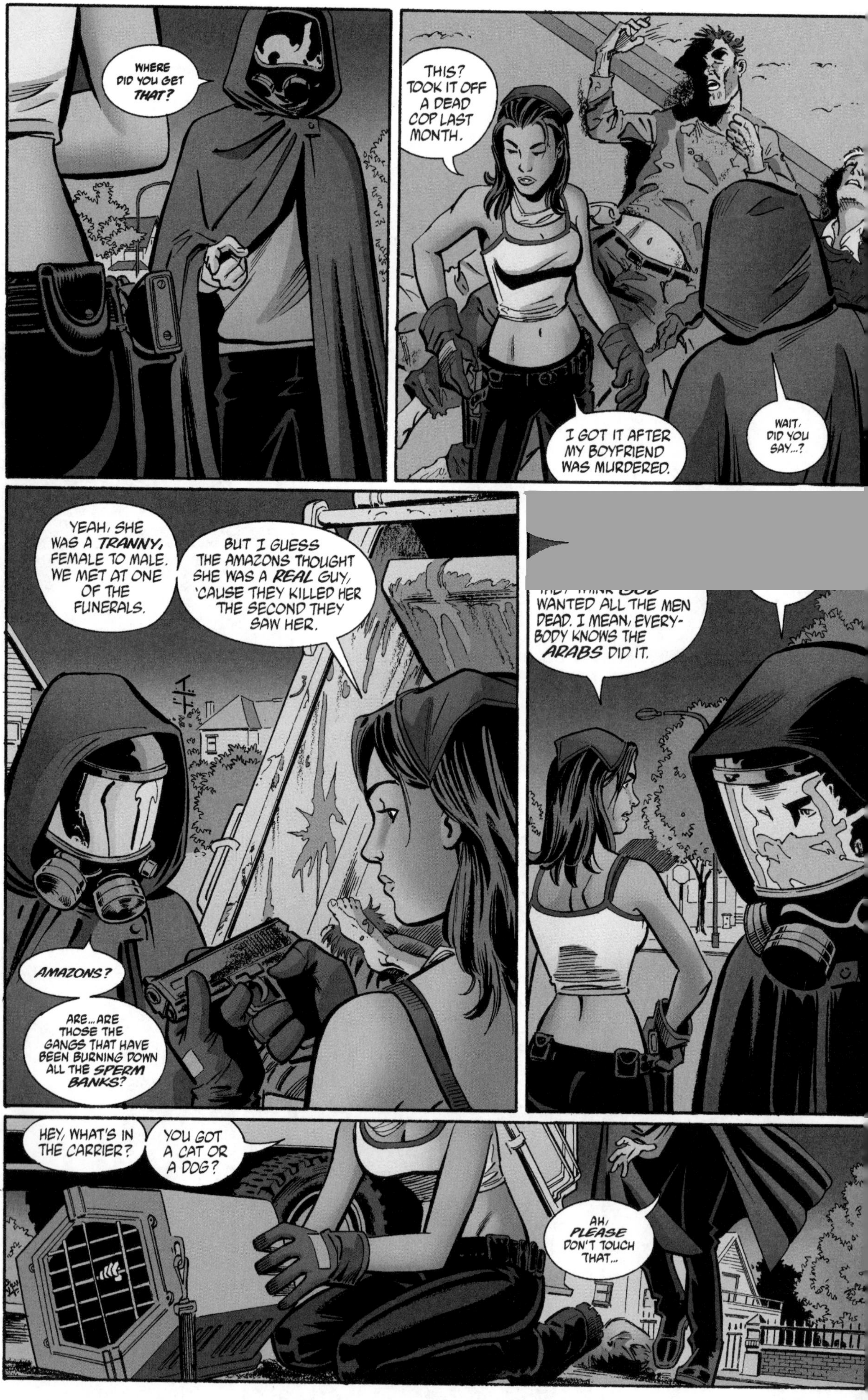
WHERE DID YOU GET *THAT?*
THIS? TOOK IT OFF A DEAD COP LAST MONTH.
I GOT IT AFTER MY BOYFRIEND WAS MURDERED.
WAIT, DID YOU SAY...?
YEAH, SHE WAS A *TRANNY,* FEMALE TO MALE. WE MET AT ONE OF THE FUNERALS.
BUT I GUESS THE AMAZONS THOUGHT SHE WAS A *REAL* GUY, 'CAUSE THEY KILLED HER THE SECOND THEY SAW HER.
AMAZONS?
ARE...ARE THOSE THE GANGS THAT HAVE BEEN BURNING DOWN ALL THE *SPERM BANKS?*
WANTED ALL THE MEN DEAD. I MEAN, EVERY-BODY KNOWS THE *ARABS* DID IT.
HEY, WHAT'S IN THE CARRIER?
YOU GOT A CAT OR A DOG?
AH, *PLEASE* DON'T TOUCH THAT...

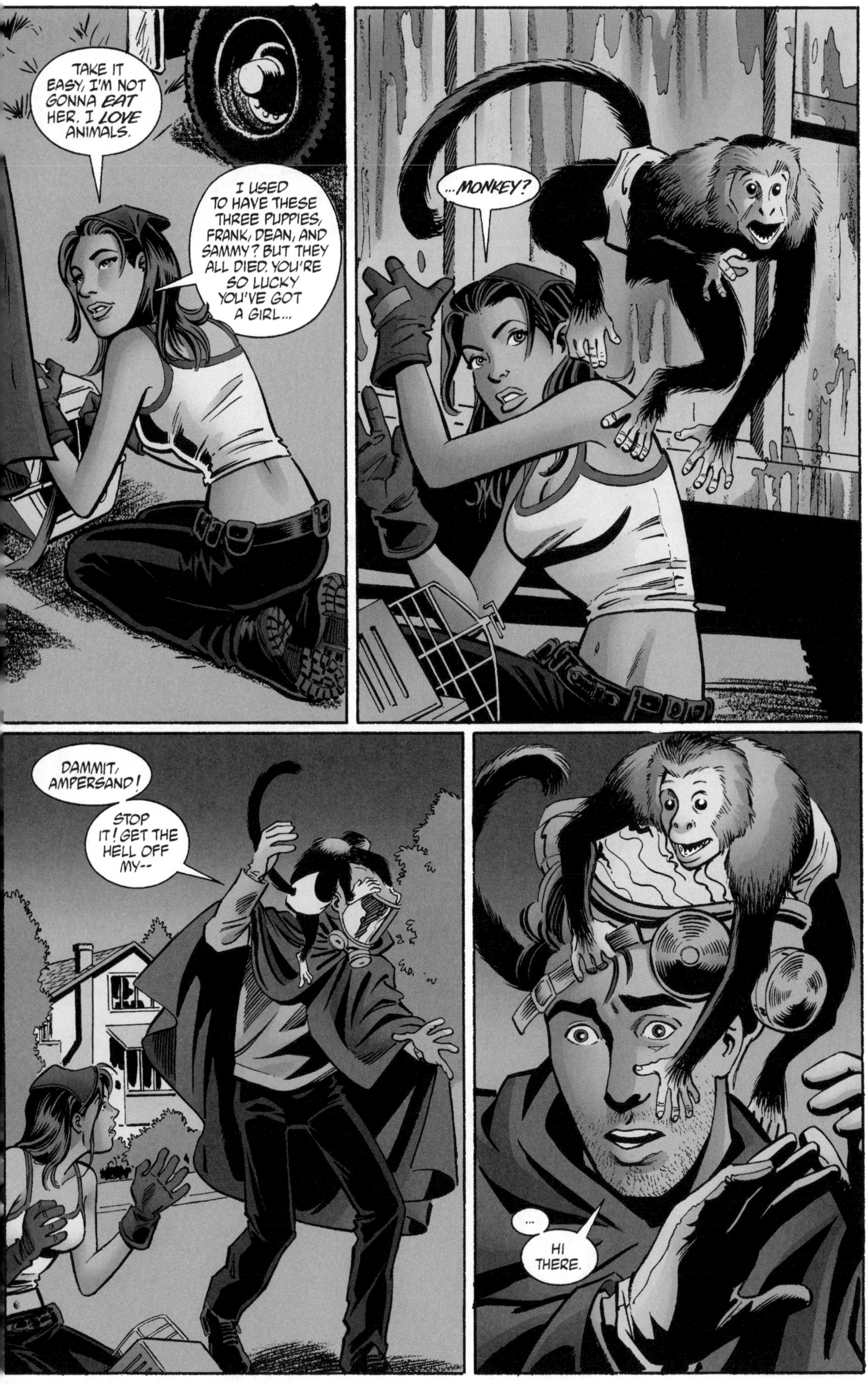
TAKE IT EASY, I'M NOT GONNA *EAT* HER. I *LOVE* ANIMALS.
I USED TO HAVE THESE THREE PUPPIES, FRANK, DEAN, AND SAMMY? BUT THEY ALL DIED. YOU'RE SO LUCKY YOU'VE GOT A GIRL...
...*MONKEY?*
DAMMIT, AMPERSAND!
STOP IT! GET THE HELL OFF MY--
...
HI THERE.

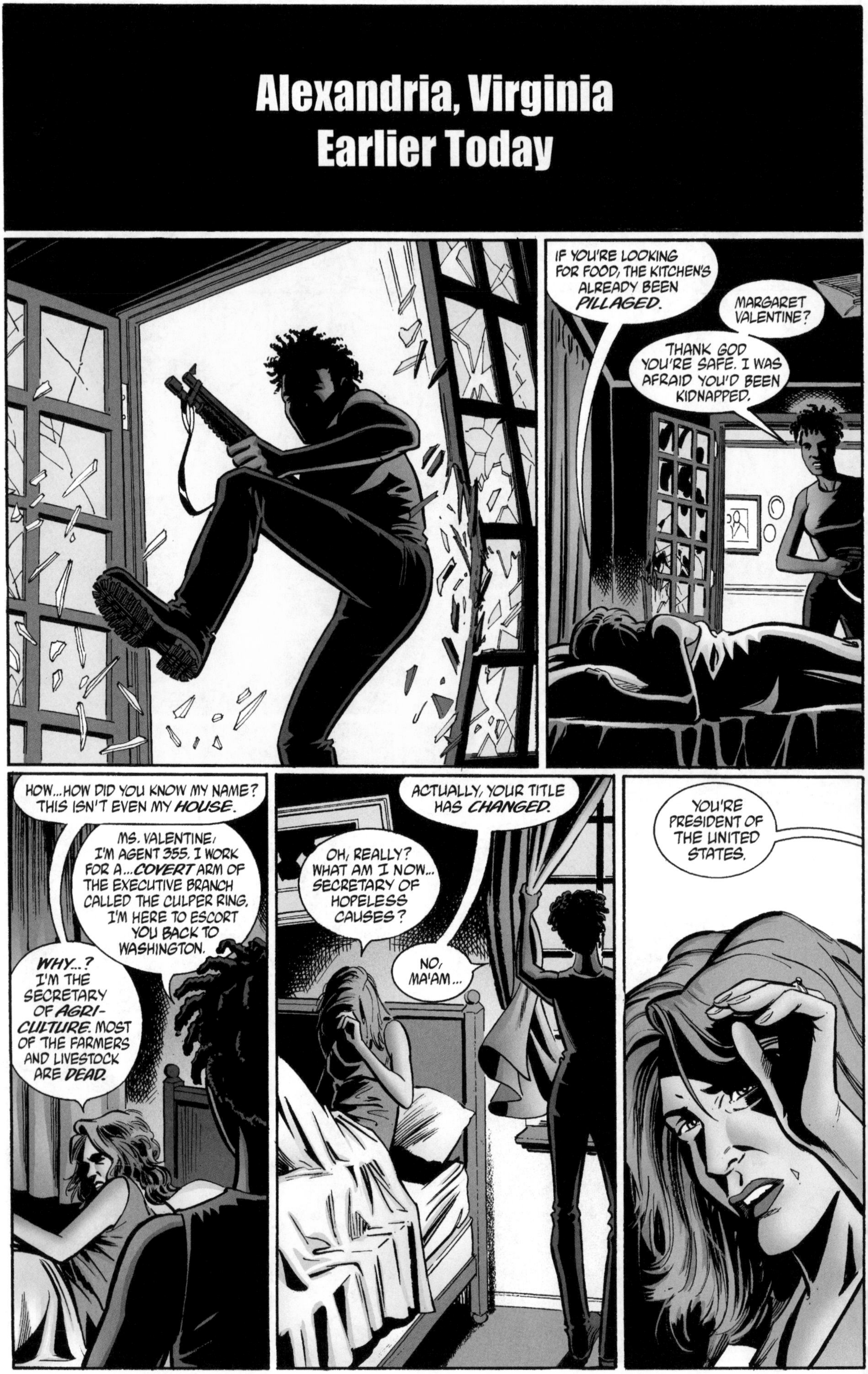
Alexandria, Virginia
Earlier Today
IF YOU'RE LOOKING FOR FOOD, THE KITCHEN'S ALREADY BEEN PILLAGED.
MARGARET VALENTINE?
THANK GOD YOU'RE SAFE. I WAS AFRAID YOU'D BEEN KIDNAPPED.
HOW...HOW DID YOU KNOW MY NAME? THIS ISN'T EVEN MY HOUSE.
MS. VALENTINE, I'M AGENT 355. I WORK FOR A...COVERT ARM OF THE EXECUTIVE BRANCH CALLED THE CULPER RING. I'M HERE TO ESCORT YOU BACK TO WASHINGTON.
WHY...? I'M THE SECRETARY OF AGRI-CULTURE. MOST OF THE FARMERS AND LIVESTOCK ARE DEAD.
ACTUALLY, YOUR TITLE HAS CHANGED.
OH, REALLY? WHAT AM I NOW... SECRETARY OF HOPELESS CAUSES?
NO, MA'AM...
YOU'RE PRESIDENT OF THE UNITED STATES.

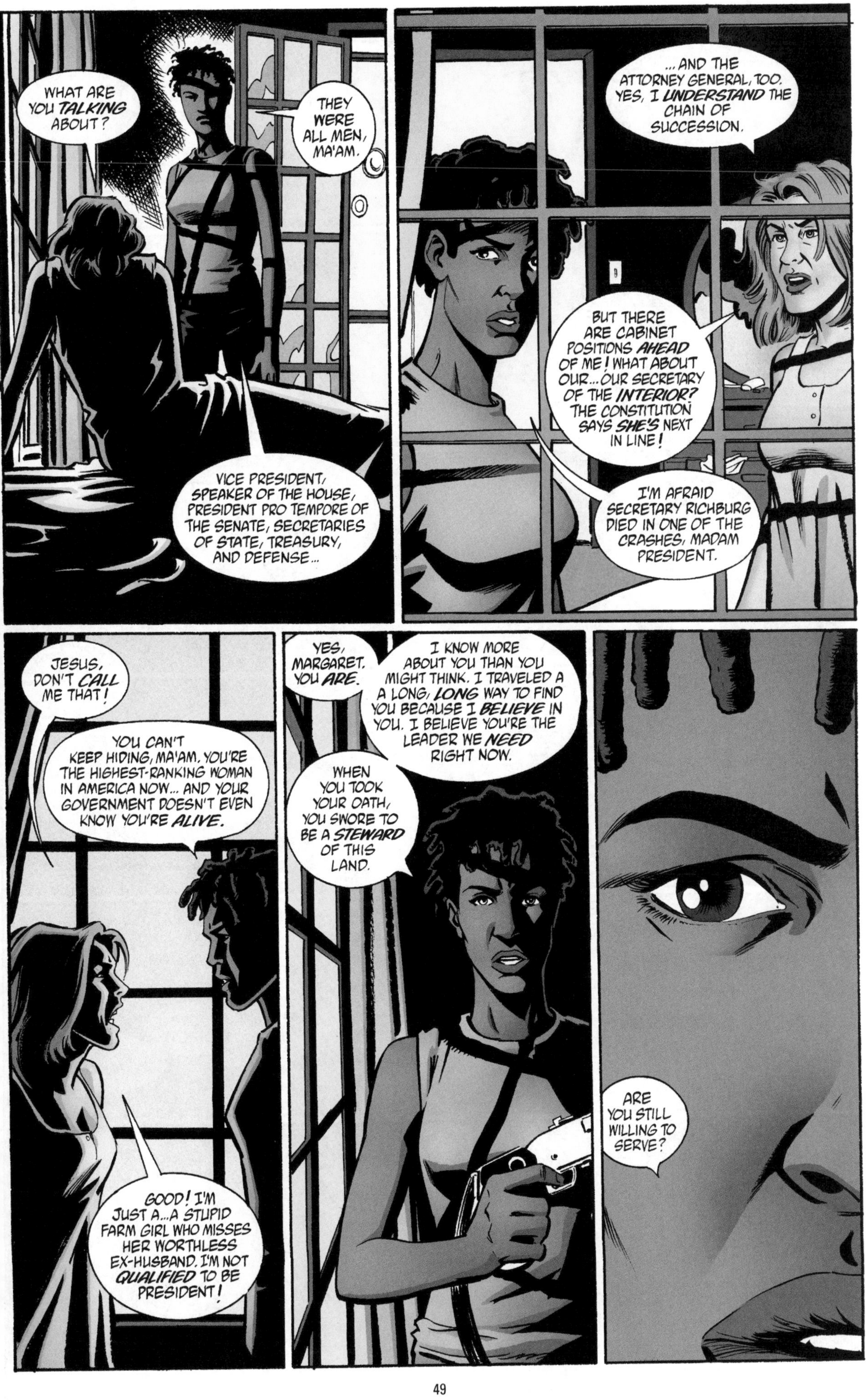
WHAT ARE YOU TALKING ABOUT?
THEY WERE ALL MEN, MA'AM.
VICE PRESIDENT, SPEAKER OF THE HOUSE, PRESIDENT PRO TEMPORE OF THE SENATE, SECRETARIES OF STATE, TREASURY, AND DEFENSE...
...AND THE ATTORNEY GENERAL, TOO. YES, I UNDERSTAND THE CHAIN OF SUCCESSION.
BUT THERE ARE CABINET POSITIONS AHEAD OF ME! WHAT ABOUT OUR... OUR SECRETARY OF THE INTERIOR? THE CONSTITUTION SAYS SHE'S NEXT IN LINE!
I'M AFRAID SECRETARY RICHBURG DIED IN ONE OF THE CRASHES, MADAM PRESIDENT.
JESUS, DON'T CALL ME THAT!
YOU CAN'T KEEP HIDING, MA'AM. YOU'RE THE HIGHEST-RANKING WOMAN IN AMERICA NOW... AND YOUR GOVERNMENT DOESN'T EVEN KNOW YOU'RE ALIVE.
GOOD! I'M JUST A... A STUPID FARM GIRL WHO MISSES HER WORTHLESS EX-HUSBAND. I'M NOT QUALIFIED TO BE PRESIDENT!
YES, MARGARET. YOU ARE.
I KNOW MORE ABOUT YOU THAN YOU MIGHT THINK. I TRAVELED A A LONG, LONG WAY TO FIND YOU BECAUSE I BELIEVE IN YOU. I BELIEVE YOU'RE THE LEADER WE NEED RIGHT NOW.
WHEN YOU TOOK YOUR OATH, YOU SWORE TO BE A STEWARD OF THIS LAND.
ARE YOU STILL WILLING TO SERVE?

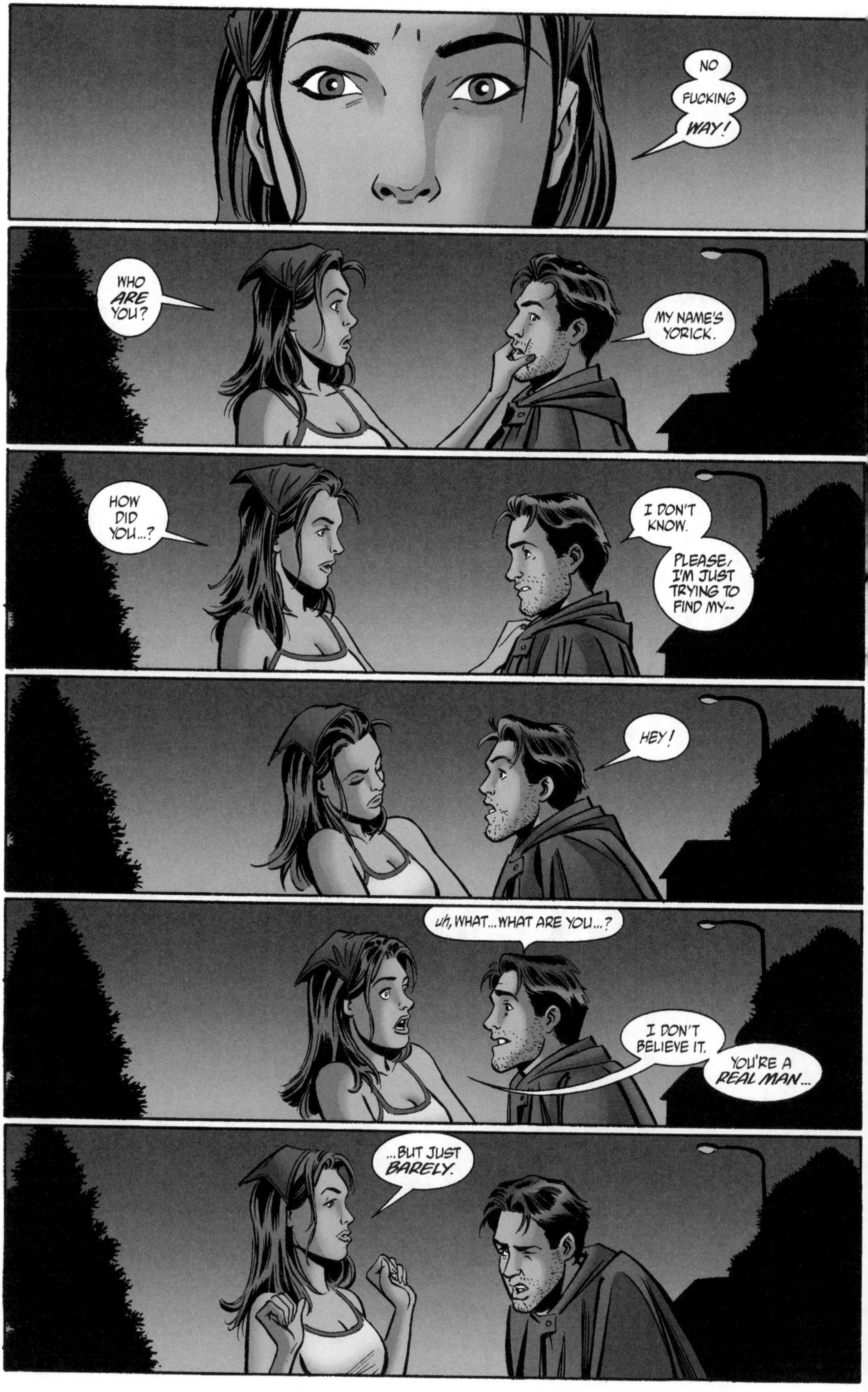
NO FUCKING WAY!
WHO ARE YOU?
MY NAME'S YORICK.
HOW DID YOU...?
I DON'T KNOW.
PLEASE, I'M JUST TRYING TO FIND MY--
HEY!
uh, WHAT...WHAT ARE YOU...?
I DON'T BELIEVE IT.
YOU'RE A REAL MAN...
...BUT JUST BARELY.

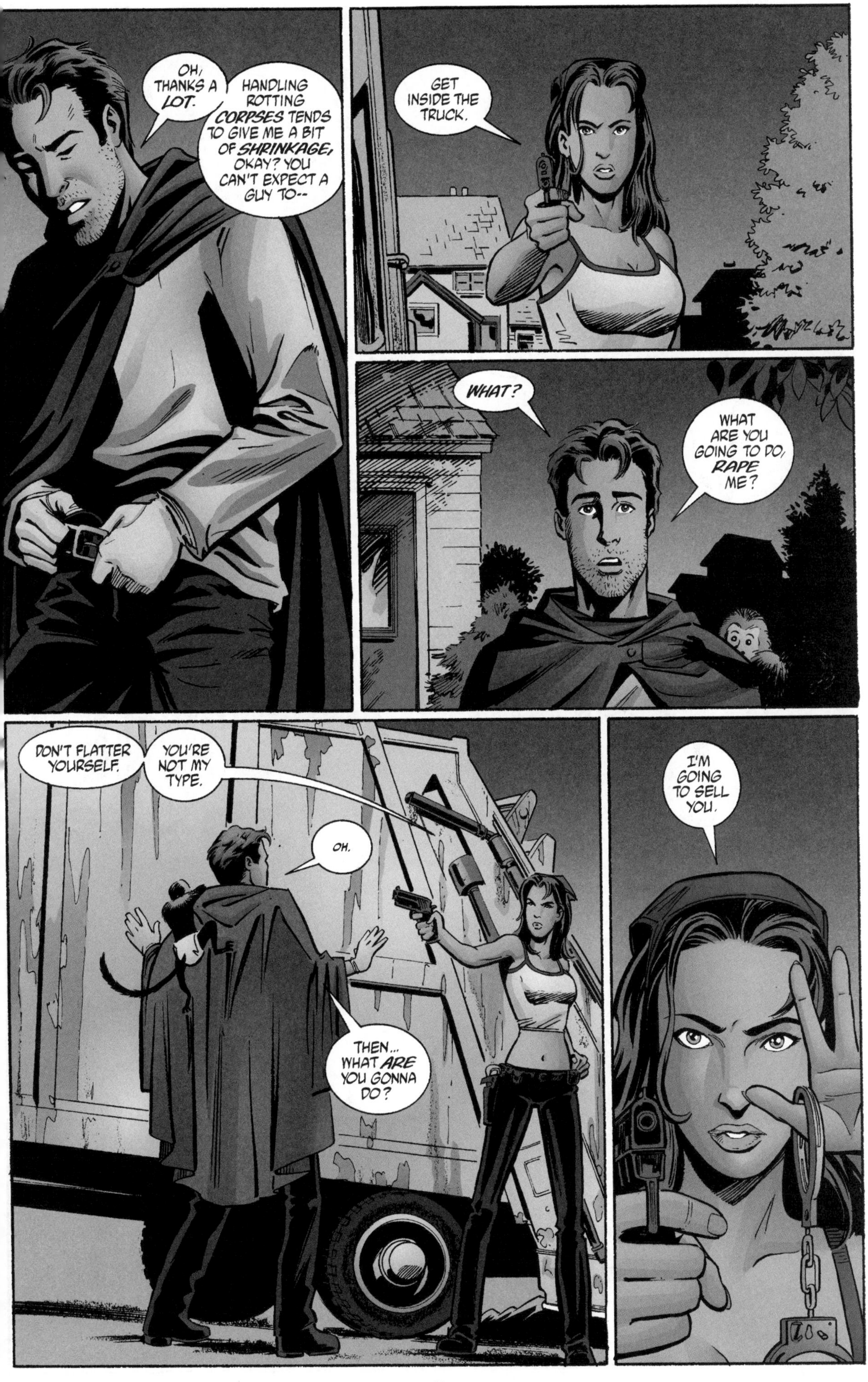
OH, THANKS A LOT.
HANDLING ROTTING CORPSES TENDS TO GIVE ME A BIT OF SHRINKAGE, OKAY? YOU CAN'T EXPECT A GUY TO--
GET INSIDE THE TRUCK.
WHAT?
WHAT ARE YOU GOING TO DO, RAPE ME?
DON'T FLATTER YOURSELF.
YOU'RE NOT MY TYPE.
OH.
THEN... WHAT ARE YOU GONNA DO?
I'M GOING TO SELL YOU.

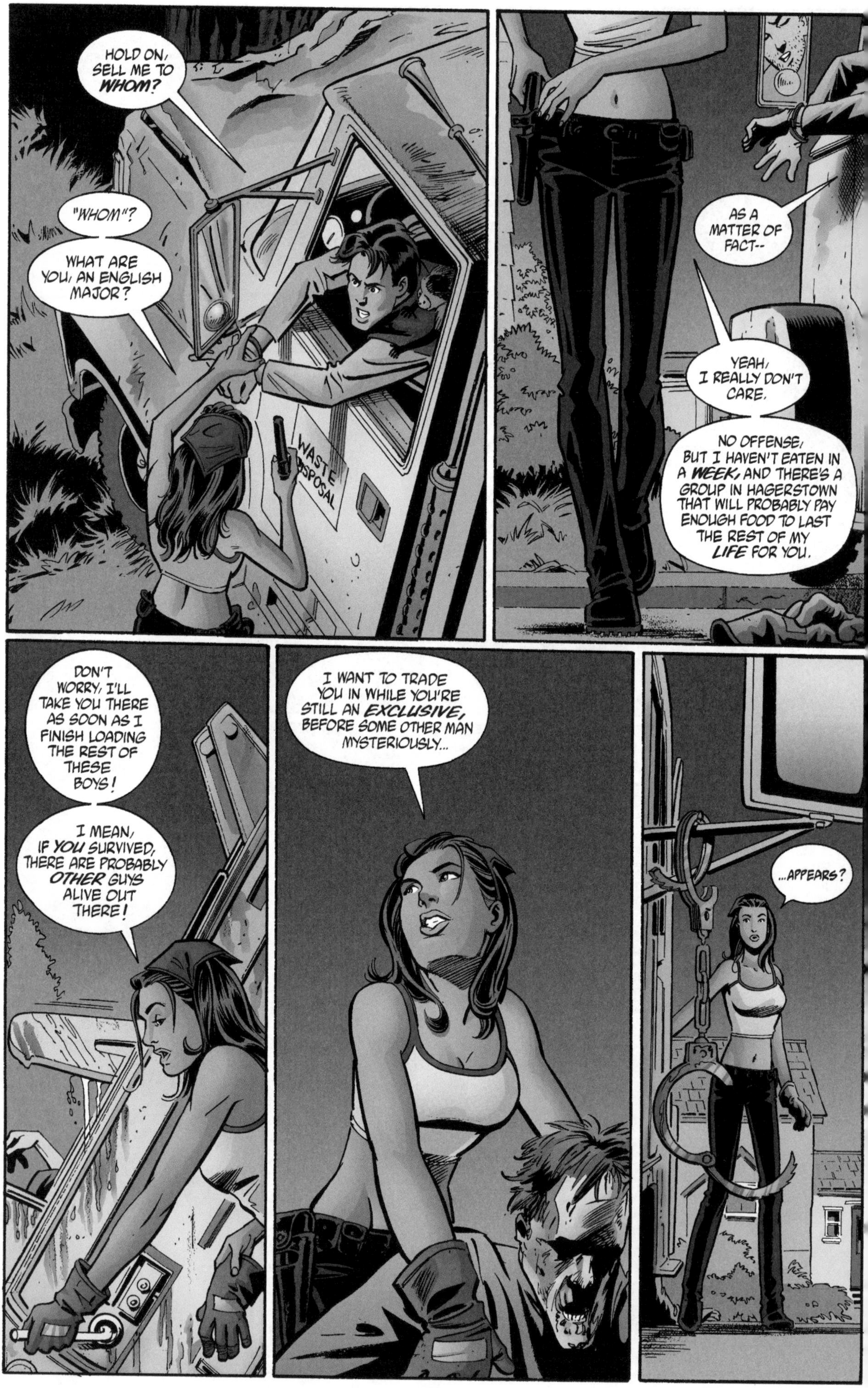
HOLD ON, SELL ME TO WHOM?
"WHOM"?
WHAT ARE YOU, AN ENGLISH MAJOR?
WASTE DISPOSAL
AS A MATTER OF FACT--
YEAH, I REALLY DON'T CARE.
NO OFFENSE, BUT I HAVEN'T EATEN IN A WEEK, AND THERE'S A GROUP IN HAGERSTOWN THAT WILL PROBABLY PAY ENOUGH FOOD TO LAST THE REST OF MY LIFE FOR YOU.
DON'T WORRY, I'LL TAKE YOU THERE AS SOON AS I FINISH LOADING THE REST OF THESE BOYS!
I MEAN, IF YOU SURVIVED, THERE ARE PROBABLY OTHER GUYS ALIVE OUT THERE!
I WANT TO TRADE YOU IN WHILE YOU'RE STILL AN EXCLUSIVE, BEFORE SOME OTHER MAN MYSTERIOUSLY...
...APPEARS?

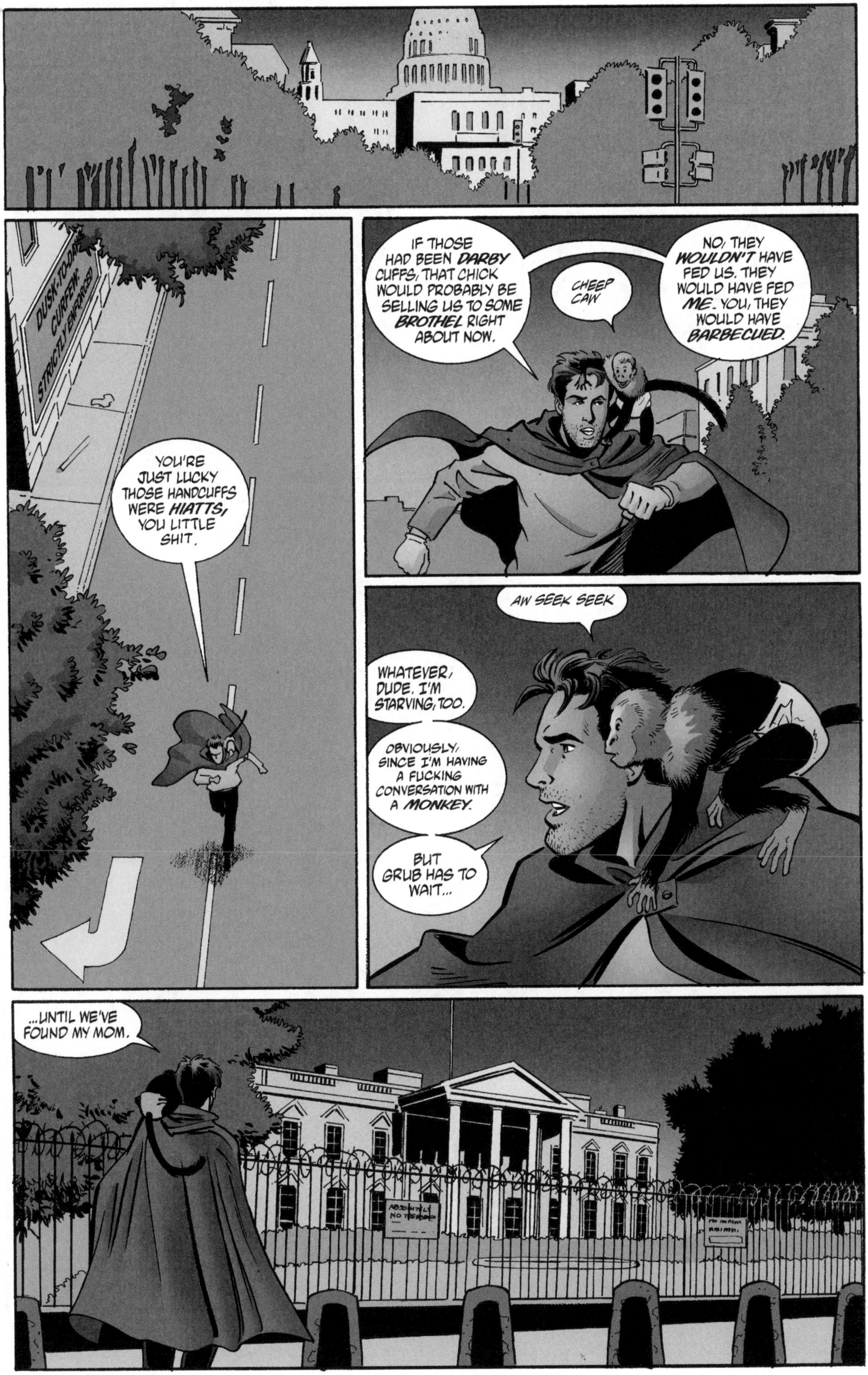
CURFEW.
STRICTLY ENFORCED
YOU'RE JUST LUCKY THOSE HANDCUFFS WERE HIATTS, YOU LITTLE SHIT.
IF THOSE HAD BEEN DARBY CUFFS, THAT CHICK WOULD PROBABLY BE SELLING US TO SOME BROTHEL RIGHT ABOUT NOW.
CHEEP CAW
NO, THEY WOULDN'T HAVE FED US. THEY WOULD HAVE FED ME. YOU, THEY WOULD HAVE BARBECUED.
AW SEEK SEEK
WHATEVER, DUDE. I'M STARVING, TOO.
OBVIOUSLY, SINCE I'M HAVING A FUCKING CONVERSATION WITH A MONKEY.
BUT GRUB HAS TO WAIT...
...UNTIL WE'VE FOUND MY MOM.

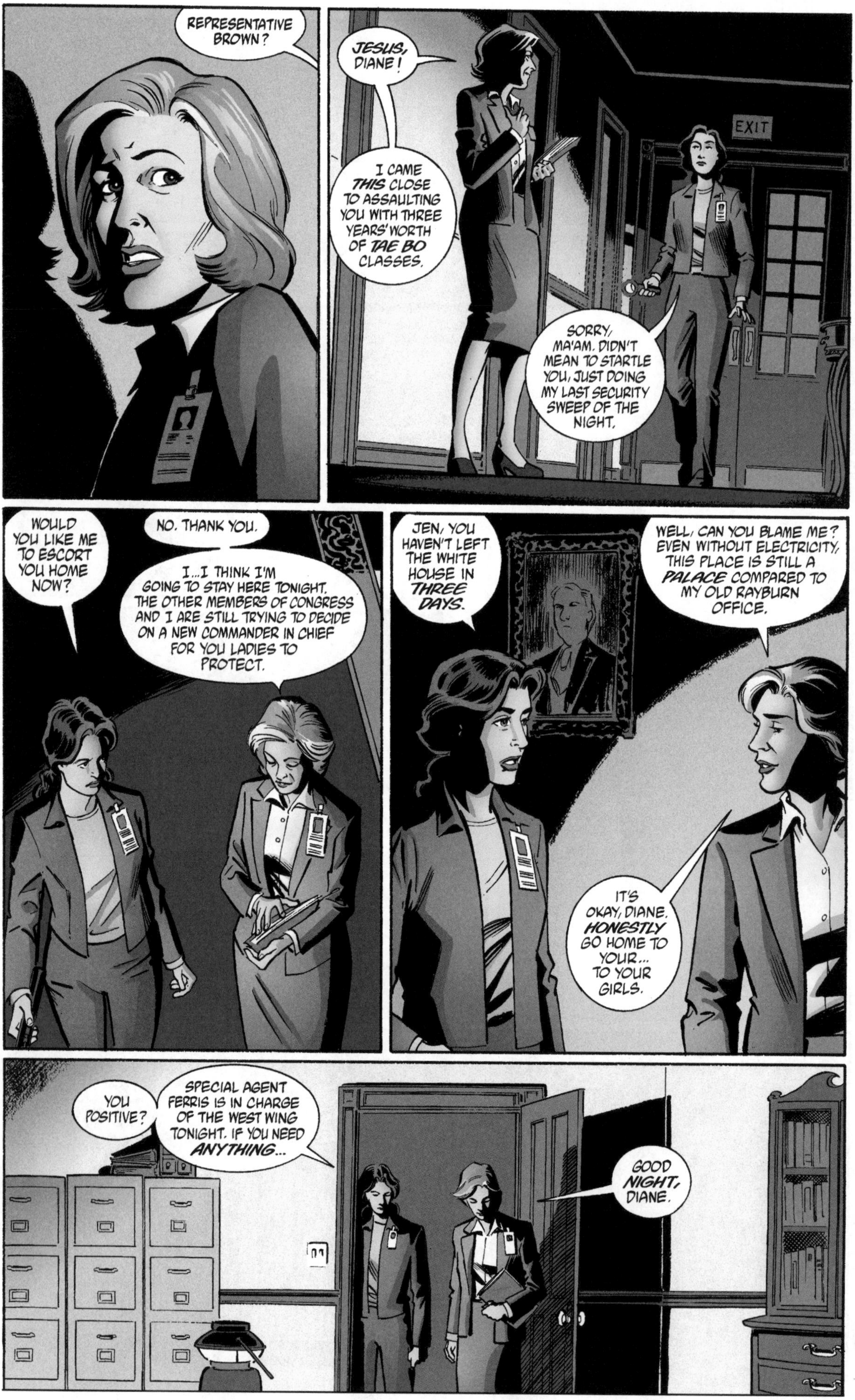
REPRESENTATIVE BROWN?
JESUS, DIANE!
I CAME THIS CLOSE TO ASSAULTING YOU WITH THREE YEARS' WORTH OF TAE BO CLASSES.
SORRY, MA'AM. DIDN'T MEAN TO STARTLE YOU, JUST DOING MY LAST SECURITY SWEEP OF THE NIGHT.
EXIT
WOULD YOU LIKE ME TO ESCORT YOU HOME NOW?
NO. THANK YOU.
I...I THINK I'M GOING TO STAY HERE TONIGHT. THE OTHER MEMBERS OF CONGRESS AND I ARE STILL TRYING TO DECIDE ON A NEW COMMANDER IN CHIEF FOR YOU LADIES TO PROTECT.
JEN, YOU HAVEN'T LEFT THE WHITE HOUSE IN THREE DAYS.
WELL, CAN YOU BLAME ME? EVEN WITHOUT ELECTRICITY, THIS PLACE IS STILL A PALACE COMPARED TO MY OLD RAYBURN OFFICE.
IT'S OKAY, DIANE. HONESTLY GO HOME TO YOUR... TO YOUR GIRLS.
YOU POSITIVE?
SPECIAL AGENT FERRIS IS IN CHARGE OF THE WEST WING TONIGHT. IF YOU NEED ANYTHING...
GOOD NIGHT, DIANE.

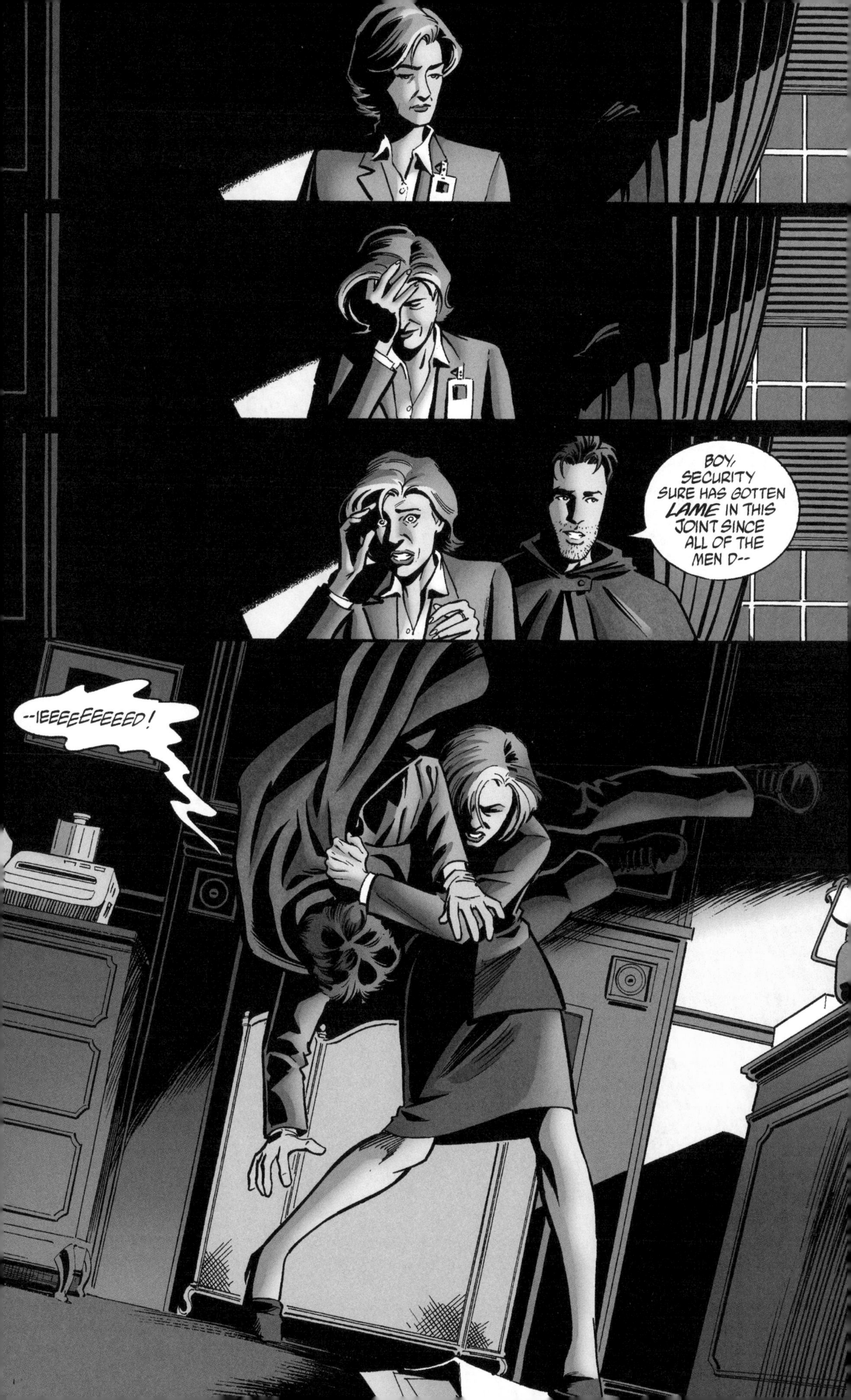
BOY, SECURITY SURE HAS GOTTEN LAME IN THIS JOINT SINCE ALL OF THE MEN D--
--IEEEEEEEEEED!

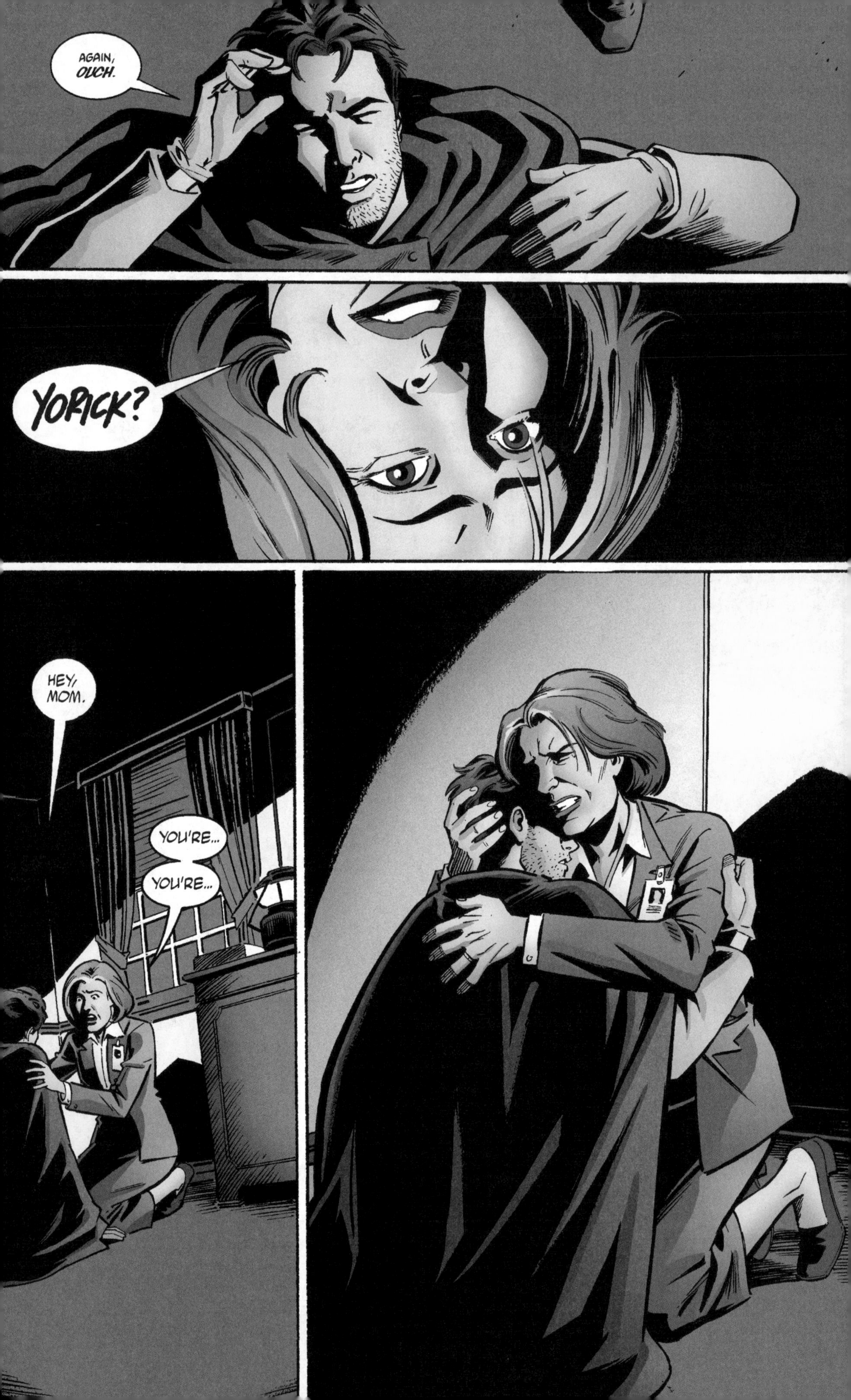
AGAIN, OUCH.
YORICK?
HEY, MOM.
YOU'RE...
YOU'RE...

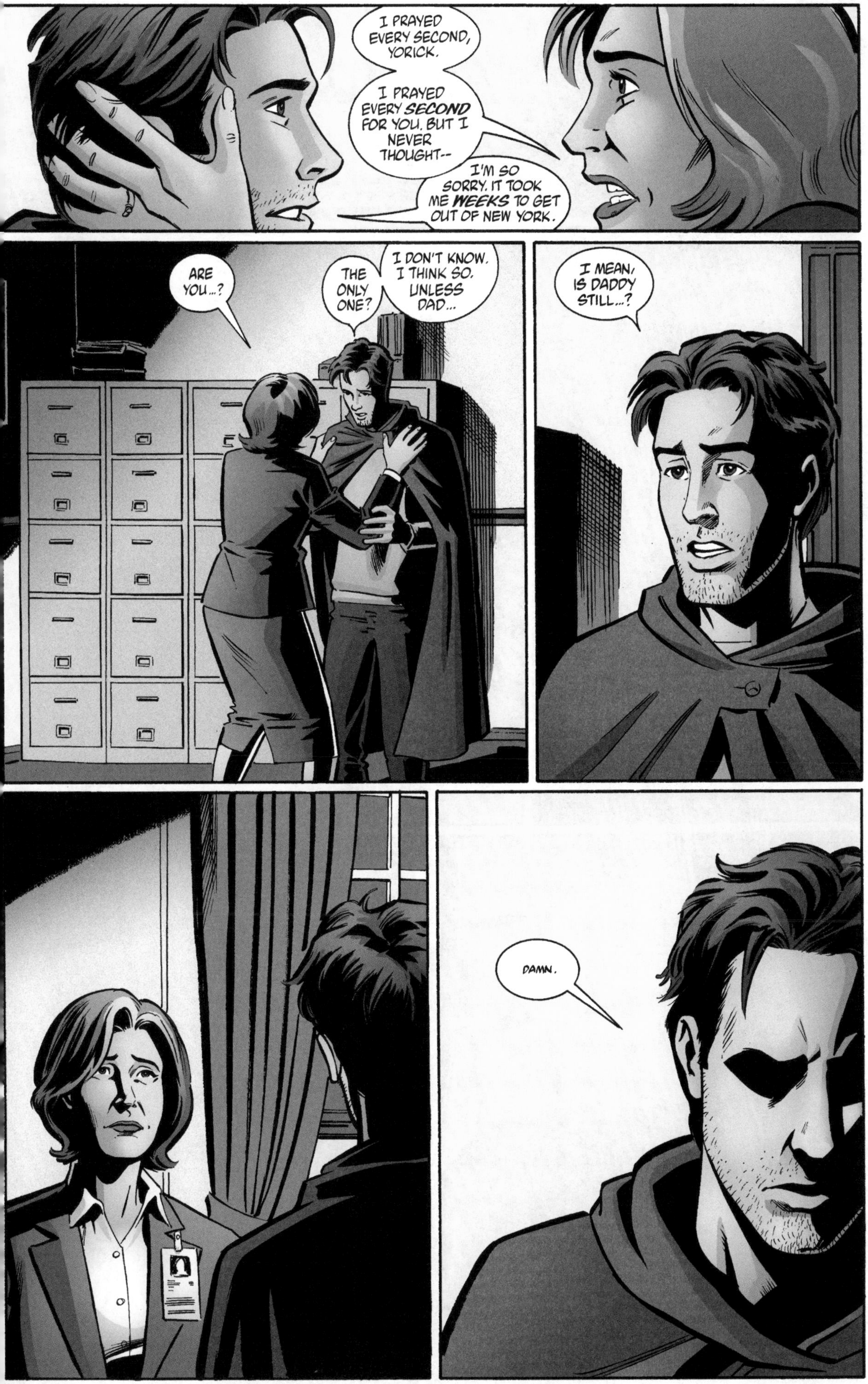
I PRAYED EVERY SECOND, YORICK.
I PRAYED EVERY SECOND FOR YOU. BUT I NEVER THOUGHT--
I'M SO SORRY. IT TOOK ME WEEKS TO GET OUT OF NEW YORK.
ARE YOU...?
THE ONLY ONE?
I DON'T KNOW. I THINK SO. UNLESS DAD...
I MEAN, IS DADDY STILL...?
DAMN.

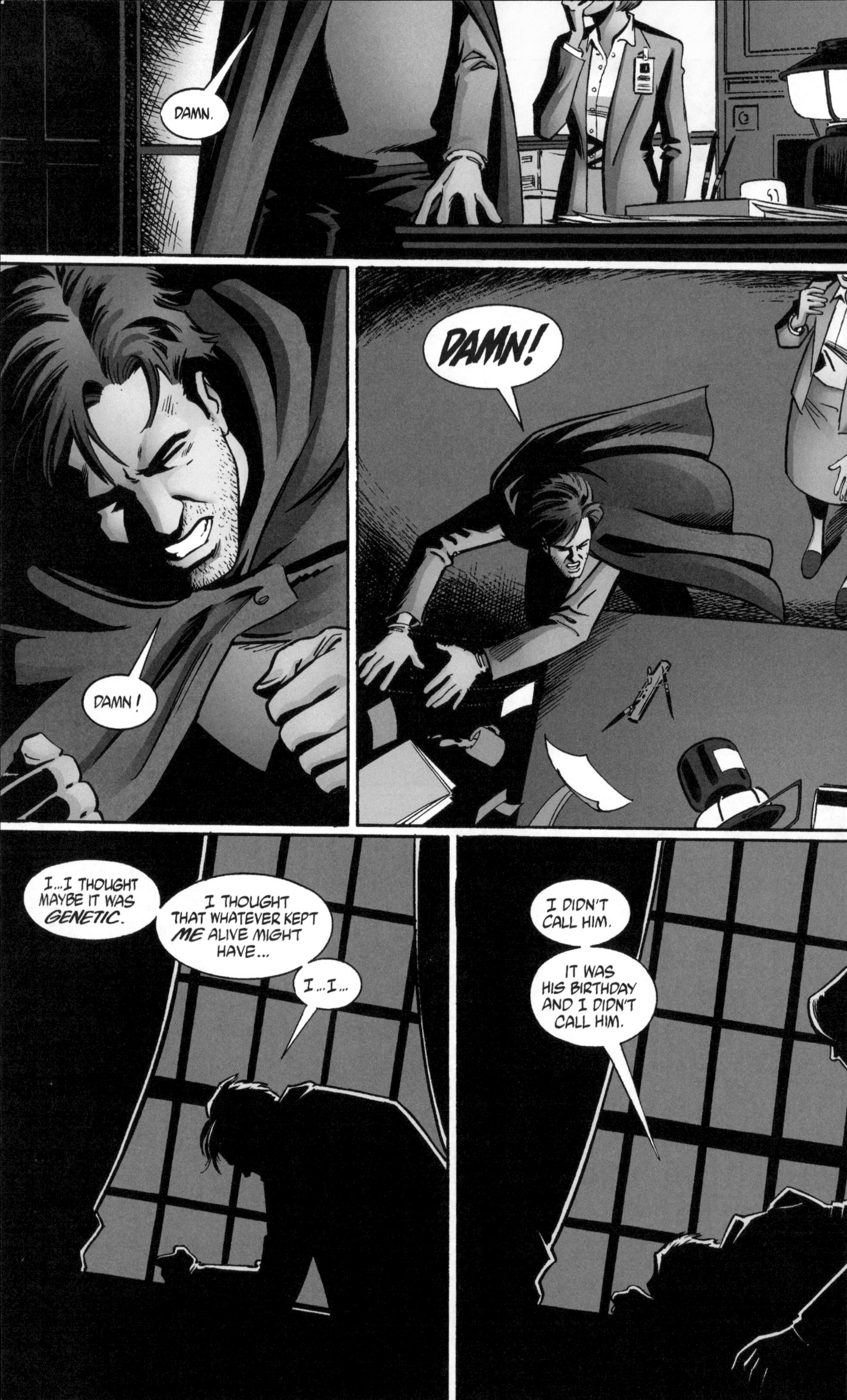
DAMN.
DAMN!
DAMN!
I...I THOUGHT MAYBE IT WAS GENETIC.
I THOUGHT THAT WHATEVER KEPT ME ALIVE MIGHT HAVE...
I...I...
I DIDN'T CALL HIM.
IT WAS HIS BIRTHDAY AND I DIDN'T CALL HIM.

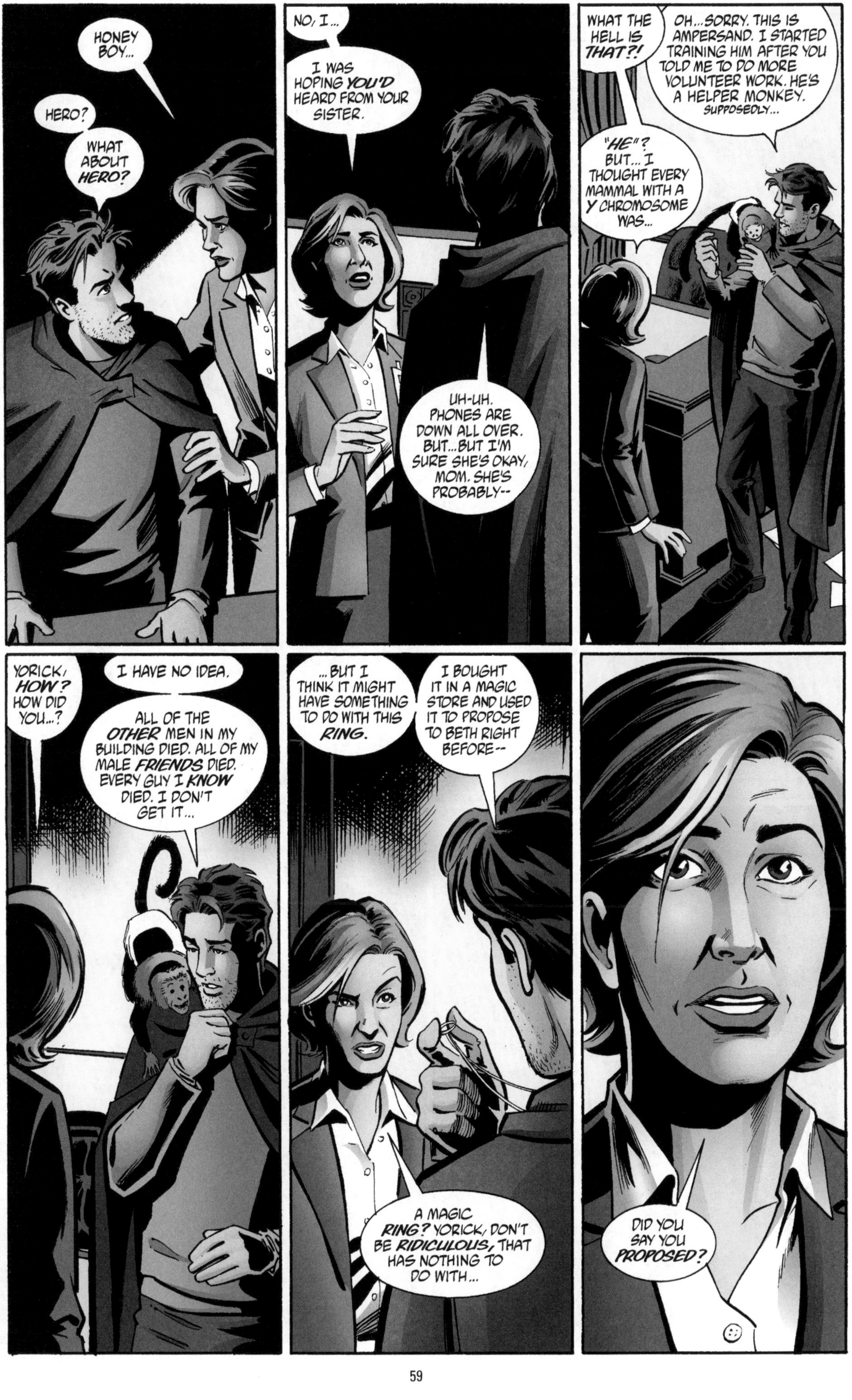
HONEY BOY...
HERO?
WHAT ABOUT HERO?
NO, I...
I WAS HOPING YOU'D HEARD FROM YOUR SISTER.
UH-UH. PHONES ARE DOWN ALL OVER. BUT...BUT I'M SURE SHE'S OKAY, MOM. SHE'S PROBABLY--
WHAT THE HELL IS THAT?!
OH...SORRY. THIS IS AMPERSAND. I STARTED TRAINING HIM AFTER YOU TOLD ME TO DO MORE VOLUNTEER WORK. HE'S A HELPER MONKEY. SUPPOSEDLY...
"HE"? BUT... I THOUGHT EVERY MAMMAL WITH A Y CHROMOSOME WAS...
YORICK, HOW? HOW DID YOU...?
I HAVE NO IDEA.
ALL OF THE OTHER MEN IN MY BUILDING DIED. ALL OF MY MALE FRIENDS DIED. EVERY GUY I KNOW DIED. I DON'T GET IT...
...BUT I THINK IT MIGHT HAVE SOMETHING TO DO WITH THIS RING.
I BOUGHT IT IN A MAGIC STORE AND USED IT TO PROPOSE TO BETH RIGHT BEFORE--
A MAGIC RING? YORICK, DON'T BE RIDICULOUS, THAT HAS NOTHING TO DO WITH...
DID YOU SAY YOU PROPOSED?

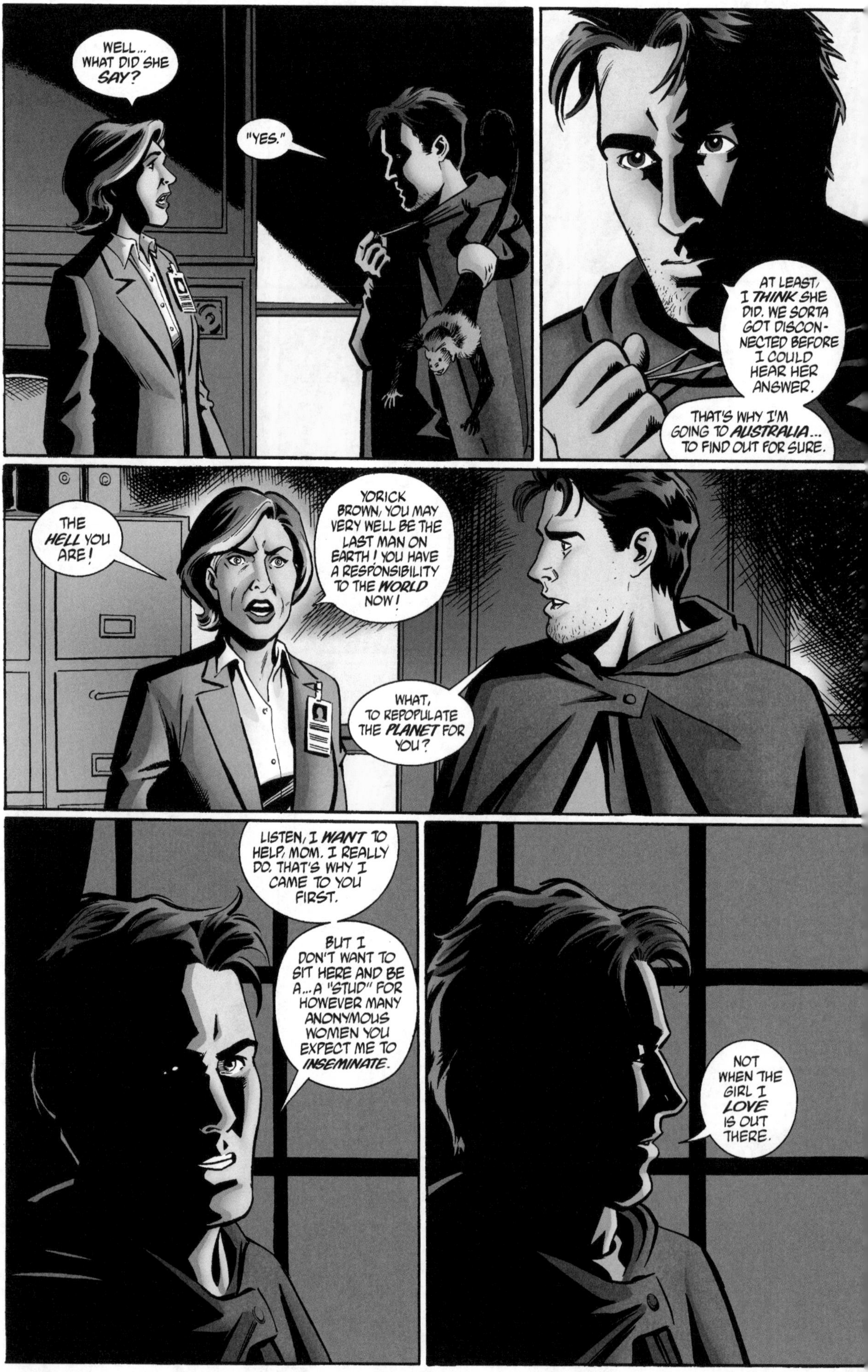
WELL... WHAT DID SHE SAY?
"YES."
AT LEAST, I THINK SHE DID. WE SORTA GOT DISCONNECTED BEFORE I COULD HEAR HER ANSWER.
THAT'S WHY I'M GOING TO AUSTRALIA... TO FIND OUT FOR SURE.
THE HELL YOU ARE!
YORICK BROWN, YOU MAY VERY WELL BE THE LAST MAN ON EARTH! YOU HAVE A RESPONSIBILITY TO THE WORLD NOW!
WHAT, TO REPOPULATE THE PLANET FOR YOU?
LISTEN, I WANT TO HELP, MOM. I REALLY DO. THAT'S WHY I CAME TO YOU FIRST.
BUT I DON'T WANT TO SIT HERE AND BE A...A "STUD" FOR HOWEVER MANY ANONYMOUS WOMEN YOU EXPECT ME TO INSEMINATE.
NOT WHEN THE GIRL I LOVE IS OUT THERE.

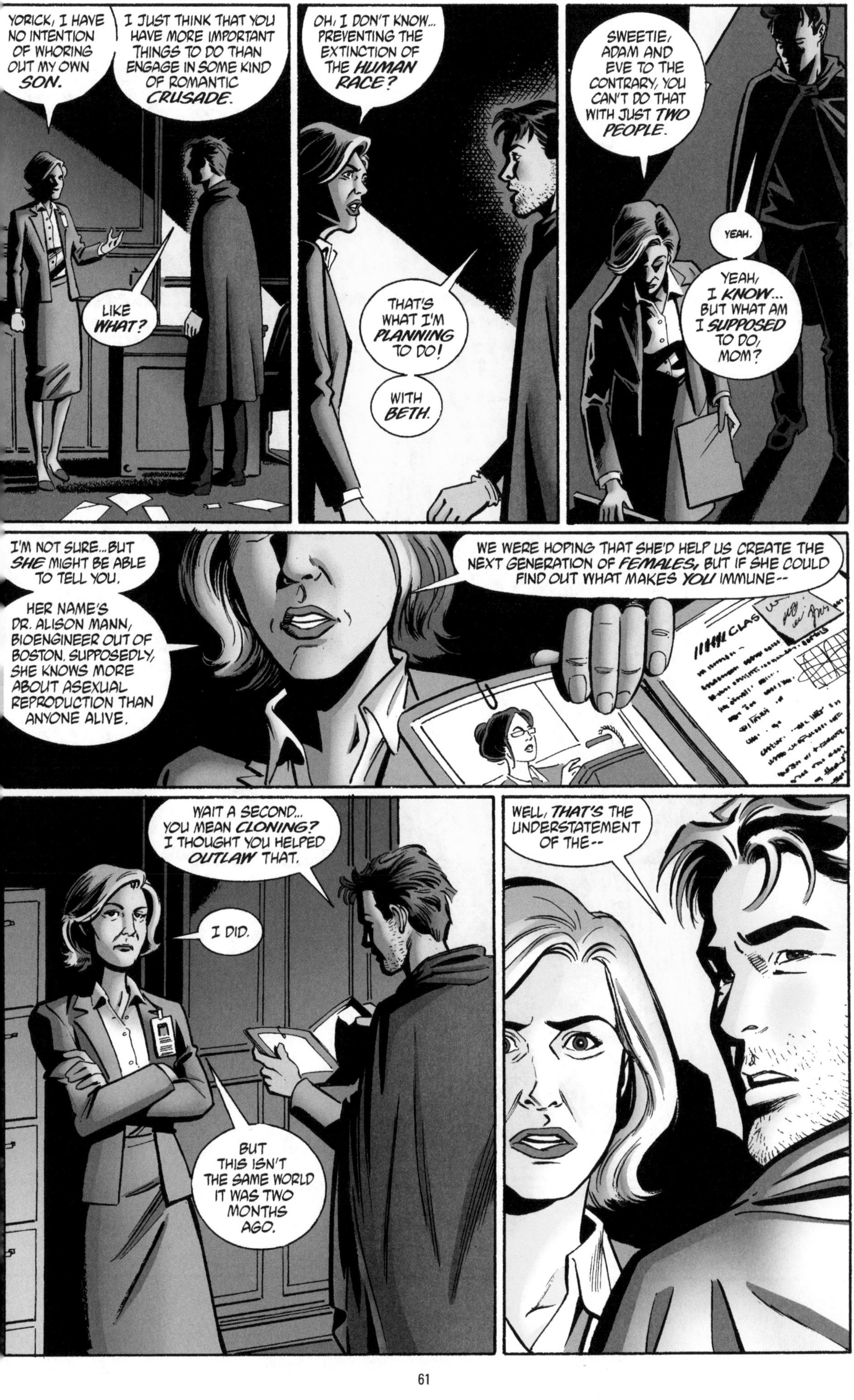
YORICK, I HAVE NO INTENTION OF WHORING OUT MY OWN SON.
I JUST THINK THAT YOU HAVE MORE IMPORTANT THINGS TO DO THAN ENGAGE IN SOME KIND OF ROMANTIC CRUSADE.
LIKE WHAT?
OH, I DON'T KNOW... PREVENTING THE EXTINCTION OF THE HUMAN RACE?
THAT'S WHAT I'M PLANNING TO DO!
WITH BETH.
SWEETIE, ADAM AND EVE TO THE CONTRARY, YOU CAN'T DO THAT WITH JUST TWO PEOPLE.
YEAH.
YEAH, I KNOW... BUT WHAT AM I SUPPOSED TO DO, MOM?
I'M NOT SURE...BUT SHE MIGHT BE ABLE TO TELL YOU.
HER NAME'S DR. ALISON MANN, BIOENGINEER OUT OF BOSTON. SUPPOSEDLY, SHE KNOWS MORE ABOUT ASEXUAL REPRODUCTION THAN ANYONE ALIVE.
WE WERE HOPING THAT SHE'D HELP US CREATE THE NEXT GENERATION OF FEMALES, BUT IF SHE COULD FIND OUT WHAT MAKES YOU IMMUNE--
WAIT A SECOND... YOU MEAN CLONING? I THOUGHT YOU HELPED OUTLAW THAT.
I DID.
BUT THIS ISN'T THE SAME WORLD IT WAS TWO MONTHS AGO.
WELL, THAT'S THE UNDERSTATEMENT OF THE--

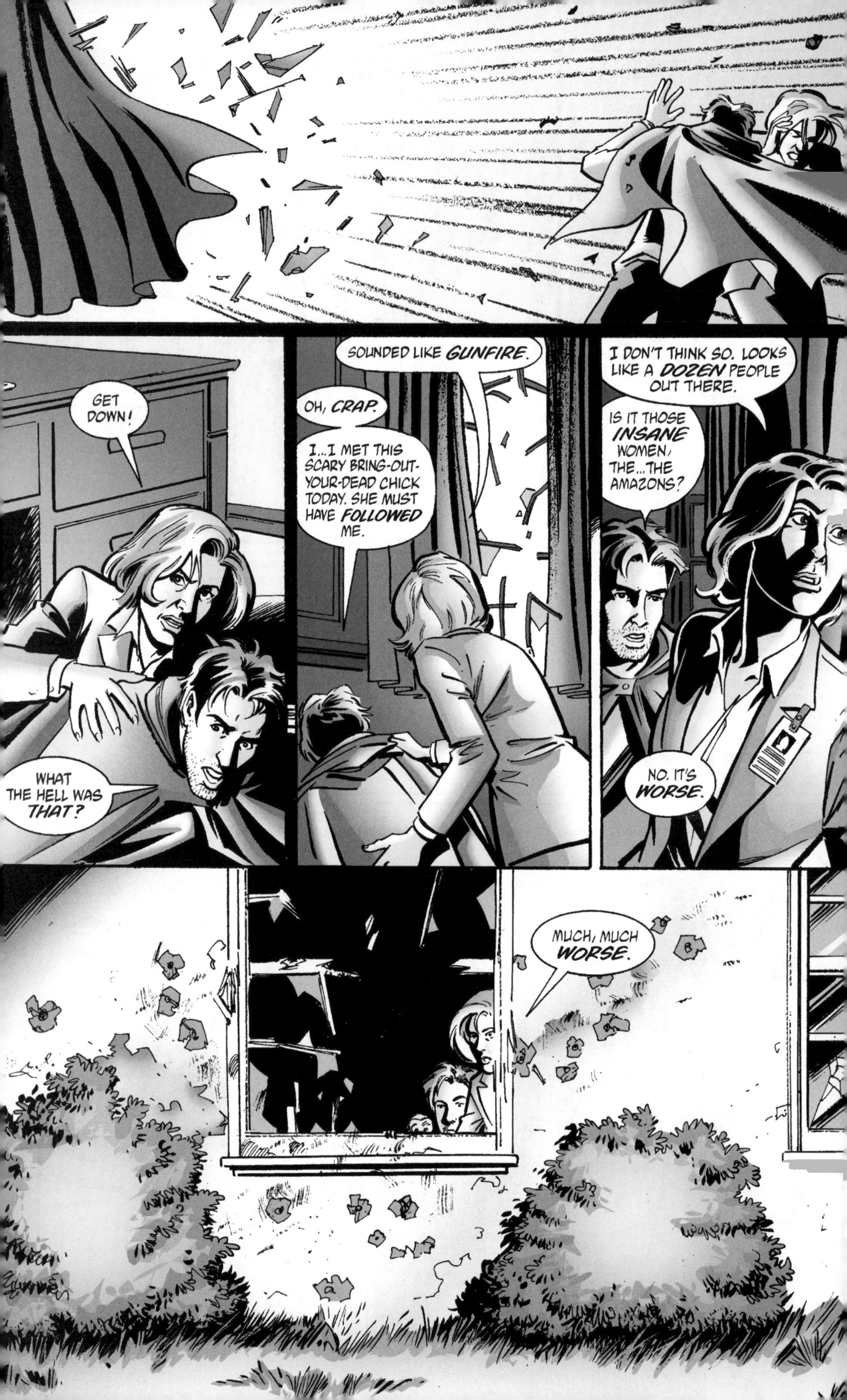
GET DOWN!
WHAT THE HELL WAS THAT?
SOUNDED LIKE GUNFIRE.
OH, CRAP.
I...I MET THIS SCARY BRING-OUT-YOUR-DEAD CHICK TODAY. SHE MUST HAVE FOLLOWED ME.
I DON'T THINK SO. LOOKS LIKE A DOZEN PEOPLE OUT THERE.
IS IT THOSE INSANE WOMEN, THE...THE AMAZONS?
NO. IT'S WORSE.
MUCH, MUCH WORSE.

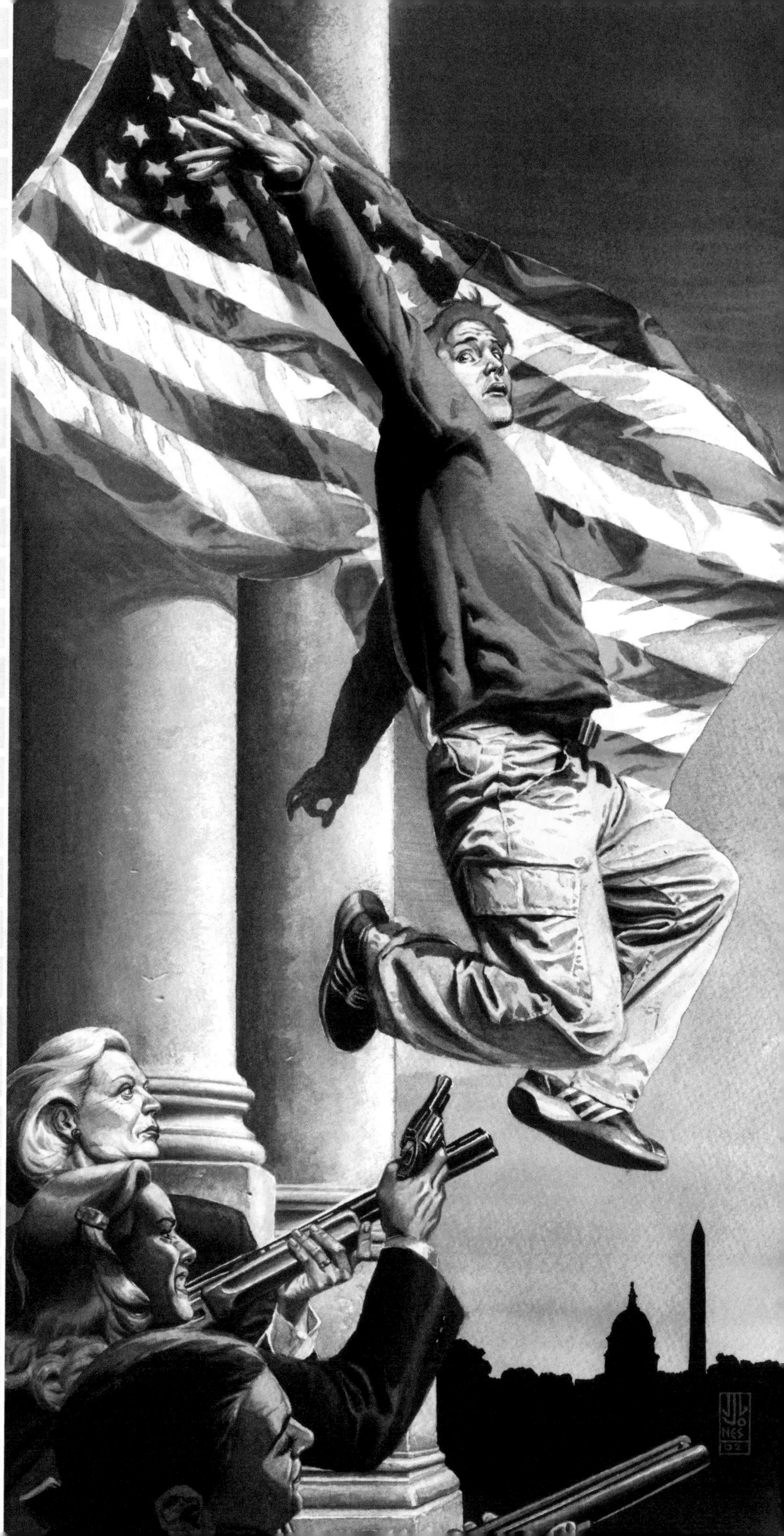

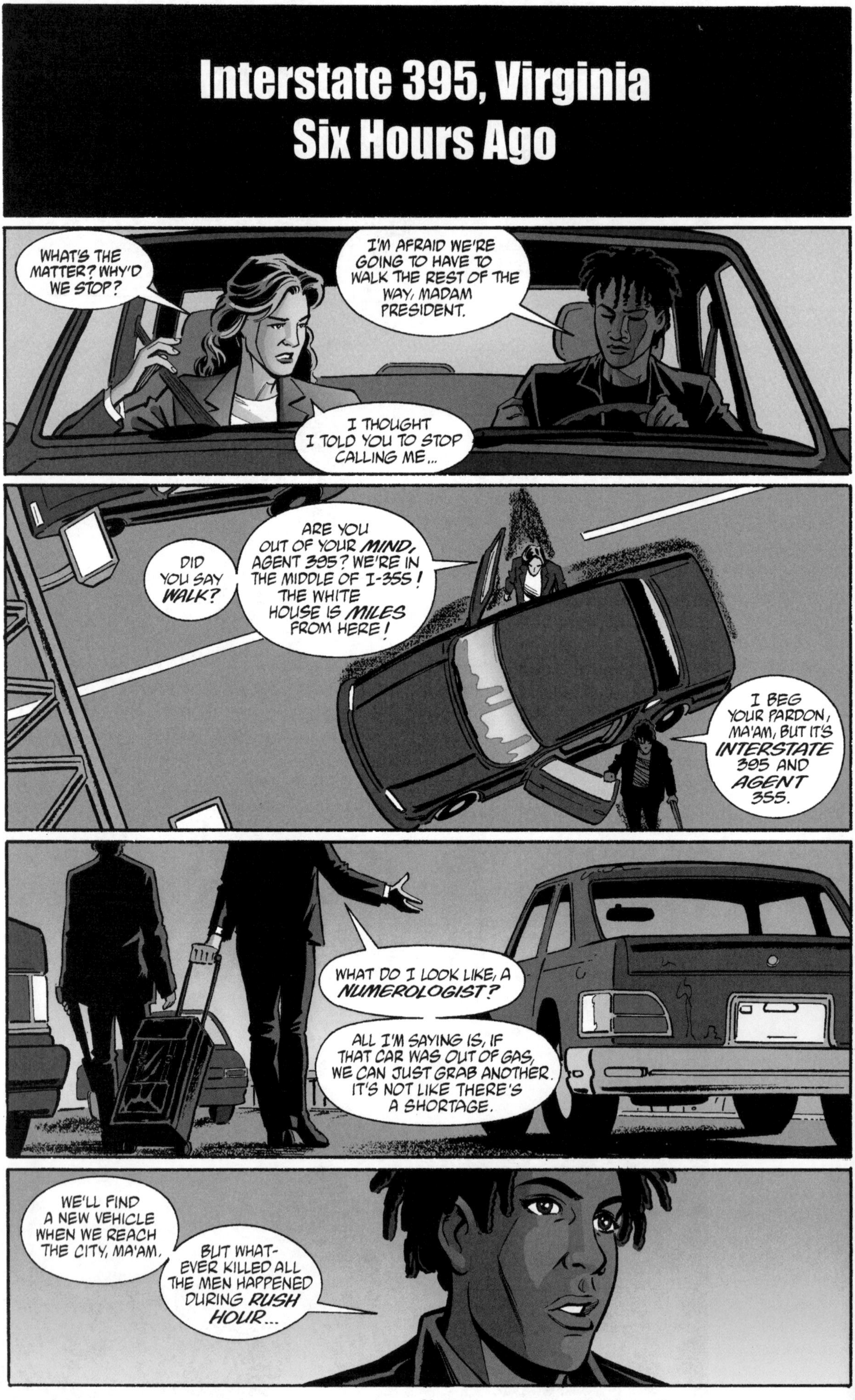
Interstate 395, Virginia
Six Hours Ago
WHAT'S THE MATTER? WHY'D WE STOP?
I'M AFRAID WE'RE GOING TO HAVE TO WALK THE REST OF THE WAY, MADAM PRESIDENT.
I THOUGHT I TOLD YOU TO STOP CALLING ME...
DID YOU SAY WALK?
ARE YOU OUT OF YOUR MIND, AGENT 395? WE'RE IN THE MIDDLE OF I-355! THE WHITE HOUSE IS MILES FROM HERE!
I BEG YOUR PARDON, MA'AM, BUT IT'S INTERSTATE 395 AND AGENT 355.
WHAT DO I LOOK LIKE, A NUMEROLOGIST?
ALL I'M SAYING IS, IF THAT CAR WAS OUT OF GAS, WE CAN JUST GRAB ANOTHER. IT'S NOT LIKE THERE'S A SHORTAGE.
WE'LL FIND A NEW VEHICLE WHEN WE REACH THE CITY, MA'AM.
BUT WHAT-EVER KILLED ALL THE MEN HAPPENED DURING RUSH HOUR...

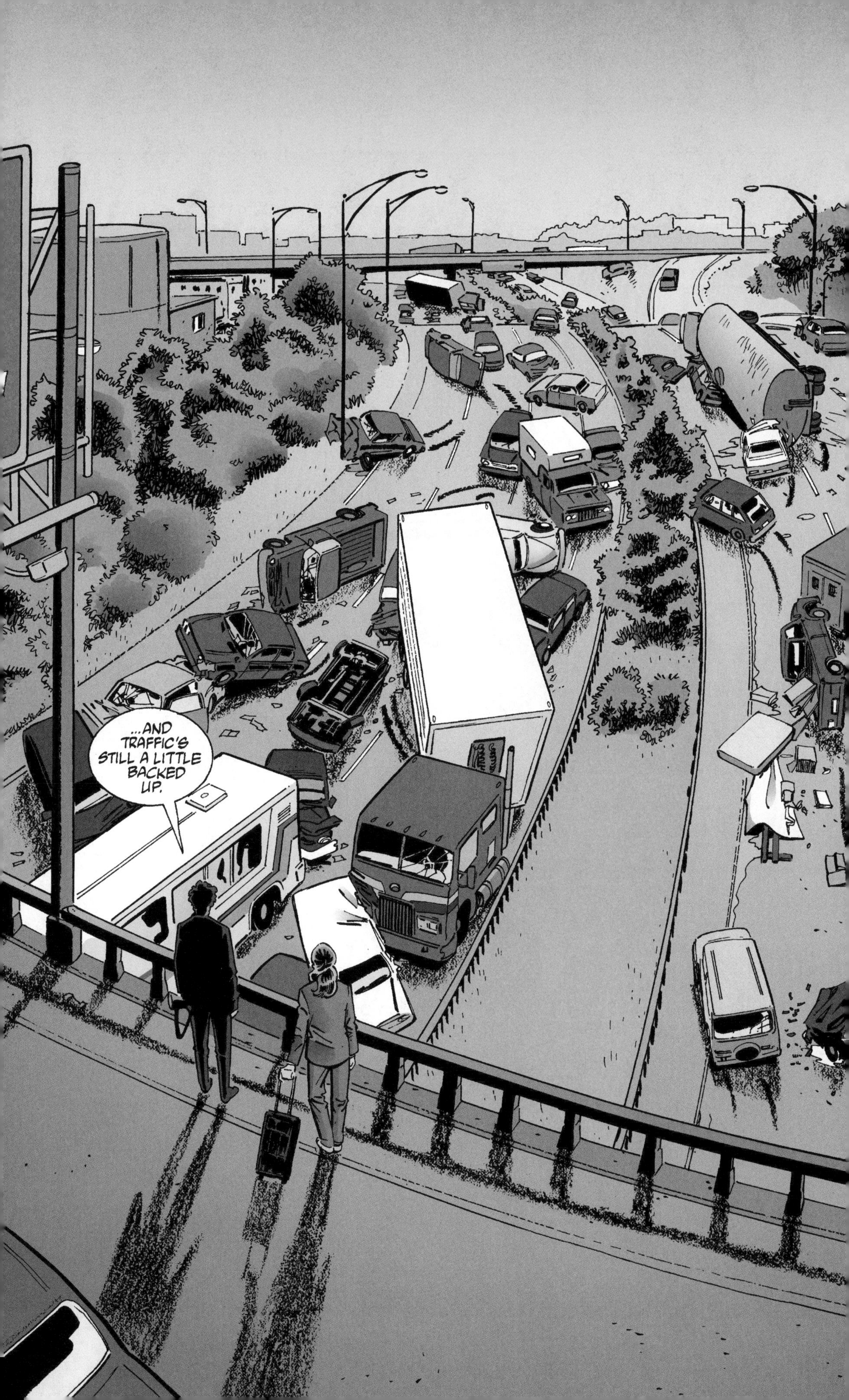
...AND TRAFFIC'S STILL A LITTLE BACKED UP.

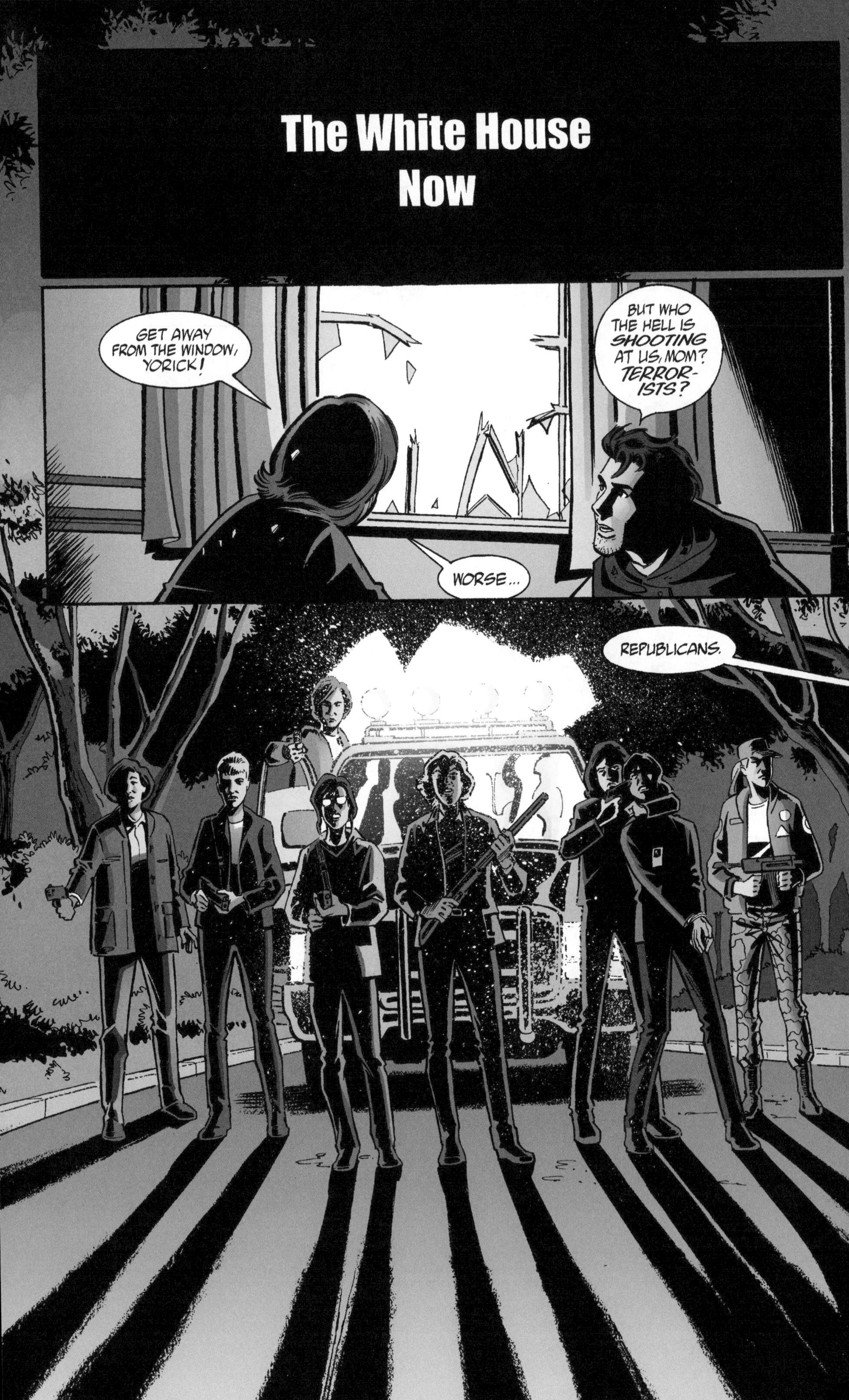
The White House
Now
GET AWAY FROM THE WINDOW, YORICK!
BUT WHO THE HELL IS SHOOTING AT US, MOM? TERRORISTS?
WORSE...
REPUBLICANS.

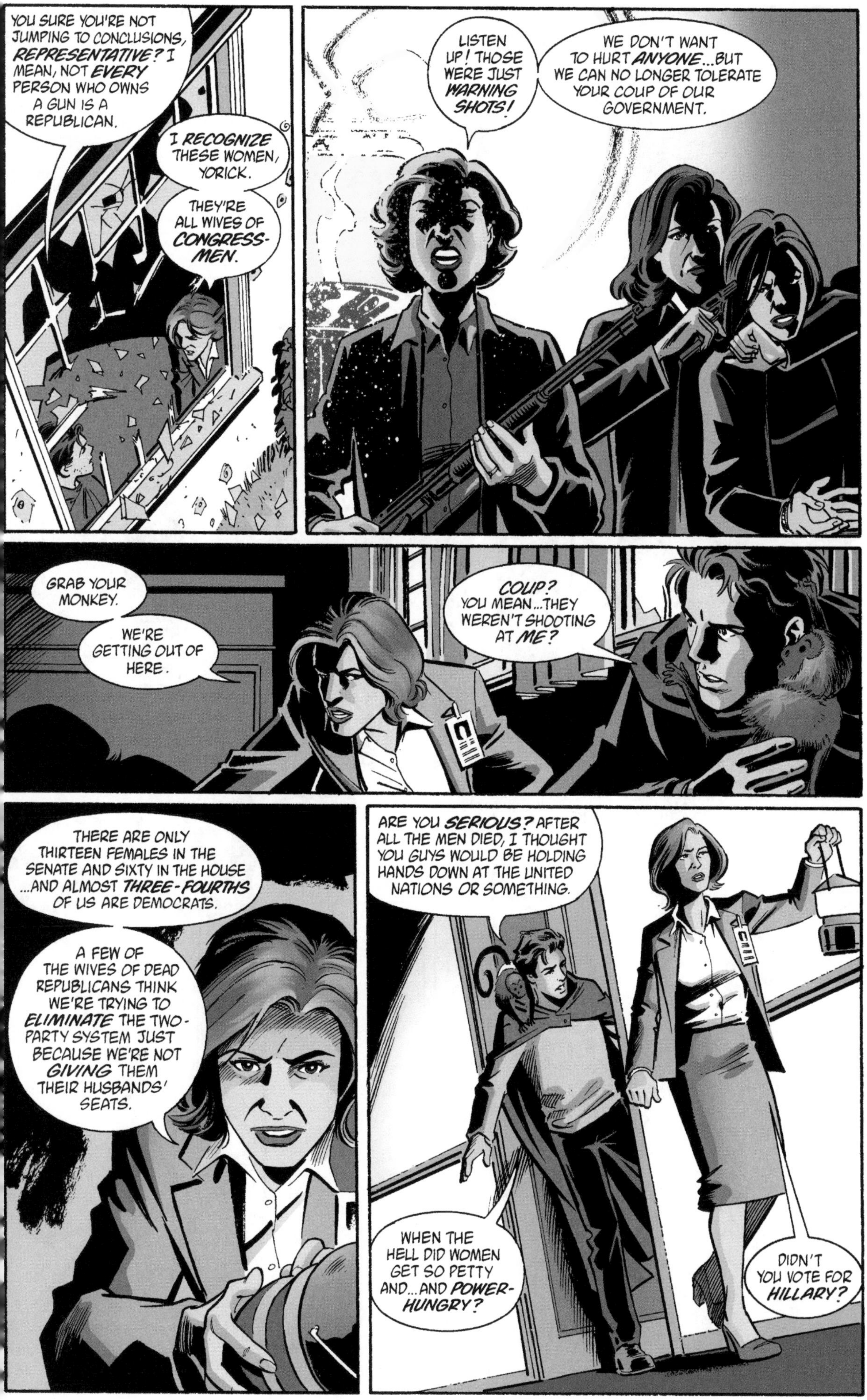
YOU SURE YOU'RE NOT JUMPING TO CONCLUSIONS, REPRESENTATIVE? I MEAN, NOT EVERY PERSON WHO OWNS A GUN IS A REPUBLICAN.
I RECOGNIZE THESE WOMEN, YORICK.
THEY'RE ALL WIVES OF CONGRESS-MEN.
LISTEN UP! THOSE WERE JUST WARNING SHOTS!
WE DON'T WANT TO HURT ANYONE...BUT WE CAN NO LONGER TOLERATE YOUR COUP OF OUR GOVERNMENT.
GRAB YOUR MONKEY.
WE'RE GETTING OUT OF HERE.
COUP? YOU MEAN...THEY WEREN'T SHOOTING AT ME?
THERE ARE ONLY THIRTEEN FEMALES IN THE SENATE AND SIXTY IN THE HOUSE ...AND ALMOST THREE-FOURTHS OF US ARE DEMOCRATS.
A FEW OF THE WIVES OF DEAD REPUBLICANS THINK WE'RE TRYING TO ELIMINATE THE TWO-PARTY SYSTEM JUST BECAUSE WE'RE NOT GIVING THEM THEIR HUSBANDS' SEATS.
ARE YOU SERIOUS? AFTER ALL THE MEN DIED, I THOUGHT YOU GUYS WOULD BE HOLDING HANDS DOWN AT THE UNITED NATIONS OR SOMETHING.
WHEN THE HELL DID WOMEN GET SO PETTY AND...AND POWER-HUNGRY?
DIDN'T YOU VOTE FOR HILLARY?

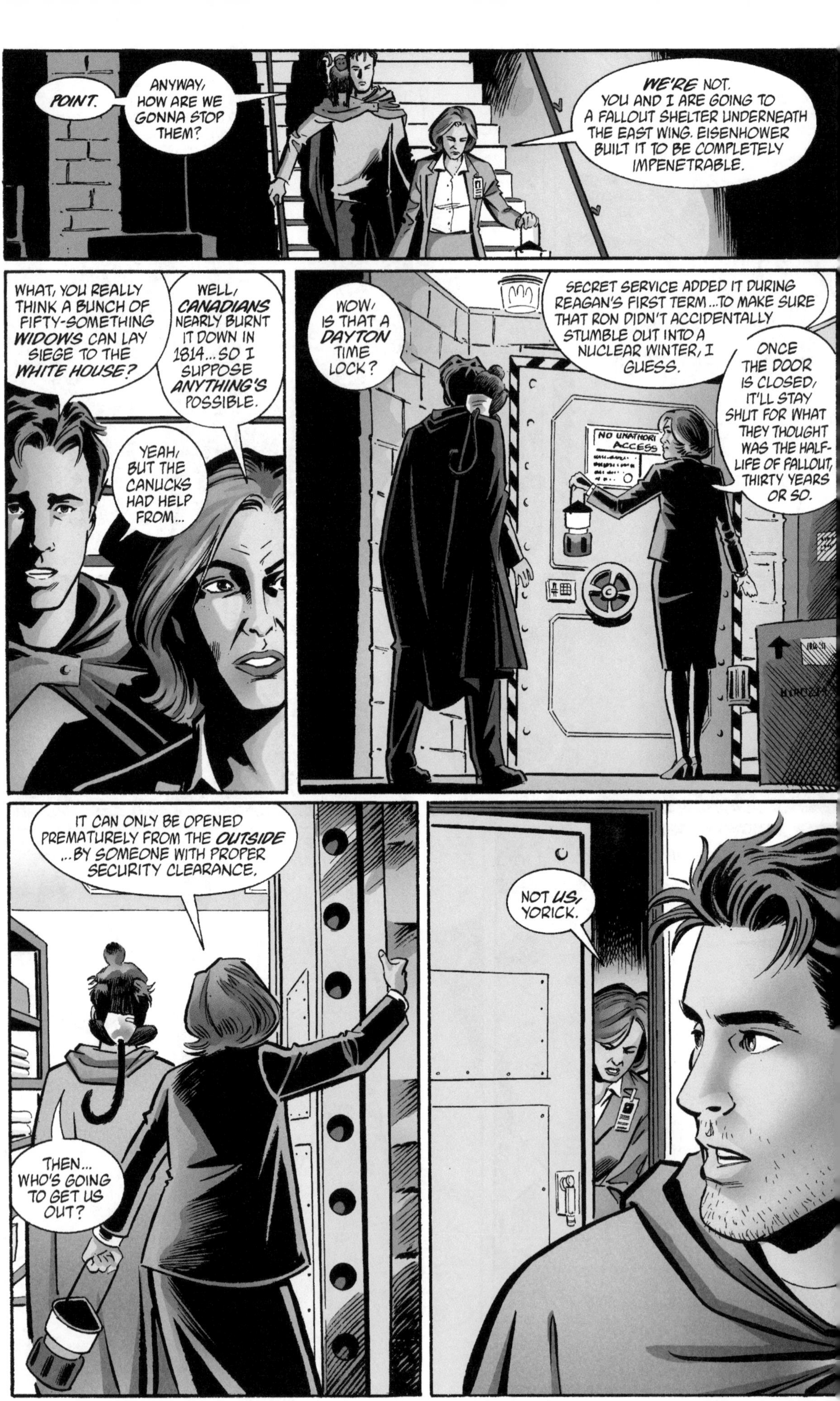
POINT.
ANYWAY, HOW ARE WE GONNA STOP THEM?
WE'RE NOT. YOU AND I ARE GOING TO A FALLOUT SHELTER UNDERNEATH THE EAST WING. EISENHOWER BUILT IT TO BE COMPLETELY IMPENETRABLE.
WHAT, YOU REALLY THINK A BUNCH OF FIFTY-SOMETHING WIDOWS CAN LAY SIEGE TO THE WHITE HOUSE?
WELL, CANADIANS NEARLY BURNT IT DOWN IN 1814... SO I SUPPOSE ANYTHING'S POSSIBLE.
YEAH, BUT THE CANUCKS HAD HELP FROM...
WOW, IS THAT A DAYTON TIME LOCK?
SECRET SERVICE ADDED IT DURING REAGAN'S FIRST TERM... TO MAKE SURE THAT RON DIDN'T ACCIDENTALLY STUMBLE OUT INTO A NUCLEAR WINTER, I GUESS.
ONCE THE DOOR IS CLOSED, IT'LL STAY SHUT FOR WHAT THEY THOUGHT WAS THE HALF-LIFE OF FALLOUT, THIRTY YEARS OR SO.
NO UNATHORI ACCESS
IT CAN ONLY BE OPENED PREMATURELY FROM THE OUTSIDE ...BY SOMEONE WITH PROPER SECURITY CLEARANCE.
THEN... WHO'S GOING TO GET US OUT?
NOT US, YORICK.

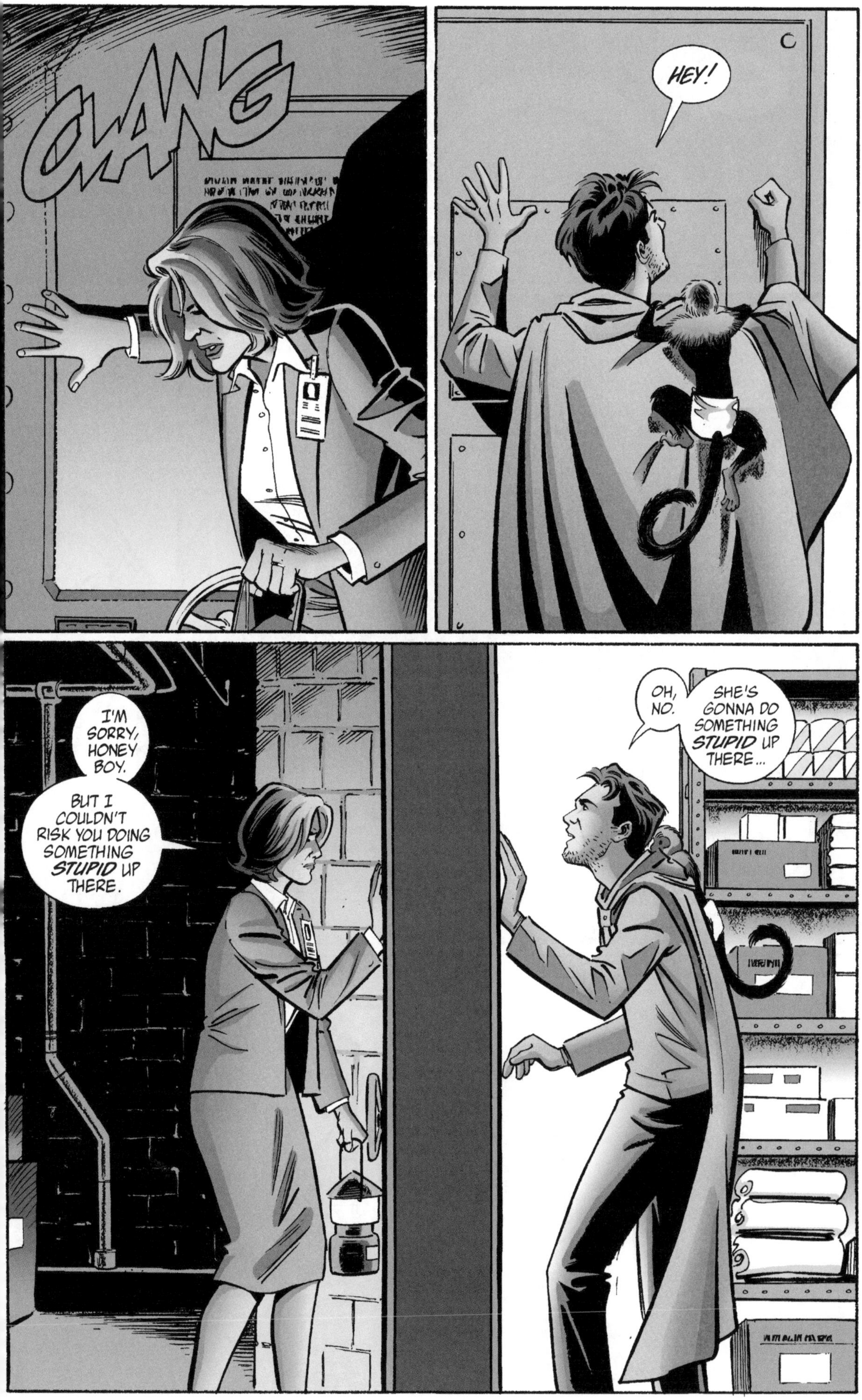
CLANG
HEY!
I'M SORRY, HONEY BOY.
BUT I COULDN'T RISK YOU DOING SOMETHING STUPID UP THERE.
OH, NO.
SHE'S GONNA DO SOMETHING STUPID UP THERE...

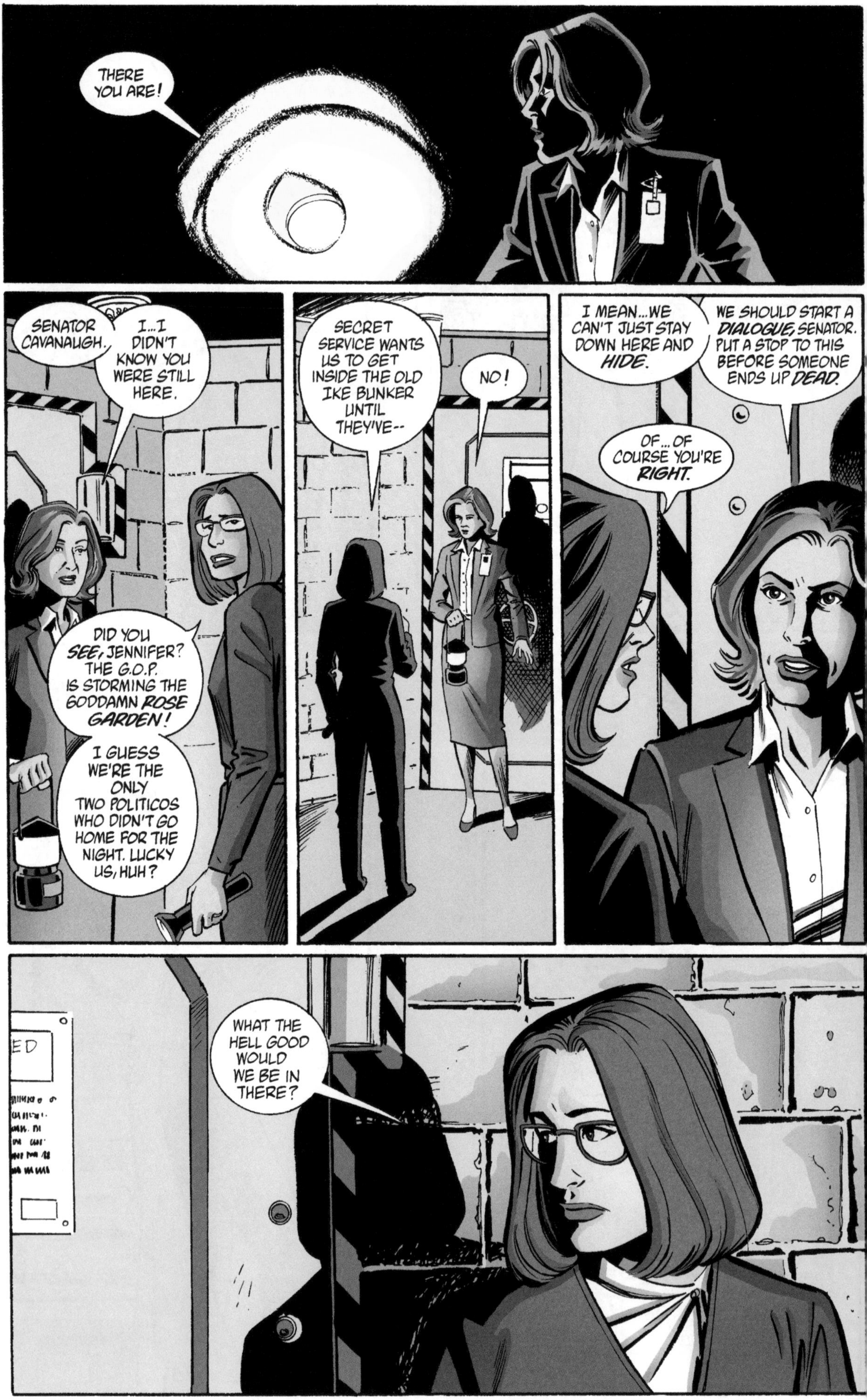
THERE YOU ARE!
SENATOR CAVANAUGH.
I...I DIDN'T KNOW YOU WERE STILL HERE.
DID YOU SEE, JENNIFER? THE G.O.P. IS STORMING THE GODDAMN ROSE GARDEN!
I GUESS WE'RE THE ONLY TWO POLITICOS WHO DIDN'T GO HOME FOR THE NIGHT. LUCKY US, HUH?
SECRET SERVICE WANTS US TO GET INSIDE THE OLD IKE BUNKER UNTIL THEY'VE--
NO!
I MEAN...WE CAN'T JUST STAY DOWN HERE AND HIDE.
WE SHOULD START A DIALOGUE, SENATOR. PUT A STOP TO THIS BEFORE SOMEONE ENDS UP DEAD.
OF... OF COURSE YOU'RE RIGHT.
WHAT THE HELL GOOD WOULD WE BE IN THERE?

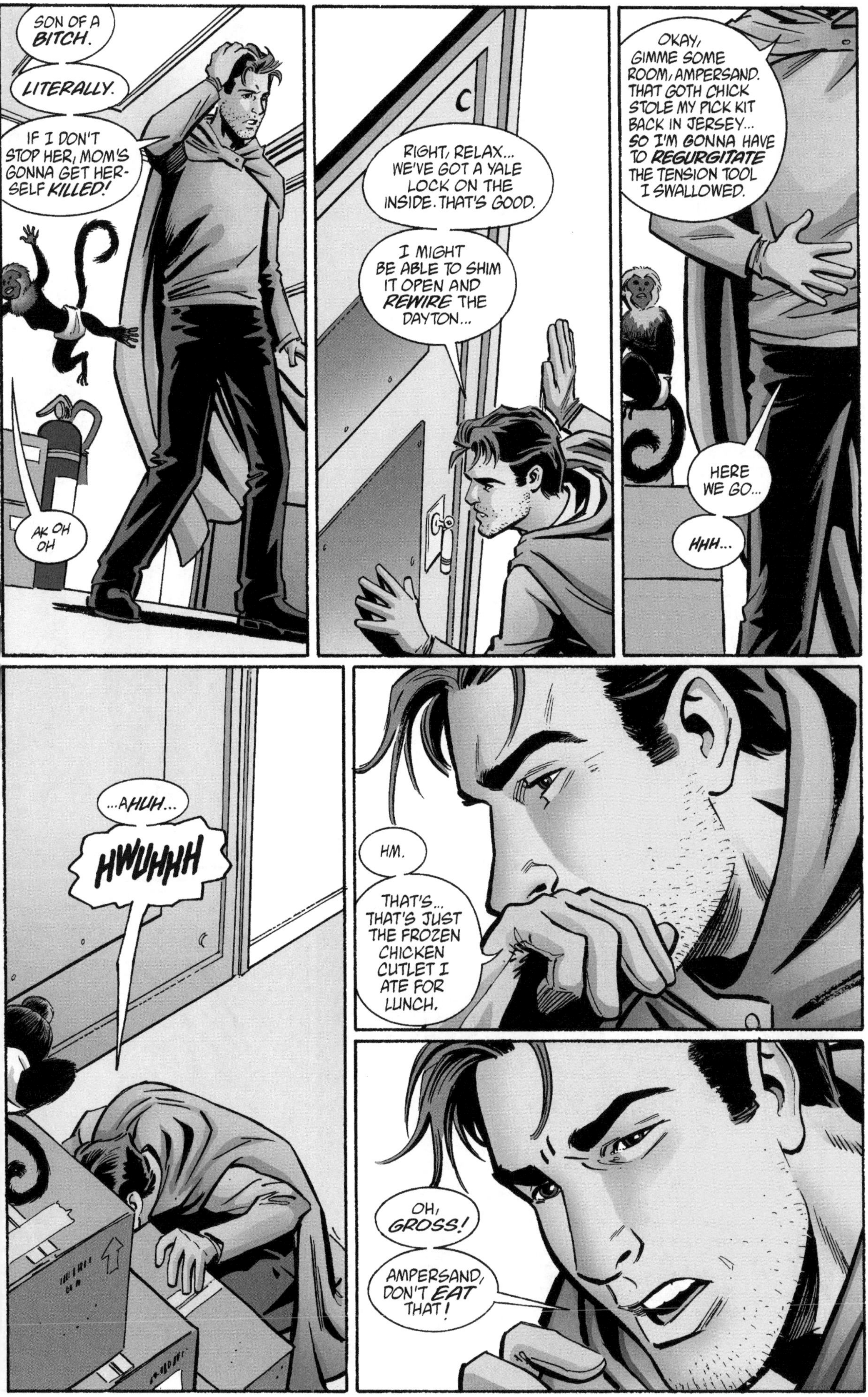
SON OF A BITCH.
LITERALLY.
IF I DON'T STOP HER, MOM'S GONNA GET HER-SELF KILLED!
AK OH OH
RIGHT, RELAX... WE'VE GOT A YALE LOCK ON THE INSIDE. THAT'S GOOD.
I MIGHT BE ABLE TO SHIM IT OPEN AND REWIRE THE DAYTON...
OKAY, GIMME SOME ROOM, AMPERSAND. THAT GOTH CHICK STOLE MY PICK KIT BACK IN JERSEY... SO I'M GONNA HAVE TO REGURGITATE THE TENSION TOOL I SWALLOWED.
HERE WE GO...
HHH...
...AHUH...
HWUHHH
HM.
THAT'S... THAT'S JUST THE FROZEN CHICKEN CUTLET I ATE FOR LUNCH.
OH, GROSS!
AMPERSAND, DON'T EAT THAT!

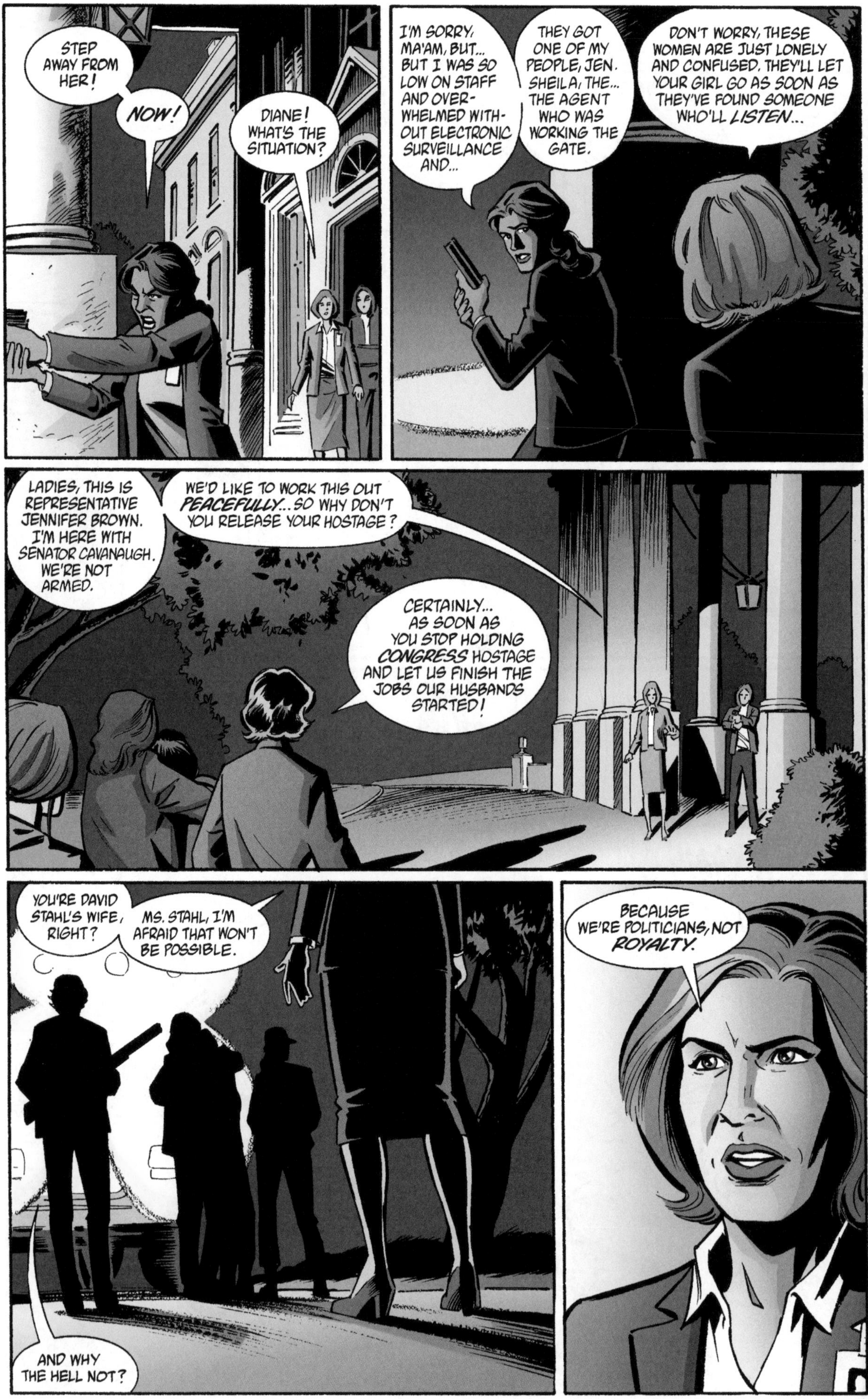
STEP AWAY FROM HER!
NOW!
DIANE! WHAT'S THE SITUATION?
I'M SORRY, MA'AM, BUT... BUT I WAS SO LOW ON STAFF AND OVER-WHELMED WITH-OUT ELECTRONIC SURVEILLANCE AND...
THEY GOT ONE OF MY PEOPLE, JEN. SHEILA, THE... THE AGENT WHO WAS WORKING THE GATE.
DON'T WORRY, THESE WOMEN ARE JUST LONELY AND CONFUSED. THEY'LL LET YOUR GIRL GO AS SOON AS THEY'VE FOUND SOMEONE WHO'LL LISTEN...
LADIES, THIS IS REPRESENTATIVE JENNIFER BROWN. I'M HERE WITH SENATOR CAVANAUGH. WE'RE NOT ARMED.
WE'D LIKE TO WORK THIS OUT PEACEFULLY... SO WHY DON'T YOU RELEASE YOUR HOSTAGE?
CERTAINLY... AS SOON AS YOU STOP HOLDING CONGRESS HOSTAGE AND LET US FINISH THE JOBS OUR HUSBANDS STARTED!
YOU'RE DAVID STAHL'S WIFE, RIGHT?
MS. STAHL, I'M AFRAID THAT WON'T BE POSSIBLE.
AND WHY THE HELL NOT?
BECAUSE WE'RE POLITICIANS, NOT ROYALTY.

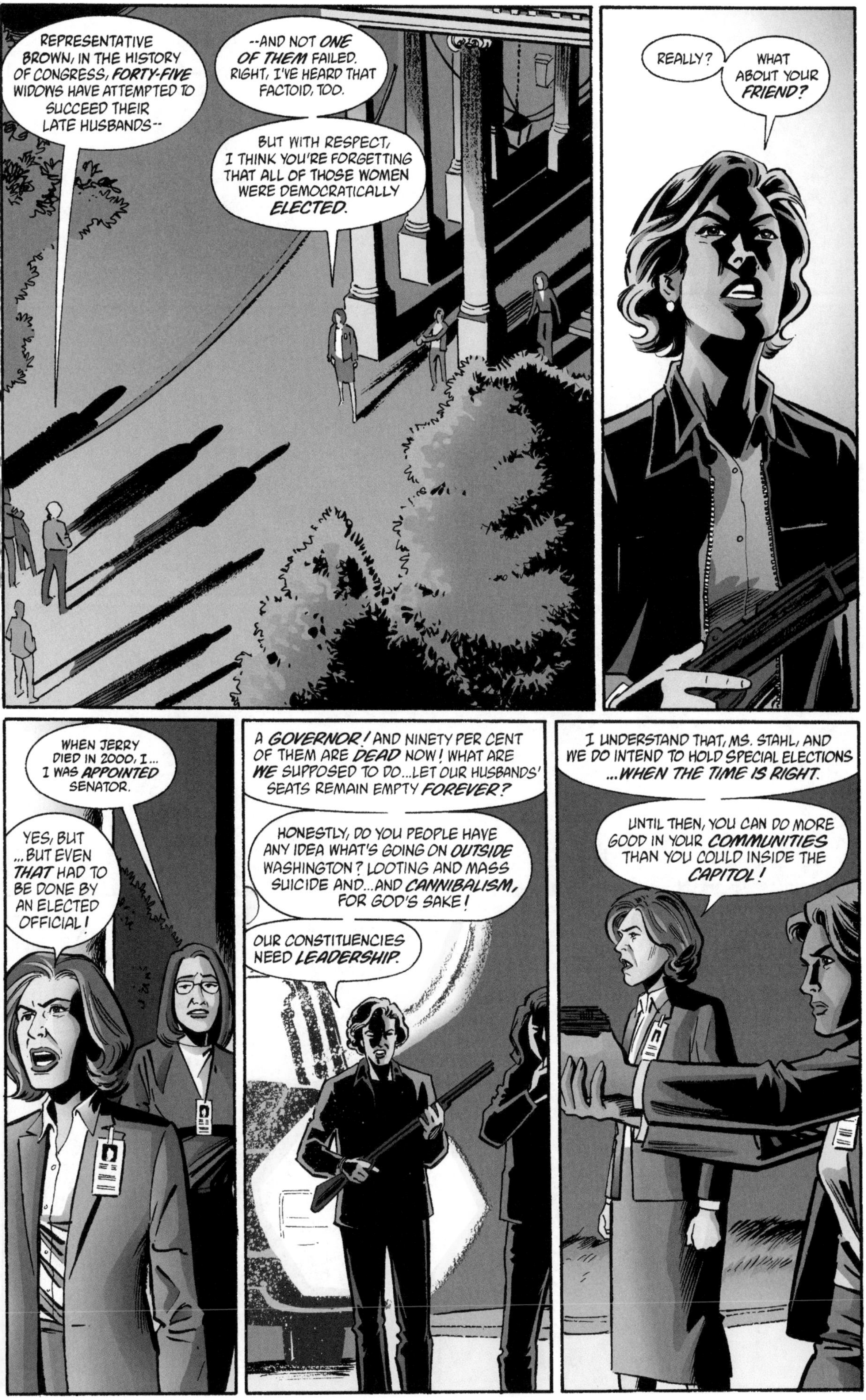
REPRESENTATIVE BROWN, IN THE HISTORY OF CONGRESS, FORTY-FIVE WIDOWS HAVE ATTEMPTED TO SUCCEED THEIR LATE HUSBANDS--
--AND NOT ONE OF THEM FAILED. RIGHT, I'VE HEARD THAT FACTOID, TOO.
BUT WITH RESPECT, I THINK YOU'RE FORGETTING THAT ALL OF THOSE WOMEN WERE DEMOCRATICALLY ELECTED.
REALLY?
WHAT ABOUT YOUR FRIEND?
WHEN JERRY DIED IN 2000, I... I WAS APPOINTED SENATOR.
YES, BUT ...BUT EVEN THAT HAD TO BE DONE BY AN ELECTED OFFICIAL!
A GOVERNOR! AND NINETY PER CENT OF THEM ARE DEAD NOW! WHAT ARE WE SUPPOSED TO DO...LET OUR HUSBANDS' SEATS REMAIN EMPTY FOREVER?
HONESTLY, DO YOU PEOPLE HAVE ANY IDEA WHAT'S GOING ON OUTSIDE WASHINGTON? LOOTING AND MASS SUICIDE AND...AND CANNIBALISM, FOR GOD'S SAKE!
OUR CONSTITUENCIES NEED LEADERSHIP.
I UNDERSTAND THAT, MS. STAHL, AND WE DO INTEND TO HOLD SPECIAL ELECTIONS ...WHEN THE TIME IS RIGHT.
UNTIL THEN, YOU CAN DO MORE GOOD IN YOUR COMMUNITIES THAN YOU COULD INSIDE THE CAPITOL!

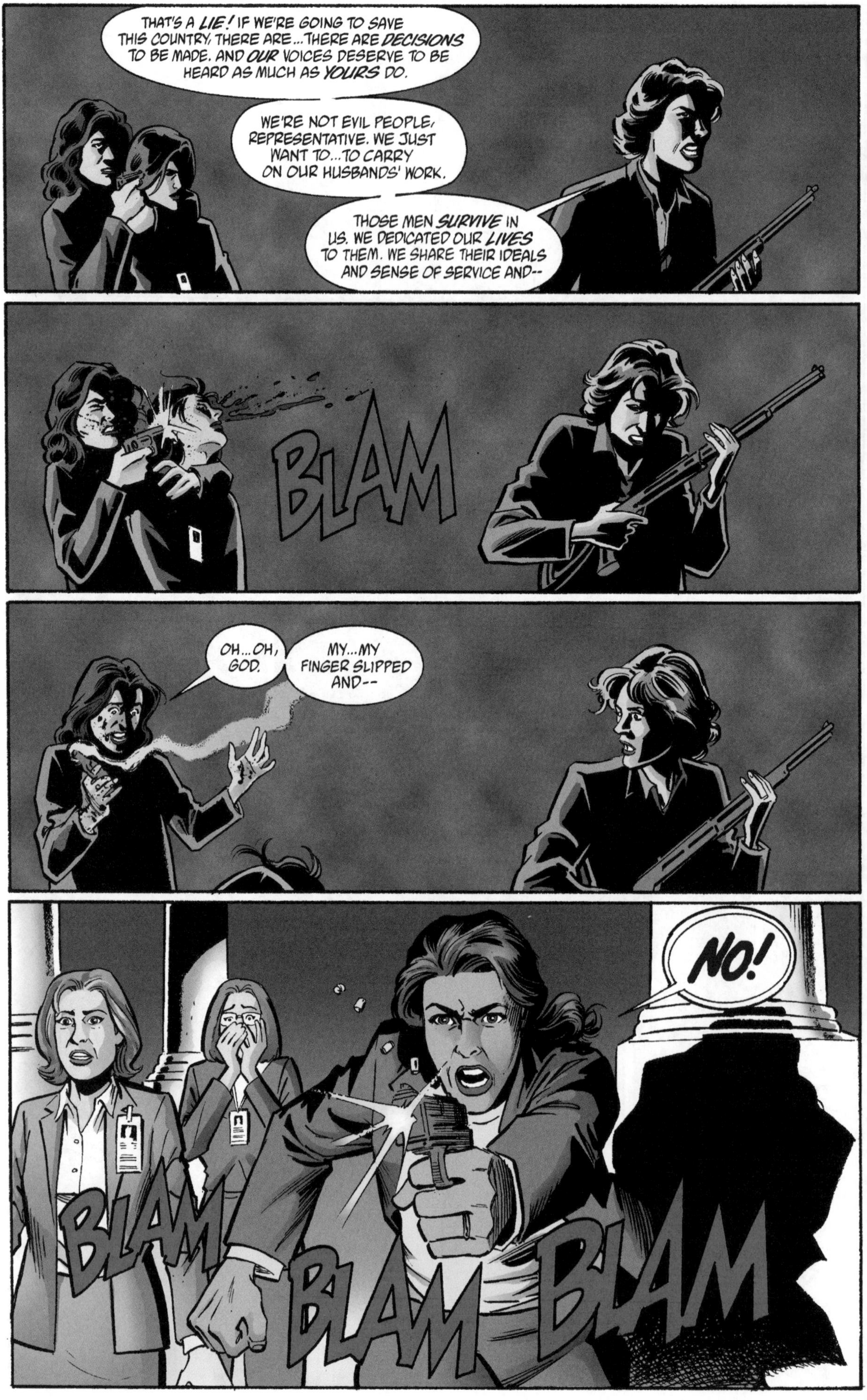
THAT'S A LIE! IF WE'RE GOING TO SAVE THIS COUNTRY, THERE ARE... THERE ARE DECISIONS TO BE MADE. AND OUR VOICES DESERVE TO BE HEARD AS MUCH AS YOURS DO.
WE'RE NOT EVIL PEOPLE, REPRESENTATIVE. WE JUST WANT TO... TO CARRY ON OUR HUSBANDS' WORK.
THOSE MEN SURVIVE IN US. WE DEDICATED OUR LIVES TO THEM. WE SHARE THEIR IDEALS AND SENSE OF SERVICE AND--
BLAM
OH... OH, GOD.
MY... MY FINGER SLIPPED AND--
NO!
BLAM
BLAM
BLAM

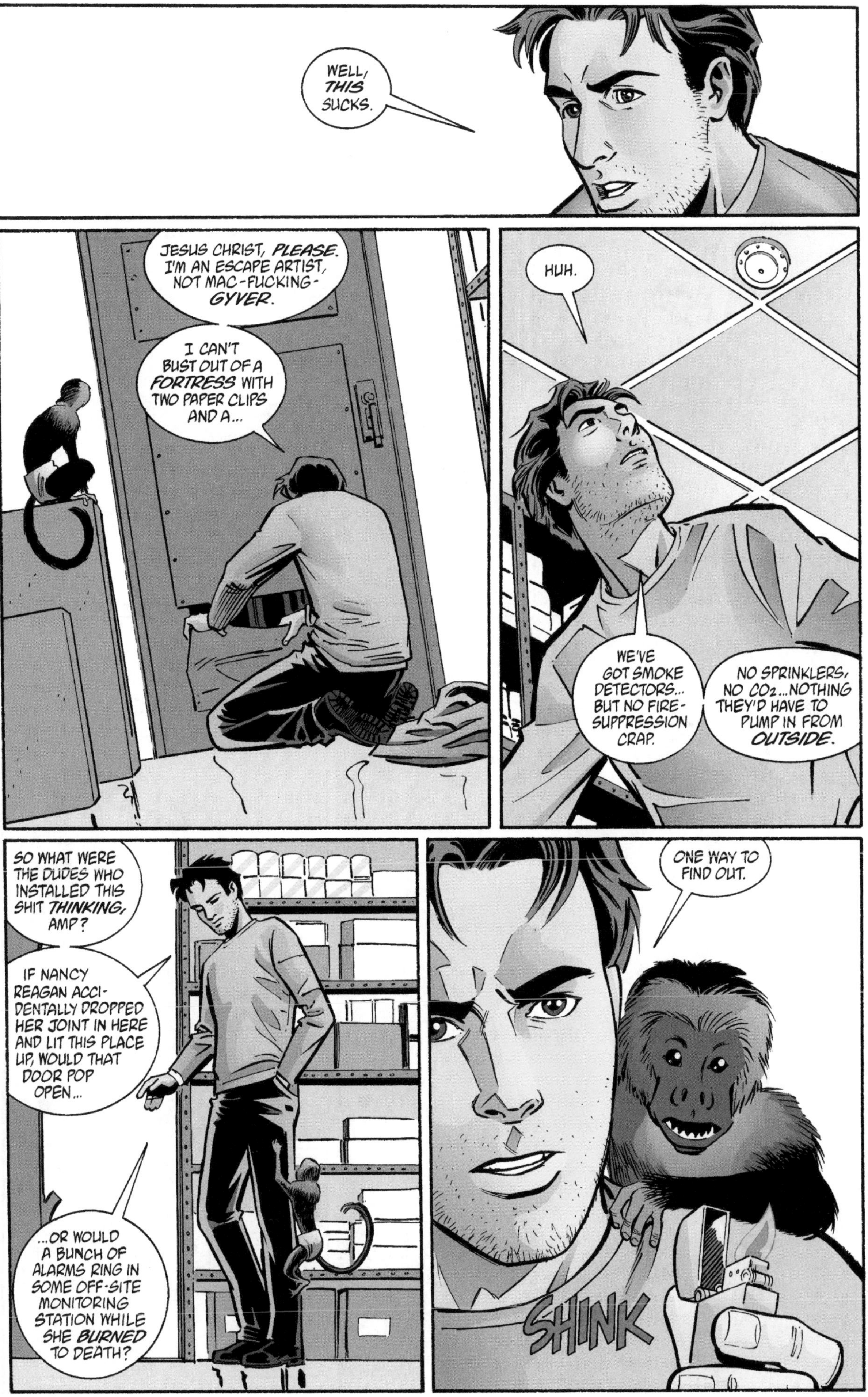
WELL, *THIS* SUCKS.
JESUS CHRIST, *PLEASE*. I'M AN ESCAPE ARTIST, NOT MAC-FUCKING-*GYVER*.
I CAN'T BUST OUT OF A *FORTRESS* WITH TWO PAPER CLIPS AND A...
HUH.
WE'VE GOT SMOKE DETECTORS... BUT NO FIRE-SUPPRESSION CRAP.
NO SPRINKLERS, NO CO2...NOTHING THEY'D HAVE TO PUMP IN FROM *OUTSIDE*.
SO WHAT WERE THE DUDES WHO INSTALLED THIS SHIT *THINKING*, AMP?
IF NANCY REAGAN ACCIDENTALLY DROPPED HER JOINT IN HERE AND LIT THIS PLACE UP, WOULD THAT DOOR POP OPEN...
...OR WOULD A BUNCH OF ALARMS RING IN SOME OFF-SITE MONITORING STATION WHILE SHE *BURNED* TO DEATH?
ONE WAY TO FIND OUT.
SHINK

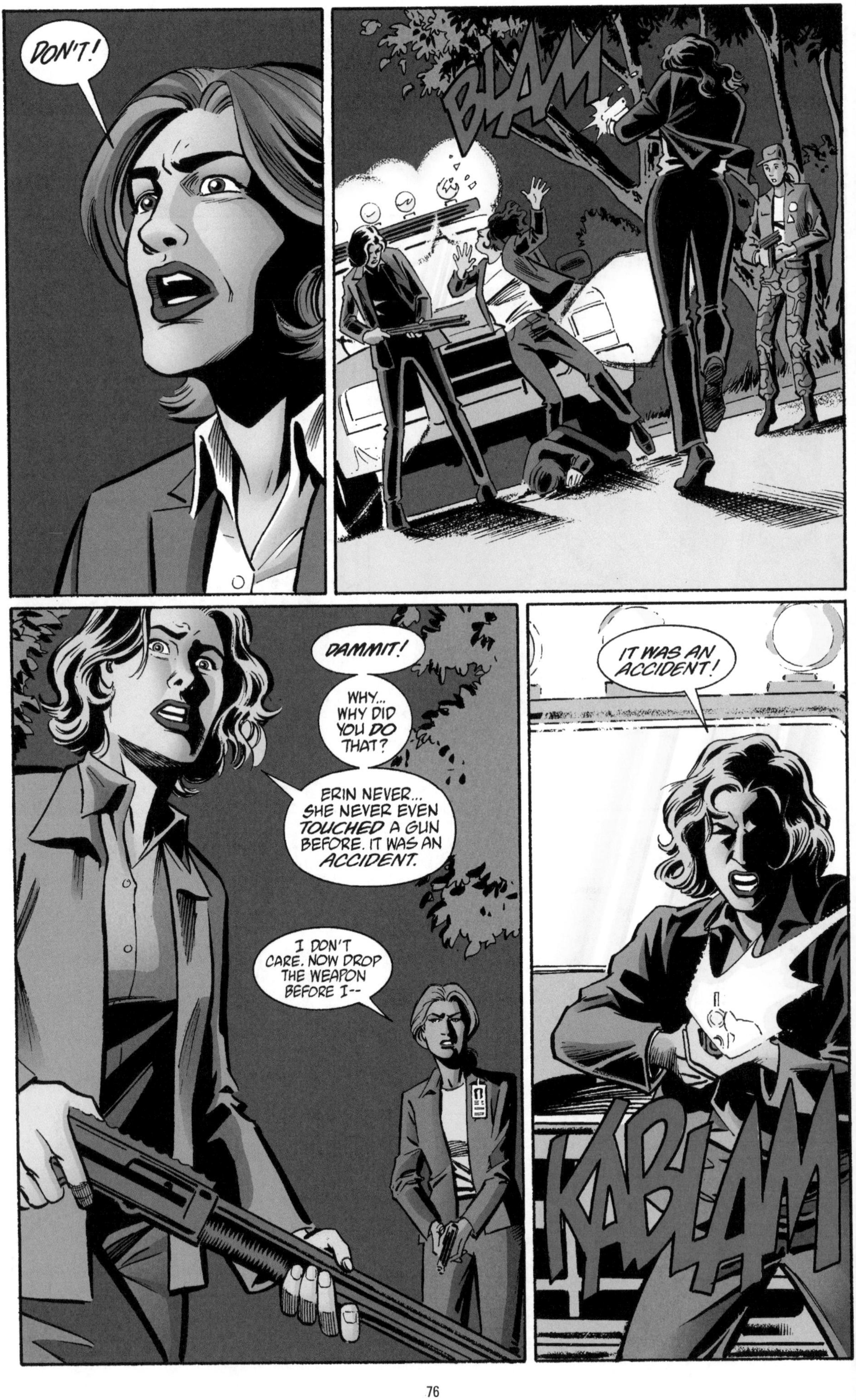
DON'T!
BLAM
DAMMIT!
WHY... WHY DID YOU DO THAT?
ERIN NEVER... SHE NEVER EVEN TOUCHED A GUN BEFORE. IT WAS AN ACCIDENT.
I DON'T CARE. NOW DROP THE WEAPON BEFORE I--
IT WAS AN ACCIDENT!
KABLAM

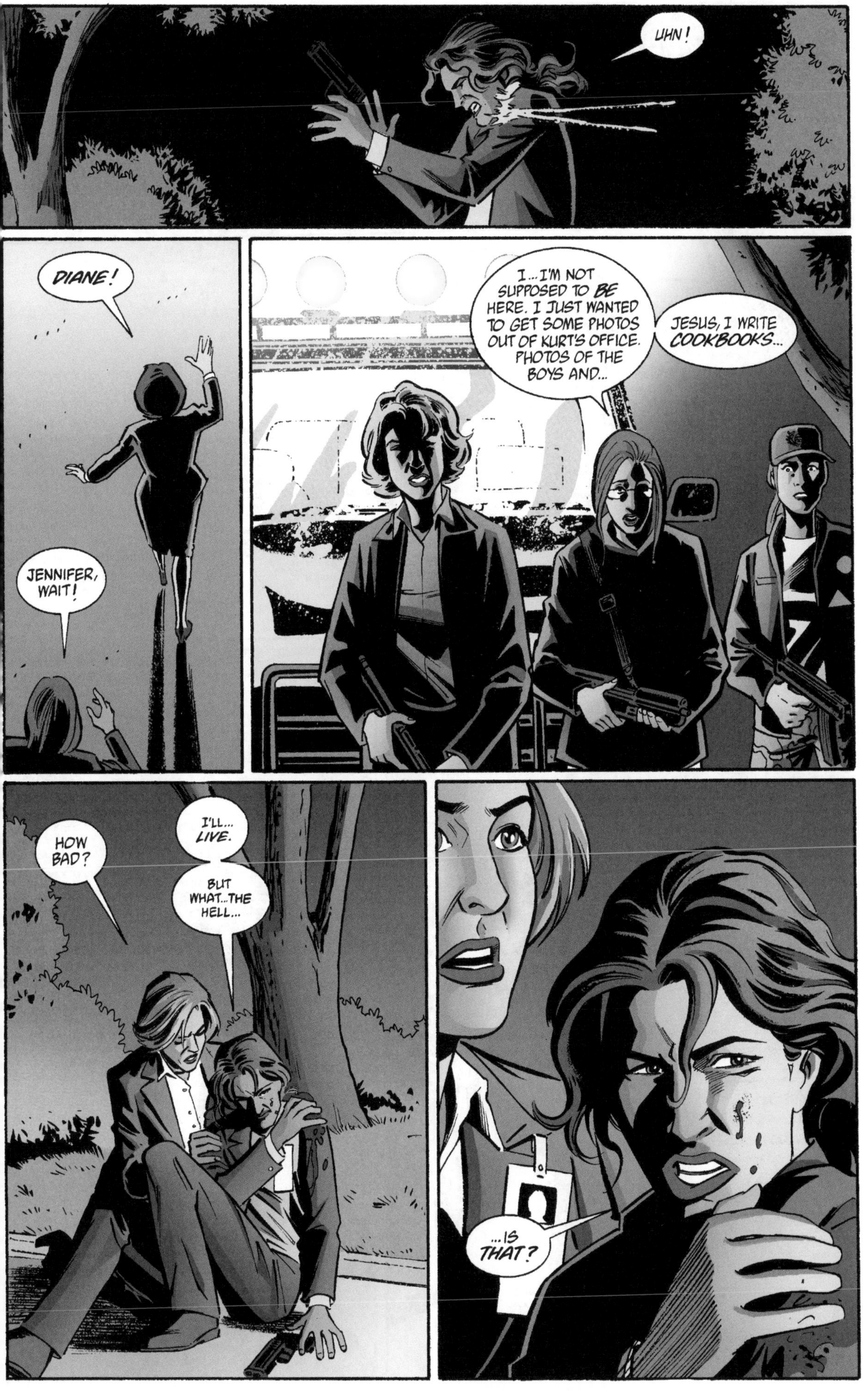
UHN!
DIANE!
JENNIFER, WAIT!
I... I'M NOT SUPPOSED TO BE HERE. I JUST WANTED TO GET SOME PHOTOS OUT OF KURT'S OFFICE. PHOTOS OF THE BOYS AND...
JESUS, I WRITE COOKBOOKS...
HOW BAD?
I'LL... LIVE.
BUT WHAT...THE HELL...
...IS THAT?

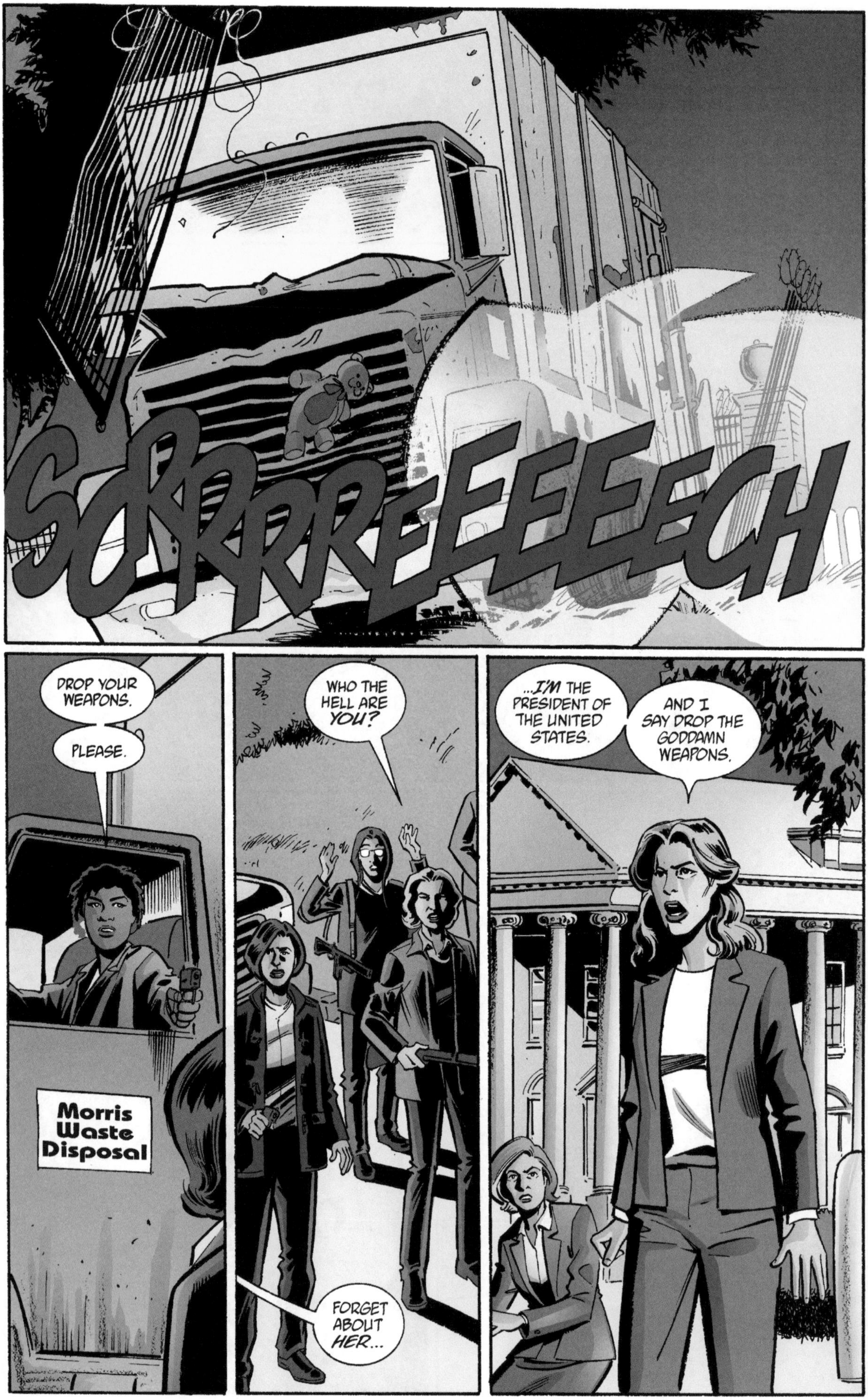
SCRRREEEEECH
DROP YOUR WEAPONS.
PLEASE.
Morris Waste Disposal
WHO THE HELL ARE YOU?
FORGET ABOUT HER...
...I'M THE PRESIDENT OF THE UNITED STATES.
AND I SAY DROP THE GODDAMN WEAPONS.

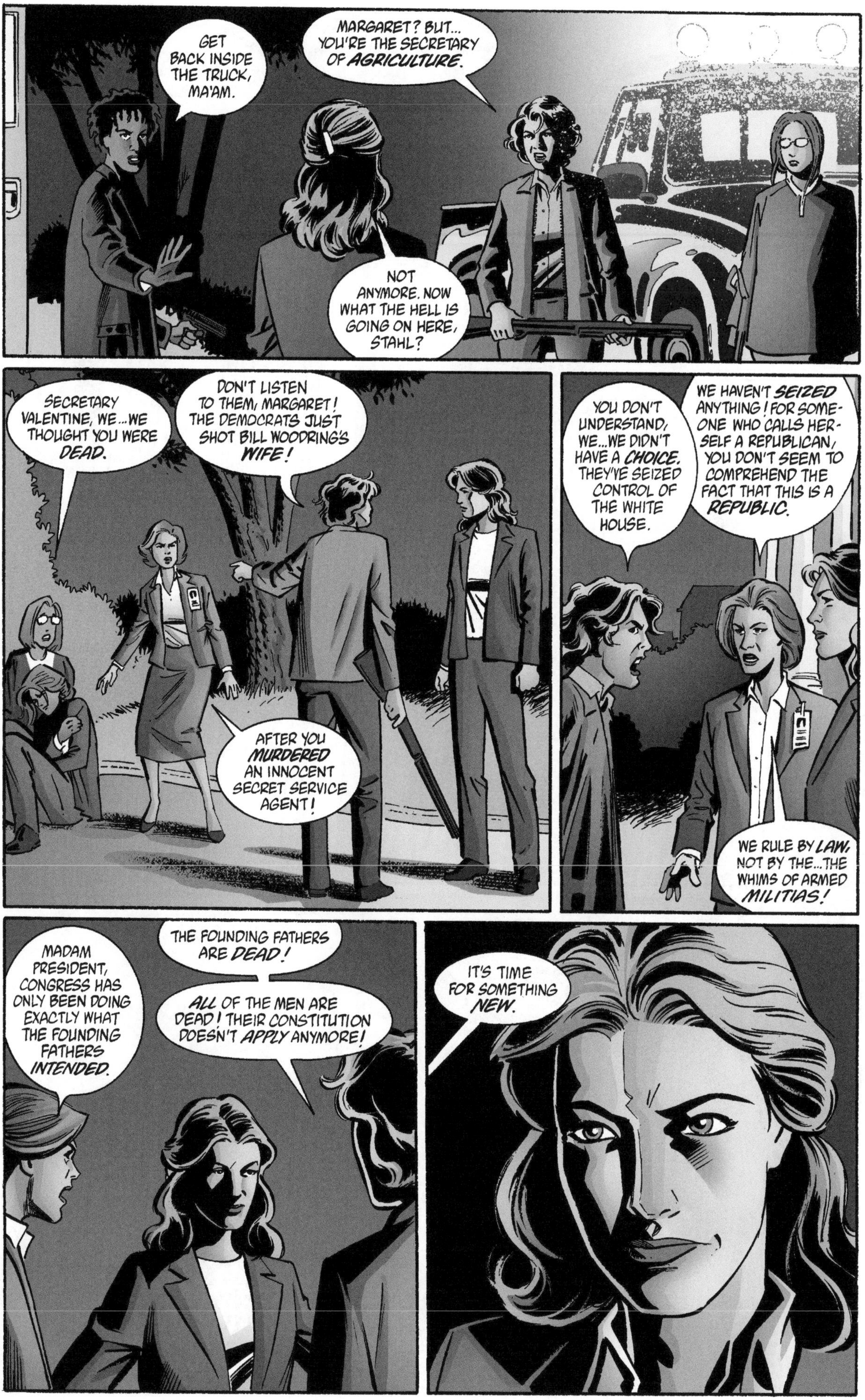

GET BACK INSIDE THE TRUCK, MA'AM.
MARGARET? BUT... YOU'RE THE SECRETARY OF AGRICULTURE.
NOT ANYMORE. NOW WHAT THE HELL IS GOING ON HERE, STAHL?
SECRETARY VALENTINE, WE...WE THOUGHT YOU WERE DEAD.
DON'T LISTEN TO THEM, MARGARET! THE DEMOCRATS JUST SHOT BILL WOODRING'S WIFE!
AFTER YOU MURDERED AN INNOCENT SECRET SERVICE AGENT!
YOU DON'T UNDERSTAND, WE...WE DIDN'T HAVE A CHOICE. THEY'VE SEIZED CONTROL OF THE WHITE HOUSE.
WE HAVEN'T SEIZED ANYTHING! FOR SOMEONE WHO CALLS HERSELF A REPUBLICAN, YOU DON'T SEEM TO COMPREHEND THE FACT THAT THIS IS A REPUBLIC.
WE RULE BY LAW, NOT BY THE...THE WHIMS OF ARMED MILITIAS!
MADAM PRESIDENT, CONGRESS HAS ONLY BEEN DOING EXACTLY WHAT THE FOUNDING FATHERS INTENDED.
THE FOUNDING FATHERS ARE DEAD!
ALL OF THE MEN ARE DEAD! THEIR CONSTITUTION DOESN'T APPLY ANYMORE!
IT'S TIME FOR SOMETHING NEW.

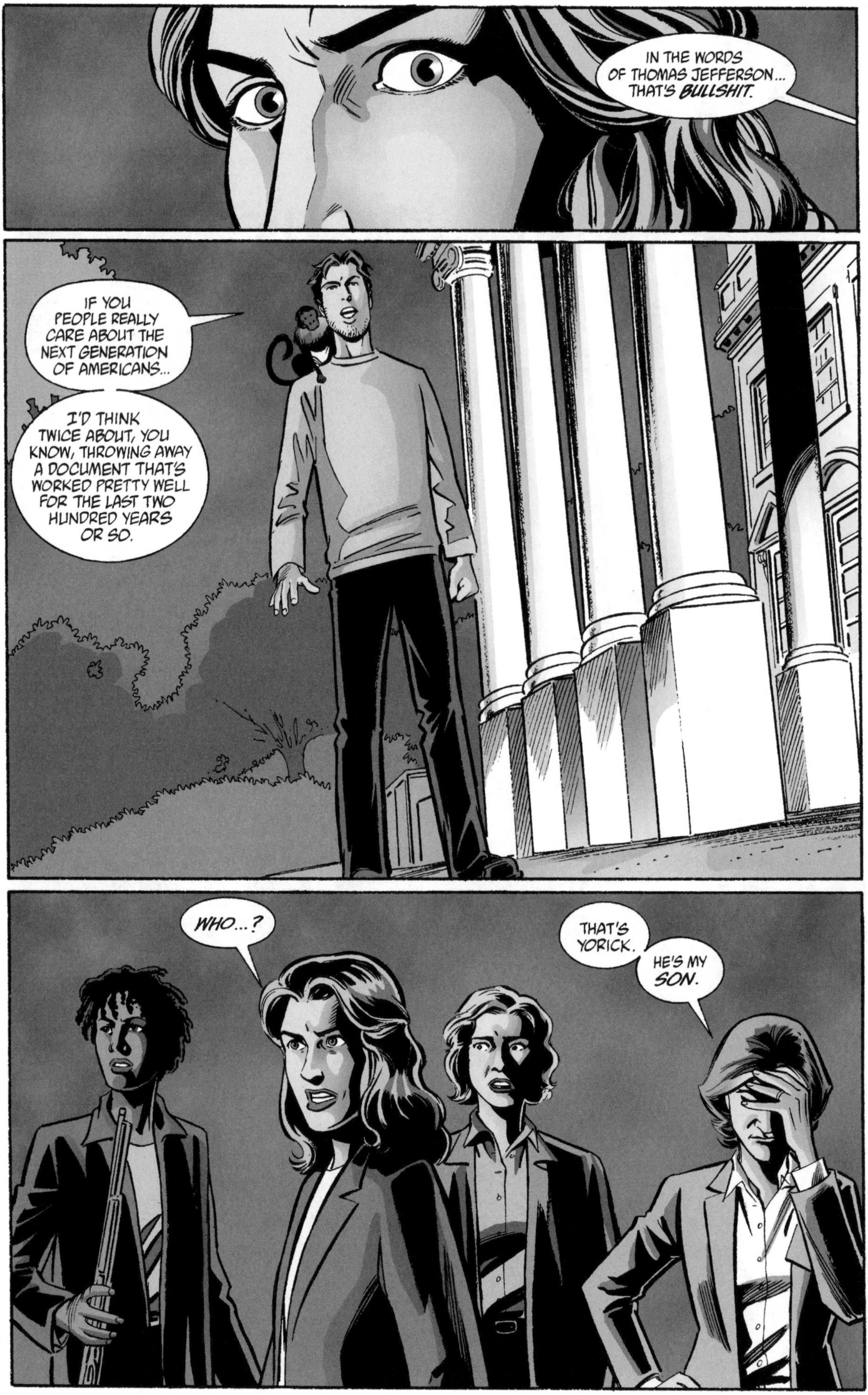
IN THE WORDS OF THOMAS JEFFERSON... THAT'S BULLSHIT.
IF YOU PEOPLE REALLY CARE ABOUT THE NEXT GENERATION OF AMERICANS...
I'D THINK TWICE ABOUT, YOU KNOW, THROWING AWAY A DOCUMENT THAT'S WORKED PRETTY WELL FOR THE LAST TWO HUNDRED YEARS OR SO.
WHO...?
THAT'S YORICK.
HE'S MY SON.

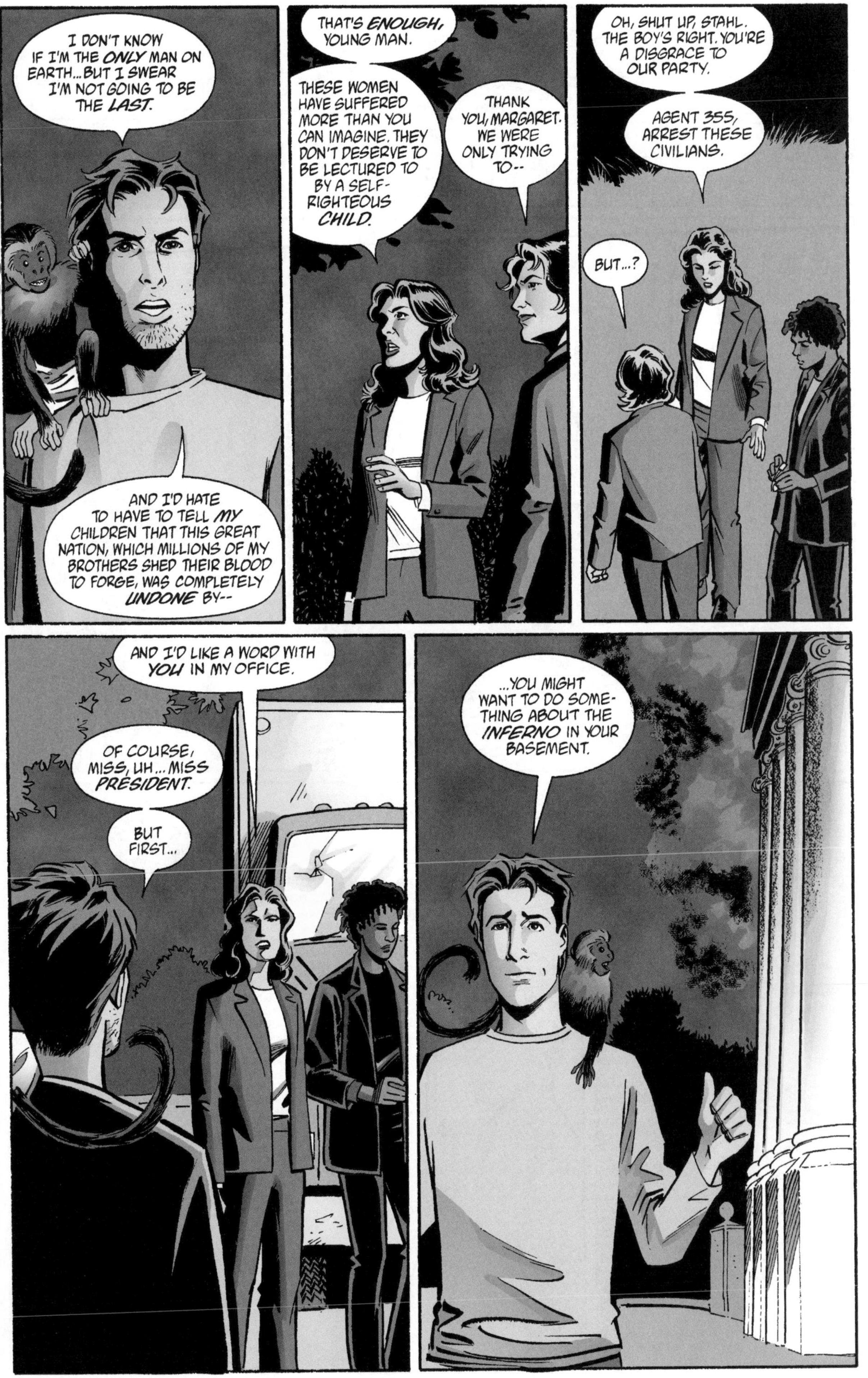
I DON'T KNOW IF I'M THE ONLY MAN ON EARTH...BUT I SWEAR I'M NOT GOING TO BE THE LAST.
AND I'D HATE TO HAVE TO TELL MY CHILDREN THAT THIS GREAT NATION, WHICH MILLIONS OF MY BROTHERS SHED THEIR BLOOD TO FORGE, WAS COMPLETELY UNDONE BY--
THAT'S ENOUGH, YOUNG MAN.
THESE WOMEN HAVE SUFFERED MORE THAN YOU CAN IMAGINE. THEY DON'T DESERVE TO BE LECTURED TO BY A SELF-RIGHTEOUS CHILD.
THANK YOU, MARGARET. WE WERE ONLY TRYING TO--
OH, SHUT UP, STAHL. THE BOY'S RIGHT. YOU'RE A DISGRACE TO OUR PARTY.
AGENT 355, ARREST THESE CIVILIANS.
BUT...?
AND I'D LIKE A WORD WITH YOU IN MY OFFICE.
OF COURSE, MISS, UH...MISS PRESIDENT.
BUT FIRST...
...YOU MIGHT WANT TO DO SOMETHING ABOUT THE INFERNO IN YOUR BASEMENT.

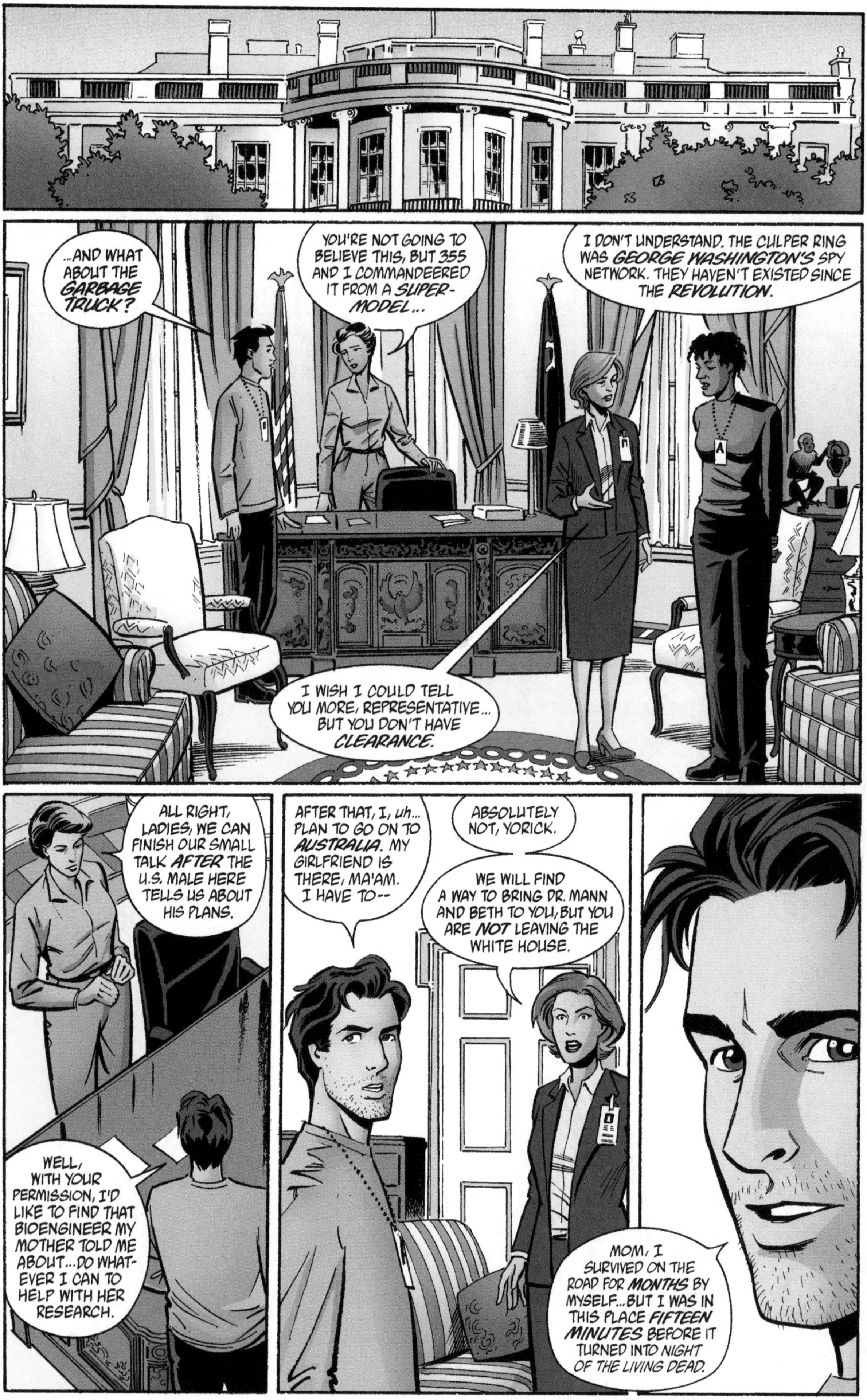
...AND WHAT ABOUT THE GARBAGE TRUCK?
YOU'RE NOT GOING TO BELIEVE THIS, BUT 355 AND I COMMANDEERED IT FROM A SUPER-MODEL...
I DON'T UNDERSTAND. THE CULPER RING WAS GEORGE WASHINGTON'S SPY NETWORK. THEY HAVEN'T EXISTED SINCE THE REVOLUTION.
I WISH I COULD TELL YOU MORE, REPRESENTATIVE... BUT YOU DON'T HAVE CLEARANCE.
ALL RIGHT, LADIES, WE CAN FINISH OUR SMALL TALK AFTER THE U.S. MALE HERE TELLS US ABOUT HIS PLANS.
WELL, WITH YOUR PERMISSION, I'D LIKE TO FIND THAT BIOENGINEER MY MOTHER TOLD ME ABOUT...DO WHAT-EVER I CAN TO HELP WITH HER RESEARCH.
AFTER THAT, I, uh... PLAN TO GO ON TO AUSTRALIA. MY GIRLFRIEND IS THERE, MA'AM. I HAVE TO--
ABSOLUTELY NOT, YORICK.
WE WILL FIND A WAY TO BRING DR. MANN AND BETH TO YOU, BUT YOU ARE NOT LEAVING THE WHITE HOUSE.
MOM, I SURVIVED ON THE ROAD FOR MONTHS BY MYSELF...BUT I WAS IN THIS PLACE FIFTEEN MINUTES BEFORE IT TURNED INTO NIGHT OF THE LIVING DEAD.

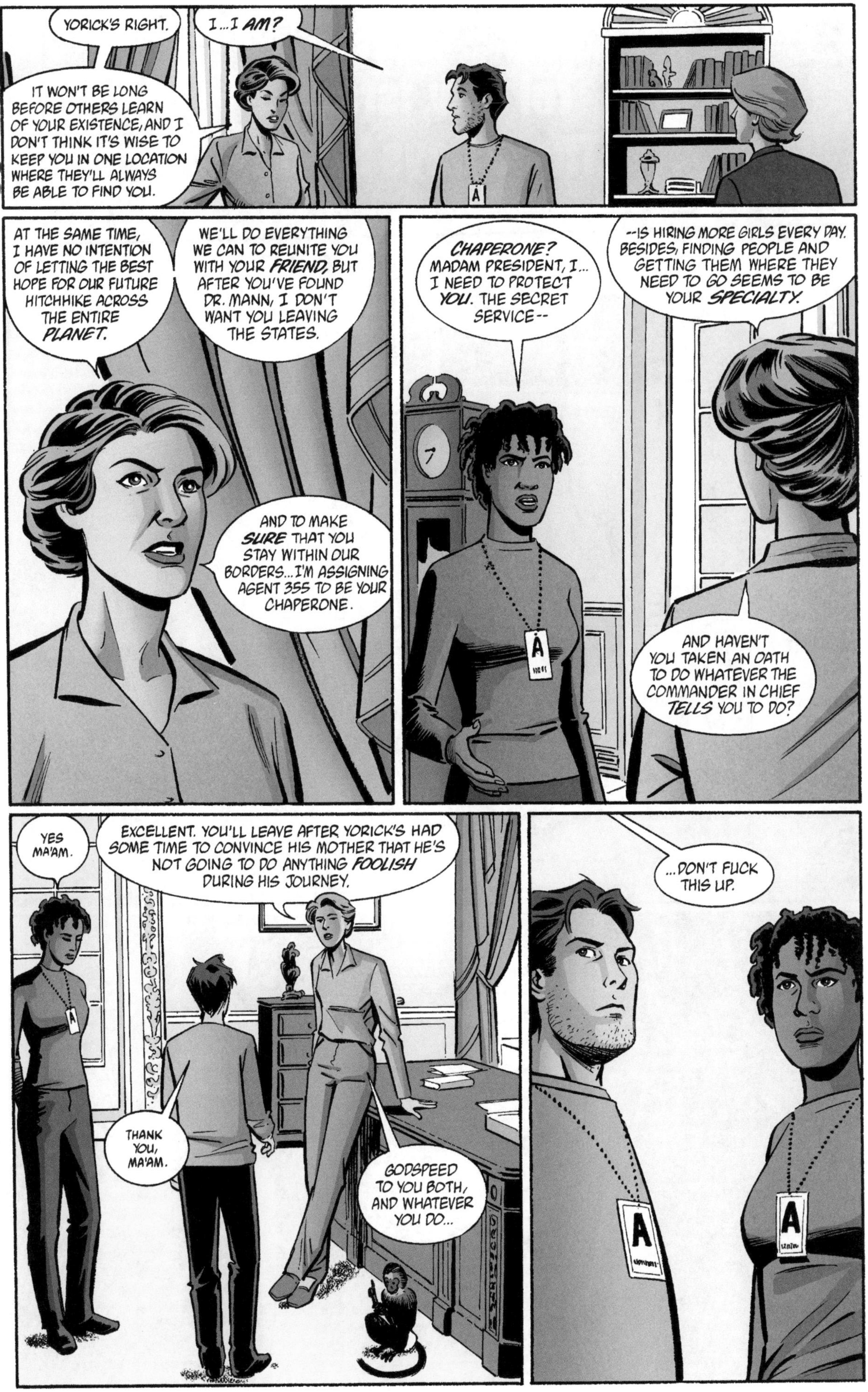
YORICK'S RIGHT.
IT WON'T BE LONG BEFORE OTHERS LEARN OF YOUR EXISTENCE, AND I DON'T THINK IT'S WISE TO KEEP YOU IN ONE LOCATION WHERE THEY'LL ALWAYS BE ABLE TO FIND YOU.
I...I AM?
AT THE SAME TIME, I HAVE NO INTENTION OF LETTING THE BEST HOPE FOR OUR FUTURE HITCHHIKE ACROSS THE ENTIRE PLANET.
WE'LL DO EVERYTHING WE CAN TO REUNITE YOU WITH YOUR FRIEND, BUT AFTER YOU'VE FOUND DR. MANN, I DON'T WANT YOU LEAVING THE STATES.
AND TO MAKE SURE THAT YOU STAY WITHIN OUR BORDERS...I'M ASSIGNING AGENT 355 TO BE YOUR CHAPERONE.
CHAPERONE? MADAM PRESIDENT, I... I NEED TO PROTECT YOU. THE SECRET SERVICE--
--IS HIRING MORE GIRLS EVERY DAY. BESIDES, FINDING PEOPLE AND GETTING THEM WHERE THEY NEED TO GO SEEMS TO BE YOUR SPECIALTY.
AND HAVEN'T YOU TAKEN AN OATH TO DO WHATEVER THE COMMANDER IN CHIEF TELLS YOU TO DO?
YES MA'AM.
EXCELLENT. YOU'LL LEAVE AFTER YORICK'S HAD SOME TIME TO CONVINCE HIS MOTHER THAT HE'S NOT GOING TO DO ANYTHING FOOLISH DURING HIS JOURNEY.
THANK YOU, MA'AM.
GODSPEED TO YOU BOTH, AND WHATEVER YOU DO...
...DON'T FUCK THIS UP.

Tel Aviv, Israel
Three Days Later

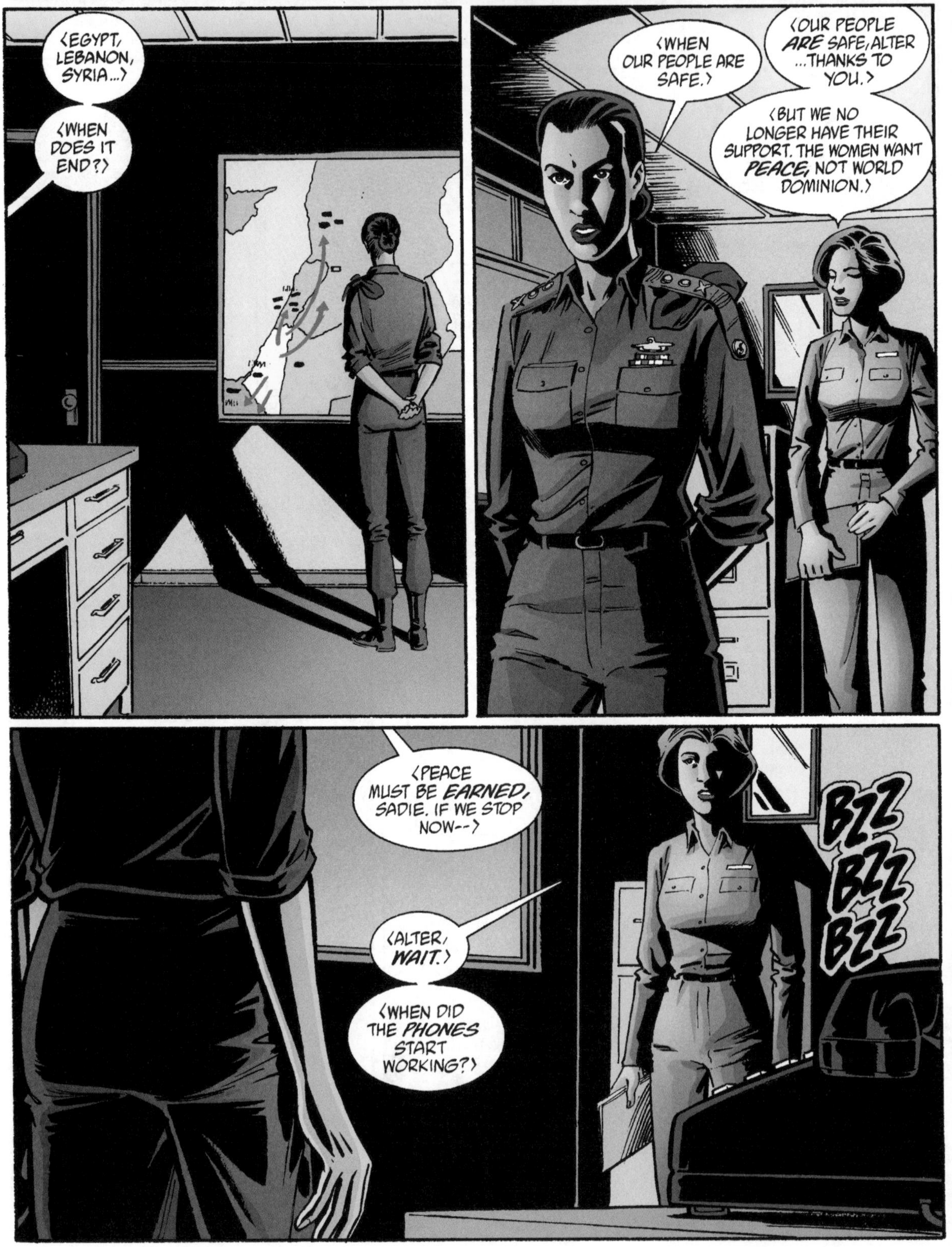

‹EGYPT, LEBANON, SYRIA...›
‹WHEN DOES IT END?›
‹WHEN OUR PEOPLE ARE SAFE.›
‹OUR PEOPLE *ARE* SAFE, ALTER ...THANKS TO YOU.›
‹BUT WE NO LONGER HAVE THEIR SUPPORT. THE WOMEN WANT *PEACE,* NOT WORLD DOMINION.›
‹PEACE MUST BE *EARNED,* SADIE. IF WE STOP NOW--›
‹ALTER, *WAIT.*›
‹WHEN DID THE *PHONES* START WORKING?›
BZZ BZZ BZZ

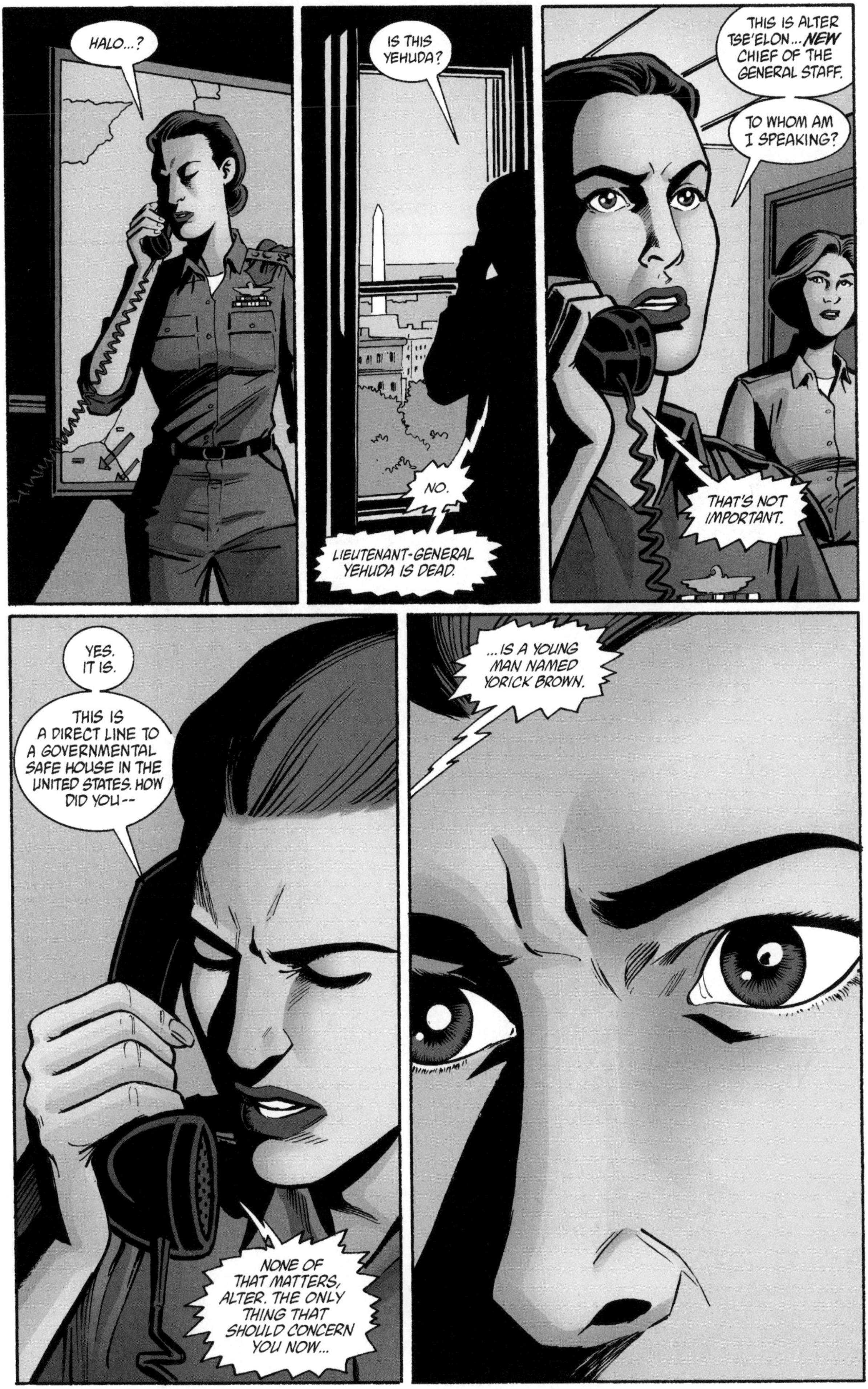
HALO...?
IS THIS YEHUDA?
NO.
LIEUTENANT-GENERAL YEHUDA IS DEAD.
THIS IS ALTER TSE'ELON... NEW CHIEF OF THE GENERAL STAFF.
TO WHOM AM I SPEAKING?
THAT'S NOT IMPORTANT.
YES. IT IS.
THIS IS A DIRECT LINE TO A GOVERNMENTAL SAFE HOUSE IN THE UNITED STATES. HOW DID YOU--
NONE OF THAT MATTERS, ALTER. THE ONLY THING THAT SHOULD CONCERN YOU NOW...
...IS A YOUNG MAN NAMED YORICK BROWN.

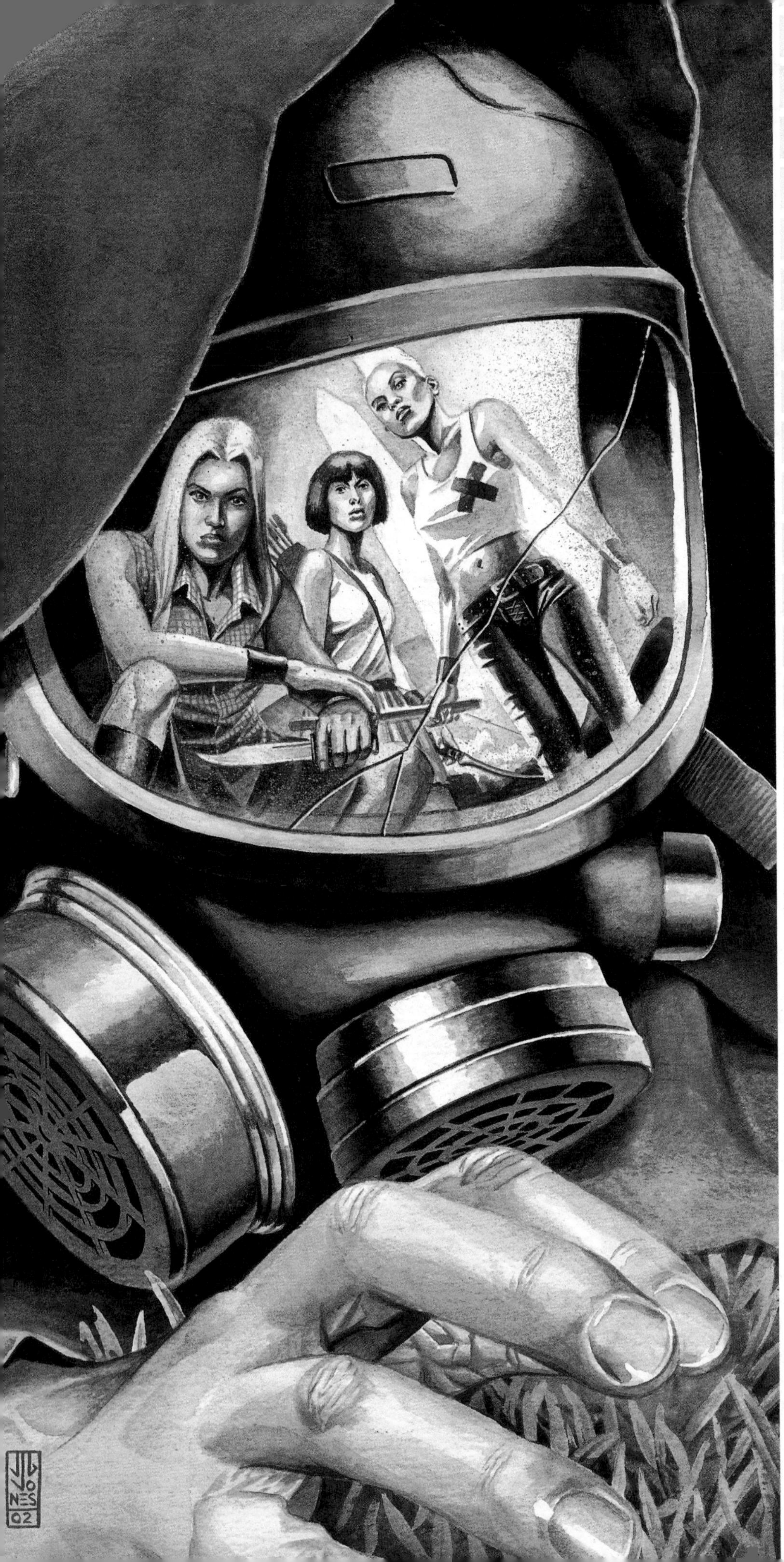
JG JONES 02

Washington, D.C.
Now

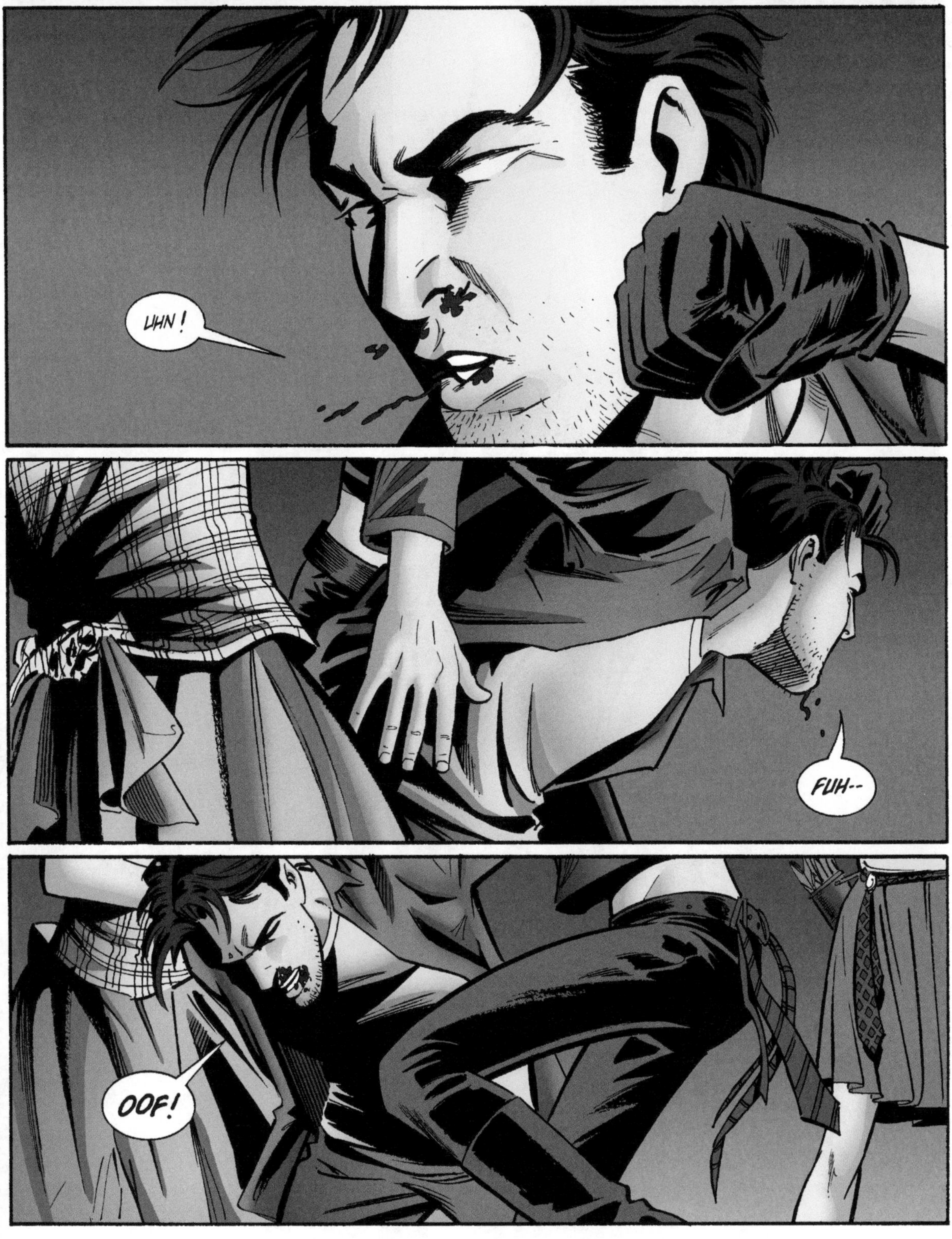
UHN!
FUH--
OOF!

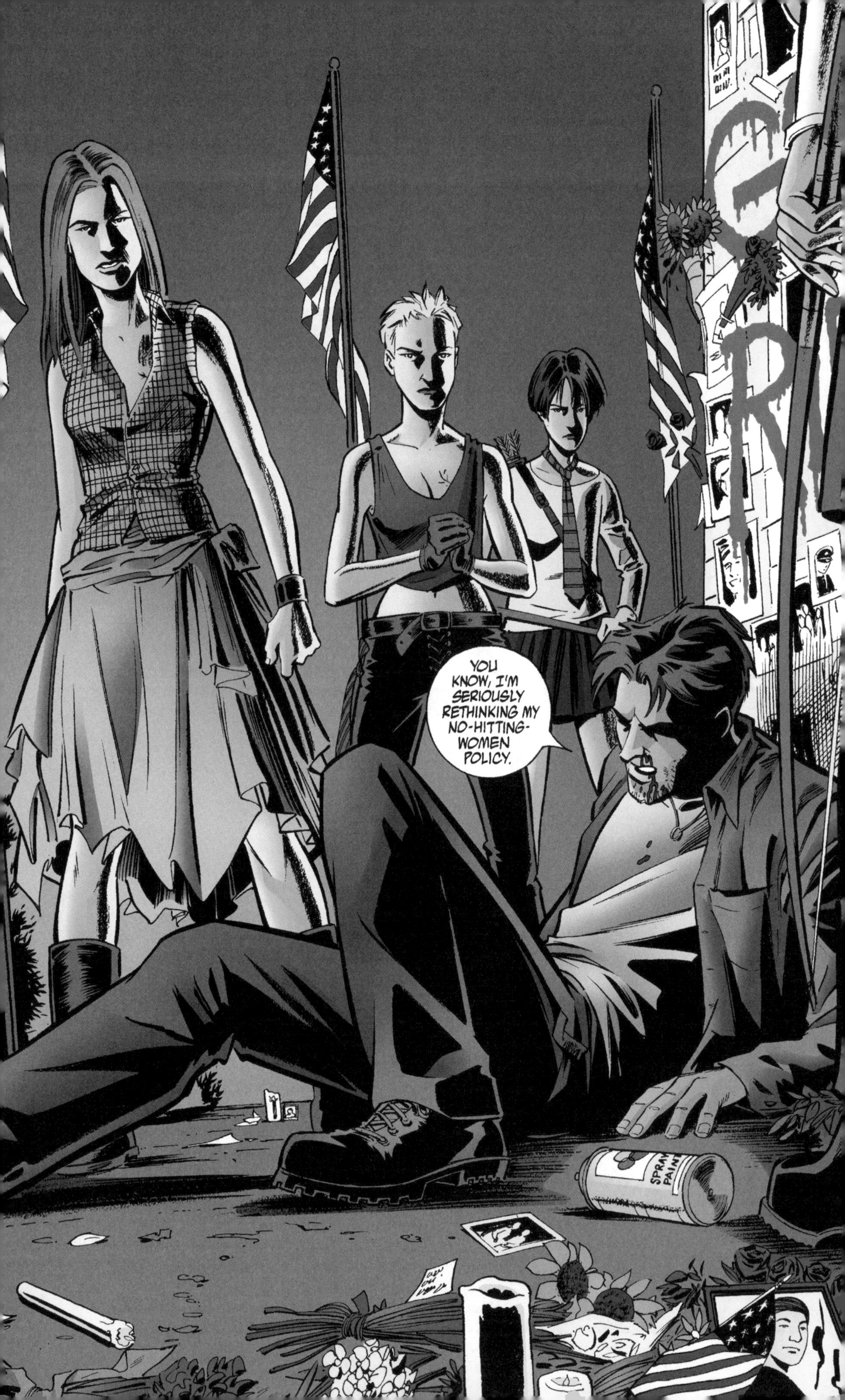
YOU KNOW, I'M SERIOUSLY RETHINKING MY NO-HITTING-WOMEN POLICY.
SPRAY PAINT

Washington, D.C.
One Hour Ago

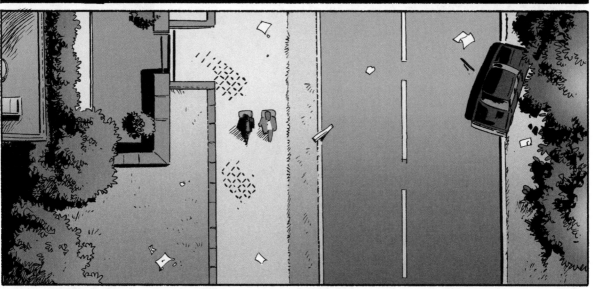

SO, uh... WHAT'S THE PLAN, FRAN?

THAT'S NOT MY NAME.

NO KIDDING. I WAS ONLY--

THERE'S A *REASON* MY REAL NAME IS CLASSIFIED, YORICK.

IF YOU HAVE TO CALL ME SOMETHING, YOU CAN CALL ME 355.

AND IF YOU'LL BE MY BODYGUARD, YOU CAN CALL ME AL?

WHAT?

FORGET IT.

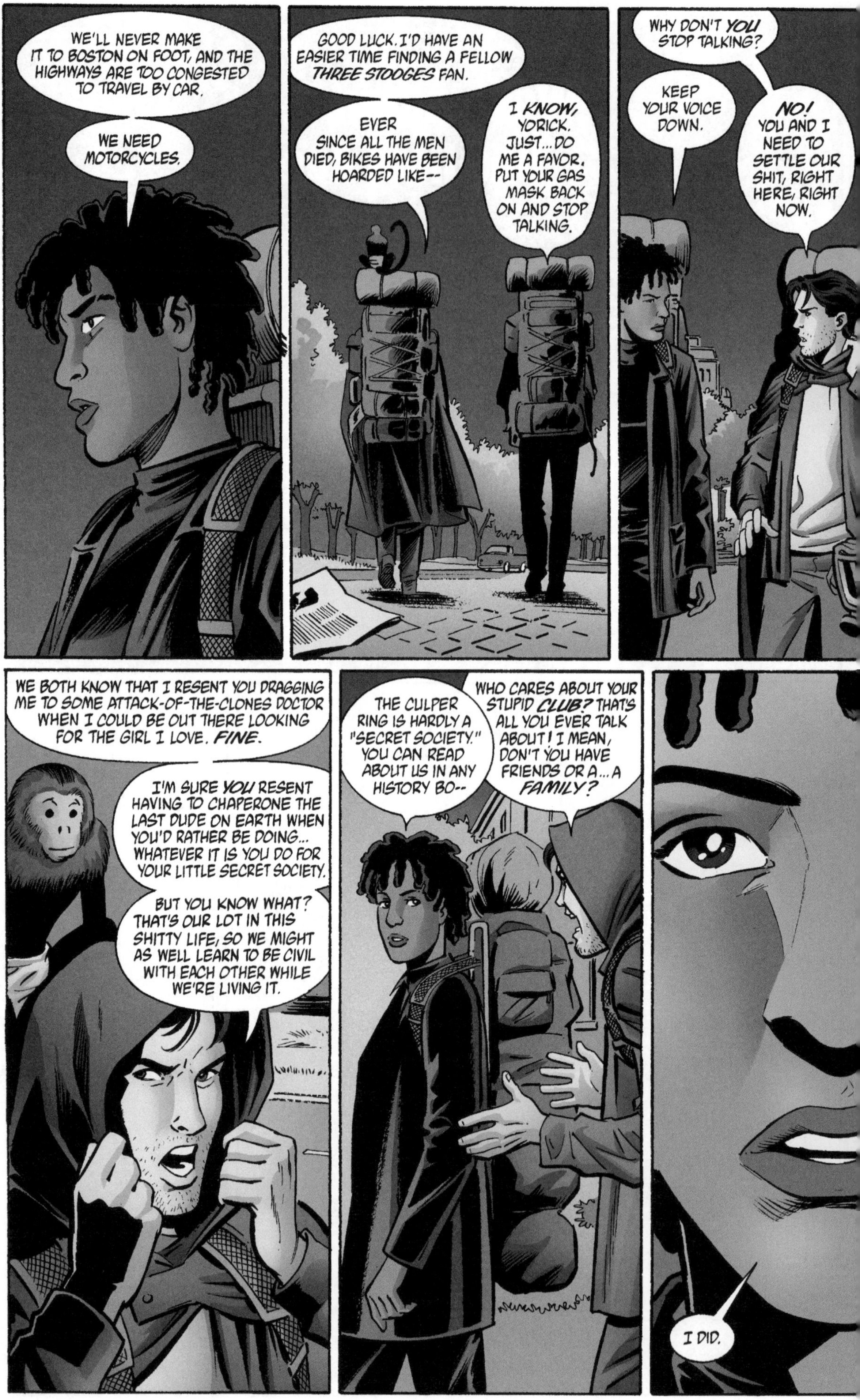
WE'LL NEVER MAKE IT TO BOSTON ON FOOT, AND THE HIGHWAYS ARE TOO CONGESTED TO TRAVEL BY CAR.
WE NEED MOTORCYCLES.
GOOD LUCK. I'D HAVE AN EASIER TIME FINDING A FELLOW THREE STOOGES FAN.
EVER SINCE ALL THE MEN DIED, BIKES HAVE BEEN HOARDED LIKE--
I KNOW, YORICK. JUST... DO ME A FAVOR. PUT YOUR GAS MASK BACK ON AND STOP TALKING.
WHY DON'T YOU STOP TALKING?
KEEP YOUR VOICE DOWN.
NO! YOU AND I NEED TO SETTLE OUR SHIT, RIGHT HERE, RIGHT NOW.
WE BOTH KNOW THAT I RESENT YOU DRAGGING ME TO SOME ATTACK-OF-THE-CLONES DOCTOR WHEN I COULD BE OUT THERE LOOKING FOR THE GIRL I LOVE. FINE.
I'M SURE YOU RESENT HAVING TO CHAPERONE THE LAST DUDE ON EARTH WHEN YOU'D RATHER BE DOING... WHATEVER IT IS YOU DO FOR YOUR LITTLE SECRET SOCIETY.
BUT YOU KNOW WHAT? THAT'S OUR LOT IN THIS SHITTY LIFE, SO WE MIGHT AS WELL LEARN TO BE CIVIL WITH EACH OTHER WHILE WE'RE LIVING IT.
THE CULPER RING IS HARDLY A "SECRET SOCIETY." YOU CAN READ ABOUT US IN ANY HISTORY BO--
WHO CARES ABOUT YOUR STUPID CLUB? THAT'S ALL YOU EVER TALK ABOUT! I MEAN, DON'T YOU HAVE FRIENDS OR A... A FAMILY?
I DID.

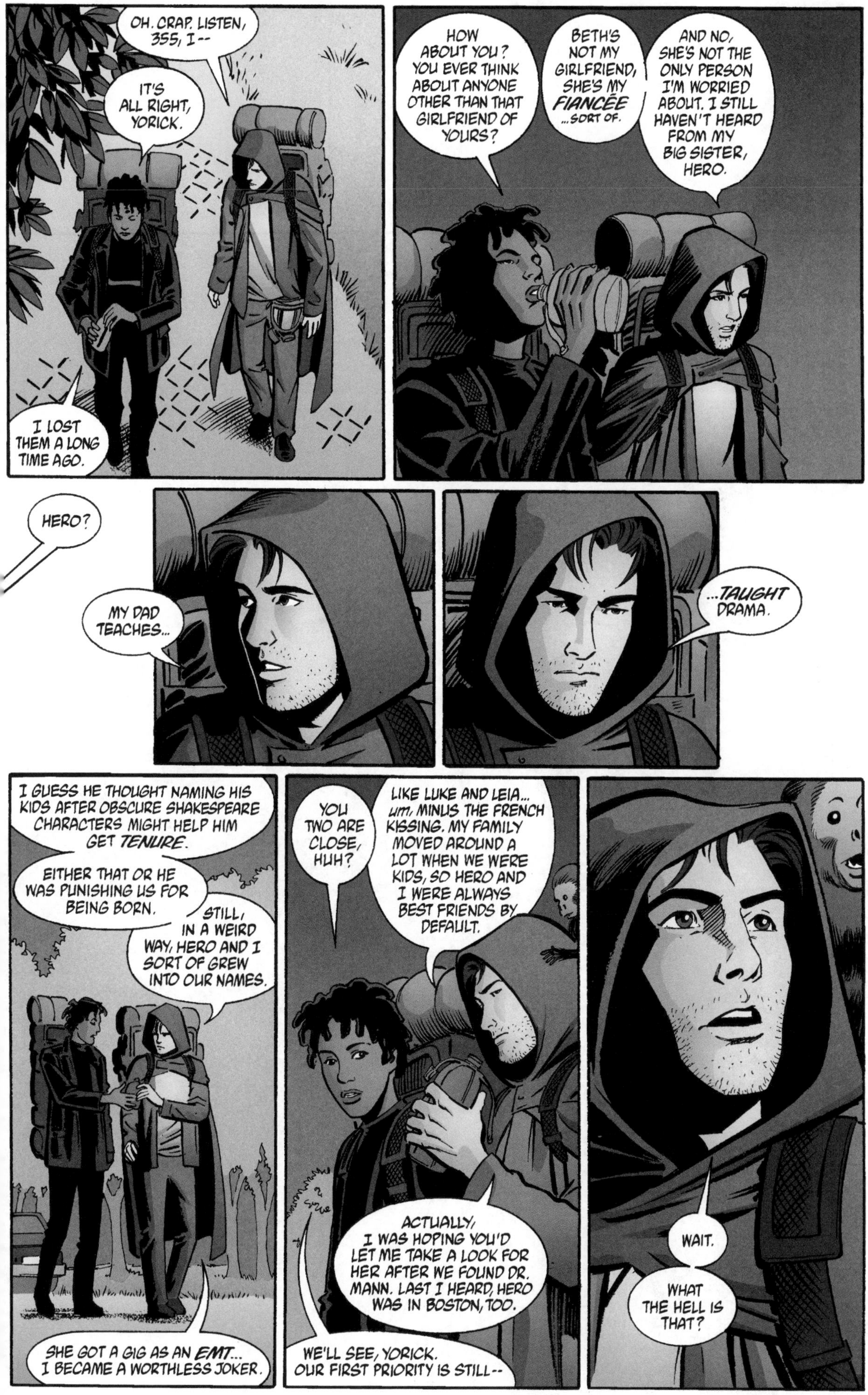
OH. CRAP. LISTEN, 355, I--
IT'S ALL RIGHT, YORICK.
I LOST THEM A LONG TIME AGO.
HOW ABOUT YOU? YOU EVER THINK ABOUT ANYONE OTHER THAN THAT GIRLFRIEND OF YOURS?
BETH'S NOT MY GIRLFRIEND, SHE'S MY FIANCÉE ...SORT OF.
AND NO, SHE'S NOT THE ONLY PERSON I'M WORRIED ABOUT. I STILL HAVEN'T HEARD FROM MY BIG SISTER, HERO.
HERO?
MY DAD TEACHES...
...TAUGHT DRAMA.
I GUESS HE THOUGHT NAMING HIS KIDS AFTER OBSCURE SHAKESPEARE CHARACTERS MIGHT HELP HIM GET TENURE.
EITHER THAT OR HE WAS PUNISHING US FOR BEING BORN.
STILL, IN A WEIRD WAY, HERO AND I SORT OF GREW INTO OUR NAMES.
SHE GOT A GIG AS AN EMT... I BECAME A WORTHLESS JOKER.
YOU TWO ARE CLOSE, HUH?
LIKE LUKE AND LEIA... UM, MINUS THE FRENCH KISSING. MY FAMILY MOVED AROUND A LOT WHEN WE WERE KIDS, SO HERO AND I WERE ALWAYS BEST FRIENDS BY DEFAULT.
ACTUALLY, I WAS HOPING YOU'D LET ME TAKE A LOOK FOR HER AFTER WE FOUND DR. MANN. LAST I HEARD, HERO WAS IN BOSTON, TOO.
WE'LL SEE, YORICK. OUR FIRST PRIORITY IS STILL--
WAIT.
WHAT THE HELL IS THAT?

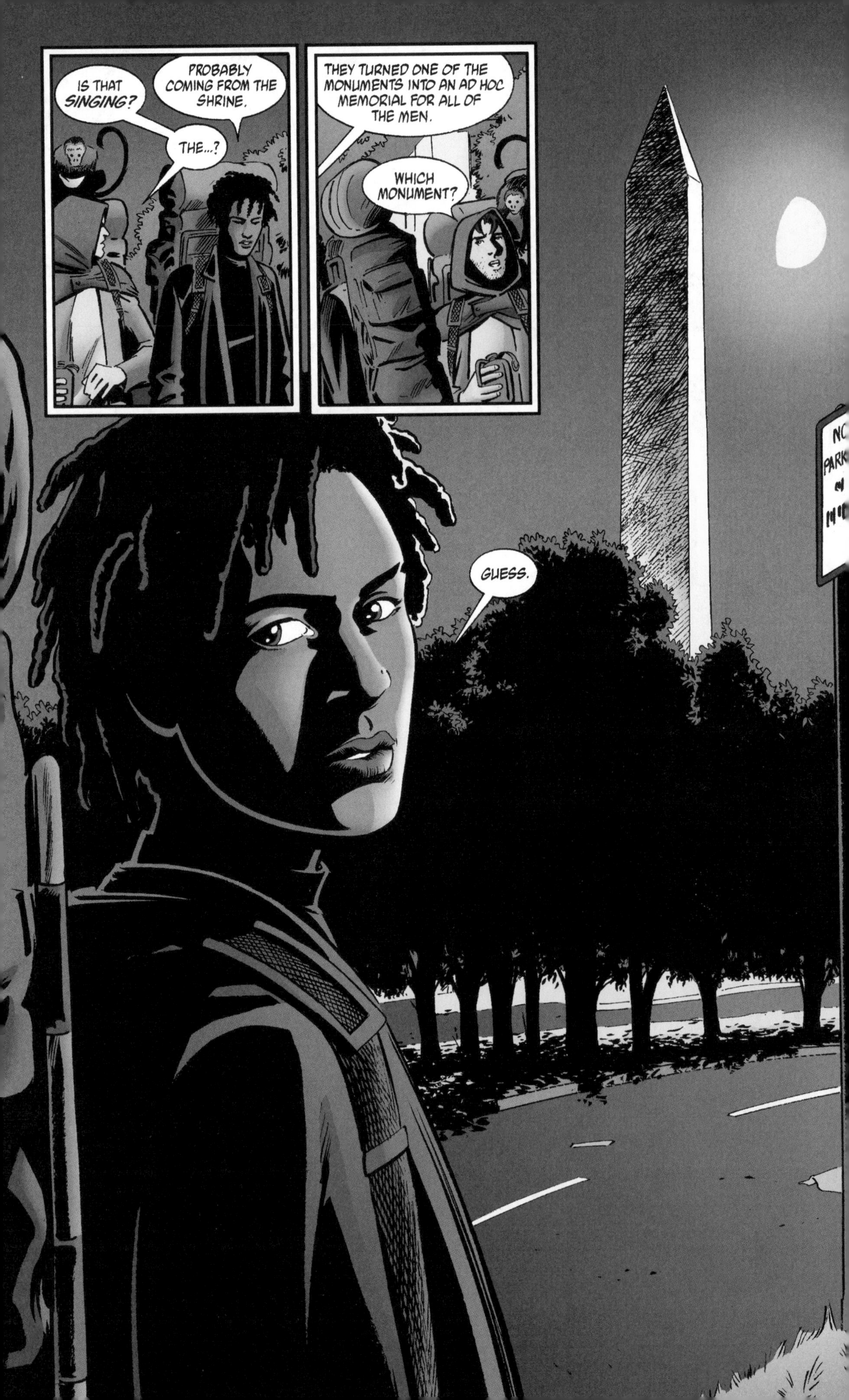
IS THAT SINGING?
PROBABLY COMING FROM THE SHRINE.
THE...?
THEY TURNED ONE OF THE MONUMENTS INTO AN AD HOC MEMORIAL FOR ALL OF THE MEN.
WHICH MONUMENT?
GUESS.

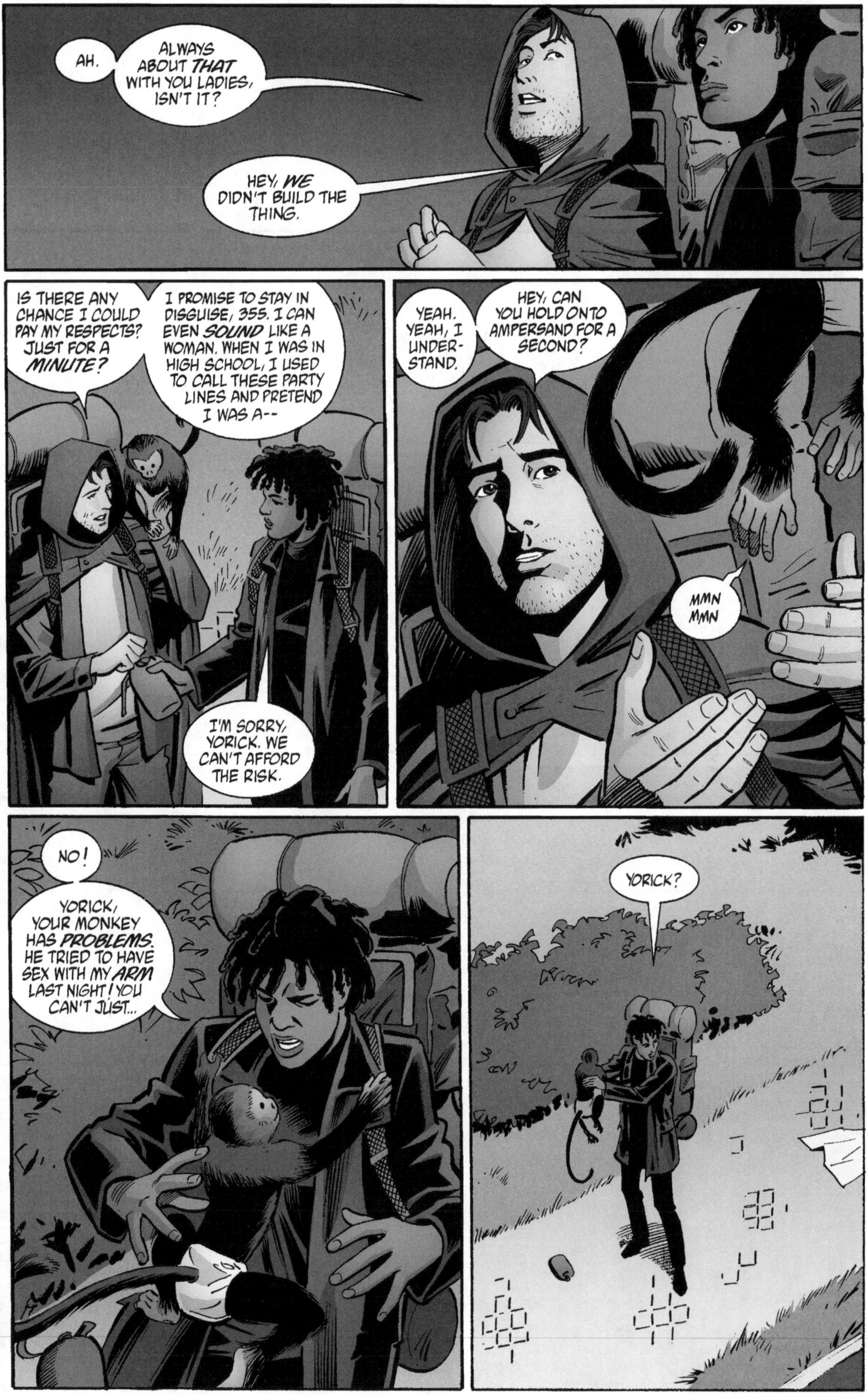
AH.
ALWAYS ABOUT THAT WITH YOU LADIES, ISN'T IT?
HEY, WE DIDN'T BUILD THE THING.
IS THERE ANY CHANCE I COULD PAY MY RESPECTS? JUST FOR A MINUTE?
I PROMISE TO STAY IN DISGUISE, 355. I CAN EVEN SOUND LIKE A WOMAN. WHEN I WAS IN HIGH SCHOOL, I USED TO CALL THESE PARTY LINES AND PRETEND I WAS A--
I'M SORRY, YORICK. WE CAN'T AFFORD THE RISK.
YEAH. YEAH, I UNDERSTAND.
HEY, CAN YOU HOLD ONTO AMPERSAND FOR A SECOND?
MMN MMN
NO!
YORICK, YOUR MONKEY HAS PROBLEMS. HE TRIED TO HAVE SEX WITH MY ARM LAST NIGHT! YOU CAN'T JUST...
YORICK?

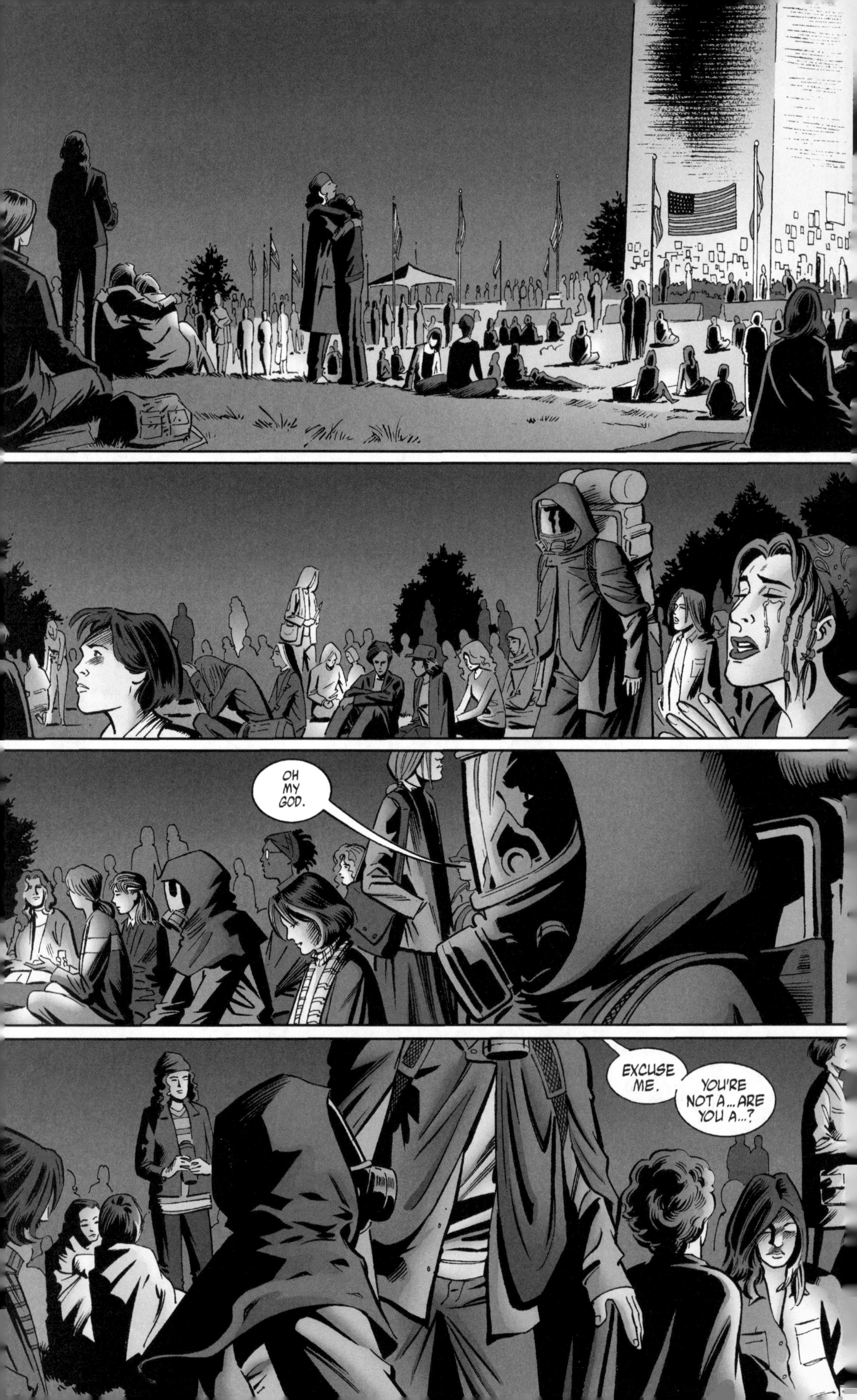
OH MY GOD.
EXCUSE ME.
YOU'RE NOT A...ARE YOU A...?

OH. I...I SAW THE GAS MASK AND I THOUGHT MAYBE YOU WERE ANOTHER...

I THOUGHT MAYBE YOU WERE SOMEONE I KNEW.

I KNOW YOU, HONEY?

SORRY. JUST GOT SO USED TO WEARING THIS DAMN THING AFTER THE PLAGUE HIT, IT'S KINDA BECOME MY SECURITY BLANKET. YOU TOO, HUH?

I'M ROSE, BY THE WAY. TAKE A LOAD OFF.

THANKS. I'M...BETH.

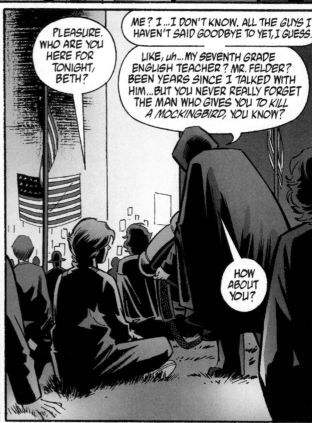

PLEASURE. WHO ARE YOU HERE FOR TONIGHT, BETH?

ME? I...I DON'T KNOW. ALL THE GUYS I HAVEN'T SAID GOODBYE TO YET, I GUESS.

LIKE, uh...MY SEVENTH GRADE ENGLISH TEACHER? MR. FELDER? BEEN YEARS SINCE I TALKED WITH HIM...BUT YOU NEVER REALLY FORGET THE MAN WHO GIVES YOU TO KILL A MOCKINGBIRD, YOU KNOW?

HOW ABOUT YOU?

MICK JAGGER.

SERIOUSLY?

ABSOLUTELY. I MEAN, DON'T GET ME WRONG, I DON'T MISS ANYONE LIKE I MISS MY PALS, BUT IT SUDDENLY HIT ME TODAY...

THE ROLLING STONES ARE DEAD.

95

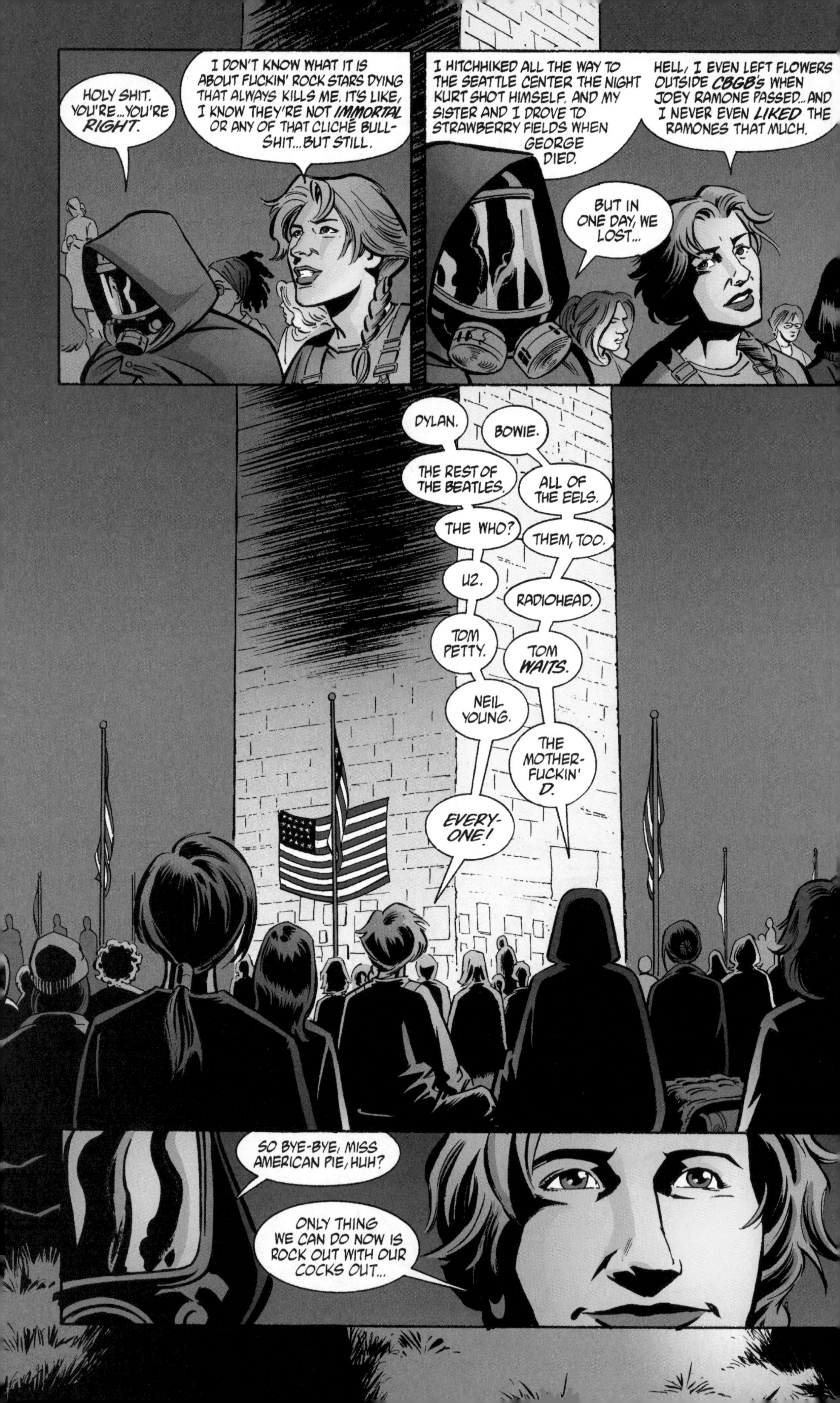
HOLY SHIT. YOU'RE...YOU'RE RIGHT.
I DON'T KNOW WHAT IT IS ABOUT FUCKIN' ROCK STARS DYING THAT ALWAYS KILLS ME. IT'S LIKE, I KNOW THEY'RE NOT IMMORTAL OR ANY OF THAT CLICHÉ BULL-SHIT...BUT STILL.
I HITCHHIKED ALL THE WAY TO THE SEATTLE CENTER THE NIGHT KURT SHOT HIMSELF. AND MY SISTER AND I DROVE TO STRAWBERRY FIELDS WHEN GEORGE DIED.
HELL, I EVEN LEFT FLOWERS OUTSIDE CBGB's WHEN JOEY RAMONE PASSED...AND I NEVER EVEN LIKED THE RAMONES THAT MUCH.
BUT IN ONE DAY, WE LOST...
DYLAN.
BOWIE.
THE REST OF THE BEATLES.
ALL OF THE EELS.
THE WHO?
THEM, TOO.
U2.
RADIOHEAD.
TOM PETTY.
TOM WAITS.
NEIL YOUNG.
THE MOTHER-FUCKIN' D.
EVERY-ONE!
SO BYE-BYE, MISS AMERICAN PIE, HUH?
ONLY THING WE CAN DO NOW IS ROCK OUT WITH OUR COCKS OUT...

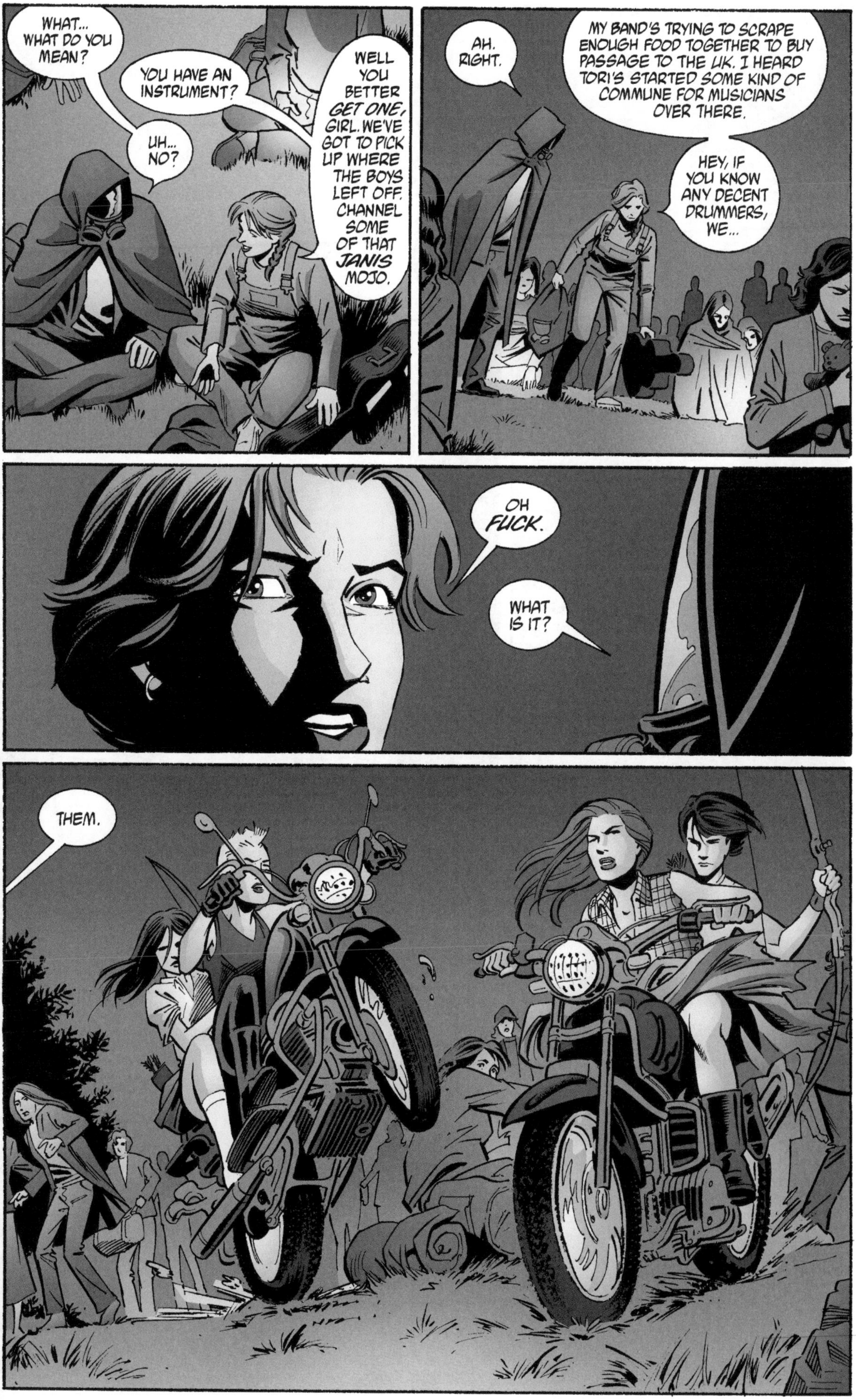

WHAT... WHAT DO YOU MEAN?
YOU HAVE AN INSTRUMENT?
UH... NO?
WELL YOU BETTER GET ONE, GIRL. WE'VE GOT TO PICK UP WHERE THE BOYS LEFT OFF. CHANNEL SOME OF THAT JANIS MOJO.
AH. RIGHT.
MY BAND'S TRYING TO SCRAPE ENOUGH FOOD TOGETHER TO BUY PASSAGE TO THE UK. I HEARD TORI'S STARTED SOME KIND OF COMMUNE FOR MUSICIANS OVER THERE.
HEY, IF YOU KNOW ANY DECENT DRUMMERS, WE...
OH FUCK.
WHAT IS IT?
THEM.

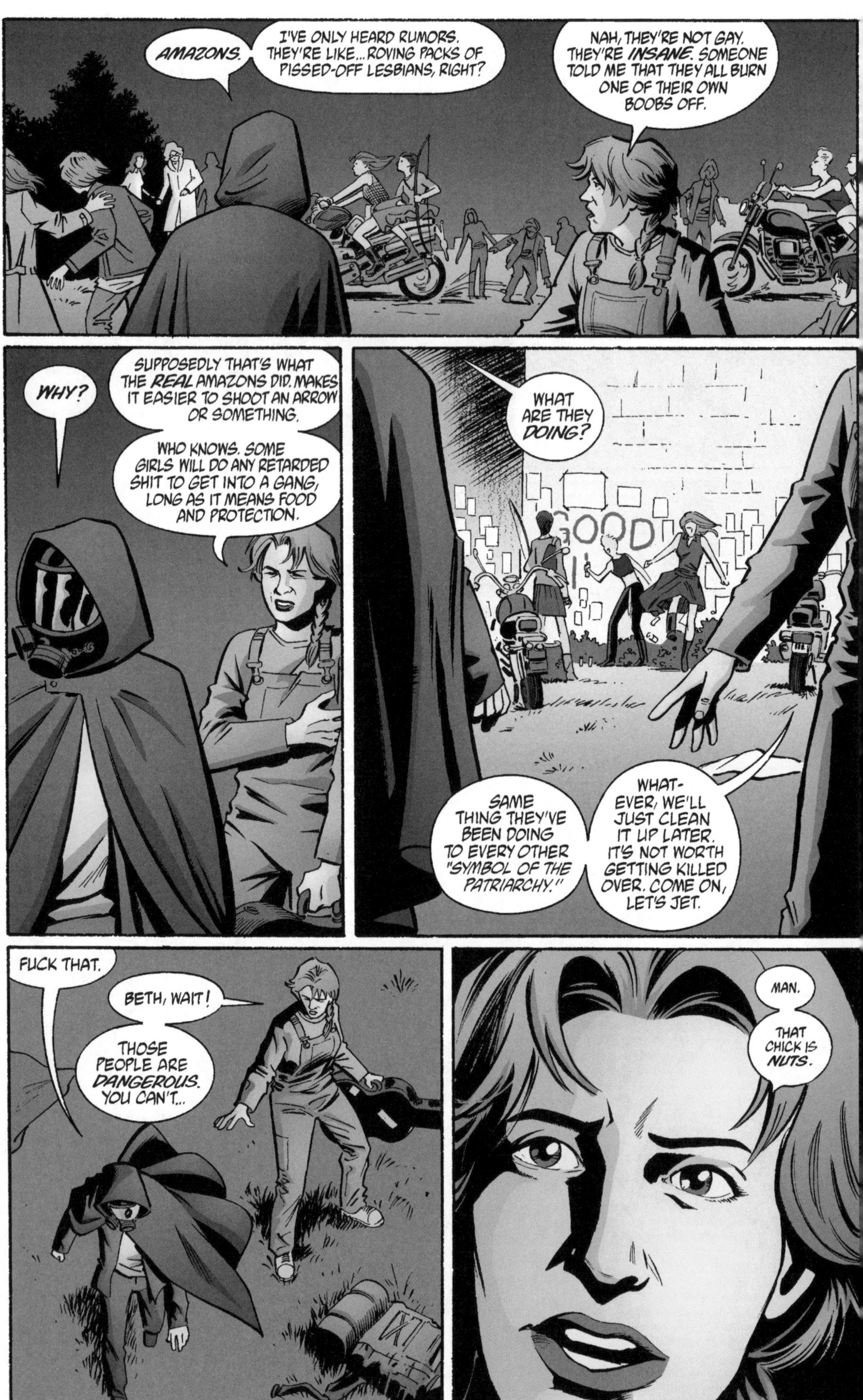

AMAZONS.
I'VE ONLY HEARD RUMORS. THEY'RE LIKE... ROVING PACKS OF PISSED-OFF LESBIANS, RIGHT?
NAH, THEY'RE NOT GAY. THEY'RE INSANE. SOMEONE TOLD ME THAT THEY ALL BURN ONE OF THEIR OWN BOOBS OFF.
WHY?
SUPPOSEDLY THAT'S WHAT THE REAL AMAZONS DID. MAKES IT EASIER TO SHOOT AN ARROW OR SOMETHING.
WHO KNOWS. SOME GIRLS WILL DO ANY RETARDED SHIT TO GET INTO A GANG, LONG AS IT MEANS FOOD AND PROTECTION.
WHAT ARE THEY DOING?
GOOD
SAME THING THEY'VE BEEN DOING TO EVERY OTHER "SYMBOL OF THE PATRIARCHY."
WHAT-EVER, WE'LL JUST CLEAN IT UP LATER. IT'S NOT WORTH GETTING KILLED OVER. COME ON, LET'S JET.
FUCK THAT.
BETH, WAIT!
THOSE PEOPLE ARE DANGEROUS. YOU CAN'T...
MAN.
THAT CHICK IS NUTS.

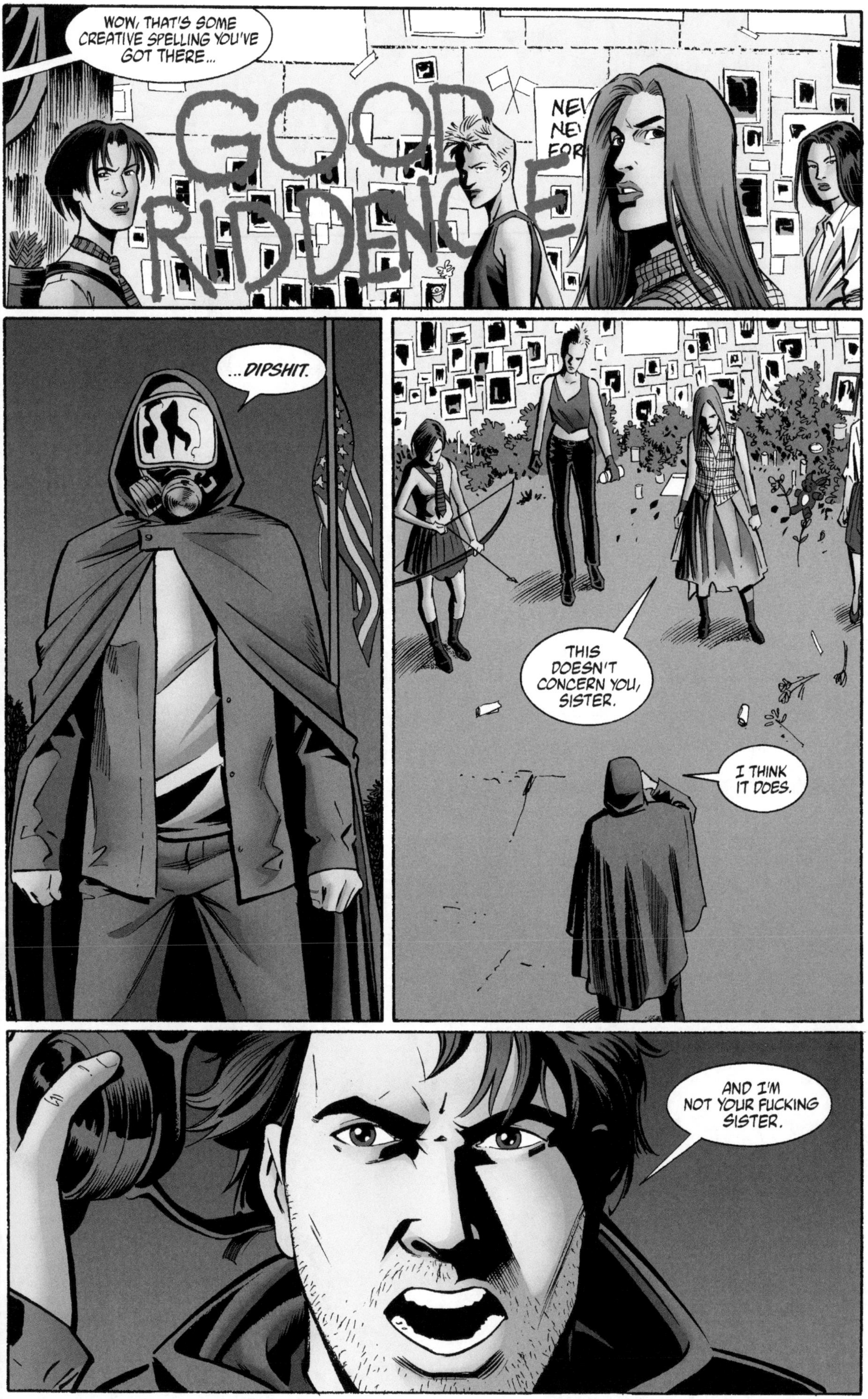
WOW, THAT'S SOME CREATIVE SPELLING YOU'VE GOT THERE...
GOOD RIDDENCE
...DIPSHIT.
THIS DOESN'T CONCERN YOU, SISTER.
I THINK IT DOES.
AND I'M NOT YOUR FUCKING SISTER.

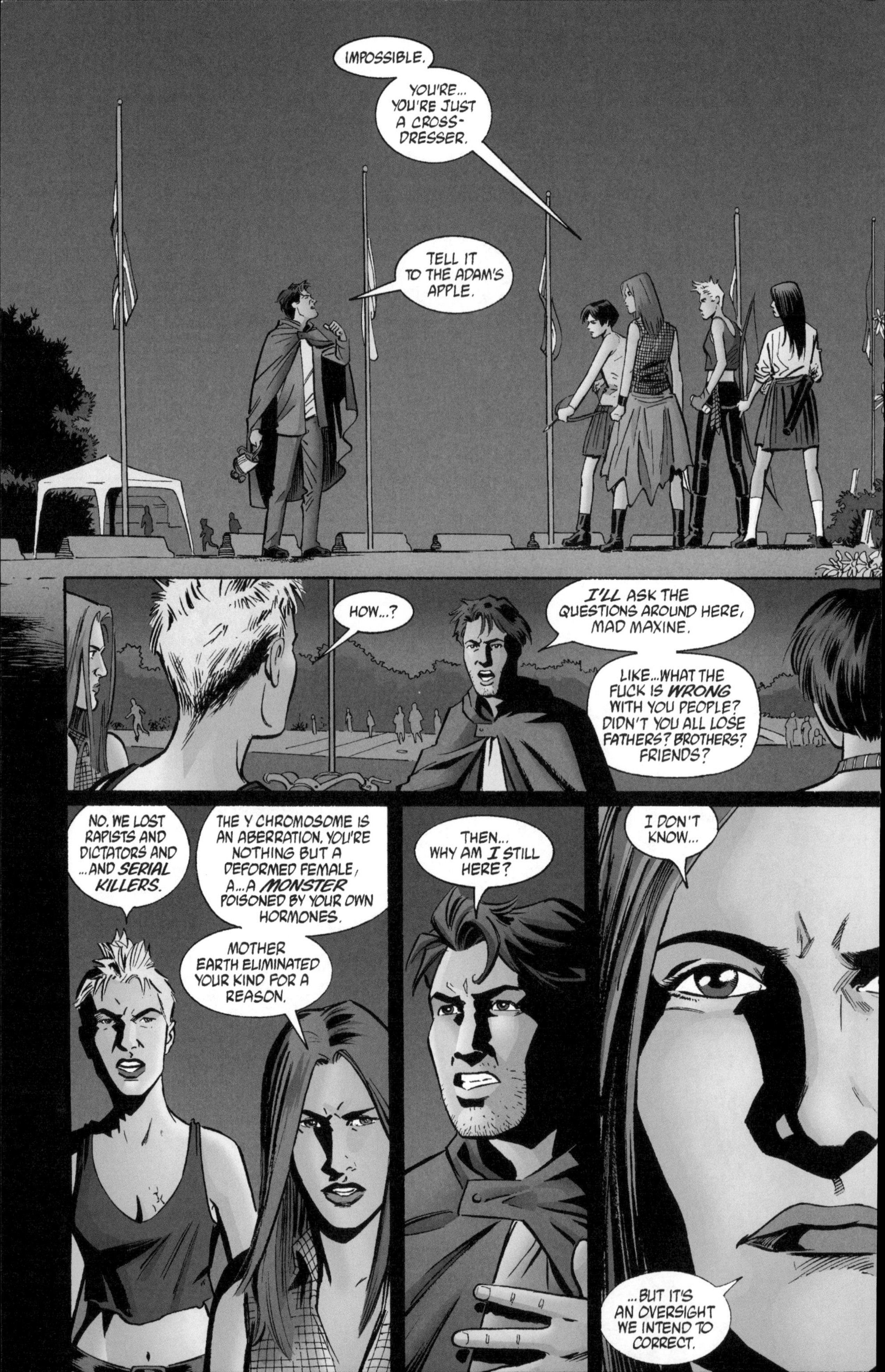
IMPOSSIBLE.
YOU'RE... YOU'RE JUST A CROSS-DRESSER.
TELL IT TO THE ADAM'S APPLE.
HOW...?
I'LL ASK THE QUESTIONS AROUND HERE, MAD MAXINE.
LIKE...WHAT THE FUCK IS WRONG WITH YOU PEOPLE? DIDN'T YOU ALL LOSE FATHERS? BROTHERS? FRIENDS?
NO. WE LOST RAPISTS AND DICTATORS AND ...AND SERIAL KILLERS.
THE Y CHROMOSOME IS AN ABERRATION. YOU'RE NOTHING BUT A DEFORMED FEMALE, A...A MONSTER POISONED BY YOUR OWN HORMONES.
MOTHER EARTH ELIMINATED YOUR KIND FOR A REASON.
THEN... WHY AM I STILL HERE?
I DON'T KNOW...
...BUT IT'S AN OVERSIGHT WE INTEND TO CORRECT.

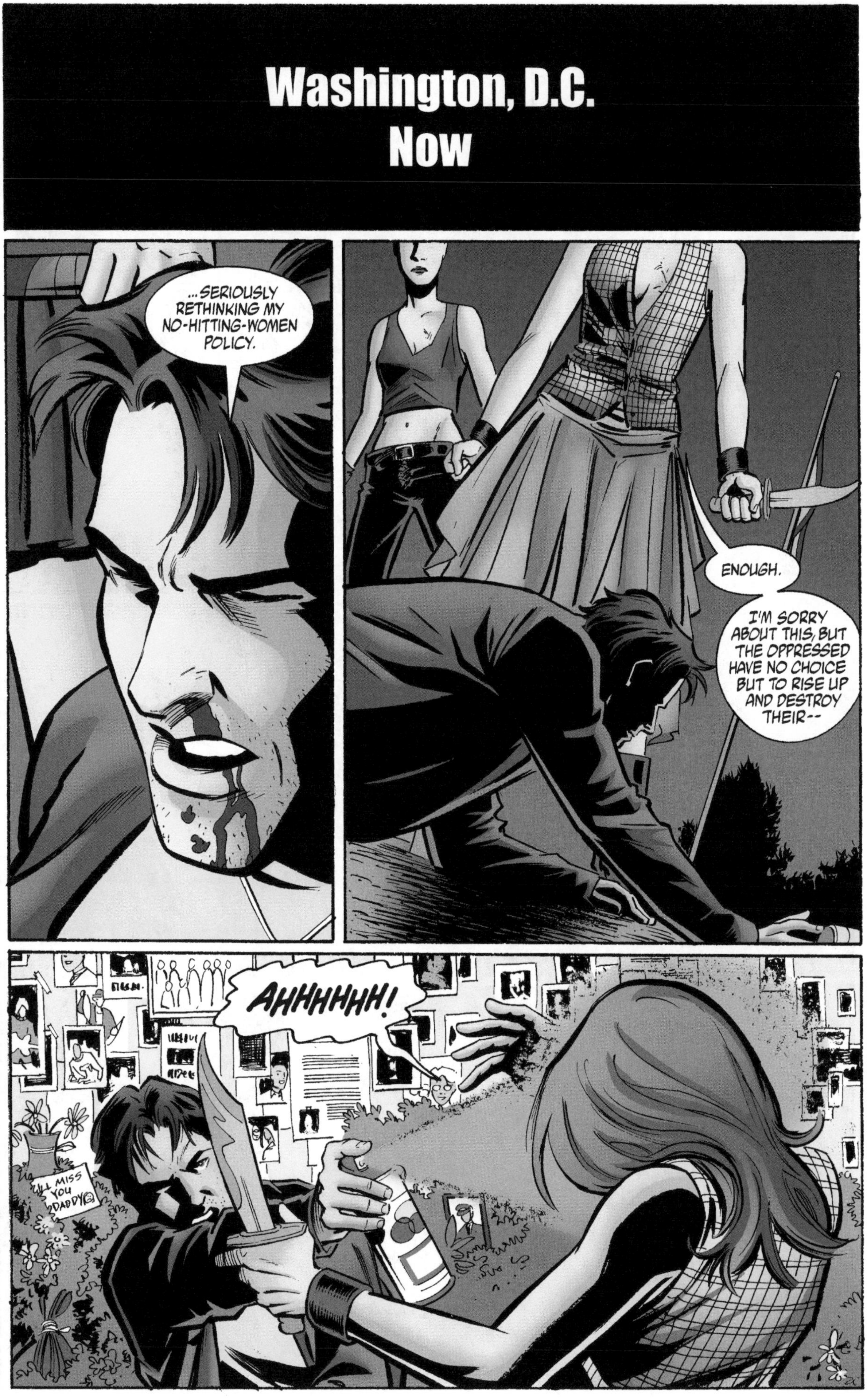
Washington, D.C.
Now
...SERIOUSLY RETHINKING MY NO-HITTING-WOMEN POLICY.
ENOUGH.
I'M SORRY ABOUT THIS, BUT THE OPPRESSED HAVE NO CHOICE BUT TO RISE UP AND DESTROY THEIR--
AHHHHHH!
MISS YOU DADDY

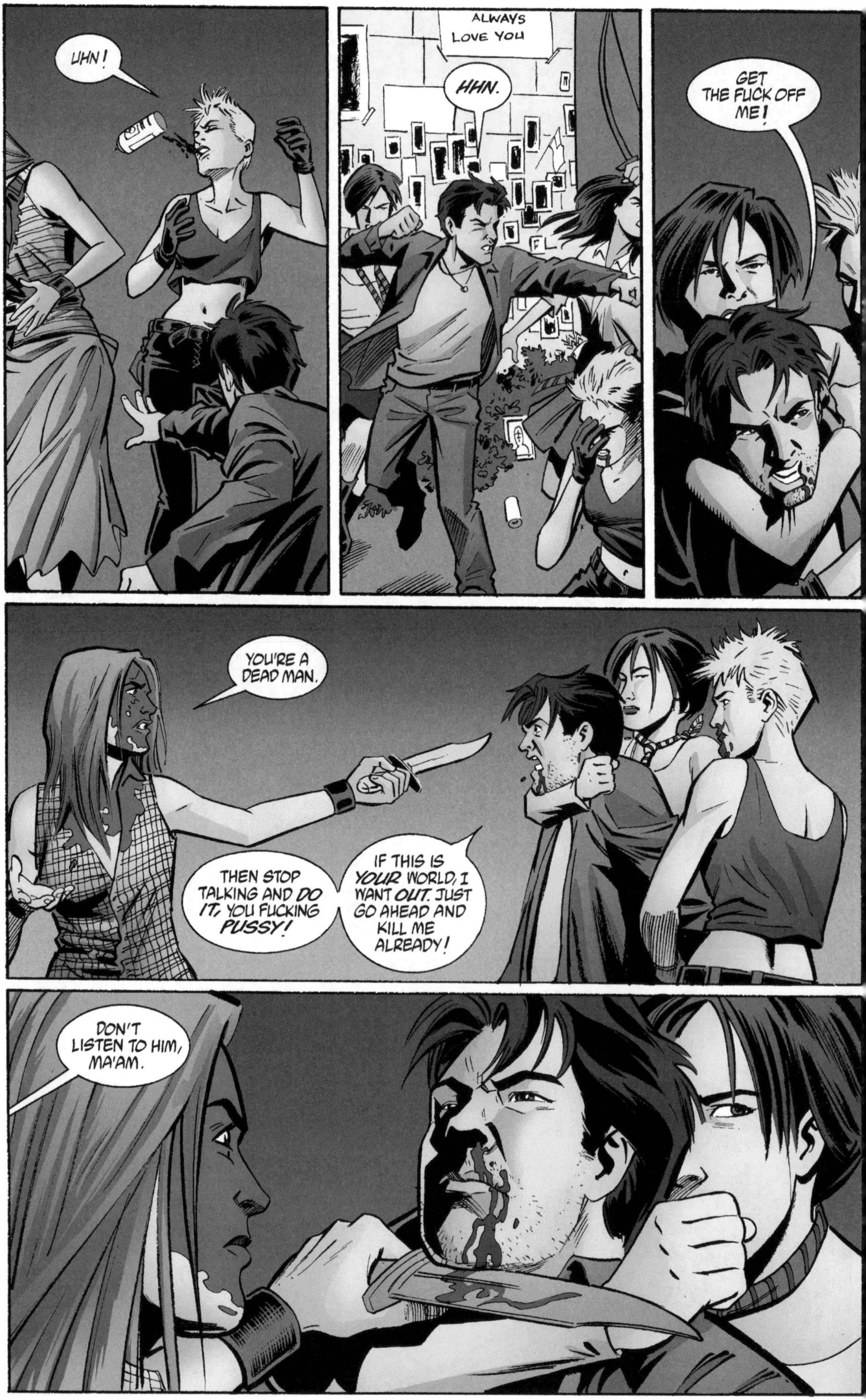
ALWAYS
LOVE YOU
UHN!
HHN.
GET THE FUCK OFF ME!
YOU'RE A DEAD MAN.
THEN STOP TALKING AND DO IT, YOU FUCKING PUSSY!
IF THIS IS YOUR WORLD, I WANT OUT. JUST GO AHEAD AND KILL ME ALREADY!
DON'T LISTEN TO HIM, MA'AM.

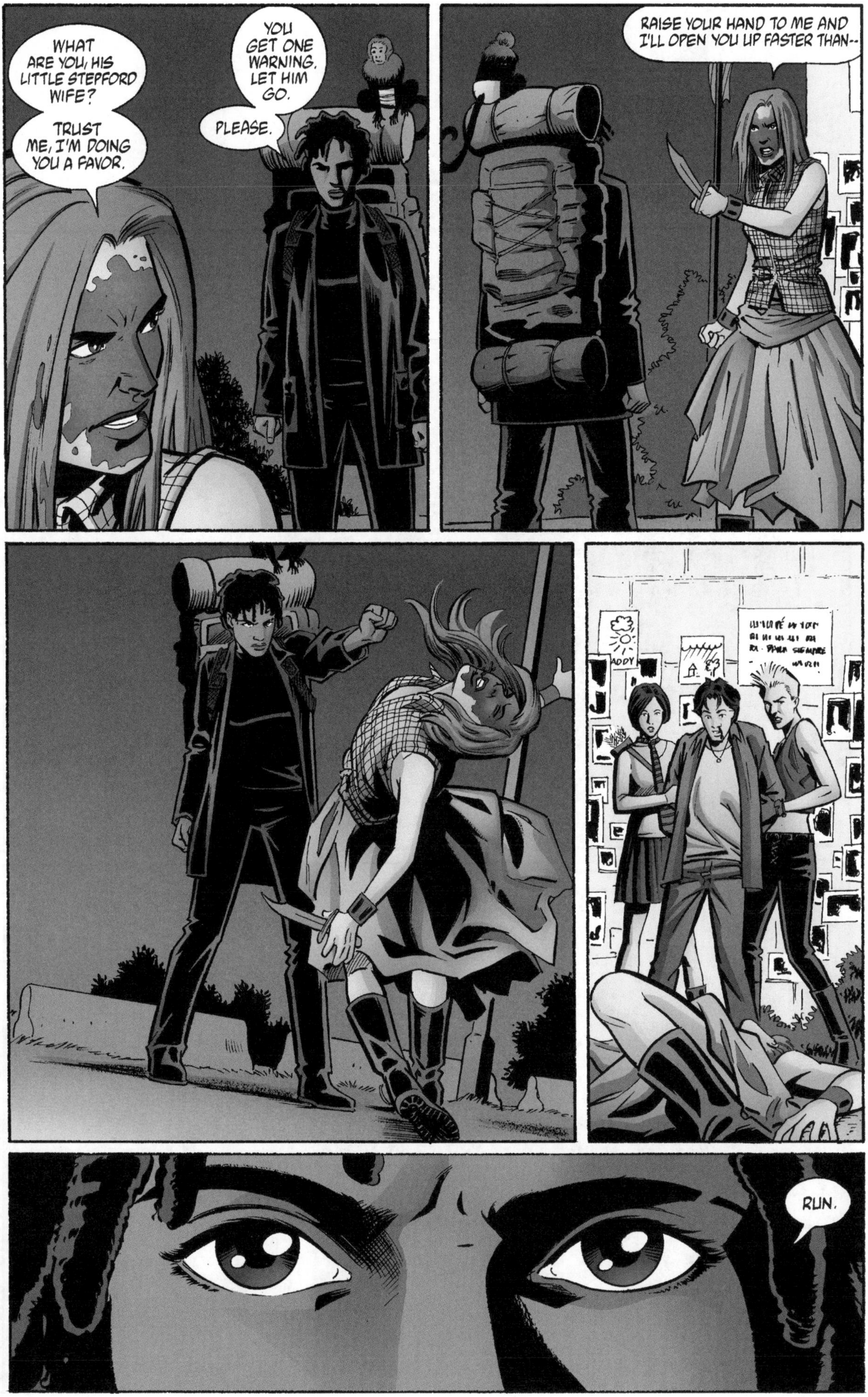
WHAT ARE YOU, HIS LITTLE STEPFORD WIFE?
TRUST ME, I'M DOING YOU A FAVOR.
YOU GET ONE WARNING. LET HIM GO.
PLEASE.
RAISE YOUR HAND TO ME AND I'LL OPEN YOU UP FASTER THAN--
RUN.

CUTTING IT A LITTLE CLOSE, AREN'T WE?

NOT REALLY. I'VE BEEN WATCHING YOU FOR THE LAST TEN MINUTES.

THE... WHAT ARE YOU *TALKING* ABOUT?

YOU JUST STOOD THERE WHILE THEY *BEAT* ME? *WHY?*

LOVE YOU

TO TEACH YOU A LESSON.

JUST BECAUSE YOU'VE GOT A *DICK* DOESN'T MEAN THAT YOU'RE *INVINCIBLE.*

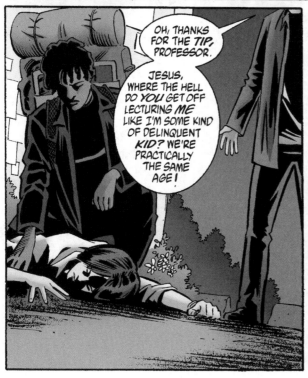

OH, THANKS FOR THE *TIP,* PROFESSOR.

JESUS, WHERE THE HELL DO *YOU* GET OFF LECTURING *ME* LIKE I'M SOME KIND OF DELINQUENT *KID?* WE'RE PRACTICALLY THE SAME AGE!

THEN START ACTING LIKE IT, YORICK!

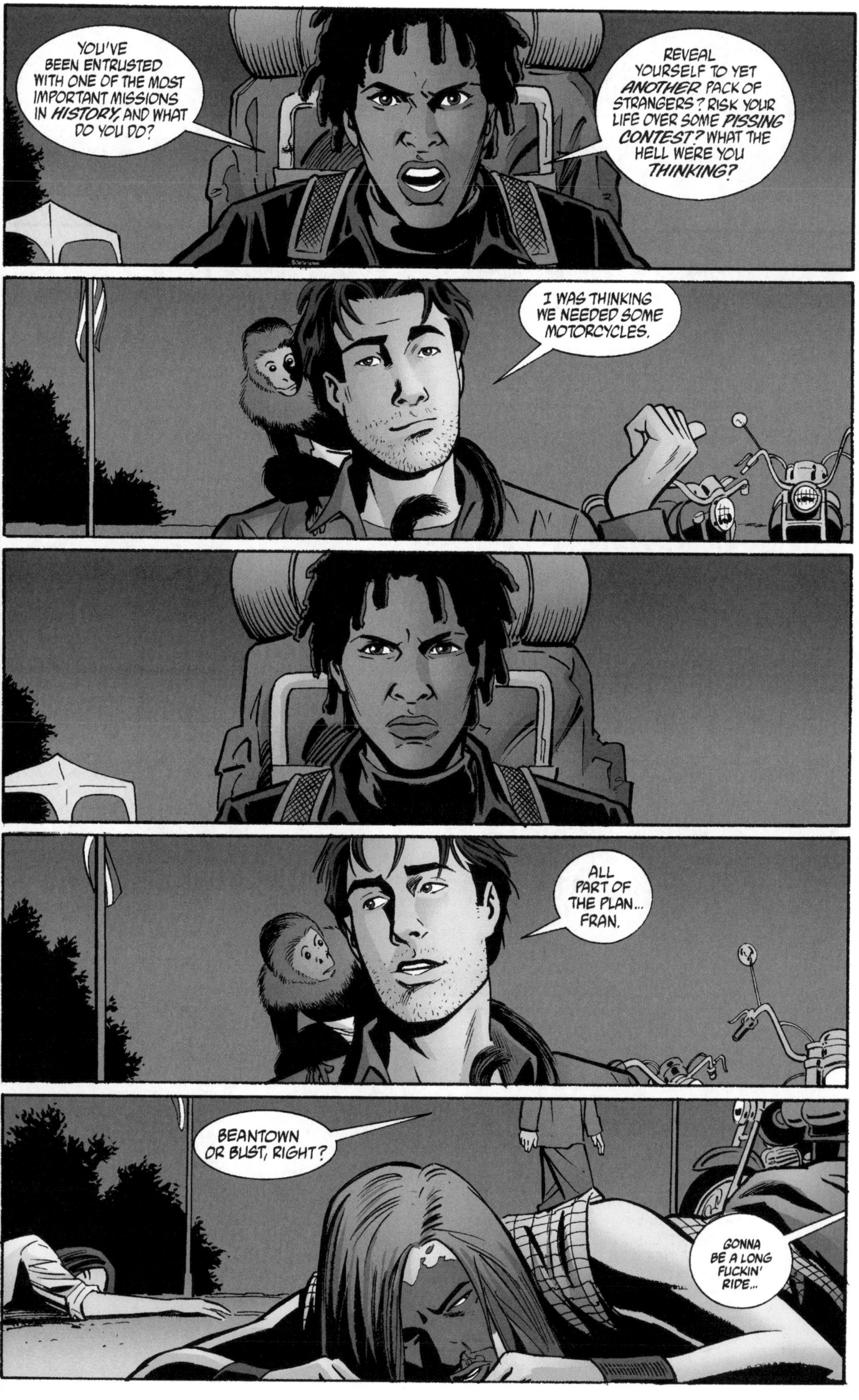
YOU'VE BEEN ENTRUSTED WITH ONE OF THE MOST IMPORTANT MISSIONS IN *HISTORY*, AND WHAT DO YOU DO?
REVEAL YOURSELF TO YET *ANOTHER* PACK OF STRANGERS? RISK YOUR LIFE OVER SOME *PISSING CONTEST?* WHAT THE HELL WERE YOU *THINKING?*
I WAS THINKING WE NEEDED SOME MOTORCYCLES.
ALL PART OF THE PLAN... FRAN.
BEANTOWN OR BUST, RIGHT?
GONNA BE A LONG FUCKIN' RIDE...

Baltimore Convention Center
Six Hours Later

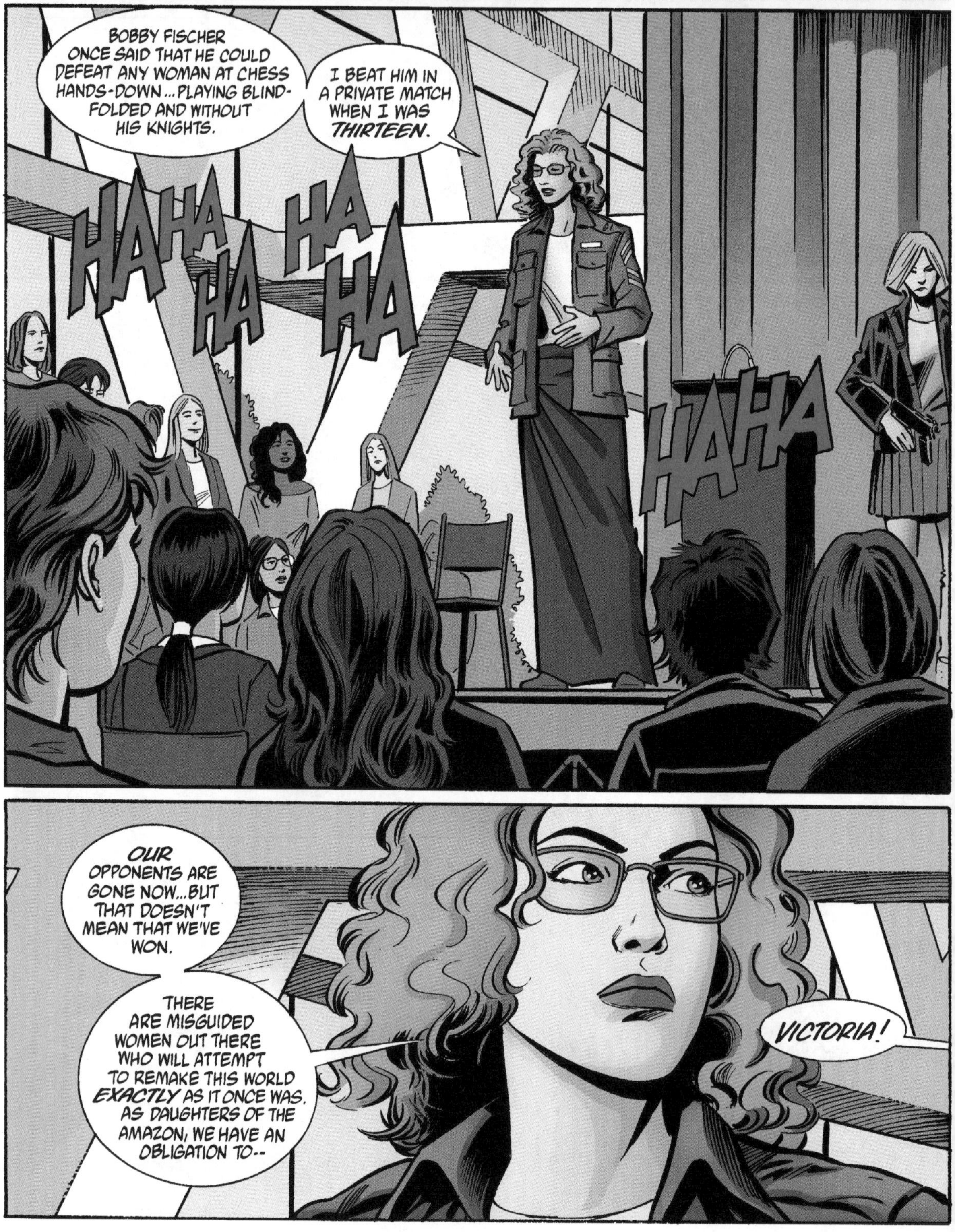
BOBBY FISCHER ONCE SAID THAT HE COULD DEFEAT ANY WOMAN AT CHESS HANDS-DOWN...PLAYING BLIND-FOLDED AND WITHOUT HIS KNIGHTS.
I BEAT HIM IN A PRIVATE MATCH WHEN I WAS THIRTEEN.
HAHA HA HA HA
HAHA
OUR OPPONENTS ARE GONE NOW...BUT THAT DOESN'T MEAN THAT WE'VE WON.
THERE ARE MISGUIDED WOMEN OUT THERE WHO WILL ATTEMPT TO REMAKE THIS WORLD EXACTLY AS IT ONCE WAS. AS DAUGHTERS OF THE AMAZON, WE HAVE AN OBLIGATION TO--
VICTORIA!

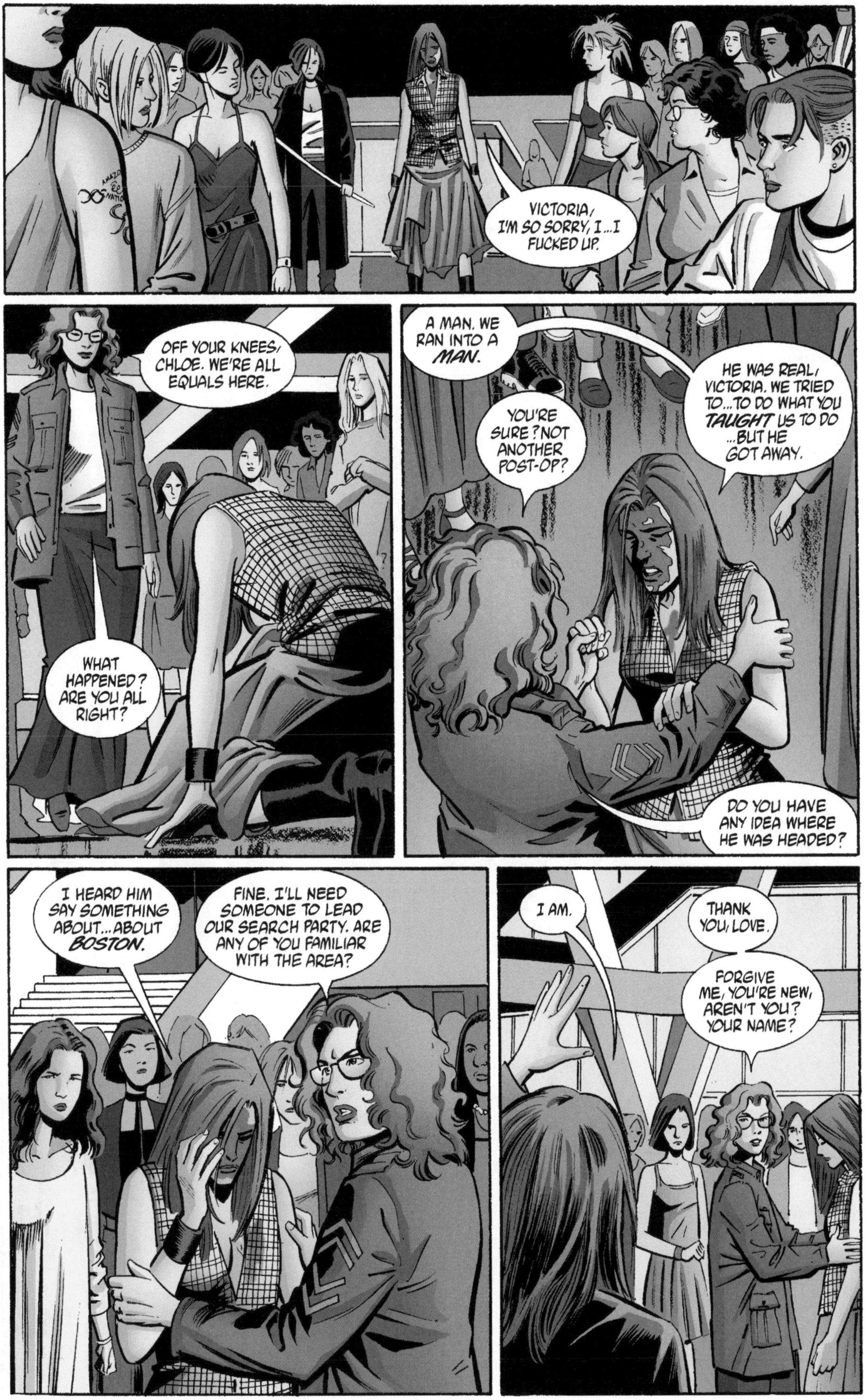
VICTORIA, I'M SO SORRY, I...I FUCKED UP.
OFF YOUR KNEES, CHLOE. WE'RE ALL EQUALS HERE.
WHAT HAPPENED? ARE YOU ALL RIGHT?
A MAN. WE RAN INTO A MAN.
YOU'RE SURE? NOT ANOTHER POST-OP?
HE WAS REAL, VICTORIA. WE TRIED TO...TO DO WHAT YOU TAUGHT US TO DO ...BUT HE GOT AWAY.
DO YOU HAVE ANY IDEA WHERE HE WAS HEADED?
I HEARD HIM SAY SOMETHING ABOUT...ABOUT BOSTON.
FINE. I'LL NEED SOMEONE TO LEAD OUR SEARCH PARTY. ARE ANY OF YOU FAMILIAR WITH THE AREA?
I AM.
THANK YOU, LOVE.
FORGIVE ME, YOU'RE NEW, AREN'T YOU? YOUR NAME?

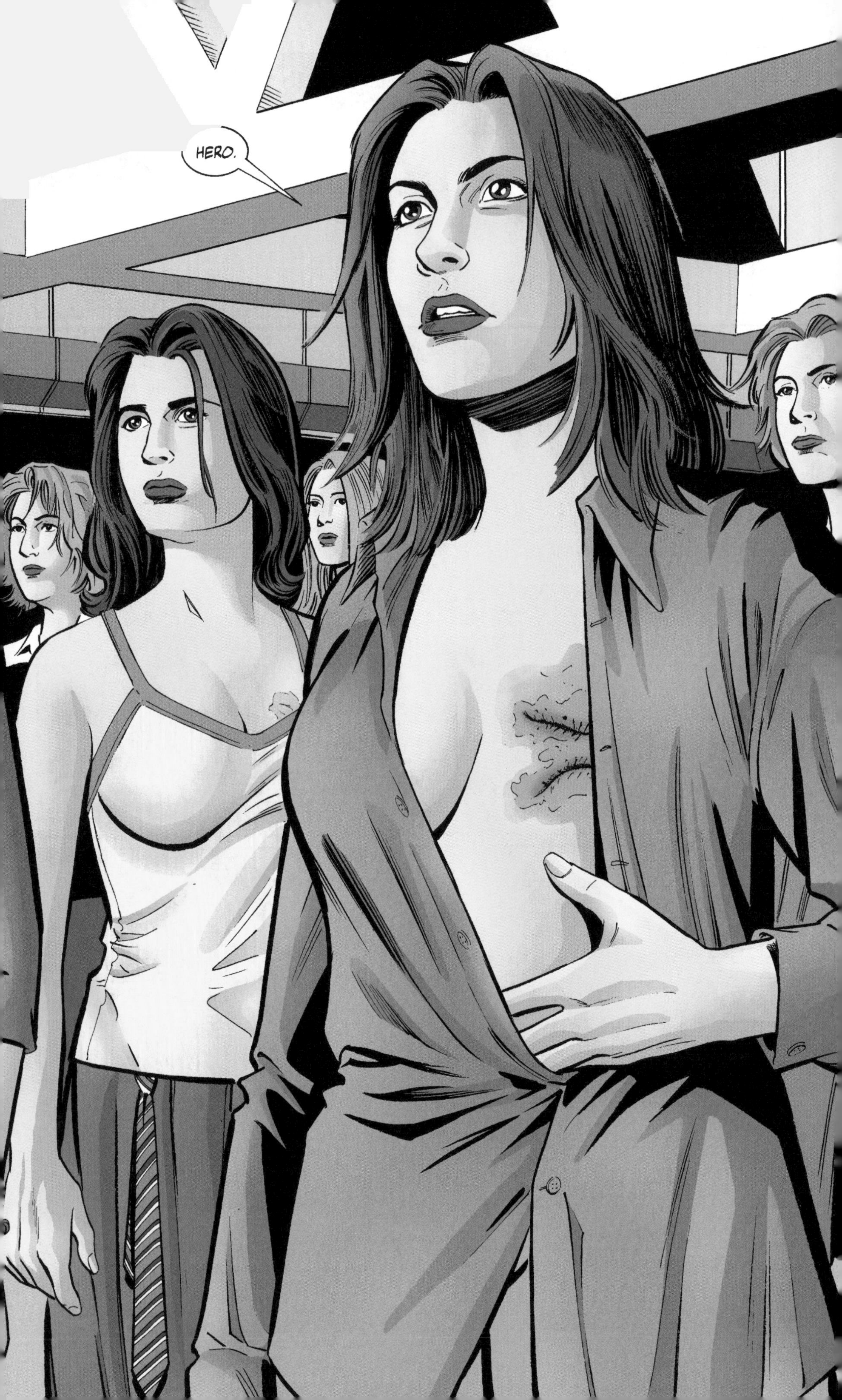
HERO.

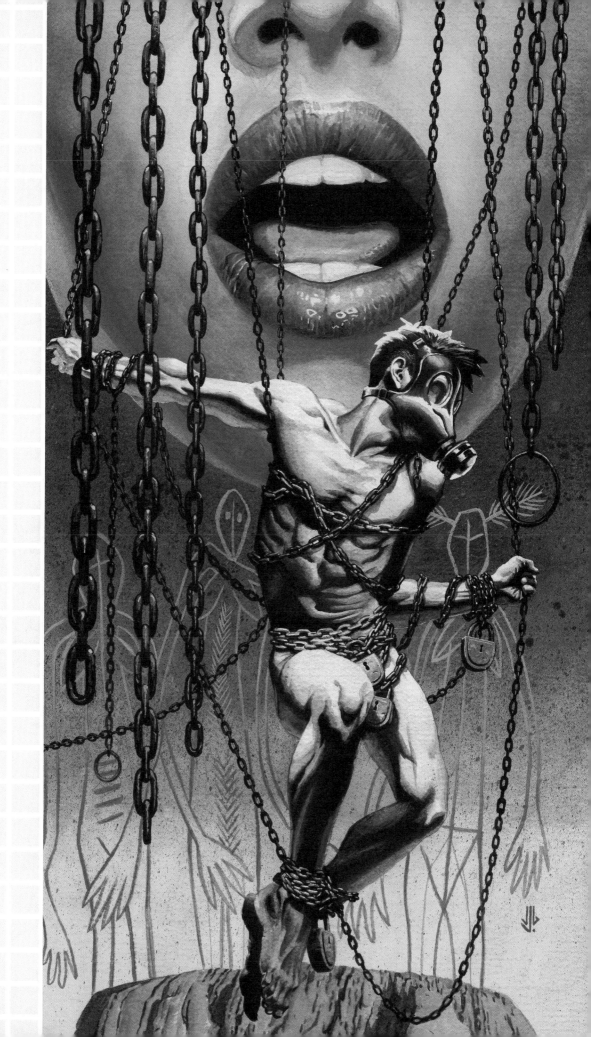

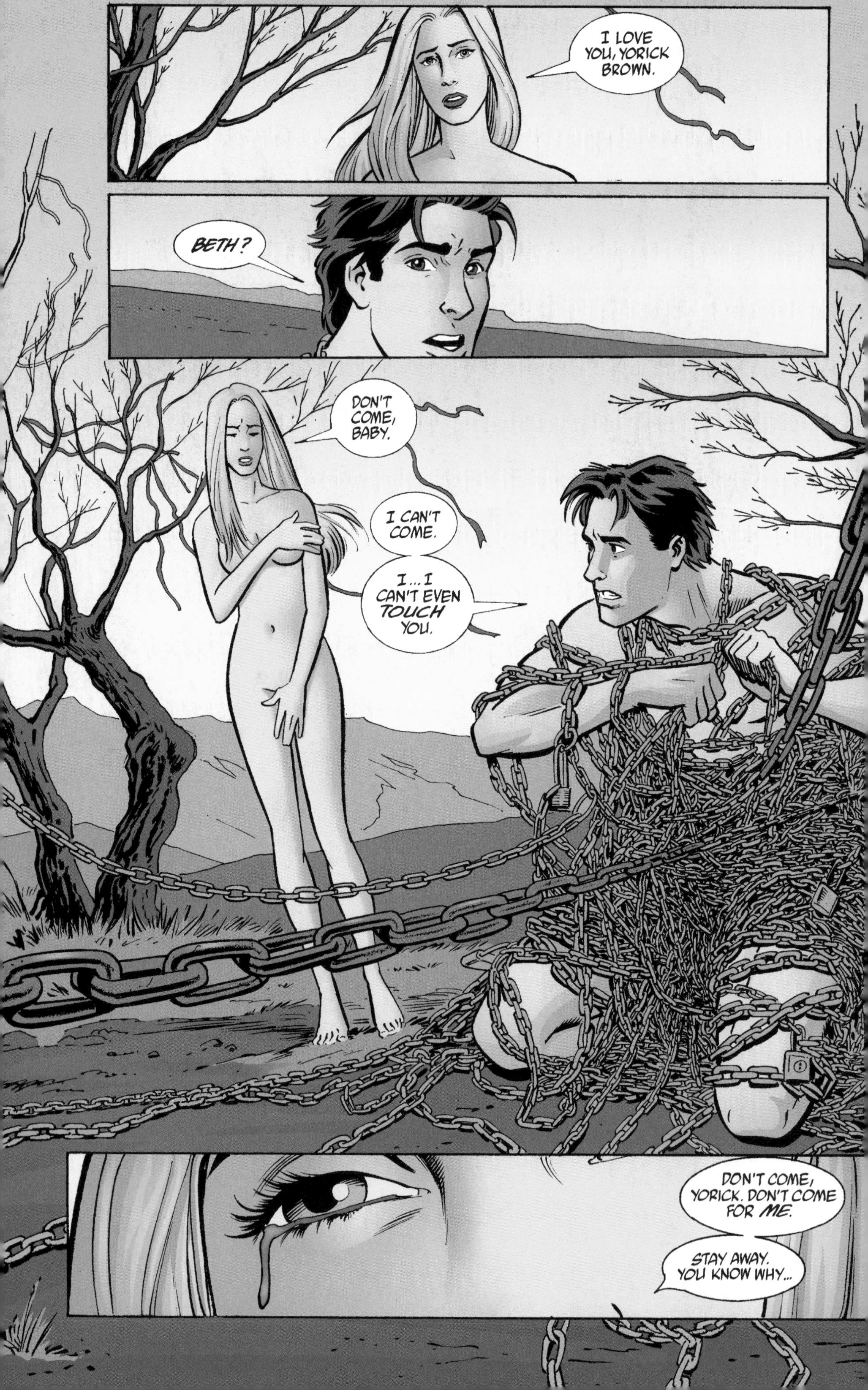
I LOVE YOU, YORICK BROWN.
BETH?
DON'T COME, BABY.
I CAN'T COME.
I... I CAN'T EVEN TOUCH YOU.
DON'T COME, YORICK. DON'T COME FOR ME.
STAY AWAY. YOU KNOW WHY...

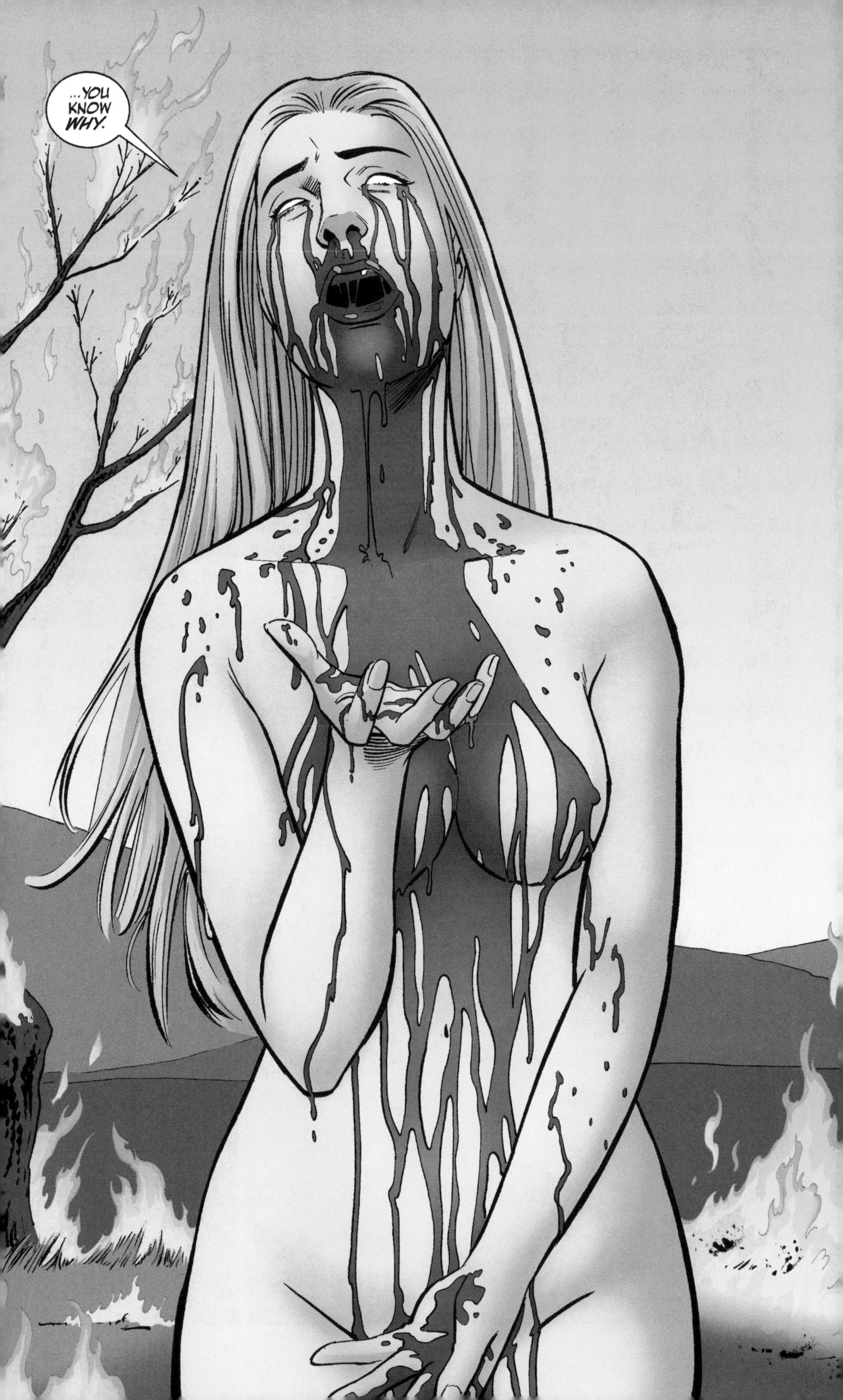
...YOU KNOW WHY.

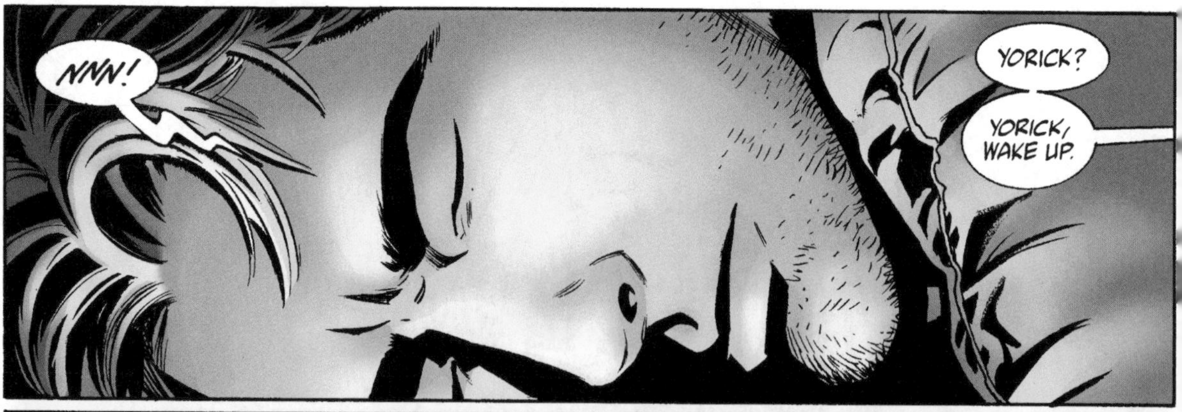
NNN!
YORICK?
YORICK, WAKE UP.

Boston, Massachusetts
Now

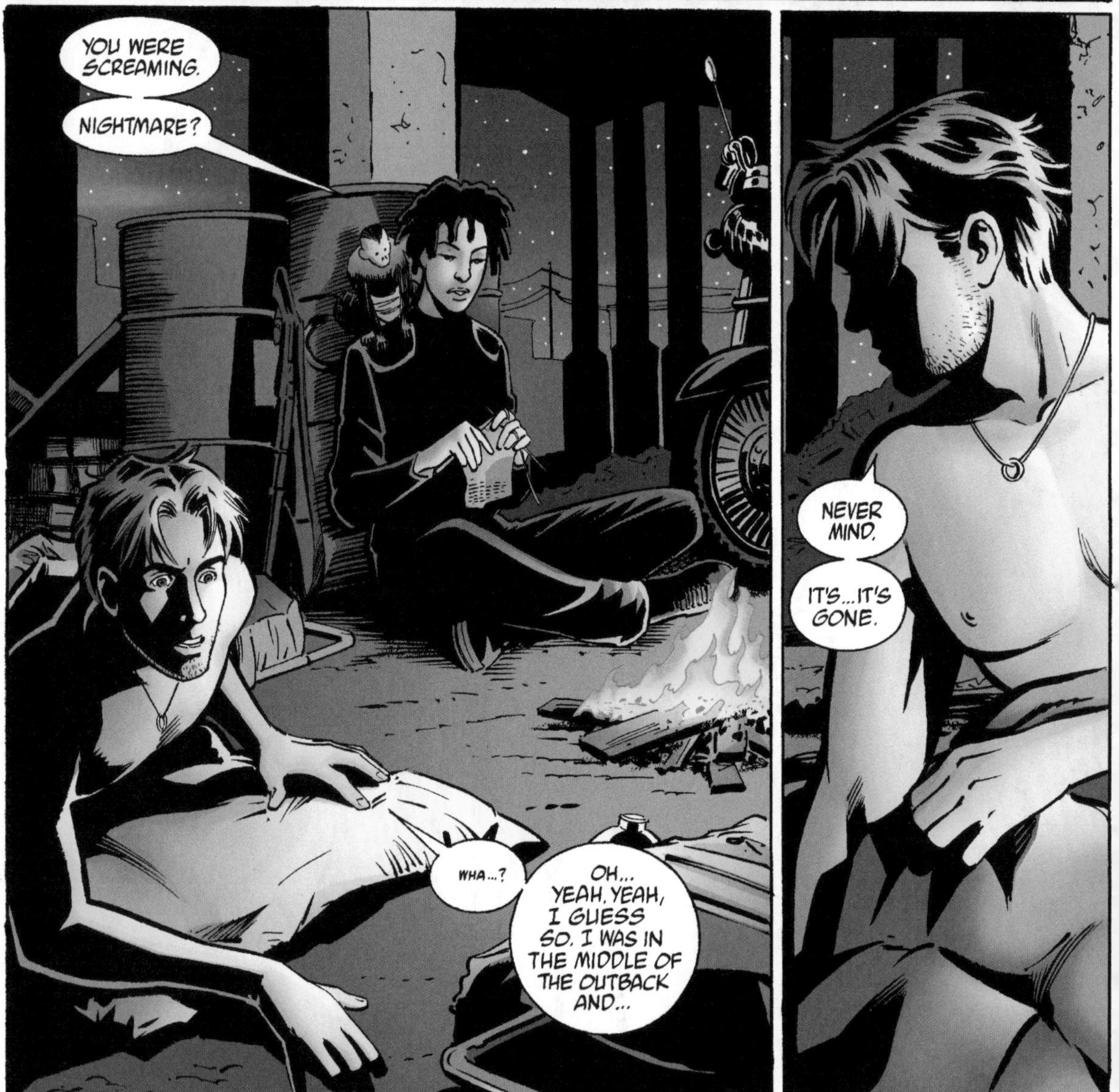
YOU WERE SCREAMING.
NIGHTMARE?
WHA...?
OH... YEAH, YEAH, I GUESS SO. I WAS IN THE MIDDLE OF THE OUTBACK AND...
NEVER MIND.
IT'S...IT'S GONE.

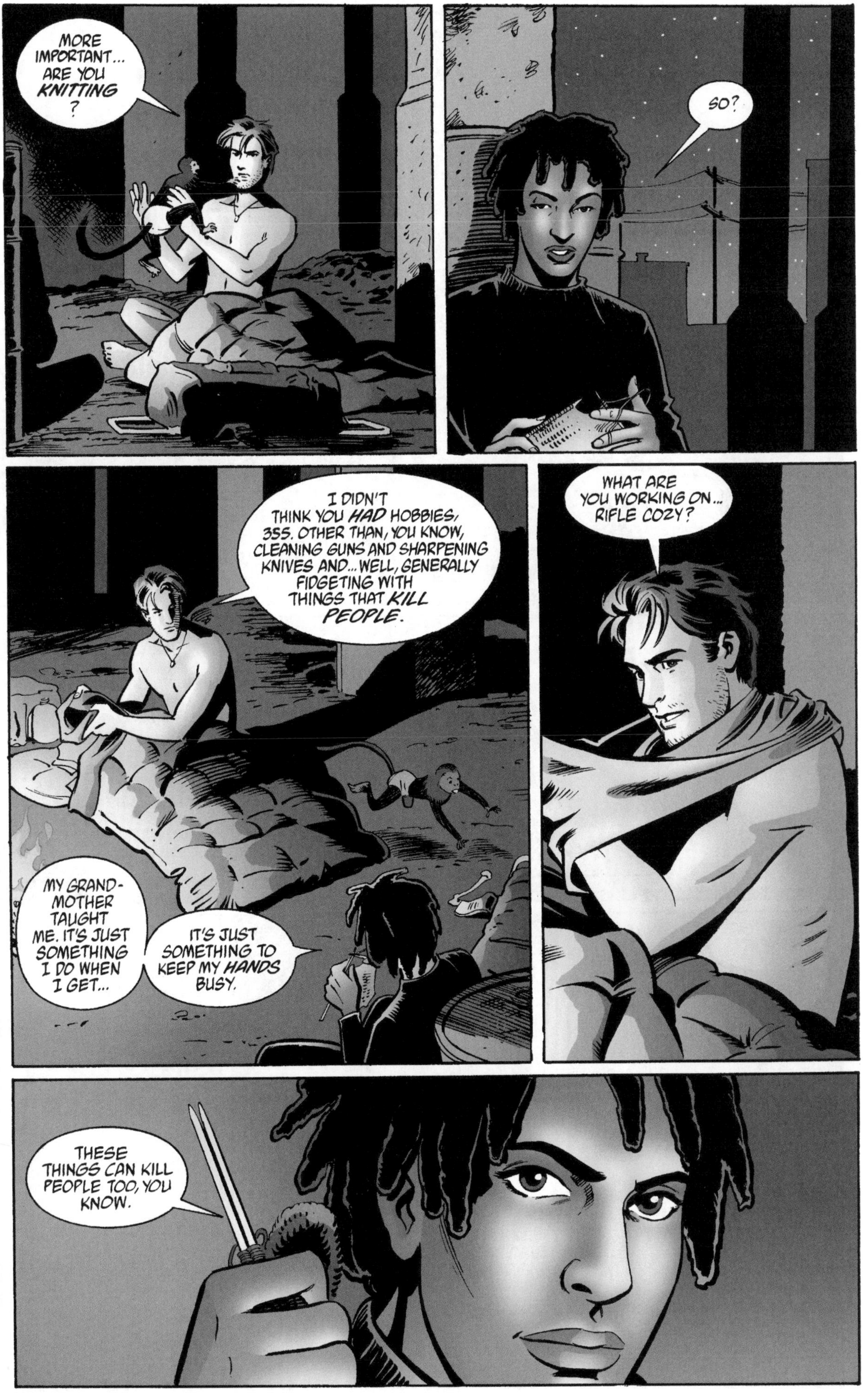
MORE IMPORTANT... ARE YOU KNITTING ?
SO?
I DIDN'T THINK YOU HAD HOBBIES, 355. OTHER THAN, YOU KNOW, CLEANING GUNS AND SHARPENING KNIVES AND... WELL, GENERALLY FIDGETING WITH THINGS THAT KILL PEOPLE.
MY GRAND-MOTHER TAUGHT ME. IT'S JUST SOMETHING I DO WHEN I GET...
IT'S JUST SOMETHING TO KEEP MY HANDS BUSY.
WHAT ARE YOU WORKING ON... RIFLE COZY?
THESE THINGS CAN KILL PEOPLE TOO, YOU KNOW.

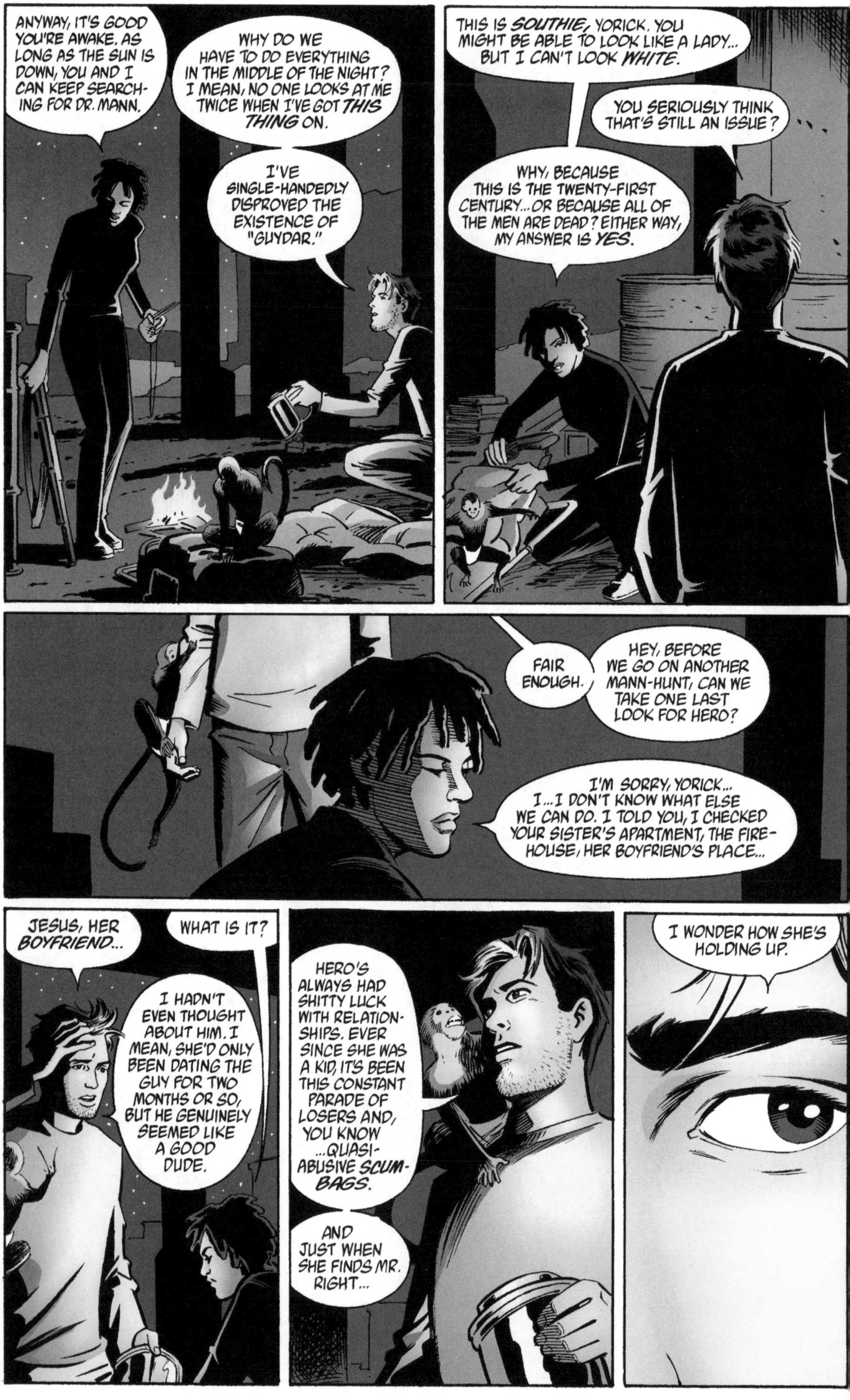
ANYWAY, IT'S GOOD YOU'RE AWAKE. AS LONG AS THE SUN IS DOWN, YOU AND I CAN KEEP SEARCHING FOR DR. MANN.
WHY DO WE HAVE TO DO EVERYTHING IN THE MIDDLE OF THE NIGHT? I MEAN, NO ONE LOOKS AT ME TWICE WHEN I'VE GOT THIS THING ON.
I'VE SINGLE-HANDEDLY DISPROVED THE EXISTENCE OF "GUYDAR."
THIS IS SOUTHIE, YORICK. YOU MIGHT BE ABLE TO LOOK LIKE A LADY... BUT I CAN'T LOOK WHITE.
YOU SERIOUSLY THINK THAT'S STILL AN ISSUE?
WHY, BECAUSE THIS IS THE TWENTY-FIRST CENTURY... OR BECAUSE ALL OF THE MEN ARE DEAD? EITHER WAY, MY ANSWER IS YES.
FAIR ENOUGH.
HEY, BEFORE WE GO ON ANOTHER MANN-HUNT, CAN WE TAKE ONE LAST LOOK FOR HERO?
I'M SORRY, YORICK... I... I DON'T KNOW WHAT ELSE WE CAN DO. I TOLD YOU, I CHECKED YOUR SISTER'S APARTMENT, THE FIRE-HOUSE, HER BOYFRIEND'S PLACE...
JESUS, HER BOYFRIEND...
WHAT IS IT?
I HADN'T EVEN THOUGHT ABOUT HIM. I MEAN, SHE'D ONLY BEEN DATING THE GUY FOR TWO MONTHS OR SO, BUT HE GENUINELY SEEMED LIKE A GOOD DUDE.
HERO'S ALWAYS HAD SHITTY LUCK WITH RELATIONSHIPS. EVER SINCE SHE WAS A KID, IT'S BEEN THIS CONSTANT PARADE OF LOSERS AND, YOU KNOW ...QUASI-ABUSIVE SCUMBAGS.
AND JUST WHEN SHE FINDS MR. RIGHT...
I WONDER HOW SHE'S HOLDING UP.

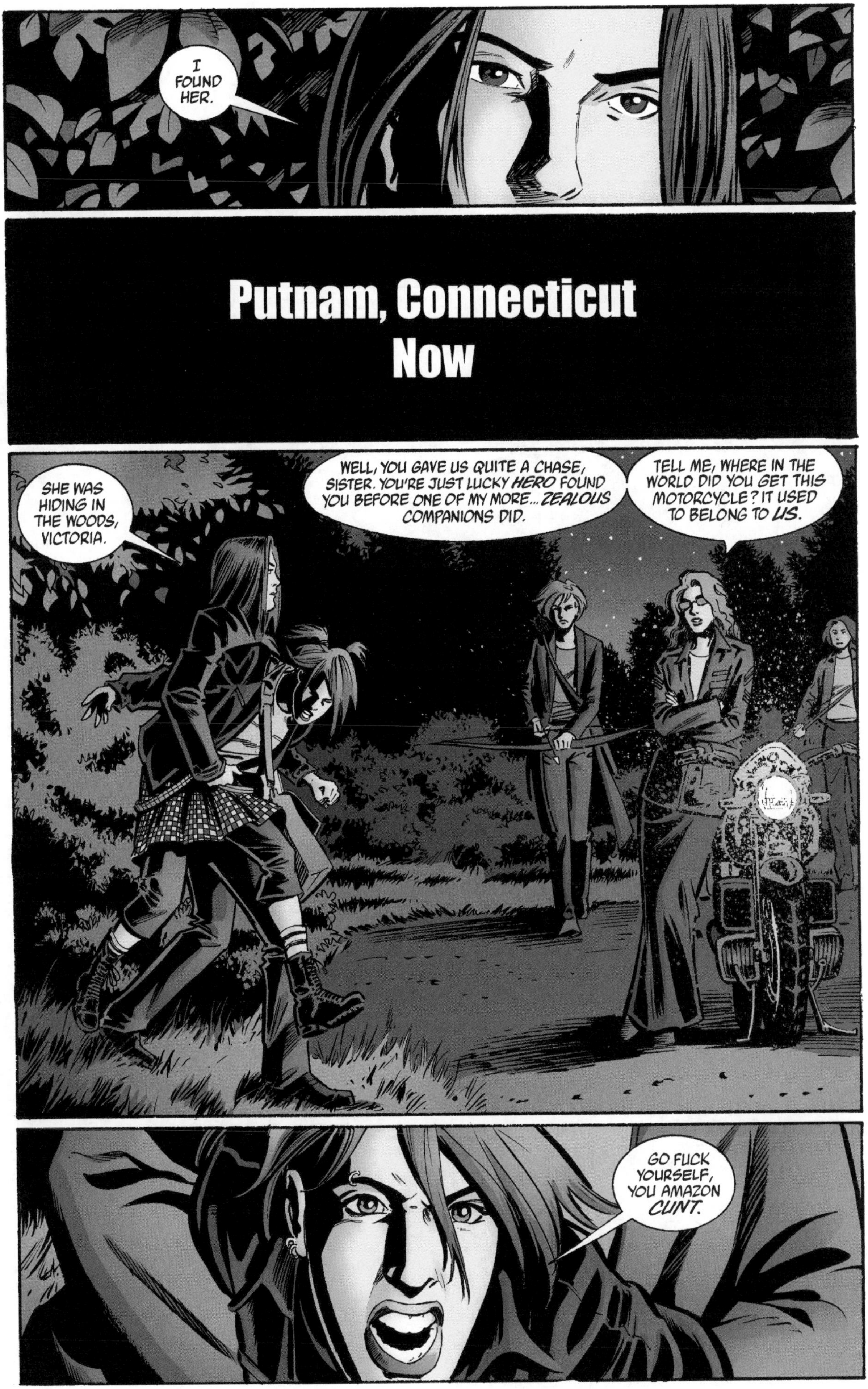
I FOUND HER.
Putnam, Connecticut
Now
SHE WAS HIDING IN THE WOODS, VICTORIA.
WELL, YOU GAVE US QUITE A CHASE, SISTER. YOU'RE JUST LUCKY HERO FOUND YOU BEFORE ONE OF MY MORE... ZEALOUS COMPANIONS DID.
TELL ME, WHERE IN THE WORLD DID YOU GET THIS MOTORCYCLE? IT USED TO BELONG TO US.
GO FUCK YOURSELF, YOU AMAZON CUNT.

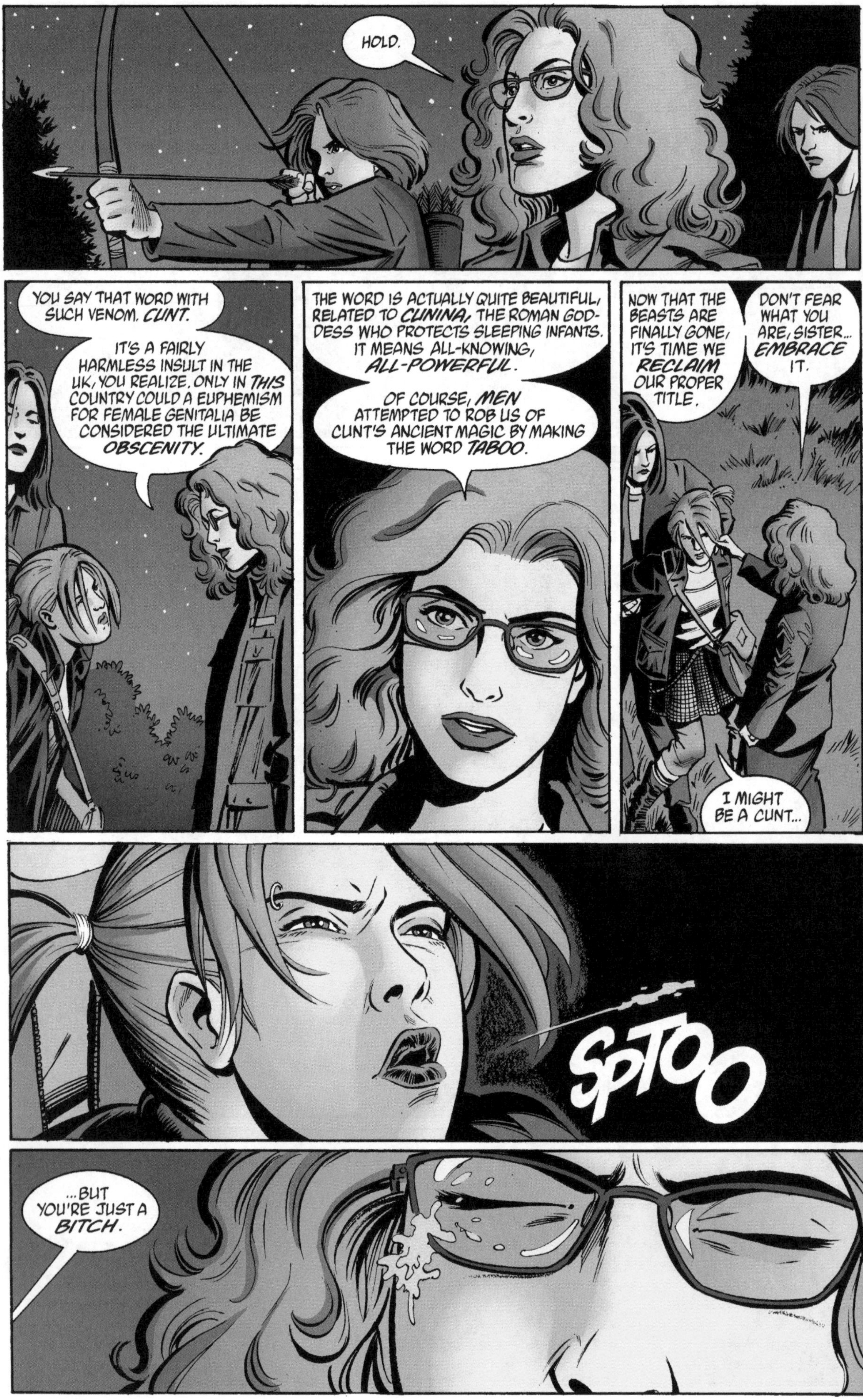
HOLD.
YOU SAY THAT WORD WITH SUCH VENOM. CUNT.
IT'S A FAIRLY HARMLESS INSULT IN THE UK, YOU REALIZE. ONLY IN THIS COUNTRY COULD A EUPHEMISM FOR FEMALE GENITALIA BE CONSIDERED THE ULTIMATE OBSCENITY.
THE WORD IS ACTUALLY QUITE BEAUTIFUL, RELATED TO CUNINA, THE ROMAN GODDESS WHO PROTECTS SLEEPING INFANTS. IT MEANS ALL-KNOWING, ALL-POWERFUL.
OF COURSE, MEN ATTEMPTED TO ROB US OF CUNT'S ANCIENT MAGIC BY MAKING THE WORD TABOO.
NOW THAT THE BEASTS ARE FINALLY GONE, IT'S TIME WE RECLAIM OUR PROPER TITLE.
DON'T FEAR WHAT YOU ARE, SISTER... EMBRACE IT.
I MIGHT BE A CUNT...
SPTOO
...BUT YOU'RE JUST A BITCH.

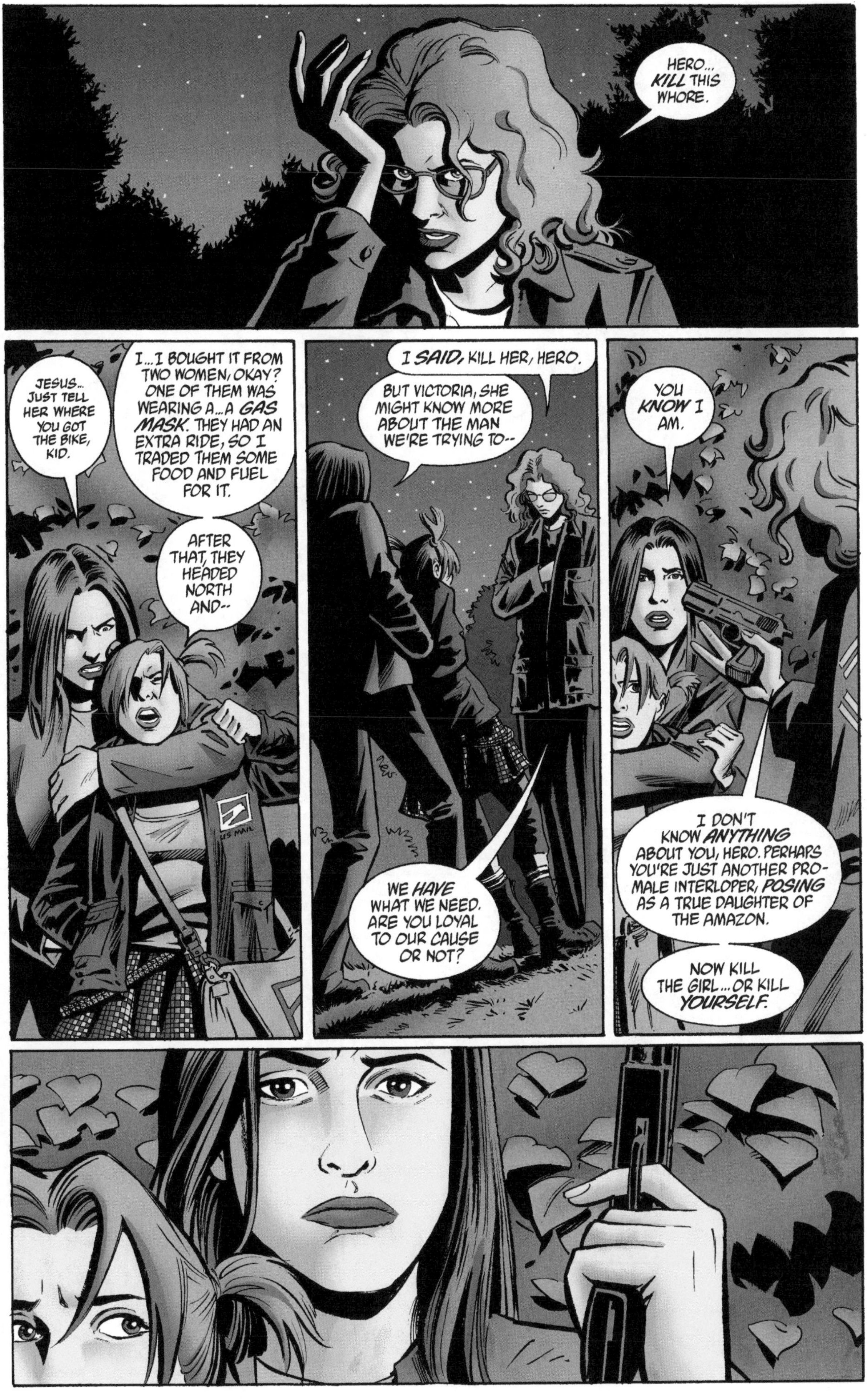
HERO... KILL THIS WHORE.
JESUS... JUST TELL HER WHERE YOU GOT THE BIKE, KID.
I...I BOUGHT IT FROM TWO WOMEN, OKAY? ONE OF THEM WAS WEARING A...A GAS MASK. THEY HAD AN EXTRA RIDE, SO I TRADED THEM SOME FOOD AND FUEL FOR IT.
AFTER THAT, THEY HEADED NORTH AND--
I SAID, KILL HER, HERO.
BUT VICTORIA, SHE MIGHT KNOW MORE ABOUT THE MAN WE'RE TRYING TO--
WE HAVE WHAT WE NEED. ARE YOU LOYAL TO OUR CAUSE OR NOT?
YOU KNOW I AM.
I DON'T KNOW ANYTHING ABOUT YOU, HERO. PERHAPS YOU'RE JUST ANOTHER PRO-MALE INTERLOPER, POSING AS A TRUE DAUGHTER OF THE AMAZON.
NOW KILL THE GIRL...OR KILL YOURSELF.

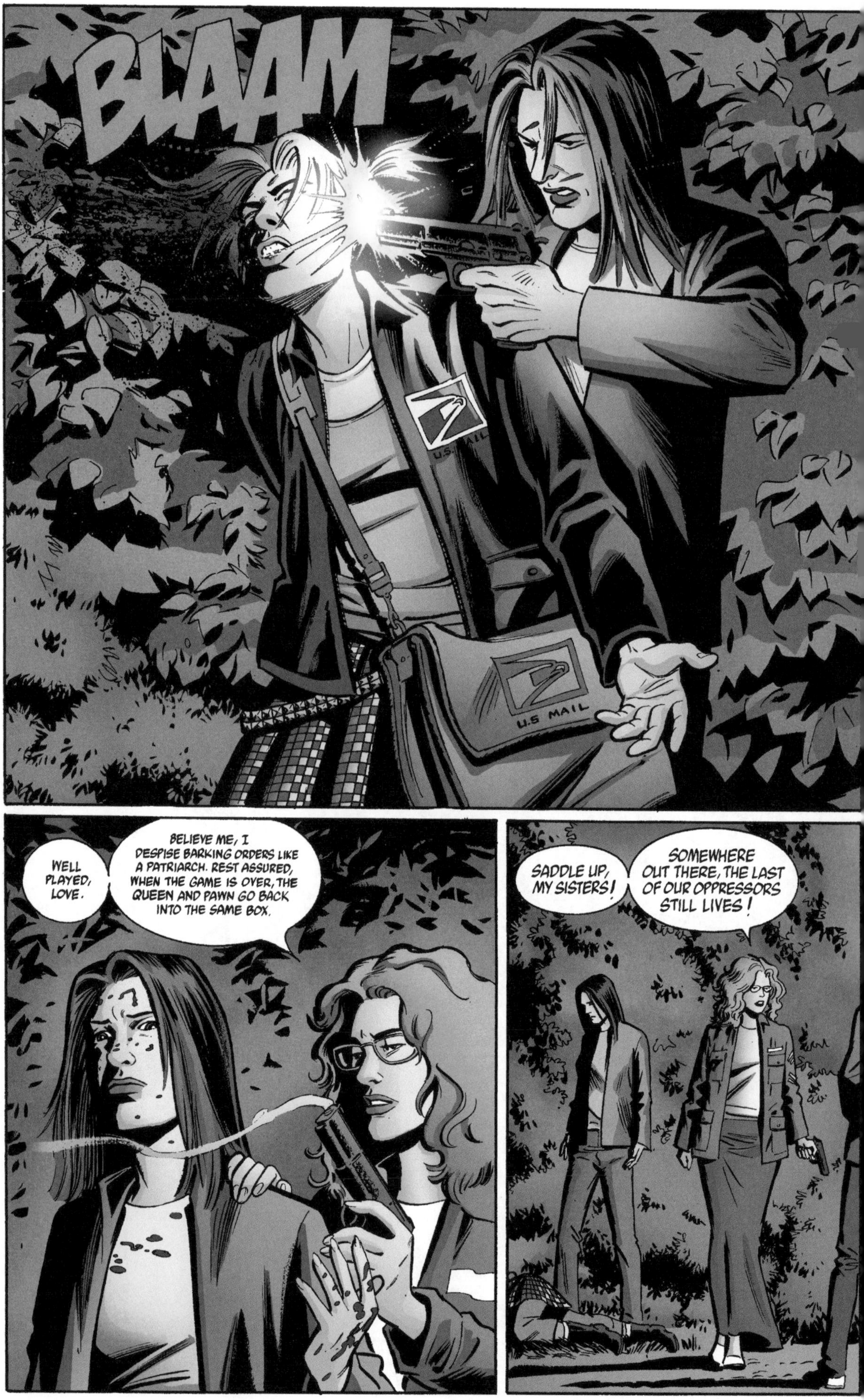
BLAAM
U.S. MAIL
U.S MAIL
WELL PLAYED, LOVE.
BELIEVE ME, I DESPISE BARKING ORDERS LIKE A PATRIARCH. REST ASSURED, WHEN THE GAME IS OVER, THE QUEEN AND PAWN GO BACK INTO THE SAME BOX.
SADDLE UP, MY SISTERS!
SOMEWHERE OUT THERE, THE LAST OF OUR OPPRESSORS STILL LIVES!

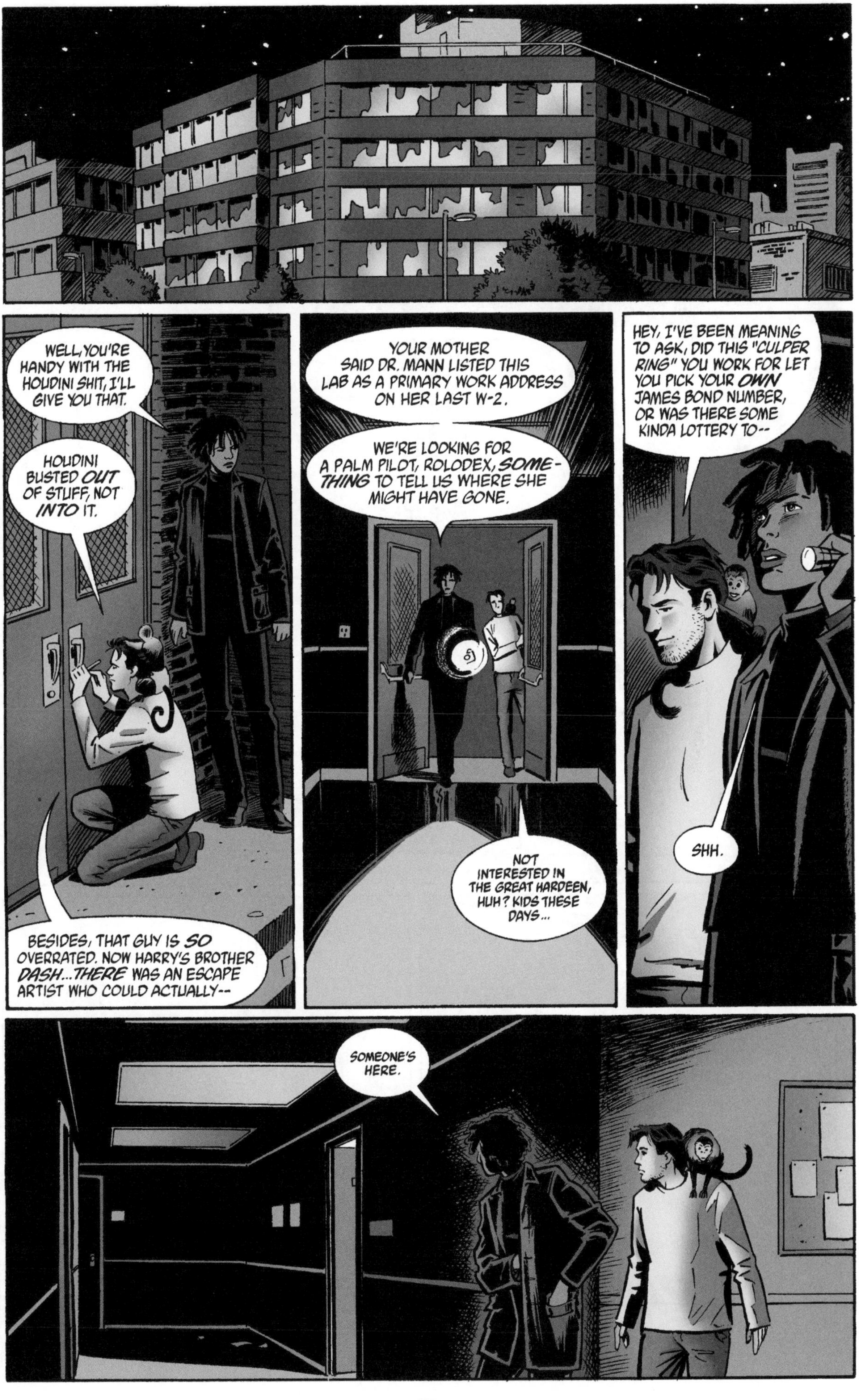
WELL, YOU'RE HANDY WITH THE HOUDINI SHIT, I'LL GIVE YOU THAT.
HOUDINI BUSTED OUT OF STUFF, NOT INTO IT.
BESIDES, THAT GUY IS SO OVERRATED. NOW HARRY'S BROTHER DASH...THERE WAS AN ESCAPE ARTIST WHO COULD ACTUALLY--
YOUR MOTHER SAID DR. MANN LISTED THIS LAB AS A PRIMARY WORK ADDRESS ON HER LAST W-2.
WE'RE LOOKING FOR A PALM PILOT, ROLODEX, SOME-THING TO TELL US WHERE SHE MIGHT HAVE GONE.
NOT INTERESTED IN THE GREAT HARDEEN, HUH? KIDS THESE DAYS...
HEY, I'VE BEEN MEANING TO ASK, DID THIS "CULPER RING" YOU WORK FOR LET YOU PICK YOUR OWN JAMES BOND NUMBER, OR WAS THERE SOME KINDA LOTTERY TO--
SHH.
SOMEONE'S HERE.

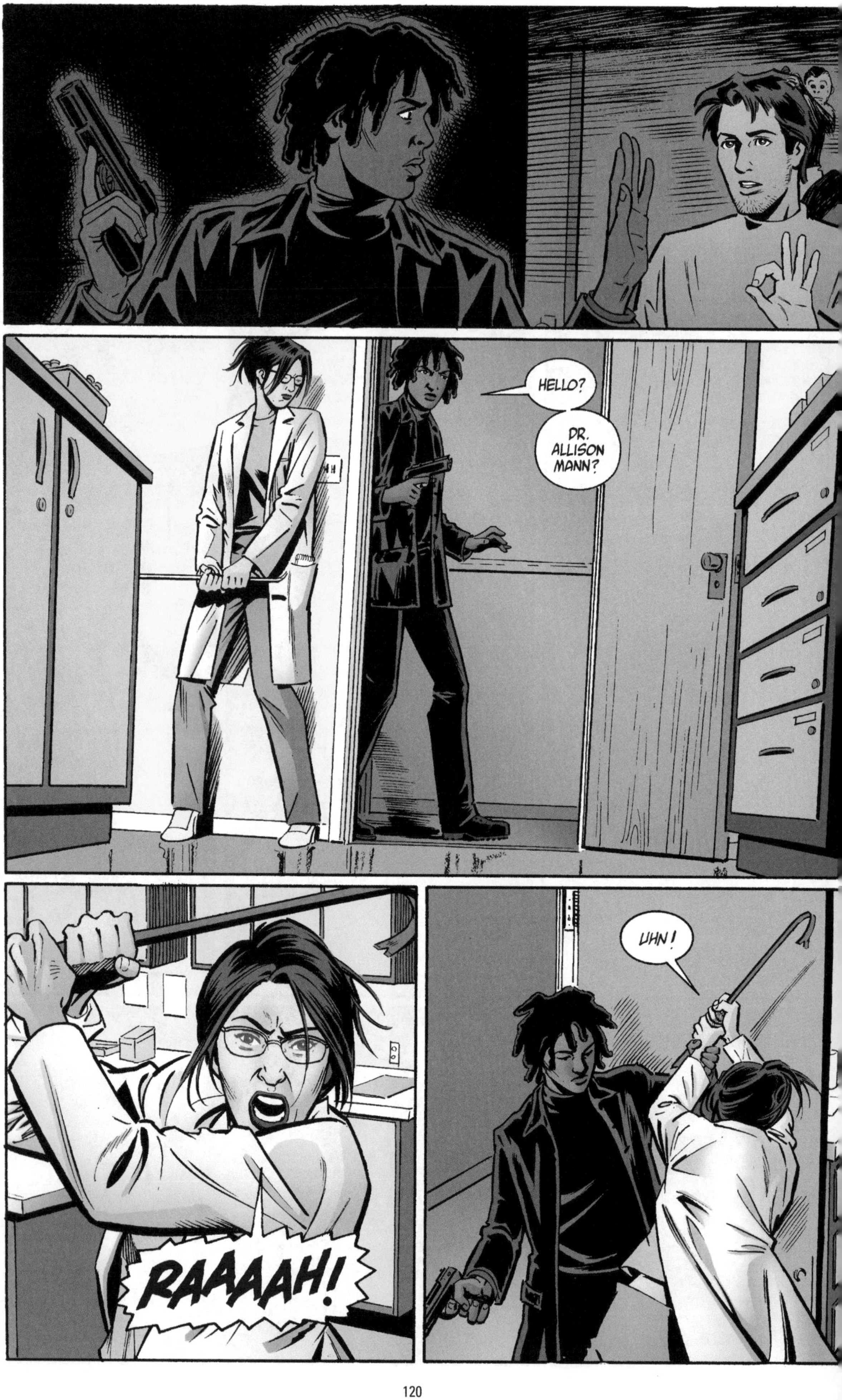
HELLO?
DR. ALLISON MANN?
RAAAAH!
UHN!

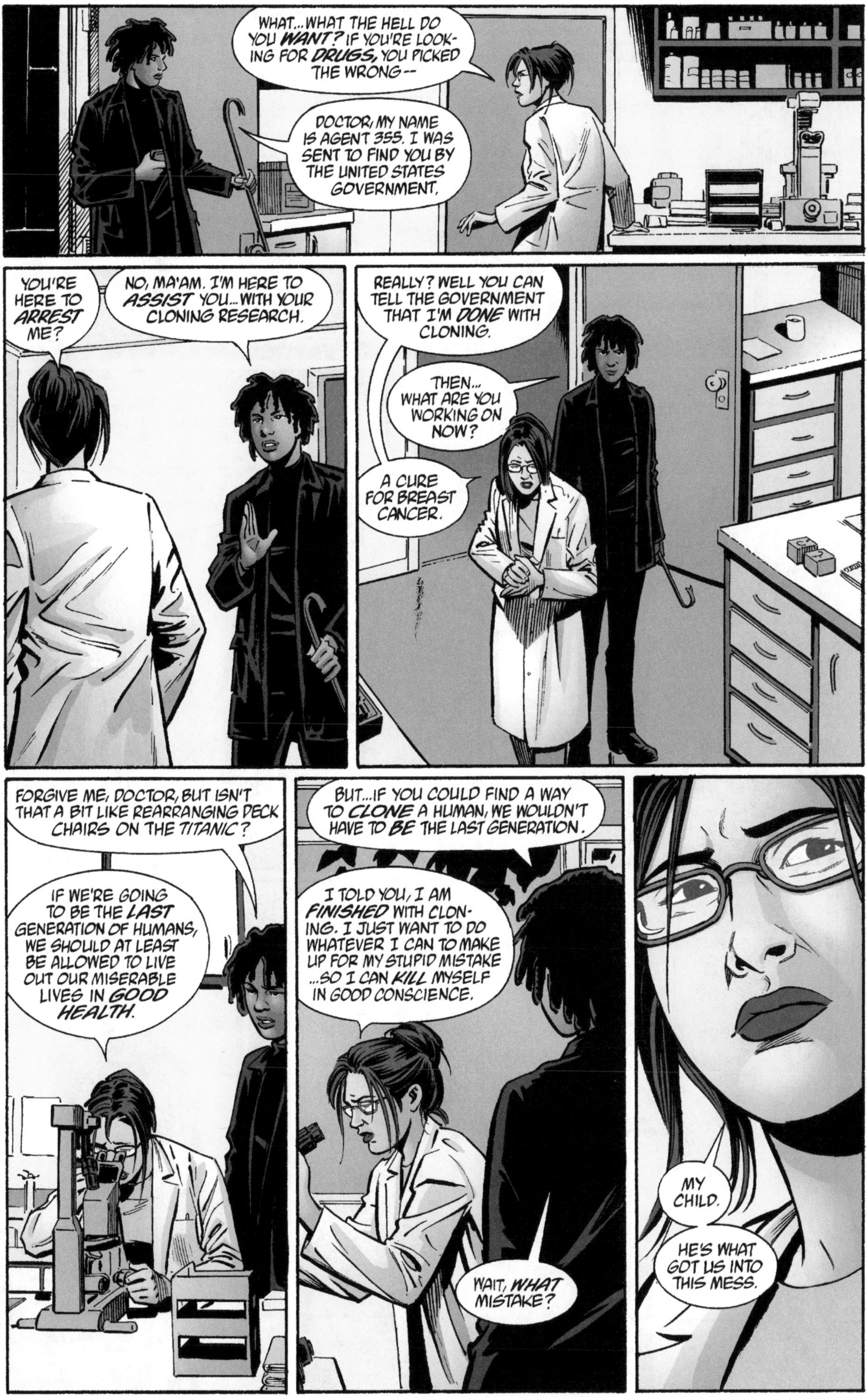

WHAT...WHAT THE HELL DO YOU WANT? IF YOU'RE LOOKING FOR DRUGS, YOU PICKED THE WRONG--
DOCTOR, MY NAME IS AGENT 355. I WAS SENT TO FIND YOU BY THE UNITED STATES GOVERNMENT.
YOU'RE HERE TO ARREST ME?
NO, MA'AM. I'M HERE TO ASSIST YOU...WITH YOUR CLONING RESEARCH.
REALLY? WELL YOU CAN TELL THE GOVERNMENT THAT I'M DONE WITH CLONING.
THEN... WHAT ARE YOU WORKING ON NOW?
A CURE FOR BREAST CANCER.
FORGIVE ME, DOCTOR, BUT ISN'T THAT A BIT LIKE REARRANGING DECK CHAIRS ON THE TITANIC?
IF WE'RE GOING TO BE THE LAST GENERATION OF HUMANS, WE SHOULD AT LEAST BE ALLOWED TO LIVE OUT OUR MISERABLE LIVES IN GOOD HEALTH.
BUT...IF YOU COULD FIND A WAY TO CLONE A HUMAN, WE WOULDN'T HAVE TO BE THE LAST GENERATION.
I TOLD YOU, I AM FINISHED WITH CLONING. I JUST WANT TO DO WHATEVER I CAN TO MAKE UP FOR MY STUPID MISTAKE ...SO I CAN KILL MYSELF IN GOOD CONSCIENCE.
WAIT, WHAT MISTAKE?
MY CHILD.
HE'S WHAT GOT US INTO THIS MESS.

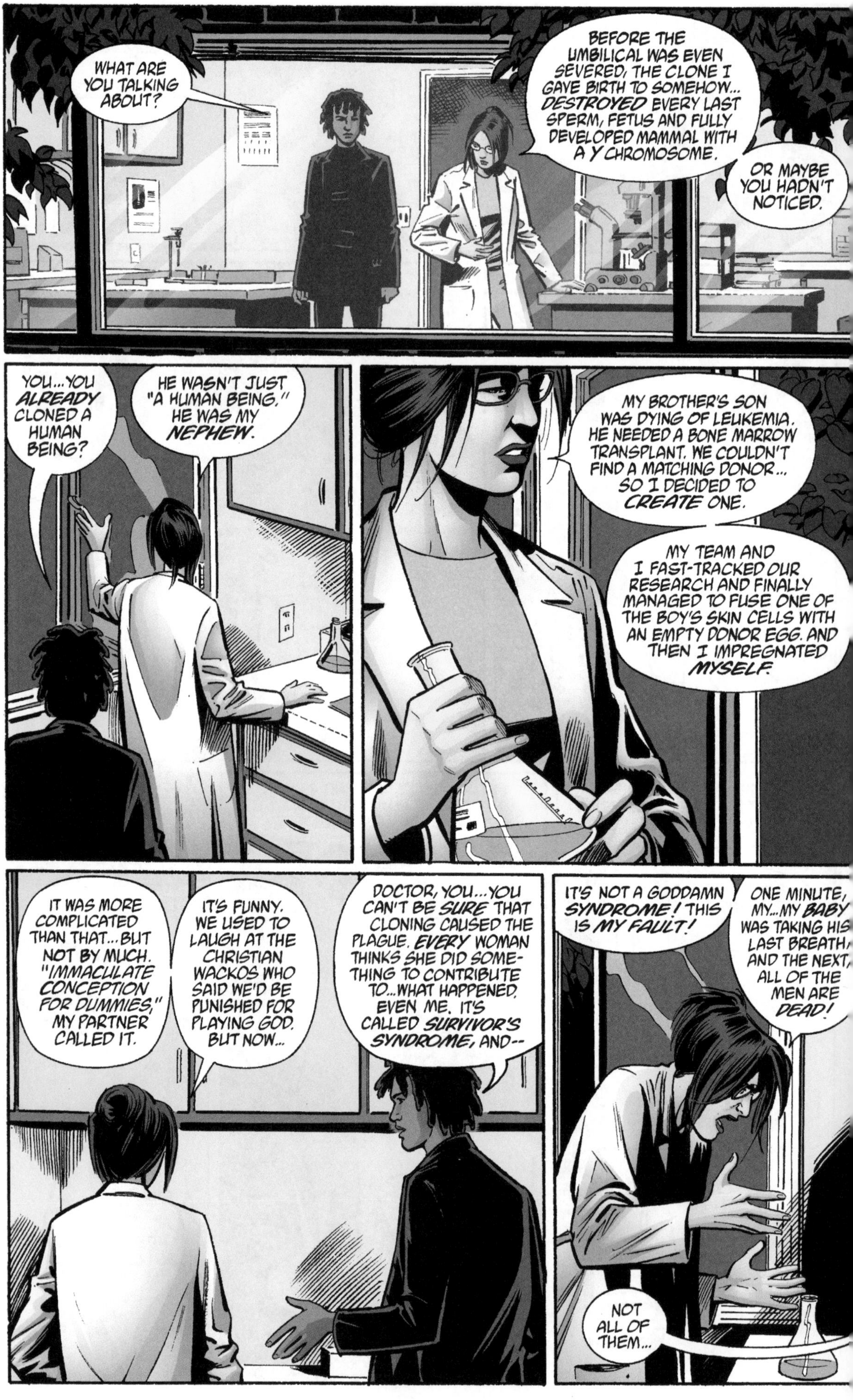
WHAT ARE YOU TALKING ABOUT?
BEFORE THE UMBILICAL WAS EVEN SEVERED, THE CLONE I GAVE BIRTH TO SOMEHOW... DESTROYED EVERY LAST SPERM, FETUS AND FULLY DEVELOPED MAMMAL WITH A Y CHROMOSOME.
OR MAYBE YOU HADN'T NOTICED.
YOU...YOU ALREADY CLONED A HUMAN BEING?
HE WASN'T JUST "A HUMAN BEING," HE WAS MY NEPHEW.
MY BROTHER'S SON WAS DYING OF LEUKEMIA. HE NEEDED A BONE MARROW TRANSPLANT. WE COULDN'T FIND A MATCHING DONOR... SO I DECIDED TO CREATE ONE.
MY TEAM AND I FAST-TRACKED OUR RESEARCH AND FINALLY MANAGED TO FUSE ONE OF THE BOY'S SKIN CELLS WITH AN EMPTY DONOR EGG. AND THEN I IMPREGNATED MYSELF.
IT WAS MORE COMPLICATED THAN THAT...BUT NOT BY MUCH. "IMMACULATE CONCEPTION FOR DUMMIES," MY PARTNER CALLED IT.
IT'S FUNNY. WE USED TO LAUGH AT THE CHRISTIAN WACKOS WHO SAID WE'D BE PUNISHED FOR PLAYING GOD. BUT NOW...
DOCTOR, YOU...YOU CAN'T BE SURE THAT CLONING CAUSED THE PLAGUE. EVERY WOMAN THINKS SHE DID SOMETHING TO CONTRIBUTE TO...WHAT HAPPENED. EVEN ME. IT'S CALLED SURVIVOR'S SYNDROME, AND--
IT'S NOT A GODDAMN SYNDROME! THIS IS MY FAULT!
ONE MINUTE, MY...MY BABY WAS TAKING HIS LAST BREATH, AND THE NEXT, ALL OF THE MEN ARE DEAD!
NOT ALL OF THEM...

WHAT'S UP, DOC?

OH MY GOD.

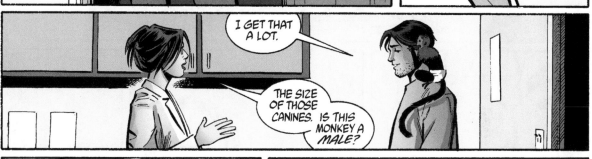

I GET THAT A LOT.

THE SIZE OF THOSE CANINES. IS THIS MONKEY A *MALE?*

uh...YEAH. ACTUALLY, I'M *ALSO--*

OBVIOUSLY. WHERE DID YOU FIND THIS ANIMAL?

AMPERSAND? HE FOUND *ME.* I VOLUNTEERED TO TRAIN A HELPER MONKEY A FEW MONTHS AGO, AND SOME GROUP FROM OUT HERE SENT ME THIS GUY.

HE'S GOT A LONG WAY TO GO BEFORE YOU COULD REALLY CALL HIM *HELPFUL* THOUGH. AMPERSAND'S MORE LIKE THAT EVIL MONKEY FROM *MONKEY SHINES,* OR THE NAZI MONKEY FROM *RAIDERS,* OR THE--

I COULD UNDERSTAND *ONE* OF YOU BEING SOME KIND OF ANOMALY ...BUT HOW DID YOU *BOTH* SURVIVE?

WE WERE HOPING *YOU* COULD EXPLAIN THAT, DOCTOR.

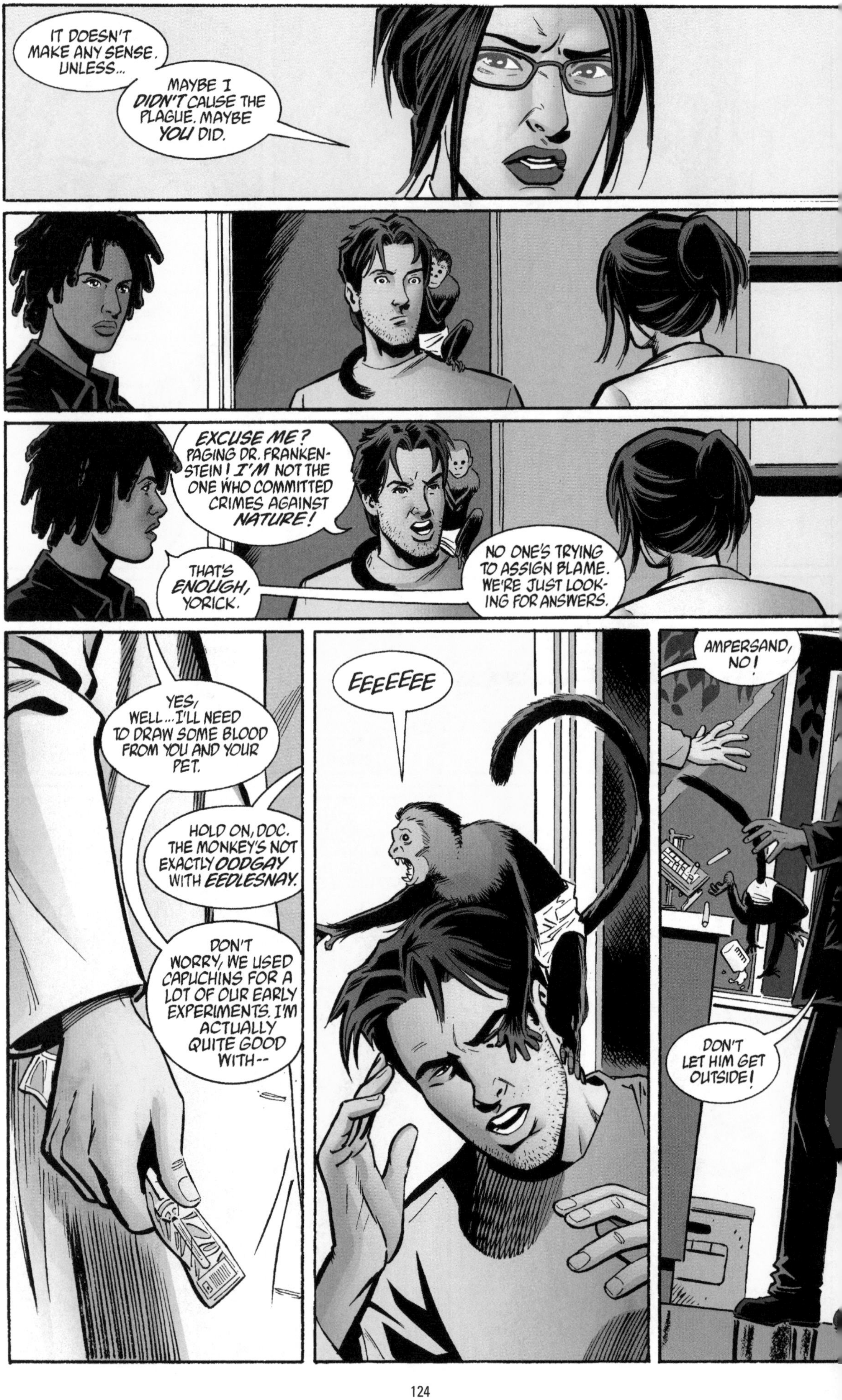
IT DOESN'T MAKE ANY SENSE. UNLESS...
MAYBE I DIDN'T CAUSE THE PLAGUE. MAYBE YOU DID.
EXCUSE ME? PAGING DR. FRANKENSTEIN! I'M NOT THE ONE WHO COMMITTED CRIMES AGAINST NATURE!
THAT'S ENOUGH, YORICK.
NO ONE'S TRYING TO ASSIGN BLAME. WE'RE JUST LOOKING FOR ANSWERS.
YES, WELL... I'LL NEED TO DRAW SOME BLOOD FROM YOU AND YOUR PET.
HOLD ON, DOC. THE MONKEY'S NOT EXACTLY OODGAY WITH EEDLESNAY.
DON'T WORRY, WE USED CAPUCHINS FOR A LOT OF OUR EARLY EXPERIMENTS. I'M ACTUALLY QUITE GOOD WITH--
EEEEEEE
AMPERSAND, NO!
DON'T LET HIM GET OUTSIDE!

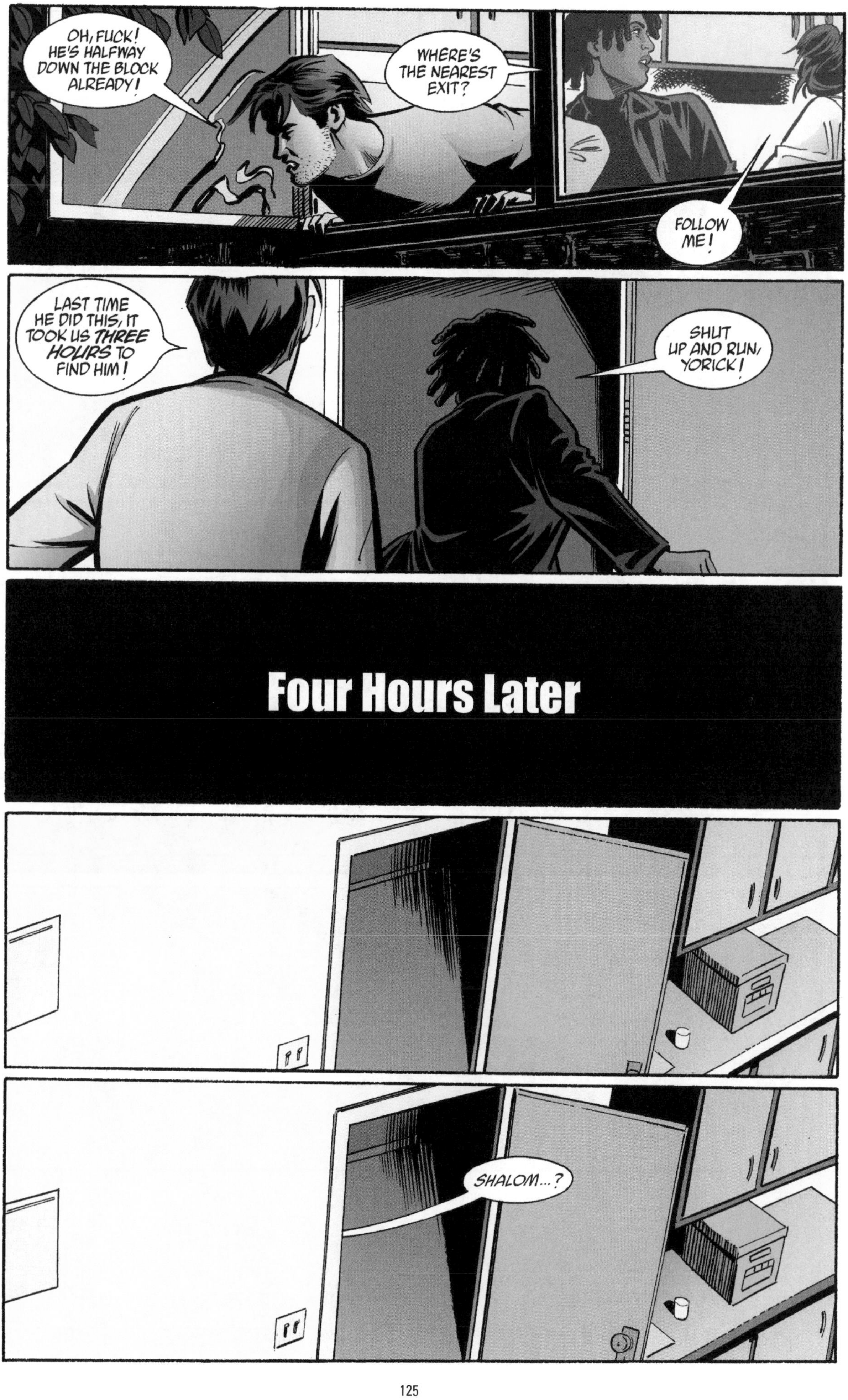
OH, FUCK! HE'S HALFWAY DOWN THE BLOCK ALREADY!
WHERE'S THE NEAREST EXIT?
FOLLOW ME!
LAST TIME HE DID THIS, IT TOOK US THREE HOURS TO FIND HIM!
SHUT UP AND RUN, YORICK!
Four Hours Later
SHALOM...?

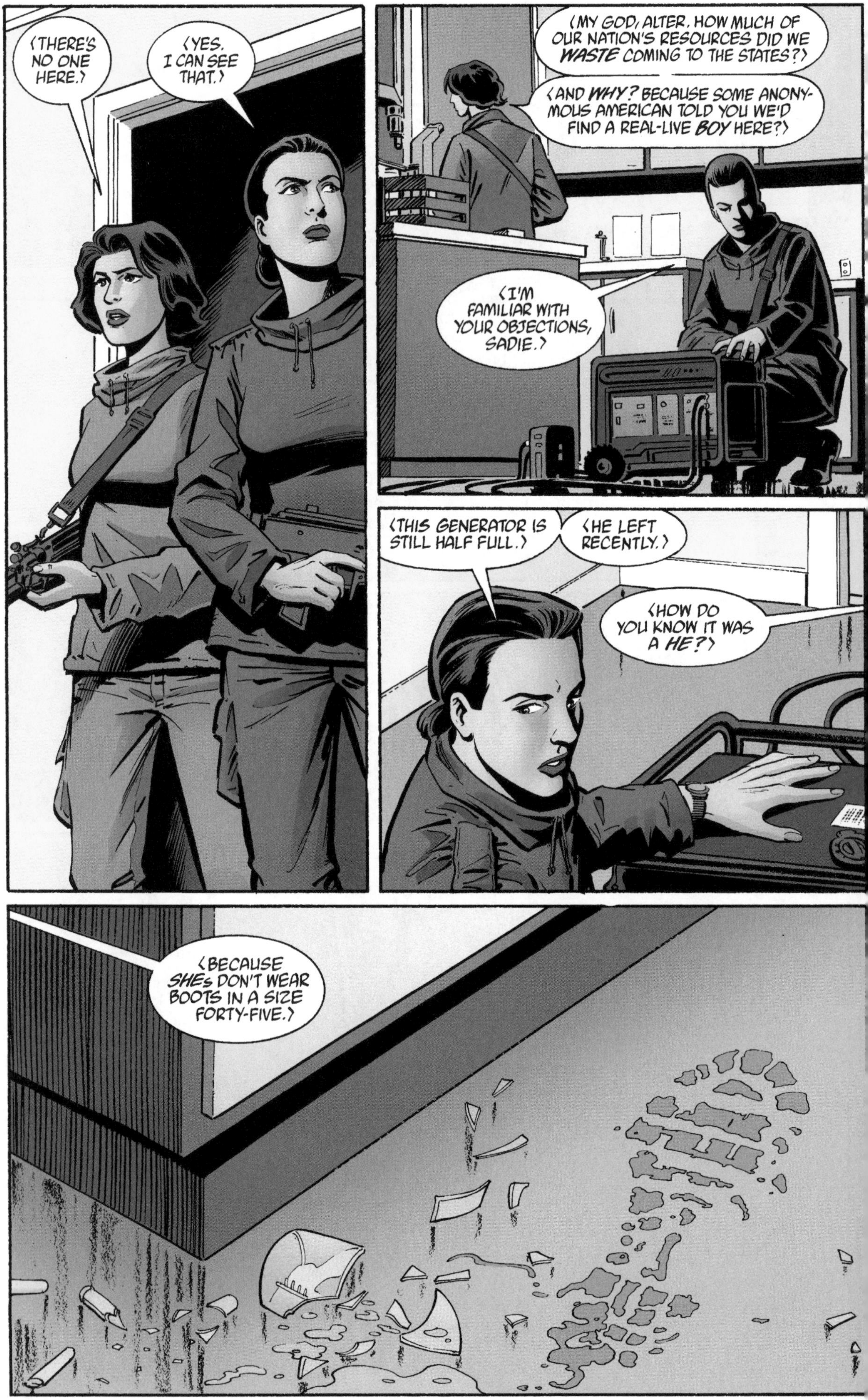

‹THERE'S NO ONE HERE.›
‹YES. I CAN SEE THAT.›
‹MY GOD, ALTER. HOW MUCH OF OUR NATION'S RESOURCES DID WE WASTE COMING TO THE STATES?›
‹AND WHY? BECAUSE SOME ANONYMOUS AMERICAN TOLD YOU WE'D FIND A REAL-LIVE BOY HERE?›
‹I'M FAMILIAR WITH YOUR OBJECTIONS, SADIE.›
‹THIS GENERATOR IS STILL HALF FULL.›
‹HE LEFT RECENTLY.›
‹HOW DO YOU KNOW IT WAS A HE?›
‹BECAUSE SHEs DON'T WEAR BOOTS IN A SIZE FORTY-FIVE.›

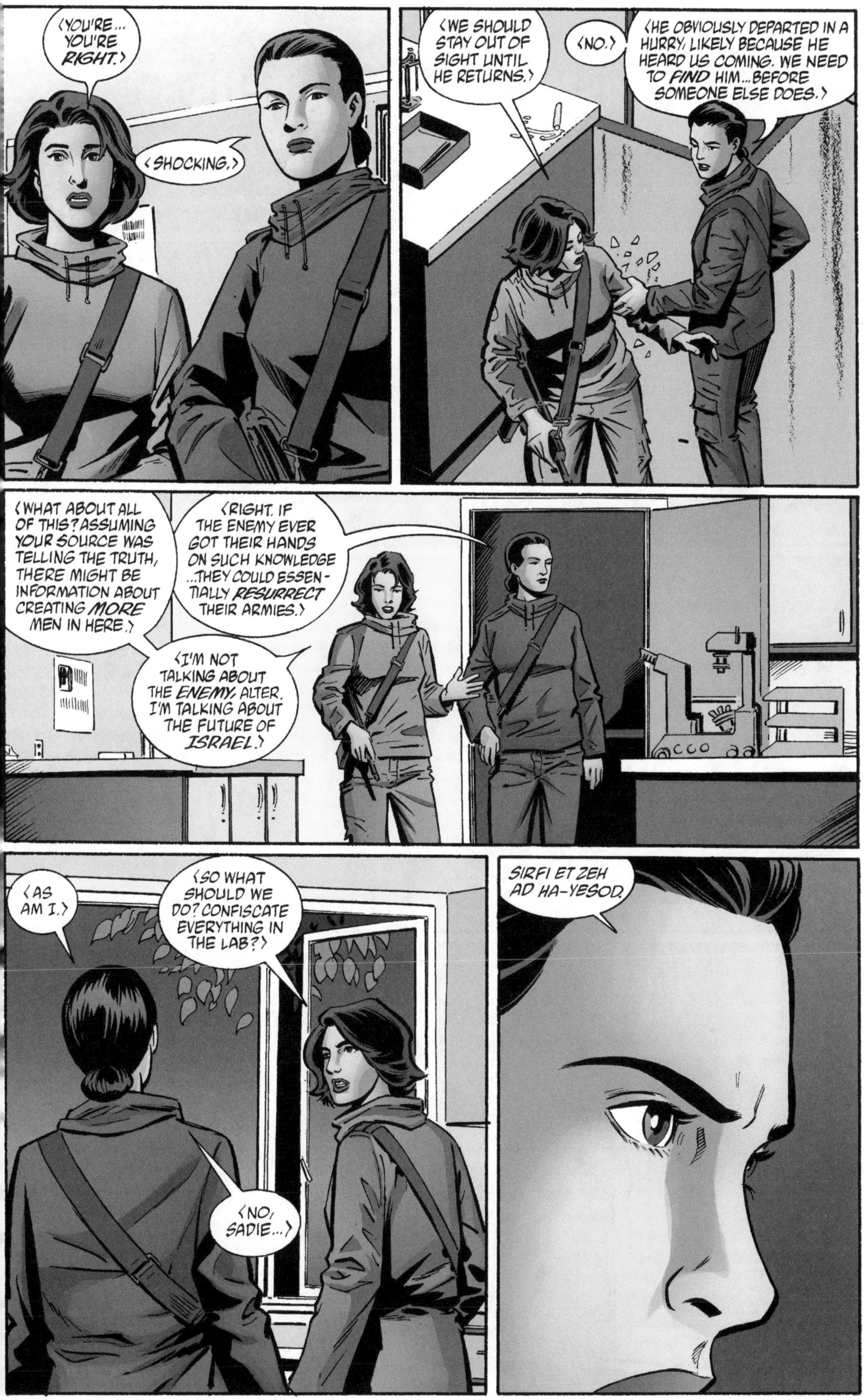
‹YOU'RE... YOU'RE RIGHT.›
‹SHOCKING.›
‹WE SHOULD STAY OUT OF SIGHT UNTIL HE RETURNS.›
‹NO.›
‹HE OBVIOUSLY DEPARTED IN A HURRY, LIKELY BECAUSE HE HEARD US COMING. WE NEED TO FIND HIM...BEFORE SOMEONE ELSE DOES.›
‹WHAT ABOUT ALL OF THIS? ASSUMING YOUR SOURCE WAS TELLING THE TRUTH, THERE MIGHT BE INFORMATION ABOUT CREATING MORE MEN IN HERE.›
‹RIGHT. IF THE ENEMY EVER GOT THEIR HANDS ON SUCH KNOWLEDGE ...THEY COULD ESSEN-TIALLY RESURRECT THEIR ARMIES.›
‹I'M NOT TALKING ABOUT THE ENEMY, ALTER. I'M TALKING ABOUT THE FUTURE OF ISRAEL.›
‹AS AM I.›
‹SO WHAT SHOULD WE DO? CONFISCATE EVERYTHING IN THE LAB?›
‹NO, SADIE...›
SIRFI ET ZEH AD HA-YESOD.

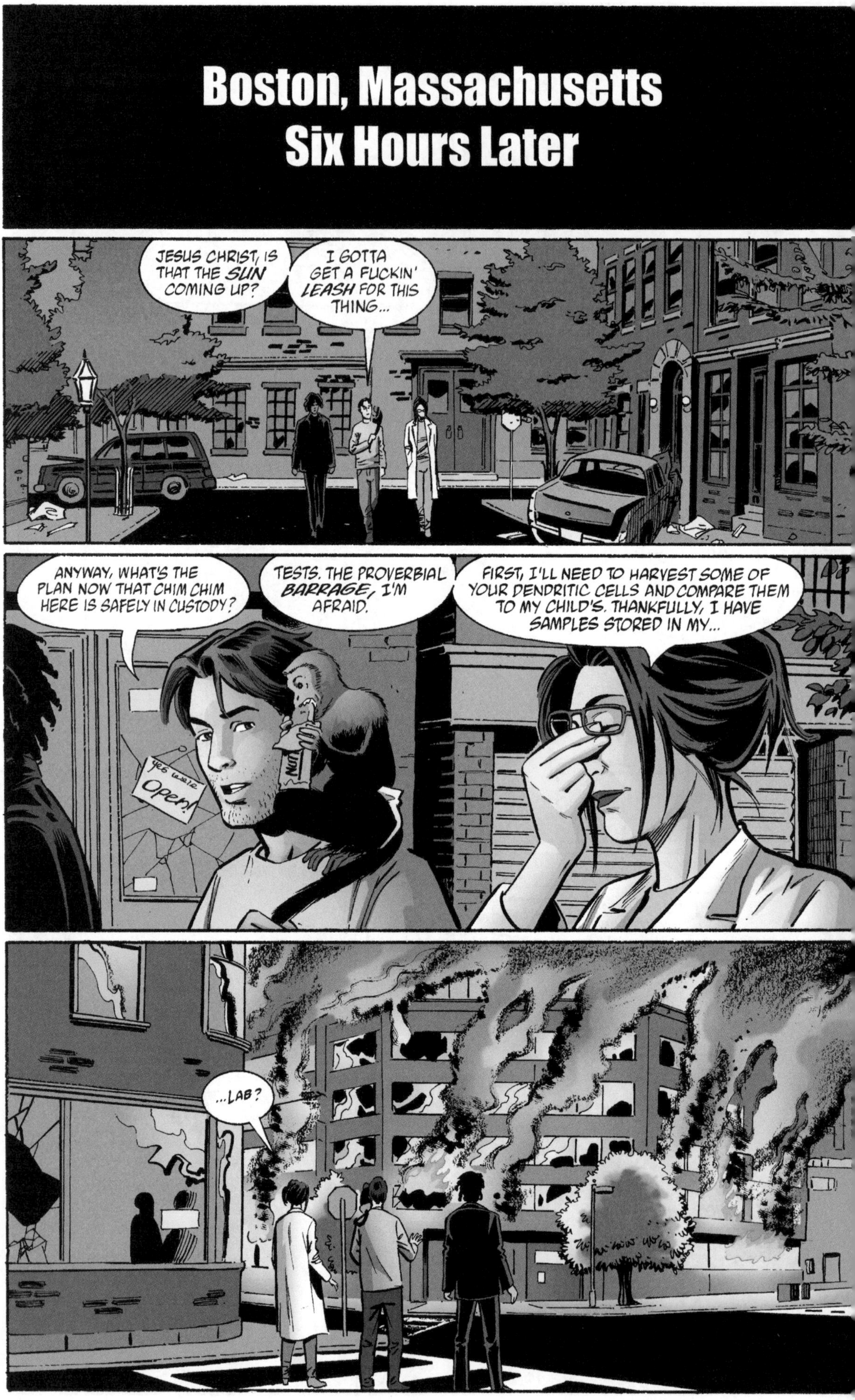
Boston, Massachusetts
Six Hours Later
JESUS CHRIST, IS THAT THE SUN COMING UP?
I GOTTA GET A FUCKIN' LEASH FOR THIS THING...
ANYWAY, WHAT'S THE PLAN NOW THAT CHIM CHIM HERE IS SAFELY IN CUSTODY?
TESTS. THE PROVERBIAL BARRAGE, I'M AFRAID.
FIRST, I'LL NEED TO HARVEST SOME OF YOUR DENDRITIC CELLS AND COMPARE THEM TO MY CHILD'S. THANKFULLY, I HAVE SAMPLES STORED IN MY...
Open!
...LAB?

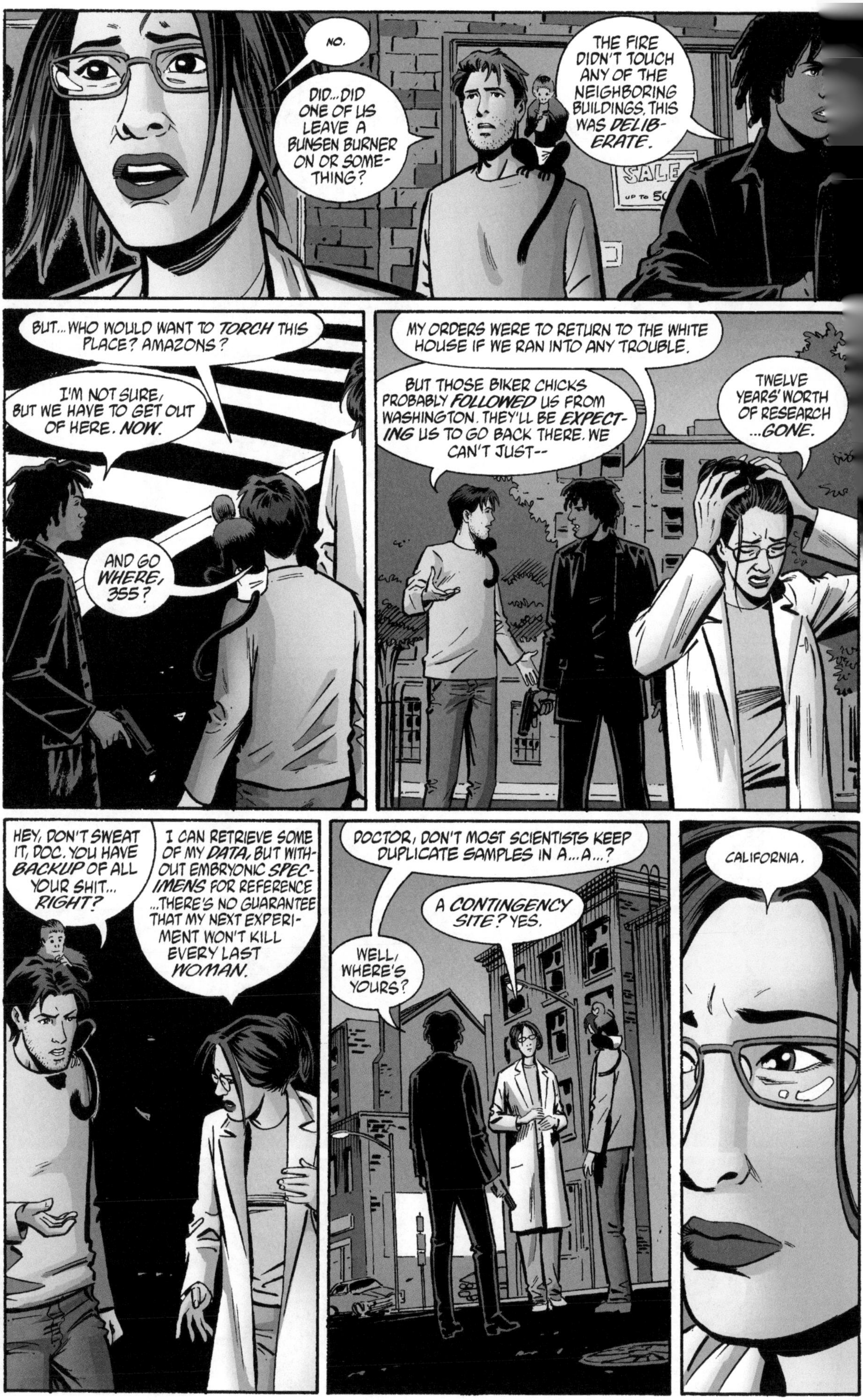
NO.
DID...DID ONE OF US LEAVE A BUNSEN BURNER ON OR SOMETHING?
THE FIRE DIDN'T TOUCH ANY OF THE NEIGHBORING BUILDINGS. THIS WAS DELIBERATE.
SALE UP TO 50
BUT...WHO WOULD WANT TO TORCH THIS PLACE? AMAZONS?
I'M NOT SURE, BUT WE HAVE TO GET OUT OF HERE. NOW.
AND GO WHERE, 355?
MY ORDERS WERE TO RETURN TO THE WHITE HOUSE IF WE RAN INTO ANY TROUBLE.
BUT THOSE BIKER CHICKS PROBABLY FOLLOWED US FROM WASHINGTON. THEY'LL BE EXPECTING US TO GO BACK THERE. WE CAN'T JUST--
TWELVE YEARS' WORTH OF RESEARCH ...GONE.
HEY, DON'T SWEAT IT, DOC. YOU HAVE BACKUP OF ALL YOUR SHIT... RIGHT?
I CAN RETRIEVE SOME OF MY DATA, BUT WITHOUT EMBRYONIC SPECIMENS FOR REFERENCE ...THERE'S NO GUARANTEE THAT MY NEXT EXPERIMENT WON'T KILL EVERY LAST WOMAN.
DOCTOR, DON'T MOST SCIENTISTS KEEP DUPLICATE SAMPLES IN A...A...?
A CONTINGENCY SITE? YES.
WELL, WHERE'S YOURS?
CALIFORNIA.

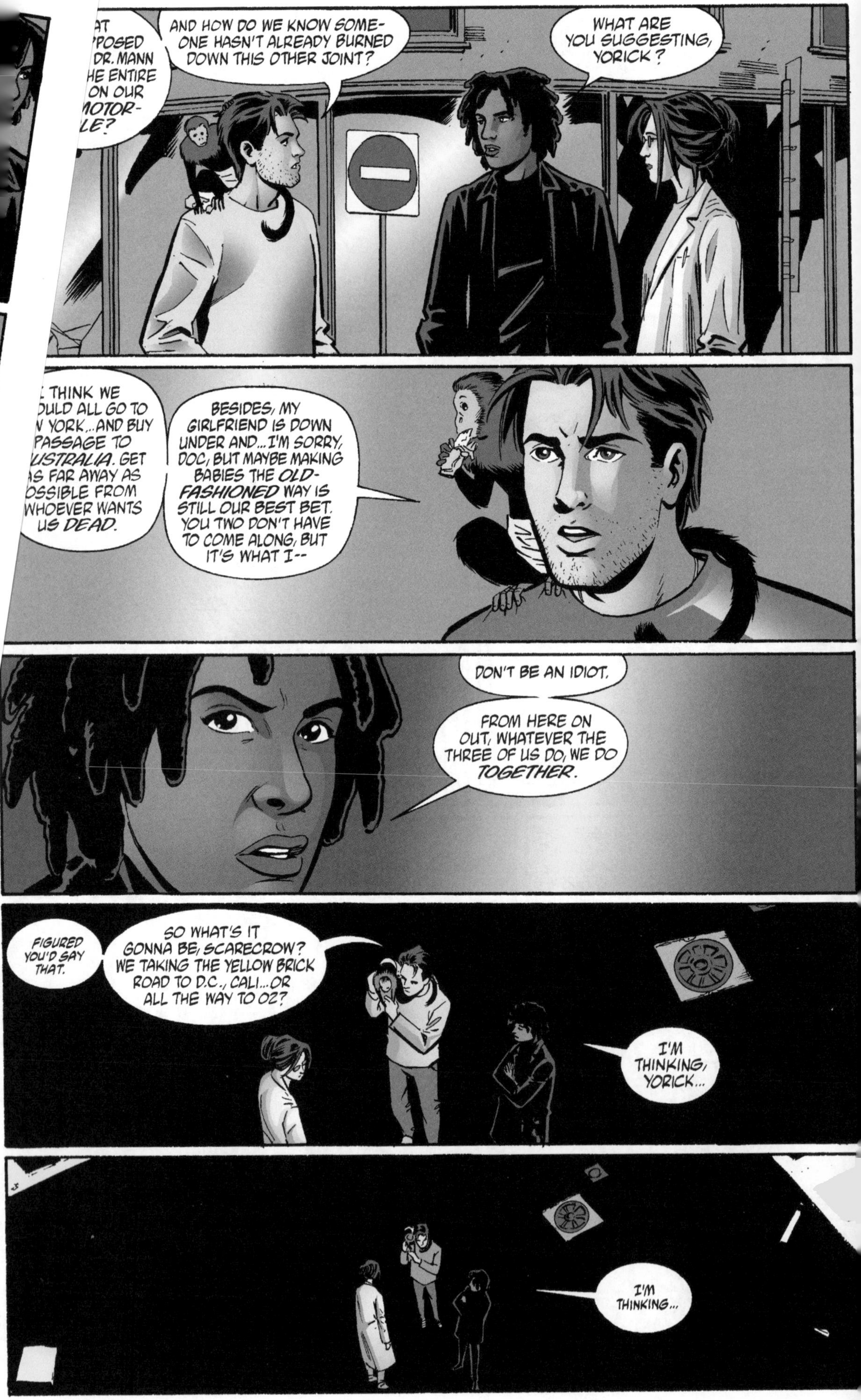
AT PPOSED DR. MANN HE ENTIRE ON OUR MOTOR- LE?
AND HOW DO WE KNOW SOME-ONE HASN'T ALREADY BURNED DOWN THIS OTHER JOINT?
WHAT ARE YOU SUGGESTING, YORICK?
THINK WE OULD ALL GO TO N YORK,...AND BUY PASSAGE TO USTRALIA. GET AS FAR AWAY AS OSSIBLE FROM WHOEVER WANTS US DEAD.
BESIDES, MY GIRLFRIEND IS DOWN UNDER AND...I'M SORRY, DOC, BUT MAYBE MAKING BABIES THE OLD-FASHIONED WAY IS STILL OUR BEST BET. YOU TWO DON'T HAVE TO COME ALONG, BUT IT'S WHAT I--
DON'T BE AN IDIOT.
FROM HERE ON OUT, WHATEVER THE THREE OF US DO, WE DO TOGETHER.
FIGURED YOU'D SAY THAT.
SO WHAT'S IT GONNA BE, SCARECROW? WE TAKING THE YELLOW BRICK ROAD TO D.C., CALI...OR ALL THE WAY TO OZ?
I'M THINKING, YORICK...
I'M THINKING...

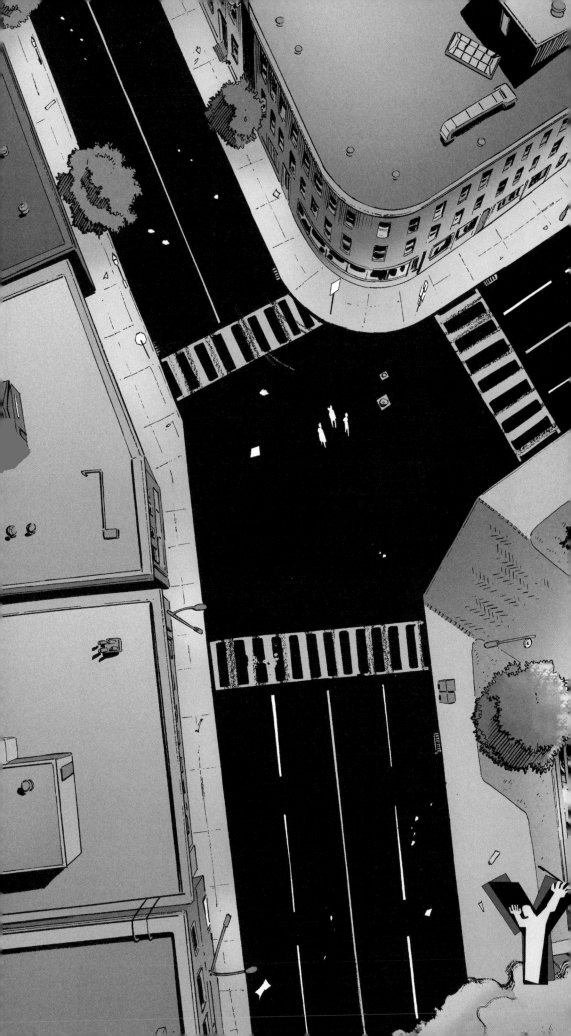

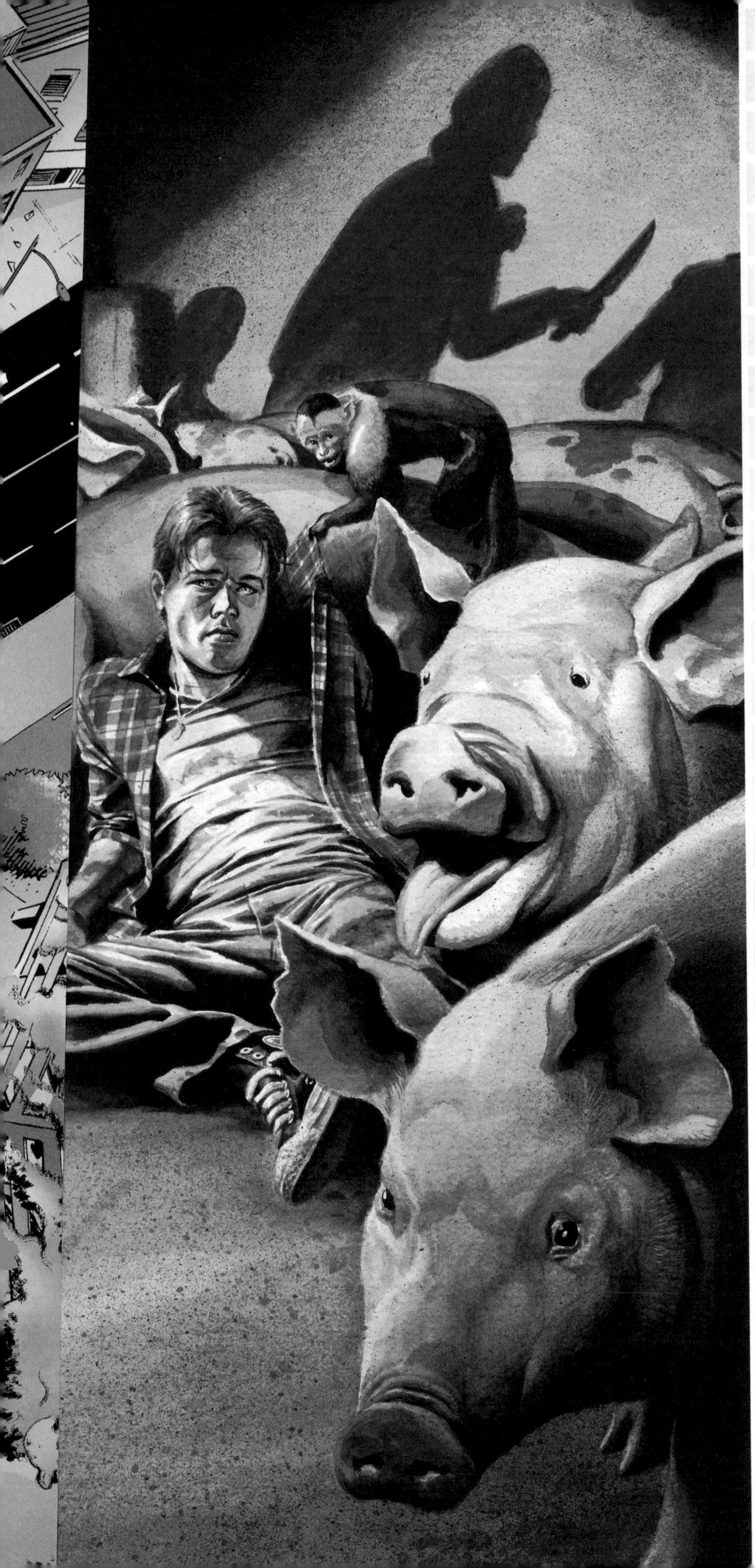

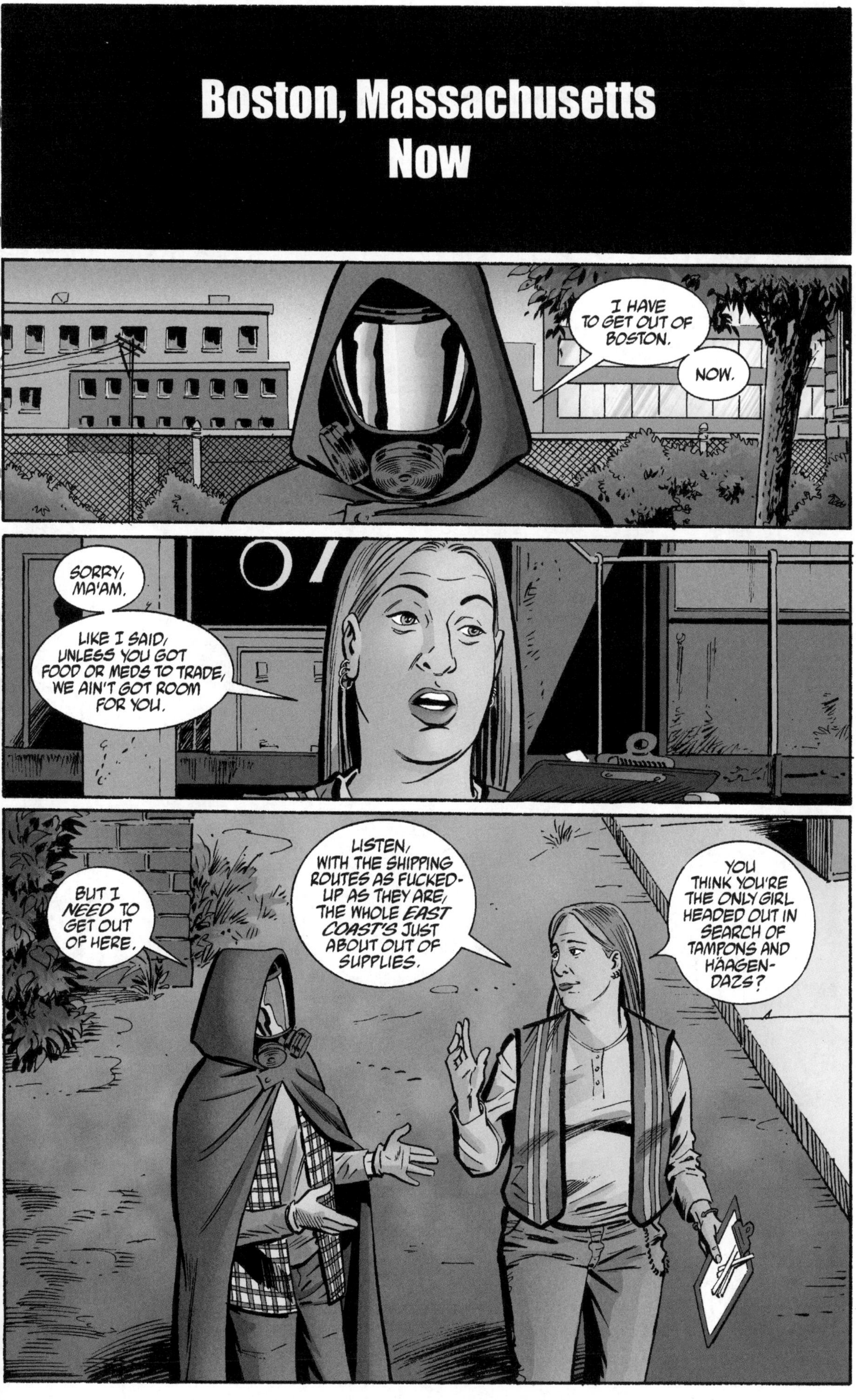
Boston, Massachusetts
Now
I HAVE TO GET OUT OF BOSTON.
NOW.
SORRY, MA'AM.
LIKE I SAID, UNLESS YOU GOT FOOD OR MEDS TO TRADE, WE AIN'T GOT ROOM FOR YOU.
BUT I NEED TO GET OUT OF HERE.
LISTEN, WITH THE SHIPPING ROUTES AS FUCKED-UP AS THEY ARE, THE WHOLE EAST COAST'S JUST ABOUT OUT OF SUPPLIES.
YOU THINK YOU'RE THE ONLY GIRL HEADED OUT IN SEARCH OF TAMPONS AND HÄAGEN-DAZS?

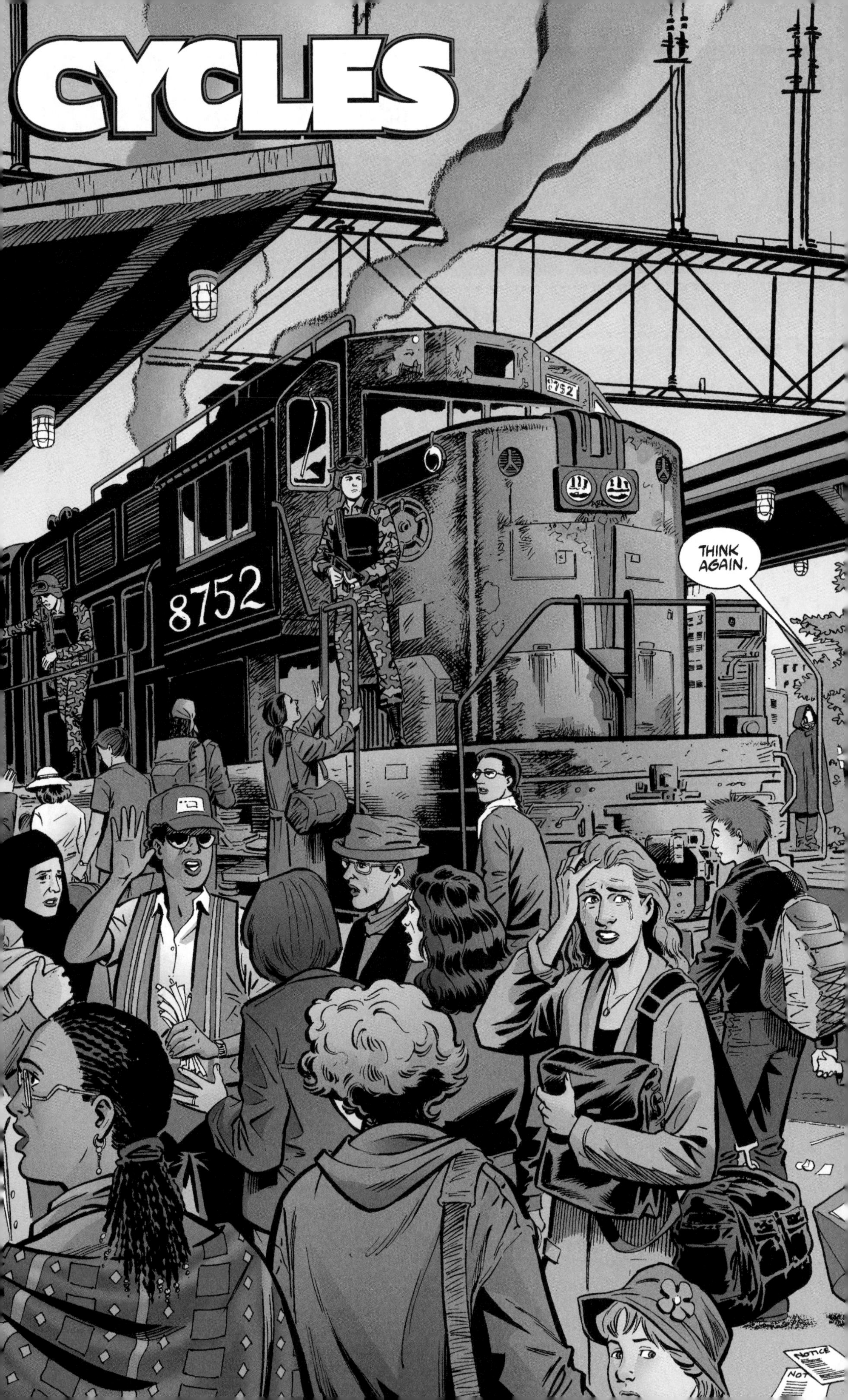
CYCLES
8752
THINK AGAIN.
NOTICE

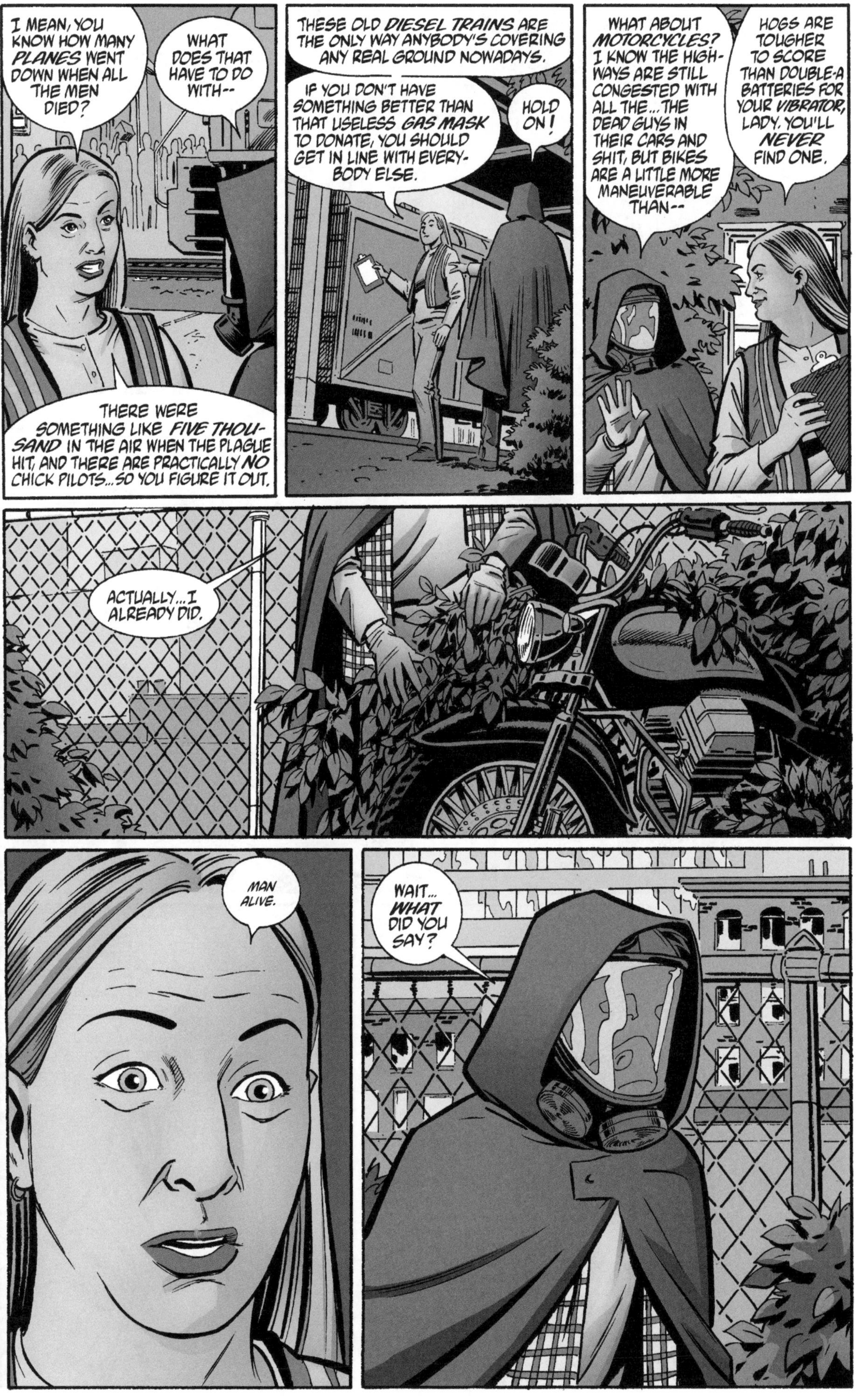
I MEAN, YOU KNOW HOW MANY PLANES WENT DOWN WHEN ALL THE MEN DIED?
WHAT DOES THAT HAVE TO DO WITH--
THERE WERE SOMETHING LIKE FIVE THOUSAND IN THE AIR WHEN THE PLAGUE HIT, AND THERE ARE PRACTICALLY NO CHICK PILOTS...SO YOU FIGURE IT OUT.
THESE OLD DIESEL TRAINS ARE THE ONLY WAY ANYBODY'S COVERING ANY REAL GROUND NOWADAYS.
IF YOU DON'T HAVE SOMETHING BETTER THAN THAT USELESS GAS MASK TO DONATE, YOU SHOULD GET IN LINE WITH EVERYBODY ELSE.
HOLD ON!
WHAT ABOUT MOTORCYCLES? I KNOW THE HIGHWAYS ARE STILL CONGESTED WITH ALL THE...THE DEAD GUYS IN THEIR CARS AND SHIT, BUT BIKES ARE A LITTLE MORE MANEUVERABLE THAN--
HOGS ARE TOUGHER TO SCORE THAN DOUBLE-A BATTERIES FOR YOUR VIBRATOR, LADY. YOU'LL NEVER FIND ONE.
ACTUALLY...I ALREADY DID.
MAN ALIVE.
WAIT... WHAT DID YOU SAY?

HUH?

OH. SORRY. OLD EXPRESSION. KINDA INAPPROPRIATE THESE DAYS, HUH?

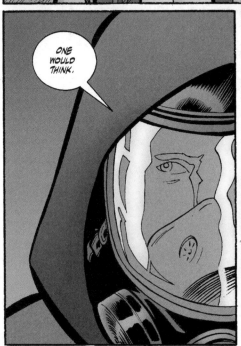

ONE WOULD THINK.

WHERE THE HELL'D YOU FIND THIS THING, ANYWAY?

MY...MY BOYFRIEND USED TO RIDE ONE JUST LIKE IT.

LONG STORY. BUT IF YOU LET ME ON BOARD, THE BIKE'S ALL YOURS. OUR LITTLE SECRET.

WELL, I...I COULDN'T GET YOU INTO PASSENGER.

CARGO, MAYBE...

DEAL.

ALL RIGHT, I'LL LEAVE A DOOR OPEN FOR YOU TOWARDS THE BACK.

BUT YOU BETTER HURRY, SHE'S PULLING OUT IN LESS THAN FIVE...

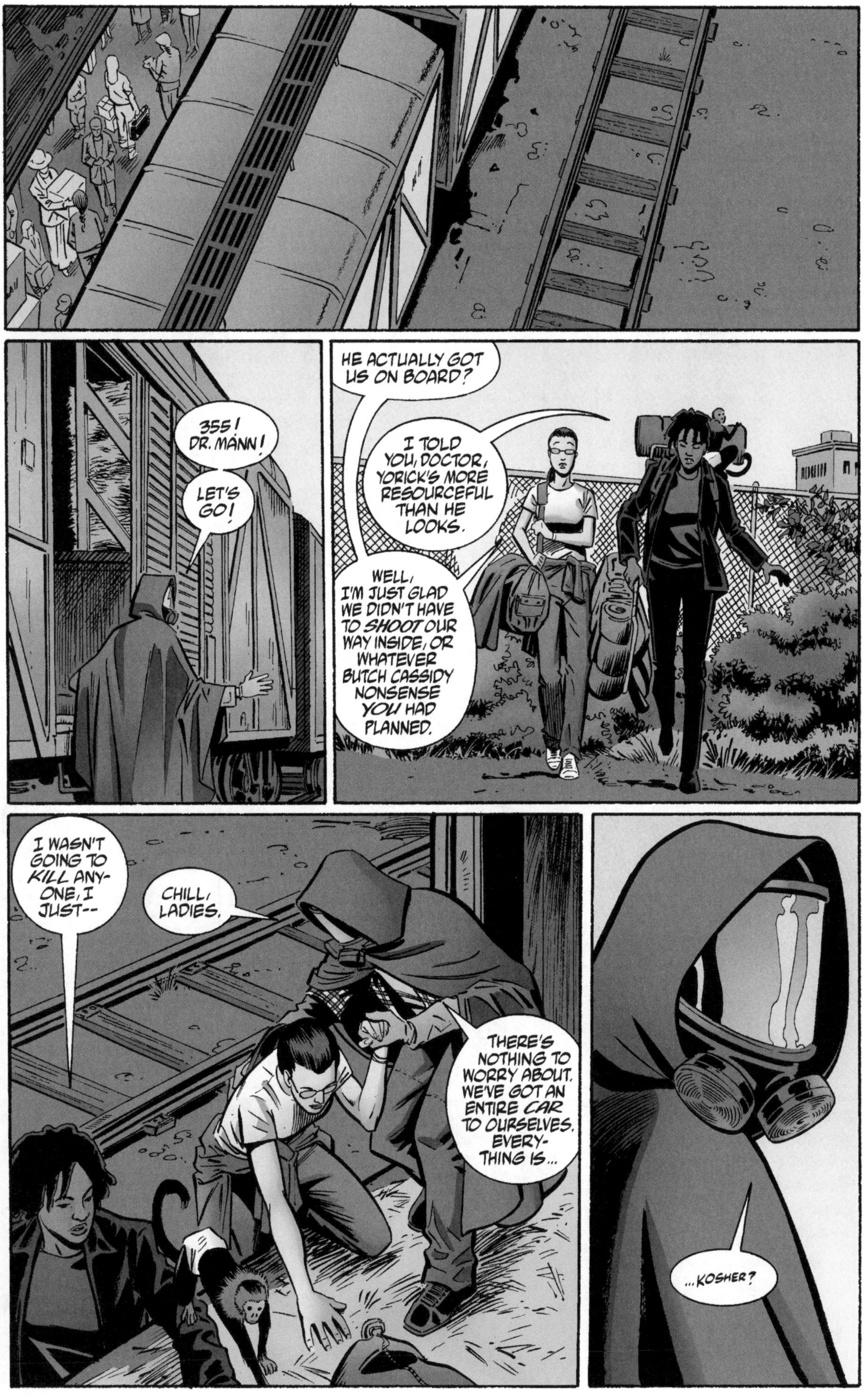
355! DR. MANN!
LET'S GO!
HE ACTUALLY GOT US ON BOARD?
I TOLD YOU, DOCTOR, YORICK'S MORE RESOURCEFUL THAN HE LOOKS.
WELL, I'M JUST GLAD WE DIDN'T HAVE TO SHOOT OUR WAY INSIDE, OR WHATEVER BUTCH CASSIDY NONSENSE YOU HAD PLANNED.
I WASN'T GOING TO KILL ANY-ONE, I JUST--
CHILL, LADIES.
THERE'S NOTHING TO WORRY ABOUT. WE'VE GOT AN ENTIRE CAR TO OURSELVES. EVERY-THING IS...
...KOSHER?

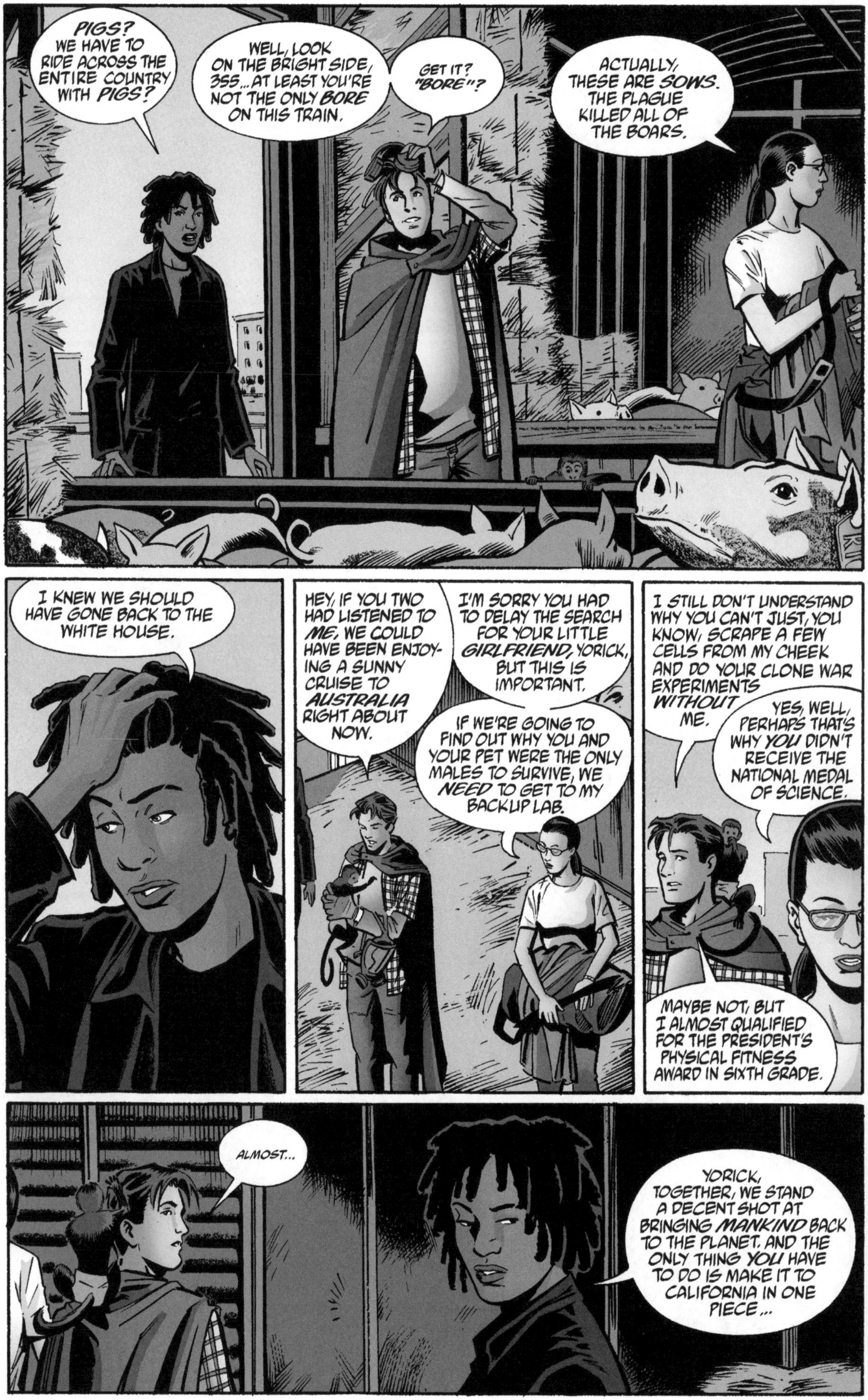
PIGS? WE HAVE TO RIDE ACROSS THE ENTIRE COUNTRY WITH PIGS?
WELL, LOOK ON THE BRIGHT SIDE, 355... AT LEAST YOU'RE NOT THE ONLY BORE ON THIS TRAIN.
GET IT? "BORE"?
ACTUALLY, THESE ARE SOWS. THE PLAGUE KILLED ALL OF THE BOARS.
I KNEW WE SHOULD HAVE GONE BACK TO THE WHITE HOUSE.
HEY, IF YOU TWO HAD LISTENED TO ME, WE COULD HAVE BEEN ENJOYING A SUNNY CRUISE TO AUSTRALIA RIGHT ABOUT NOW.
I'M SORRY YOU HAD TO DELAY THE SEARCH FOR YOUR LITTLE GIRLFRIEND, YORICK, BUT THIS IS IMPORTANT.
IF WE'RE GOING TO FIND OUT WHY YOU AND YOUR PET WERE THE ONLY MALES TO SURVIVE, WE NEED TO GET TO MY BACKUP LAB.
I STILL DON'T UNDERSTAND WHY YOU CAN'T JUST, YOU KNOW, SCRAPE A FEW CELLS FROM MY CHEEK AND DO YOUR CLONE WAR EXPERIMENTS WITHOUT ME.
YES, WELL, PERHAPS THAT'S WHY YOU DIDN'T RECEIVE THE NATIONAL MEDAL OF SCIENCE.
MAYBE NOT, BUT I ALMOST QUALIFIED FOR THE PRESIDENT'S PHYSICAL FITNESS AWARD IN SIXTH GRADE.
ALMOST...
YORICK, TOGETHER, WE STAND A DECENT SHOT AT BRINGING MANKIND BACK TO THE PLANET. AND THE ONLY THING YOU HAVE TO DO IS MAKE IT TO CALIFORNIA IN ONE PIECE...

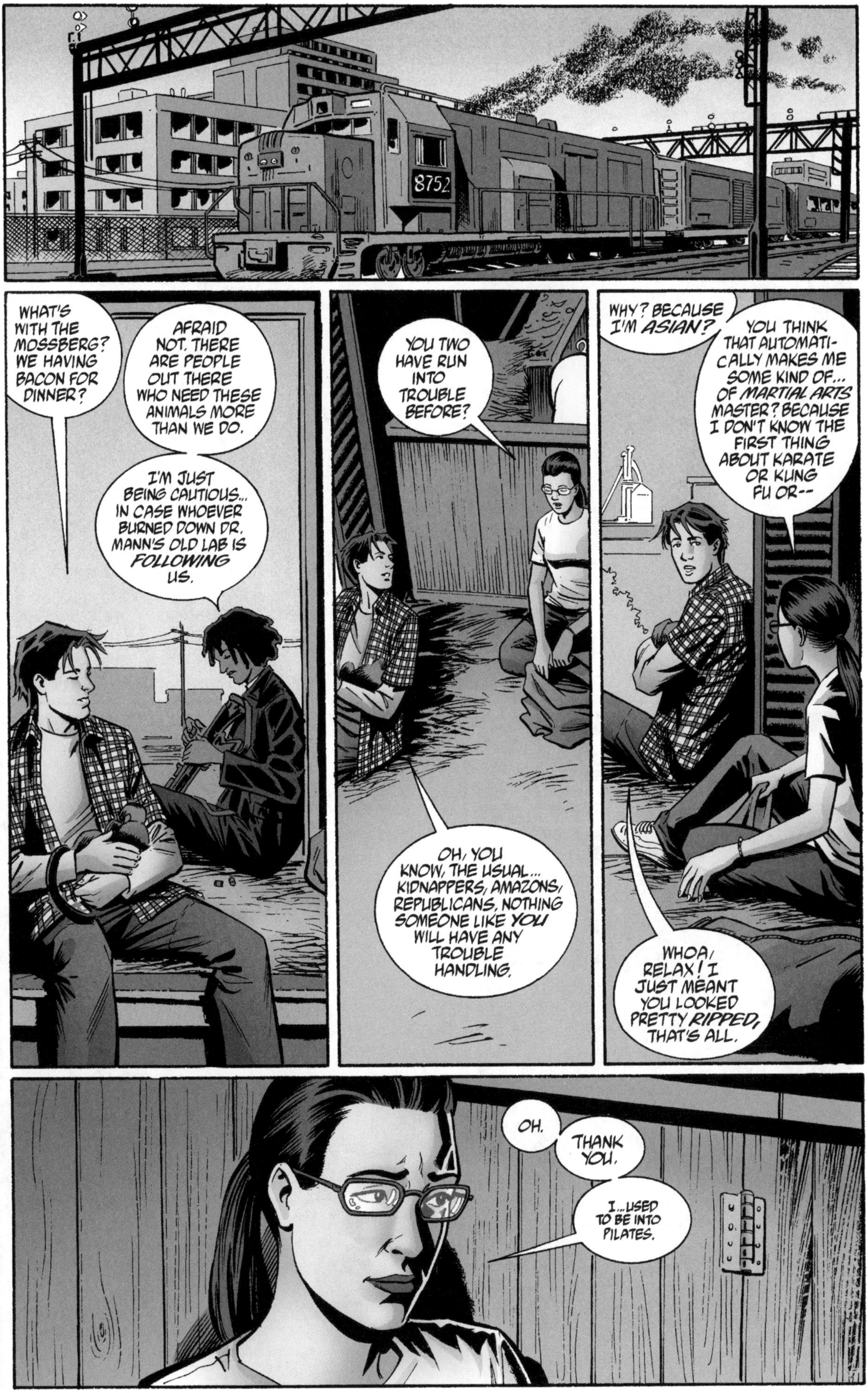
8752
WHAT'S WITH THE MOSSBERG? WE HAVING BACON FOR DINNER?
AFRAID NOT. THERE ARE PEOPLE OUT THERE WHO NEED THESE ANIMALS MORE THAN WE DO.
I'M JUST BEING CAUTIOUS... IN CASE WHOEVER BURNED DOWN DR. MANN'S OLD LAB IS FOLLOWING US.
YOU TWO HAVE RUN INTO TROUBLE BEFORE?
OH, YOU KNOW, THE USUAL... KIDNAPPERS, AMAZONS, REPUBLICANS, NOTHING SOMEONE LIKE YOU WILL HAVE ANY TROUBLE HANDLING.
WHY? BECAUSE I'M ASIAN?
YOU THINK THAT AUTOMATICALLY MAKES ME SOME KIND OF... OF MARTIAL ARTS MASTER? BECAUSE I DON'T KNOW THE FIRST THING ABOUT KARATE OR KUNG FU OR--
WHOA, RELAX! I JUST MEANT YOU LOOKED PRETTY RIPPED, THAT'S ALL.
OH.
THANK YOU.
I...USED TO BE INTO PILATES.

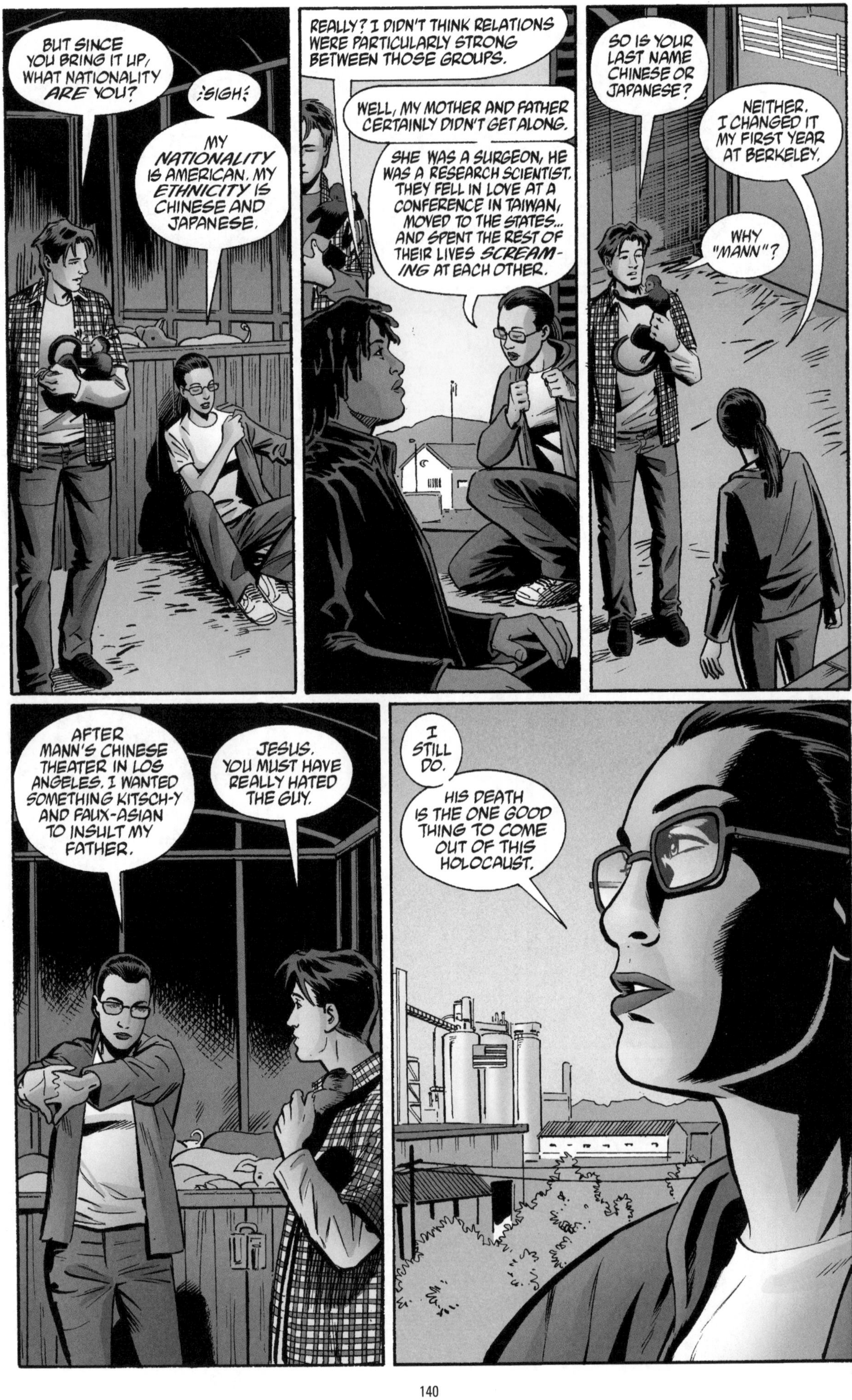
BUT SINCE YOU BRING IT UP, WHAT NATIONALITY ARE YOU?
:SIGH:
MY NATIONALITY IS AMERICAN. MY ETHNICITY IS CHINESE AND JAPANESE.
REALLY? I DIDN'T THINK RELATIONS WERE PARTICULARLY STRONG BETWEEN THOSE GROUPS.
WELL, MY MOTHER AND FATHER CERTAINLY DIDN'T GET ALONG.
SHE WAS A SURGEON, HE WAS A RESEARCH SCIENTIST. THEY FELL IN LOVE AT A CONFERENCE IN TAIWAN, MOVED TO THE STATES... AND SPENT THE REST OF THEIR LIVES SCREAMING AT EACH OTHER.
SO IS YOUR LAST NAME CHINESE OR JAPANESE?
NEITHER. I CHANGED IT MY FIRST YEAR AT BERKELEY.
WHY "MANN"?
AFTER MANN'S CHINESE THEATER IN LOS ANGELES. I WANTED SOMETHING KITSCH-Y AND FAUX-ASIAN TO INSULT MY FATHER.
JESUS. YOU MUST HAVE REALLY HATED THE GUY.
I STILL DO.
HIS DEATH IS THE ONE GOOD THING TO COME OUT OF THIS HOLOCAUST.

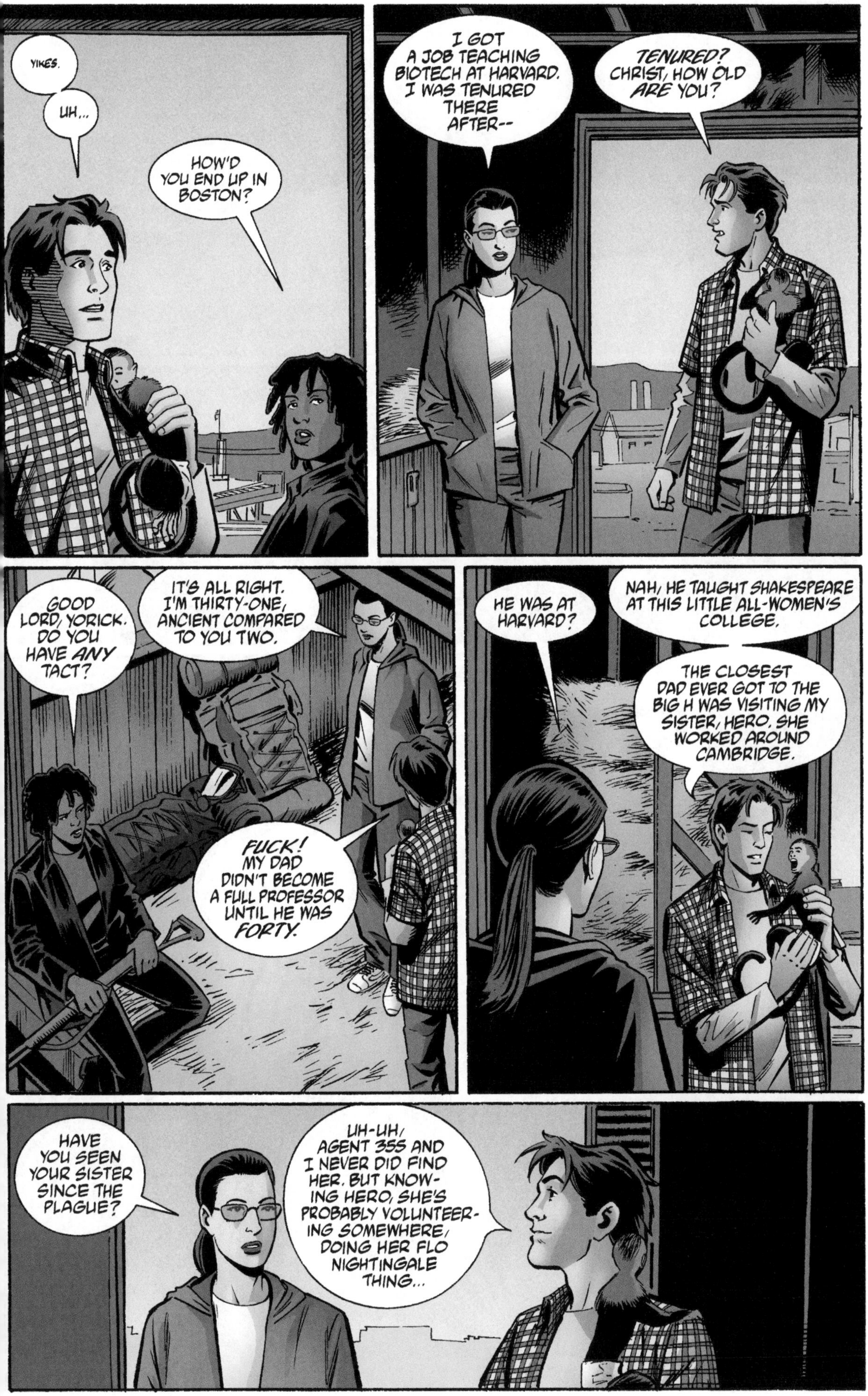
YIKES.
UH...
HOW'D YOU END UP IN BOSTON?
I GOT A JOB TEACHING BIOTECH AT HARVARD. I WAS TENURED THERE AFTER--
TENURED? CHRIST, HOW OLD ARE YOU?
GOOD LORD, YORICK. DO YOU HAVE ANY TACT?
IT'S ALL RIGHT. I'M THIRTY-ONE, ANCIENT COMPARED TO YOU TWO.
FUCK! MY DAD DIDN'T BECOME A FULL PROFESSOR UNTIL HE WAS FORTY.
HE WAS AT HARVARD?
NAH, HE TAUGHT SHAKESPEARE AT THIS LITTLE ALL-WOMEN'S COLLEGE.
THE CLOSEST DAD EVER GOT TO THE BIG H WAS VISITING MY SISTER, HERO. SHE WORKED AROUND CAMBRIDGE.
HAVE YOU SEEN YOUR SISTER SINCE THE PLAGUE?
UH-UH, AGENT 355 AND I NEVER DID FIND HER. BUT KNOWING HERO, SHE'S PROBABLY VOLUNTEERING SOMEWHERE, DOING HER FLO NIGHTINGALE THING...

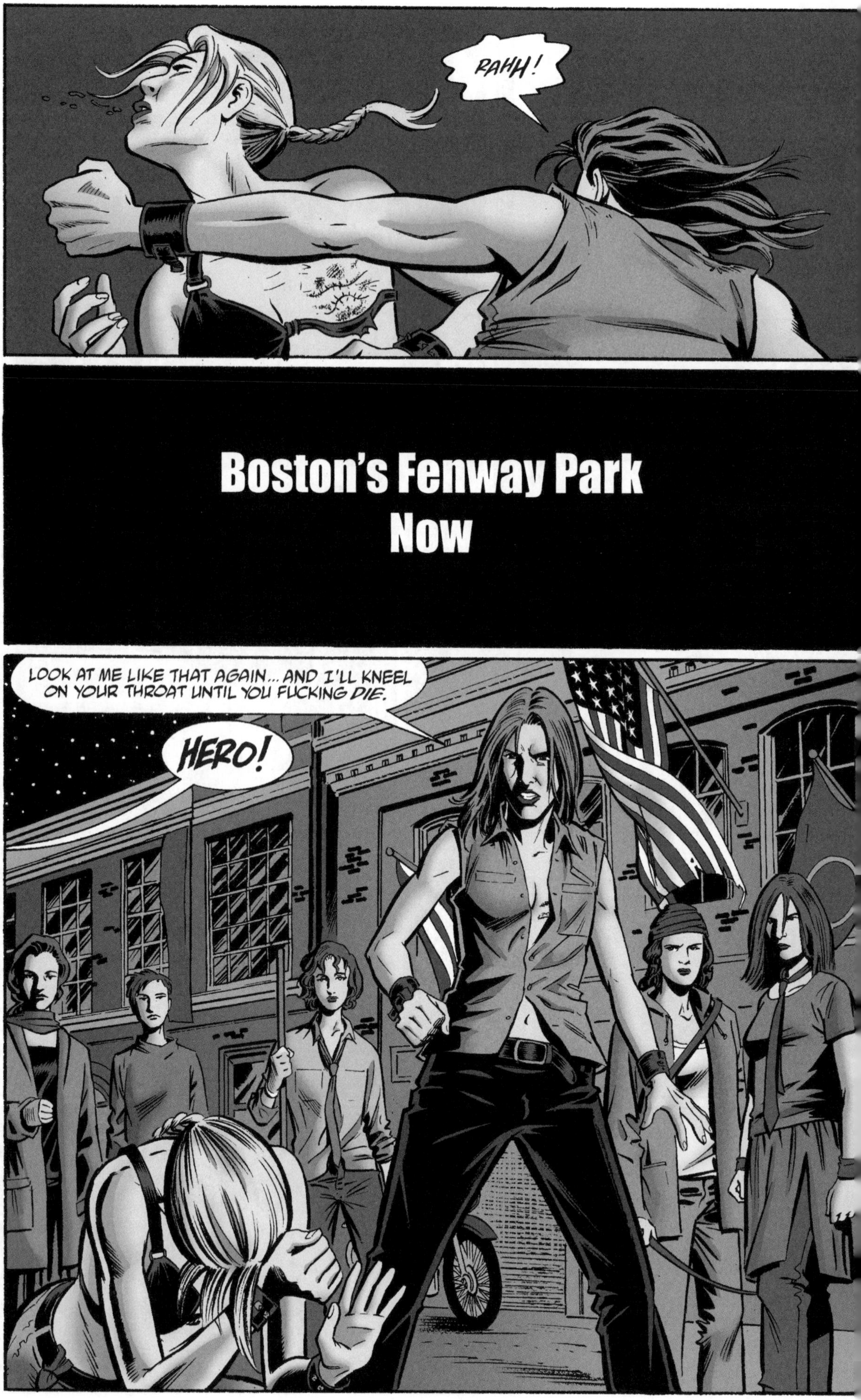
RAHH!
Boston's Fenway Park
Now
LOOK AT ME LIKE THAT AGAIN... AND I'LL KNEEL ON YOUR THROAT UNTIL YOU FUCKING DIE.
HERO!

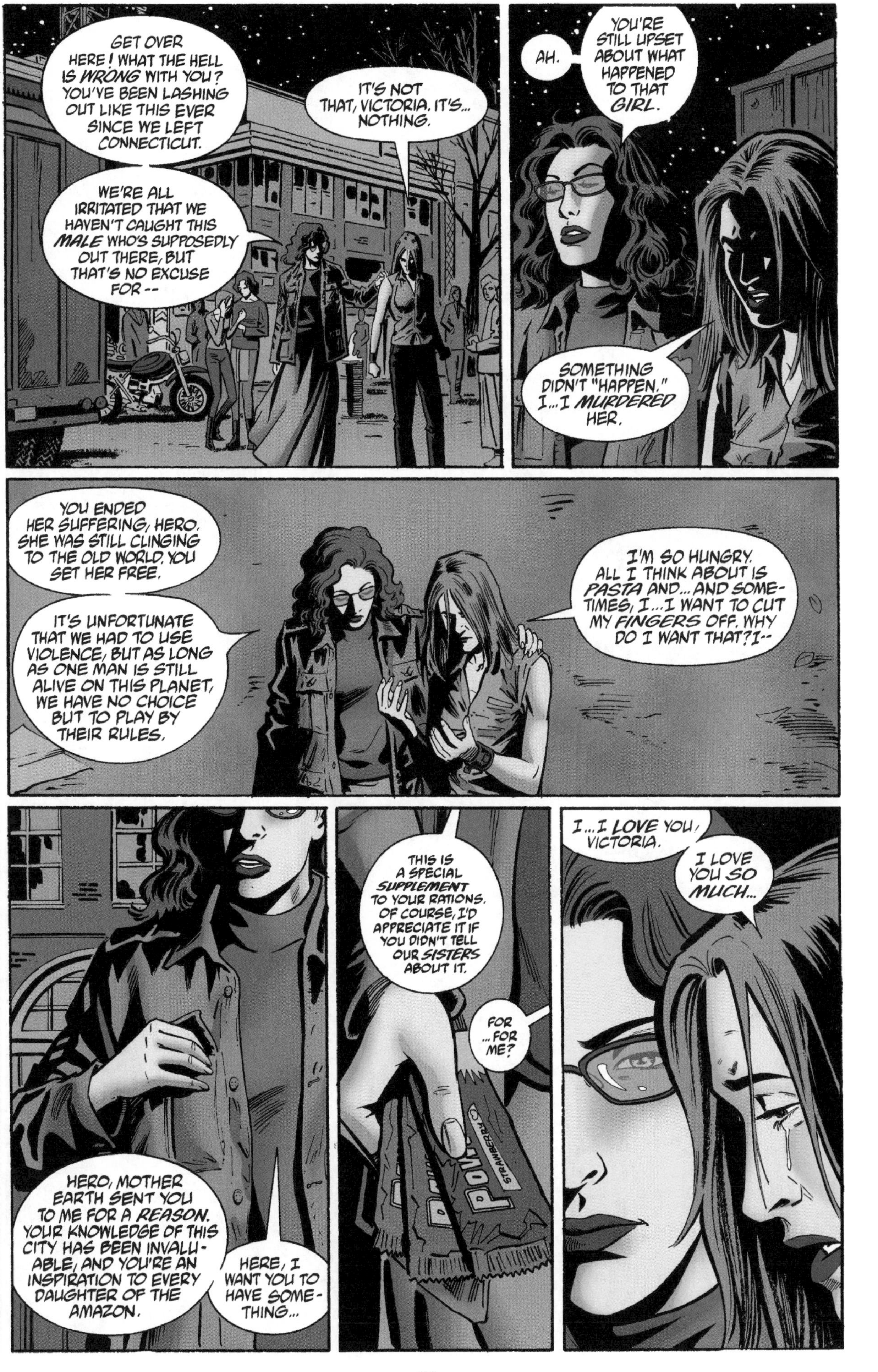
GET OVER HERE! WHAT THE HELL IS WRONG WITH YOU? YOU'VE BEEN LASHING OUT LIKE THIS EVER SINCE WE LEFT CONNECTICUT.
WE'RE ALL IRRITATED THAT WE HAVEN'T CAUGHT THIS MALE WHO'S SUPPOSEDLY OUT THERE, BUT THAT'S NO EXCUSE FOR --
IT'S NOT THAT, VICTORIA. IT'S... NOTHING.
AH.
YOU'RE STILL UPSET ABOUT WHAT HAPPENED TO THAT GIRL.
SOMETHING DIDN'T "HAPPEN." I...I MURDERED HER.
YOU ENDED HER SUFFERING, HERO. SHE WAS STILL CLINGING TO THE OLD WORLD. YOU SET HER FREE.
IT'S UNFORTUNATE THAT WE HAD TO USE VIOLENCE, BUT AS LONG AS ONE MAN IS STILL ALIVE ON THIS PLANET, WE HAVE NO CHOICE BUT TO PLAY BY THEIR RULES.
I'M SO HUNGRY. ALL I THINK ABOUT IS PASTA AND... AND SOMETIMES, I... I WANT TO CUT MY FINGERS OFF. WHY DO I WANT THAT? I--
HERO, MOTHER EARTH SENT YOU TO ME FOR A REASON. YOUR KNOWLEDGE OF THIS CITY HAS BEEN INVALUABLE, AND YOU'RE AN INSPIRATION TO EVERY DAUGHTER OF THE AMAZON.
HERE, I WANT YOU TO HAVE SOMETHING...
THIS IS A SPECIAL SUPPLEMENT TO YOUR RATIONS. OF COURSE, I'D APPRECIATE IT IF YOU DIDN'T TELL OUR SISTERS ABOUT IT.
FOR ...FOR ME?
STRAWBERRY
I...I LOVE YOU, VICTORIA.
I LOVE YOU SO MUCH...

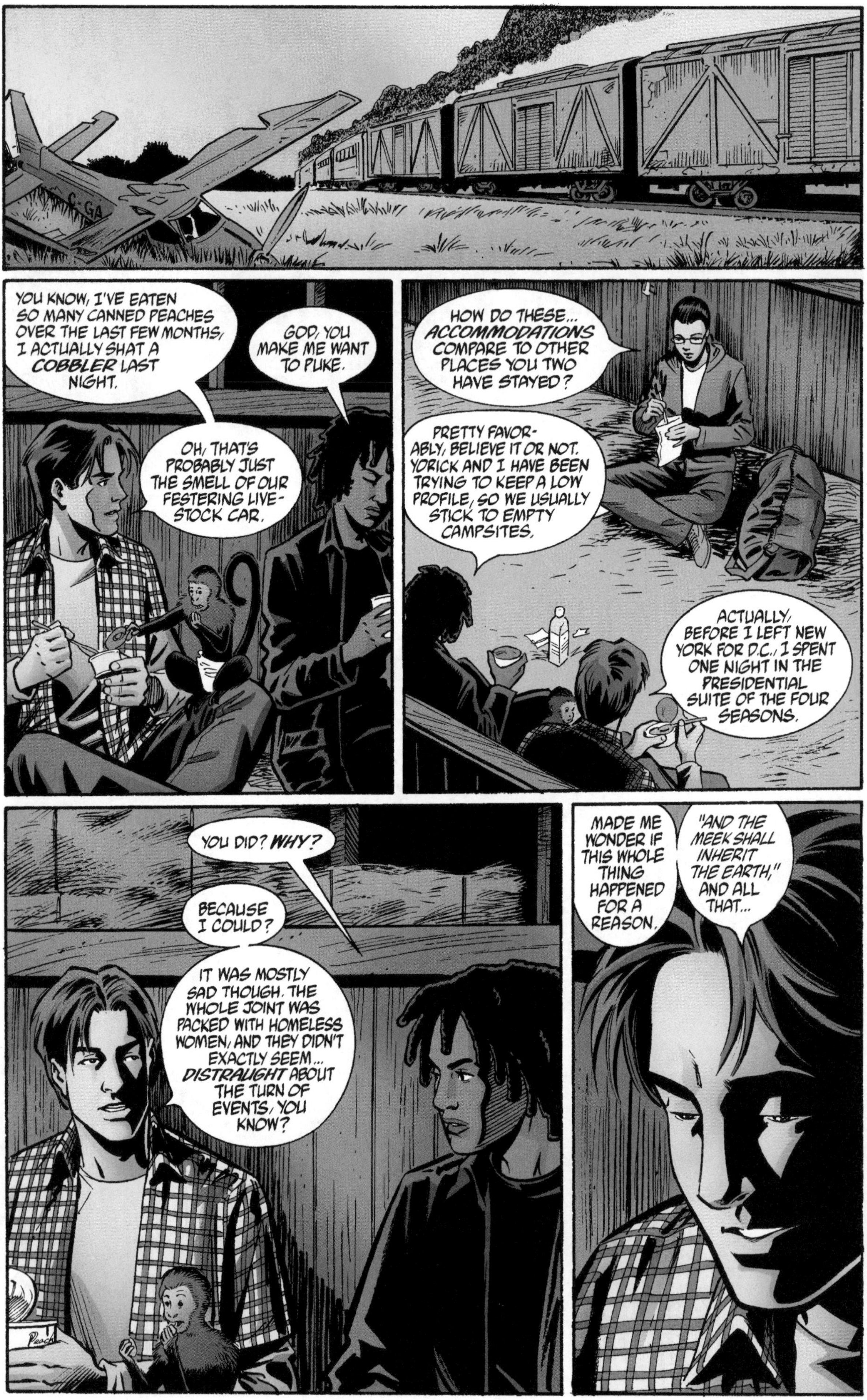
C-GA
YOU KNOW, I'VE EATEN SO MANY CANNED PEACHES OVER THE LAST FEW MONTHS, I ACTUALLY SHAT A COBBLER LAST NIGHT.
GOD, YOU MAKE ME WANT TO PUKE.
OH, THAT'S PROBABLY JUST THE SMELL OF OUR FESTERING LIVE-STOCK CAR.
HOW DO THESE... ACCOMMODATIONS COMPARE TO OTHER PLACES YOU TWO HAVE STAYED?
PRETTY FAVOR-ABLY, BELIEVE IT OR NOT. YORICK AND I HAVE BEEN TRYING TO KEEP A LOW PROFILE, SO WE USUALLY STICK TO EMPTY CAMPSITES.
ACTUALLY, BEFORE I LEFT NEW YORK FOR D.C., I SPENT ONE NIGHT IN THE PRESIDENTIAL SUITE OF THE FOUR SEASONS.
YOU DID? WHY?
BECAUSE I COULD?
IT WAS MOSTLY SAD THOUGH. THE WHOLE JOINT WAS PACKED WITH HOMELESS WOMEN, AND THEY DIDN'T EXACTLY SEEM... DISTRAUGHT ABOUT THE TURN OF EVENTS, YOU KNOW?
Peach
MADE ME WONDER IF THIS WHOLE THING HAPPENED FOR A REASON.
"AND THE MEEK SHALL INHERIT THE EARTH," AND ALL THAT...

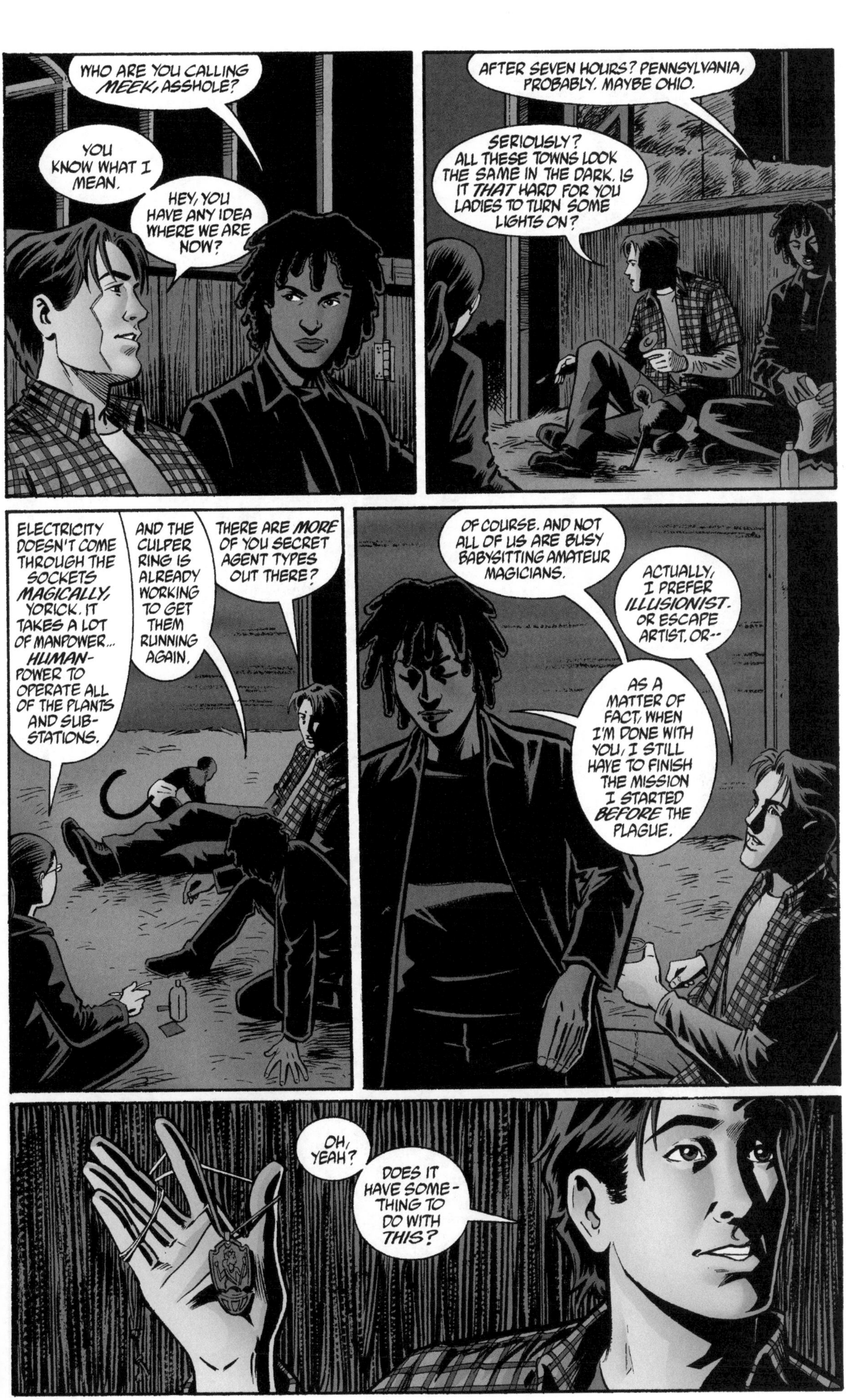
WHO ARE YOU CALLING MEEK, ASSHOLE?
YOU KNOW WHAT I MEAN.
HEY, YOU HAVE ANY IDEA WHERE WE ARE NOW?
AFTER SEVEN HOURS? PENNSYLVANIA, PROBABLY. MAYBE OHIO.
SERIOUSLY? ALL THESE TOWNS LOOK THE SAME IN THE DARK. IS IT THAT HARD FOR YOU LADIES TO TURN SOME LIGHTS ON?
ELECTRICITY DOESN'T COME THROUGH THE SOCKETS MAGICALLY, YORICK. IT TAKES A LOT OF MANPOWER... HUMAN-POWER TO OPERATE ALL OF THE PLANTS AND SUB-STATIONS.
AND THE CULPER RING IS ALREADY WORKING TO GET THEM RUNNING AGAIN.
THERE ARE MORE OF YOU SECRET AGENT TYPES OUT THERE?
OF COURSE. AND NOT ALL OF US ARE BUSY BABYSITTING AMATEUR MAGICIANS.
ACTUALLY, I PREFER ILLUSIONIST-OR ESCAPE ARTIST, OR--
AS A MATTER OF FACT, WHEN I'M DONE WITH YOU, I STILL HAVE TO FINISH THE MISSION I STARTED BEFORE THE PLAGUE.
OH, YEAH?
DOES IT HAVE SOME-THING TO DO WITH THIS?

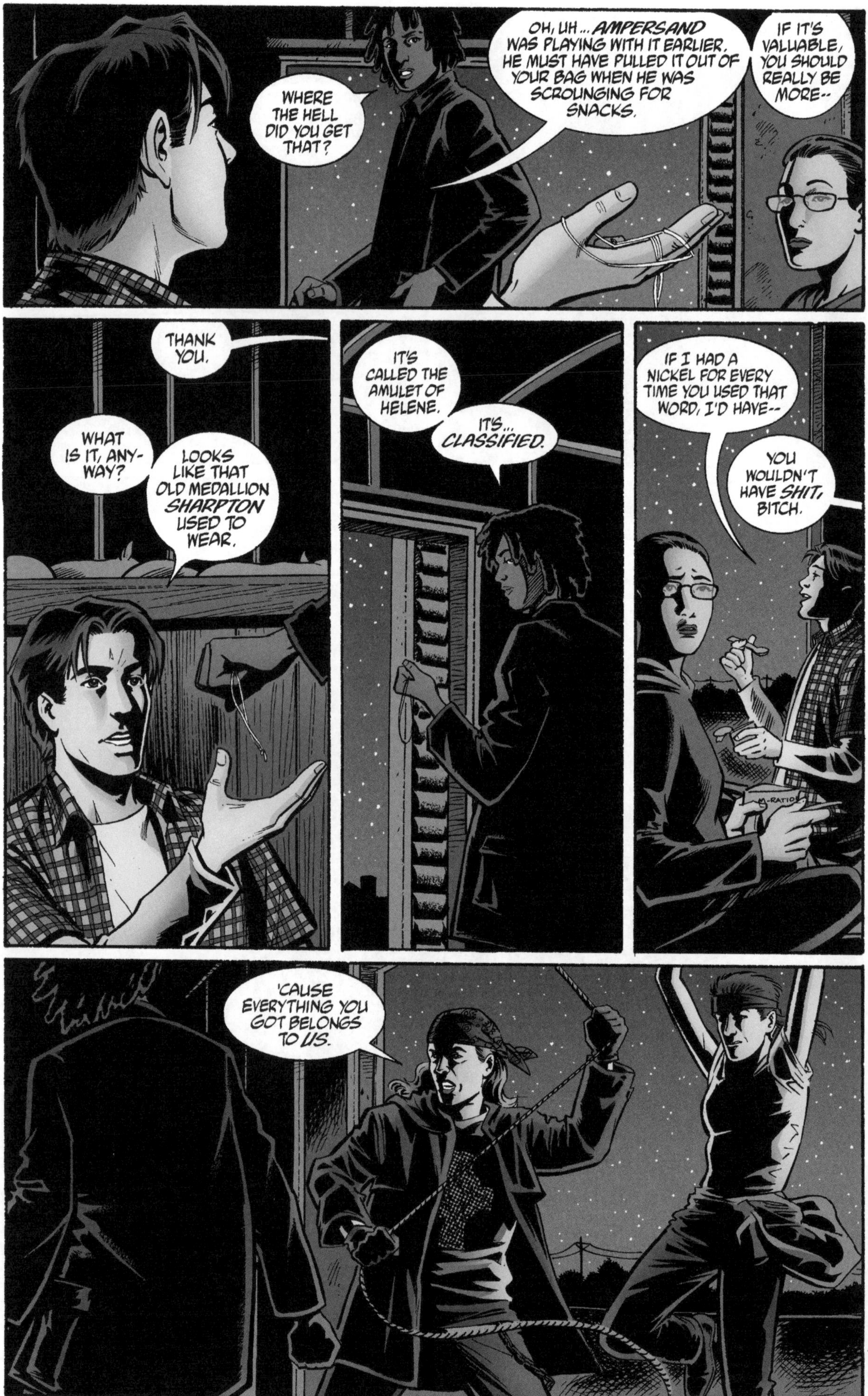
WHERE THE HELL DID YOU GET THAT?
OH, UH... AMPERSAND WAS PLAYING WITH IT EARLIER. HE MUST HAVE PULLED IT OUT OF YOUR BAG WHEN HE WAS SCROUNGING FOR SNACKS.
IF IT'S VALUABLE, YOU SHOULD REALLY BE MORE--
THANK YOU.
WHAT IS IT, ANY-WAY?
LOOKS LIKE THAT OLD MEDALLION SHARPTON USED TO WEAR.
IT'S CALLED THE AMULET OF HELENE.
IT'S... CLASSIFIED.
IF I HAD A NICKEL FOR EVERY TIME YOU USED THAT WORD, I'D HAVE--
YOU WOULDN'T HAVE SHIT, BITCH.
'CAUSE EVERYTHING YOU GOT BELONGS TO US.

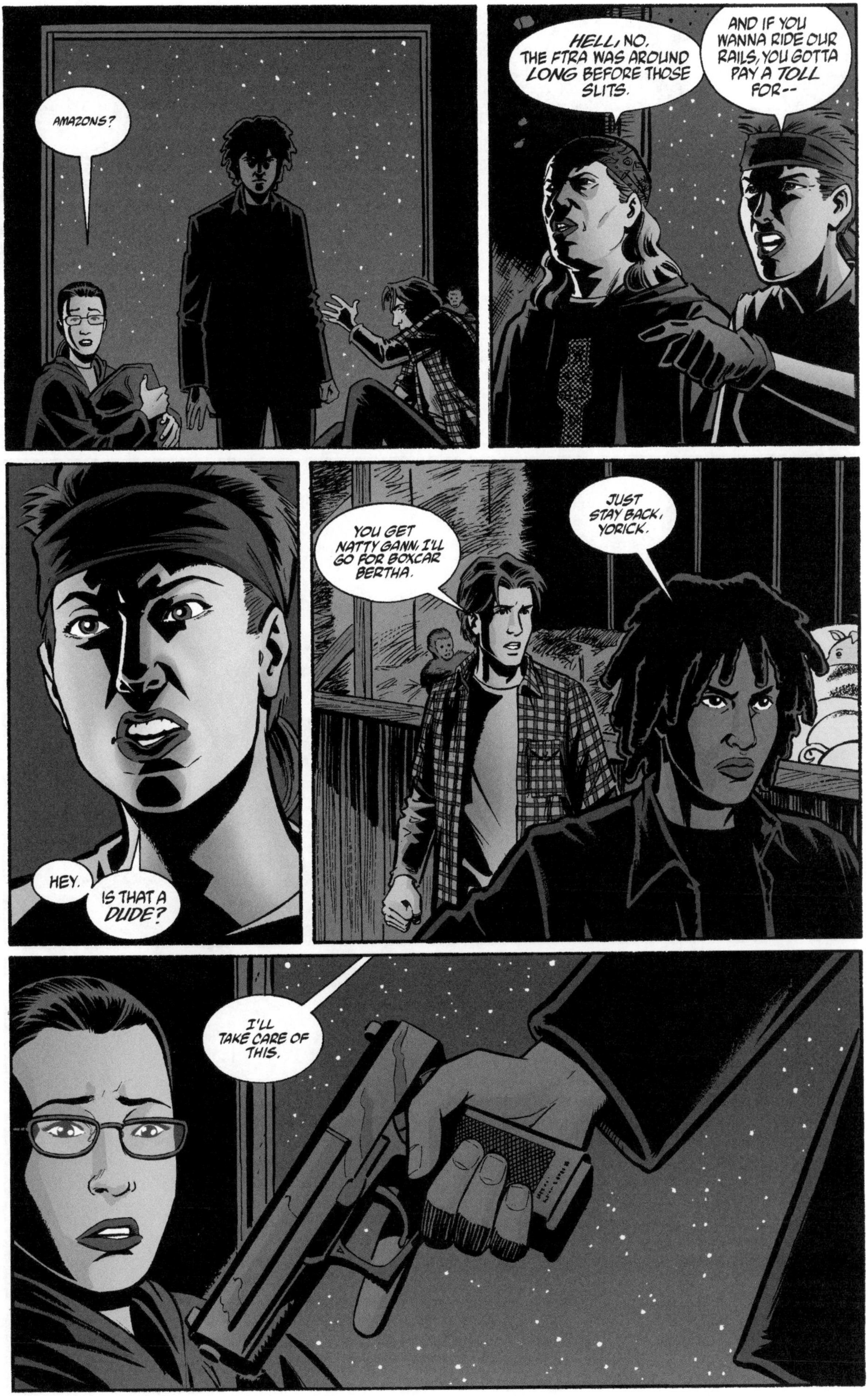
AMAZONS?
HELL, NO. THE FTRA WAS AROUND LONG BEFORE THOSE SLITS.
AND IF YOU WANNA RIDE OUR RAILS, YOU GOTTA PAY A TOLL FOR--
HEY.
IS THAT A DUDE?
YOU GET NATTY GANN, I'LL GO FOR BOXCAR BERTHA.
JUST STAY BACK, YORICK.
I'LL TAKE CARE OF THIS.

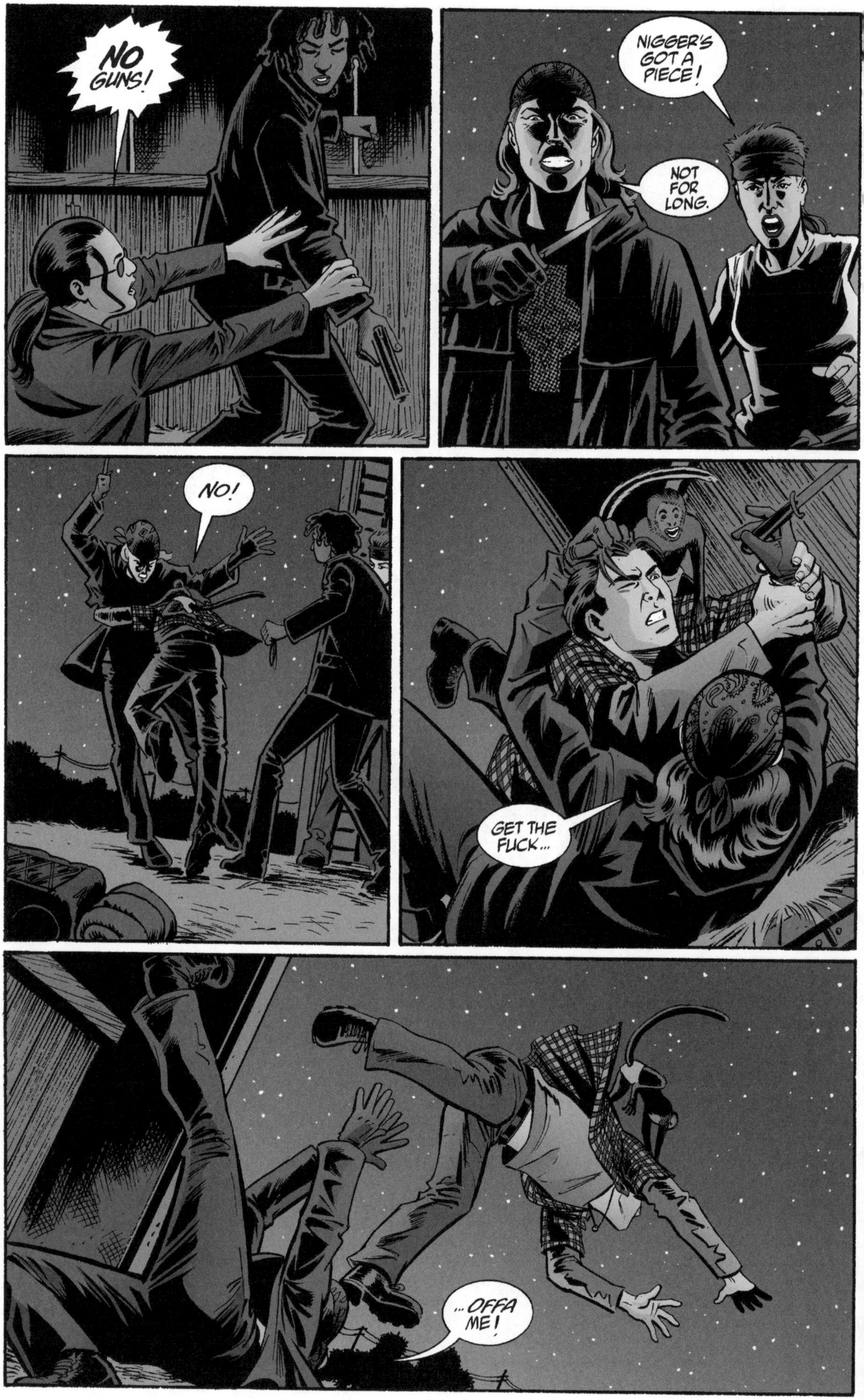
NO GUNS!
NIGGER'S GOT A PIECE!
NOT FOR LONG.
NO!
GET THE FUCK...
...OFFA ME!

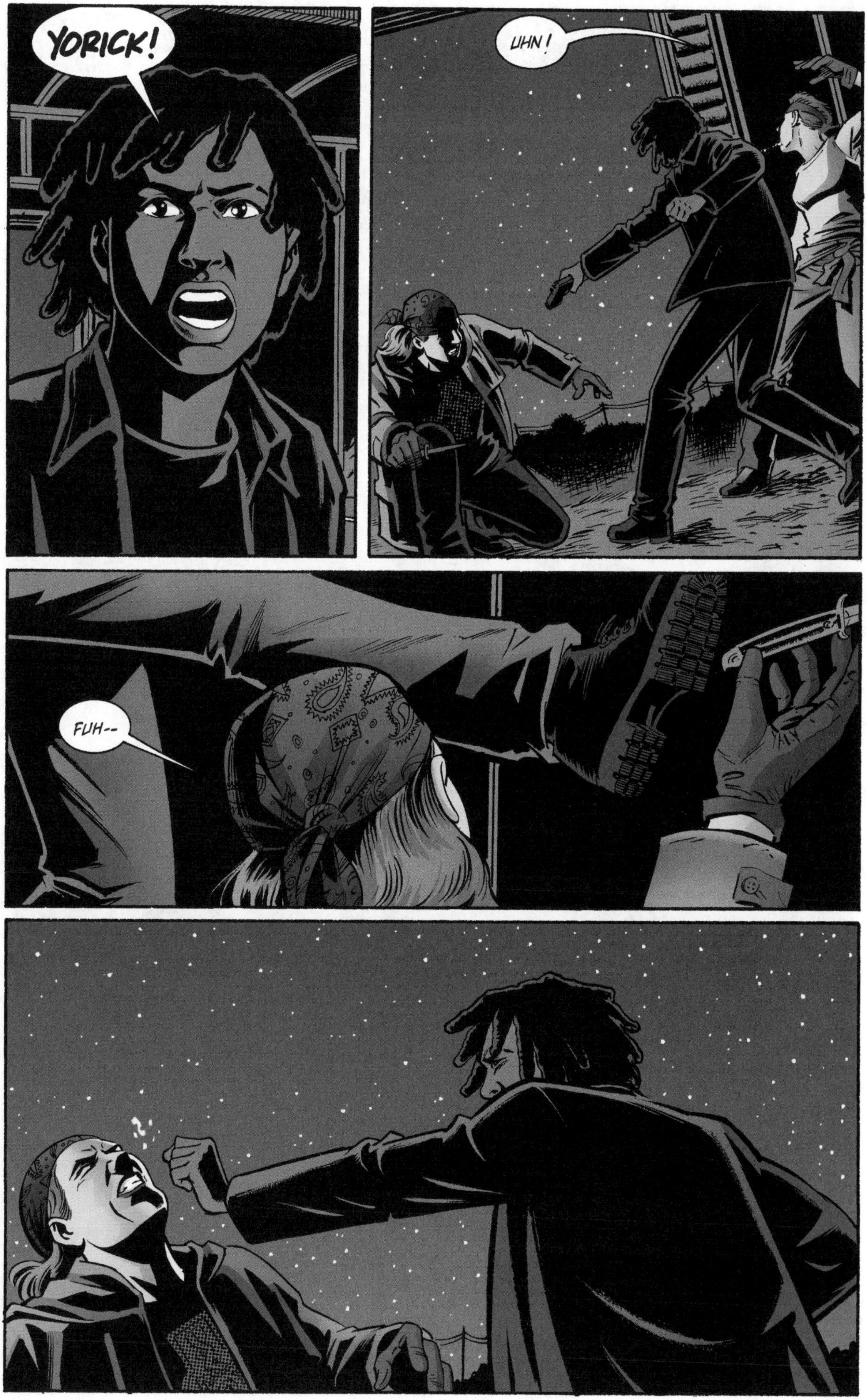
YORICK!
UHN!
FUH--

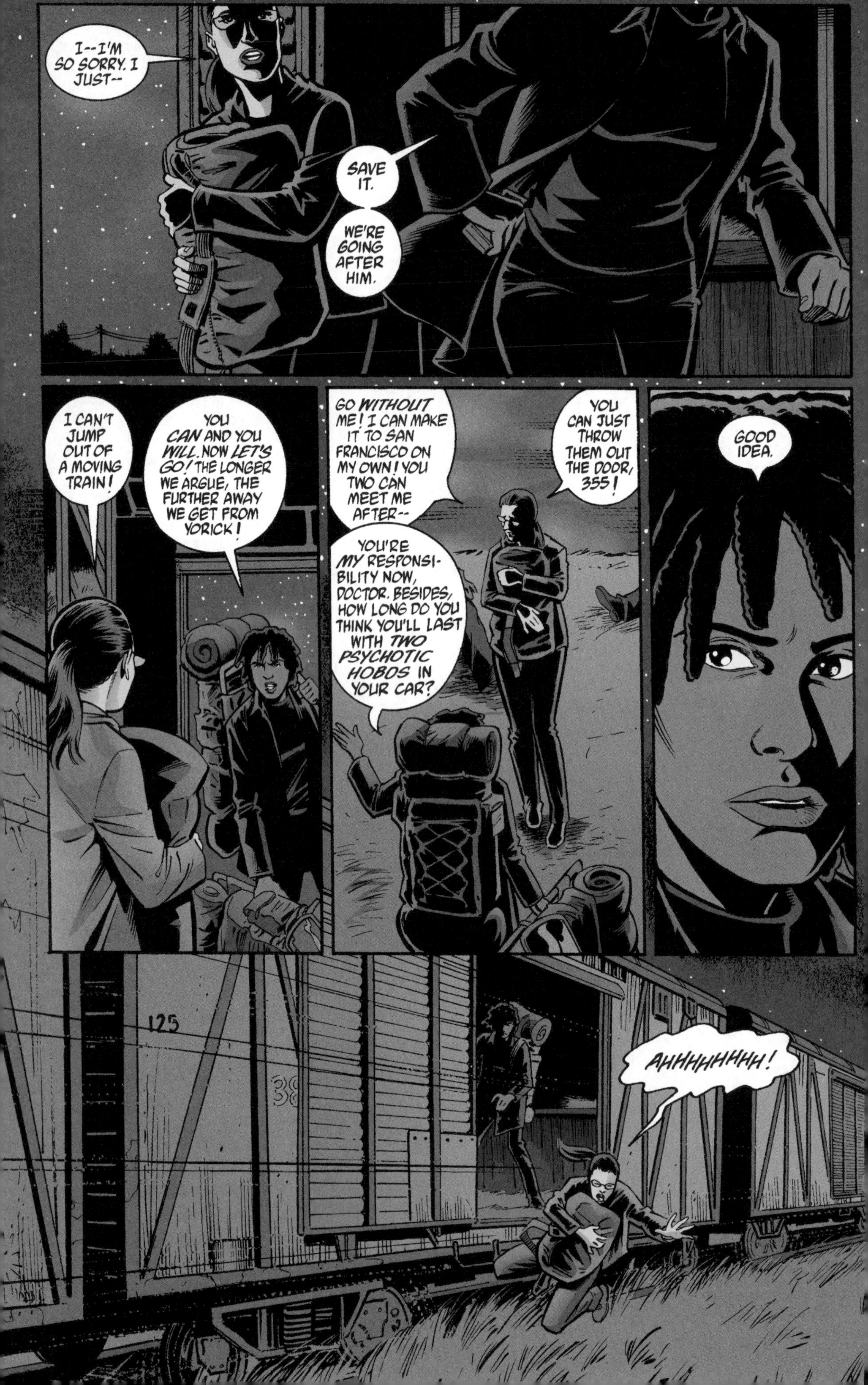
I--I'M SO SORRY. I JUST--
SAVE IT.
WE'RE GOING AFTER HIM.
I CAN'T JUMP OUT OF A MOVING TRAIN!
YOU CAN AND YOU WILL. NOW LET'S GO! THE LONGER WE ARGUE, THE FURTHER AWAY WE GET FROM YORICK!
GO WITHOUT ME! I CAN MAKE IT TO SAN FRANCISCO ON MY OWN! YOU TWO CAN MEET ME AFTER--
YOU CAN JUST THROW THEM OUT THE DOOR, 355!
YOU'RE MY RESPONSIBILITY NOW, DOCTOR. BESIDES, HOW LONG DO YOU THINK YOU'LL LAST WITH TWO PSYCHOTIC HOBOS IN YOUR CAR?
GOOD IDEA.
125
AHHHHHHHH!

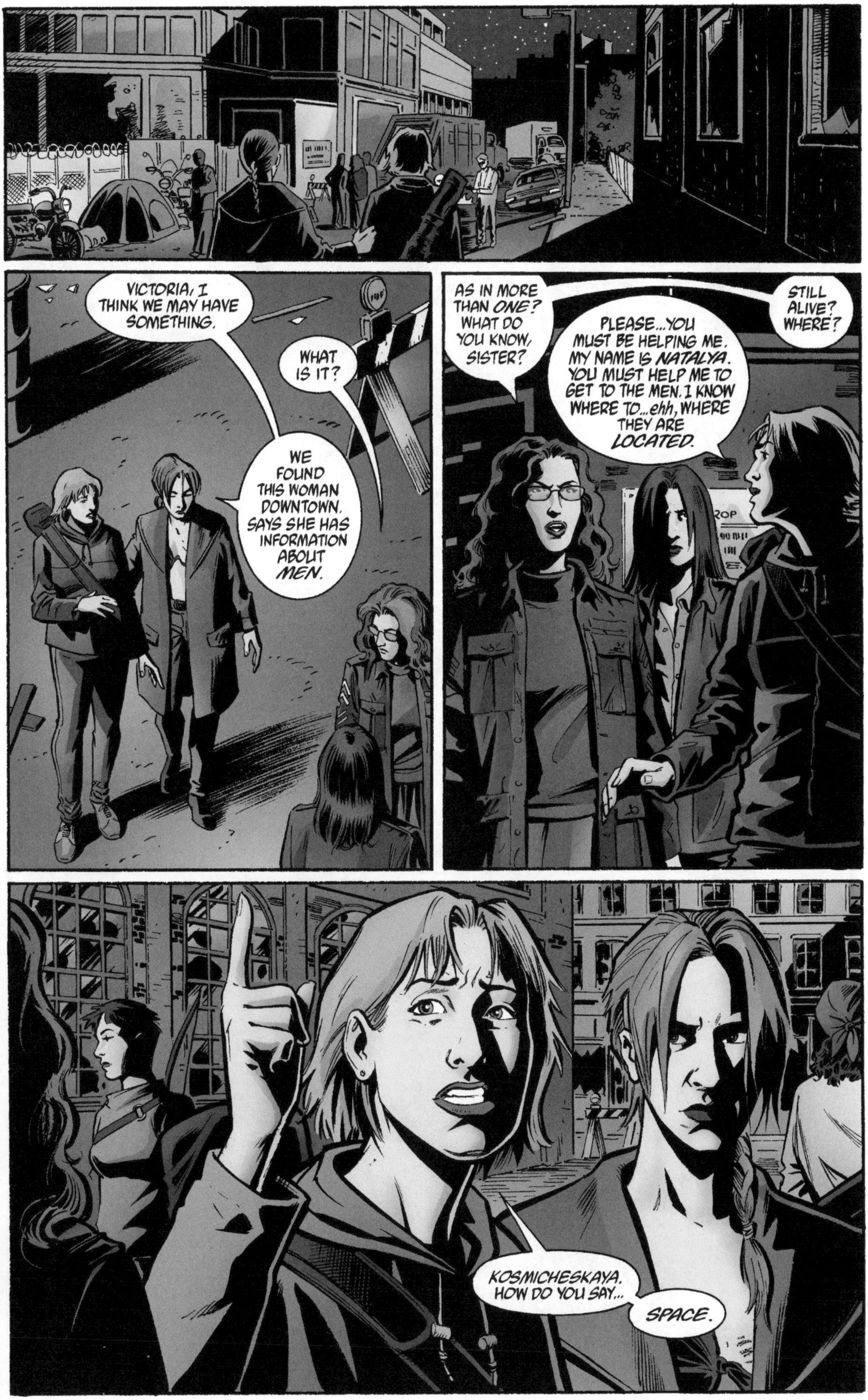
VICTORIA, I THINK WE MAY HAVE SOMETHING.
WHAT IS IT?
WE FOUND THIS WOMAN DOWNTOWN. SAYS SHE HAS INFORMATION ABOUT *MEN*.
STILL ALIVE? WHERE?
PLEASE...YOU MUST BE HELPING ME. MY NAME IS *NATALYA*. YOU MUST HELP ME TO GET TO THE MEN. I KNOW WHERE TO...*ehh*, WHERE THEY ARE *LOCATED*.
AS IN MORE THAN *ONE*? WHAT DO YOU KNOW, SISTER?
KOSMICHESKAYA. HOW DO YOU SAY...
SPACE.

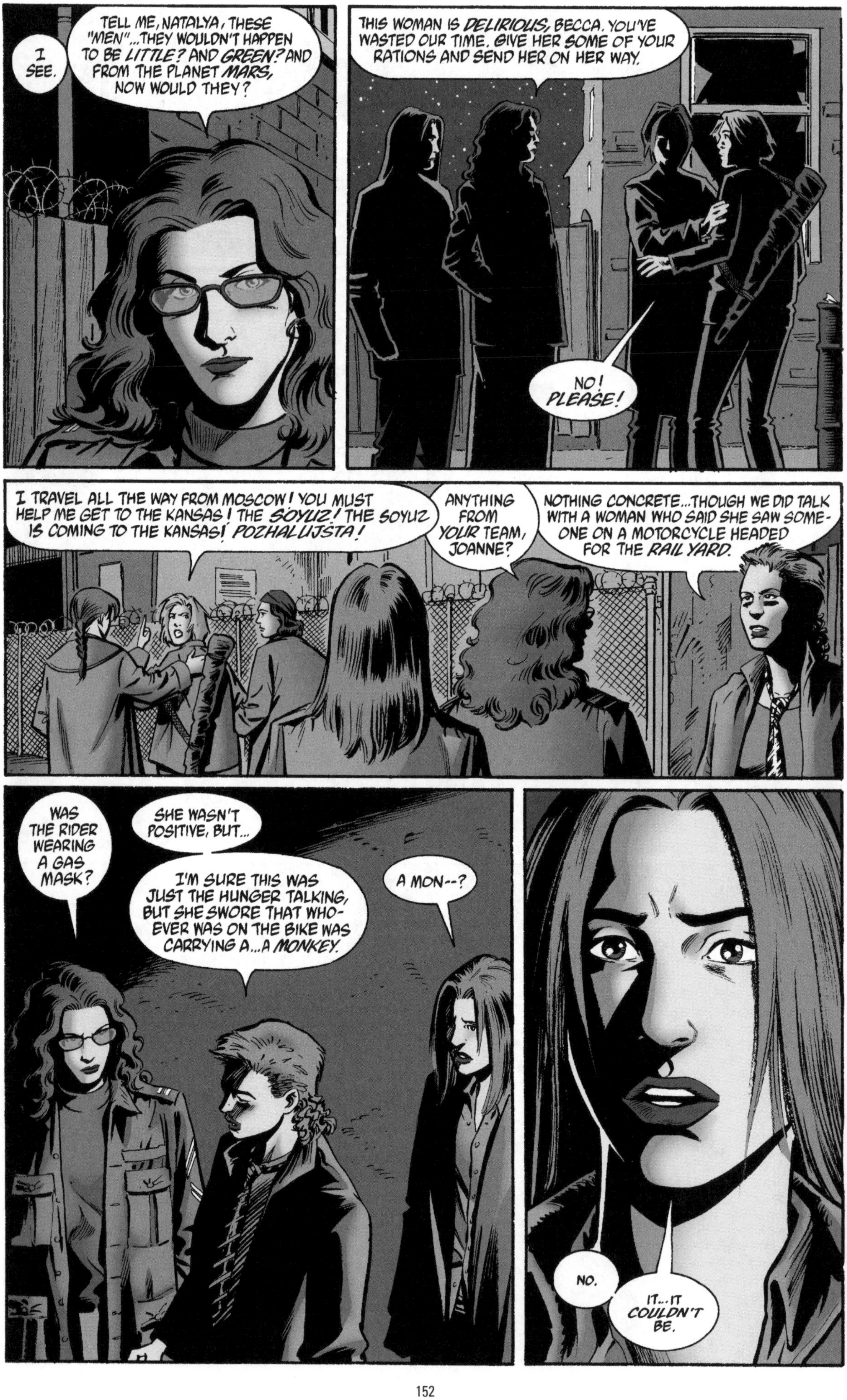

I SEE.
TELL ME, NATALYA, THESE "MEN"...THEY WOULDN'T HAPPEN TO BE LITTLE? AND GREEN? AND FROM THE PLANET MARS, NOW WOULD THEY?
THIS WOMAN IS DELIRIOUS, BECCA. YOU'VE WASTED OUR TIME. GIVE HER SOME OF YOUR RATIONS AND SEND HER ON HER WAY.
NO! PLEASE!
I TRAVEL ALL THE WAY FROM MOSCOW! YOU MUST HELP ME GET TO THE KANSAS! THE SOYUZ! THE SOYUZ IS COMING TO THE KANSAS! POZHALUJSTA!
ANYTHING FROM YOUR TEAM, JOANNE?
NOTHING CONCRETE...THOUGH WE DID TALK WITH A WOMAN WHO SAID SHE SAW SOME-ONE ON A MOTORCYCLE HEADED FOR THE RAIL YARD.
WAS THE RIDER WEARING A GAS MASK?
SHE WASN'T POSITIVE, BUT...
I'M SURE THIS WAS JUST THE HUNGER TALKING, BUT SHE SWORE THAT WHO-EVER WAS ON THE BIKE WAS CARRYING A...A MONKEY.
A MON--?
NO.
IT...IT COULDN'T BE.

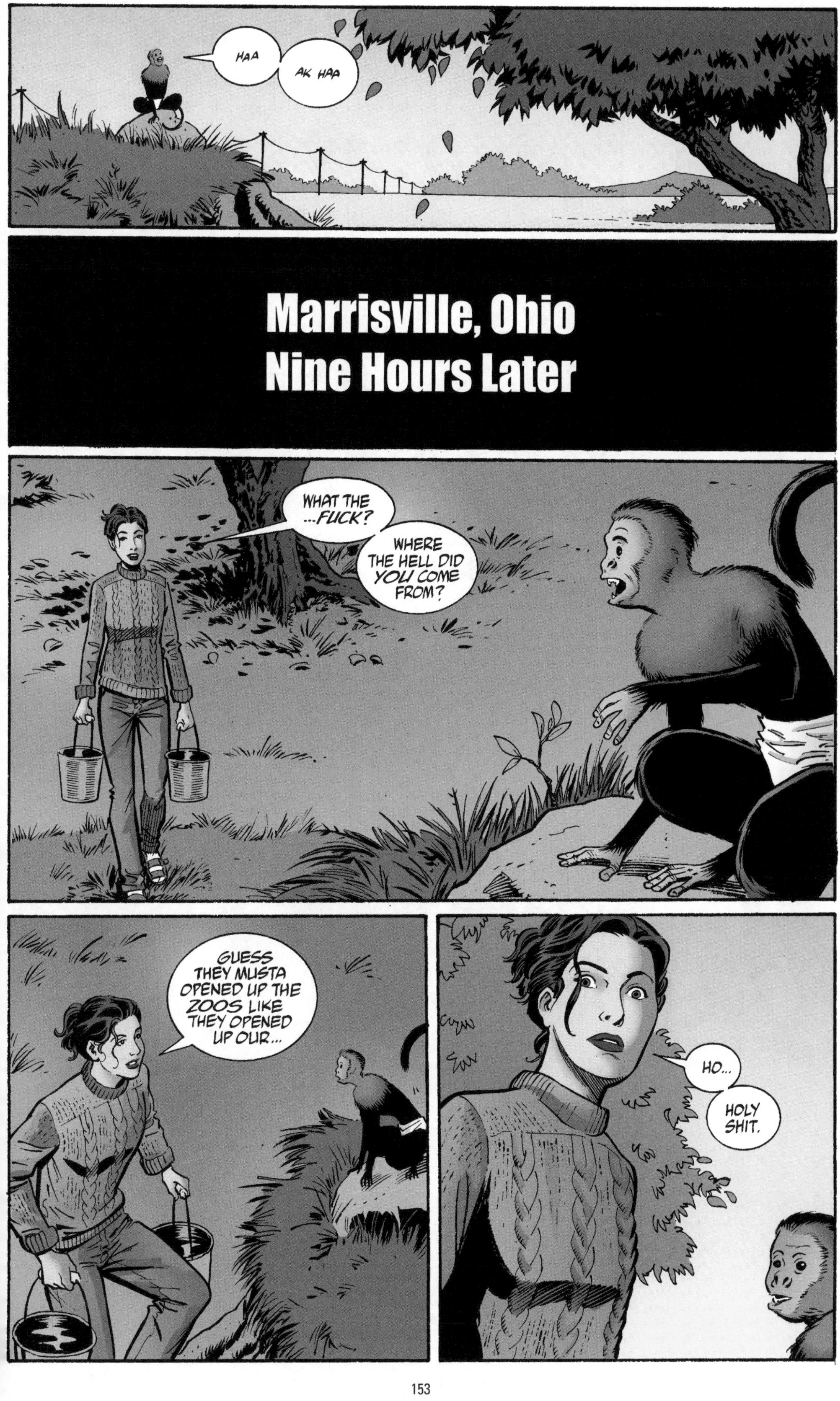
HAA
AK HAA
Marrisville, Ohio
Nine Hours Later
WHAT THE ...FUCK?
WHERE THE HELL DID YOU COME FROM?
GUESS THEY MUSTA OPENED UP THE ZOOS LIKE THEY OPENED UP OUR...
HO...
HOLY SHIT.

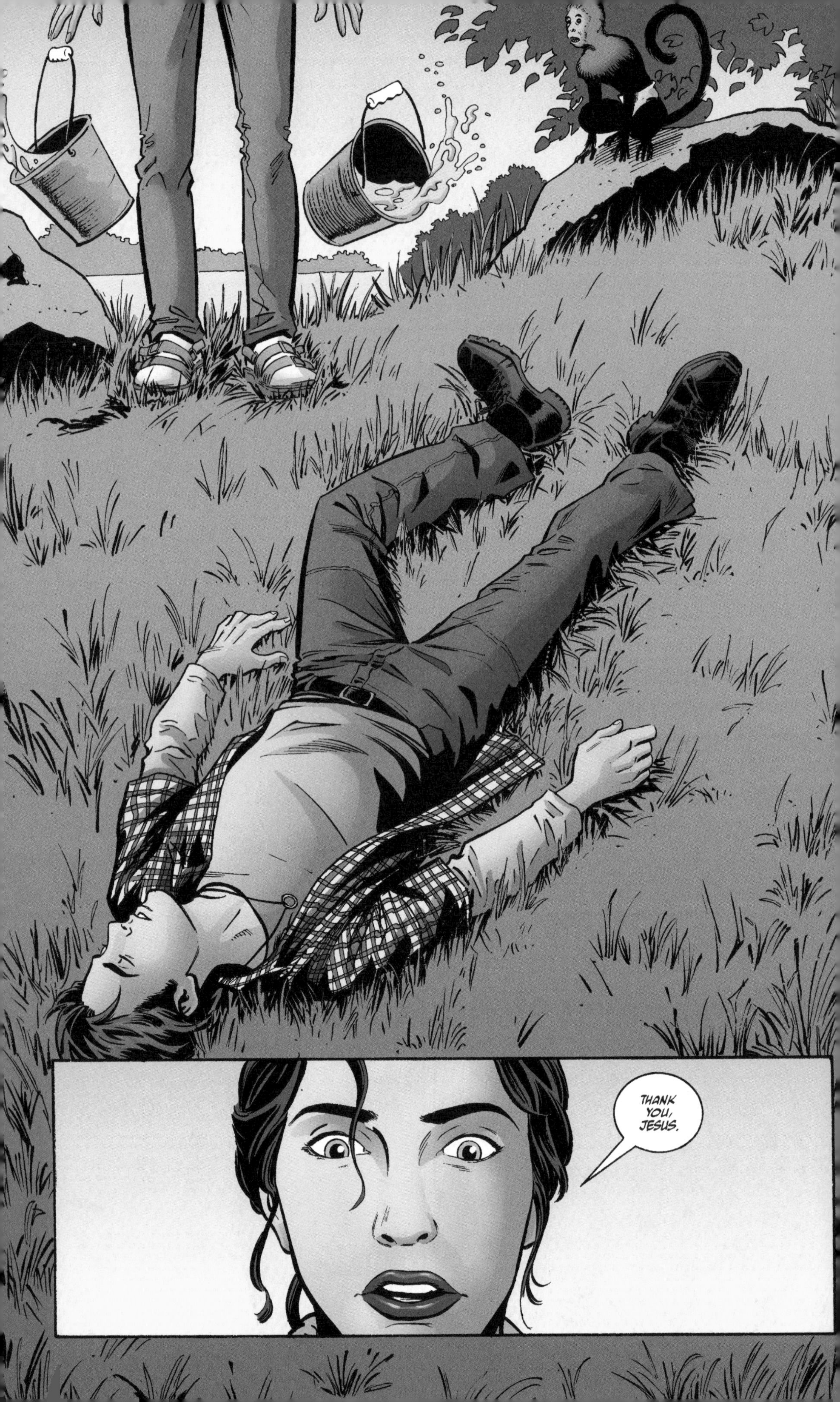
THANK YOU, JESUS.

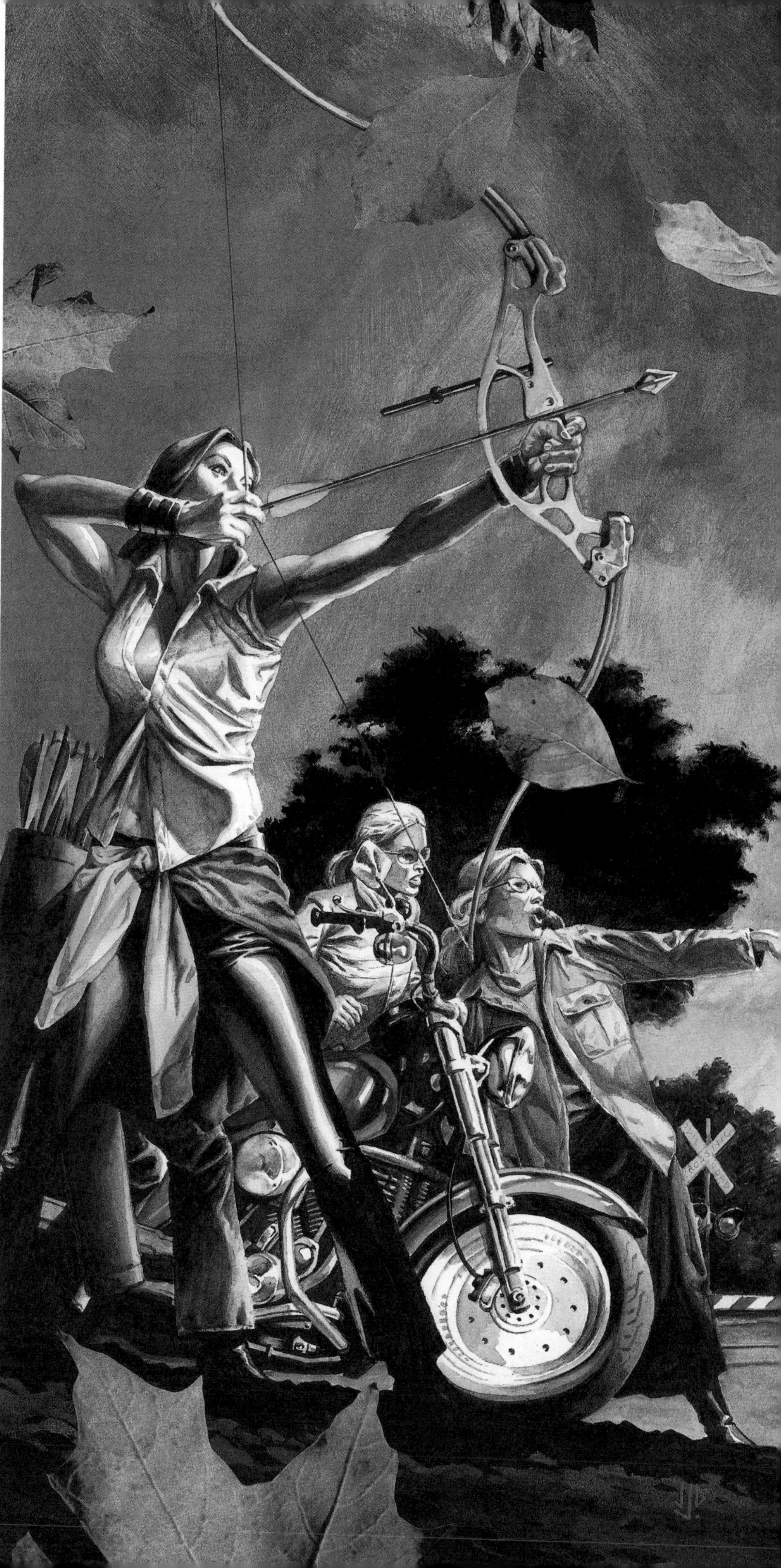

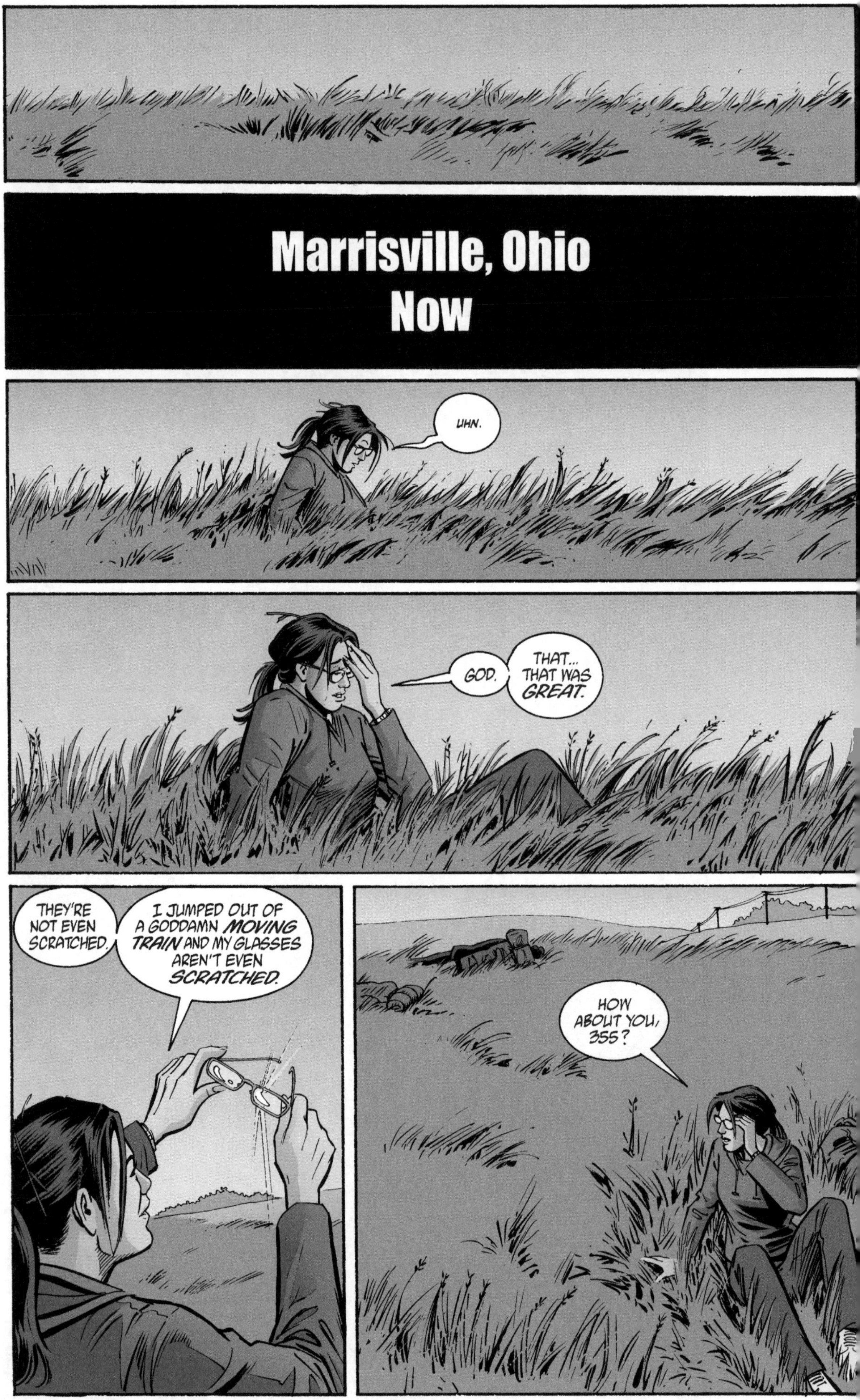
Marrisville, Ohio
Now
UHN.
GOD.
THAT... THAT WAS GREAT.
THEY'RE NOT EVEN SCRATCHED.
I JUMPED OUT OF A GODDAMN MOVING TRAIN AND MY GLASSES AREN'T EVEN SCRATCHED.
HOW ABOUT YOU, 355?

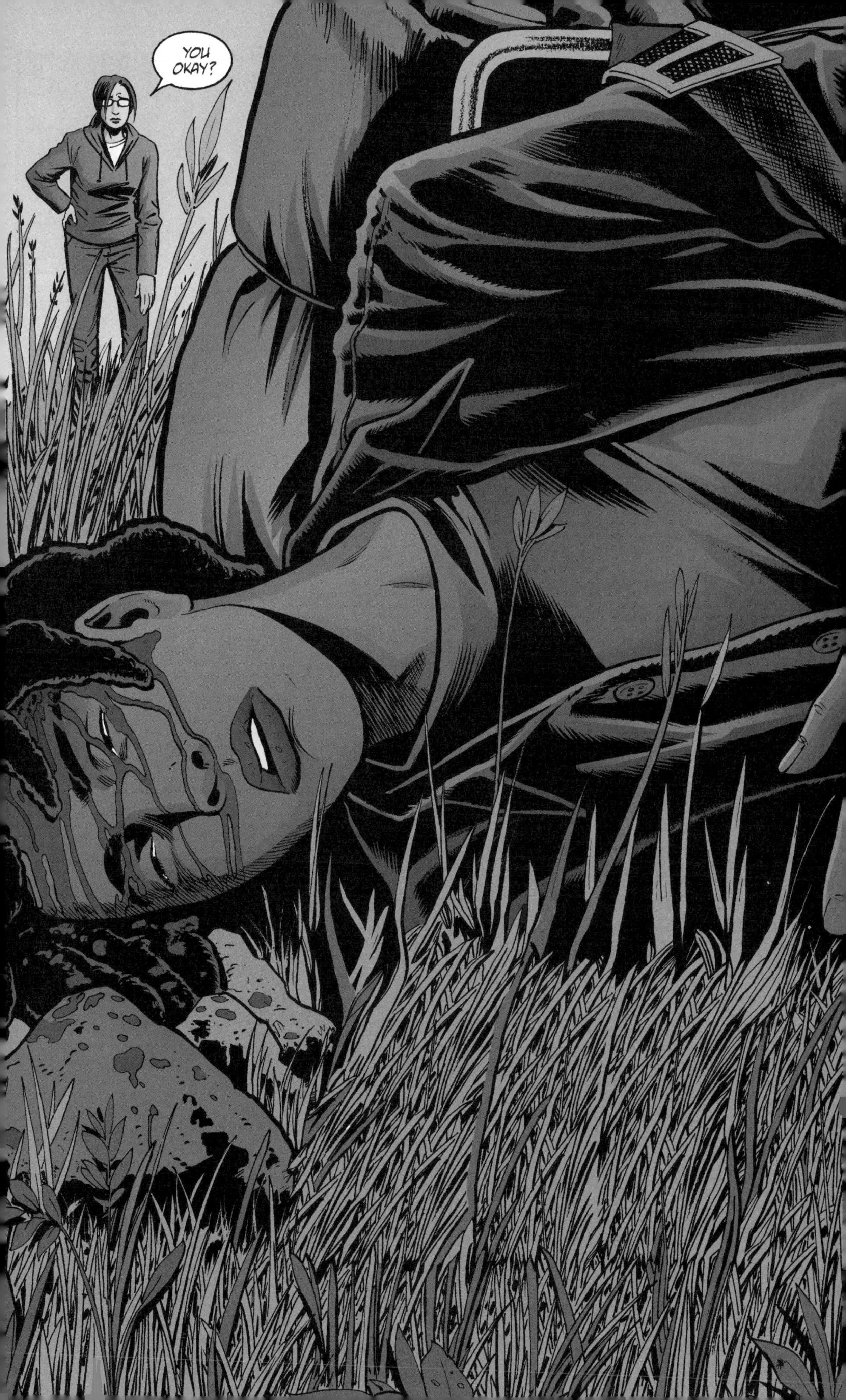
YOU OKAY?

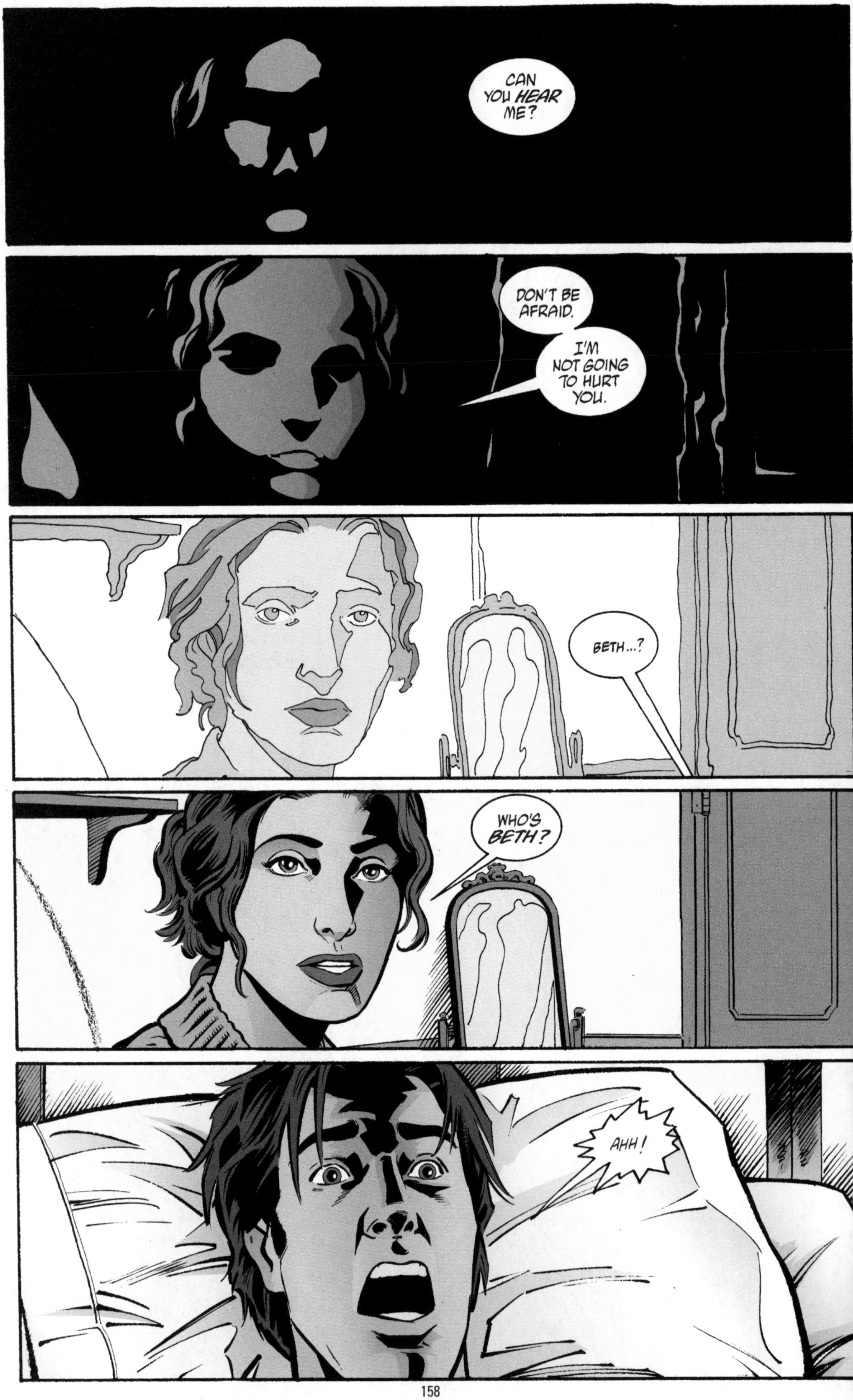
CAN YOU HEAR ME?
DON'T BE AFRAID.
I'M NOT GOING TO HURT YOU.
BETH...?
WHO'S BETH?
AHH!

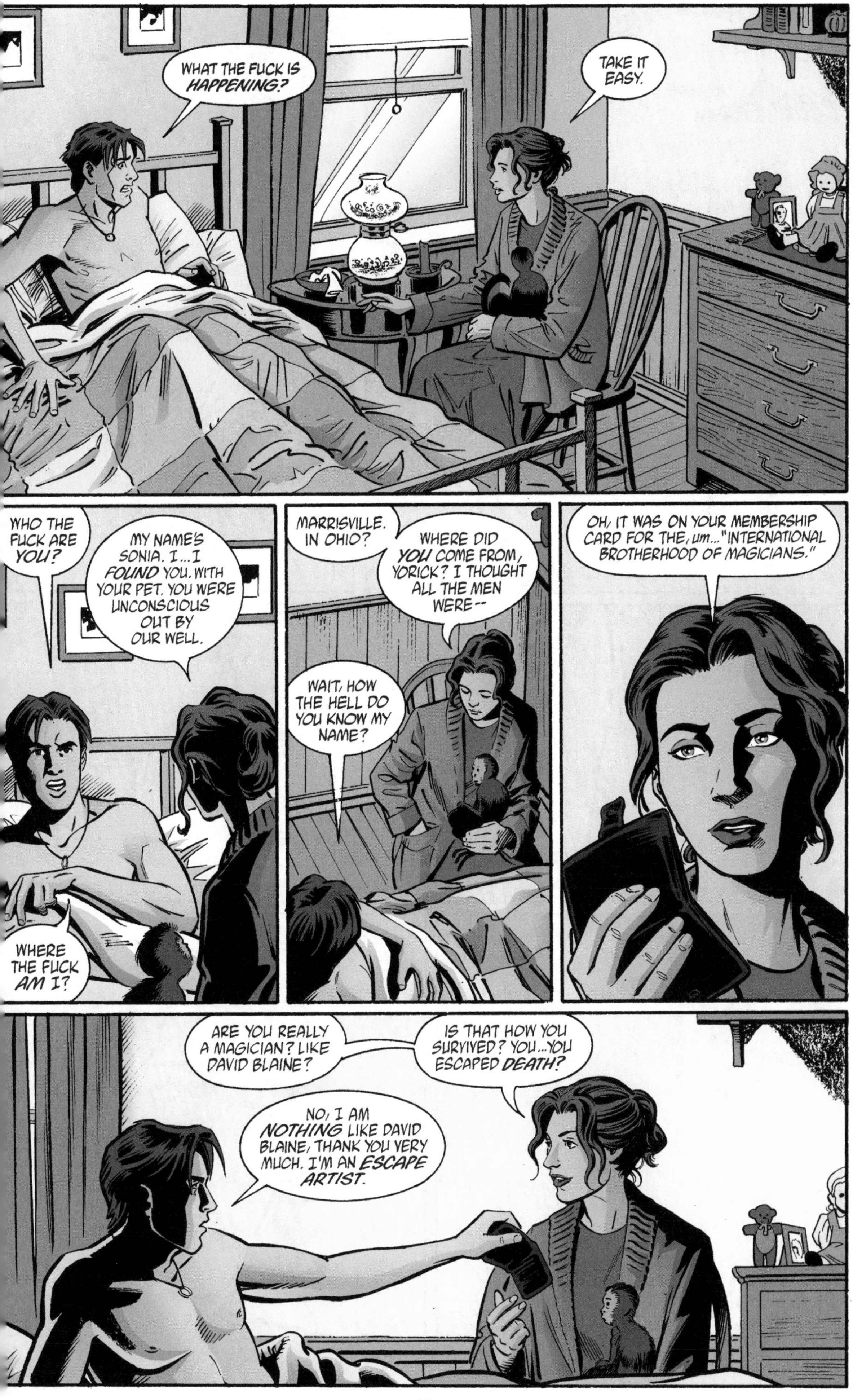
WHAT THE FUCK IS HAPPENING?
TAKE IT EASY.
WHO THE FUCK ARE YOU?
MY NAME'S SONIA. I...I FOUND YOU. WITH YOUR PET. YOU WERE UNCONSCIOUS OUT BY OUR WELL.
WHERE THE FUCK AM I?
MARRISVILLE. IN OHIO?
WHERE DID YOU COME FROM, YORICK? I THOUGHT ALL THE MEN WERE--
WAIT, HOW THE HELL DO YOU KNOW MY NAME?
OH, IT WAS ON YOUR MEMBERSHIP CARD FOR THE, um..."INTERNATIONAL BROTHERHOOD OF MAGICIANS."
ARE YOU REALLY A MAGICIAN? LIKE DAVID BLAINE?
IS THAT HOW YOU SURVIVED? YOU...YOU ESCAPED DEATH?
NO, I AM NOTHING LIKE DAVID BLAINE, THANK YOU VERY MUCH. I'M AN ESCAPE ARTIST.

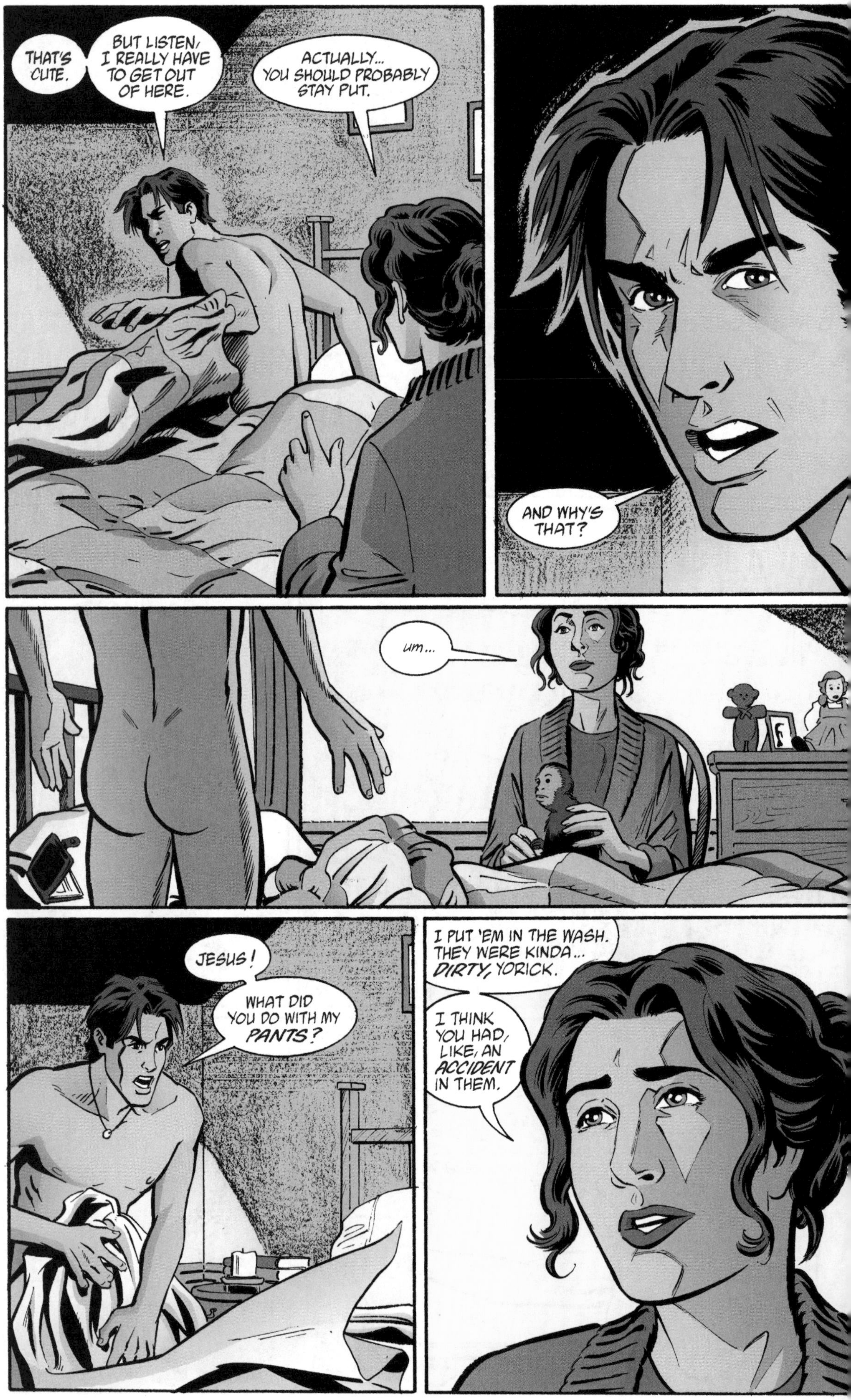
THAT'S CUTE.
BUT LISTEN, I REALLY HAVE TO GET OUT OF HERE.
ACTUALLY... YOU SHOULD PROBABLY STAY PUT.
AND WHY'S THAT?
um...
JESUS!
WHAT DID YOU DO WITH MY *PANTS?*
I PUT 'EM IN THE WASH. THEY WERE KINDA... *DIRTY,* YORICK.
I THINK YOU HAD, LIKE, AN *ACCIDENT* IN THEM.

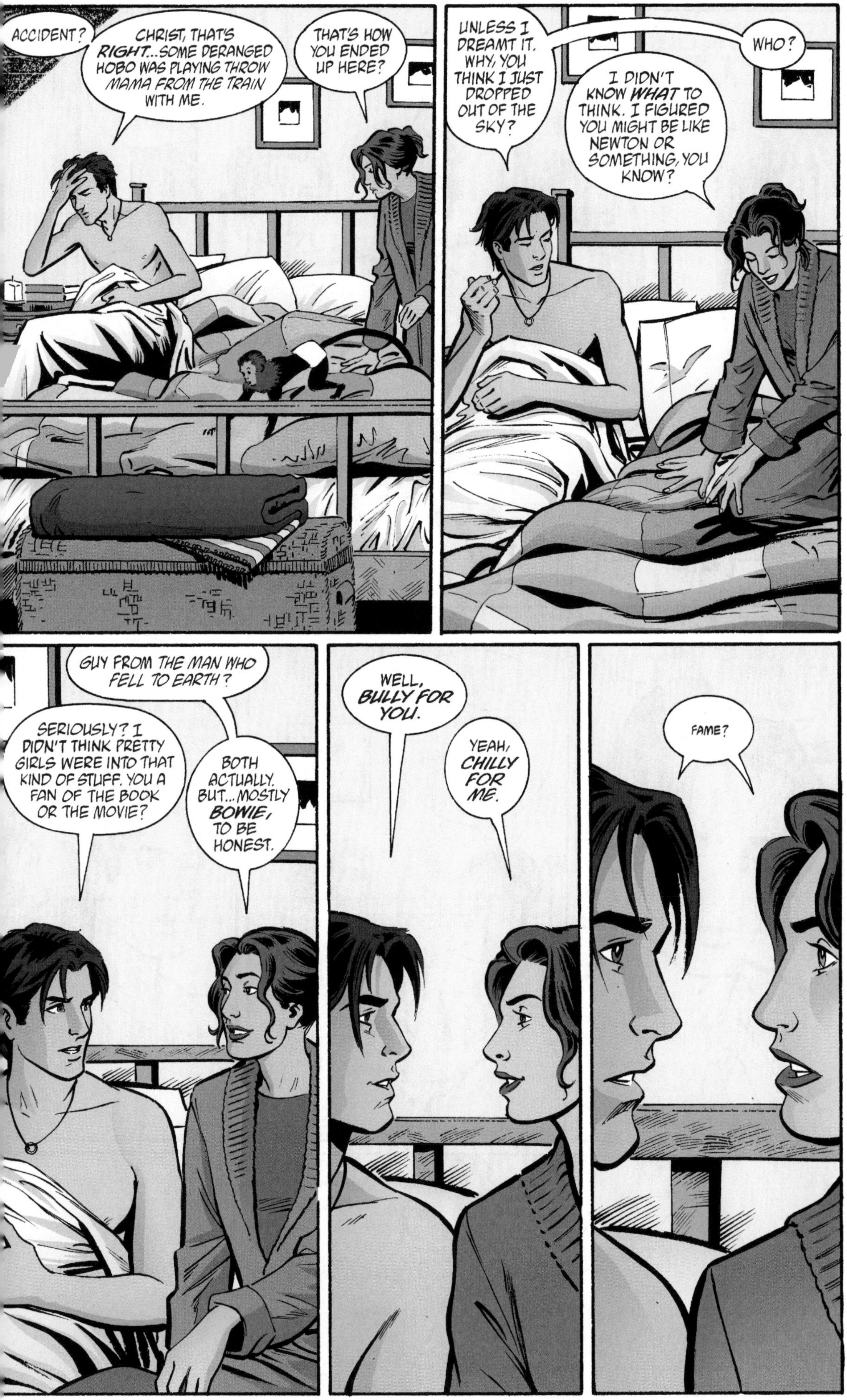
ACCIDENT?
CHRIST, THAT'S RIGHT...SOME DERANGED HOBO WAS PLAYING THROW MAMA FROM THE TRAIN WITH ME.
THAT'S HOW YOU ENDED UP HERE?
UNLESS I DREAMT IT. WHY, YOU THINK I JUST DROPPED OUT OF THE SKY?
I DIDN'T KNOW WHAT TO THINK. I FIGURED YOU MIGHT BE LIKE NEWTON OR SOMETHING, YOU KNOW?
WHO?
GUY FROM THE MAN WHO FELL TO EARTH?
SERIOUSLY? I DIDN'T THINK PRETTY GIRLS WERE INTO THAT KIND OF STUFF. YOU A FAN OF THE BOOK OR THE MOVIE?
BOTH ACTUALLY. BUT...MOSTLY BOWIE, TO BE HONEST.
WELL, BULLY FOR YOU.
YEAH, CHILLY FOR ME.
FAME?

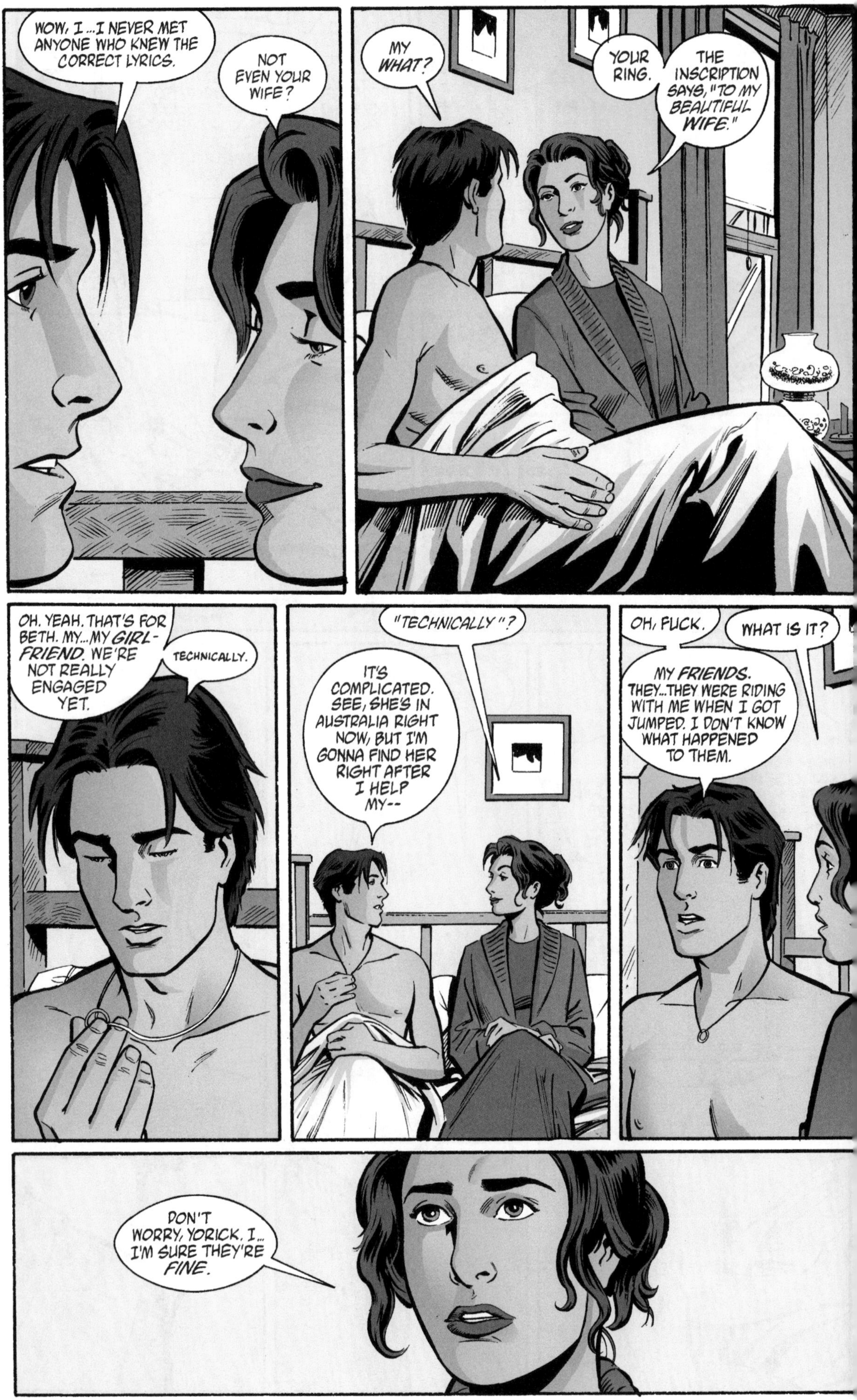
WOW, I ...I NEVER MET ANYONE WHO KNEW THE CORRECT LYRICS.
NOT EVEN YOUR WIFE?
MY WHAT?
YOUR RING.
THE INSCRIPTION SAYS, "TO MY BEAUTIFUL WIFE."
OH. YEAH. THAT'S FOR BETH. MY...MY GIRL-FRIEND. WE'RE NOT REALLY ENGAGED YET.
TECHNICALLY.
"TECHNICALLY"?
IT'S COMPLICATED. SEE, SHE'S IN AUSTRALIA RIGHT NOW, BUT I'M GONNA FIND HER RIGHT AFTER I HELP MY--
OH, FUCK.
WHAT IS IT?
MY FRIENDS. THEY...THEY WERE RIDING WITH ME WHEN I GOT JUMPED. I DON'T KNOW WHAT HAPPENED TO THEM.
DON'T WORRY, YORICK. I... I'M SURE THEY'RE FINE.

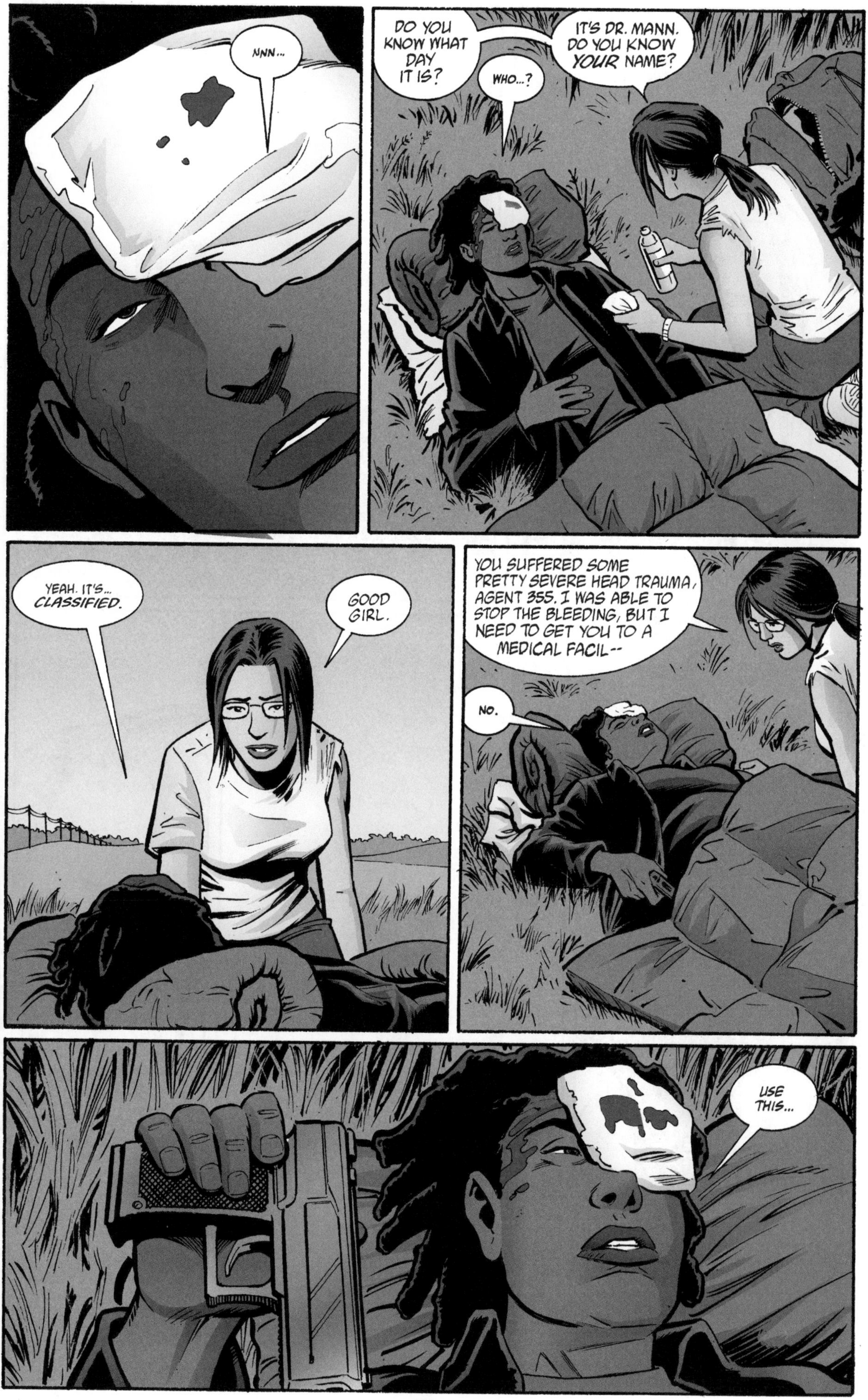
NNN...
DO YOU KNOW WHAT DAY IT IS?
WHO...?
IT'S DR. MANN. DO YOU KNOW YOUR NAME?
YEAH. IT'S... CLASSIFIED.
GOOD GIRL.
YOU SUFFERED SOME PRETTY SEVERE HEAD TRAUMA, AGENT 355. I WAS ABLE TO STOP THE BLEEDING, BUT I NEED TO GET YOU TO A MEDICAL FACIL--
NO.
USE THIS...

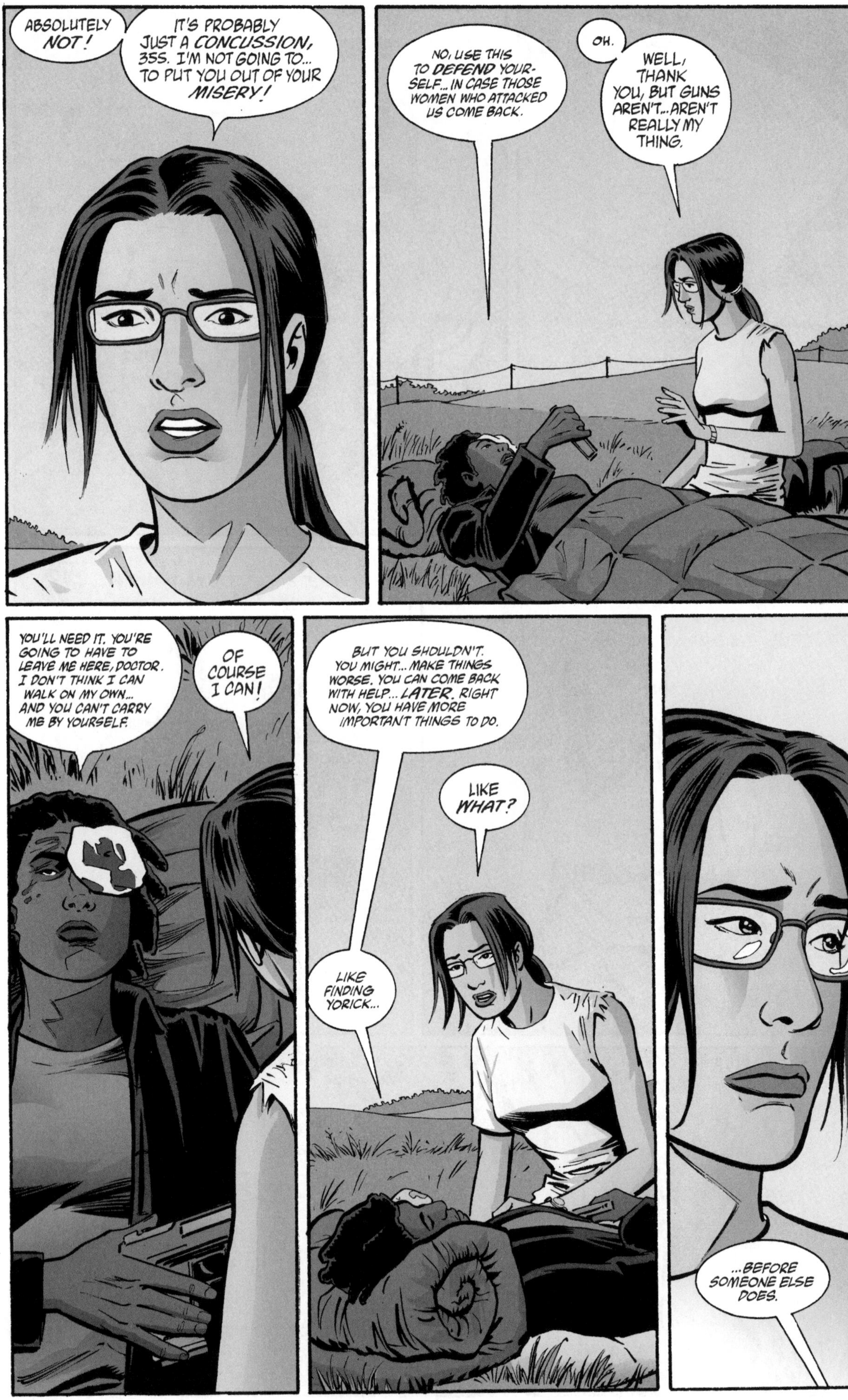
ABSOLUTELY NOT!
IT'S PROBABLY JUST A CONCUSSION, 355. I'M NOT GOING TO... TO PUT YOU OUT OF YOUR MISERY!
NO, USE THIS TO DEFEND YOURSELF... IN CASE THOSE WOMEN WHO ATTACKED US COME BACK.
OH.
WELL, THANK YOU, BUT GUNS AREN'T... AREN'T REALLY MY THING.
YOU'LL NEED IT. YOU'RE GOING TO HAVE TO LEAVE ME HERE, DOCTOR. I DON'T THINK I CAN WALK ON MY OWN... AND YOU CAN'T CARRY ME BY YOURSELF.
OF COURSE I CAN!
BUT YOU SHOULDN'T. YOU MIGHT... MAKE THINGS WORSE. YOU CAN COME BACK WITH HELP... LATER. RIGHT NOW, YOU HAVE MORE IMPORTANT THINGS TO DO.
LIKE WHAT?
LIKE FINDING YORICK...
...BEFORE SOMEONE ELSE DOES.

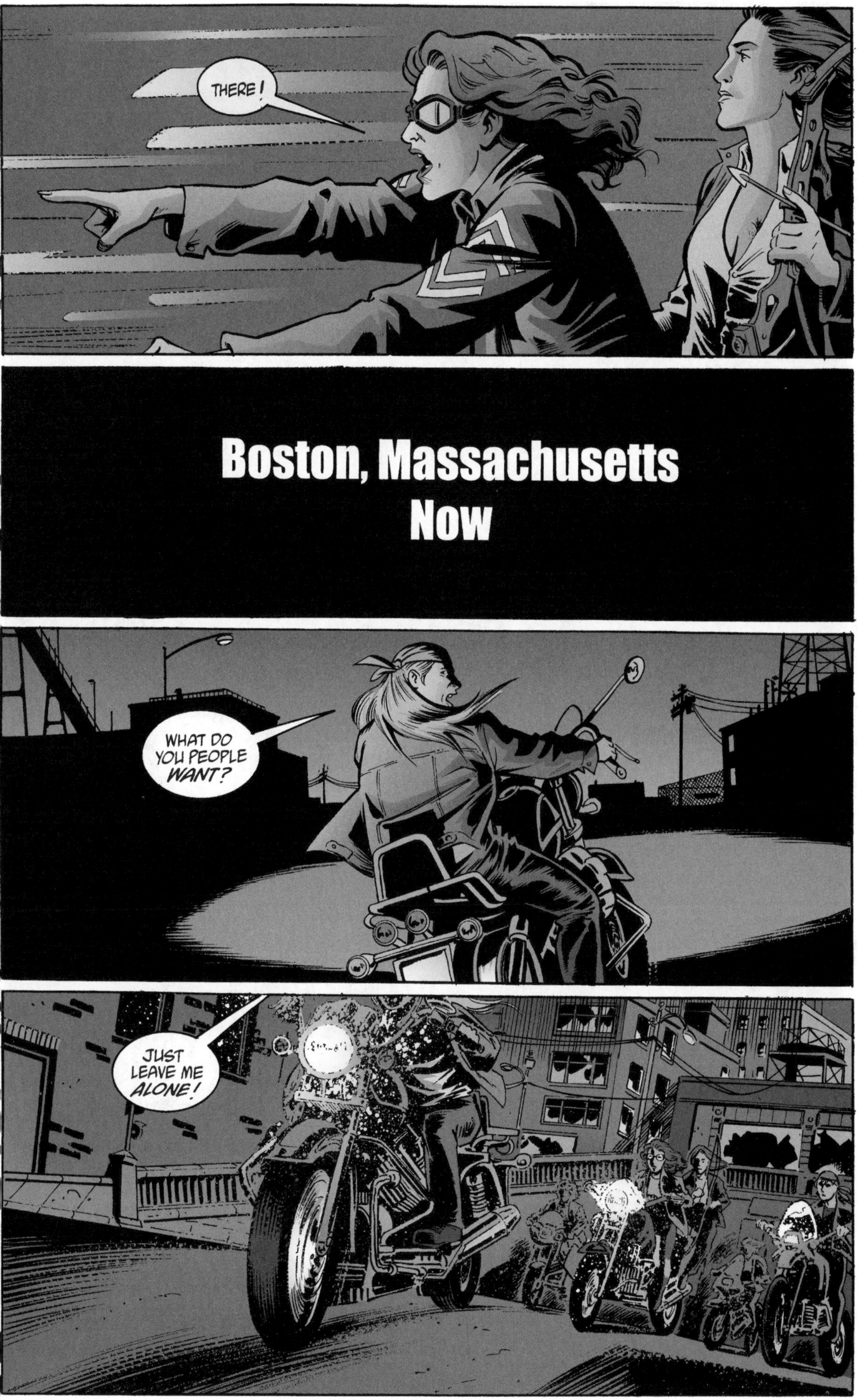
THERE!
Boston, Massachusetts
Now
WHAT DO YOU PEOPLE WANT?
JUST LEAVE ME ALONE!

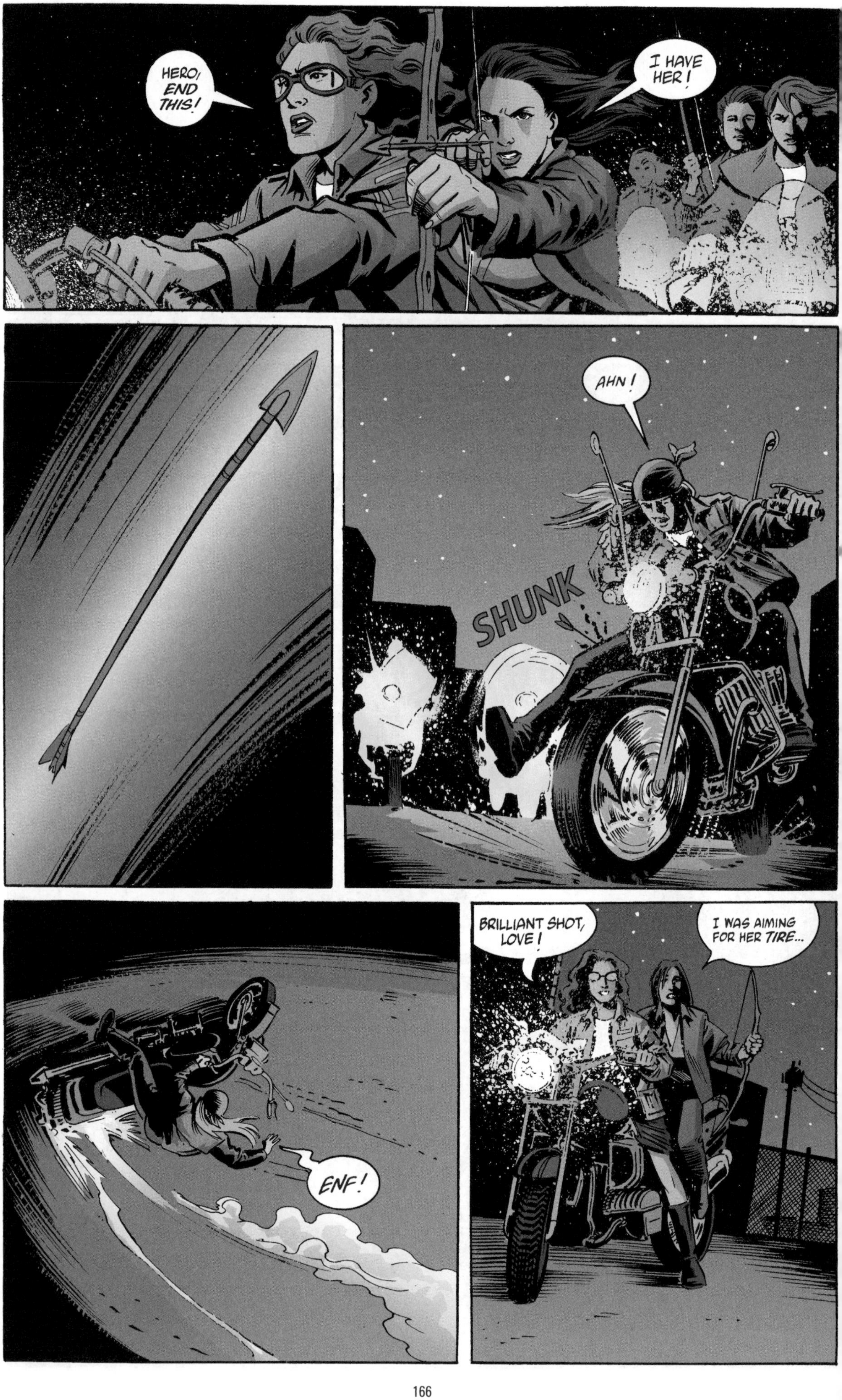
HERO, END THIS!
I HAVE HER!
AHN!
SHUNK
ENF!
BRILLIANT SHOT, LOVE!
I WAS AIMING FOR HER TIRE...

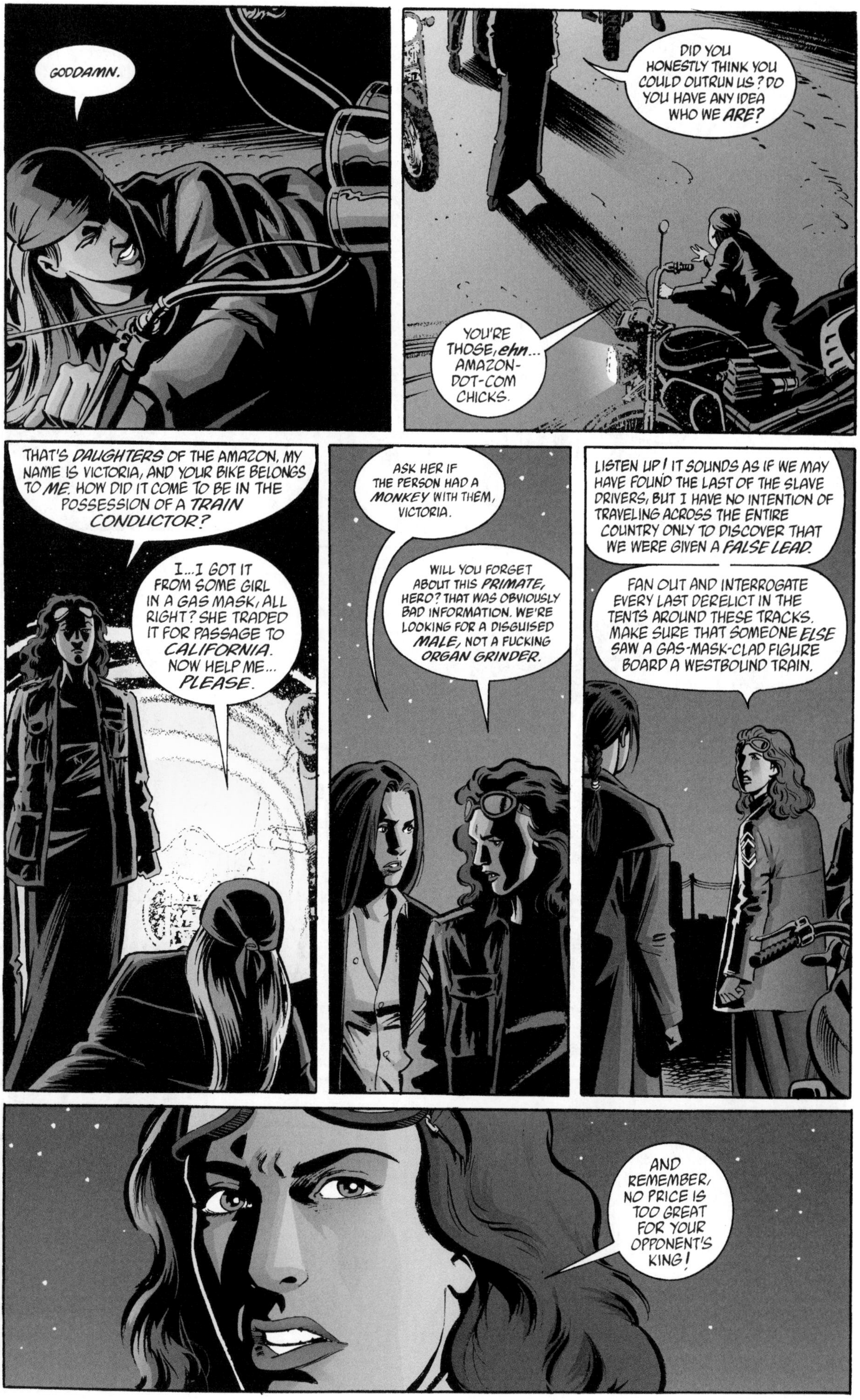
GODDAMN.
DID YOU HONESTLY THINK YOU COULD OUTRUN US? DO YOU HAVE ANY IDEA WHO WE ARE?
YOU'RE THOSE, ehn... AMAZON-DOT-COM CHICKS.
THAT'S DAUGHTERS OF THE AMAZON. MY NAME IS VICTORIA, AND YOUR BIKE BELONGS TO ME. HOW DID IT COME TO BE IN THE POSSESSION OF A TRAIN CONDUCTOR?
I...I GOT IT FROM SOME GIRL IN A GAS MASK, ALL RIGHT? SHE TRADED IT FOR PASSAGE TO CALIFORNIA. NOW HELP ME... PLEASE.
ASK HER IF THE PERSON HAD A MONKEY WITH THEM, VICTORIA.
WILL YOU FORGET ABOUT THIS PRIMATE, HERO? THAT WAS OBVIOUSLY BAD INFORMATION. WE'RE LOOKING FOR A DISGUISED MALE, NOT A FUCKING ORGAN GRINDER.
LISTEN UP! IT SOUNDS AS IF WE MAY HAVE FOUND THE LAST OF THE SLAVE DRIVERS, BUT I HAVE NO INTENTION OF TRAVELING ACROSS THE ENTIRE COUNTRY ONLY TO DISCOVER THAT WE WERE GIVEN A FALSE LEAD.
FAN OUT AND INTERROGATE EVERY LAST DERELICT IN THE TENTS AROUND THESE TRACKS. MAKE SURE THAT SOMEONE ELSE SAW A GAS-MASK-CLAD FIGURE BOARD A WESTBOUND TRAIN.
AND REMEMBER, NO PRICE IS TOO GREAT FOR YOUR OPPONENT'S KING!

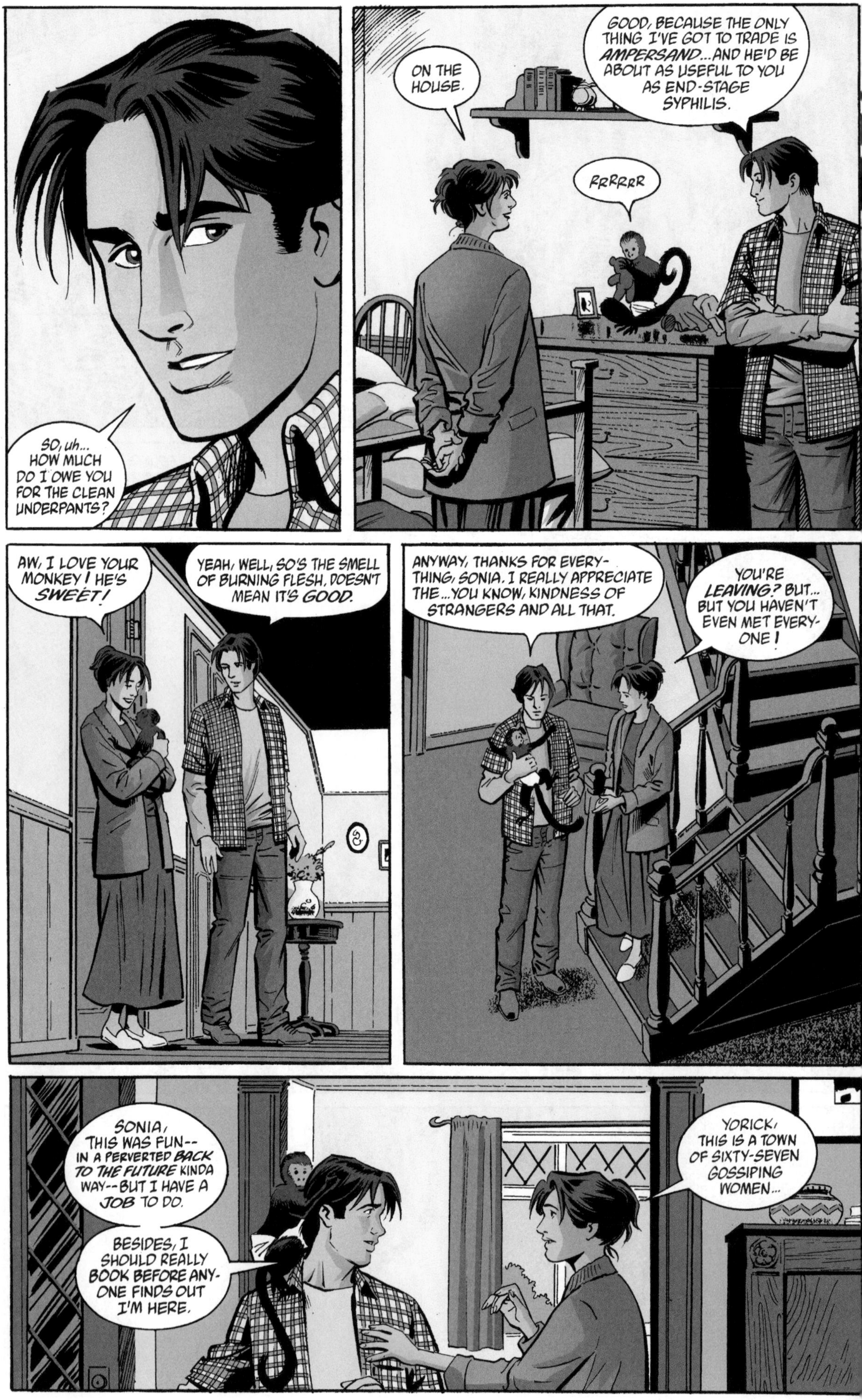
SO, uh... HOW MUCH DO I OWE YOU FOR THE CLEAN UNDERPANTS?
ON THE HOUSE.
GOOD, BECAUSE THE ONLY THING I'VE GOT TO TRADE IS AMPERSAND...AND HE'D BE ABOUT AS USEFUL TO YOU AS END-STAGE SYPHILIS.
RRRRRR
AW, I LOVE YOUR MONKEY! HE'S SWEET!
YEAH, WELL, SO'S THE SMELL OF BURNING FLESH. DOESN'T MEAN IT'S GOOD.
ANYWAY, THANKS FOR EVERYTHING, SONIA. I REALLY APPRECIATE THE...YOU KNOW, KINDNESS OF STRANGERS AND ALL THAT.
YOU'RE LEAVING? BUT... BUT YOU HAVEN'T EVEN MET EVERYONE!
SONIA, THIS WAS FUN-- IN A PERVERTED BACK TO THE FUTURE KINDA WAY--BUT I HAVE A JOB TO DO.
BESIDES, I SHOULD REALLY BOOK BEFORE ANYONE FINDS OUT I'M HERE.
YORICK, THIS IS A TOWN OF SIXTY-SEVEN GOSSIPING WOMEN...

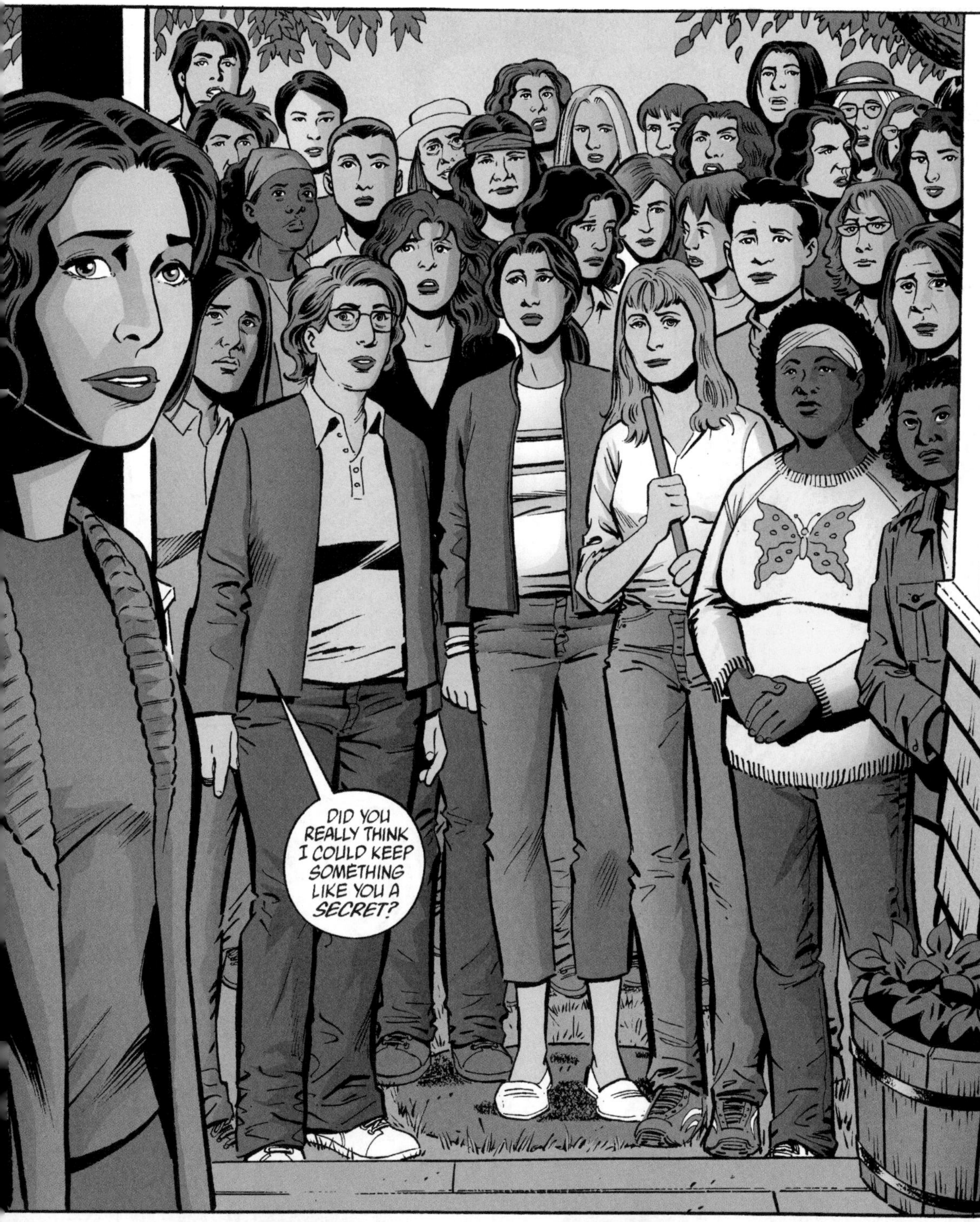
DID YOU REALLY THINK I COULD KEEP SOMETHING LIKE YOU A SECRET?

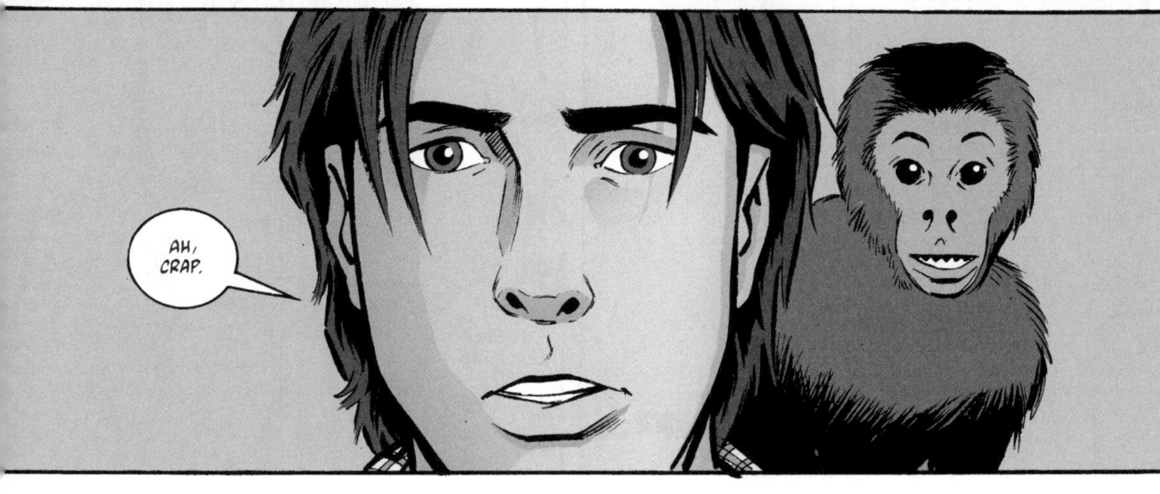
AH, CRAP.

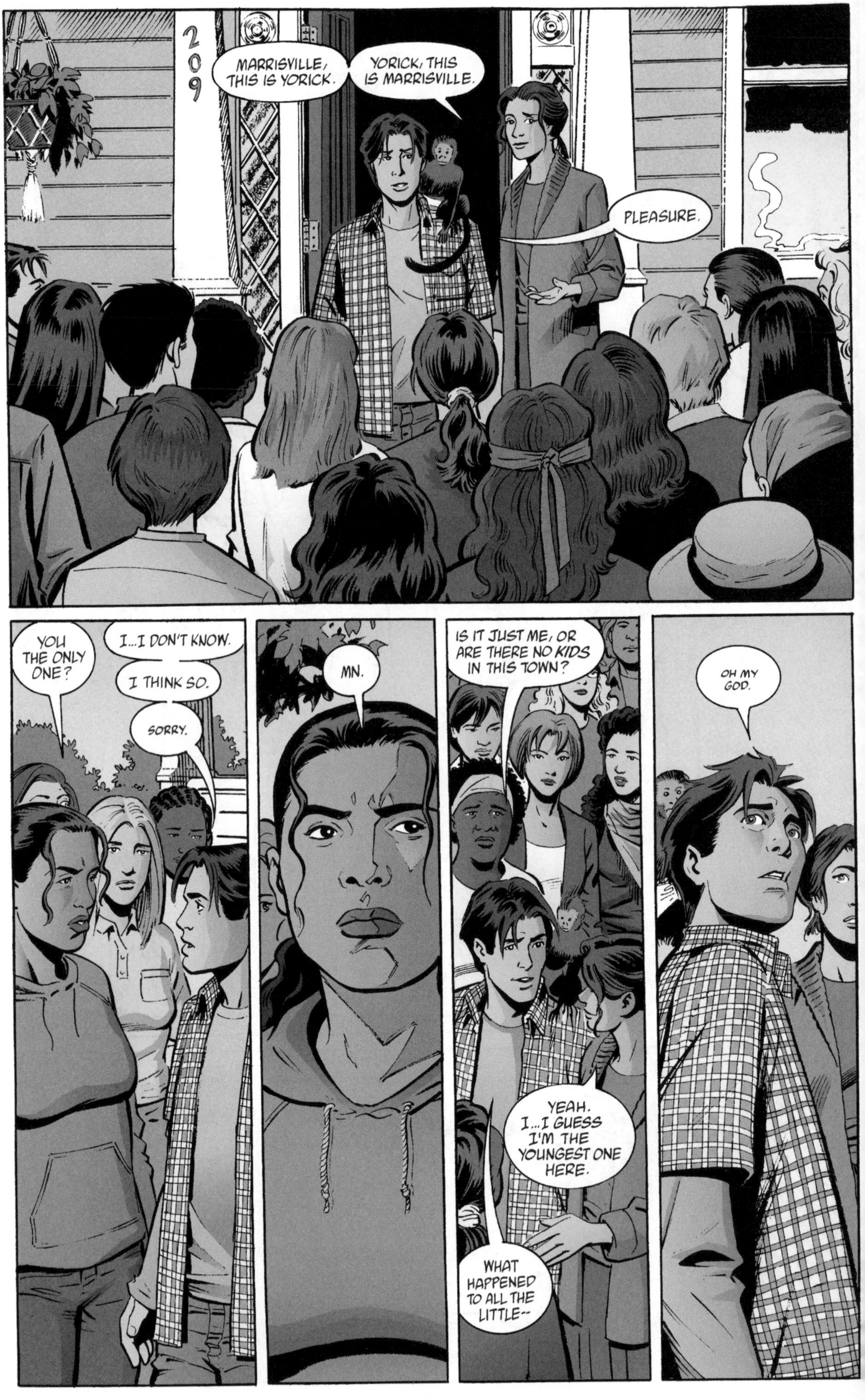

209
MARRISVILLE, THIS IS YORICK.
YORICK, THIS IS MARRISVILLE.
PLEASURE.
YOU THE ONLY ONE?
I...I DON'T KNOW.
I THINK SO.
SORRY.
MN.
IS IT JUST ME, OR ARE THERE NO KIDS IN THIS TOWN?
YEAH. I...I GUESS I'M THE YOUNGEST ONE HERE.
WHAT HAPPENED TO ALL THE LITTLE--
OH MY GOD.

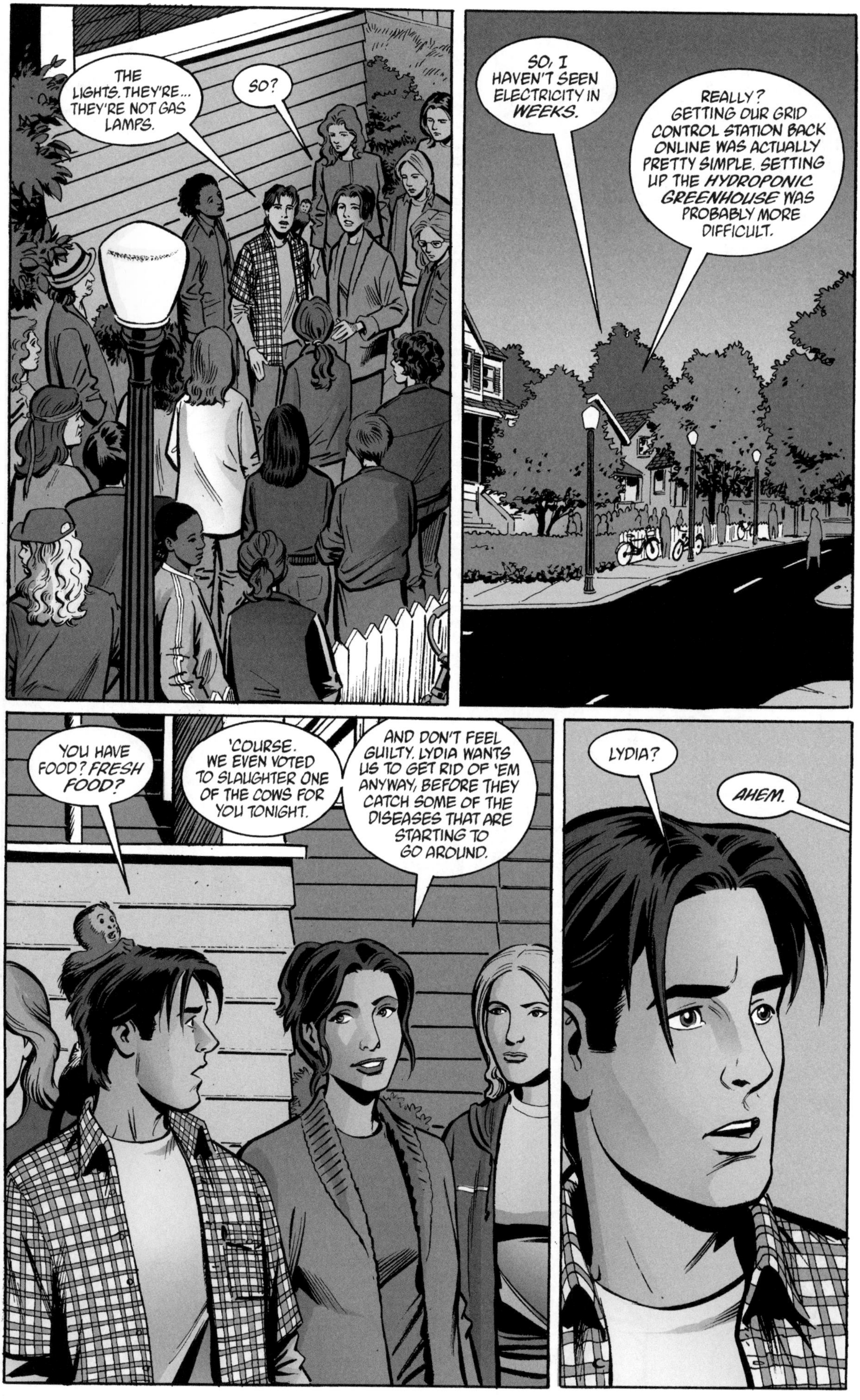
THE LIGHTS. THEY'RE... THEY'RE NOT GAS LAMPS.
SO?
SO, I HAVEN'T SEEN ELECTRICITY IN *WEEKS.*
REALLY? GETTING OUR GRID CONTROL STATION BACK ONLINE WAS ACTUALLY PRETTY SIMPLE. SETTING UP THE *HYDROPONIC GREENHOUSE* WAS PROBABLY MORE DIFFICULT.
YOU HAVE FOOD? *FRESH FOOD?*
'COURSE. WE EVEN VOTED TO SLAUGHTER ONE OF THE COWS FOR YOU TONIGHT.
AND DON'T FEEL GUILTY. LYDIA WANTS US TO GET RID OF 'EM ANYWAY, BEFORE THEY CATCH SOME OF THE DISEASES THAT ARE STARTING TO GO AROUND.
LYDIA?
AHEM.

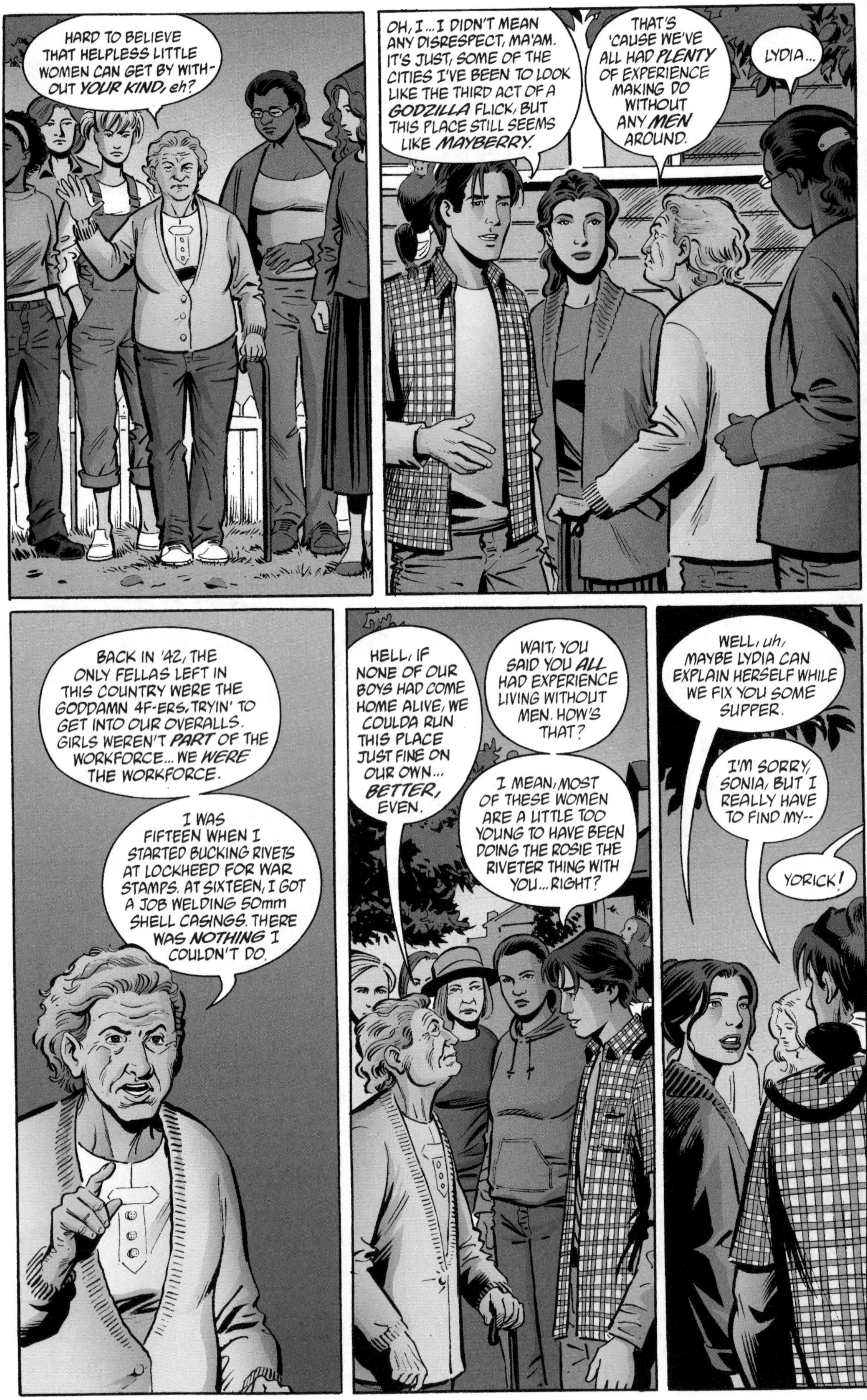

HARD TO BELIEVE THAT HELPLESS LITTLE WOMEN CAN GET BY WITH-OUT YOUR KIND, eh?
OH, I... I DIDN'T MEAN ANY DISRESPECT, MA'AM. IT'S JUST, SOME OF THE CITIES I'VE BEEN TO LOOK LIKE THE THIRD ACT OF A GODZILLA FLICK, BUT THIS PLACE STILL SEEMS LIKE MAYBERRY.
THAT'S 'CAUSE WE'VE ALL HAD PLENTY OF EXPERIENCE MAKING DO WITHOUT ANY MEN AROUND.
LYDIA...
BACK IN '42, THE ONLY FELLAS LEFT IN THIS COUNTRY WERE THE GODDAMN 4F-ERS, TRYIN' TO GET INTO OUR OVERALLS. GIRLS WEREN'T PART OF THE WORKFORCE... WE WERE THE WORKFORCE.
I WAS FIFTEEN WHEN I STARTED BUCKING RIVETS AT LOCKHEED FOR WAR STAMPS. AT SIXTEEN, I GOT A JOB WELDING 50mm SHELL CASINGS. THERE WAS NOTHING I COULDN'T DO.
HELL, IF NONE OF OUR BOYS HAD COME HOME ALIVE, WE COULDA RUN THIS PLACE JUST FINE ON OUR OWN... BETTER, EVEN.
WAIT, YOU SAID YOU ALL HAD EXPERIENCE LIVING WITHOUT MEN. HOW'S THAT?
I MEAN, MOST OF THESE WOMEN ARE A LITTLE TOO YOUNG TO HAVE BEEN DOING THE ROSIE THE RIVETER THING WITH YOU... RIGHT?
WELL, uh, MAYBE LYDIA CAN EXPLAIN HERSELF WHILE WE FIX YOU SOME SUPPER.
I'M SORRY, SONIA, BUT I REALLY HAVE TO FIND MY--
YORICK!

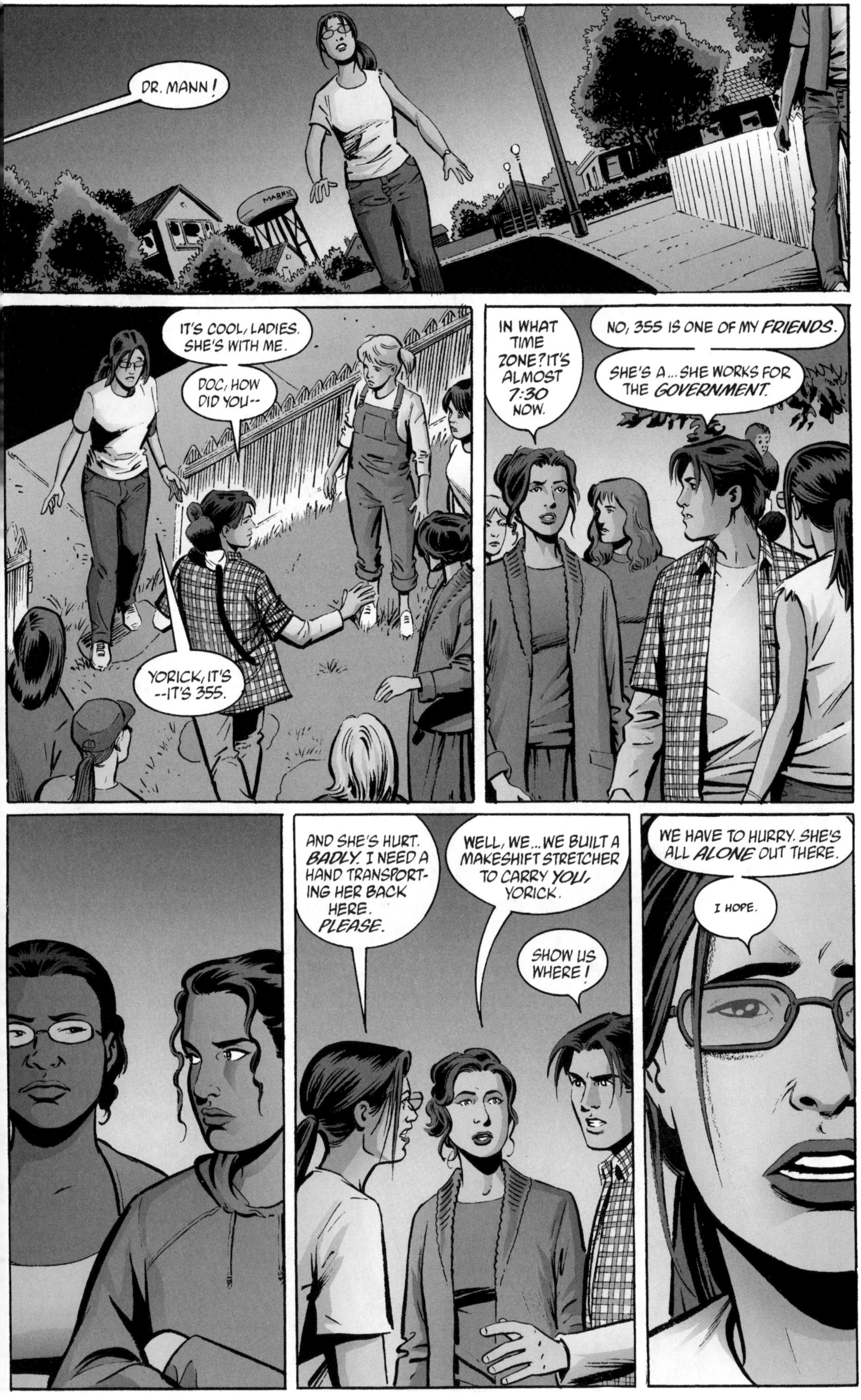
DR. MANN!
IT'S COOL, LADIES. SHE'S WITH ME.
DOC, HOW DID YOU--
YORICK, IT'S --IT'S 355.
IN WHAT TIME ZONE? IT'S ALMOST 7:30 NOW.
NO, 355 IS ONE OF MY FRIENDS.
SHE'S A... SHE WORKS FOR THE GOVERNMENT.
AND SHE'S HURT. BADLY. I NEED A HAND TRANSPORTING HER BACK HERE. PLEASE.
WELL, WE... WE BUILT A MAKESHIFT STRETCHER TO CARRY YOU, YORICK.
SHOW US WHERE!
WE HAVE TO HURRY. SHE'S ALL ALONE OUT THERE.
I HOPE.

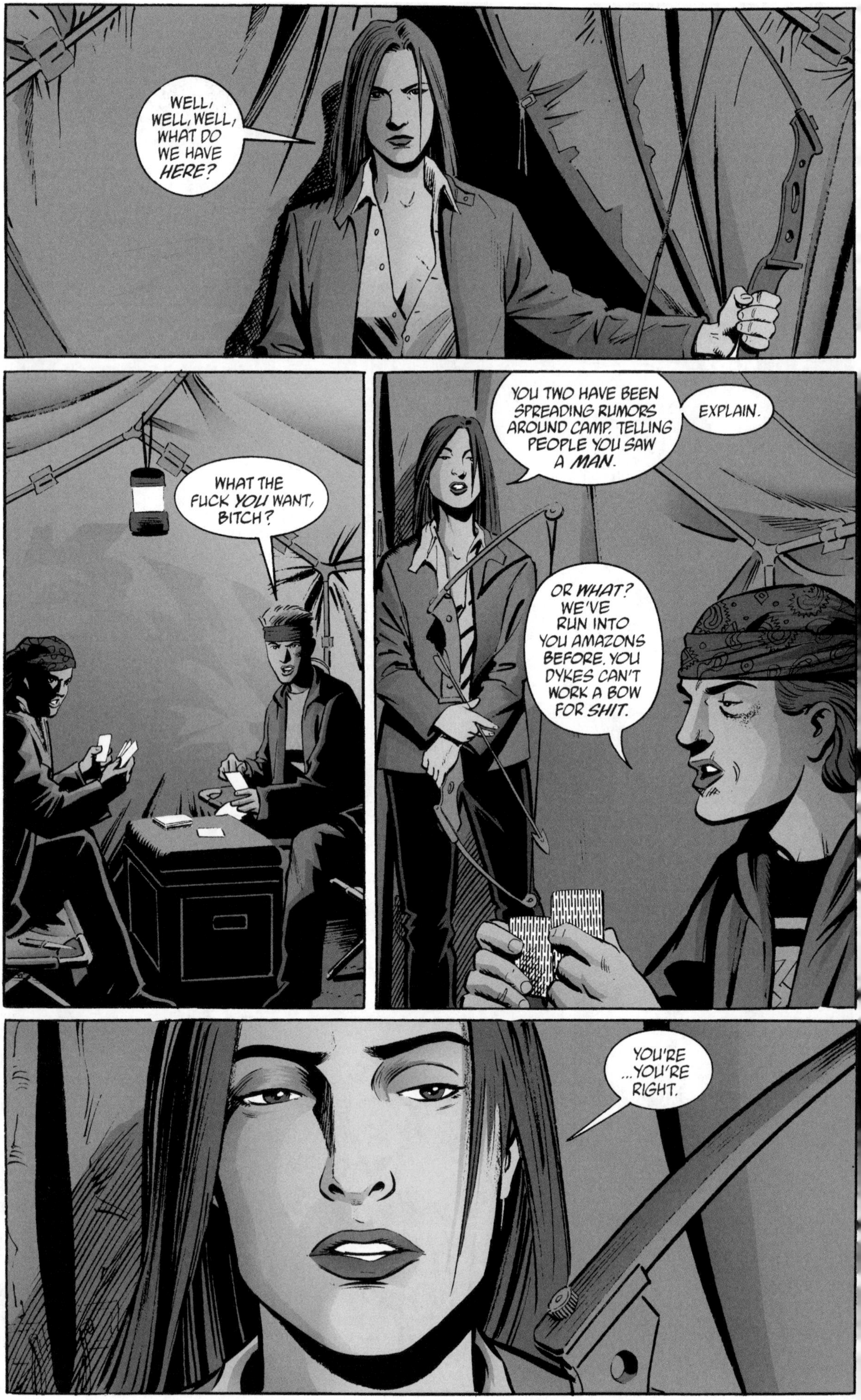
WELL, WELL, WELL, WHAT DO WE HAVE *HERE?*
WHAT THE FUCK *YOU* WANT, BITCH?
YOU TWO HAVE BEEN SPREADING RUMORS AROUND CAMP, TELLING PEOPLE YOU SAW A *MAN*.
EXPLAIN.
OR *WHAT?* WE'VE RUN INTO YOU AMAZONS BEFORE. YOU DYKES CAN'T WORK A BOW FOR *SHIT*.
YOU'RE ...YOU'RE RIGHT.

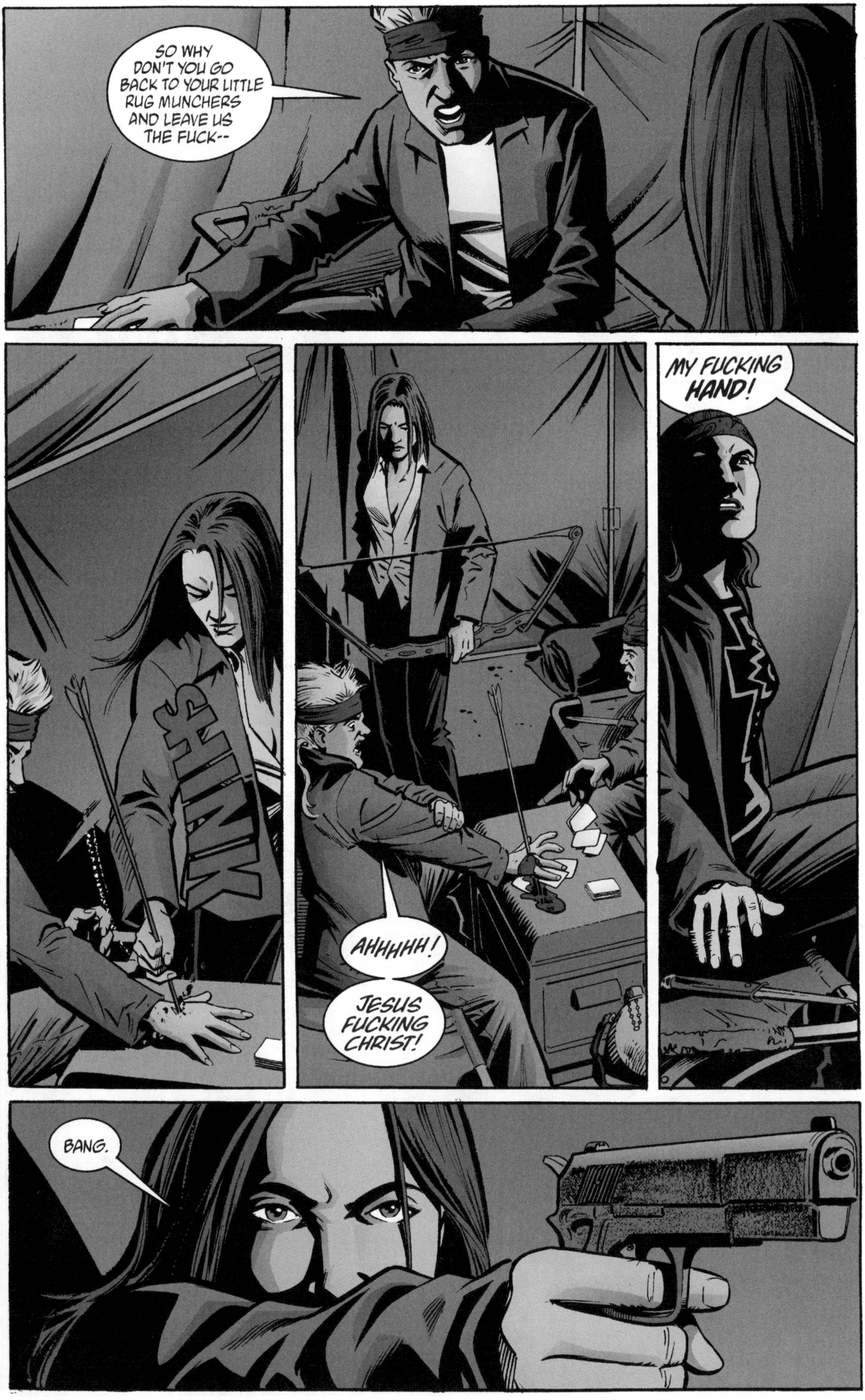

SO WHY DON'T YOU GO BACK TO YOUR LITTLE RUG MUNCHERS AND LEAVE US THE FUCK--
SHINK
AHHHHH!
JESUS FUCKING CHRIST!
MY FUCKING HAND!
BANG.

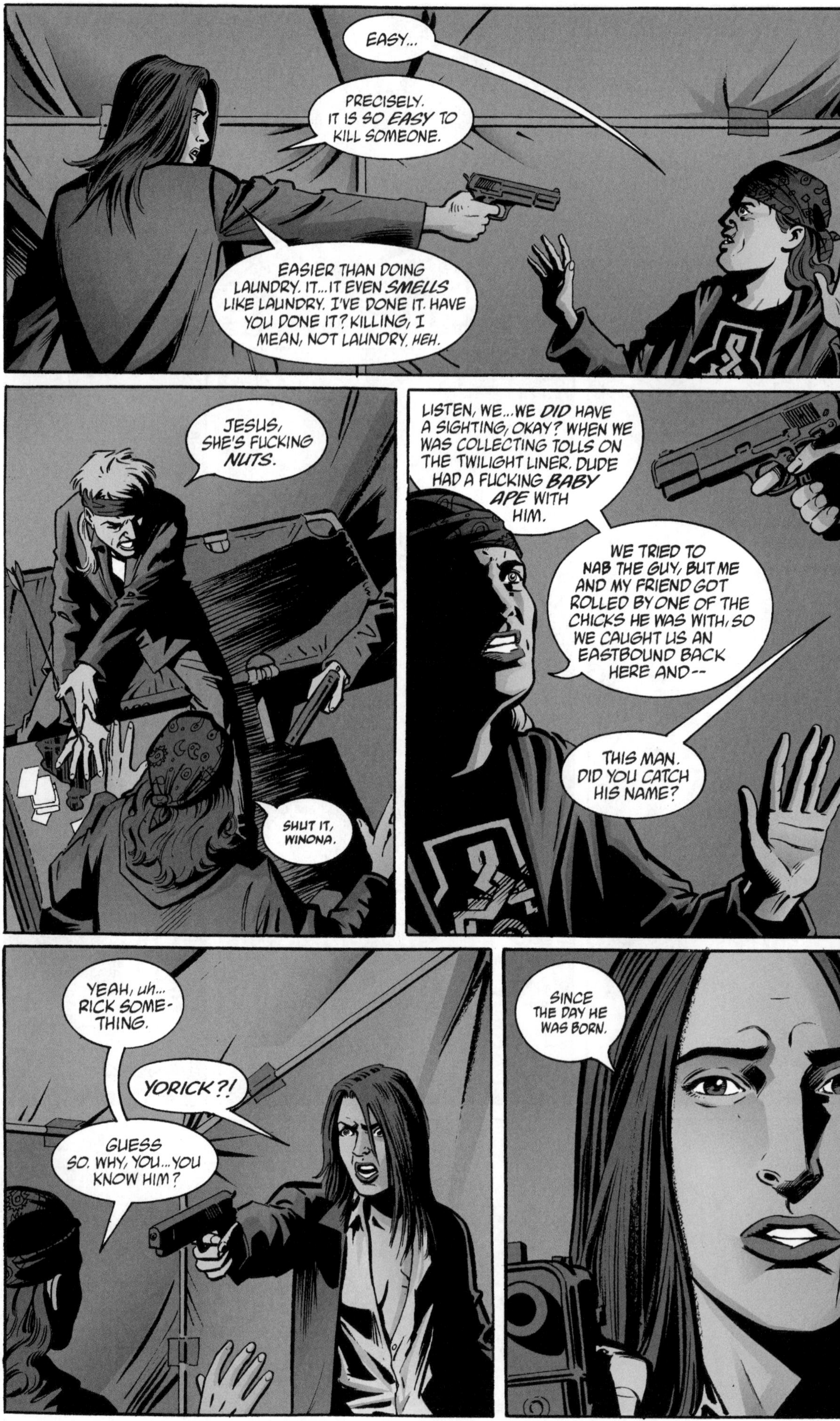
EASY...
PRECISELY. IT IS SO EASY TO KILL SOMEONE.
EASIER THAN DOING LAUNDRY. IT...IT EVEN SMELLS LIKE LAUNDRY. I'VE DONE IT. HAVE YOU DONE IT? KILLING, I MEAN, NOT LAUNDRY. HEH.
JESUS, SHE'S FUCKING NUTS.
SHUT IT, WINONA.
LISTEN, WE...WE DID HAVE A SIGHTING, OKAY? WHEN WE WAS COLLECTING TOLLS ON THE TWILIGHT LINER. DUDE HAD A FUCKING BABY APE WITH HIM.
WE TRIED TO NAB THE GUY, BUT ME AND MY FRIEND GOT ROLLED BY ONE OF THE CHICKS HE WAS WITH, SO WE CAUGHT US AN EASTBOUND BACK HERE AND--
THIS MAN. DID YOU CATCH HIS NAME?
YEAH, uh... RICK SOME-THING.
YORICK?!
GUESS SO. WHY, YOU...YOU KNOW HIM?
SINCE THE DAY HE WAS BORN.

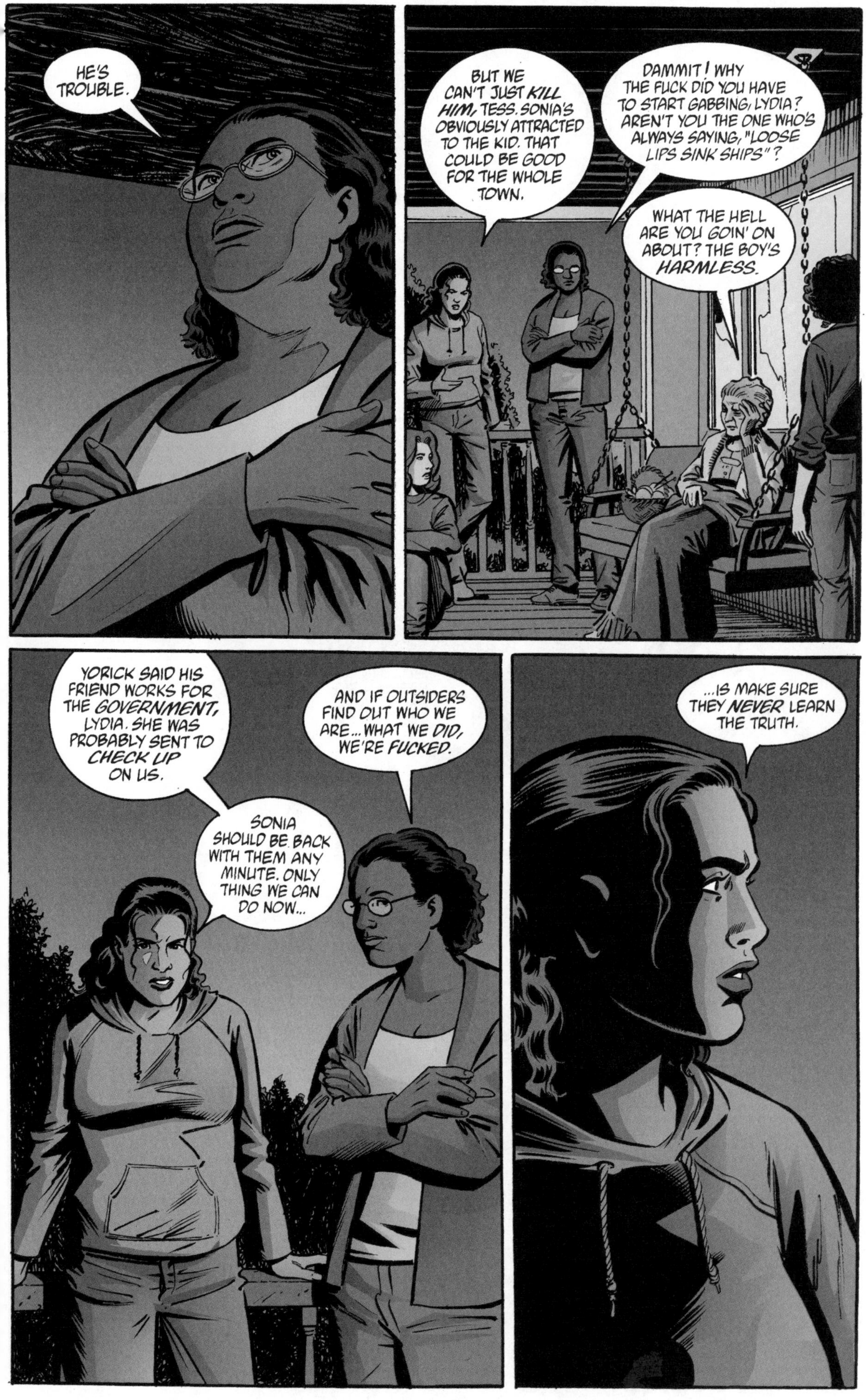
HE'S TROUBLE.
BUT WE CAN'T JUST KILL HIM, TESS. SONIA'S OBVIOUSLY ATTRACTED TO THE KID. THAT COULD BE GOOD FOR THE WHOLE TOWN.
DAMMIT! WHY THE FUCK DID YOU HAVE TO START GABBING, LYDIA? AREN'T YOU THE ONE WHO'S ALWAYS SAYING, "LOOSE LIPS SINK SHIPS"?
WHAT THE HELL ARE YOU GOIN' ON ABOUT? THE BOY'S HARMLESS.
YORICK SAID HIS FRIEND WORKS FOR THE GOVERNMENT, LYDIA. SHE WAS PROBABLY SENT TO CHECK UP ON US.
AND IF OUTSIDERS FIND OUT WHO WE ARE... WHAT WE DID, WE'RE FUCKED.
SONIA SHOULD BE BACK WITH THEM ANY MINUTE. ONLY THING WE CAN DO NOW...
...IS MAKE SURE THEY NEVER LEARN THE TRUTH.

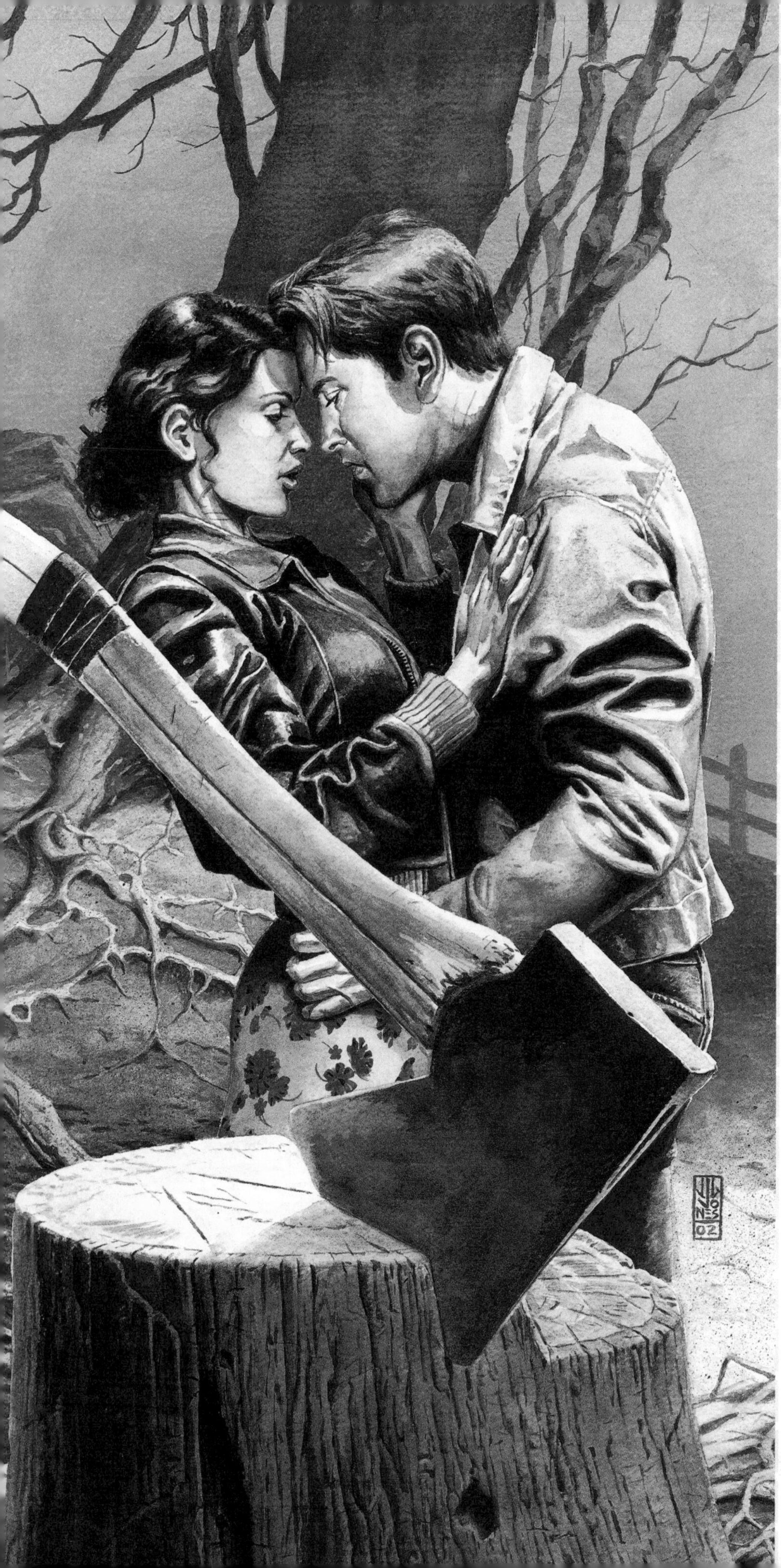

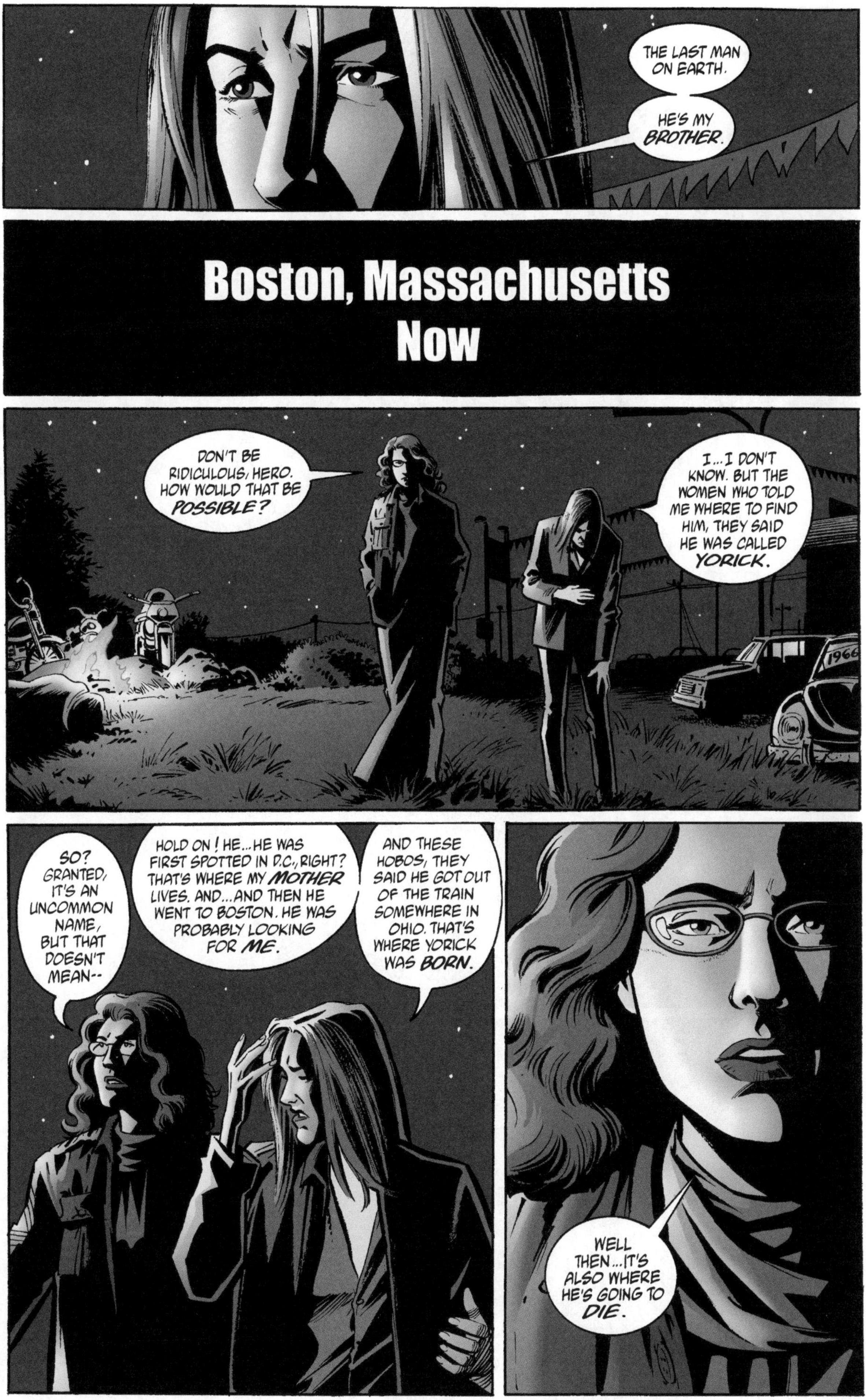
THE LAST MAN ON EARTH.
HE'S MY BROTHER.
Boston, Massachusetts
Now
DON'T BE RIDICULOUS, HERO. HOW WOULD THAT BE POSSIBLE?
I...I DON'T KNOW. BUT THE WOMEN WHO TOLD ME WHERE TO FIND HIM, THEY SAID HE WAS CALLED YORICK.
1966
SO? GRANTED, IT'S AN UNCOMMON NAME, BUT THAT DOESN'T MEAN--
HOLD ON! HE...HE WAS FIRST SPOTTED IN D.C., RIGHT? THAT'S WHERE MY MOTHER LIVES. AND...AND THEN HE WENT TO BOSTON. HE WAS PROBABLY LOOKING FOR ME.
AND THESE HOBOS, THEY SAID HE GOT OUT OF THE TRAIN SOMEWHERE IN OHIO. THAT'S WHERE YORICK WAS BORN.
WELL THEN...IT'S ALSO WHERE HE'S GOING TO DIE.

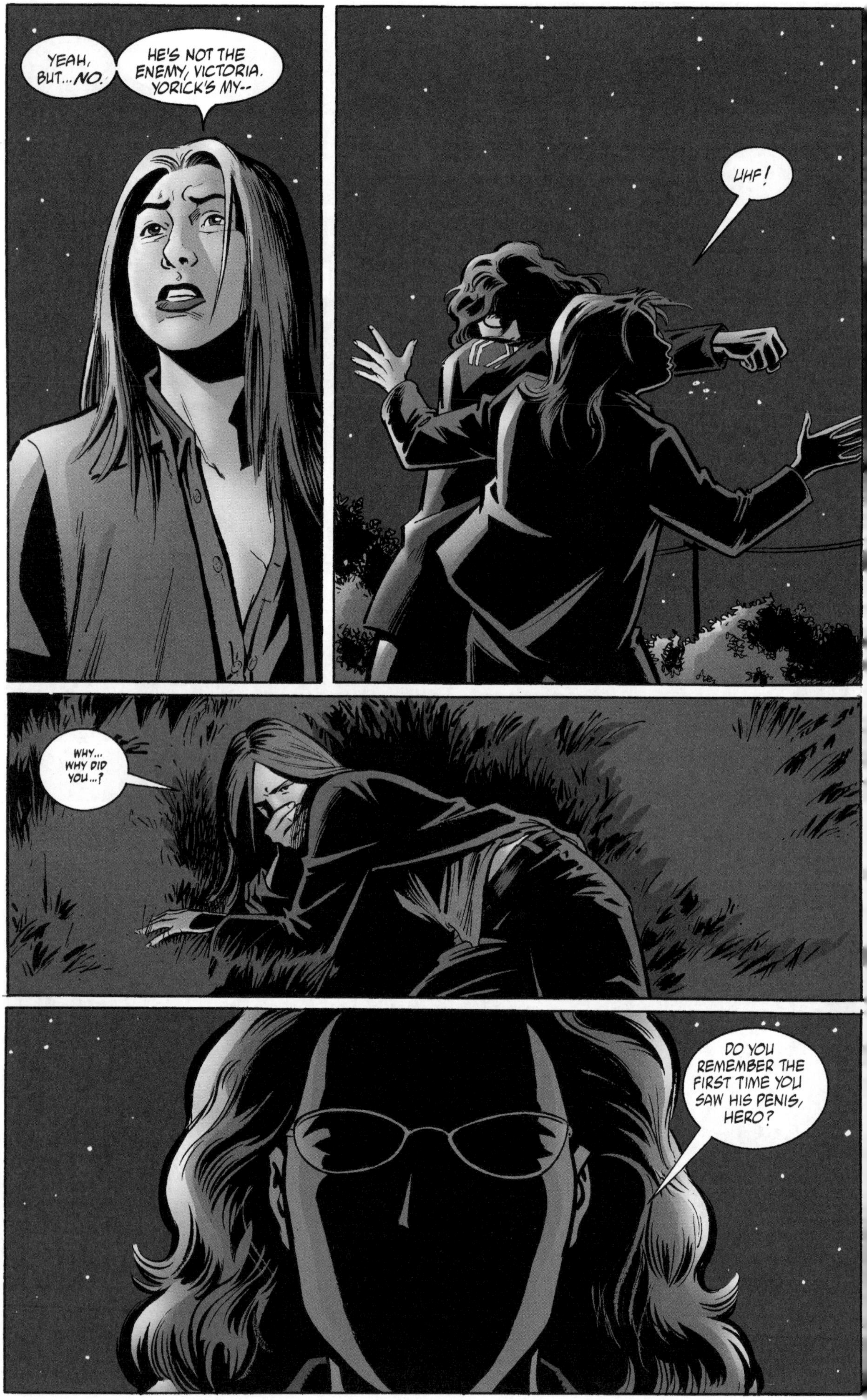

YEAH, BUT... NO.
HE'S NOT THE ENEMY, VICTORIA. YORICK'S MY--
UHF!
WHY... WHY DID YOU...?
DO YOU REMEMBER THE FIRST TIME YOU SAW HIS PENIS, HERO?

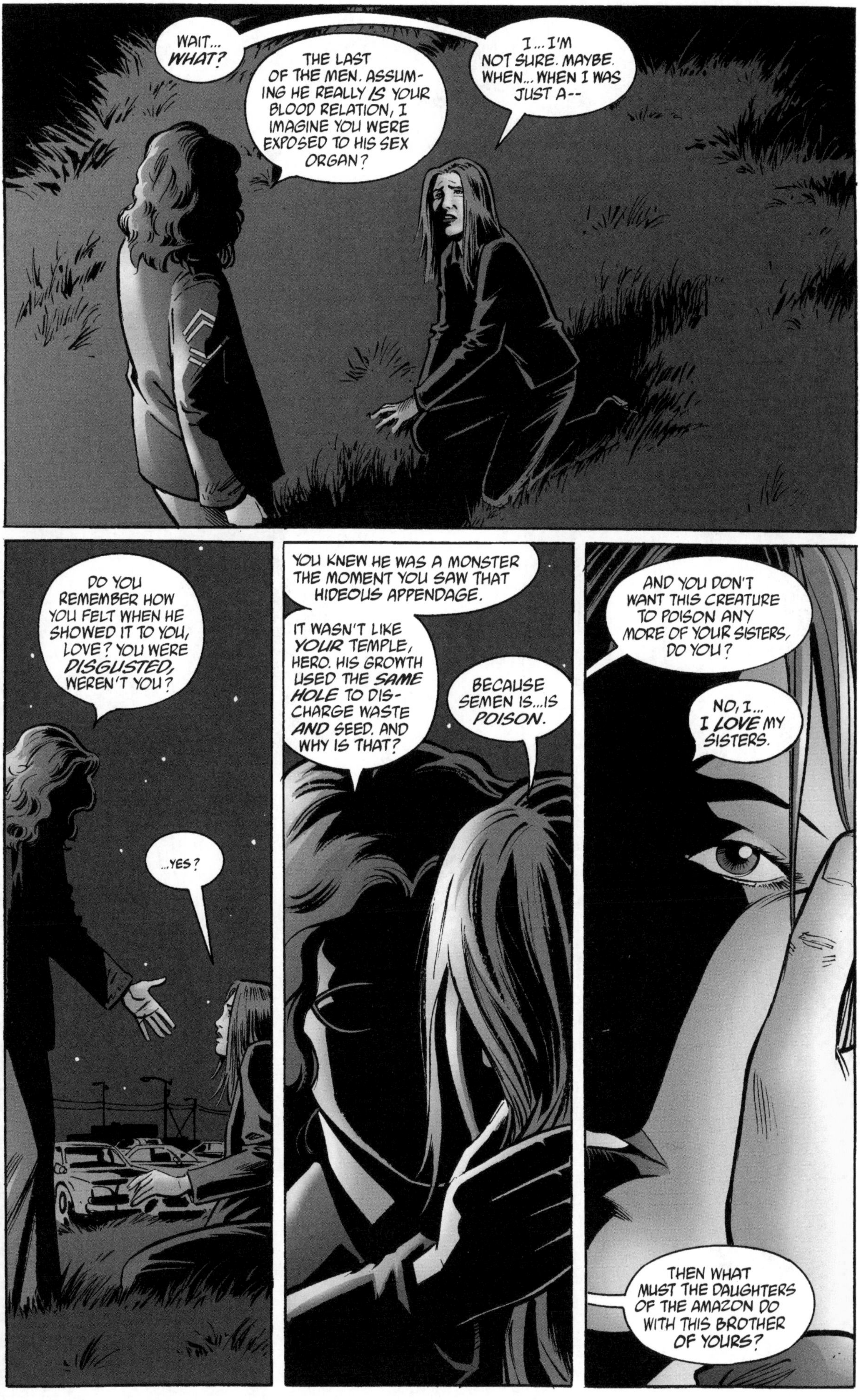
WAIT... WHAT?
THE LAST OF THE MEN. ASSUMING HE REALLY IS YOUR BLOOD RELATION, I IMAGINE YOU WERE EXPOSED TO HIS SEX ORGAN?
I... I'M NOT SURE. MAYBE. WHEN... WHEN I WAS JUST A--
DO YOU REMEMBER HOW YOU FELT WHEN HE SHOWED IT TO YOU, LOVE? YOU WERE DISGUSTED, WEREN'T YOU?
...YES?
YOU KNEW HE WAS A MONSTER THE MOMENT YOU SAW THAT HIDEOUS APPENDAGE.
IT WASN'T LIKE YOUR TEMPLE, HERO. HIS GROWTH USED THE SAME HOLE TO DISCHARGE WASTE AND SEED. AND WHY IS THAT?
BECAUSE SEMEN IS...IS POISON.
AND YOU DON'T WANT THIS CREATURE TO POISON ANY MORE OF YOUR SISTERS, DO YOU?
NO, I... I LOVE MY SISTERS.
THEN WHAT MUST THE DAUGHTERS OF THE AMAZON DO WITH THIS BROTHER OF YOURS?

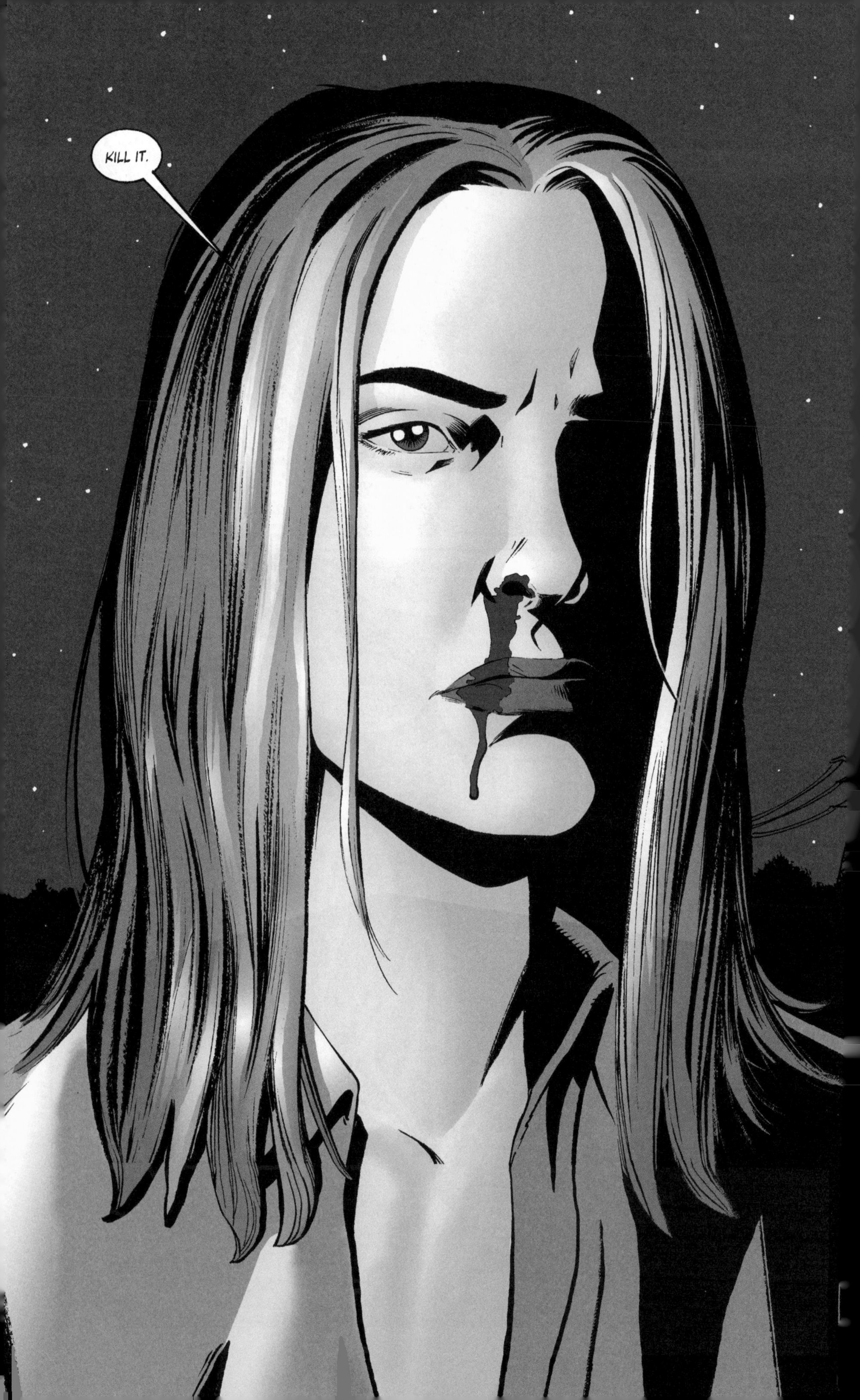
KILL IT.

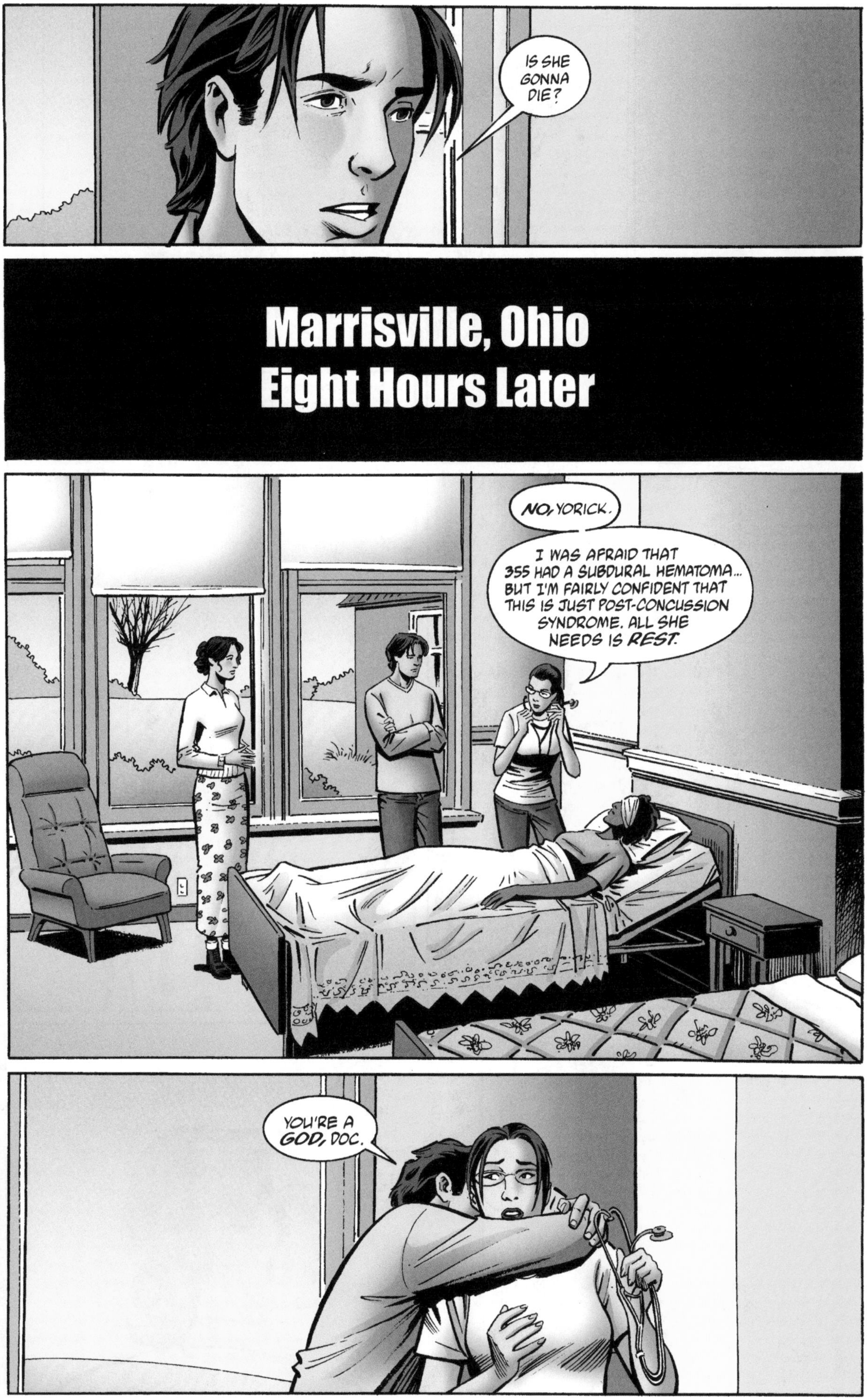
IS SHE GONNA DIE?
Marrisville, Ohio
Eight Hours Later
NO, YORICK.
I WAS AFRAID THAT 355 HAD A SUBDURAL HEMATOMA... BUT I'M FAIRLY CONFIDENT THAT THIS IS JUST POST-CONCUSSION SYNDROME. ALL SHE NEEDS IS REST.
YOU'RE A GOD, DOC.

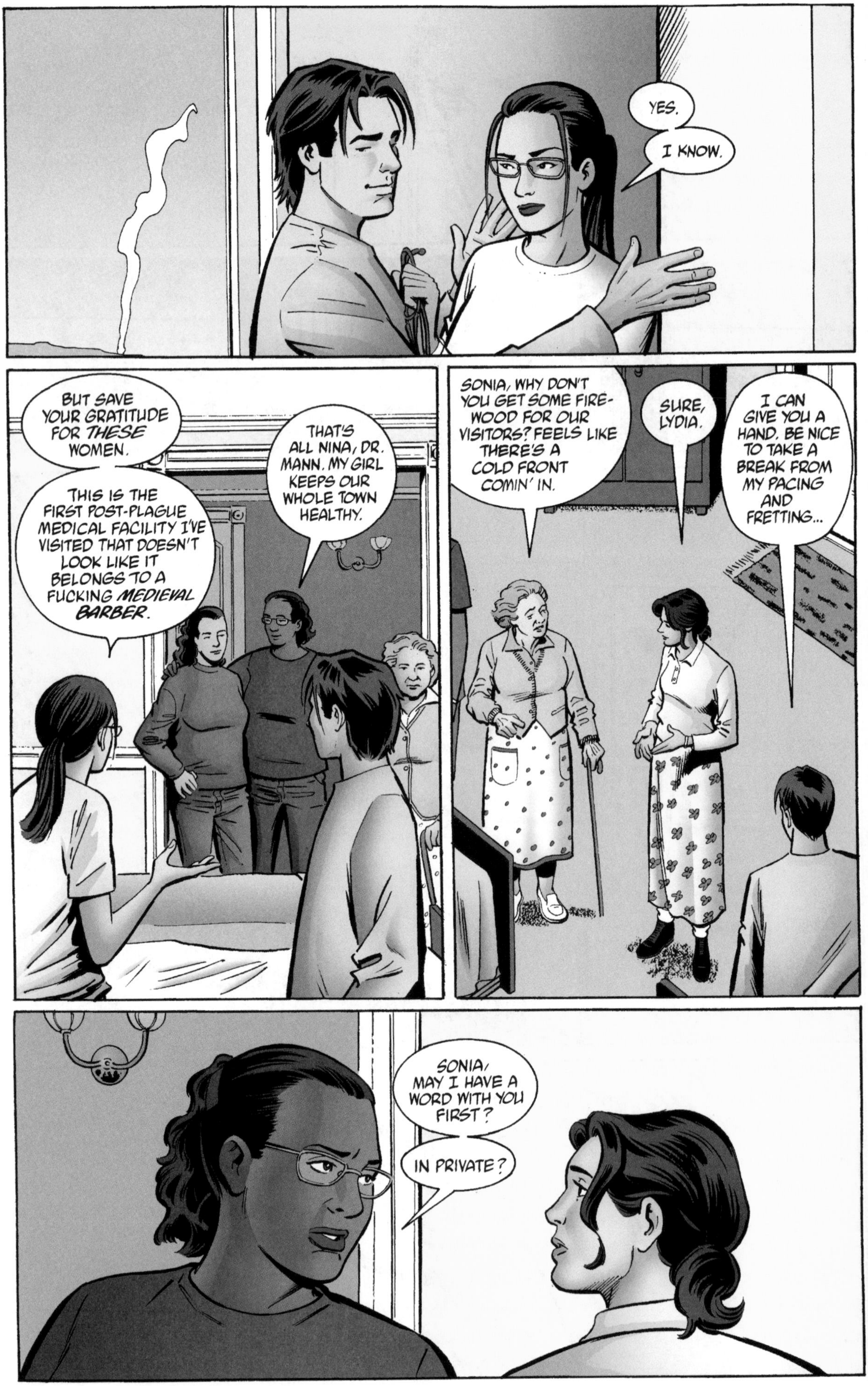
YES.
I KNOW.
BUT SAVE YOUR GRATITUDE FOR *THESE* WOMEN.
THIS IS THE FIRST POST-PLAGUE MEDICAL FACILITY I'VE VISITED THAT DOESN'T LOOK LIKE IT BELONGS TO A FUCKING *MEDIEVAL BARBER*.
THAT'S ALL NINA, DR. MANN. MY GIRL KEEPS OUR WHOLE TOWN HEALTHY.
SONIA, WHY DON'T YOU GET SOME FIRE-WOOD FOR OUR VISITORS? FEELS LIKE THERE'S A COLD FRONT COMIN' IN.
SURE, LYDIA.
I CAN GIVE YOU A HAND. BE NICE TO TAKE A BREAK FROM MY PACING AND FRETTING...
SONIA, MAY I HAVE A WORD WITH YOU FIRST?
IN PRIVATE?

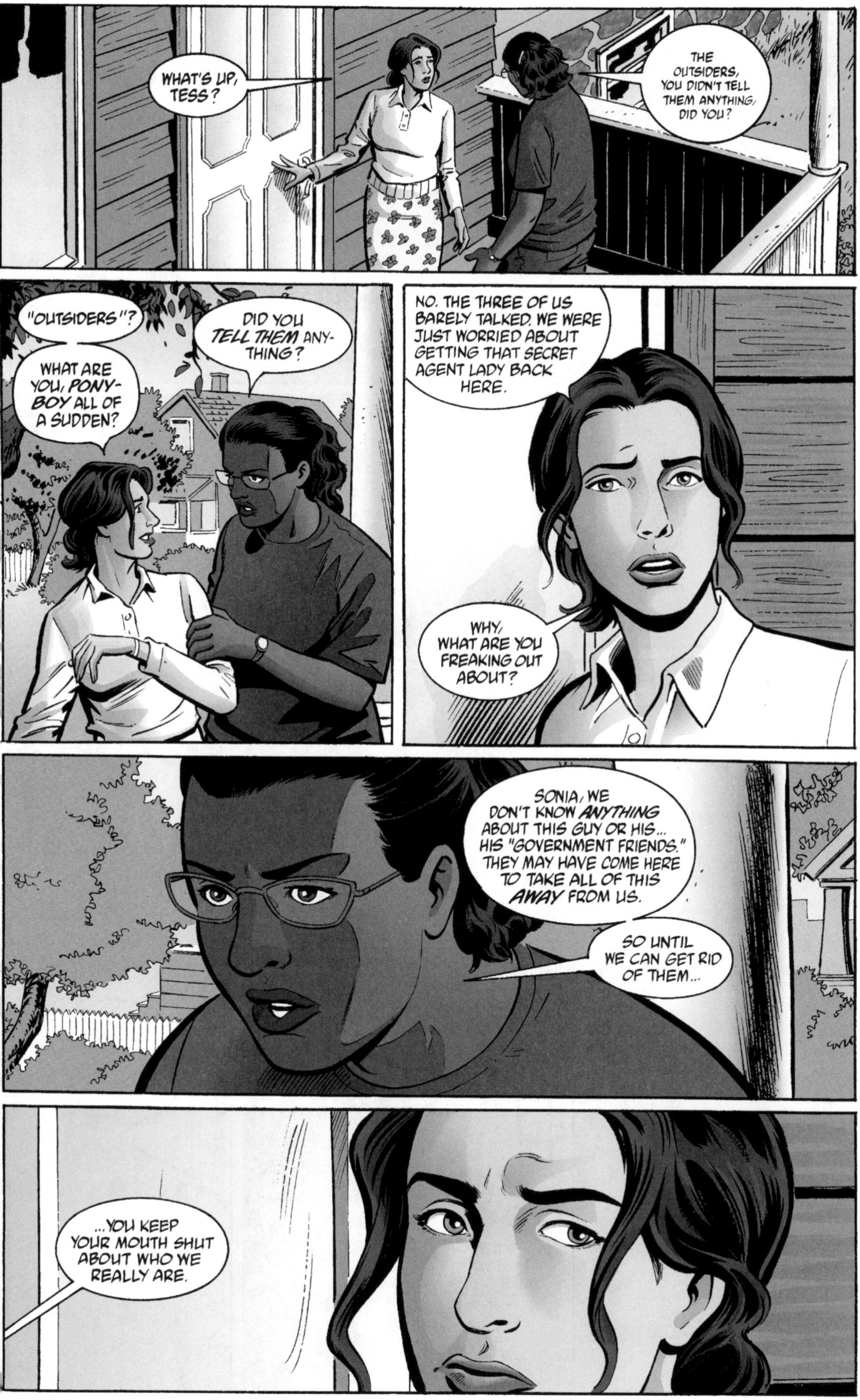
WHAT'S UP, TESS?
THE OUTSIDERS, YOU DIDN'T TELL THEM ANYTHING, DID YOU?
"OUTSIDERS"?
WHAT ARE YOU, PONY-BOY ALL OF A SUDDEN?
DID YOU TELL THEM ANY-THING?
NO. THE THREE OF US BARELY TALKED. WE WERE JUST WORRIED ABOUT GETTING THAT SECRET AGENT LADY BACK HERE.
WHY, WHAT ARE YOU FREAKING OUT ABOUT?
SONIA, WE DON'T KNOW ANYTHING ABOUT THIS GUY OR HIS... HIS "GOVERNMENT FRIENDS." THEY MAY HAVE COME HERE TO TAKE ALL OF THIS AWAY FROM US.
SO UNTIL WE CAN GET RID OF THEM...
...YOU KEEP YOUR MOUTH SHUT ABOUT WHO WE REALLY ARE.

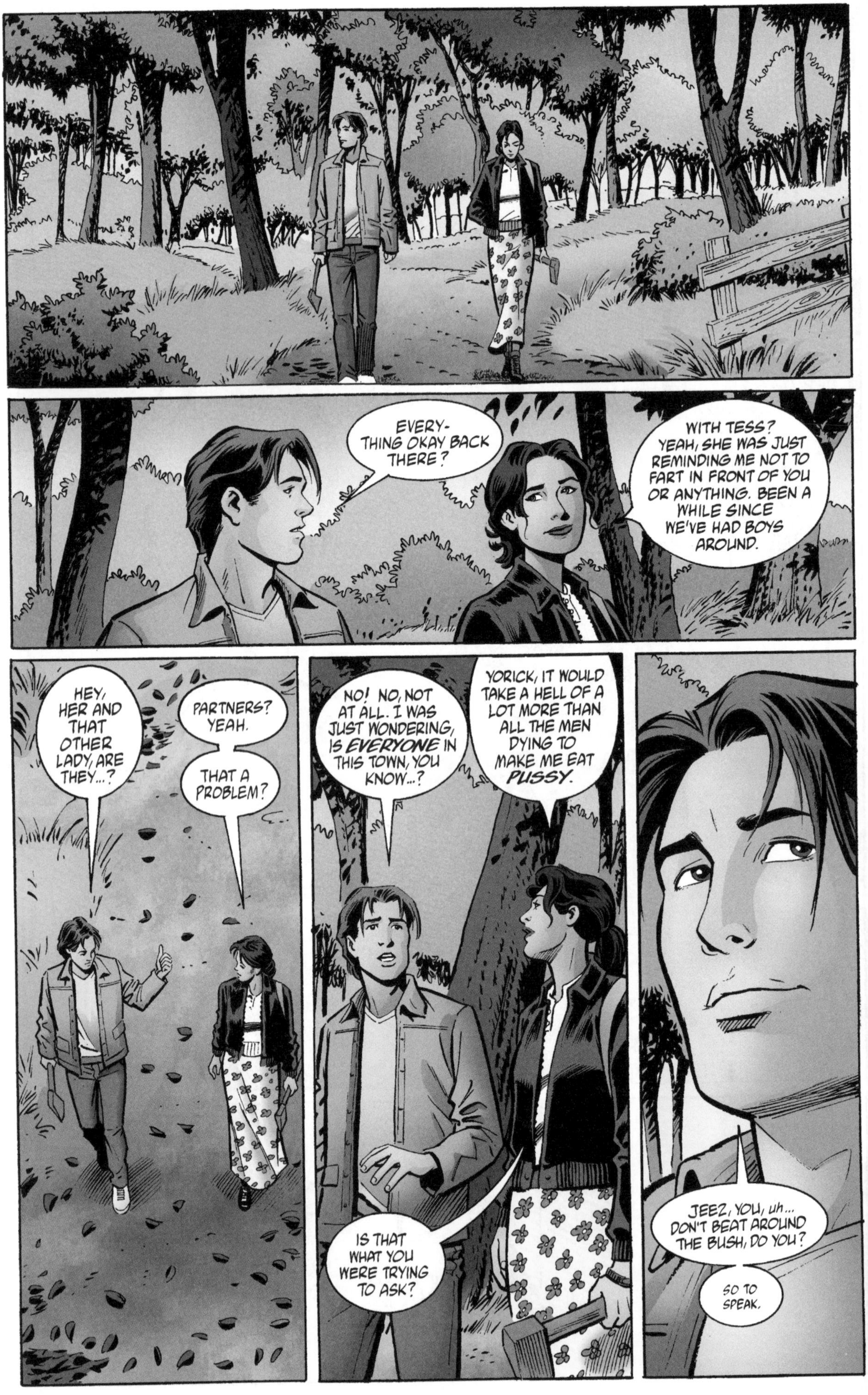
EVERY-THING OKAY BACK THERE?
WITH TESS? YEAH, SHE WAS JUST REMINDING ME NOT TO FART IN FRONT OF YOU OR ANYTHING. BEEN A WHILE SINCE WE'VE HAD BOYS AROUND.
HEY, HER AND THAT OTHER LADY, ARE THEY...?
PARTNERS? YEAH.
THAT A PROBLEM?
NO! NO, NOT AT ALL. I WAS JUST WONDERING, IS *EVERYONE* IN THIS TOWN, YOU KNOW...?
YORICK, IT WOULD TAKE A HELL OF A LOT MORE THAN ALL THE MEN DYING TO MAKE ME EAT ***PUSSY***.
IS THAT WHAT YOU WERE TRYING TO ASK?
JEEZ, YOU, uh... DON'T BEAT AROUND THE BUSH, DO YOU?
SO TO SPEAK.

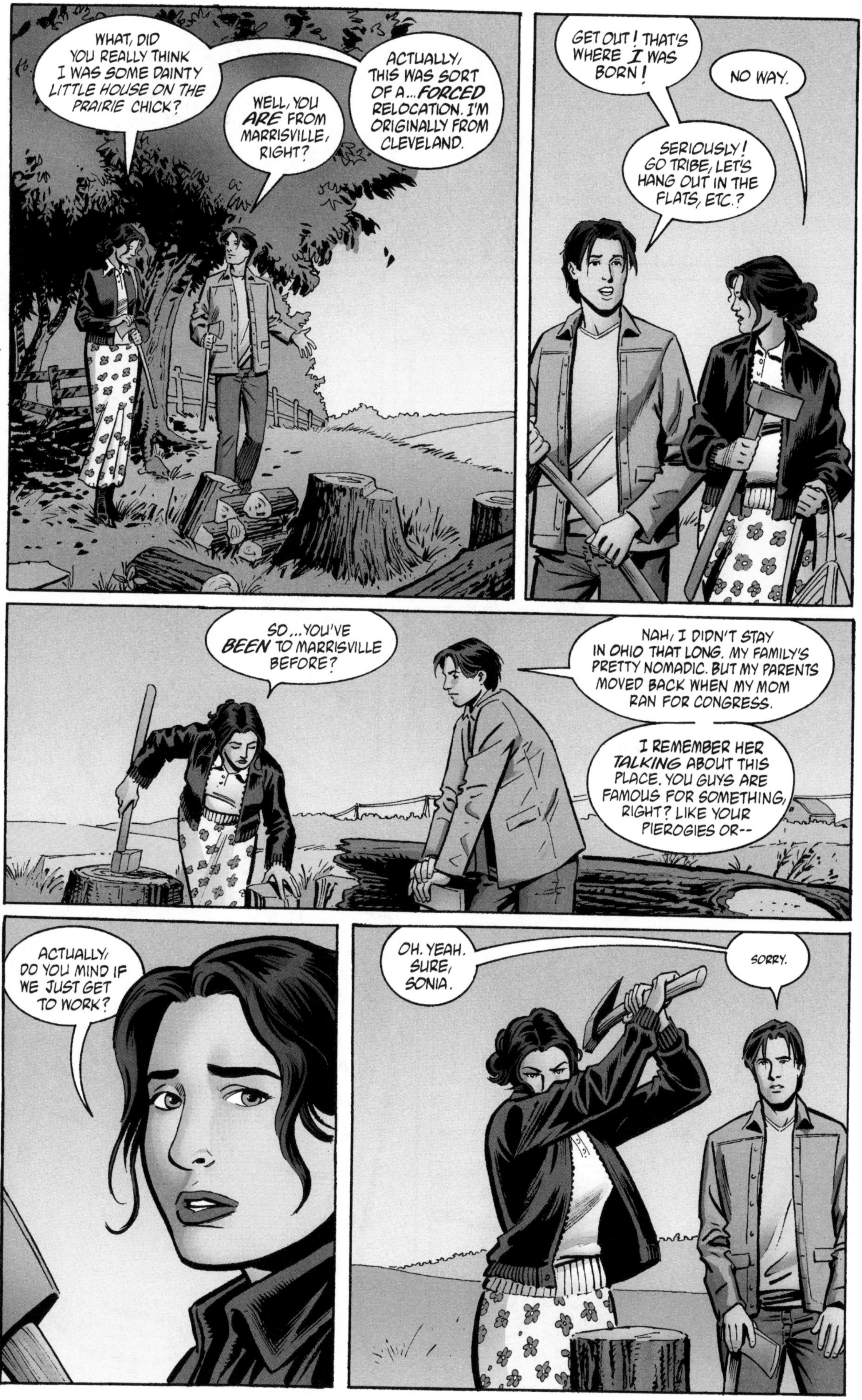
WHAT, DID YOU REALLY THINK I WAS SOME DAINTY LITTLE HOUSE ON THE PRAIRIE CHICK?
WELL, YOU ARE FROM MARRISVILLE, RIGHT?
ACTUALLY, THIS WAS SORT OF A...FORCED RELOCATION. I'M ORIGINALLY FROM CLEVELAND.
GET OUT! THAT'S WHERE I WAS BORN!
NO WAY.
SERIOUSLY! GO TRIBE, LET'S HANG OUT IN THE FLATS, ETC.?
SO...YOU'VE BEEN TO MARRISVILLE BEFORE?
NAH, I DIDN'T STAY IN OHIO THAT LONG. MY FAMILY'S PRETTY NOMADIC. BUT MY PARENTS MOVED BACK WHEN MY MOM RAN FOR CONGRESS.
I REMEMBER HER TALKING ABOUT THIS PLACE. YOU GUYS ARE FAMOUS FOR SOMETHING, RIGHT? LIKE YOUR PIEROGIES OR--
ACTUALLY, DO YOU MIND IF WE JUST GET TO WORK?
OH. YEAH. SURE, SONIA.
SORRY.

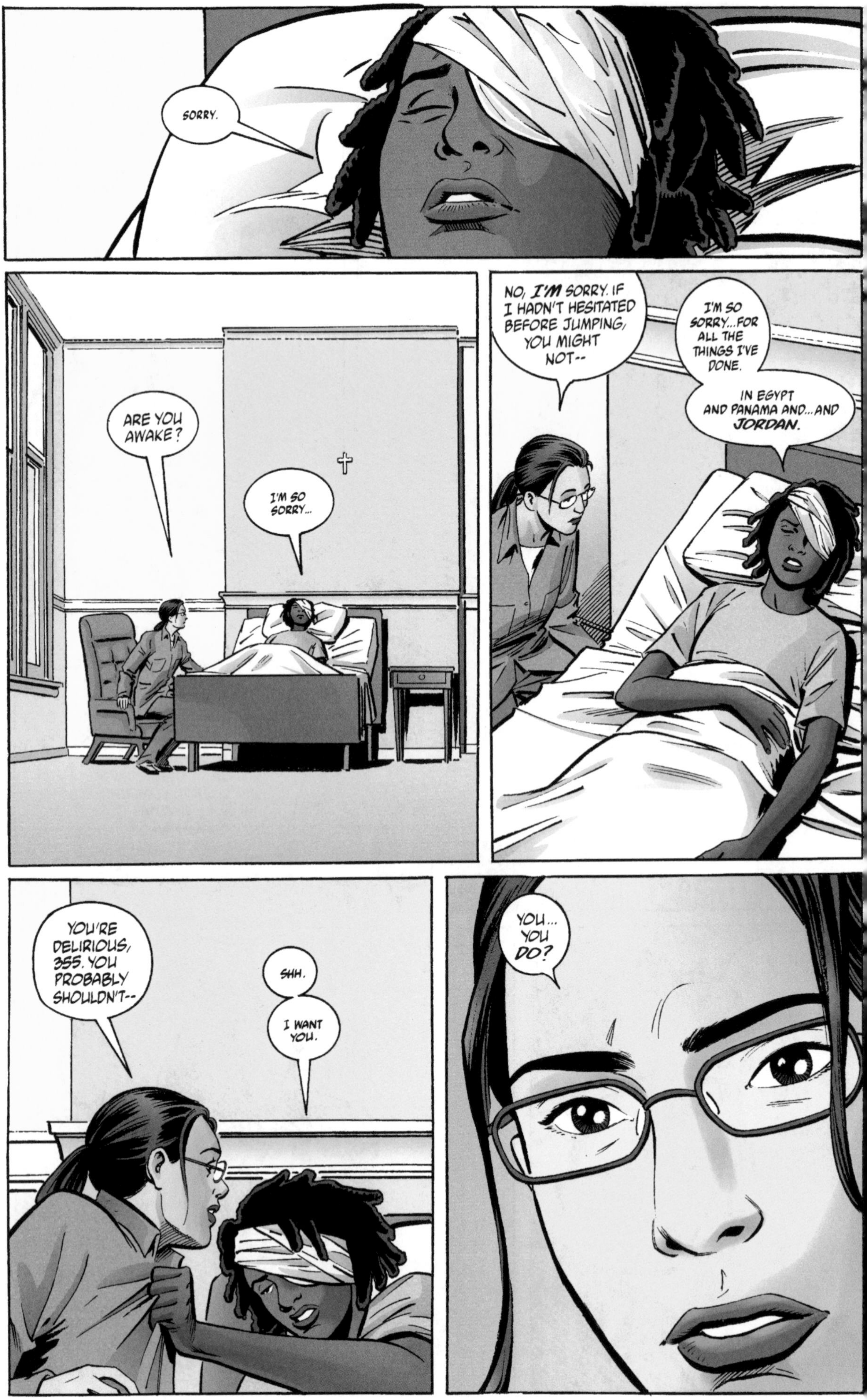
SORRY.
ARE YOU AWAKE?
I'M SO SORRY...
NO, I'M SORRY. IF I HADN'T HESITATED BEFORE JUMPING, YOU MIGHT NOT--
I'M SO SORRY...FOR ALL THE THINGS I'VE DONE.
IN EGYPT AND PANAMA AND...AND JORDAN.
YOU'RE DELIRIOUS, 355. YOU PROBABLY SHOULDN'T--
SHH.
I WANT YOU.
YOU... YOU DO?

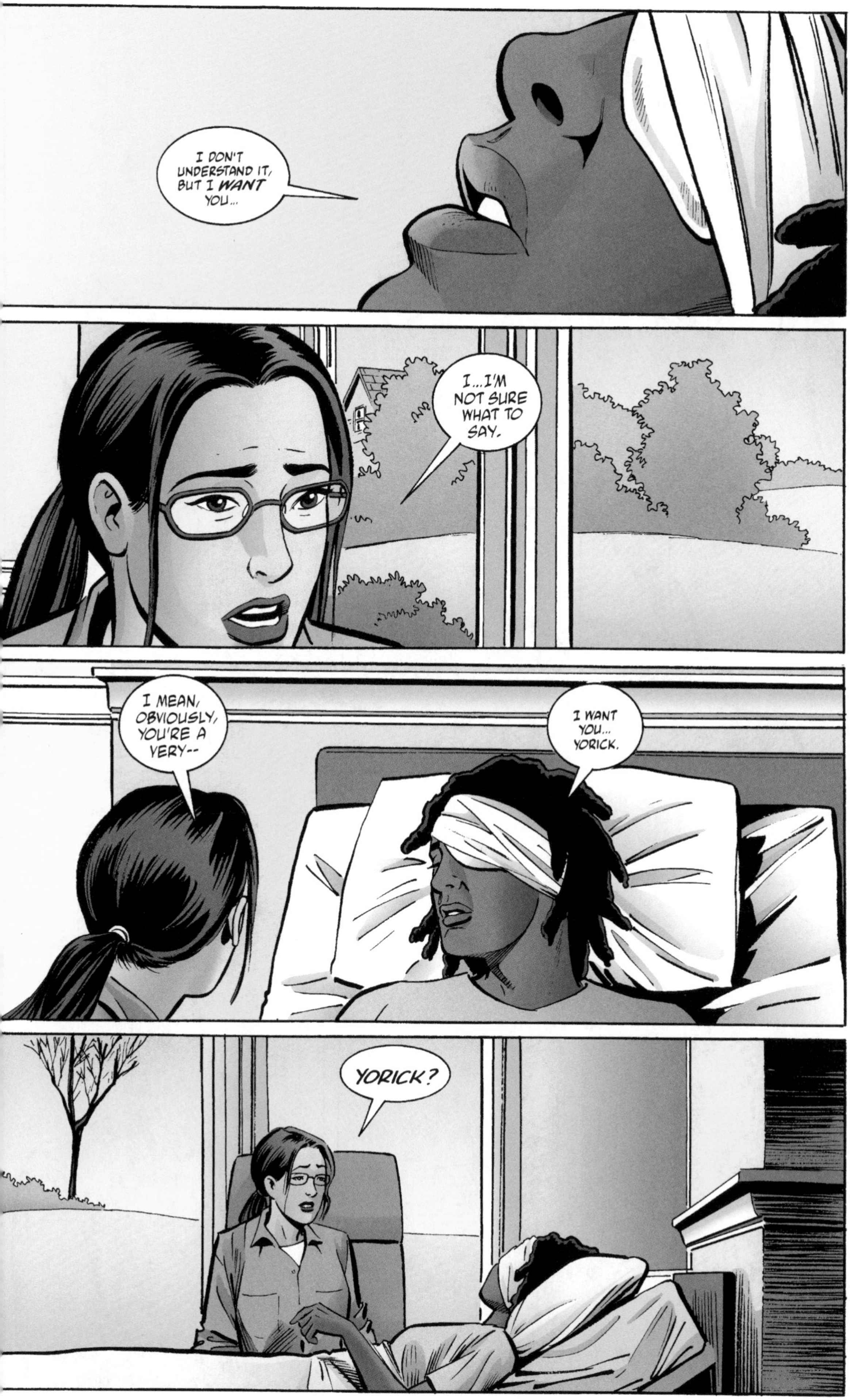
I DON'T UNDERSTAND IT, BUT I *WANT* YOU...
I...I'M NOT SURE WHAT TO SAY.
I MEAN, OBVIOUSLY, YOU'RE A VERY--
I WANT YOU... YORICK.
YORICK?

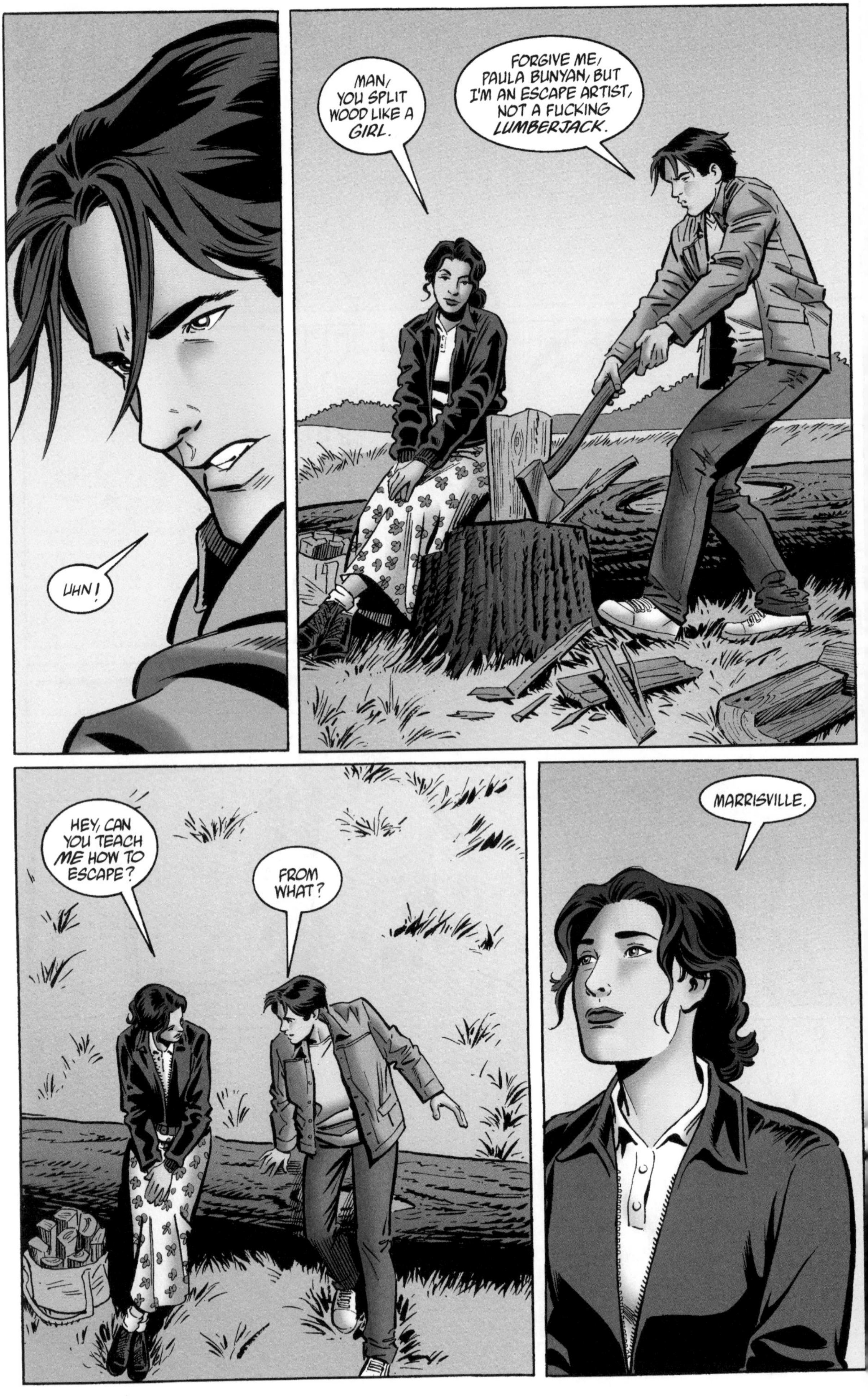
UHN!
MAN, YOU SPLIT WOOD LIKE A GIRL.
FORGIVE ME, PAULA BUNYAN, BUT I'M AN ESCAPE ARTIST, NOT A FUCKING LUMBERJACK.
HEY, CAN YOU TEACH ME HOW TO ESCAPE?
FROM WHAT?
MARRISVILLE.

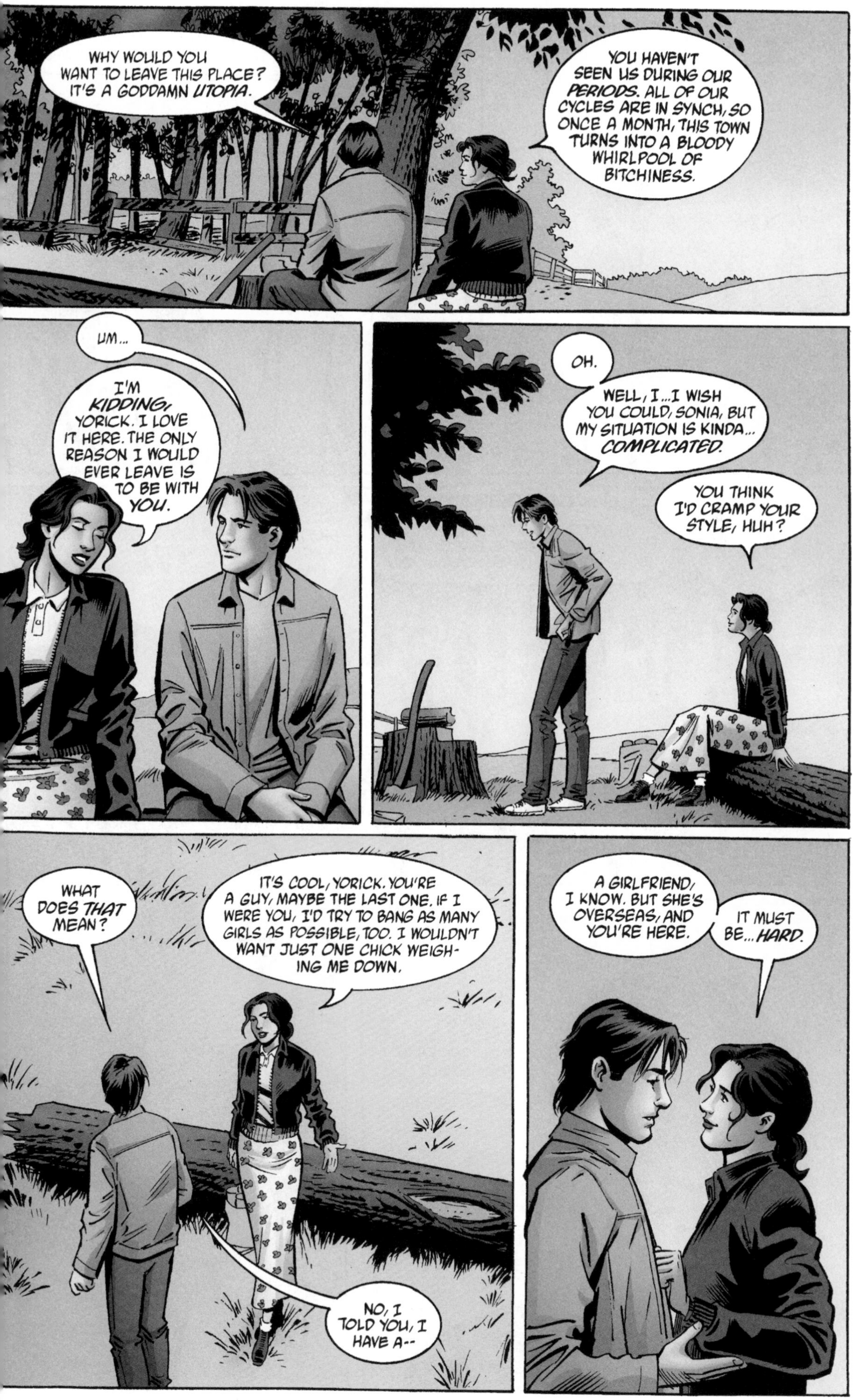
WHY WOULD YOU WANT TO LEAVE THIS PLACE? IT'S A GODDAMN *UTOPIA*.
YOU HAVEN'T SEEN US DURING OUR *PERIODS*. ALL OF OUR CYCLES ARE IN SYNCH, SO ONCE A MONTH, THIS TOWN TURNS INTO A BLOODY WHIRLPOOL OF BITCHINESS.
UM...
I'M *KIDDING*, YORICK. I LOVE IT HERE. THE ONLY REASON I WOULD EVER LEAVE IS TO BE WITH *YOU*.
OH.
WELL, I...I WISH YOU COULD, SONIA, BUT MY SITUATION IS KINDA... *COMPLICATED*.
YOU THINK I'D CRAMP YOUR STYLE, HUH?
WHAT DOES *THAT* MEAN?
IT'S COOL, YORICK. YOU'RE A GUY, MAYBE THE LAST ONE. IF I WERE YOU, I'D TRY TO BANG AS MANY GIRLS AS POSSIBLE, TOO. I WOULDN'T WANT JUST ONE CHICK WEIGHING ME DOWN.
NO, I TOLD YOU, I HAVE A--
A GIRLFRIEND, I KNOW. BUT SHE'S OVERSEAS, AND YOU'RE HERE.
IT MUST BE... *HARD*.

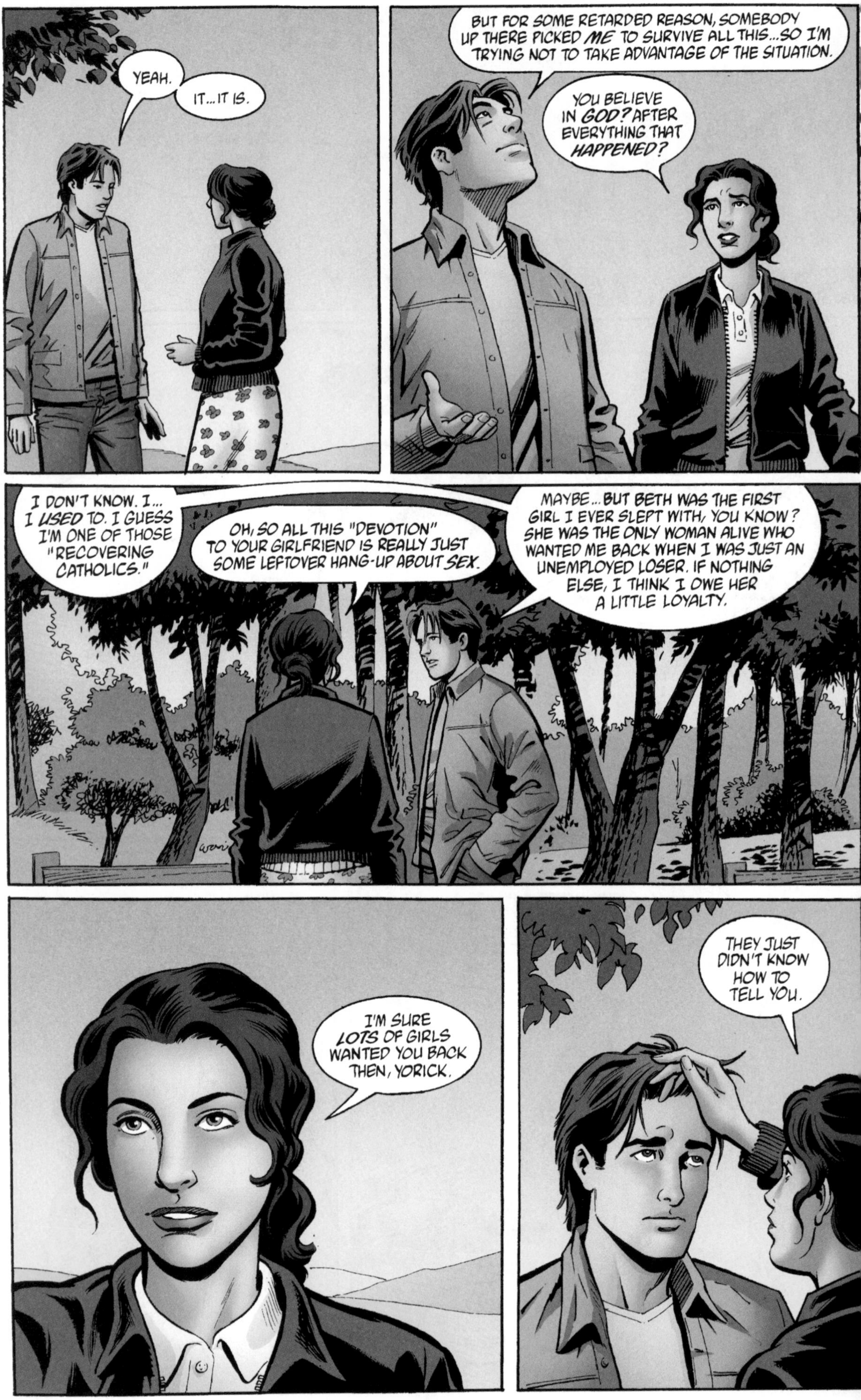
YEAH.
IT... IT IS.
BUT FOR SOME RETARDED REASON, SOMEBODY UP THERE PICKED ME TO SURVIVE ALL THIS... SO I'M TRYING NOT TO TAKE ADVANTAGE OF THE SITUATION.
YOU BELIEVE IN GOD? AFTER EVERYTHING THAT HAPPENED?
I DON'T KNOW. I... I USED TO. I GUESS I'M ONE OF THOSE "RECOVERING CATHOLICS."
OH, SO ALL THIS "DEVOTION" TO YOUR GIRLFRIEND IS REALLY JUST SOME LEFTOVER HANG-UP ABOUT SEX.
MAYBE... BUT BETH WAS THE FIRST GIRL I EVER SLEPT WITH, YOU KNOW? SHE WAS THE ONLY WOMAN ALIVE WHO WANTED ME BACK WHEN I WAS JUST AN UNEMPLOYED LOSER. IF NOTHING ELSE, I THINK I OWE HER A LITTLE LOYALTY.
I'M SURE LOTS OF GIRLS WANTED YOU BACK THEN, YORICK.
THEY JUST DIDN'T KNOW HOW TO TELL YOU.

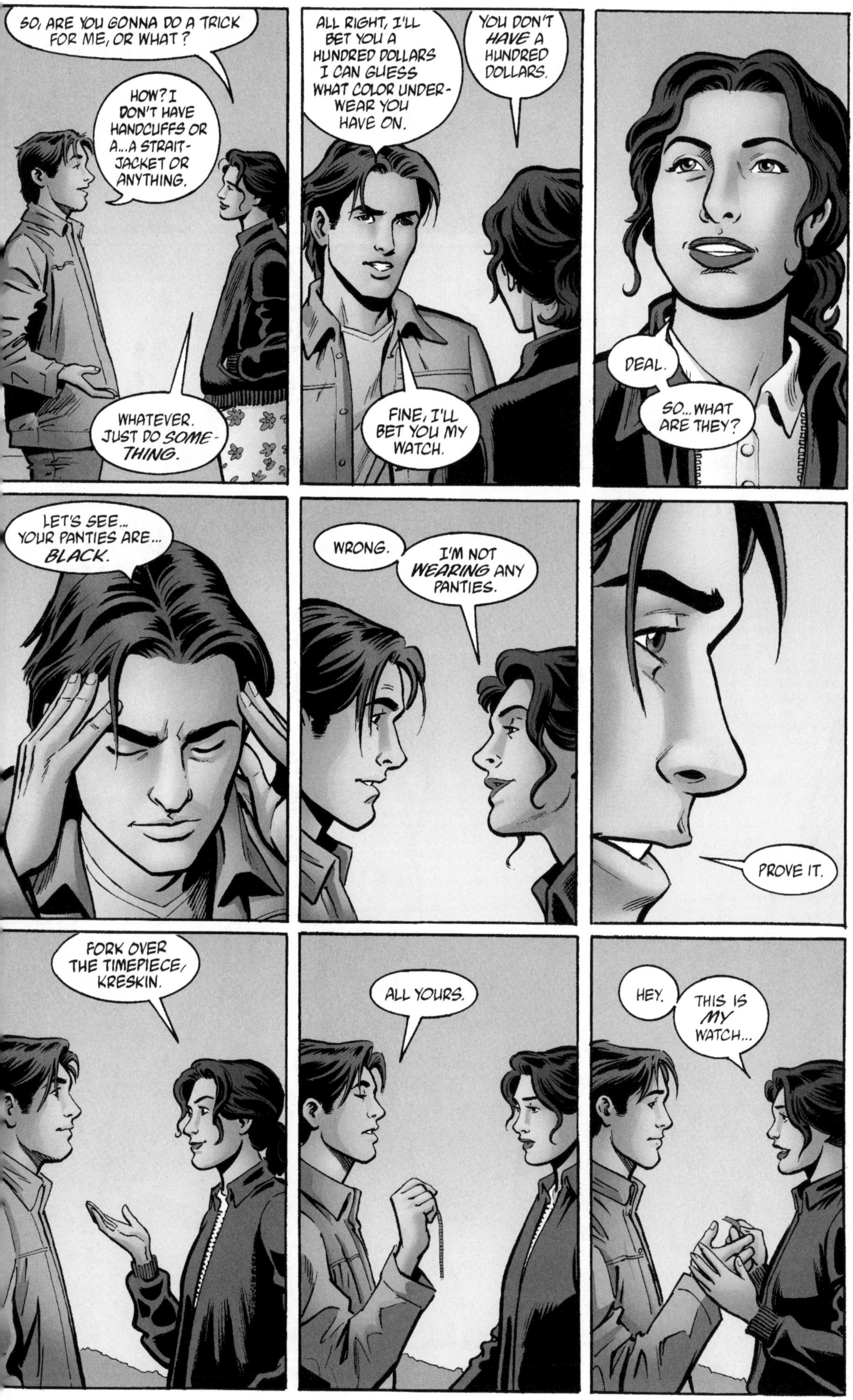
SO, ARE YOU GONNA DO A TRICK FOR ME, OR WHAT?
HOW? I DON'T HAVE HANDCUFFS OR A...A STRAIT-JACKET OR ANYTHING.
WHATEVER. JUST DO SOME-THING.
ALL RIGHT, I'LL BET YOU A HUNDRED DOLLARS I CAN GUESS WHAT COLOR UNDER-WEAR YOU HAVE ON.
YOU DON'T HAVE A HUNDRED DOLLARS.
FINE, I'LL BET YOU MY WATCH.
DEAL.
SO...WHAT ARE THEY?
LET'S SEE... YOUR PANTIES ARE... BLACK.
WRONG.
I'M NOT WEARING ANY PANTIES.
PROVE IT.
FORK OVER THE TIMEPIECE, KRESKIN.
ALL YOURS.
HEY.
THIS IS MY WATCH...

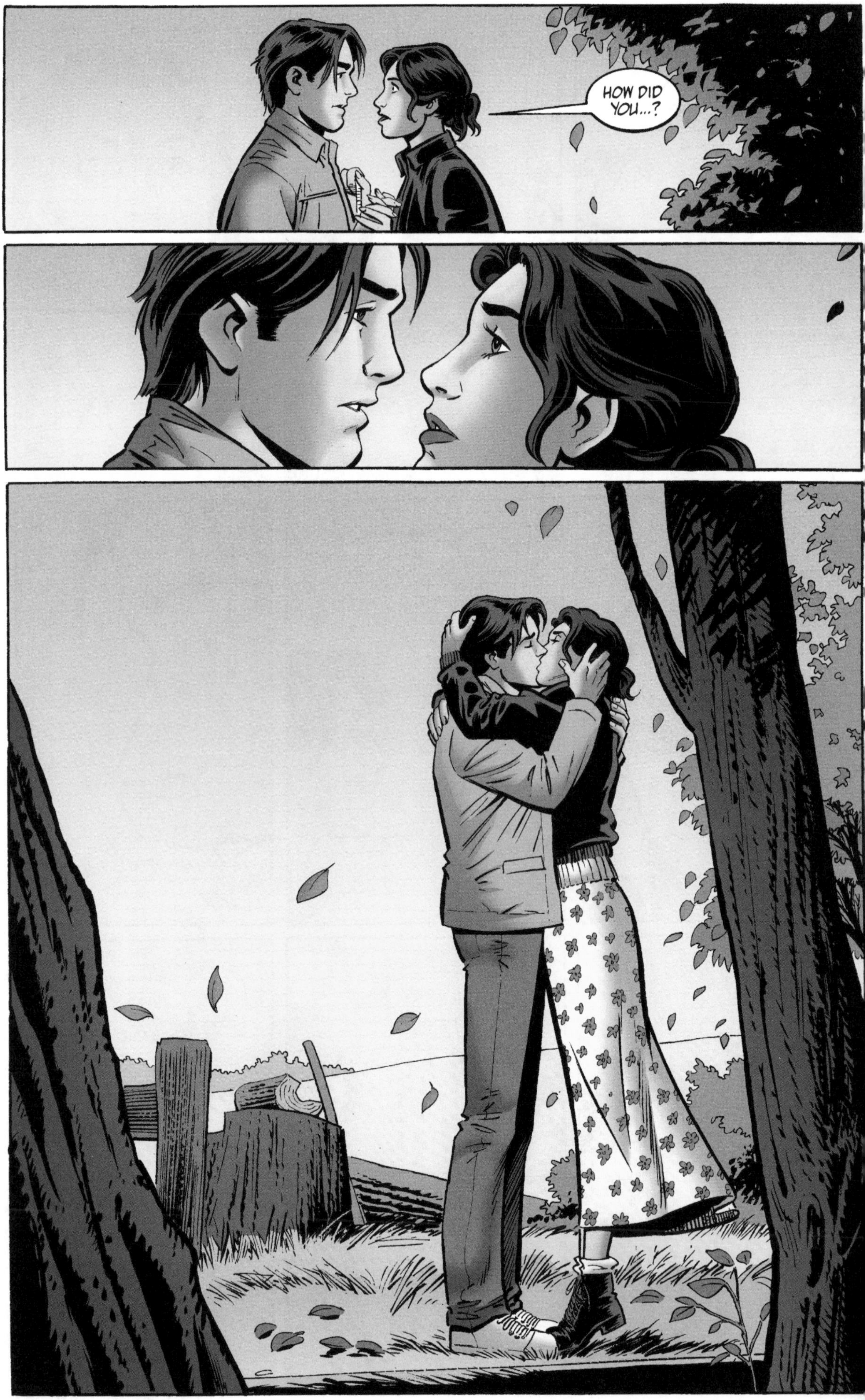
HOW DID YOU...?

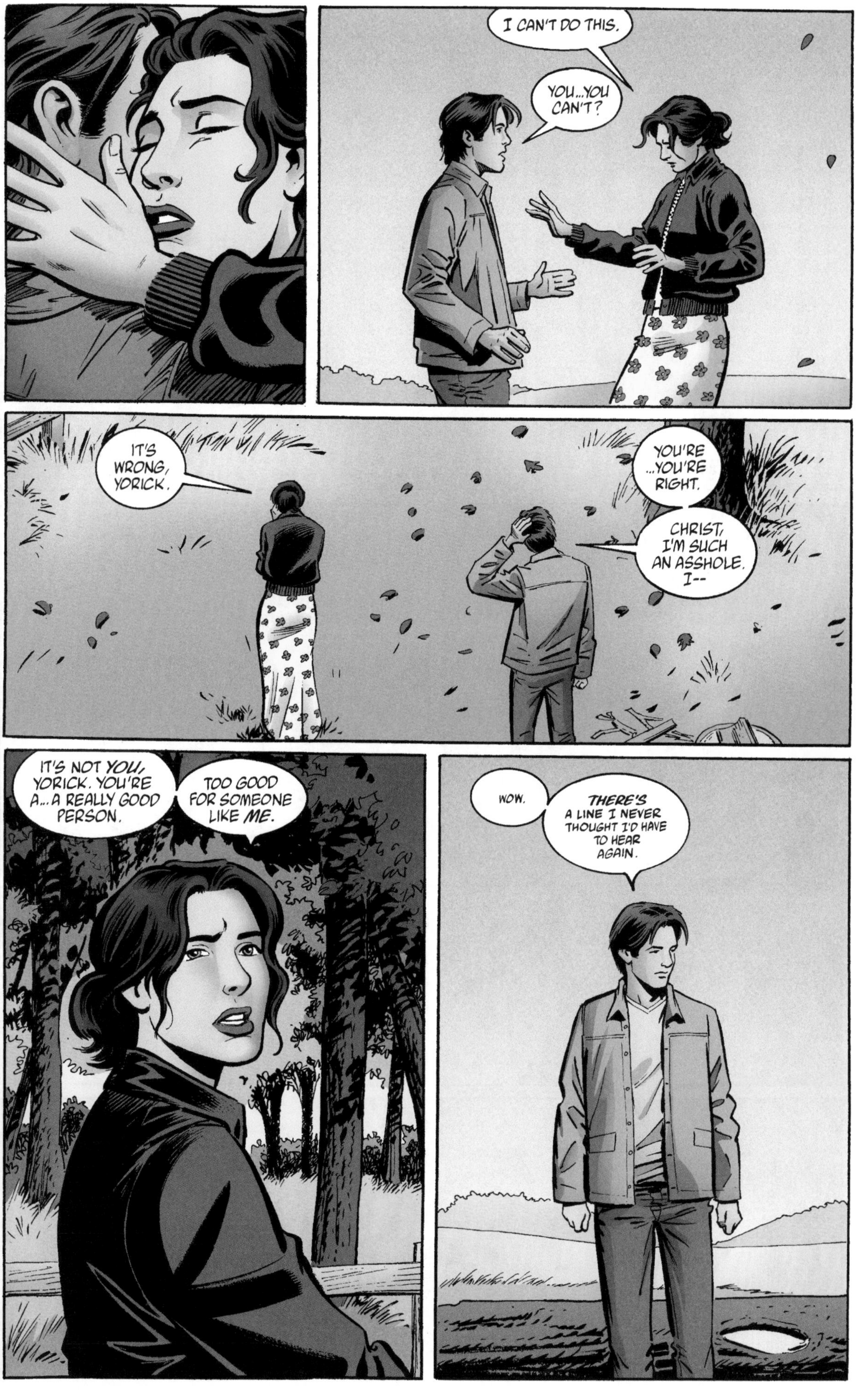
I CAN'T DO THIS.
YOU...YOU CAN'T?
IT'S WRONG, YORICK.
YOU'RE ...YOU'RE RIGHT.
CHRIST, I'M SUCH AN ASSHOLE. I--
IT'S NOT YOU, YORICK. YOU'RE A... A REALLY GOOD PERSON.
TOO GOOD FOR SOMEONE LIKE ME.
WOW.
THERE'S A LINE I NEVER THOUGHT I'D HAVE TO HEAR AGAIN.

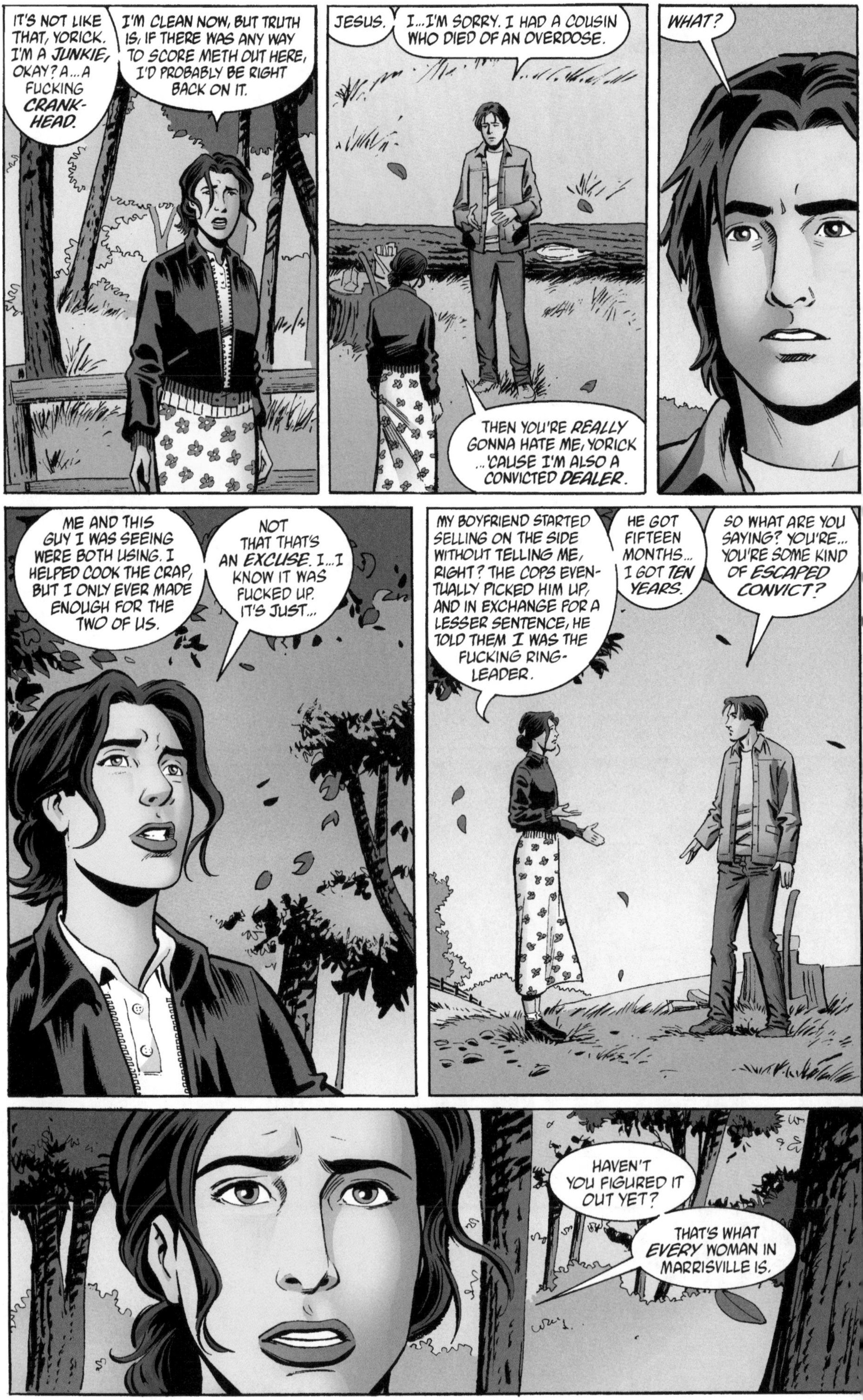
IT'S NOT LIKE THAT, YORICK. I'M A JUNKIE, OKAY? A...A FUCKING CRANK-HEAD.
I'M CLEAN NOW, BUT TRUTH IS, IF THERE WAS ANY WAY TO SCORE METH OUT HERE, I'D PROBABLY BE RIGHT BACK ON IT.
JESUS.
I...I'M SORRY. I HAD A COUSIN WHO DIED OF AN OVERDOSE.
THEN YOU'RE REALLY GONNA HATE ME, YORICK ...'CAUSE I'M ALSO A CONVICTED DEALER.
WHAT?
ME AND THIS GUY I WAS SEEING WERE BOTH USING. I HELPED COOK THE CRAP, BUT I ONLY EVER MADE ENOUGH FOR THE TWO OF US.
NOT THAT THAT'S AN EXCUSE. I...I KNOW IT WAS FUCKED UP. IT'S JUST...
MY BOYFRIEND STARTED SELLING ON THE SIDE WITHOUT TELLING ME, RIGHT? THE COPS EVEN-TUALLY PICKED HIM UP, AND IN EXCHANGE FOR A LESSER SENTENCE, HE TOLD THEM I WAS THE FUCKING RING-LEADER.
HE GOT FIFTEEN MONTHS... I GOT TEN YEARS.
SO WHAT ARE YOU SAYING? YOU'RE... YOU'RE SOME KIND OF ESCAPED CONVICT?
HAVEN'T YOU FIGURED IT OUT YET?
THAT'S WHAT EVERY WOMAN IN MARRISVILLE IS.

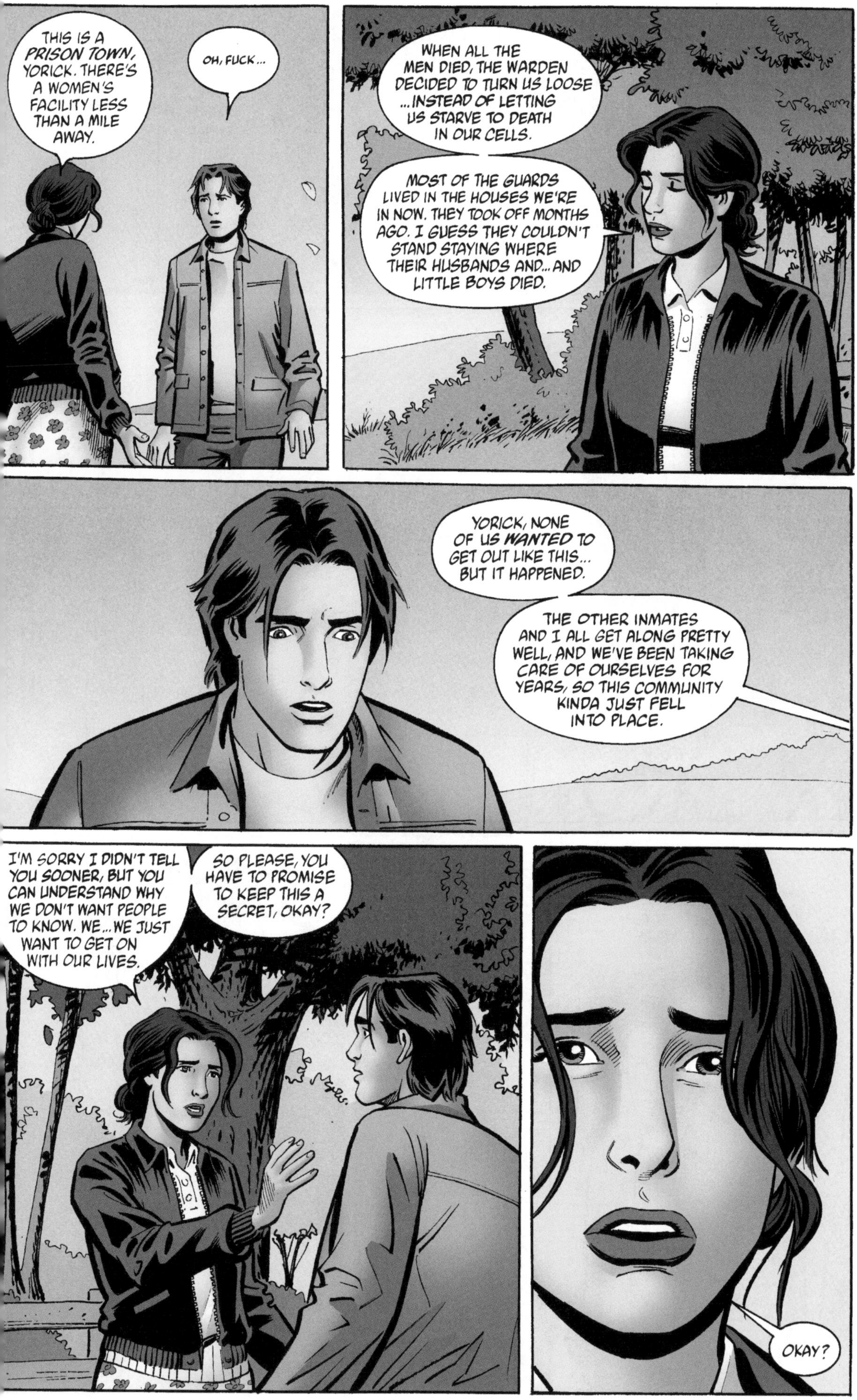

THIS IS A *PRISON TOWN,* YORICK. THERE'S A WOMEN'S FACILITY LESS THAN A MILE AWAY.
OH, FUCK...
WHEN ALL THE MEN DIED, THE WARDEN DECIDED TO TURN US LOOSE ...INSTEAD OF LETTING US STARVE TO DEATH IN OUR CELLS.
MOST OF THE GUARDS LIVED IN THE HOUSES WE'RE IN NOW. THEY TOOK OFF MONTHS AGO. I GUESS THEY COULDN'T STAND STAYING WHERE THEIR HUSBANDS AND... AND LITTLE BOYS DIED.
YORICK, NONE OF US *WANTED* TO GET OUT LIKE THIS... BUT IT HAPPENED.
THE OTHER INMATES AND I ALL GET ALONG PRETTY WELL, AND WE'VE BEEN TAKING CARE OF OURSELVES FOR YEARS, SO THIS COMMUNITY KINDA JUST FELL INTO PLACE.
I'M SORRY I DIDN'T TELL YOU SOONER, BUT YOU CAN UNDERSTAND WHY WE DON'T WANT PEOPLE TO KNOW. WE... WE JUST WANT TO GET ON WITH OUR LIVES.
SO PLEASE, YOU HAVE TO PROMISE TO KEEP THIS A SECRET, OKAY?
OKAY?

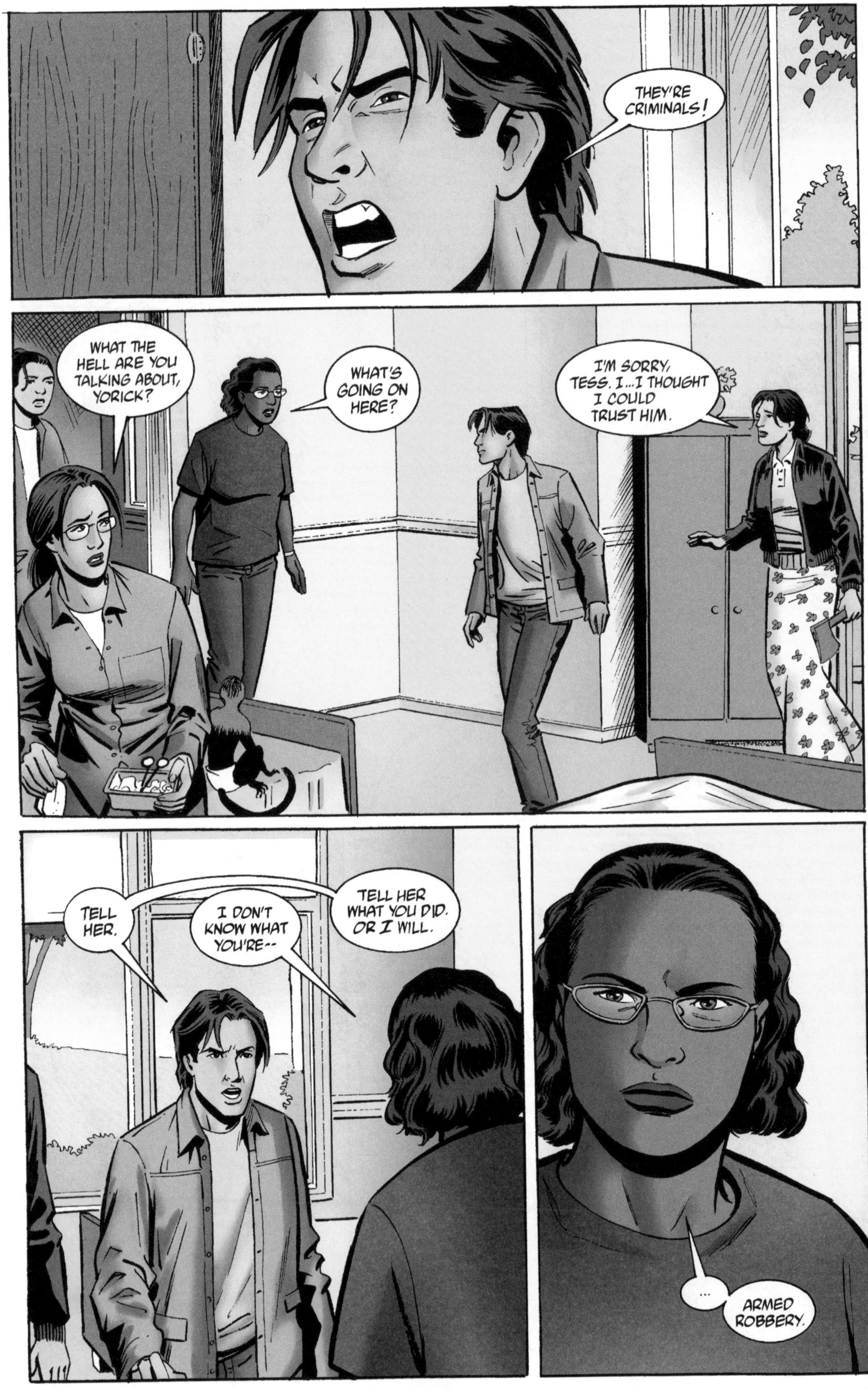
THEY'RE CRIMINALS!
WHAT THE HELL ARE YOU TALKING ABOUT, YORICK?
WHAT'S GOING ON HERE?
I'M SORRY, TESS. I...I THOUGHT I COULD TRUST HIM.
TELL HER.
I DON'T KNOW WHAT YOU'RE--
TELL HER WHAT YOU DID. OR I WILL.
...
ARMED ROBBERY.

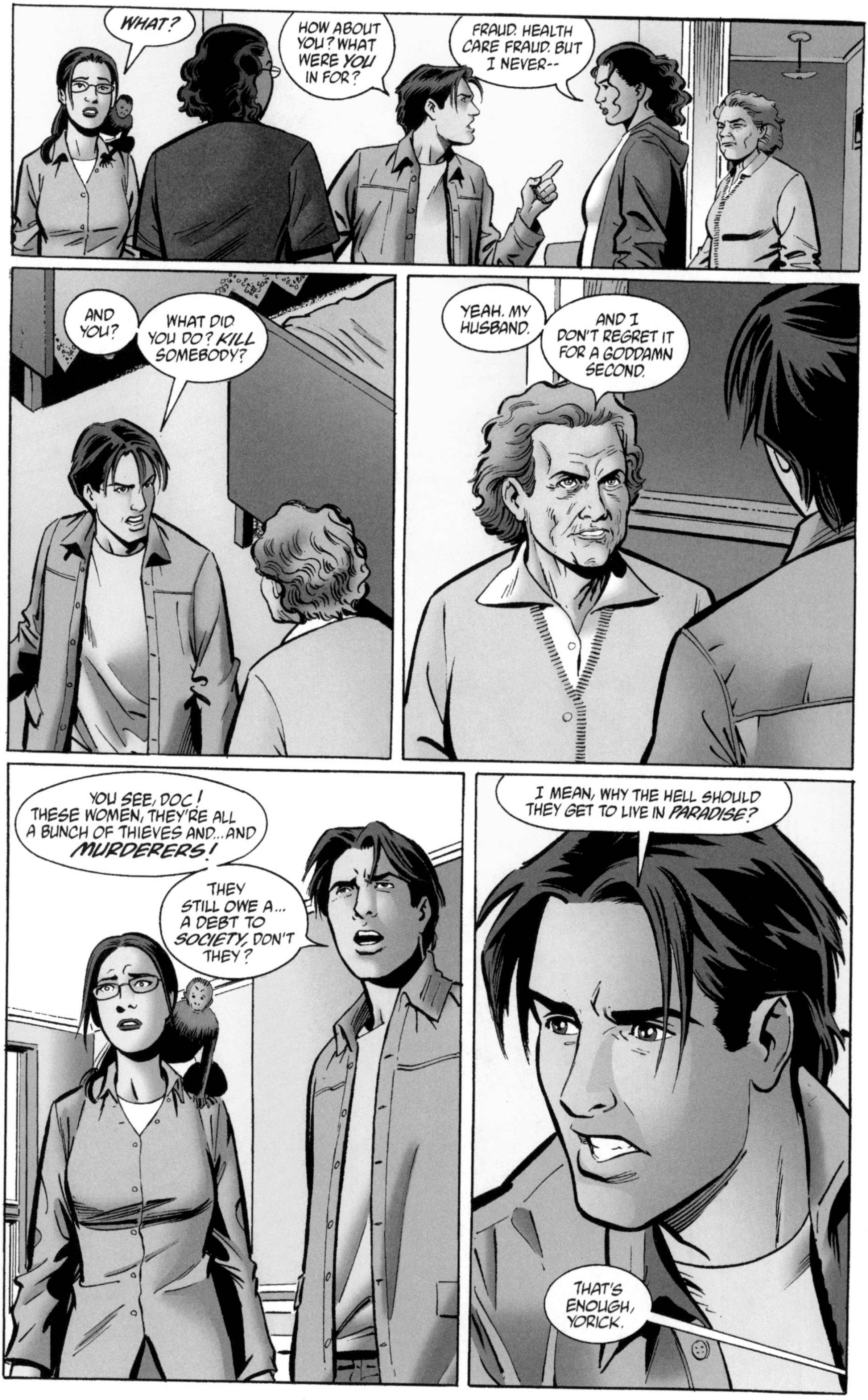
WHAT?
HOW ABOUT YOU? WHAT WERE YOU IN FOR?
FRAUD. HEALTH CARE FRAUD. BUT I NEVER--
AND YOU?
WHAT DID YOU DO? KILL SOMEBODY?
YEAH. MY HUSBAND.
AND I DON'T REGRET IT FOR A GODDAMN SECOND.
YOU SEE, DOC! THESE WOMEN, THEY'RE ALL A BUNCH OF THIEVES AND... AND MURDERERS!
THEY STILL OWE A... A DEBT TO SOCIETY, DON'T THEY?
I MEAN, WHY THE HELL SHOULD THEY GET TO LIVE IN PARADISE?
THAT'S ENOUGH, YORICK.

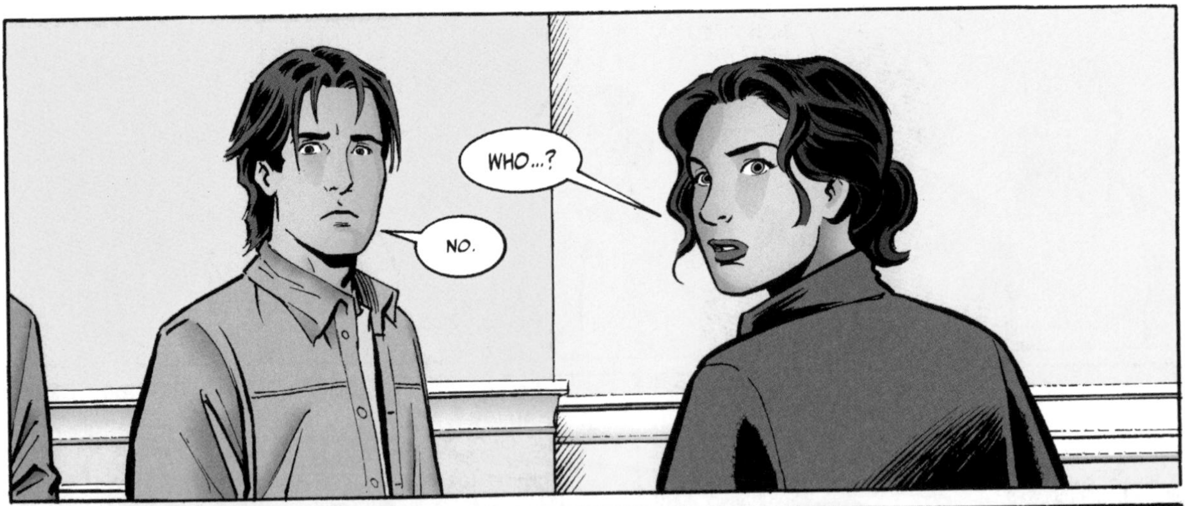
WHO...?
NO.

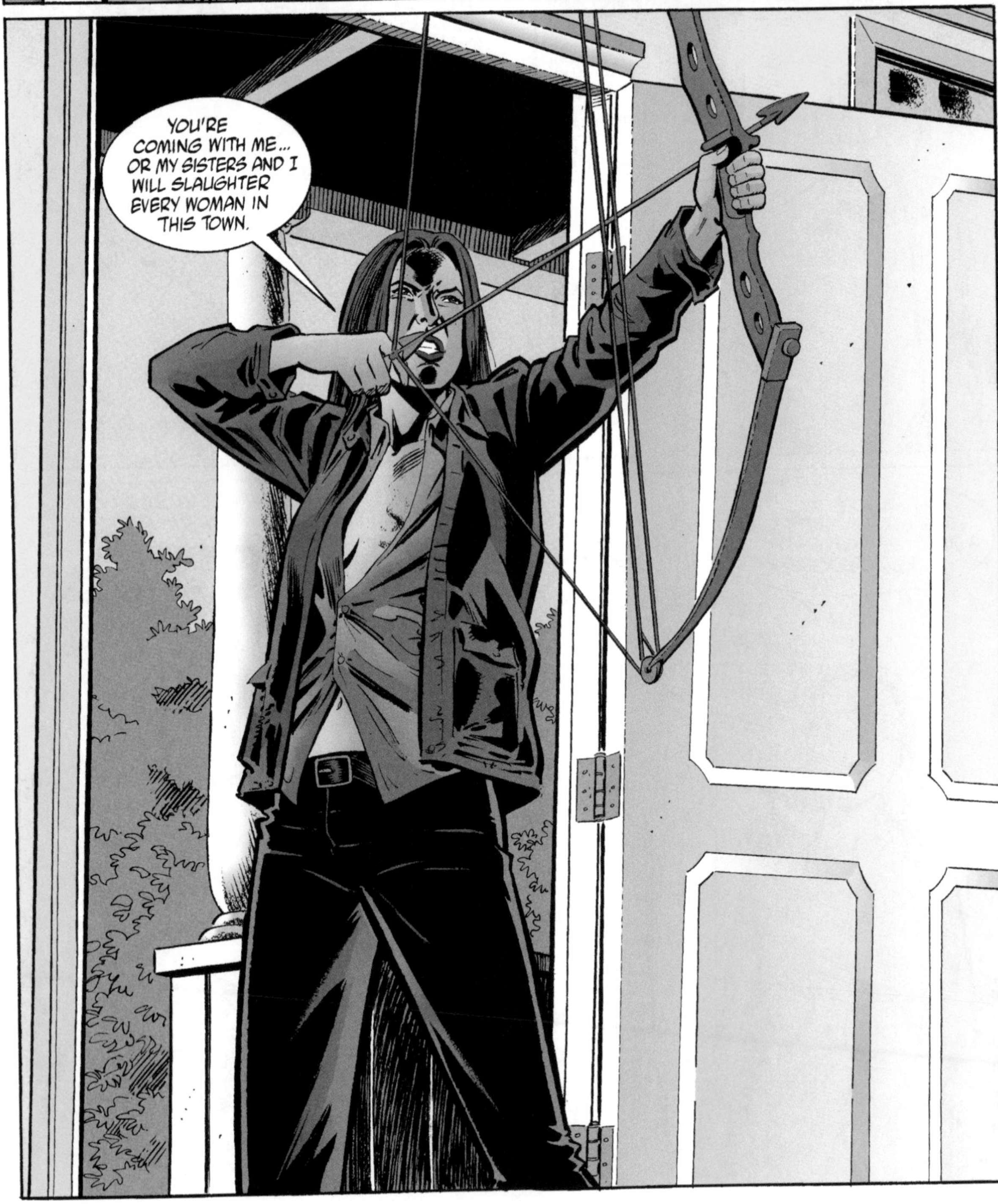
YOU'RE COMING WITH ME... OR MY SISTERS AND I WILL SLAUGHTER EVERY WOMAN IN THIS TOWN.

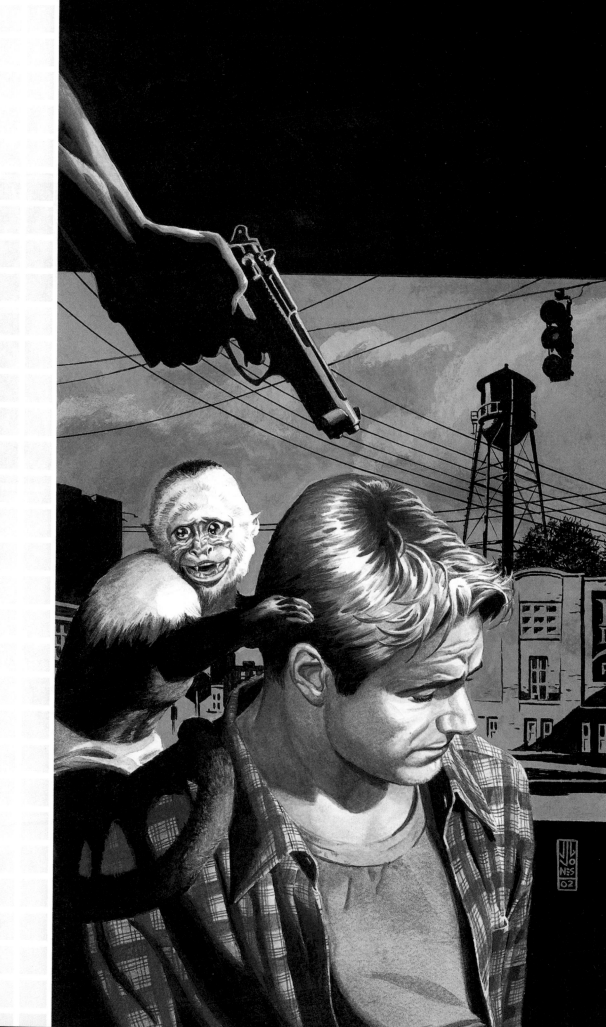

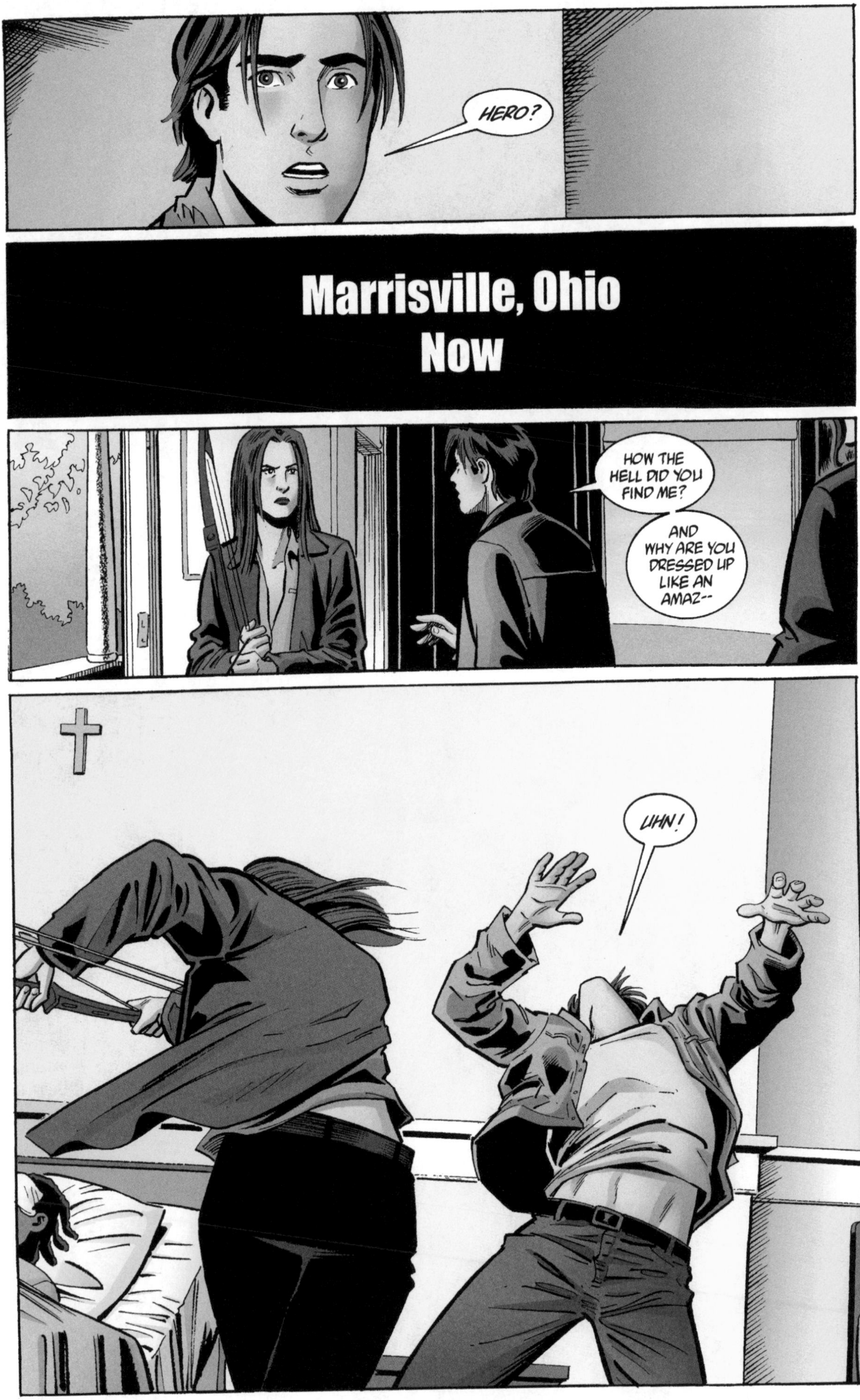
HERO?
Marrisville, Ohio
Now
HOW THE HELL DID YOU FIND ME?
AND WHY ARE YOU DRESSED UP LIKE AN AMAZ--
UHN!

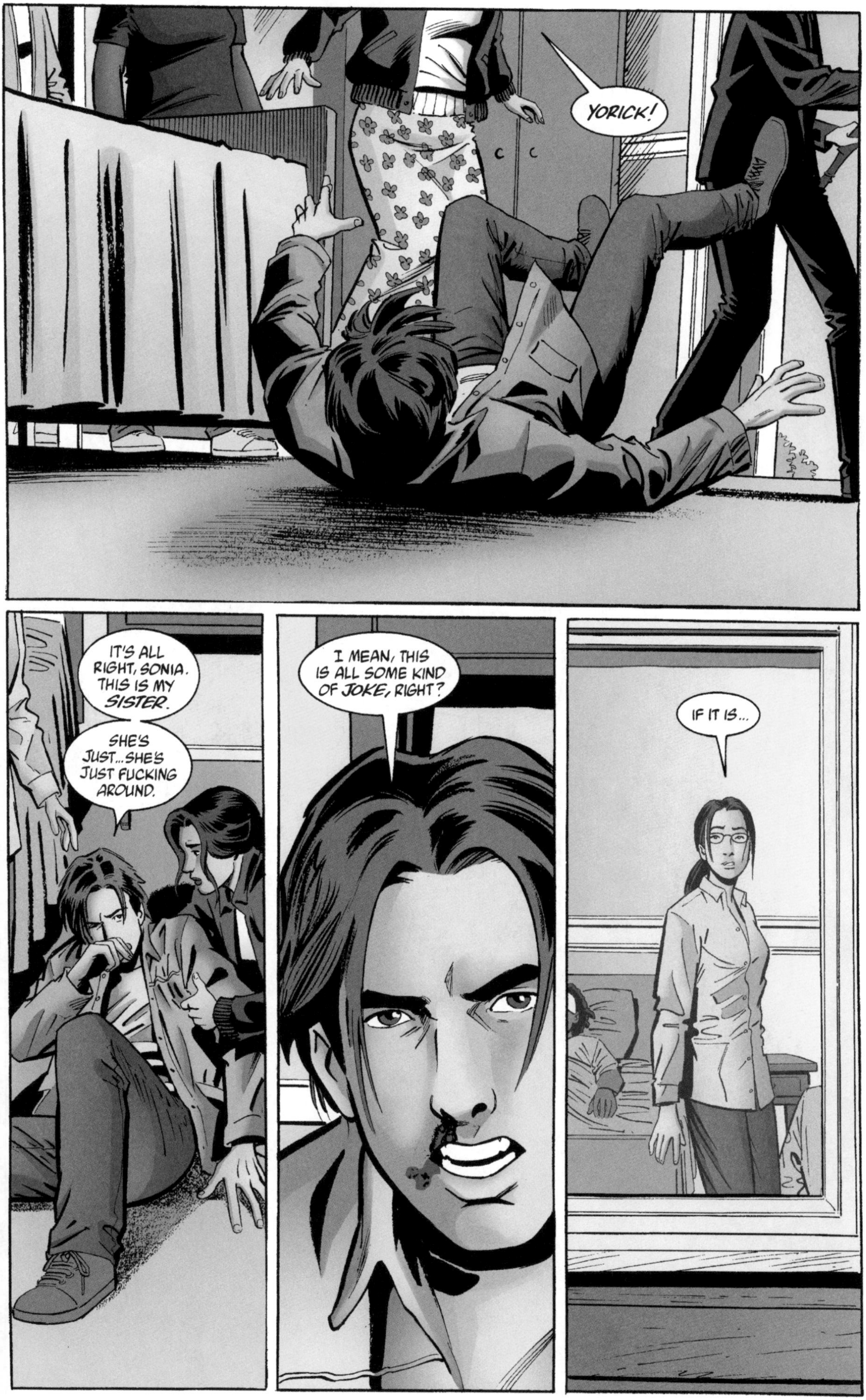
YORICK!
IT'S ALL RIGHT, SONIA. THIS IS MY SISTER.
SHE'S JUST...SHE'S JUST FUCKING AROUND.
I MEAN, THIS IS ALL SOME KIND OF JOKE, RIGHT?
IF IT IS...

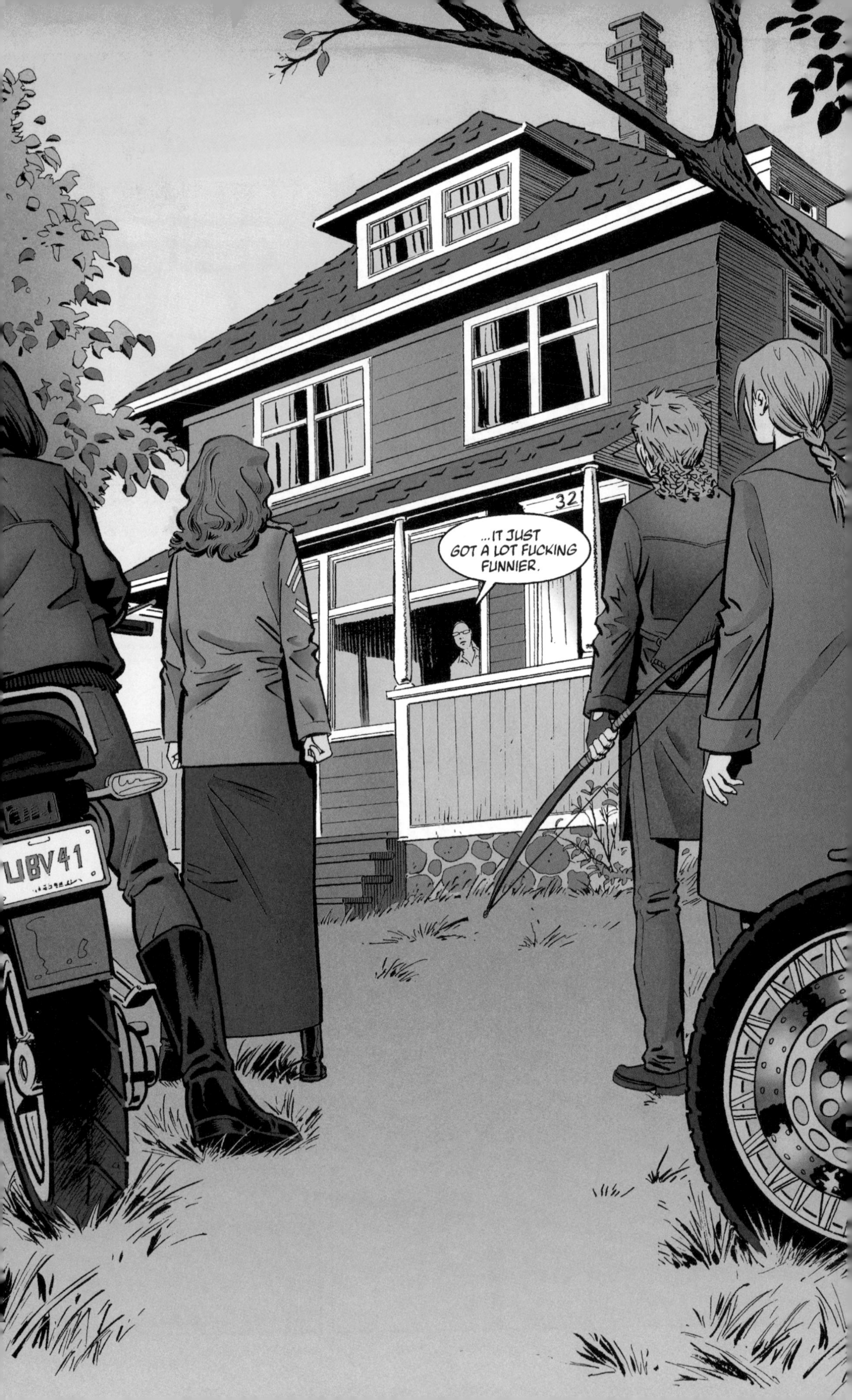
32
...IT JUST GOT A LOT FUCKING FUNNIER.
UBV41

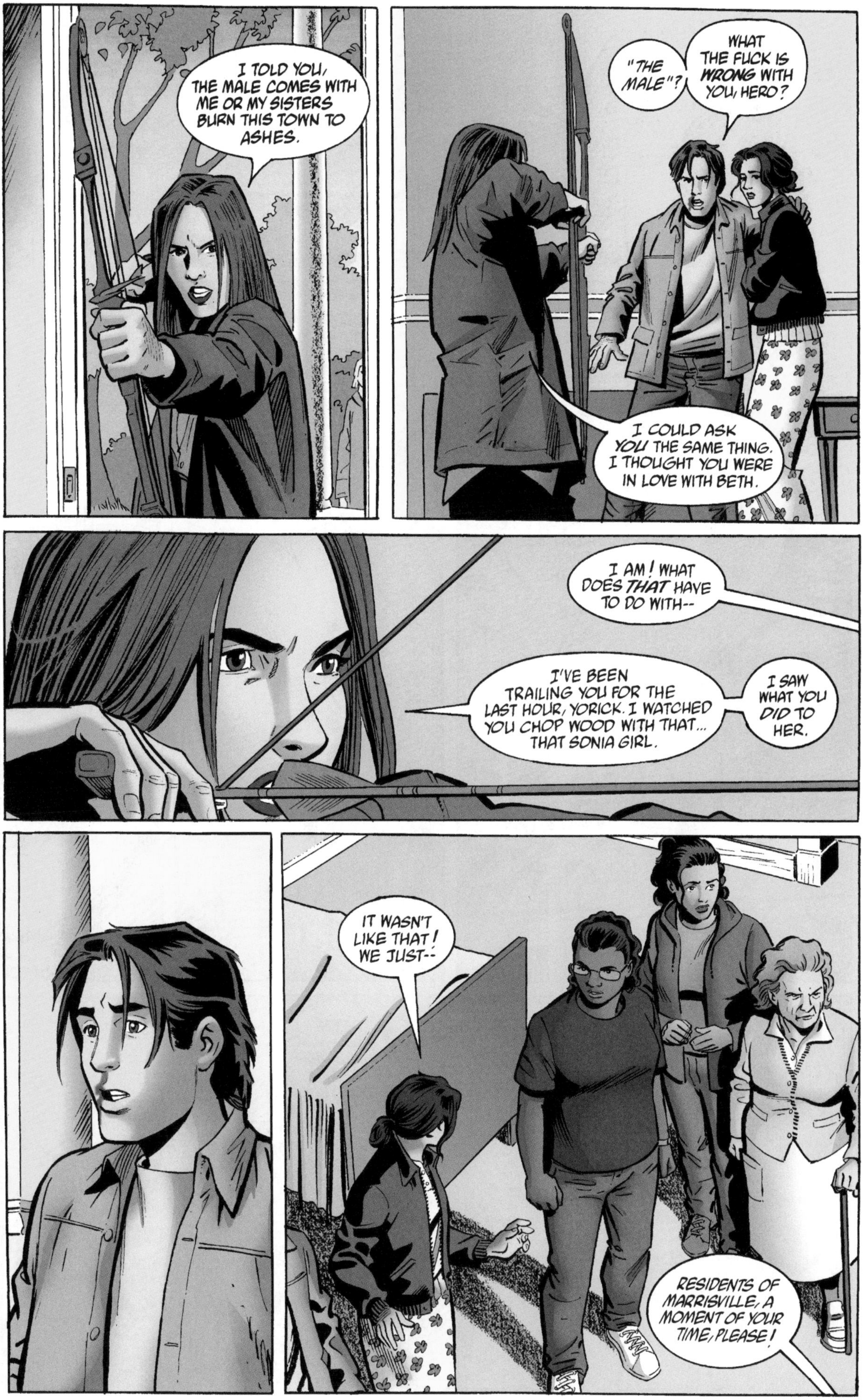
I TOLD YOU, THE MALE COMES WITH ME OR MY SISTERS BURN THIS TOWN TO ASHES.
"THE MALE"?
WHAT THE FUCK IS WRONG WITH YOU, HERO?
I COULD ASK YOU THE SAME THING. I THOUGHT YOU WERE IN LOVE WITH BETH.
I AM! WHAT DOES THAT HAVE TO DO WITH--
I'VE BEEN TRAILING YOU FOR THE LAST HOUR, YORICK. I WATCHED YOU CHOP WOOD WITH THAT... THAT SONIA GIRL.
I SAW WHAT YOU DID TO HER.
IT WASN'T LIKE THAT! WE JUST--
RESIDENTS OF MARRISVILLE, A MOMENT OF YOUR TIME, PLEASE!

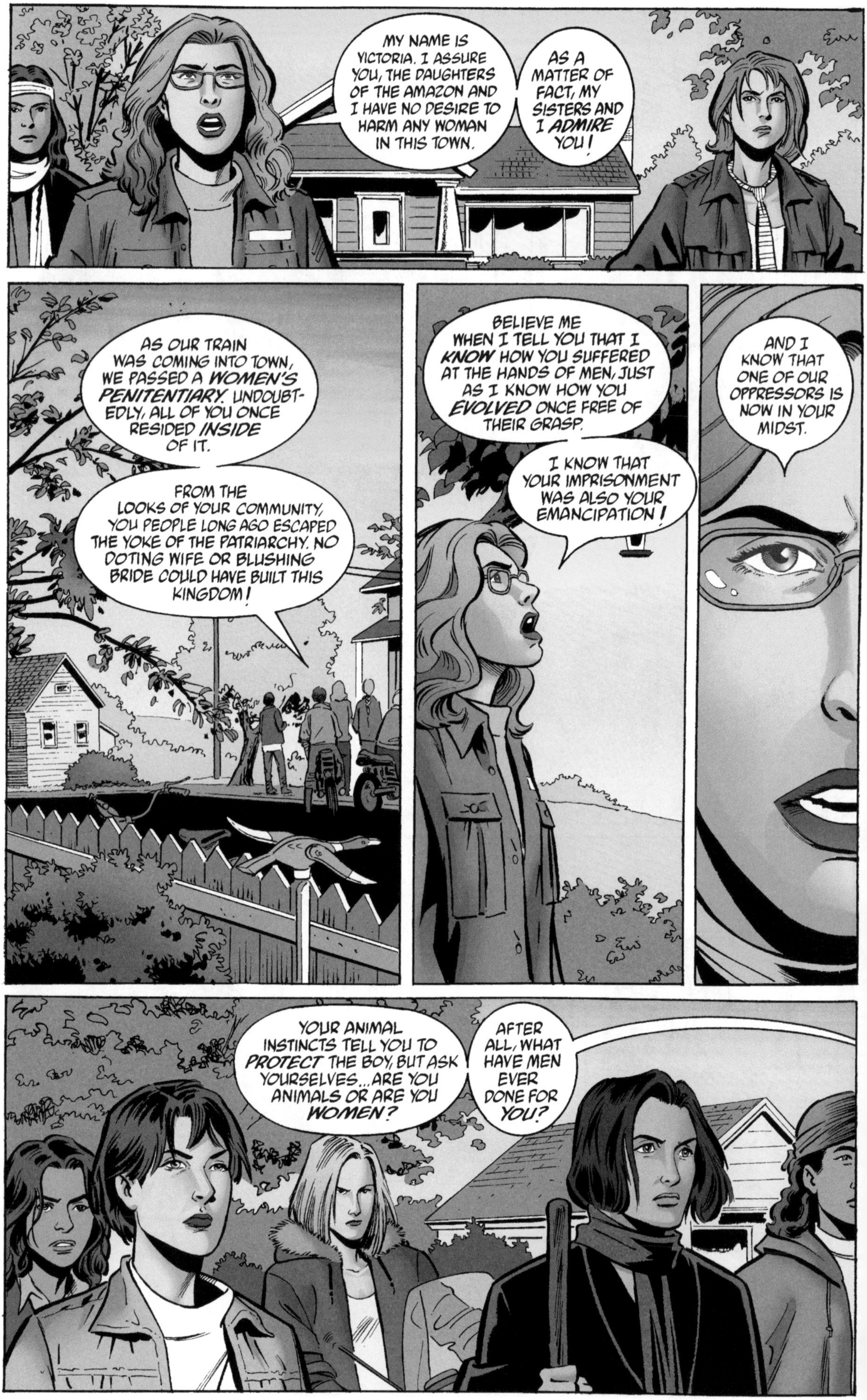
MY NAME IS VICTORIA. I ASSURE YOU, THE DAUGHTERS OF THE AMAZON AND I HAVE NO DESIRE TO HARM ANY WOMAN IN THIS TOWN.
AS A MATTER OF FACT, MY SISTERS AND I ADMIRE YOU!
AS OUR TRAIN WAS COMING INTO TOWN, WE PASSED A WOMEN'S PENITENTIARY. UNDOUBTEDLY, ALL OF YOU ONCE RESIDED INSIDE OF IT.
FROM THE LOOKS OF YOUR COMMUNITY, YOU PEOPLE LONG AGO ESCAPED THE YOKE OF THE PATRIARCHY. NO DOTING WIFE OR BLUSHING BRIDE COULD HAVE BUILT THIS KINGDOM!
BELIEVE ME WHEN I TELL YOU THAT I KNOW HOW YOU SUFFERED AT THE HANDS OF MEN, JUST AS I KNOW HOW YOU EVOLVED ONCE FREE OF THEIR GRASP.
I KNOW THAT YOUR IMPRISONMENT WAS ALSO YOUR EMANCIPATION!
AND I KNOW THAT ONE OF OUR OPPRESSORS IS NOW IN YOUR MIDST.
YOUR ANIMAL INSTINCTS TELL YOU TO PROTECT THE BOY, BUT ASK YOURSELVES... ARE YOU ANIMALS OR ARE YOU WOMEN?
AFTER ALL, WHAT HAVE MEN EVER DONE FOR YOU?

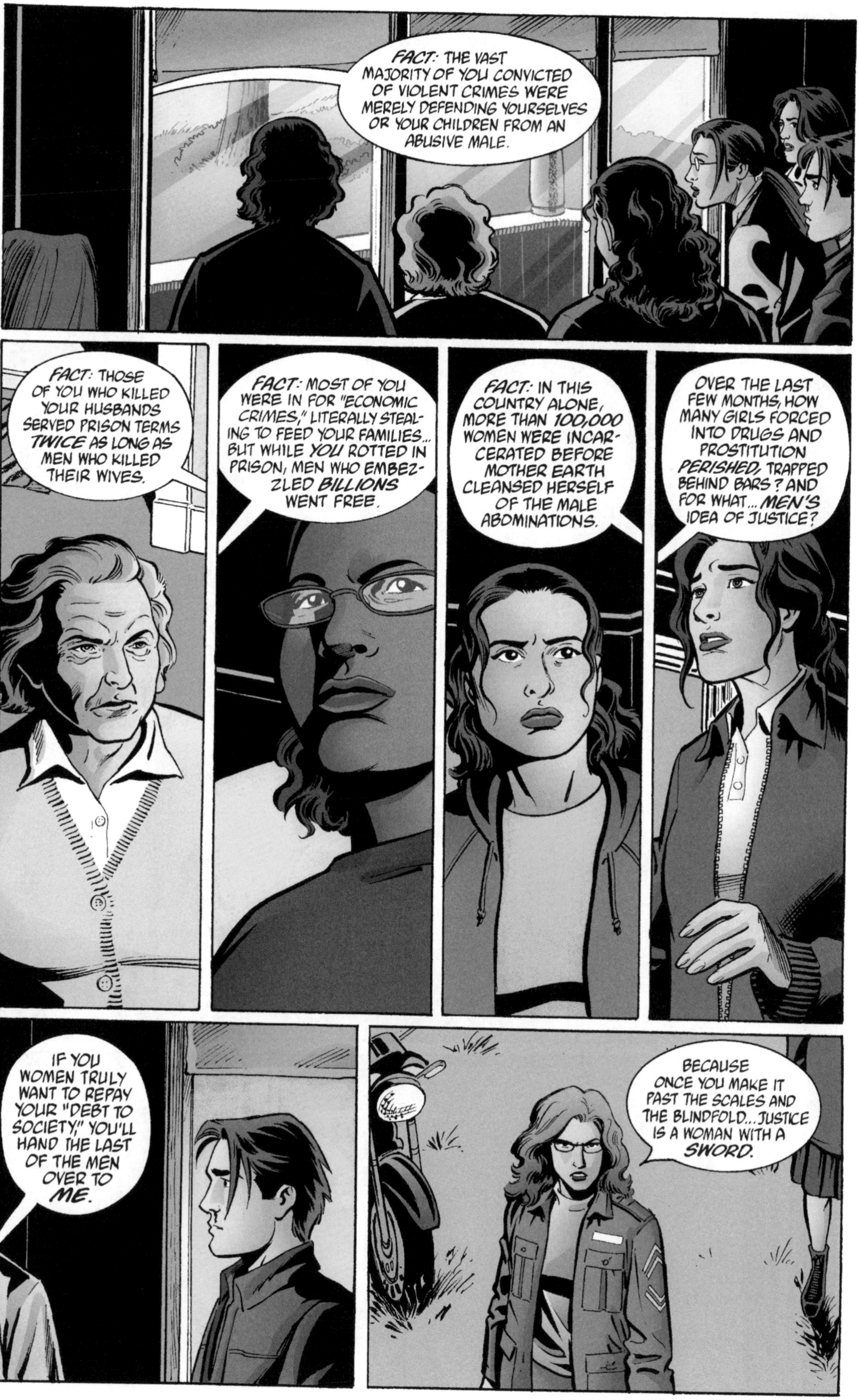
FACT: THE VAST MAJORITY OF YOU CONVICTED OF VIOLENT CRIMES WERE MERELY DEFENDING YOURSELVES OR YOUR CHILDREN FROM AN ABUSIVE MALE.
FACT: THOSE OF YOU WHO KILLED YOUR HUSBANDS SERVED PRISON TERMS TWICE AS LONG AS MEN WHO KILLED THEIR WIVES.
FACT: MOST OF YOU WERE IN FOR "ECONOMIC CRIMES," LITERALLY STEALING TO FEED YOUR FAMILIES... BUT WHILE YOU ROTTED IN PRISON, MEN WHO EMBEZZLED BILLIONS WENT FREE.
FACT: IN THIS COUNTRY ALONE, MORE THAN 100,000 WOMEN WERE INCARCERATED BEFORE MOTHER EARTH CLEANSED HERSELF OF THE MALE ABOMINATIONS.
OVER THE LAST FEW MONTHS, HOW MANY GIRLS FORCED INTO DRUGS AND PROSTITUTION PERISHED, TRAPPED BEHIND BARS? AND FOR WHAT... MEN'S IDEA OF JUSTICE?
IF YOU WOMEN TRULY WANT TO REPAY YOUR "DEBT TO SOCIETY," YOU'LL HAND THE LAST OF THE MEN OVER TO ME.
BECAUSE ONCE YOU MAKE IT PAST THE SCALES AND THE BLINDFOLD... JUSTICE IS A WOMAN WITH A SWORD.

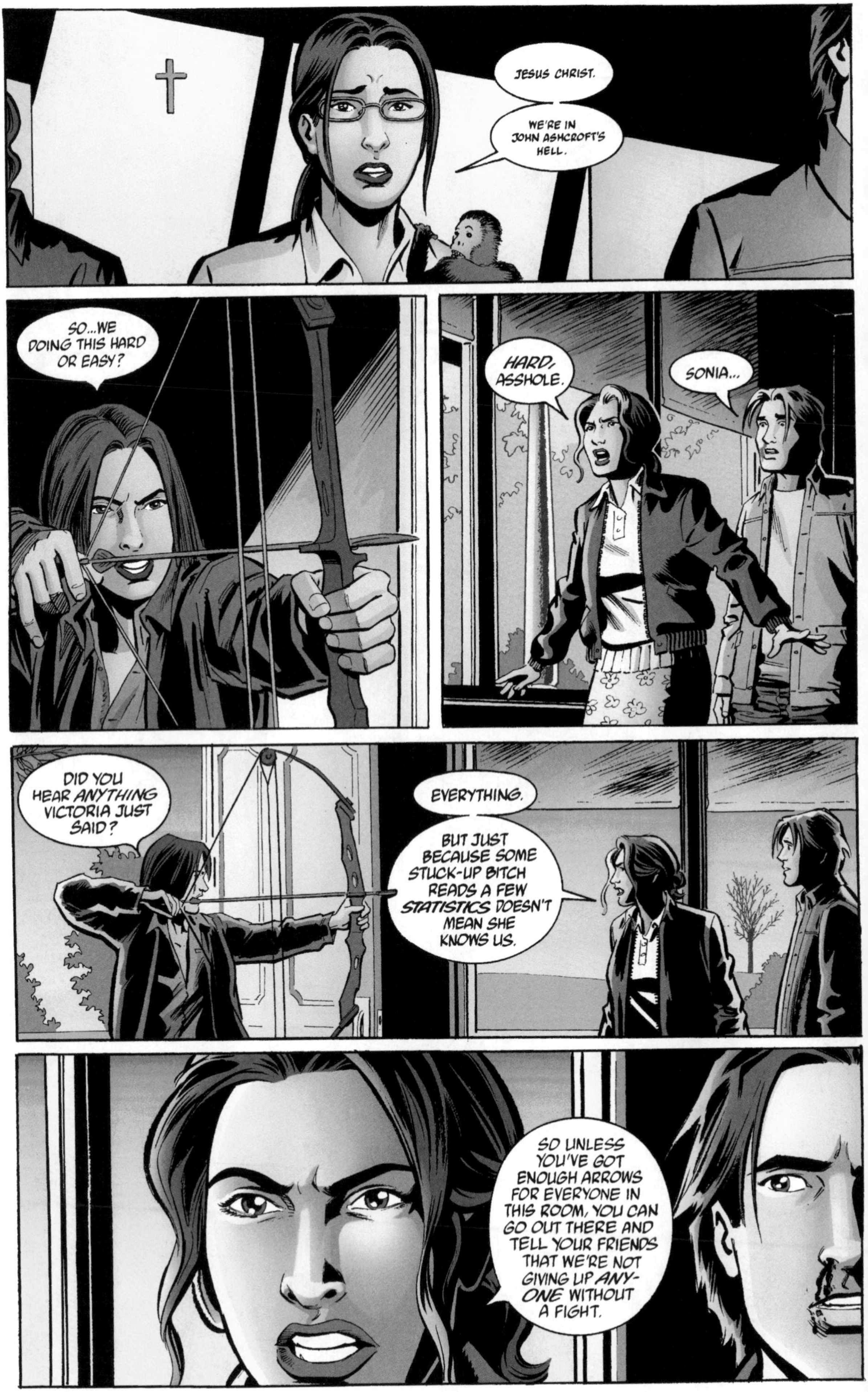
JESUS CHRIST.
WE'RE IN JOHN ASHCROFT'S HELL.
SO...WE DOING THIS HARD OR EASY?
HARD, ASSHOLE.
SONIA...
DID YOU HEAR ANYTHING VICTORIA JUST SAID?
EVERYTHING.
BUT JUST BECAUSE SOME STUCK-UP BITCH READS A FEW STATISTICS DOESN'T MEAN SHE KNOWS US.
SO UNLESS YOU'VE GOT ENOUGH ARROWS FOR EVERYONE IN THIS ROOM, YOU CAN GO OUT THERE AND TELL YOUR FRIENDS THAT WE'RE NOT GIVING UP ANYONE WITHOUT A FIGHT.

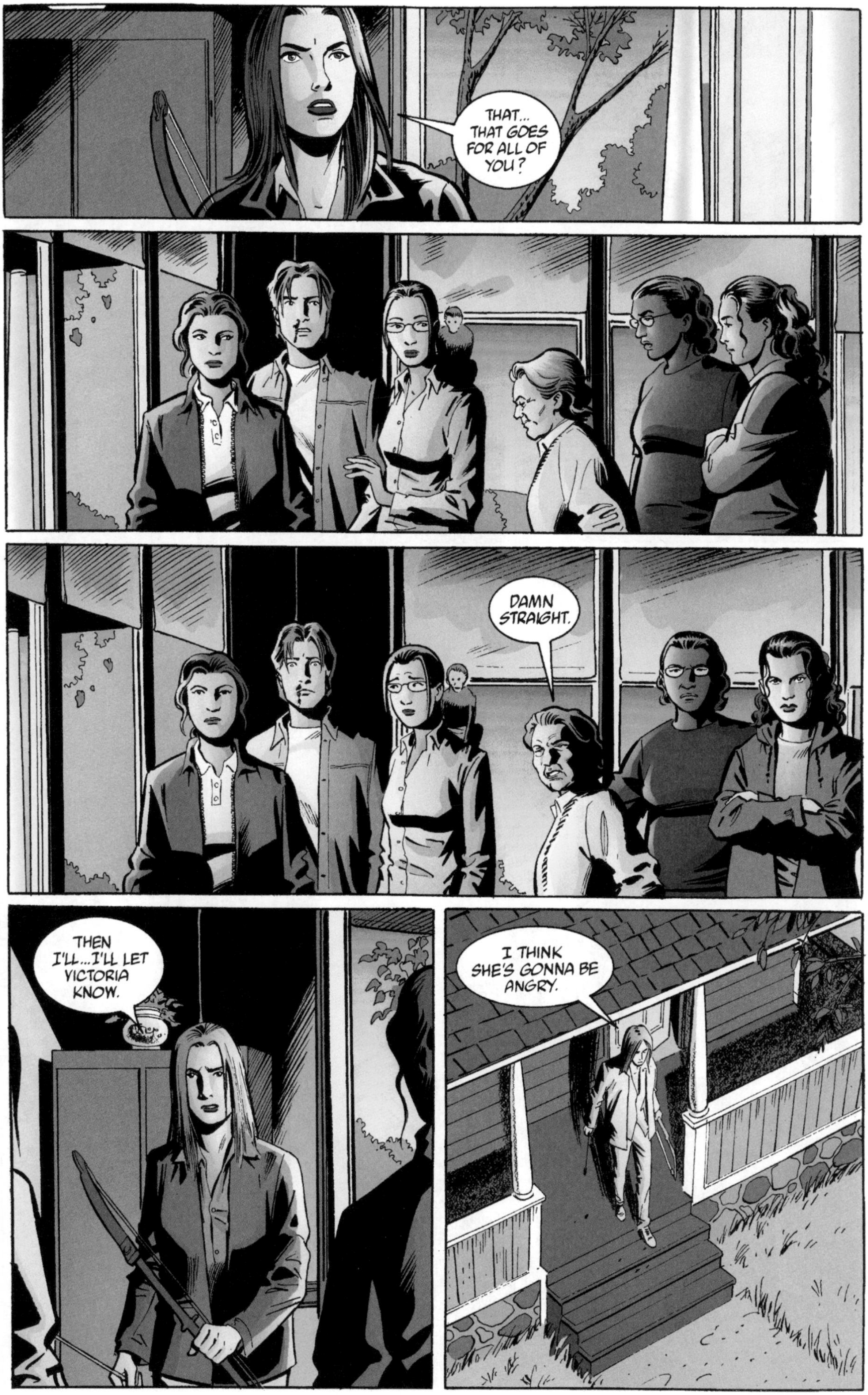
THAT... THAT GOES FOR ALL OF YOU?
DAMN STRAIGHT.
THEN I'LL...I'LL LET VICTORIA KNOW.
I THINK SHE'S GONNA BE ANGRY.

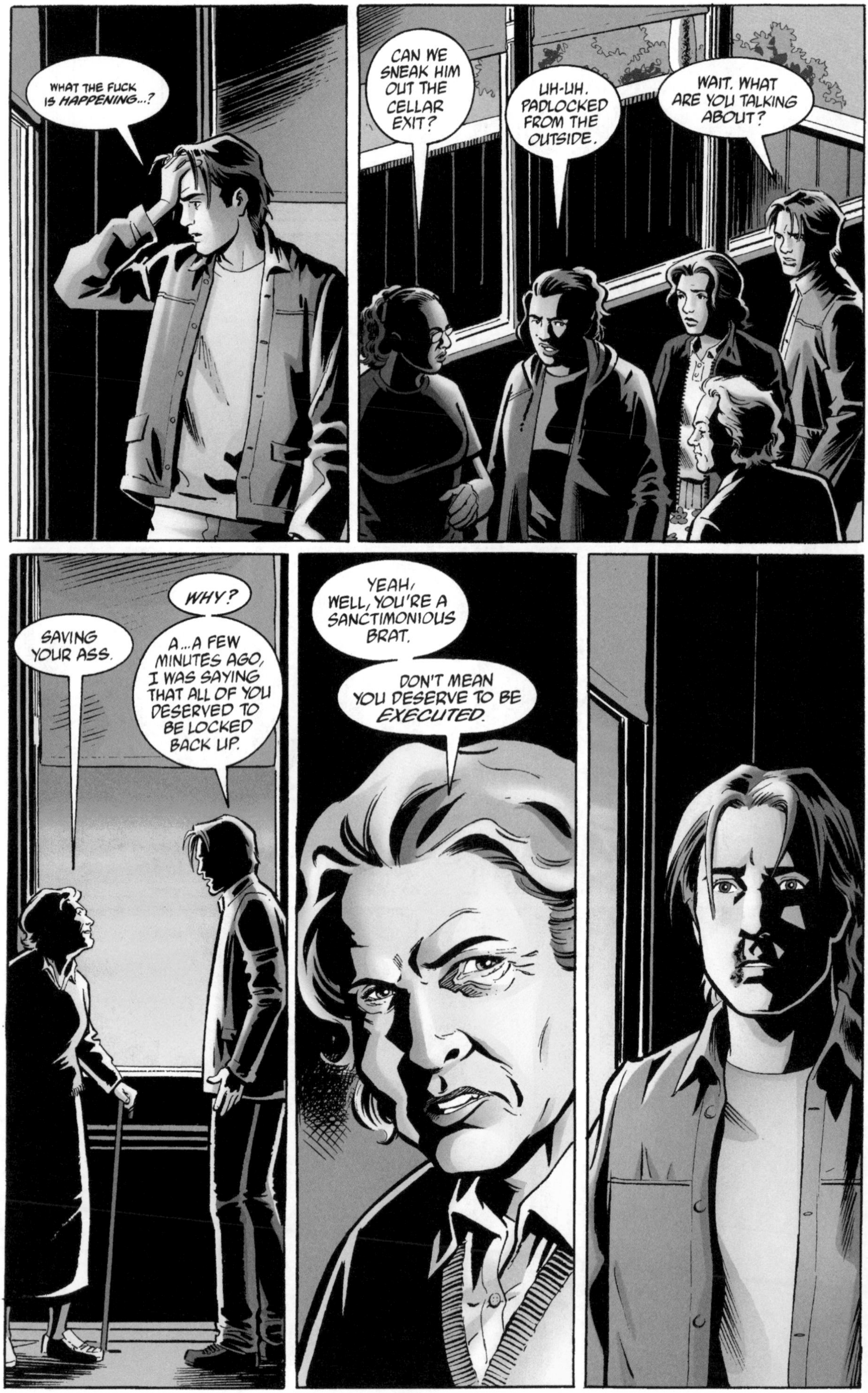
WHAT THE FUCK IS *HAPPENING*...?
CAN WE SNEAK HIM OUT THE CELLAR EXIT?
UH-UH. PADLOCKED FROM THE OUTSIDE.
WAIT. WHAT ARE YOU TALKING ABOUT?
SAVING YOUR ASS.
WHY?
A...A FEW MINUTES AGO, I WAS SAYING THAT ALL OF YOU DESERVED TO BE LOCKED BACK UP.
YEAH, WELL, YOU'RE A SANCTIMONIOUS BRAT.
DON'T MEAN YOU DESERVE TO BE *EXECUTED*.

SO WHAT DO WE DO NOW?

RALLY THE TROOPS.

RIGHT. THERE ARE FOUR OF US FOR EVERY ONE OF THEM.

BUT THE BRA BURNERS OUT THERE HAVE *WEAPONS*.

DO...DO YOU?

NO ARMS IN MARRISVILLE.

IT WAS THE FIRST RULE IN OUR CHARTER.

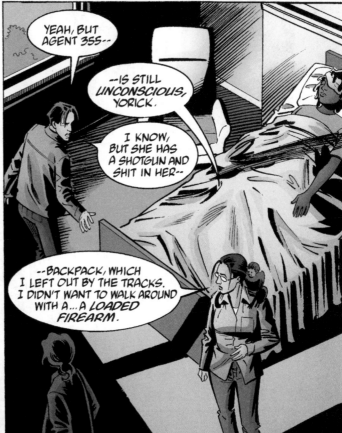

YEAH, BUT AGENT 355--

--IS STILL *UNCONSCIOUS*, YORICK.

I KNOW, BUT SHE HAS A SHOTGUN AND SHIT IN HER--

--BACKPACK, WHICH I LEFT OUT BY THE TRACKS. I DIDN'T WANT TO WALK AROUND WITH A...A *LOADED FIREARM*.

I WAS AFRAID SOMEONE MIGHT GET HURT.

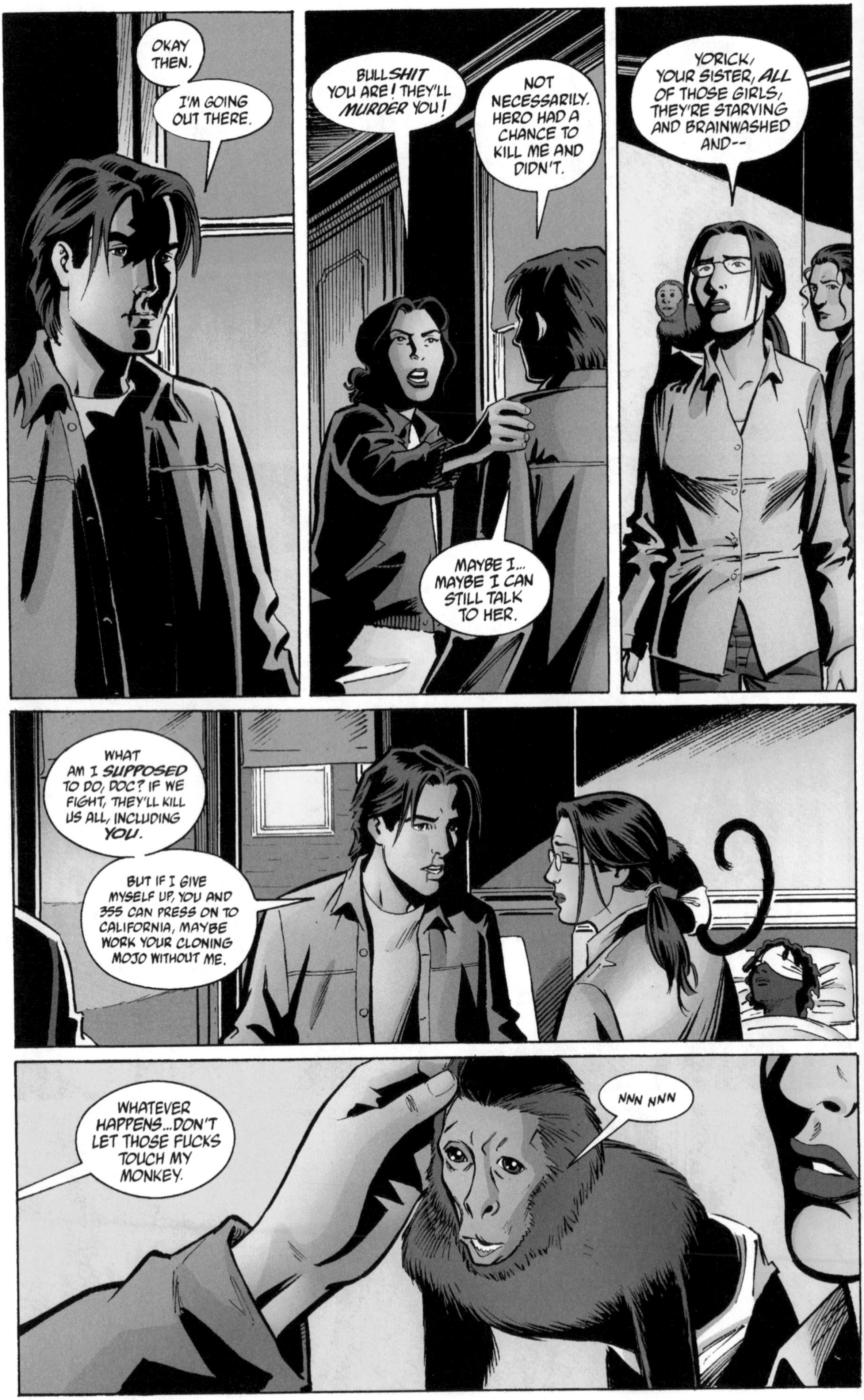
OKAY THEN.
I'M GOING OUT THERE.
BULLSHIT YOU ARE! THEY'LL MURDER YOU!
NOT NECESSARILY. HERO HAD A CHANCE TO KILL ME AND DIDN'T.
MAYBE I... MAYBE I CAN STILL TALK TO HER.
YORICK, YOUR SISTER, ALL OF THOSE GIRLS, THEY'RE STARVING AND BRAINWASHED AND--
WHAT AM I SUPPOSED TO DO, DOC? IF WE FIGHT, THEY'LL KILL US ALL, INCLUDING YOU.
BUT IF I GIVE MYSELF UP, YOU AND 355 CAN PRESS ON TO CALIFORNIA, MAYBE WORK YOUR CLONING MOJO WITHOUT ME.
WHATEVER HAPPENS...DON'T LET THOSE FUCKS TOUCH MY MONKEY.
NNN NNN

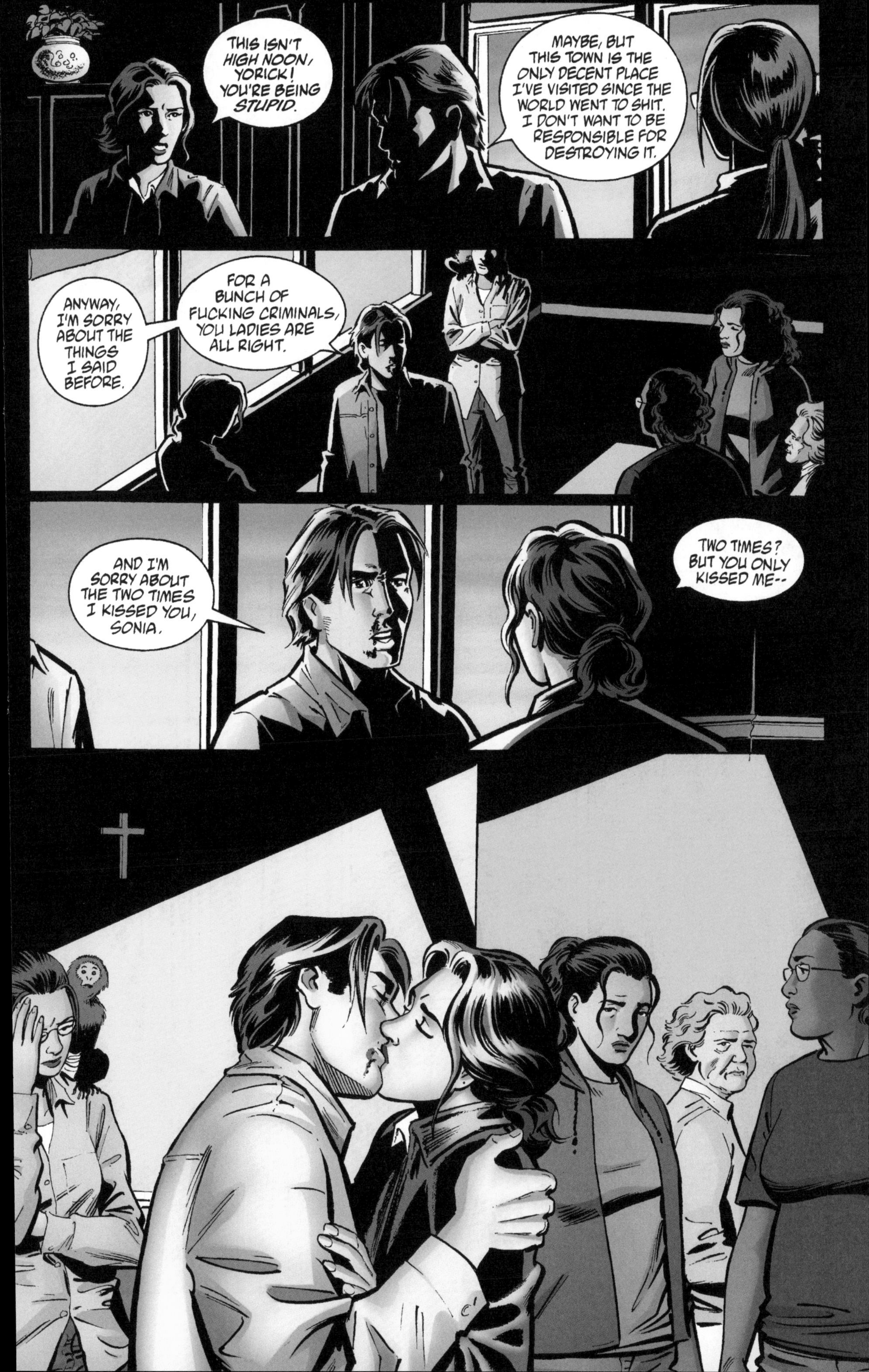
THIS ISN'T HIGH NOON, YORICK! YOU'RE BEING STUPID.
MAYBE, BUT THIS TOWN IS THE ONLY DECENT PLACE I'VE VISITED SINCE THE WORLD WENT TO SHIT. I DON'T WANT TO BE RESPONSIBLE FOR DESTROYING IT.
ANYWAY, I'M SORRY ABOUT THE THINGS I SAID BEFORE.
FOR A BUNCH OF FUCKING CRIMINALS, YOU LADIES ARE ALL RIGHT.
AND I'M SORRY ABOUT THE TWO TIMES I KISSED YOU, SONIA.
TWO TIMES? BUT YOU ONLY KISSED ME--

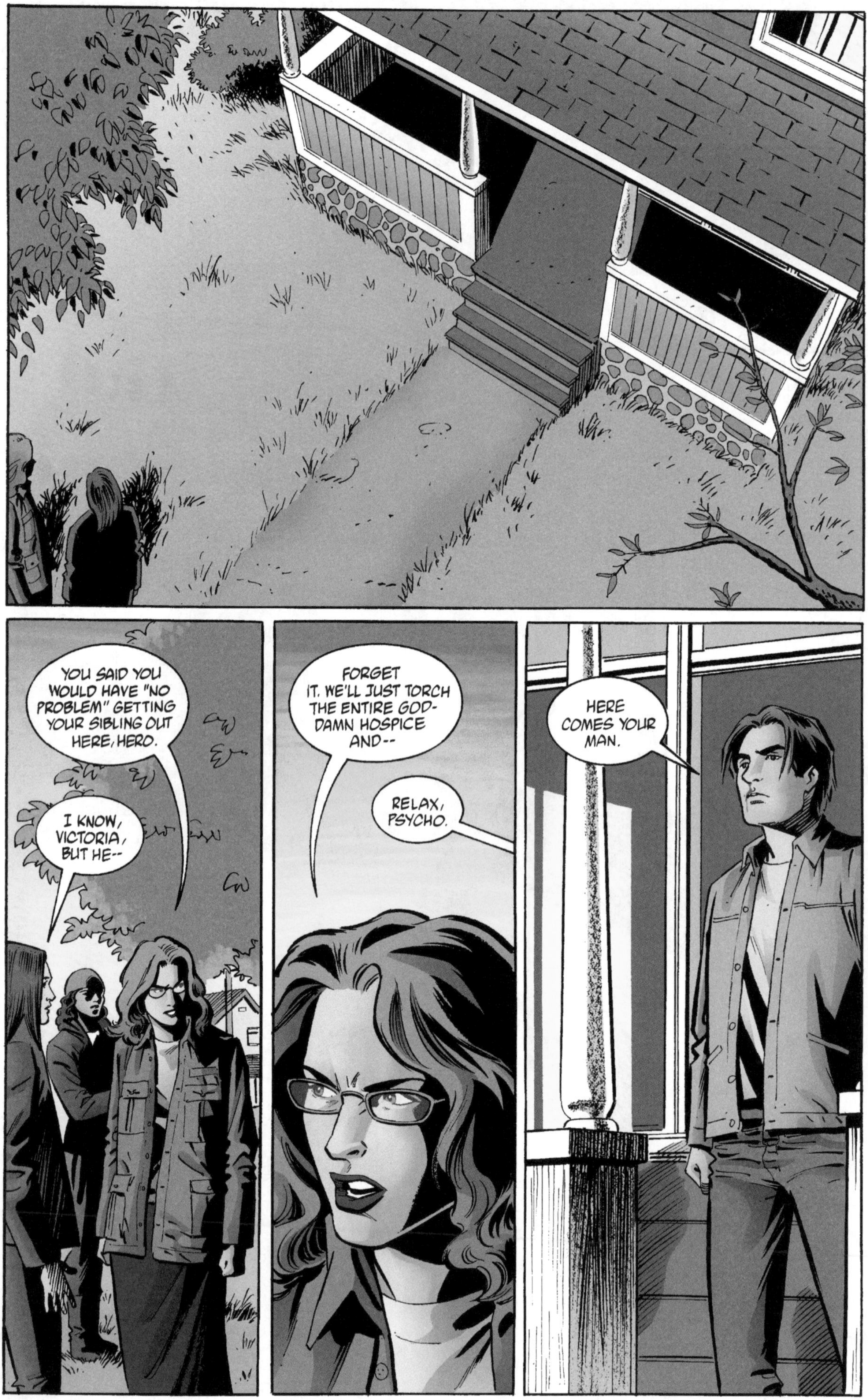
YOU SAID YOU WOULD HAVE "NO PROBLEM" GETTING YOUR SIBLING OUT HERE, HERO.
I KNOW, VICTORIA, BUT HE--
FORGET IT. WE'LL JUST TORCH THE ENTIRE GOD-DAMN HOSPICE AND--
RELAX, PSYCHO.
HERE COMES YOUR MAN.

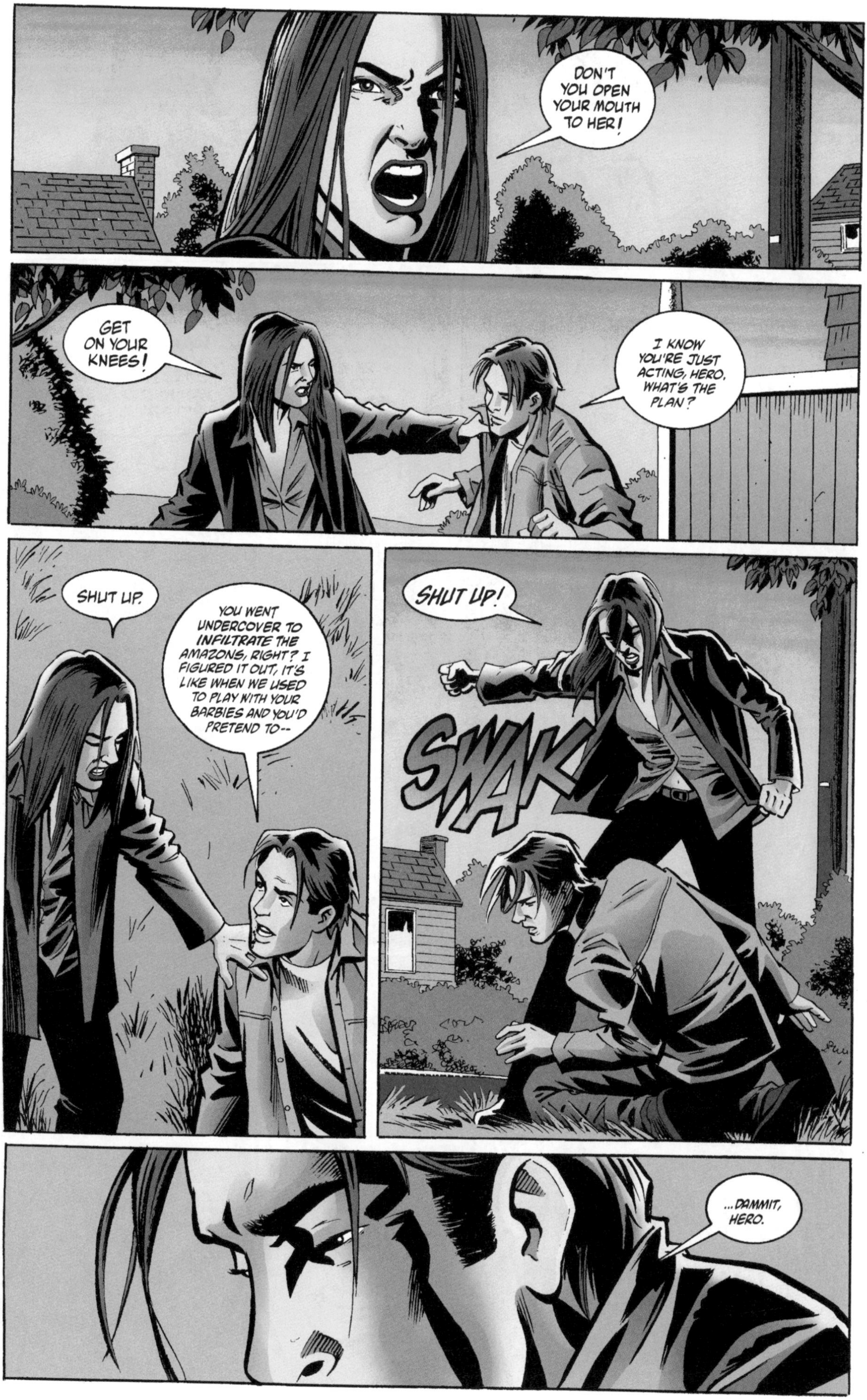
DON'T YOU OPEN YOUR MOUTH TO HER!
GET ON YOUR KNEES!
I KNOW YOU'RE JUST ACTING, HERO. WHAT'S THE PLAN?
SHUT UP.
YOU WENT UNDERCOVER TO INFILTRATE THE AMAZONS, RIGHT? I FIGURED IT OUT, IT'S LIKE WHEN WE USED TO PLAY WITH YOUR BARBIES AND YOU'D PRETEND TO--
SHUT UP!
SWAK
...DAMMIT, HERO.

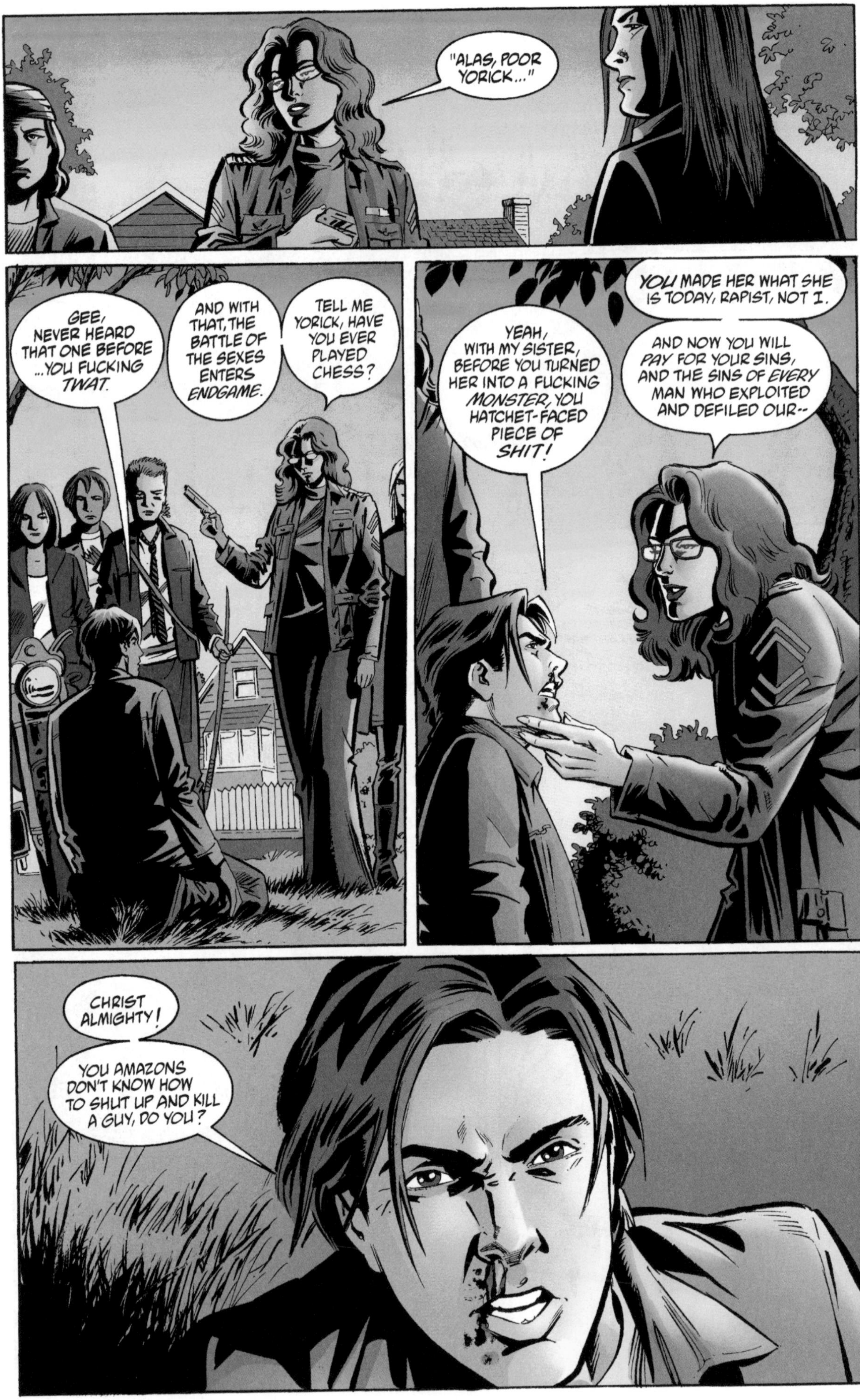
"ALAS, POOR YORICK..."
GEE, NEVER HEARD THAT ONE BEFORE ...YOU FUCKING TWAT.
AND WITH THAT, THE BATTLE OF THE SEXES ENTERS ENDGAME.
TELL ME YORICK, HAVE YOU EVER PLAYED CHESS?
YEAH, WITH MY SISTER, BEFORE YOU TURNED HER INTO A FUCKING MONSTER, YOU HATCHET-FACED PIECE OF SHIT!
YOU MADE HER WHAT SHE IS TODAY, RAPIST, NOT I.
AND NOW YOU WILL PAY FOR YOUR SINS, AND THE SINS OF EVERY MAN WHO EXPLOITED AND DEFILED OUR--
CHRIST ALMIGHTY!
YOU AMAZONS DON'T KNOW HOW TO SHUT UP AND KILL A GUY, DO YOU?

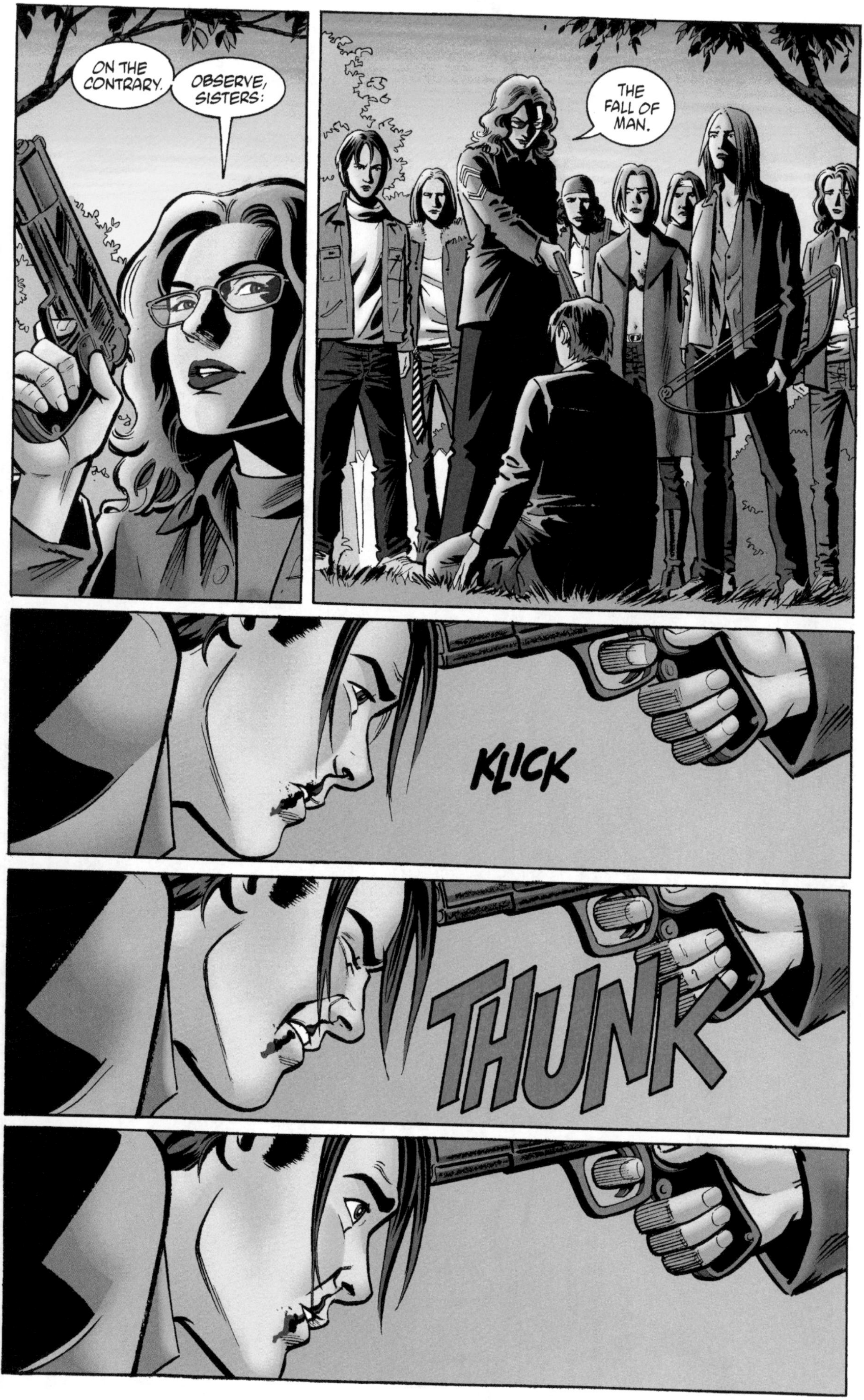
ON THE CONTRARY.
OBSERVE, SISTERS:
THE FALL OF MAN.
KLICK
THUNK

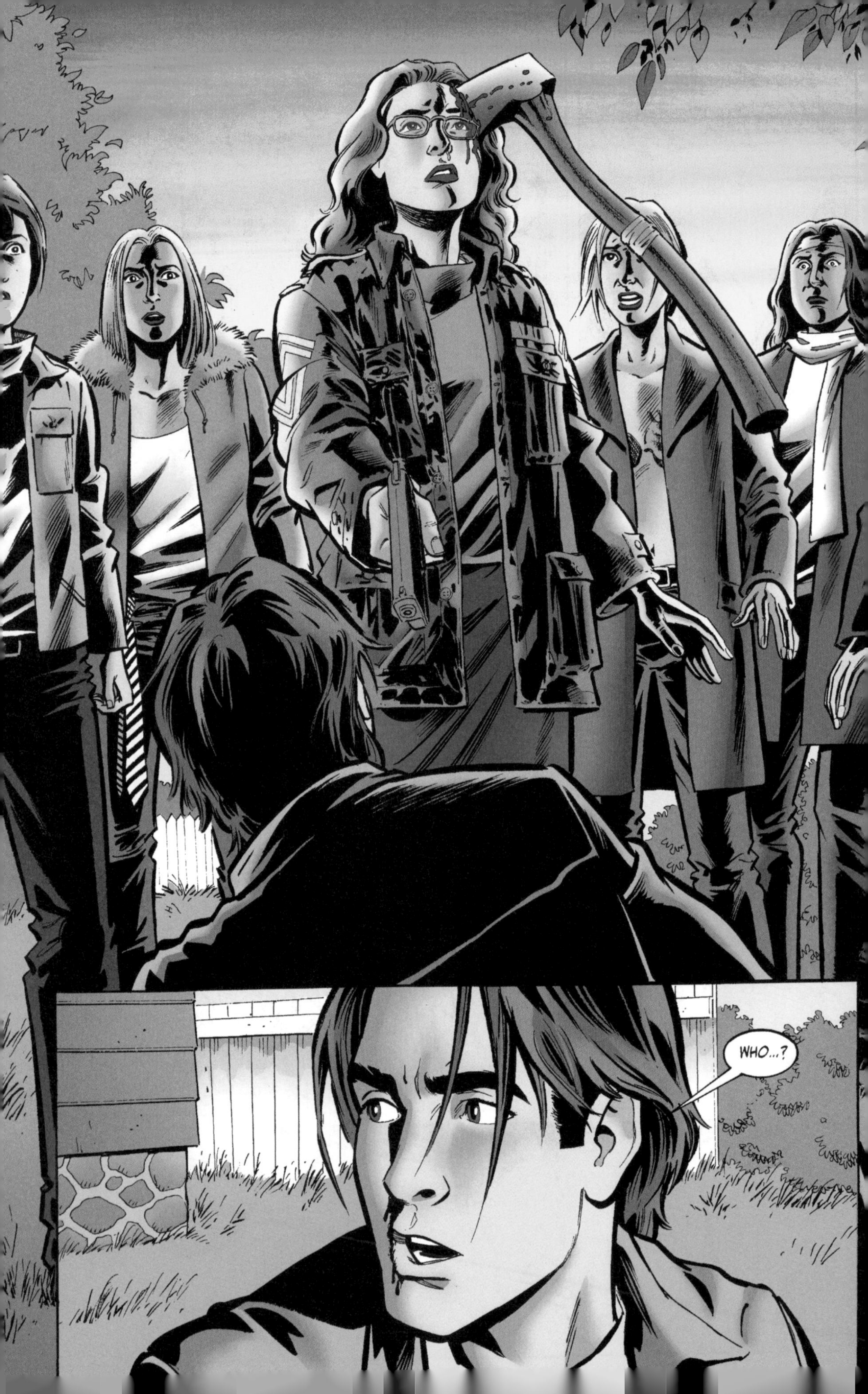
WHO...?

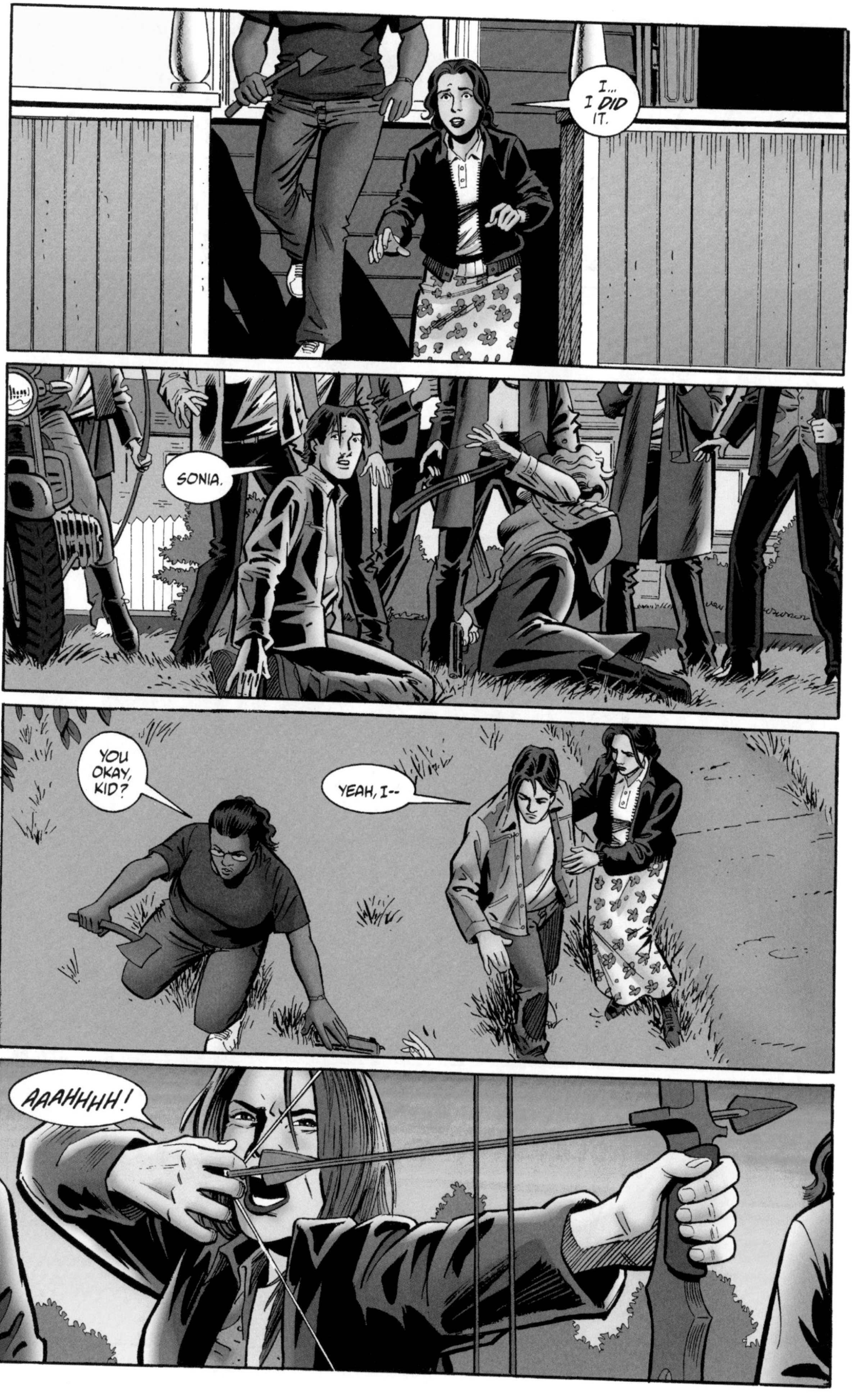
I... I DID IT.
SONIA.
YOU OKAY, KID?
YEAH, I--
AAAHHHH!

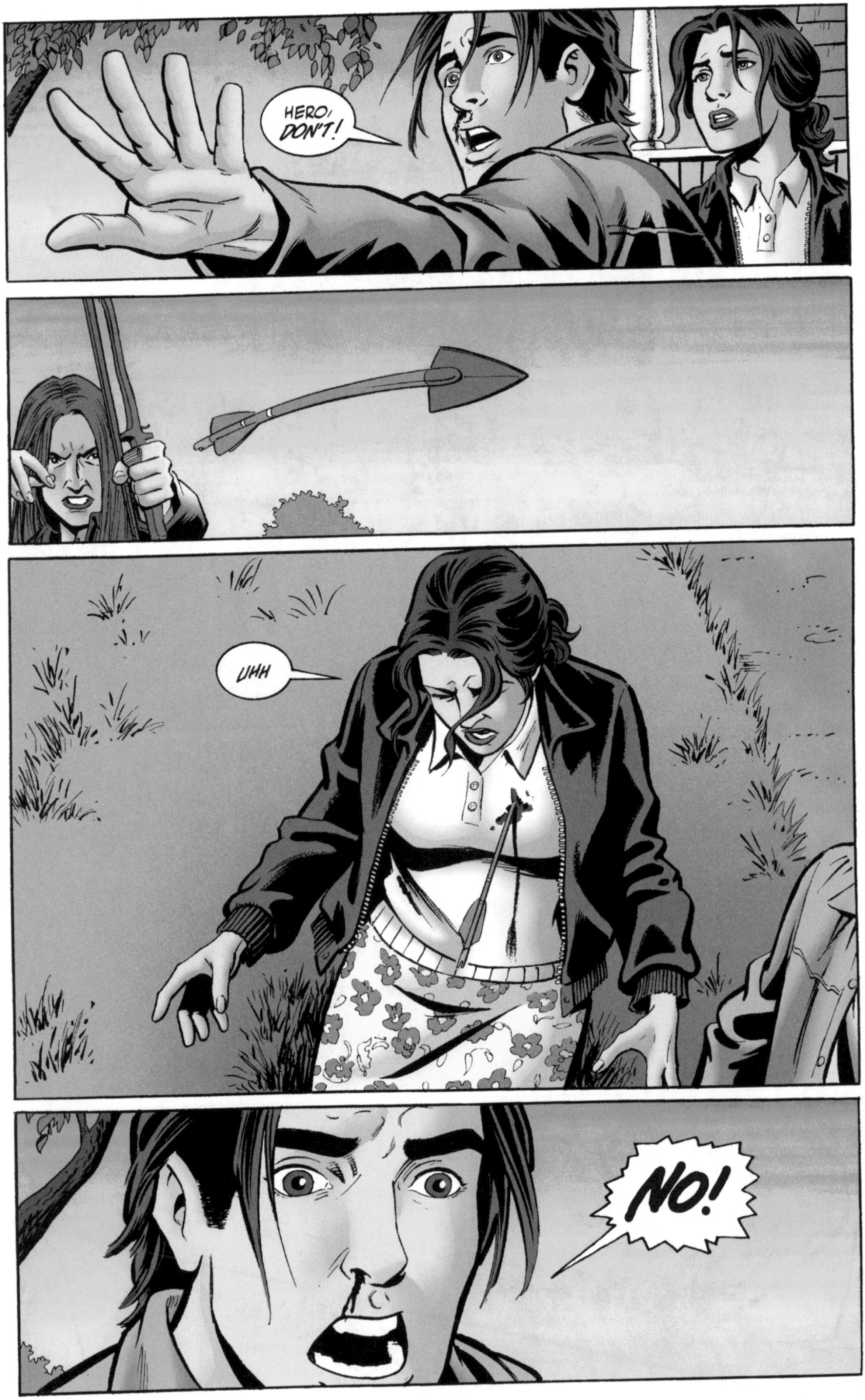

HERO, DON'T!
UHH
NO!

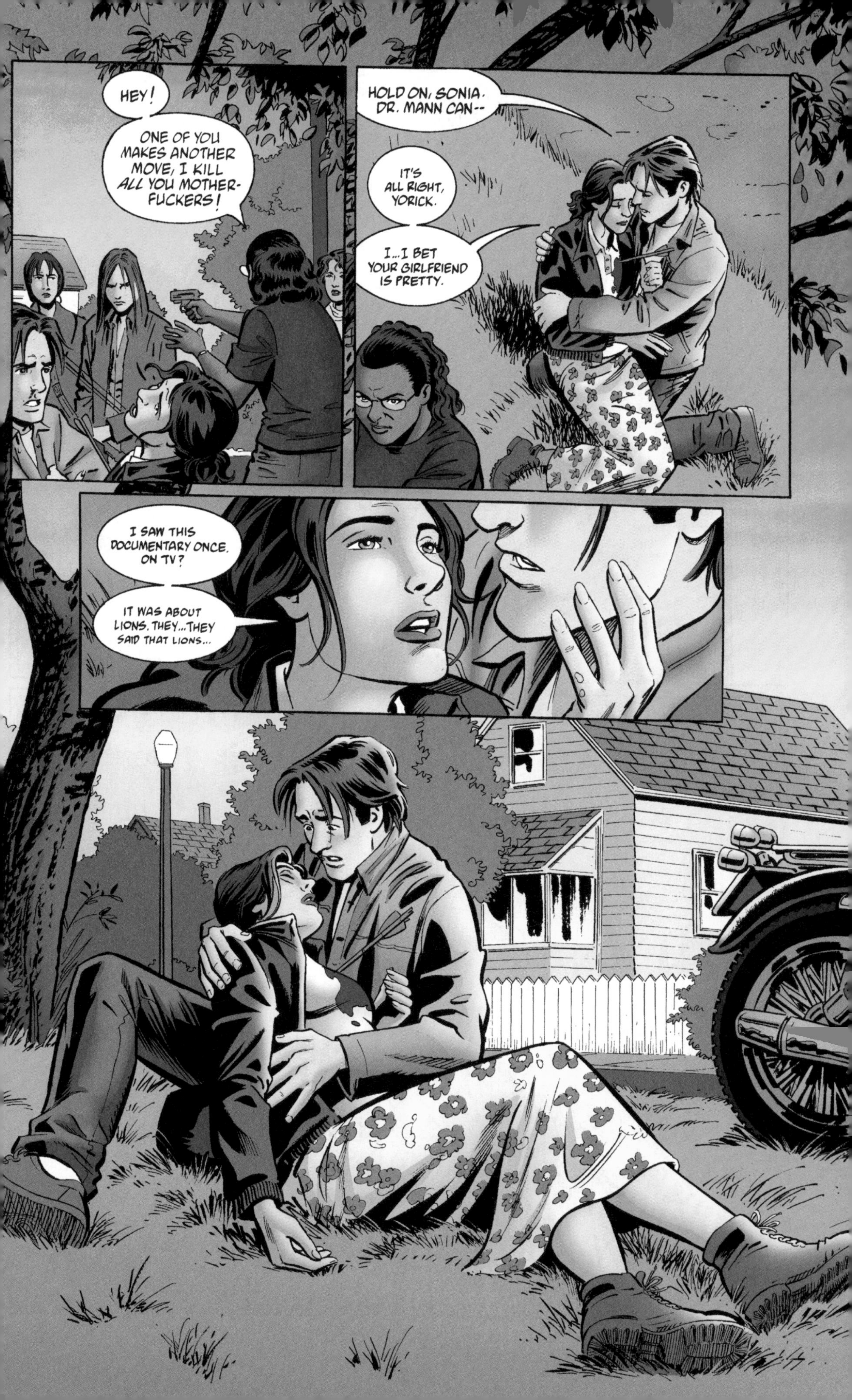
HEY!
ONE OF YOU MAKES ANOTHER MOVE, I KILL ALL YOU MOTHER-FUCKERS!
HOLD ON, SONIA. DR. MANN CAN--
IT'S ALL RIGHT, YORICK.
I...I BET YOUR GIRLFRIEND IS PRETTY.
I SAW THIS DOCUMENTARY ONCE. ON TV?
IT WAS ABOUT LIONS. THEY...THEY SAID THAT LIONS...

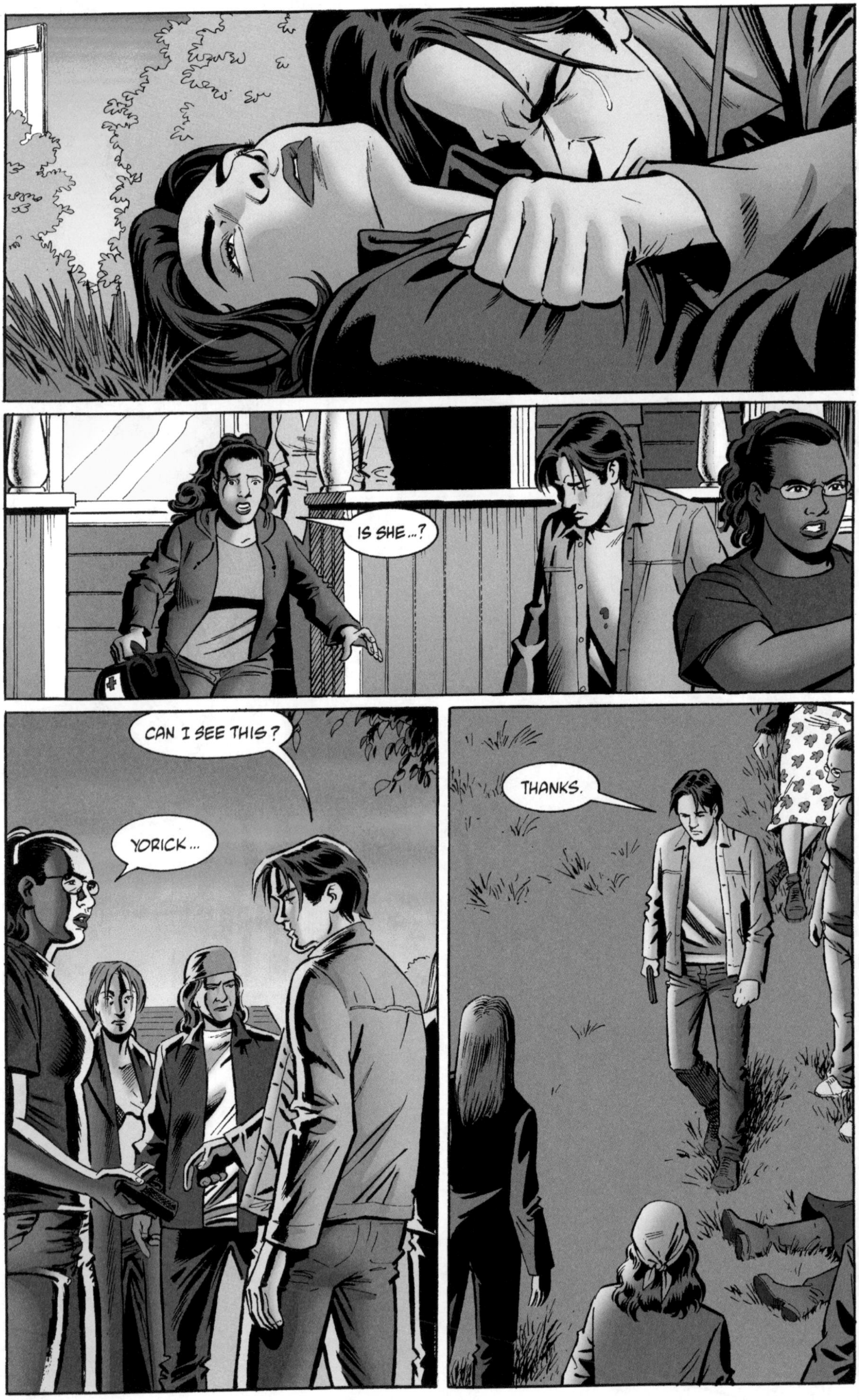
IS SHE...?
CAN I SEE THIS?
YORICK...
THANKS.

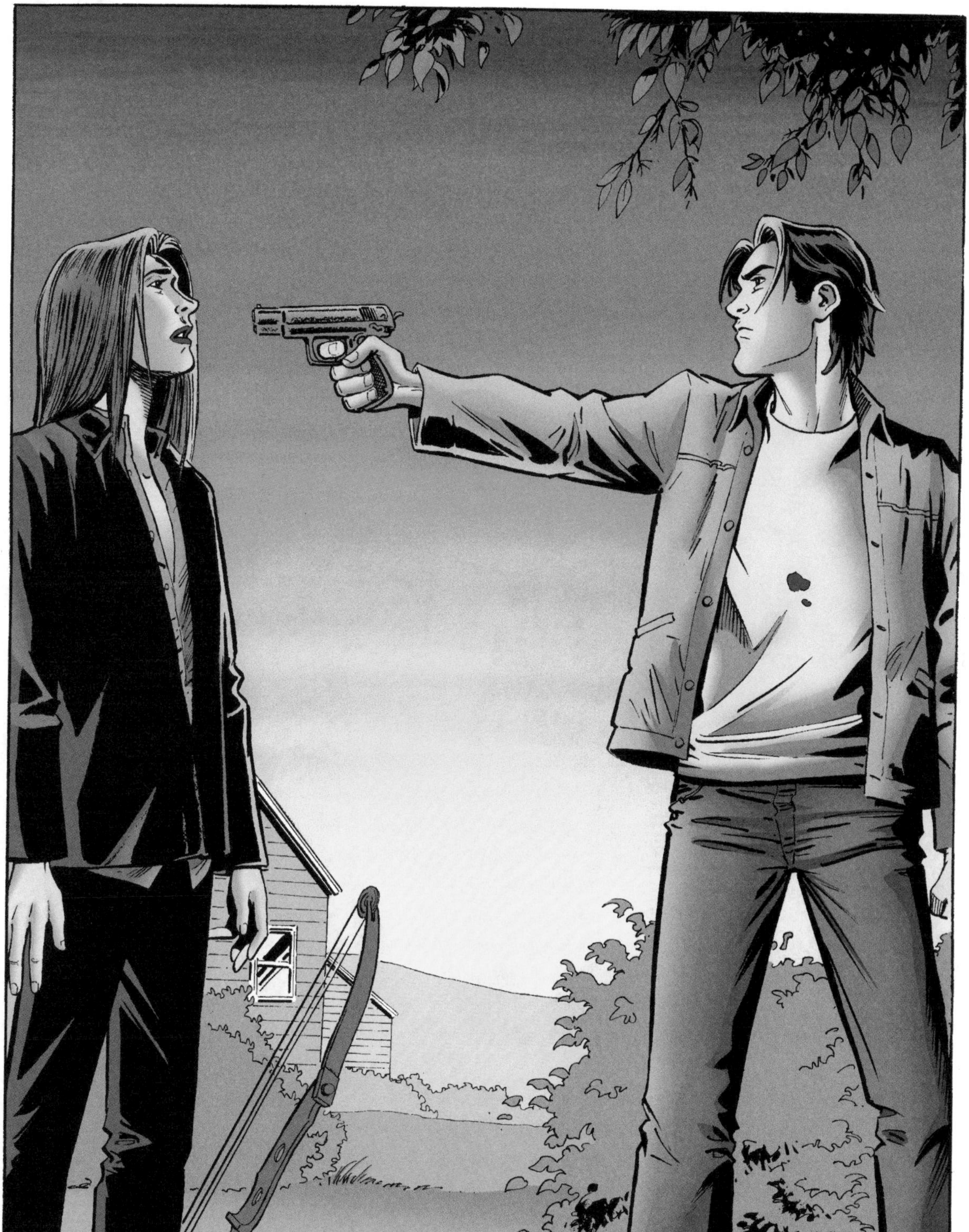

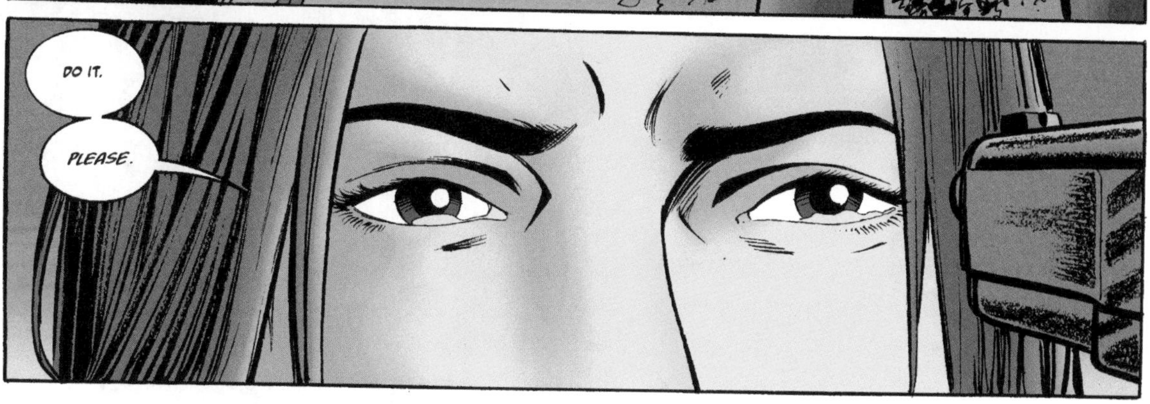
DO IT.
PLEASE.

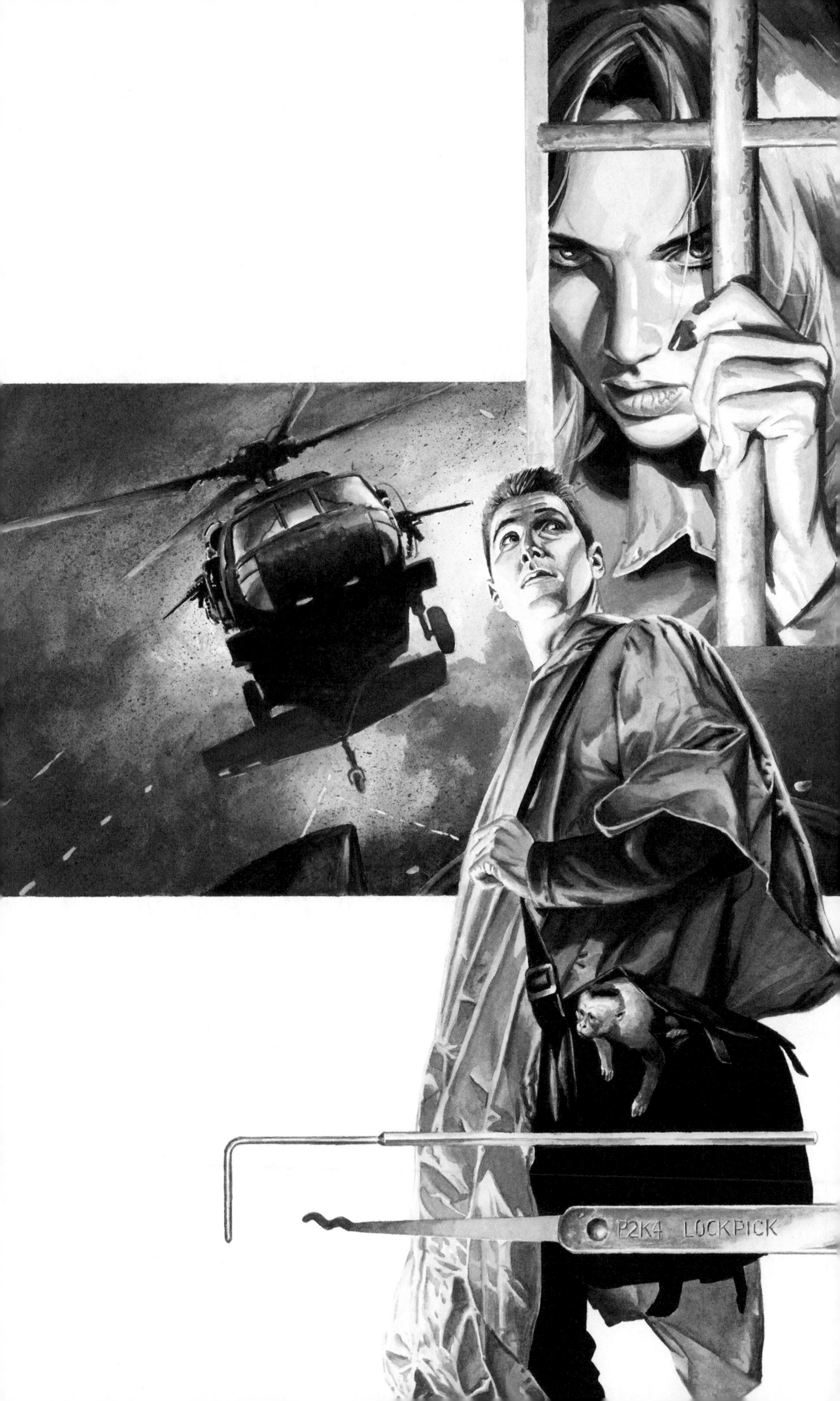
P2K4 LOCKPICK

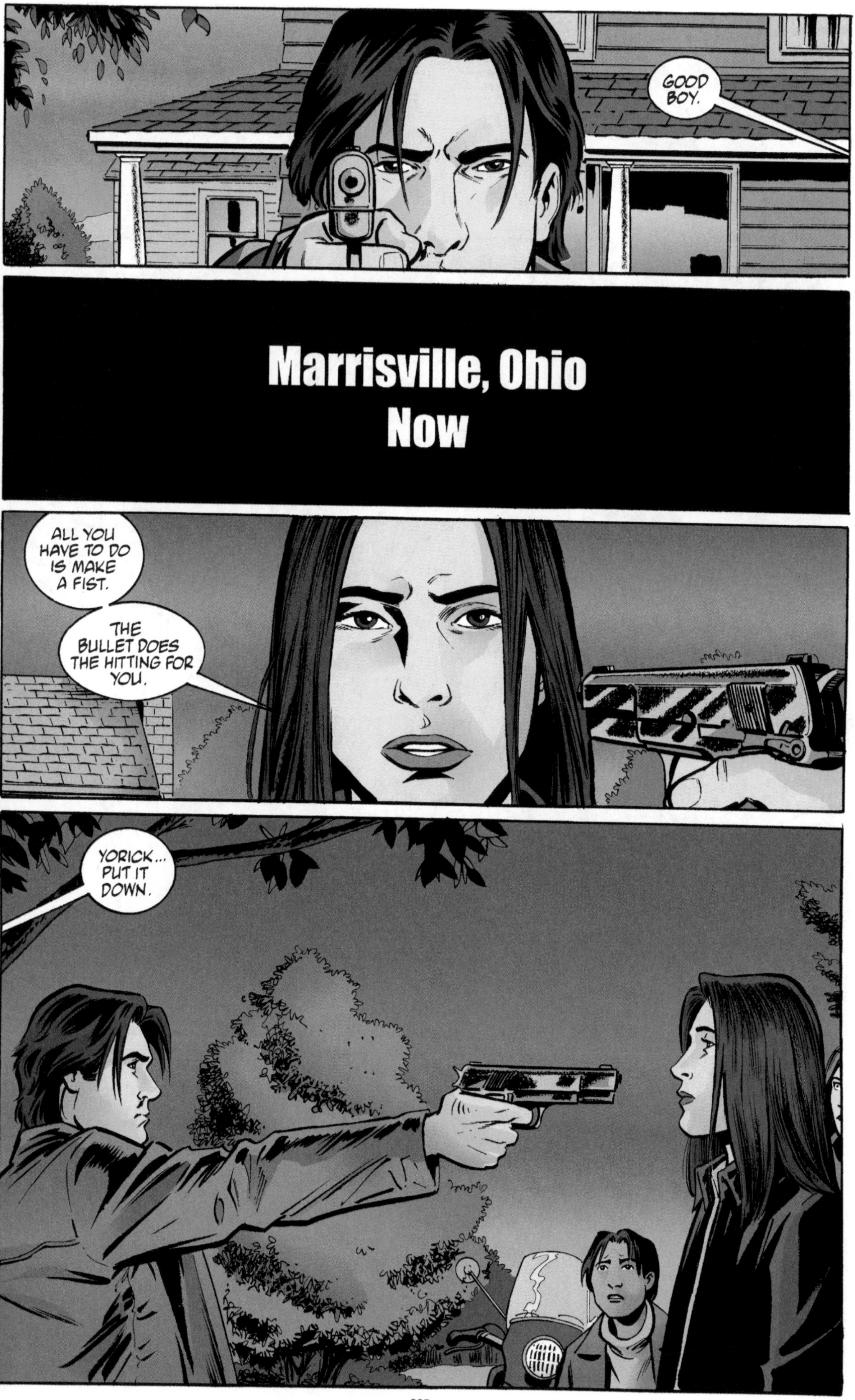
GOOD BOY.
Marrisville, Ohio
Now
ALL YOU HAVE TO DO IS MAKE A FIST.
THE BULLET DOES THE HITTING FOR YOU.
YORICK... PUT IT DOWN.

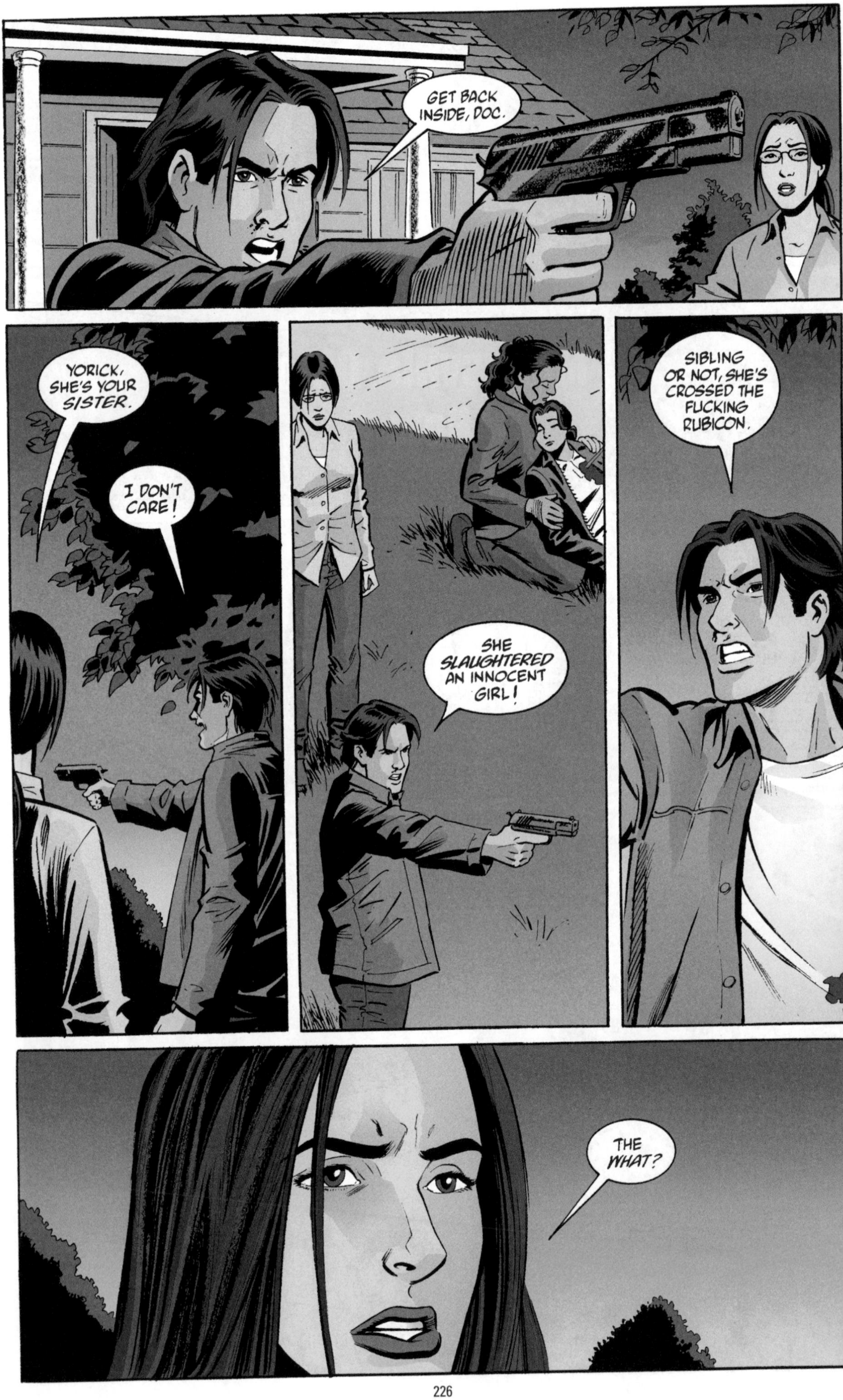
GET BACK INSIDE, DOC.
YORICK, SHE'S YOUR SISTER.
I DON'T CARE!
SHE SLAUGHTERED AN INNOCENT GIRL!
SIBLING OR NOT, SHE'S CROSSED THE FUCKING RUBICON.
THE WHAT?

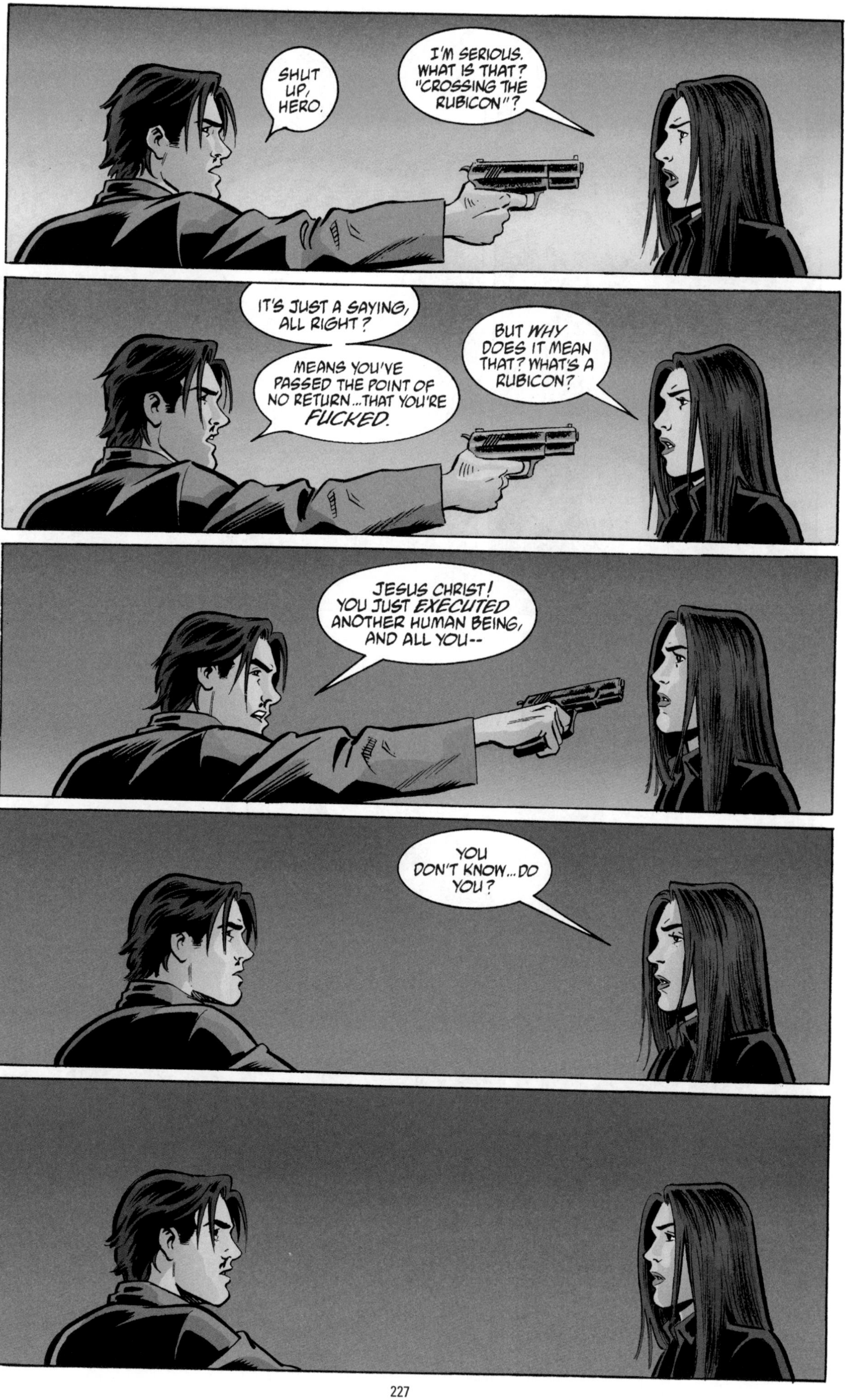
SHUT UP, HERO.
I'M SERIOUS. WHAT IS THAT? "CROSSING THE RUBICON"?
IT'S JUST A SAYING, ALL RIGHT?
MEANS YOU'VE PASSED THE POINT OF NO RETURN...THAT YOU'RE FUCKED.
BUT WHY DOES IT MEAN THAT? WHAT'S A RUBICON?
JESUS CHRIST! YOU JUST EXECUTED ANOTHER HUMAN BEING, AND ALL YOU--
YOU DON'T KNOW...DO YOU?

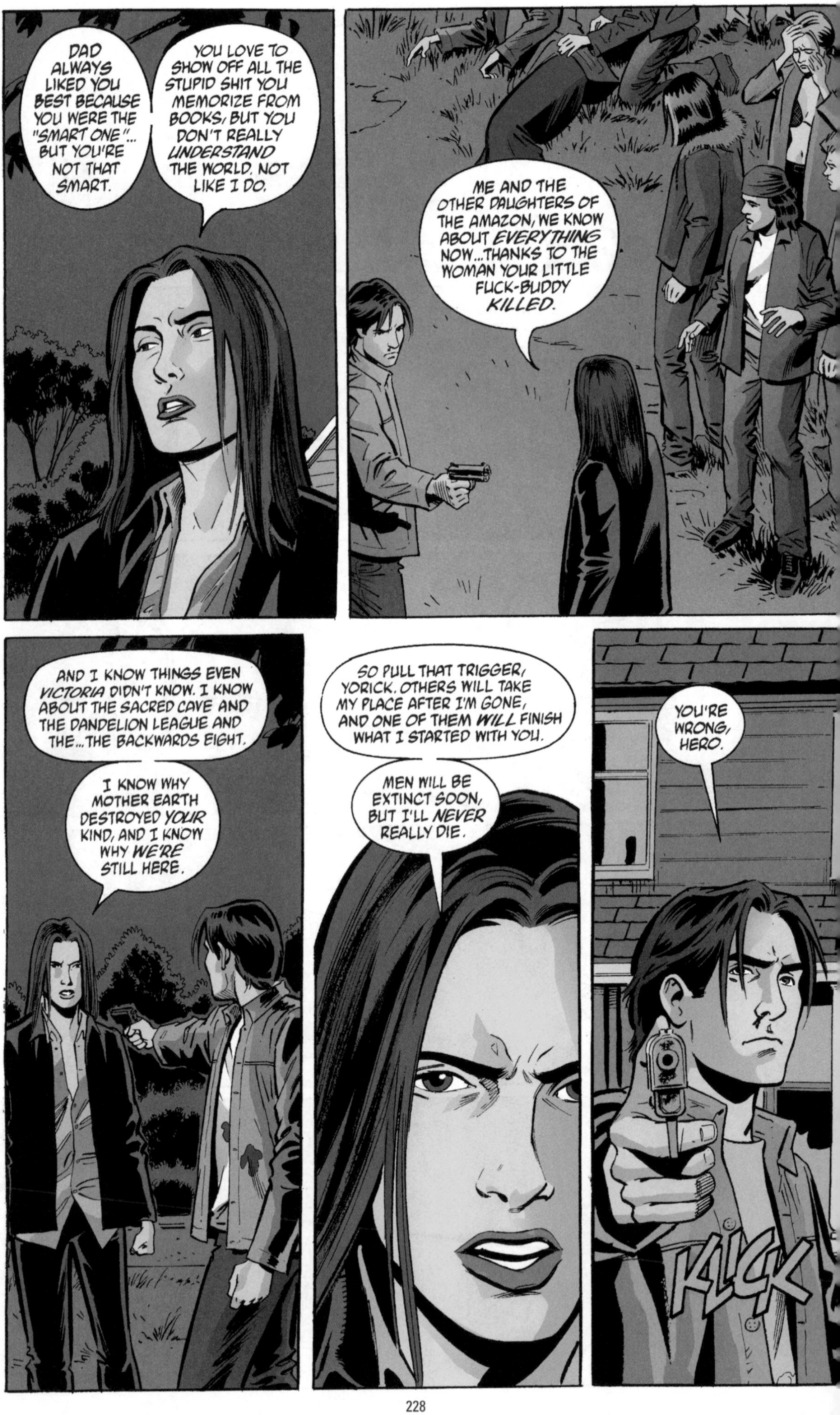
DAD ALWAYS LIKED YOU BEST BECAUSE YOU WERE THE "SMART ONE"... BUT YOU'RE NOT THAT SMART.
YOU LOVE TO SHOW OFF ALL THE STUPID SHIT YOU MEMORIZE FROM BOOKS, BUT YOU DON'T REALLY *UNDERSTAND* THE WORLD. NOT LIKE I DO.
ME AND THE OTHER DAUGHTERS OF THE AMAZON, WE KNOW ABOUT *EVERYTHING* NOW...THANKS TO THE WOMAN YOUR LITTLE FUCK-BUDDY *KILLED*.
AND I KNOW THINGS EVEN *VICTORIA* DIDN'T KNOW. I KNOW ABOUT THE SACRED CAVE AND THE DANDELION LEAGUE AND THE...THE BACKWARDS EIGHT.
I KNOW WHY MOTHER EARTH DESTROYED *YOUR* KIND, AND I KNOW WHY *WE'RE* STILL HERE.
SO PULL THAT TRIGGER, YORICK. OTHERS WILL TAKE MY PLACE AFTER I'M GONE, AND ONE OF THEM *WILL* FINISH WHAT I STARTED WITH YOU.
MEN WILL BE EXTINCT SOON, BUT I'LL *NEVER* REALLY DIE.
YOU'RE WRONG, HERO.
KLICK

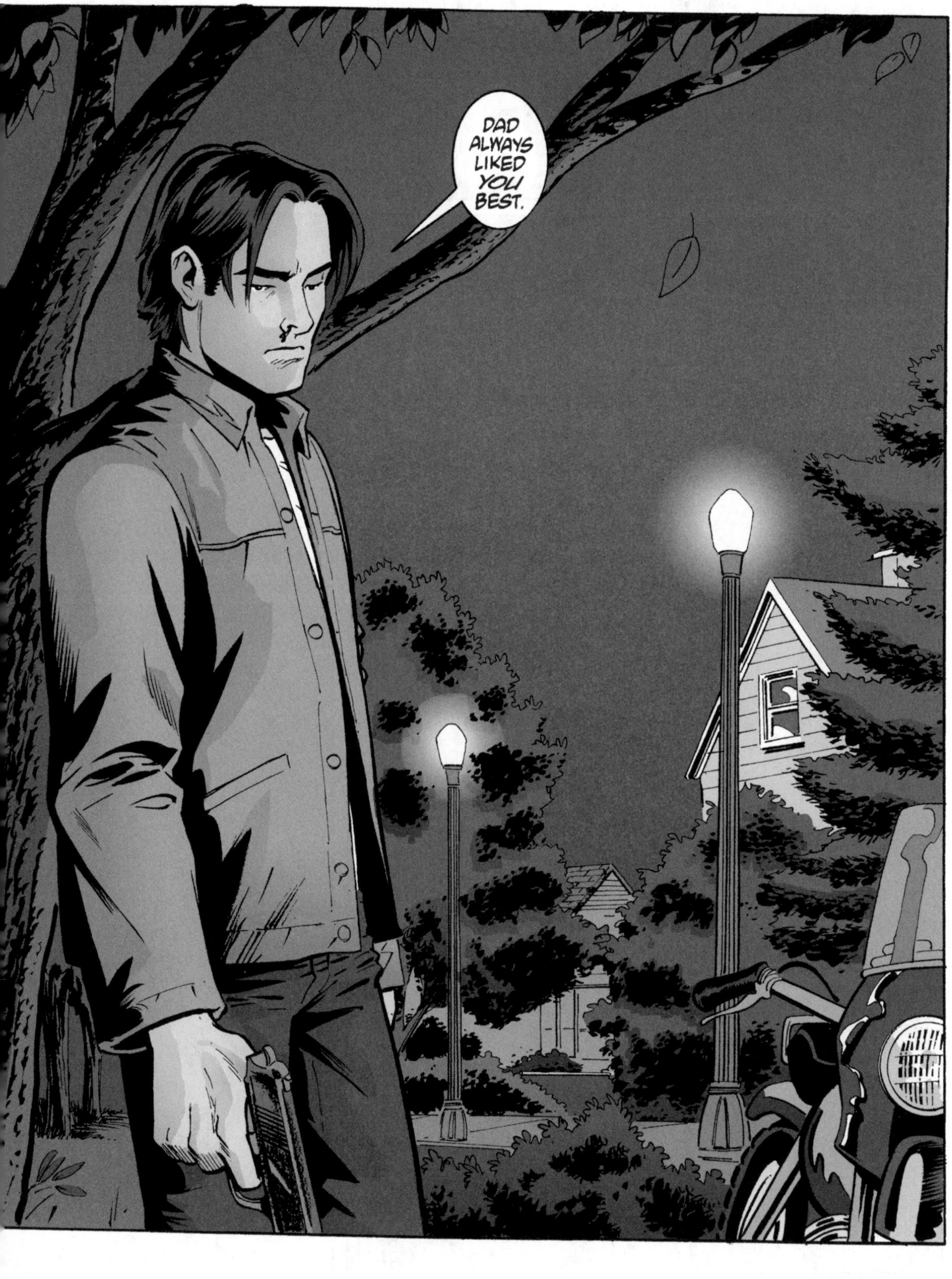
DAD ALWAYS LIKED YOU BEST.

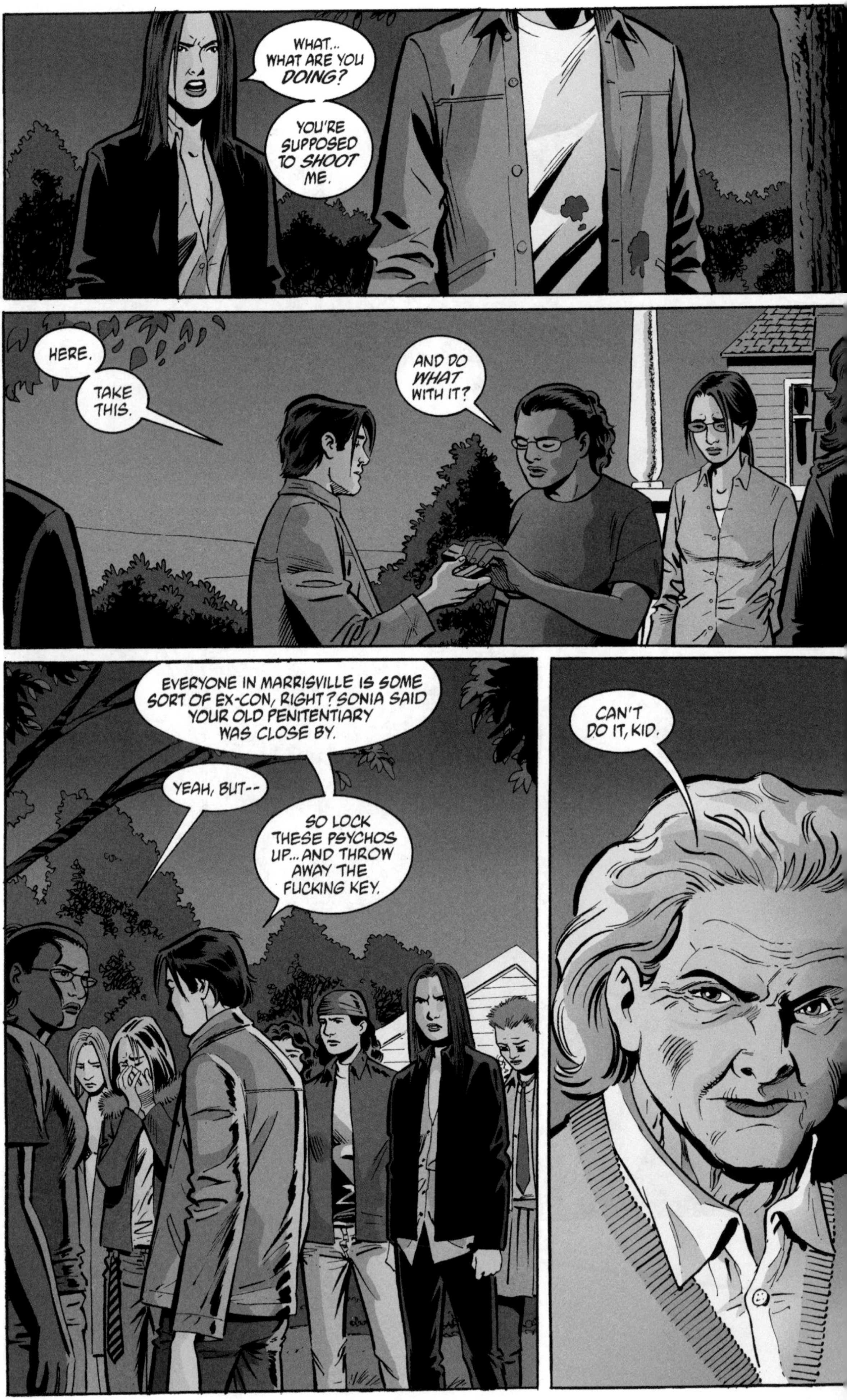
WHAT... WHAT ARE YOU DOING?
YOU'RE SUPPOSED TO SHOOT ME.
HERE.
TAKE THIS.
AND DO WHAT WITH IT?
EVERYONE IN MARRISVILLE IS SOME SORT OF EX-CON, RIGHT? SONIA SAID YOUR OLD PENITENTIARY WAS CLOSE BY.
YEAH, BUT--
SO LOCK THESE PSYCHOS UP... AND THROW AWAY THE FUCKING KEY.
CAN'T DO IT, KID.

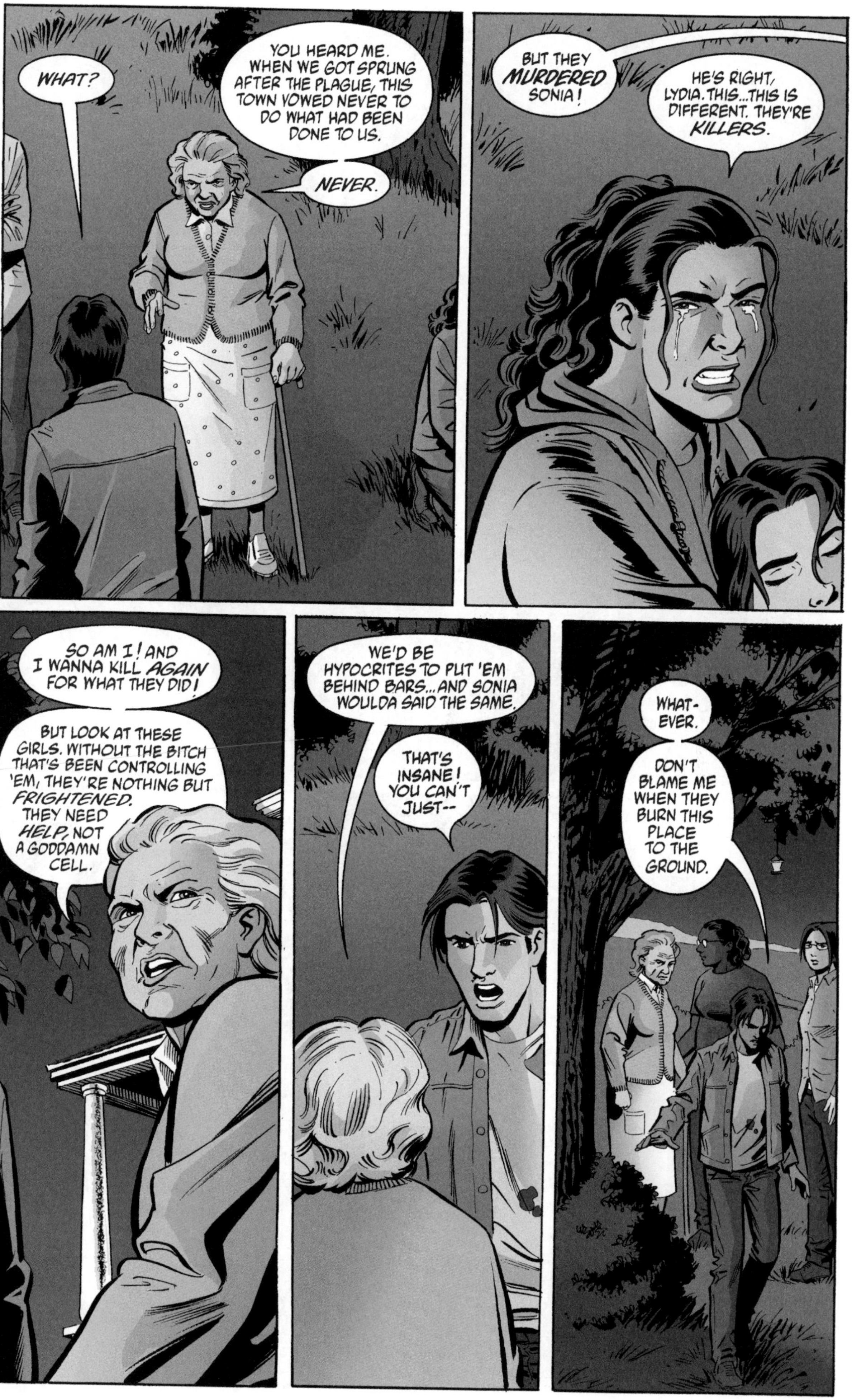

WHAT?
YOU HEARD ME. WHEN WE GOT SPRUNG AFTER THE PLAGUE, THIS TOWN VOWED NEVER TO DO WHAT HAD BEEN DONE TO US.
NEVER.
BUT THEY MURDERED SONIA!
HE'S RIGHT, LYDIA. THIS...THIS IS DIFFERENT. THEY'RE KILLERS.
SO AM I! AND I WANNA KILL AGAIN FOR WHAT THEY DID!
BUT LOOK AT THESE GIRLS. WITHOUT THE BITCH THAT'S BEEN CONTROLLING 'EM, THEY'RE NOTHING BUT FRIGHTENED. THEY NEED HELP, NOT A GODDAMN CELL.
WE'D BE HYPOCRITES TO PUT 'EM BEHIND BARS...AND SONIA WOULDA SAID THE SAME.
THAT'S INSANE! YOU CAN'T JUST--
WHAT-EVER.
DON'T BLAME ME WHEN THEY BURN THIS PLACE TO THE GROUND.

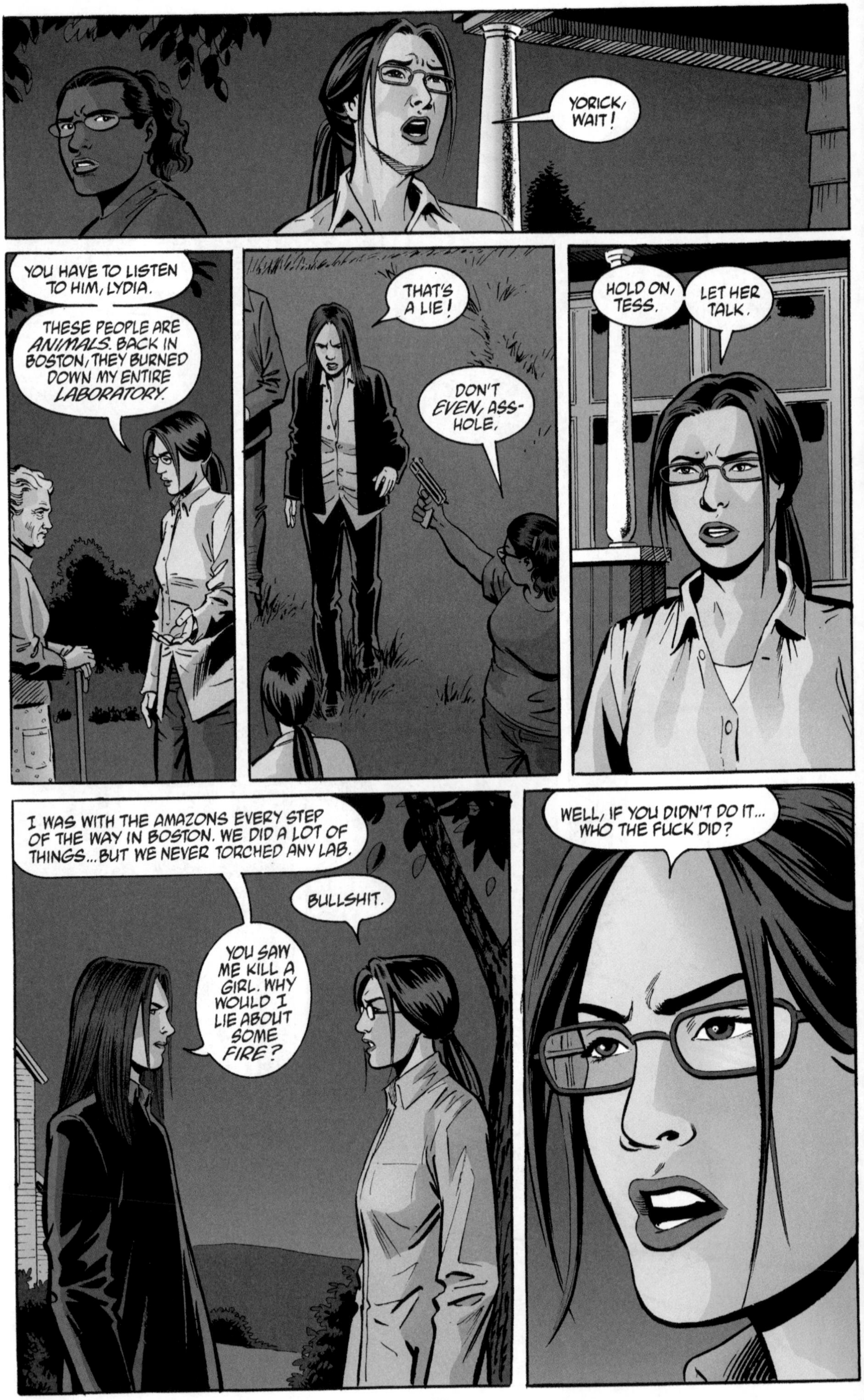
YORICK, WAIT!
YOU HAVE TO LISTEN TO HIM, LYDIA.
THESE PEOPLE ARE ANIMALS. BACK IN BOSTON, THEY BURNED DOWN MY ENTIRE LABORATORY.
THAT'S A LIE!
DON'T EVEN, ASS-HOLE.
HOLD ON, TESS.
LET HER TALK.
I WAS WITH THE AMAZONS EVERY STEP OF THE WAY IN BOSTON. WE DID A LOT OF THINGS... BUT WE NEVER TORCHED ANY LAB.
BULLSHIT.
YOU SAW ME KILL A GIRL. WHY WOULD I LIE ABOUT SOME FIRE?
WELL, IF YOU DIDN'T DO IT... WHO THE FUCK DID?

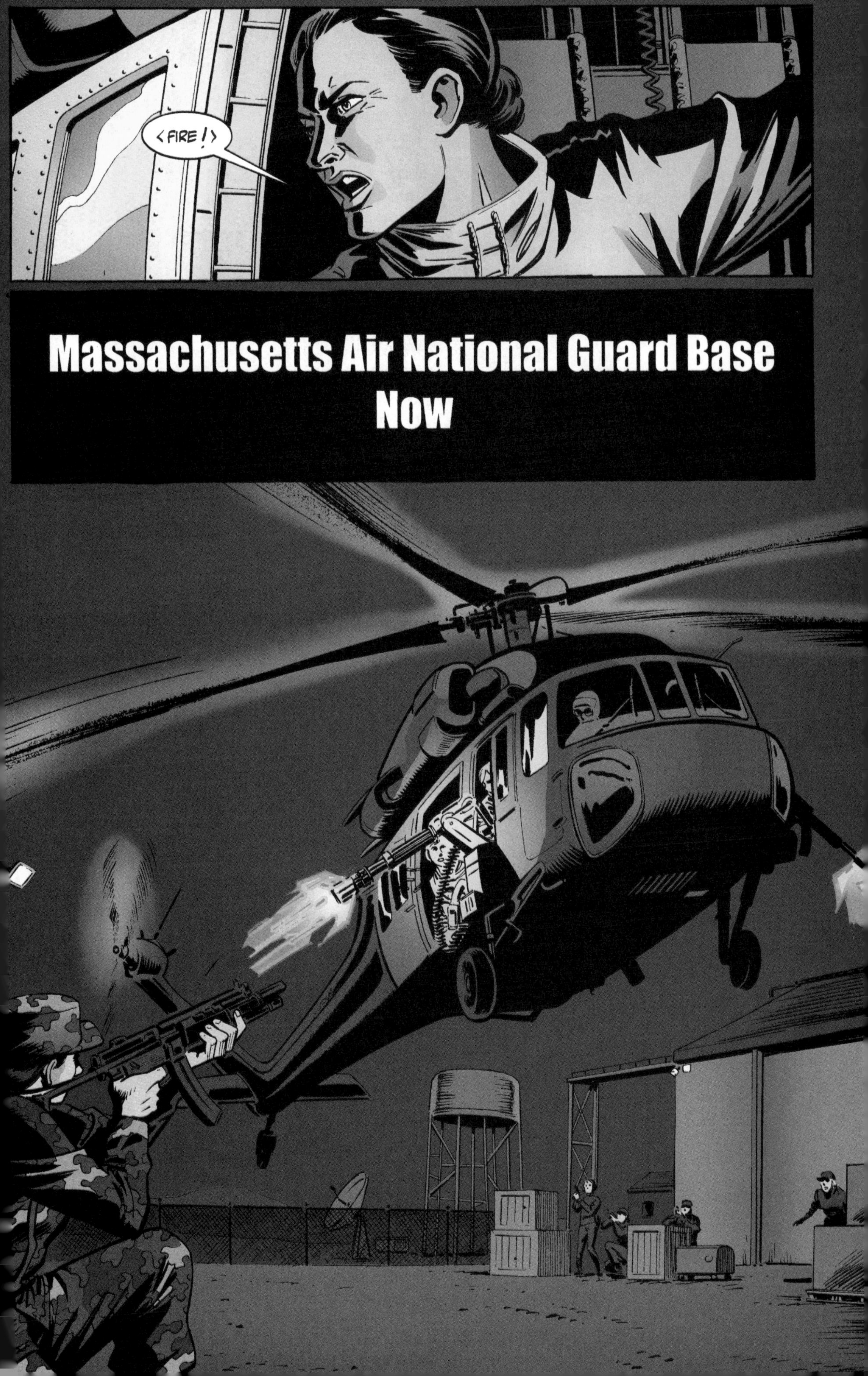
<FIRE!>
Massachusetts Air National Guard Base
Now

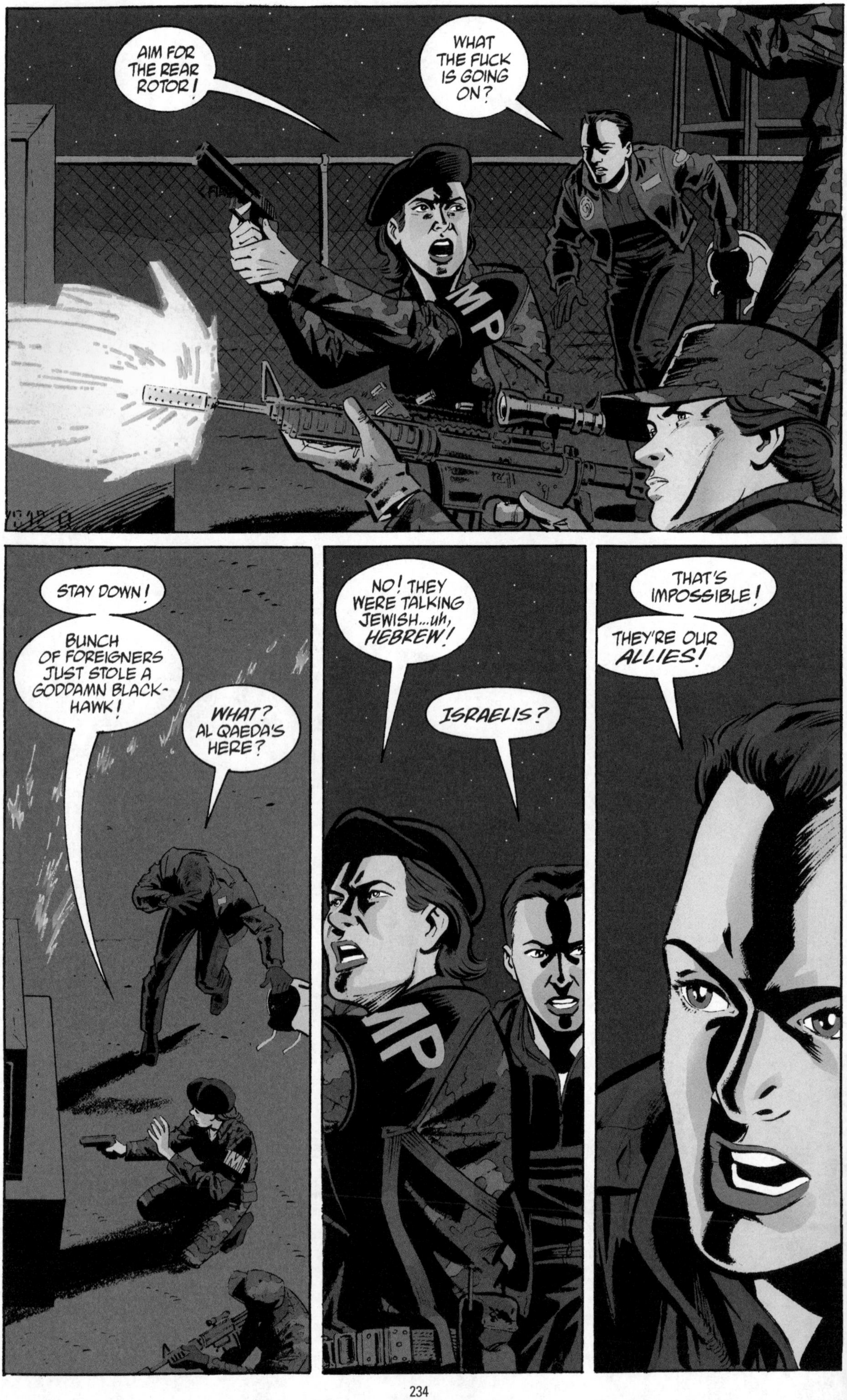
AIM FOR THE REAR ROTOR!
WHAT THE FUCK IS GOING ON?
STAY DOWN!
BUNCH OF FOREIGNERS JUST STOLE A GODDAMN BLACK-HAWK!
WHAT? AL QAEDA'S HERE?
NO! THEY WERE TALKING JEWISH...uh, HEBREW!
ISRAELIS?
THAT'S IMPOSSIBLE!
THEY'RE OUR ALLIES!

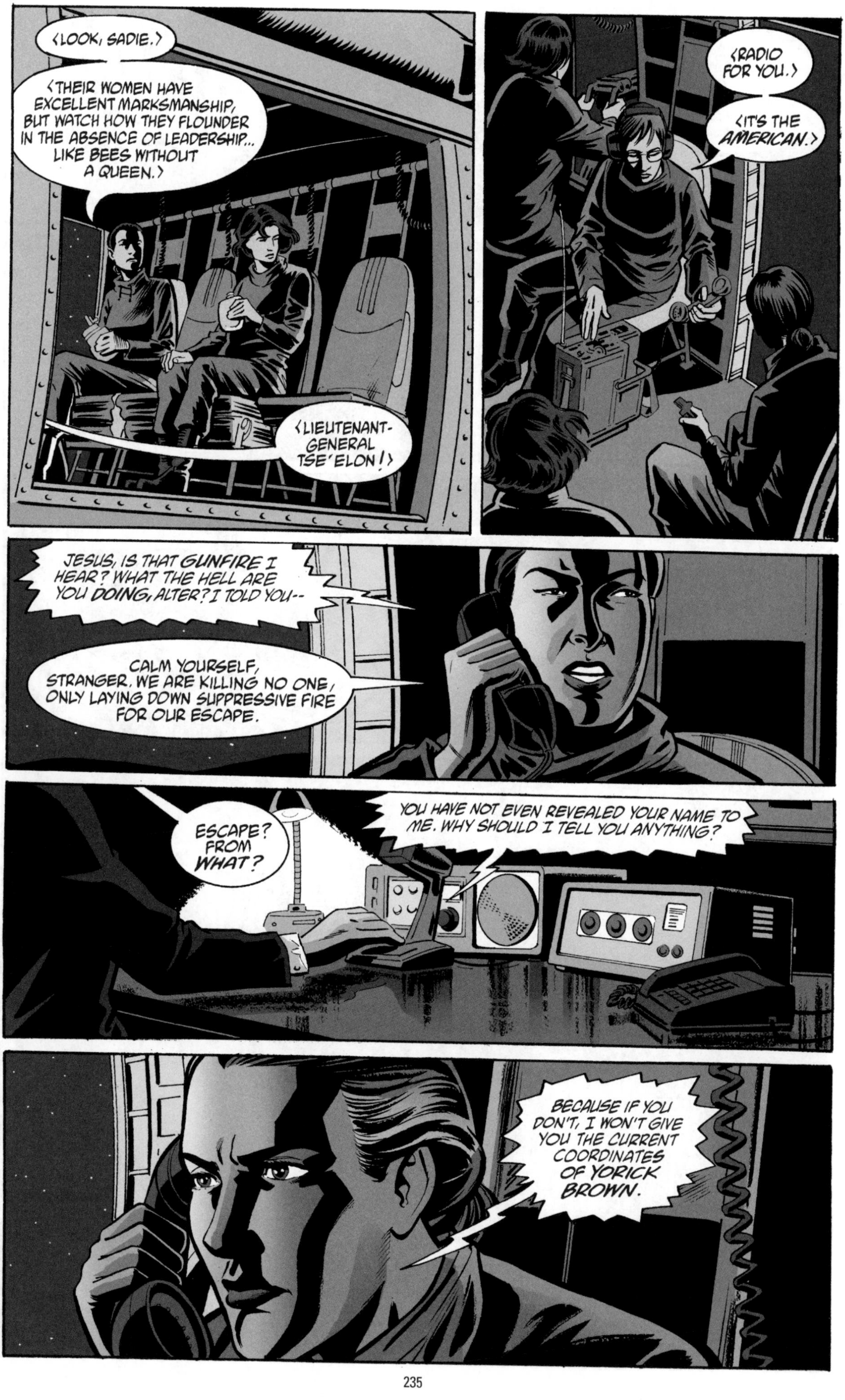

‹LOOK, SADIE.›
‹THEIR WOMEN HAVE EXCELLENT MARKSMANSHIP, BUT WATCH HOW THEY FLOUNDER IN THE ABSENCE OF LEADERSHIP... LIKE BEES WITHOUT A QUEEN.›
‹LIEUTENANT-GENERAL TSE'ELON!›
‹RADIO FOR YOU.›
‹IT'S THE AMERICAN.›
JESUS, IS THAT GUNFIRE I HEAR? WHAT THE HELL ARE YOU DOING, ALTER? I TOLD YOU--
CALM YOURSELF, STRANGER. WE ARE KILLING NO ONE, ONLY LAYING DOWN SUPPRESSIVE FIRE FOR OUR ESCAPE.
ESCAPE? FROM WHAT?
YOU HAVE NOT EVEN REVEALED YOUR NAME TO ME. WHY SHOULD I TELL YOU ANYTHING?
BECAUSE IF YOU DON'T, I WON'T GIVE YOU THE CURRENT COORDINATES OF YORICK BROWN.

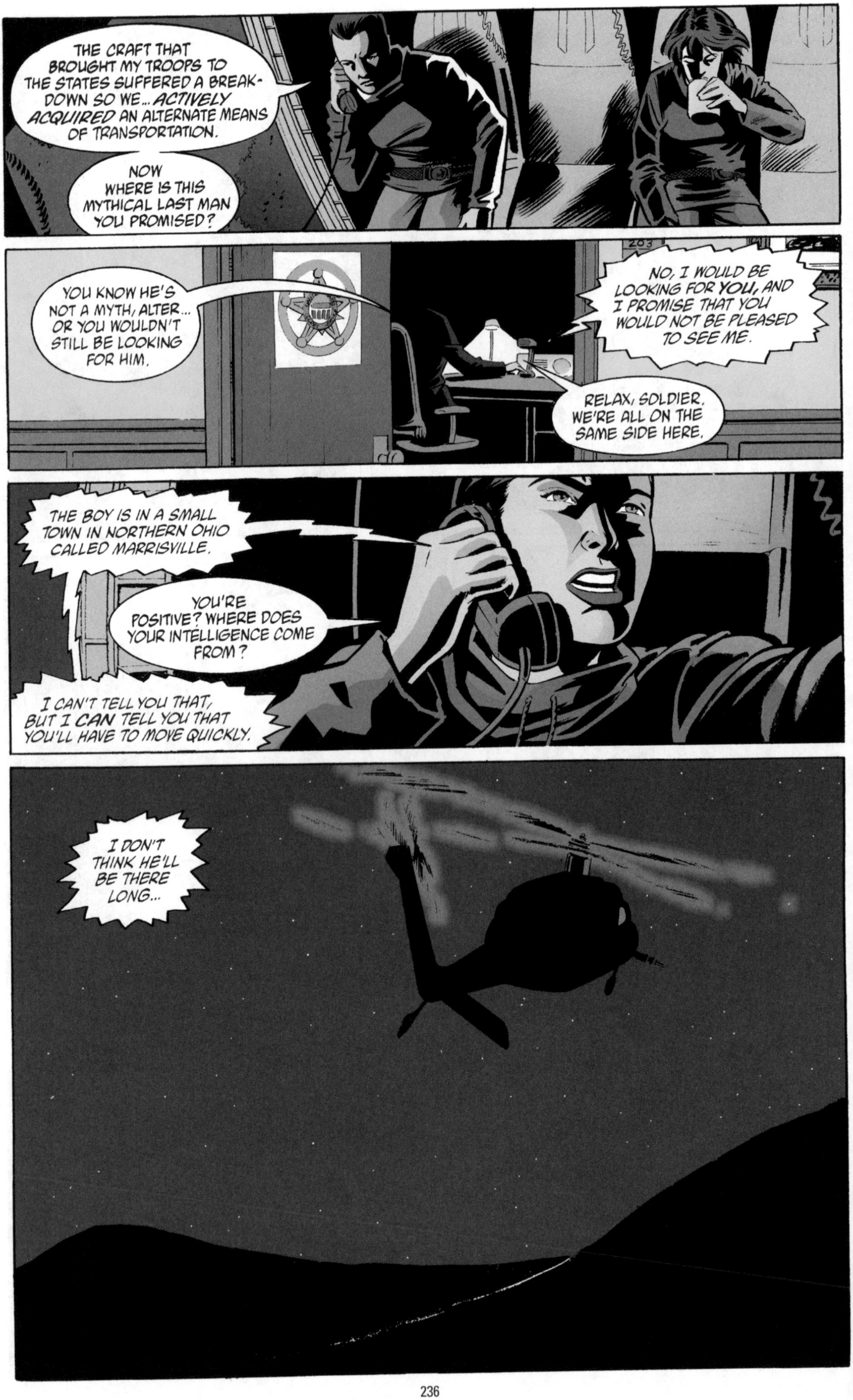
THE CRAFT THAT BROUGHT MY TROOPS TO THE STATES SUFFERED A BREAK-DOWN SO WE... ACTIVELY ACQUIRED AN ALTERNATE MEANS OF TRANSPORTATION.
NOW WHERE IS THIS MYTHICAL LAST MAN YOU PROMISED?
YOU KNOW HE'S NOT A MYTH, ALTER... OR YOU WOULDN'T STILL BE LOOKING FOR HIM.
NO, I WOULD BE LOOKING FOR YOU, AND I PROMISE THAT YOU WOULD NOT BE PLEASED TO SEE ME.
RELAX, SOLDIER. WE'RE ALL ON THE SAME SIDE HERE.
THE BOY IS IN A SMALL TOWN IN NORTHERN OHIO CALLED MARRISVILLE.
YOU'RE POSITIVE? WHERE DOES YOUR INTELLIGENCE COME FROM?
I CAN'T TELL YOU THAT, BUT I CAN TELL YOU THAT YOU'LL HAVE TO MOVE QUICKLY.
I DON'T THINK HE'LL BE THERE LONG...

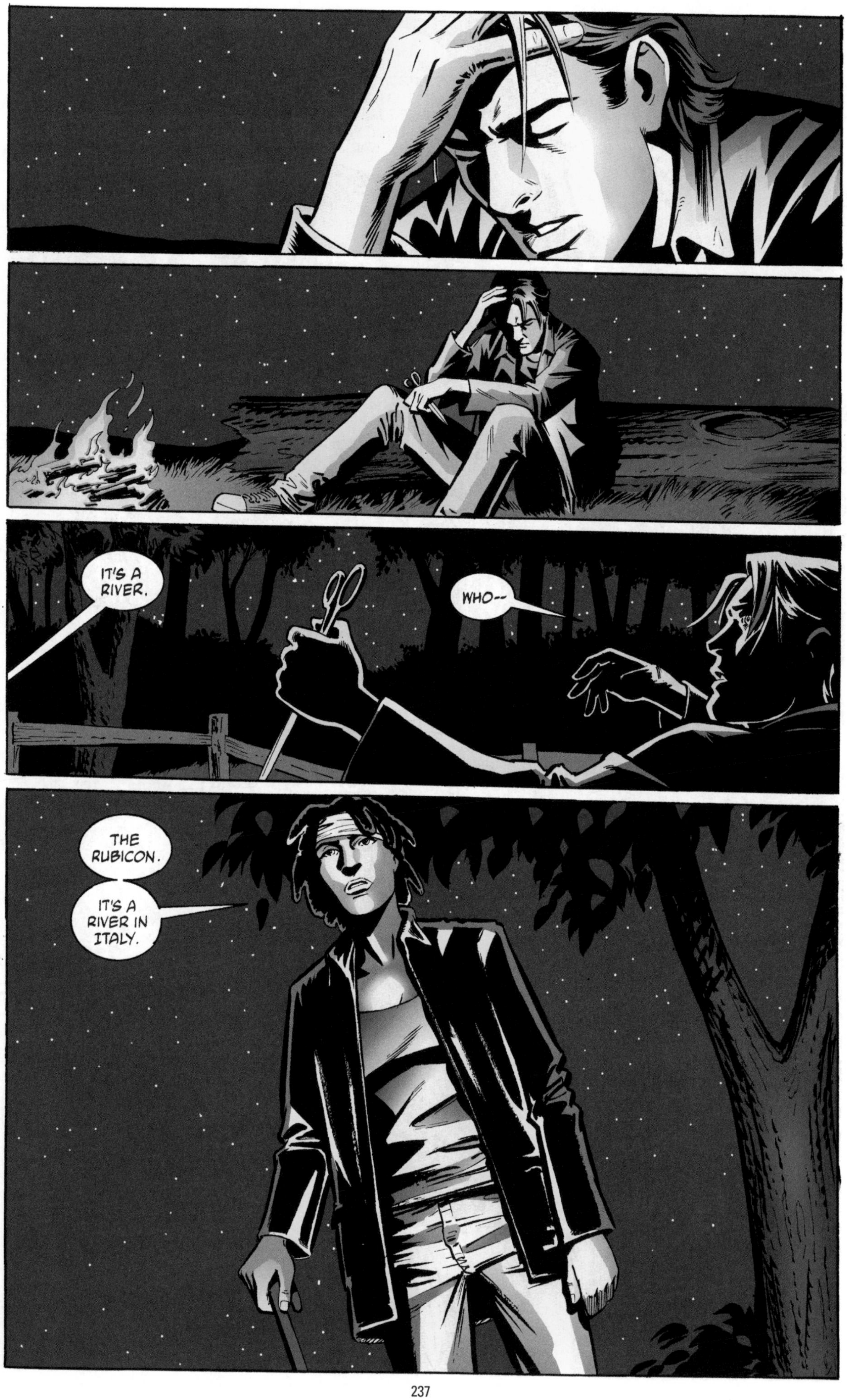

IT'S A RIVER.
WHO--
THE RUBICON.
IT'S A RIVER IN ITALY.

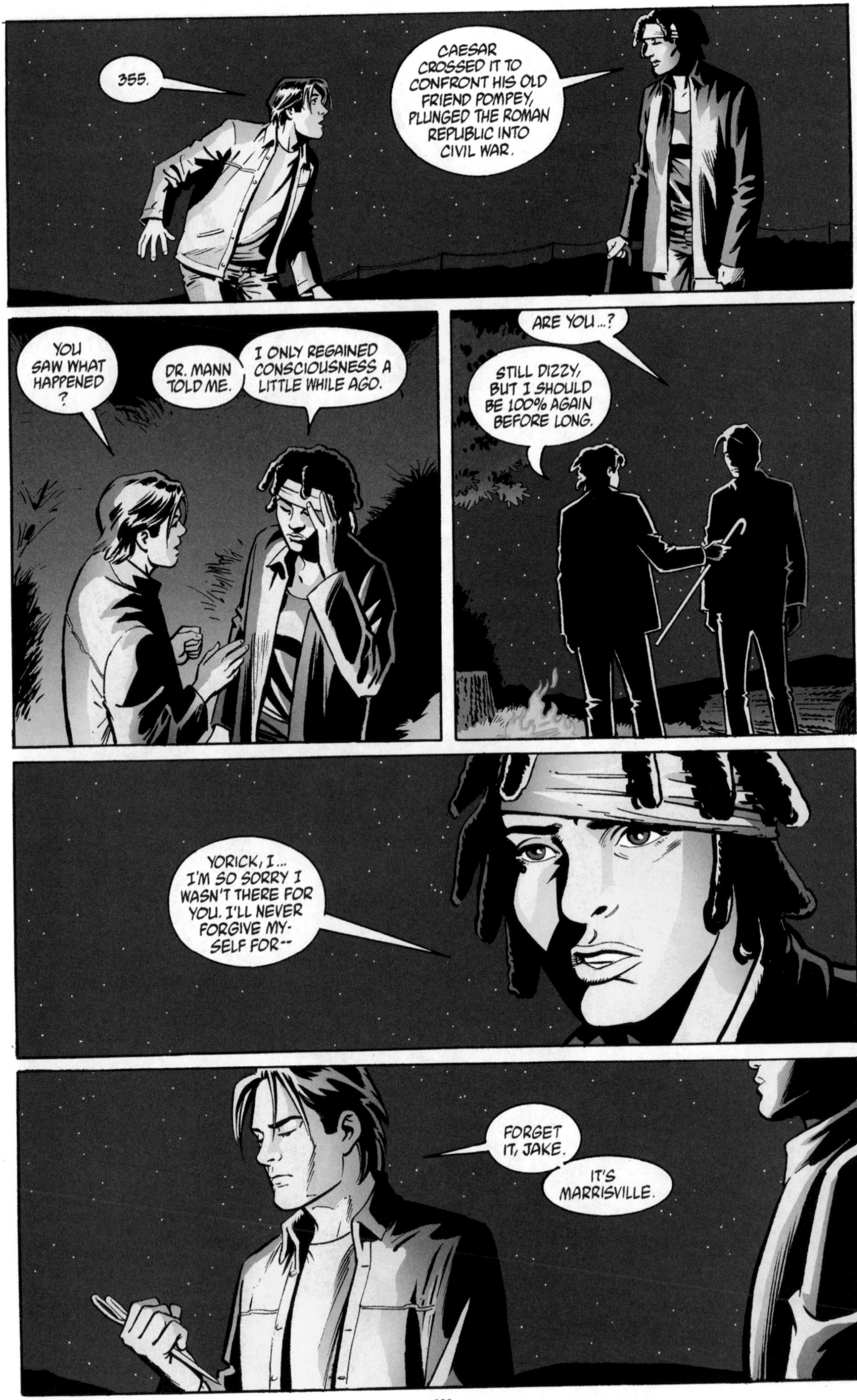
355.
CAESAR CROSSED IT TO CONFRONT HIS OLD FRIEND POMPEY, PLUNGED THE ROMAN REPUBLIC INTO CIVIL WAR.
YOU SAW WHAT HAPPENED ?
DR. MANN TOLD ME.
I ONLY REGAINED CONSCIOUSNESS A LITTLE WHILE AGO.
ARE YOU ...?
STILL DIZZY, BUT I SHOULD BE 100% AGAIN BEFORE LONG.
YORICK, I... I'M SO SORRY I WASN'T THERE FOR YOU. I'LL NEVER FORGIVE MY-SELF FOR--
FORGET IT, JAKE.
IT'S MARRISVILLE.

"JAKE"?

HOW CAN SOMEONE KNOW RUBICON BUT NOT CHINATOWN?

WHAT'S WITH THE SCISSORS?

HUH? OH. I FOUND 'EM IN SONIA'S ROOM AND I THOUGHT... WHATEVER. IT'S STUPID.

I HAVEN'T GOTTEN MY HAIR CUT SINCE ALL THE BARBERS DIED, AND FOR SOME REASON I SUD- DENLY FELT LIKE--

HERE. LET ME.

YOU HAVE TIME TO PLAY *STYLIST*? SHOULDN'T YOU BE BACK IN TOWN, MAK- ING SURE THE ROAD WARRIORS DON'T START RAPING AND PILLAGING?

THE LOCALS ALREADY INCAR- CERATED THEM, YORICK.

SERIOUSLY?

APPARENTLY, EVERYONE REACHED A COMPROMISE. THEY'RE GOING TO DETAIN ALL THE AMAZONS FOR THE TIME BEING, AND STAGGER RELEASES AS INDIVIDUALS ARE DEEMED READY TO BE REINTRODUCED TO SOCIETY.

AND YOU'RE *OKAY* WITH THAT? I THOUGHT YOU WERE SUPPOSED TO BE MS. LAW & ORDER!

YORICK, THIS COUNTRY'S PRISON SYSTEM WAS AN EMBARRASSMENT. I'D CONSIDER JUST ABOUT ANY ALTERNATIVE MORE REASONABLE.

HOW CAN YOU *SAY* THAT? A FEW HOURS AGO, I WAS STANDING HERE TALKING WITH A GIRL, AND NOW SHE'S FUCKING *GONE!* ALL BECAUSE OF ONE OF THOSE *SAVAGES...*

ALL BECAUSE OF MY SISTER.

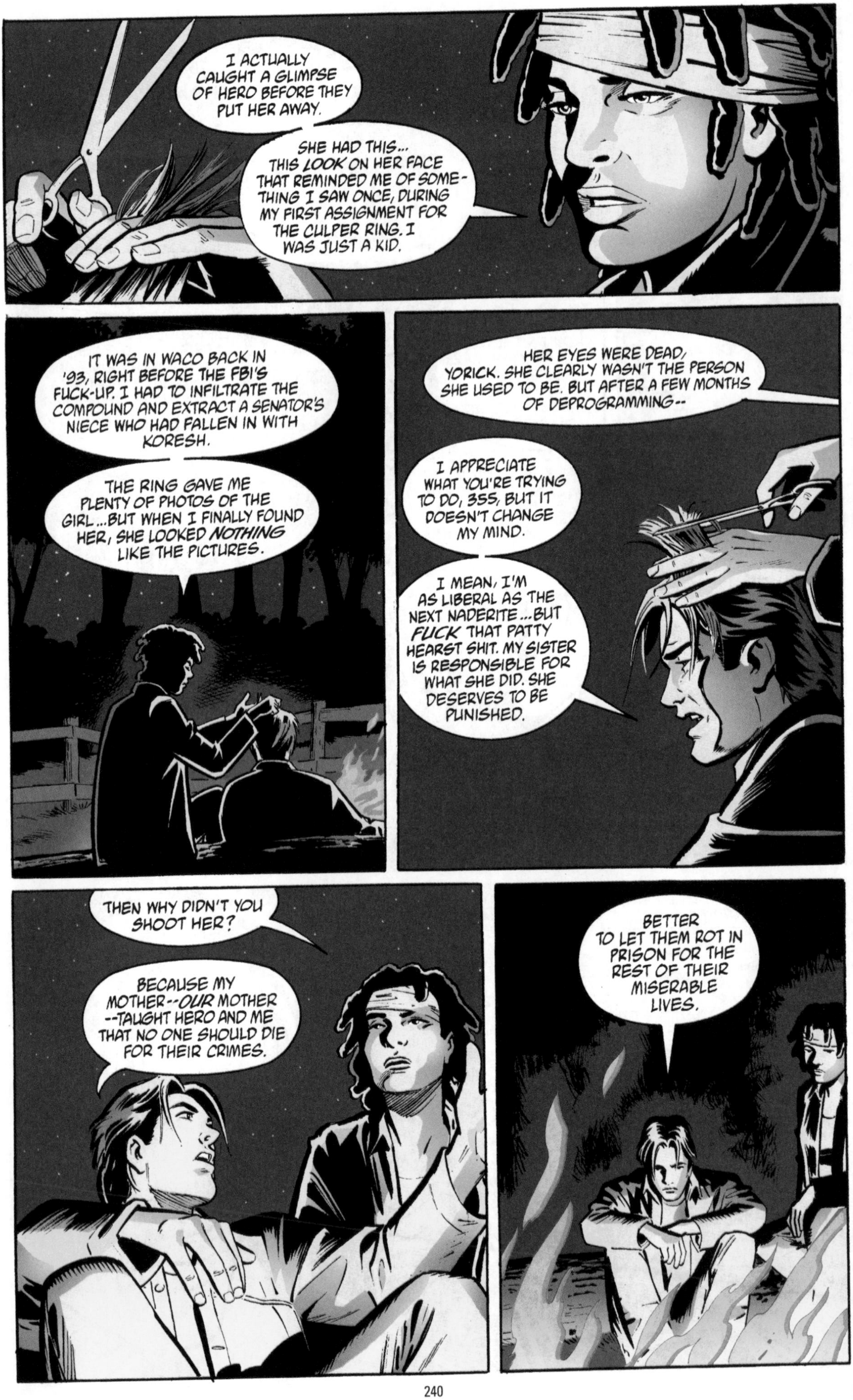
I ACTUALLY CAUGHT A GLIMPSE OF HERO BEFORE THEY PUT HER AWAY.
SHE HAD THIS... THIS *LOOK* ON HER FACE THAT REMINDED ME OF SOME-THING I SAW ONCE, DURING MY FIRST ASSIGNMENT FOR THE CULPER RING. I WAS JUST A KID.
IT WAS IN WACO BACK IN '93, RIGHT BEFORE THE FBI'S FUCK-UP. I HAD TO INFILTRATE THE COMPOUND AND EXTRACT A SENATOR'S NIECE WHO HAD FALLEN IN WITH KORESH.
THE RING GAVE ME PLENTY OF PHOTOS OF THE GIRL...BUT WHEN I FINALLY FOUND HER, SHE LOOKED *NOTHING* LIKE THE PICTURES.
HER EYES WERE DEAD, YORICK. SHE CLEARLY WASN'T THE PERSON SHE USED TO BE. BUT AFTER A FEW MONTHS OF DEPROGRAMMING--
I APPRECIATE WHAT YOU'RE TRYING TO DO, 355, BUT IT DOESN'T CHANGE MY MIND.
I MEAN, I'M AS LIBERAL AS THE NEXT NADERITE...BUT *FUCK* THAT PATTY HEARST SHIT. MY SISTER IS RESPONSIBLE FOR WHAT SHE DID. SHE DESERVES TO BE PUNISHED.
THEN WHY DIDN'T YOU SHOOT HER?
BECAUSE MY MOTHER--*OUR* MOTHER--TAUGHT HERO AND ME THAT NO ONE SHOULD DIE FOR THEIR CRIMES.
BETTER TO LET THEM ROT IN PRISON FOR THE REST OF THEIR MISERABLE LIVES.

HHH... AHUH...

HWUHHH

HERO, ARE ...ARE YOU *PUKING*?

MY...MY BROTHER...

I KNOW. WE'LL FIND A WAY TO GET HIM, HERO. AS SOON AS THEY LET US OUT OF HERE, WE'LL--

YOU DON'T UNDERSTAND. MY BROTHER...IS AN *ESCAPE ARTIST*.

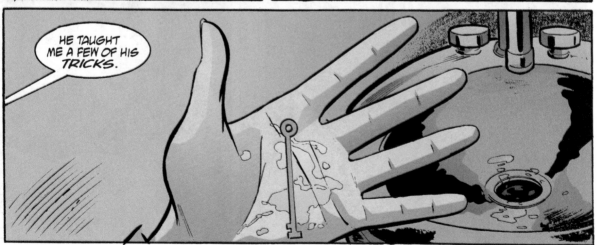

HE TAUGHT ME A FEW OF HIS *TRICKS*.

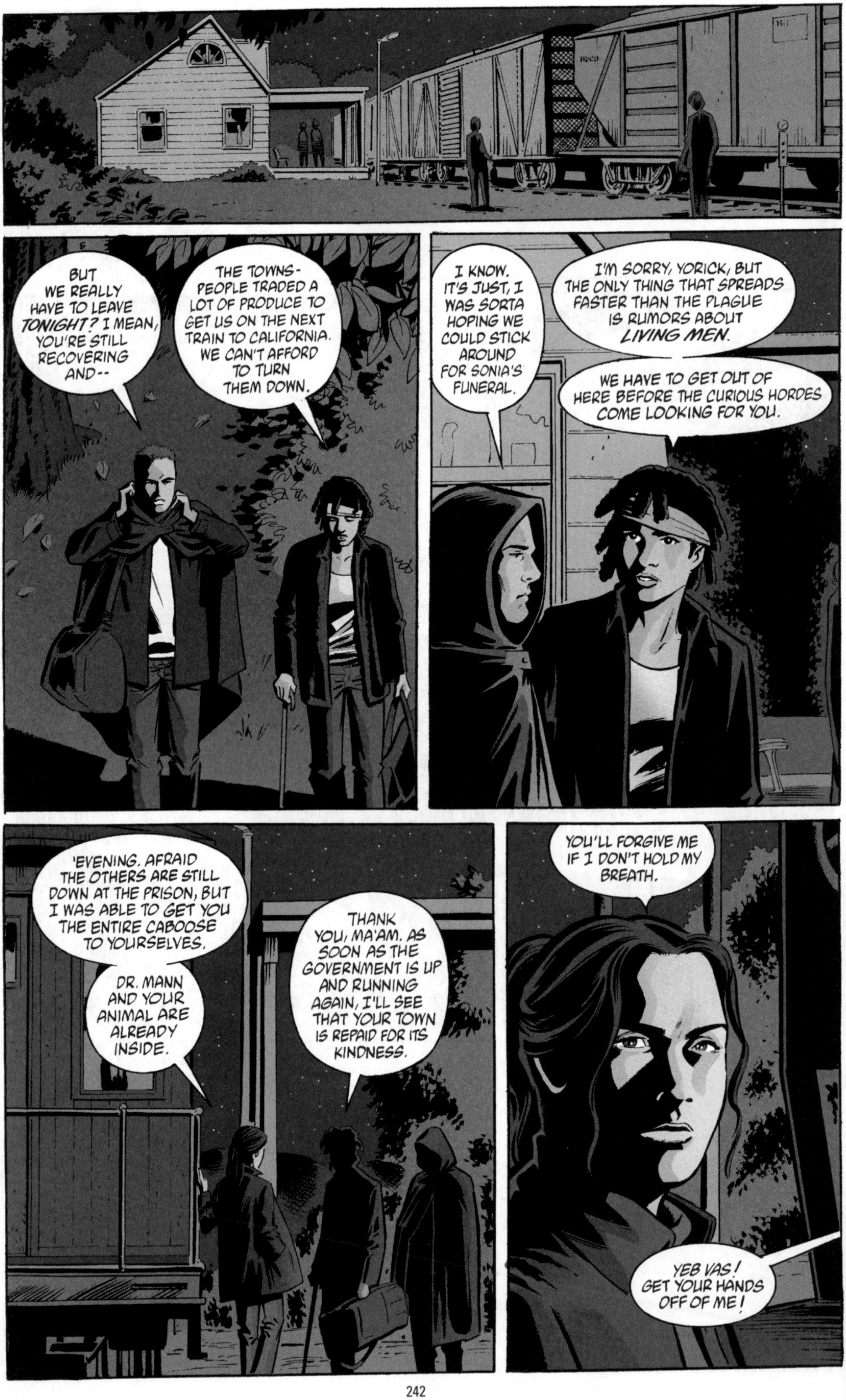
BUT WE REALLY HAVE TO LEAVE TONIGHT? I MEAN, YOU'RE STILL RECOVERING AND--
THE TOWNSPEOPLE TRADED A LOT OF PRODUCE TO GET US ON THE NEXT TRAIN TO CALIFORNIA. WE CAN'T AFFORD TO TURN THEM DOWN.
I KNOW. IT'S JUST, I WAS SORTA HOPING WE COULD STICK AROUND FOR SONIA'S FUNERAL.
I'M SORRY, YORICK, BUT THE ONLY THING THAT SPREADS FASTER THAN THE PLAGUE IS RUMORS ABOUT LIVING MEN.
WE HAVE TO GET OUT OF HERE BEFORE THE CURIOUS HORDES COME LOOKING FOR YOU.
'EVENING. AFRAID THE OTHERS ARE STILL DOWN AT THE PRISON, BUT I WAS ABLE TO GET YOU THE ENTIRE CABOOSE TO YOURSELVES.
DR. MANN AND YOUR ANIMAL ARE ALREADY INSIDE.
THANK YOU, MA'AM. AS SOON AS THE GOVERNMENT IS UP AND RUNNING AGAIN, I'LL SEE THAT YOUR TOWN IS REPAID FOR ITS KINDNESS.
YOU'LL FORGIVE ME IF I DON'T HOLD MY BREATH.
YEB VAS! GET YOUR HANDS OFF OF ME!

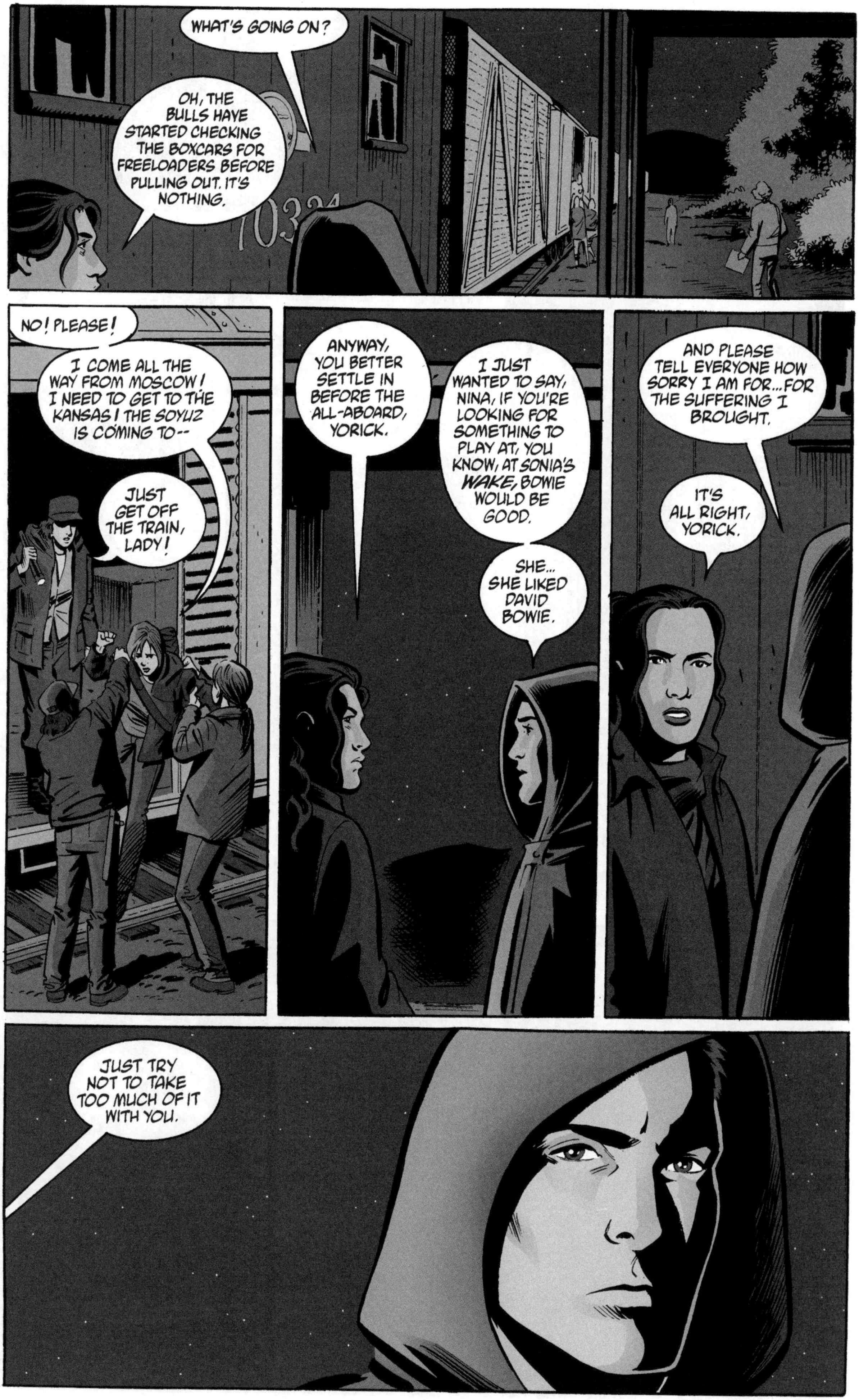
WHAT'S GOING ON?
OH, THE BULLS HAVE STARTED CHECKING THE BOXCARS FOR FREELOADERS BEFORE PULLING OUT. IT'S NOTHING.
NO! PLEASE!
I COME ALL THE WAY FROM MOSCOW! I NEED TO GET TO THE KANSAS! THE SOYUZ IS COMING TO--
JUST GET OFF THE TRAIN, LADY!
ANYWAY, YOU BETTER SETTLE IN BEFORE THE ALL-ABOARD, YORICK.
I JUST WANTED TO SAY, NINA, IF YOU'RE LOOKING FOR SOMETHING TO PLAY AT, YOU KNOW, AT SONIA'S *WAKE*, BOWIE WOULD BE GOOD.
SHE... SHE LIKED DAVID BOWIE.
AND PLEASE TELL EVERYONE HOW SORRY I AM FOR...FOR THE SUFFERING I BROUGHT.
IT'S ALL RIGHT, YORICK.
JUST TRY NOT TO TAKE TOO MUCH OF IT WITH YOU.

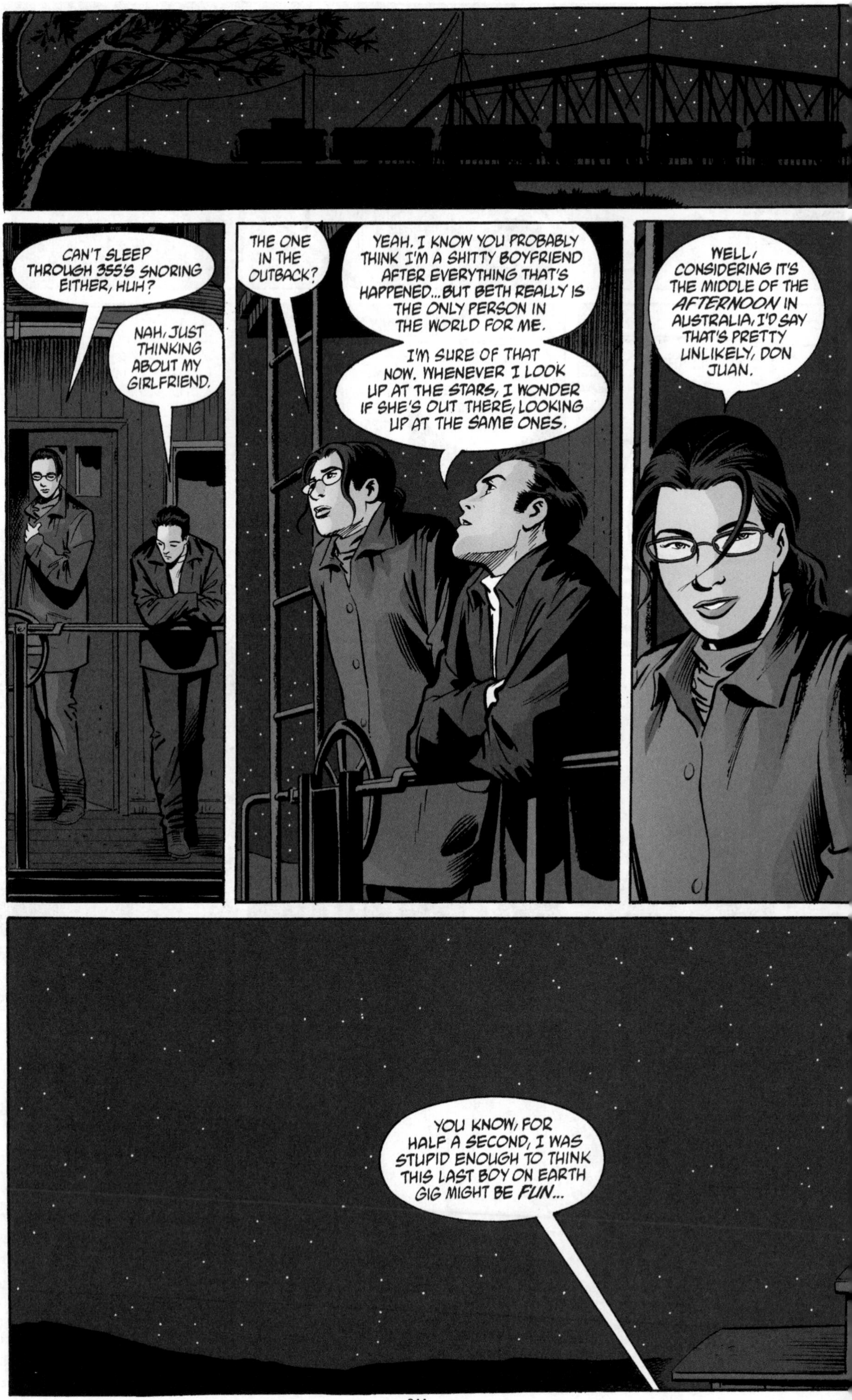
CAN'T SLEEP THROUGH 355'S SNORING EITHER, HUH?
NAH, JUST THINKING ABOUT MY GIRLFRIEND.
THE ONE IN THE OUTBACK?
YEAH. I KNOW YOU PROBABLY THINK I'M A SHITTY BOYFRIEND AFTER EVERYTHING THAT'S HAPPENED... BUT BETH REALLY IS THE ONLY PERSON IN THE WORLD FOR ME.
I'M SURE OF THAT NOW. WHENEVER I LOOK UP AT THE STARS, I WONDER IF SHE'S OUT THERE, LOOKING UP AT THE SAME ONES.
WELL, CONSIDERING IT'S THE MIDDLE OF THE AFTERNOON IN AUSTRALIA, I'D SAY THAT'S PRETTY UNLIKELY, DON JUAN.
YOU KNOW, FOR HALF A SECOND, I WAS STUPID ENOUGH TO THINK THIS LAST BOY ON EARTH GIG MIGHT BE FUN...

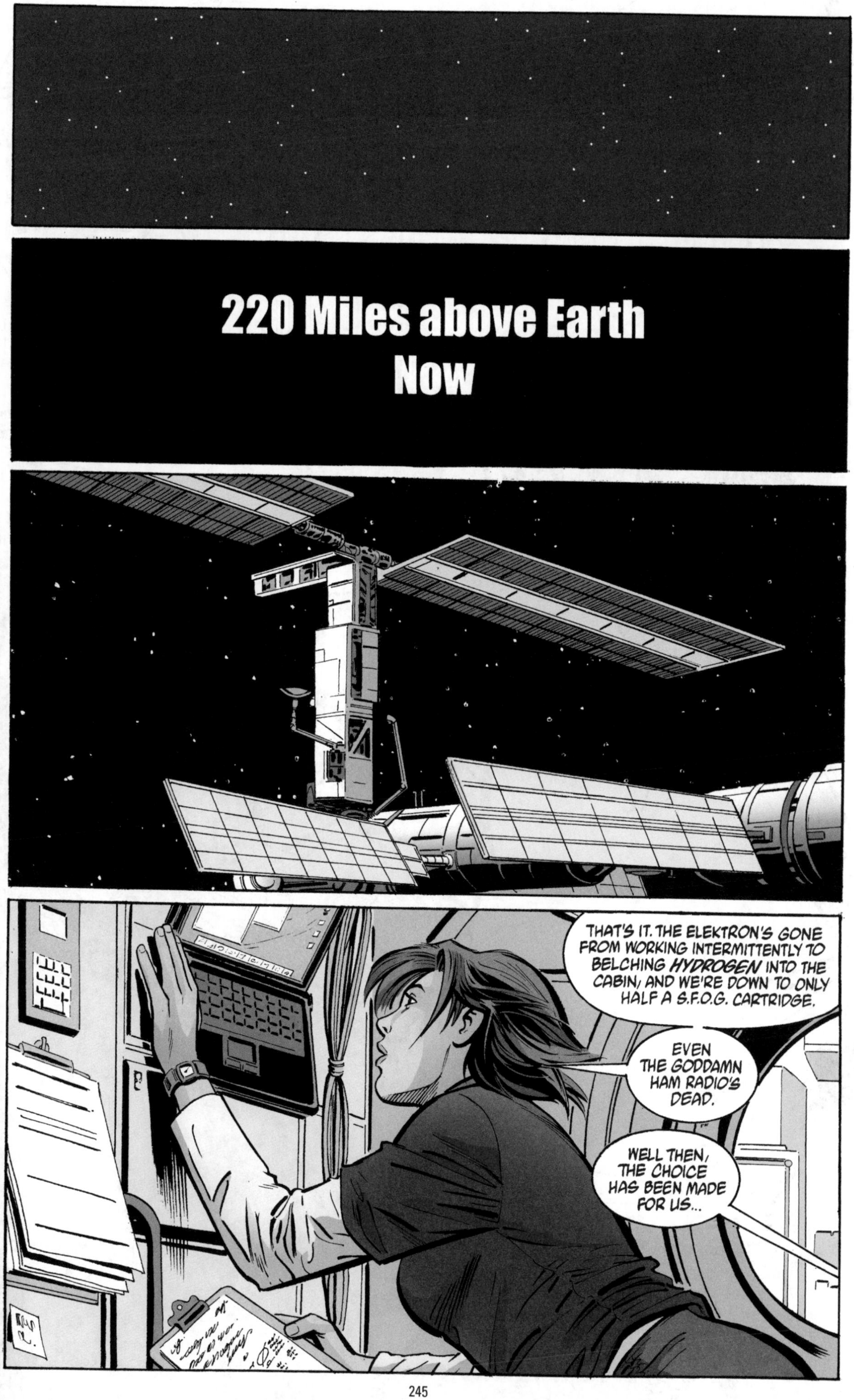
220 Miles above Earth
Now
THAT'S IT. THE ELEKTRON'S GONE FROM WORKING INTERMITTENTLY TO BELCHING HYDROGEN INTO THE CABIN, AND WE'RE DOWN TO ONLY HALF A S.F.O.G. CARTRIDGE.
EVEN THE GODDAMN HAM RADIO'S DEAD.
WELL THEN, THE CHOICE HAS BEEN MADE FOR US...

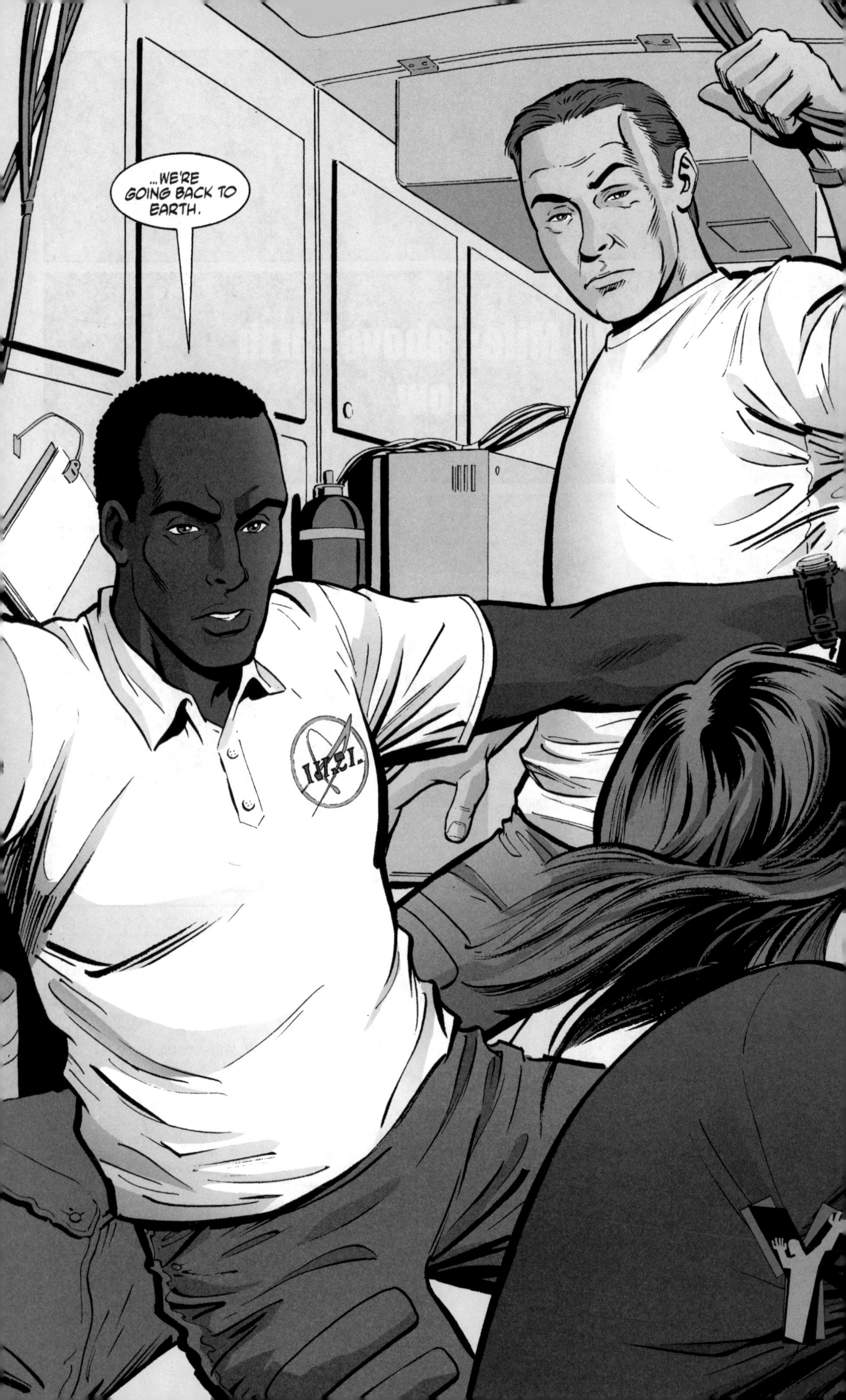
...WE'RE GOING BACK TO EARTH.

Y: THE SKETCHBOOK

Preliminary character designs and sketches from co-creator and penciller Pia Guerra.

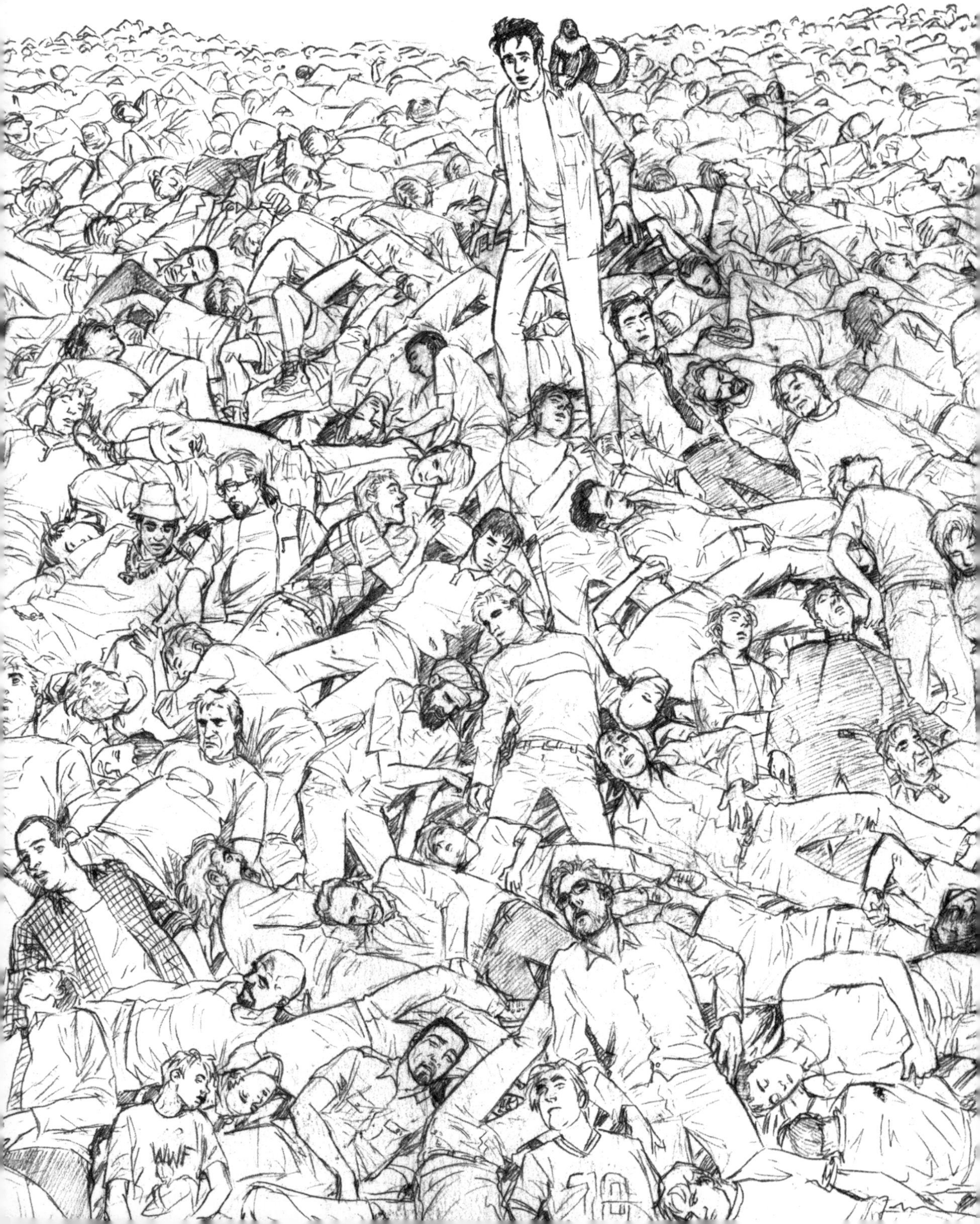
WWF

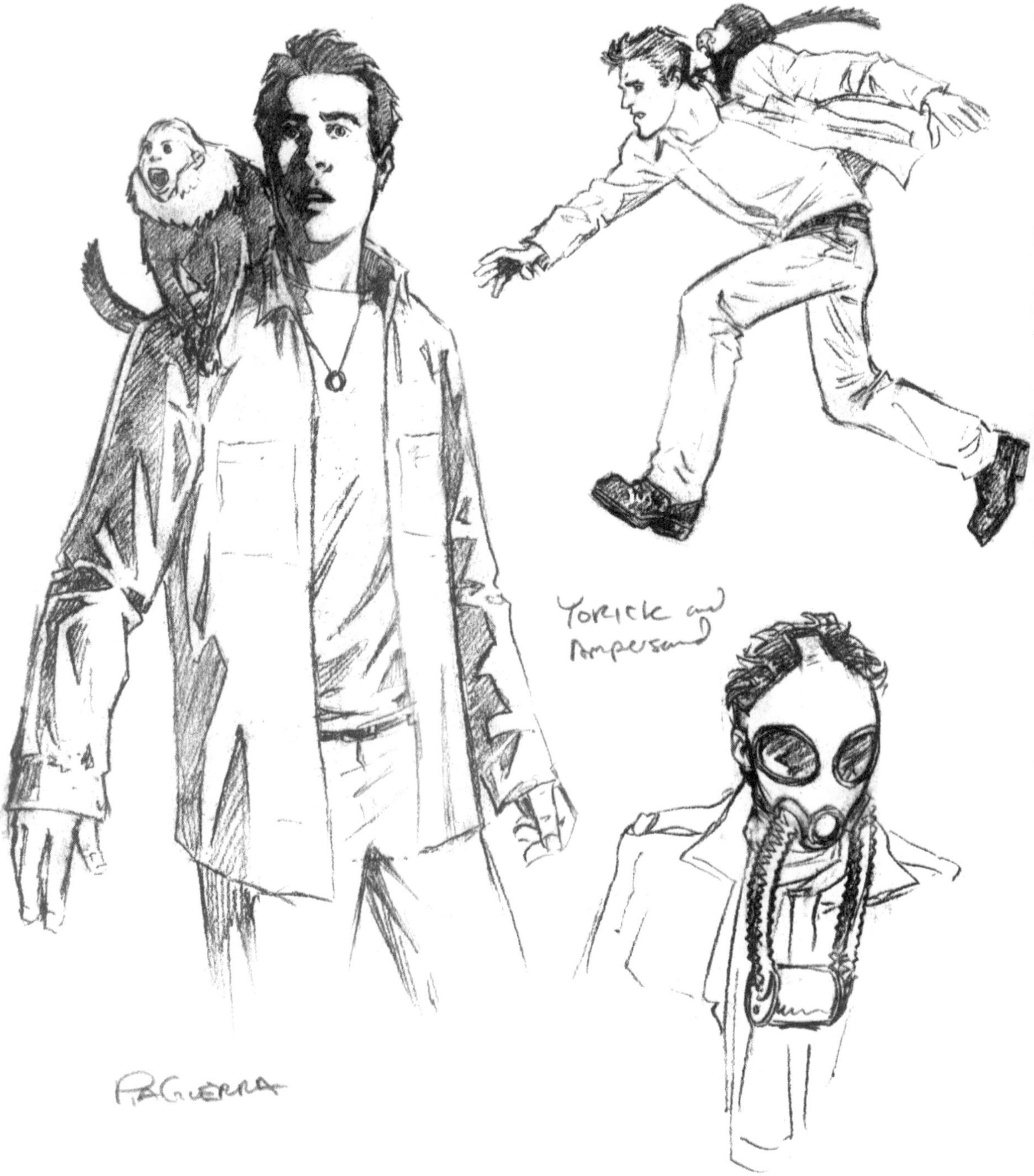
Yorick and Ampersand
PAGuerra

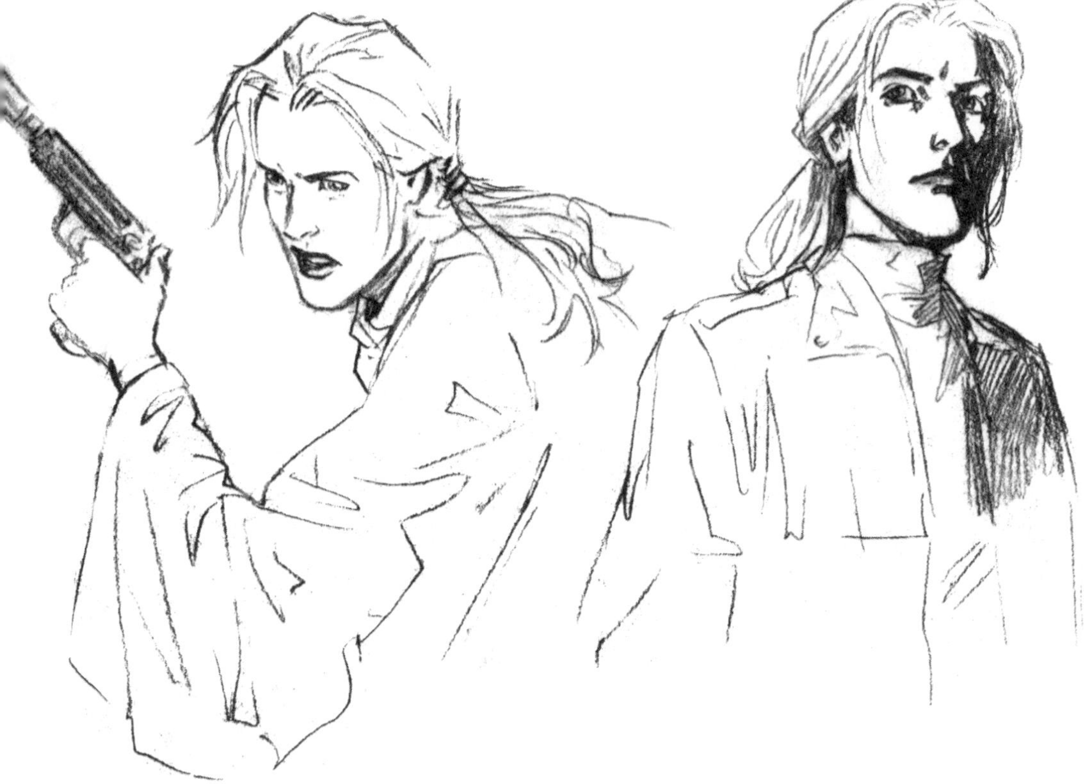

First design for 355

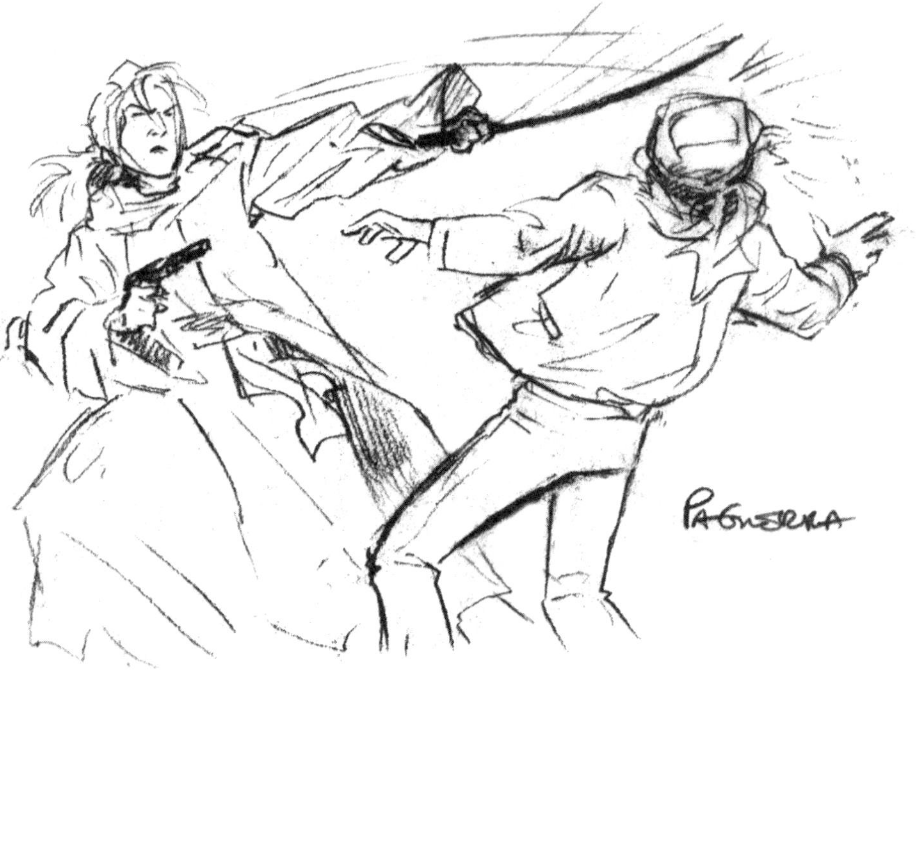
PAGUERRA

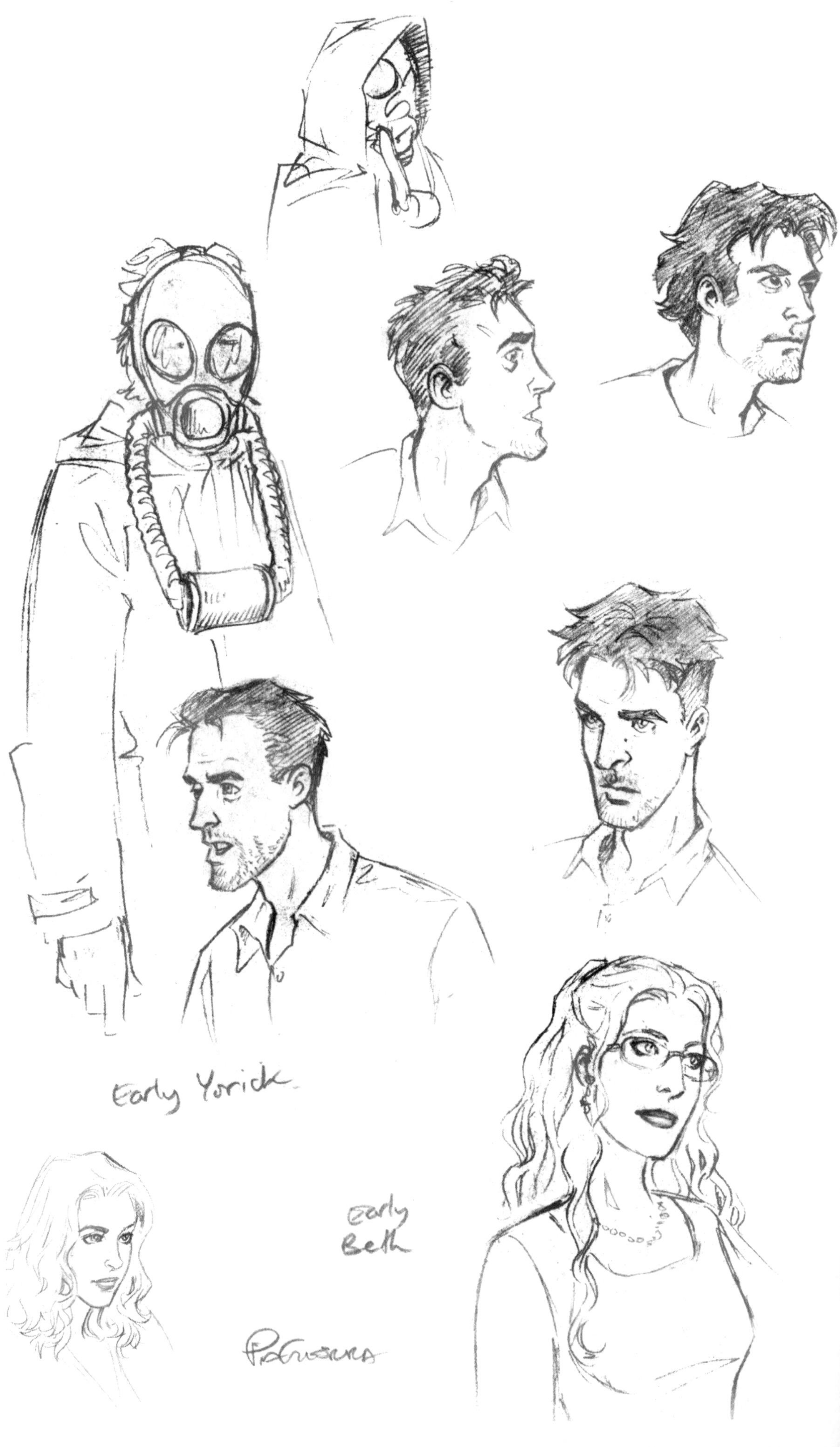
Early Yorick
Early Beth
PGuerra

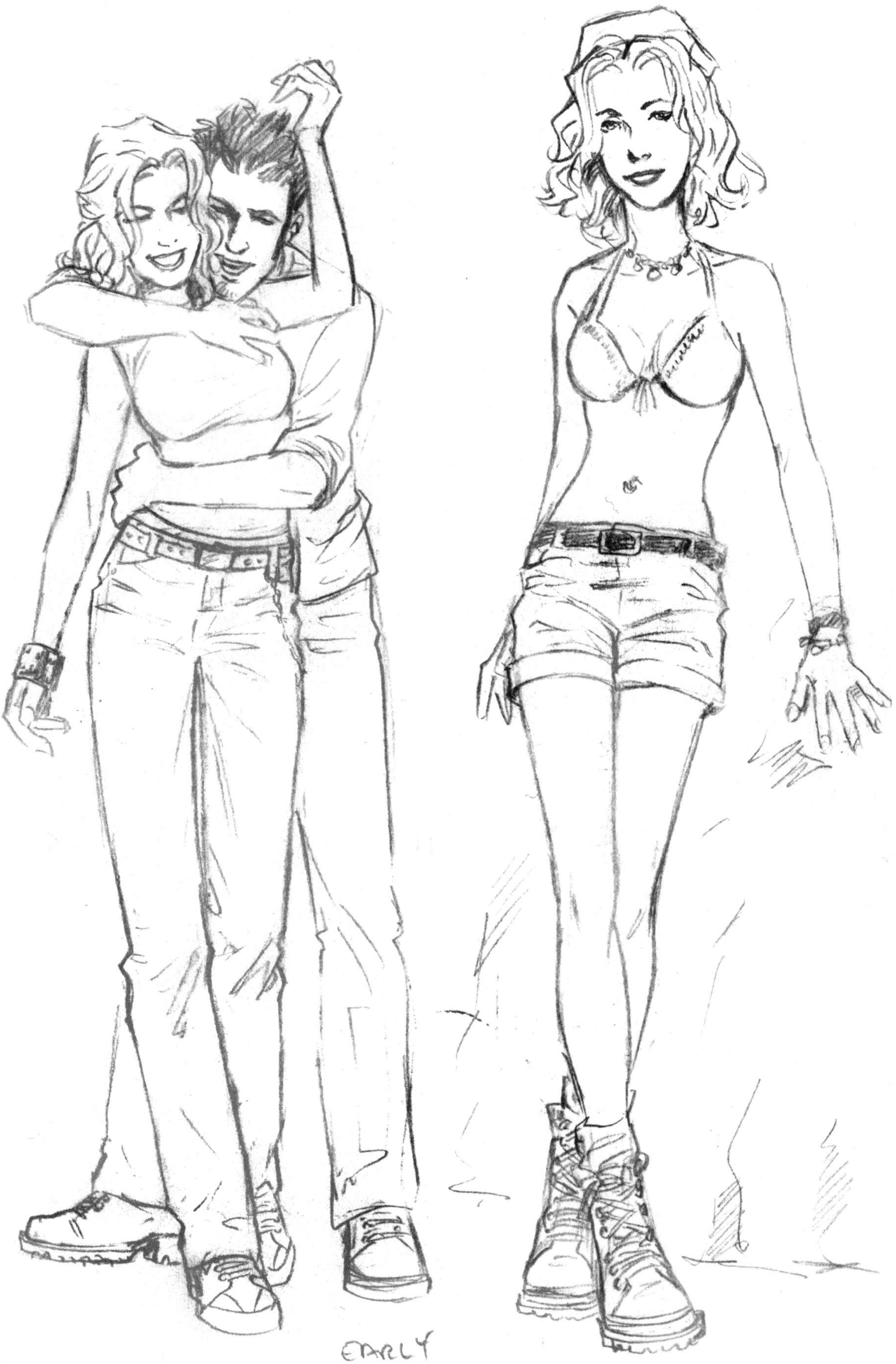

EARLY
BETH
AND YORICK

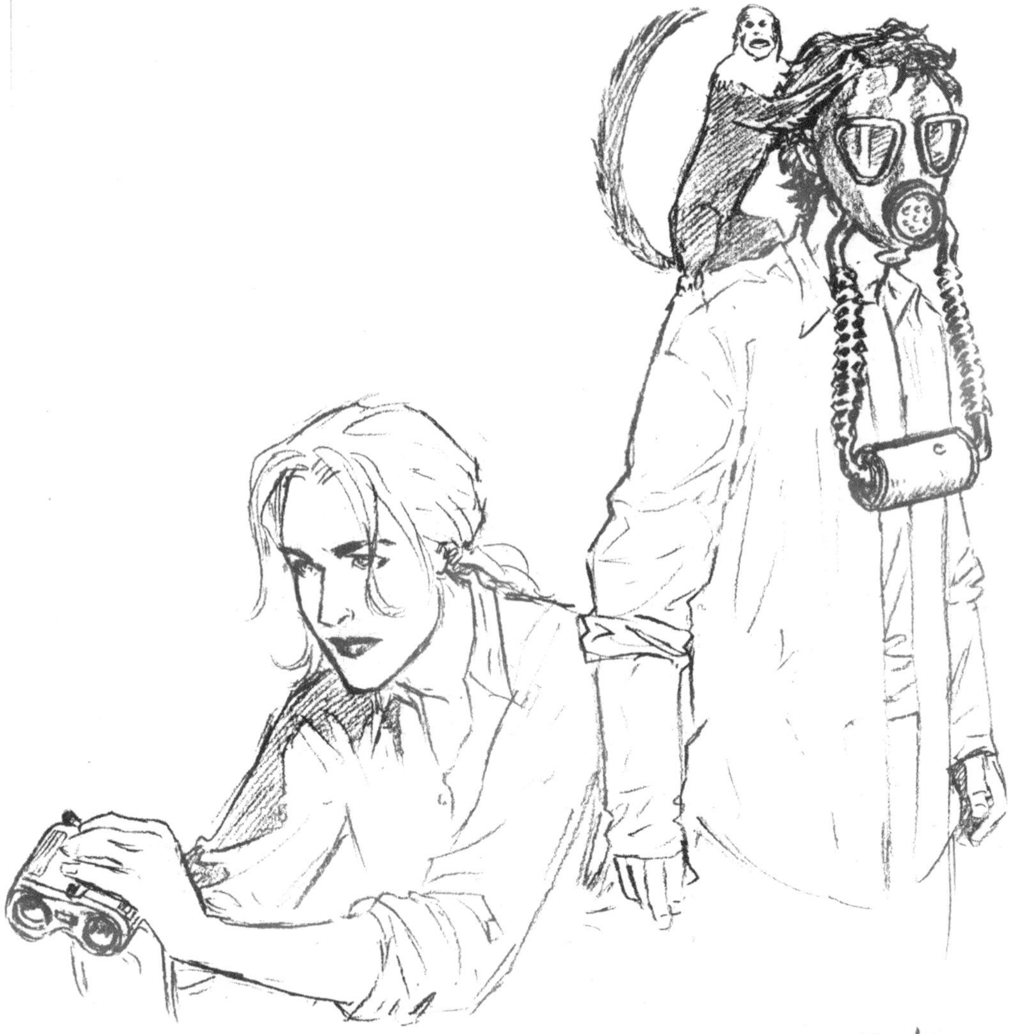

Early
355 + Yorick + Amp.

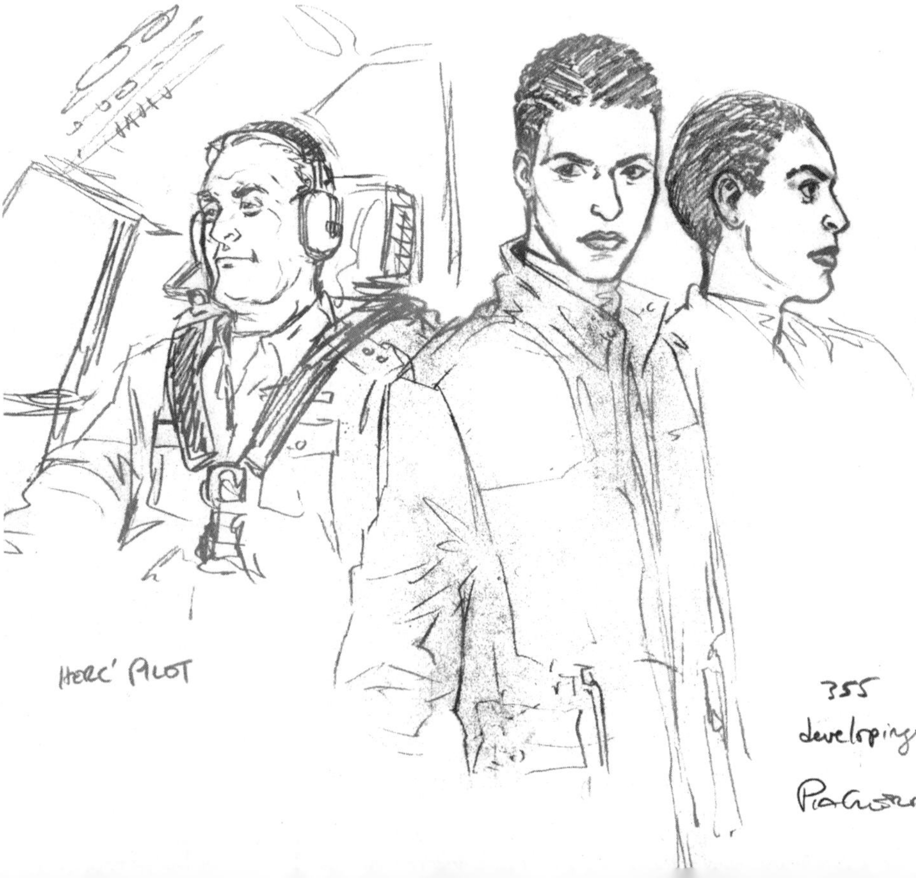

Herc' Pilot

355
developing

PiaGuerra

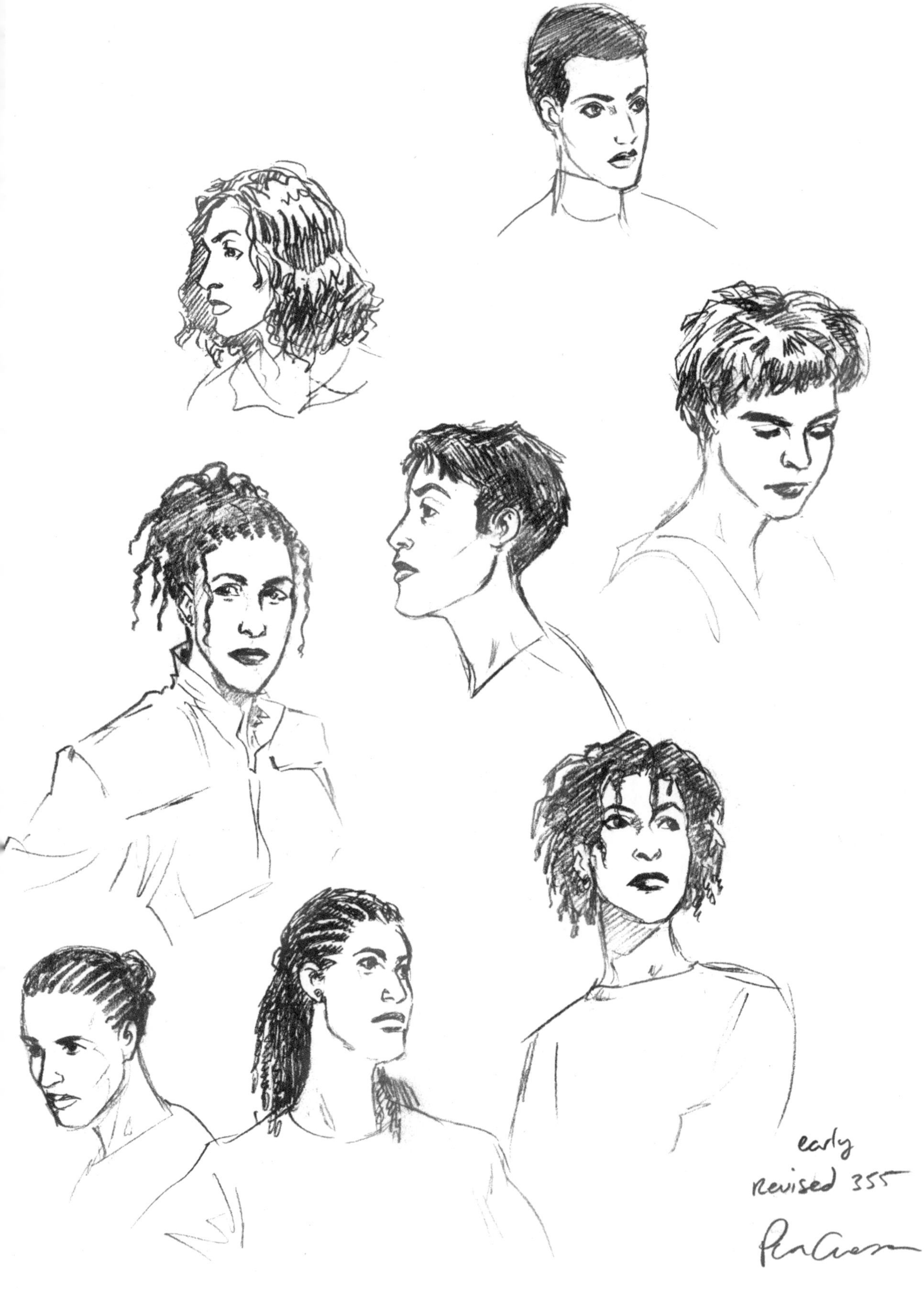
early
Revised 355

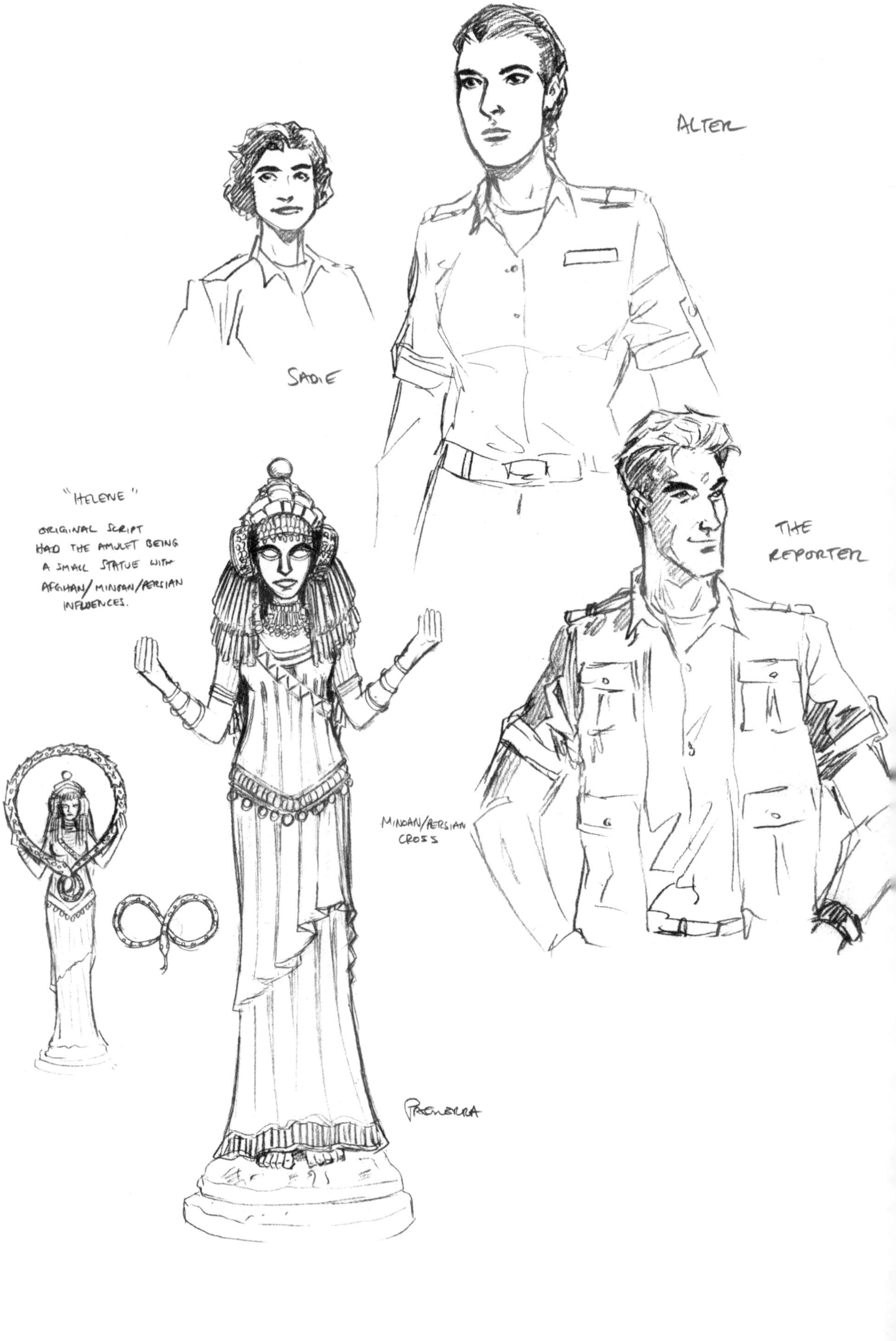
ALTER
SADIE
"HELENE"
ORIGINAL SCRIPT HAD THE AMULET BEING A SMALL STATUE WITH AFGHAN/MINOAN/PERSIAN INFLUENCES.
THE REPORTER
MINOAN/PERSIAN CROSS

FIRST SKETCH
DR MANN

Pia Guerra

FROZAN HAMAD
and "Helene"

Pia Guerra

Amazons

Pia Guerra